Fundamentals of
Systems Engineering

Fundamentals of
Systems Engineering
with Economics, Probability,
and Statistics

C. Jotin Khisty
Illinois Institute of Technology, Chicago

Jamshid Mohammadi
Illinois Institute of Technology, Chicago

Prentice Hall
Prentice Hall
Upper Saddle River, N J 07458

Library of Congress Cataloging-in-Publication Data

Khisty, C. Jotin, 1928-
  Fundamentals of systems engineering / C. Jotin Khisty and Jamshid Mohammadi.
    p. cm.
  Includes bibliographical references and index.
  ISBN 0-13-010649-6
    1. Systems engineering. I. Mohammadi, Jamshid. II. Title.

TA168 .K46 2000
620'.001'1—dc21   00-037360

Vice-president and editorial director of ECS: *Marcia Horton*
Aquisitions editor: *Laura Curless*
Editorial assistant: *Christine Ragosta*
Production Supervision: *Scott Disanno*
Executive managing editor: *Vince O'Brien*
Managing editor: *David A. George*
Vice-president of production and manufacturing: *David W. Riccardi*
Art director: *Gus Vibal*
Art editor: *Adam Velthaus*
Cover design: *Bruce Kenselaar*
Manufacturing buyer: *Pat Brown*

© 2001 by Prentice Hall
Prentice-Hall, Inc.
Upper Saddle River, New Jersey 07458

The author and publisher of this book have used their best efforts in preparing this book. These efforts include the development, research, and testing of the theories and programs to determine their effectiveness. The author and publisher make no warranty of any kind, expressed or implied, with regard to these programs or the documentation contained in this book. The author and publisher shall not be liable in any event for incidental or consequential damages in connection with, or arising out of, the furnishing, performance, or use of these programs.

Printed in the United States of America
10 9 8 7 6 5 4 3 2 1

ISBN: 0-13-010649-6

Prentice-Hall International (UK) Limited, *London*
Prentice-Hall of Australia Pty. Limited, *Sydney*
Prentice-Hall of Canada, Inc., *Toronto*
Prentice-Hall Hispanoamericana, S.A., *Mexico*
Prentice-Hall of India Private Limited, *New Delhi*
Prentice-Hall of Japan, Inc., *Tokyo*
Pearson Education Asia Pte. Ltd., *Singapore*
Editora Prentice-Hall do Brasil, Ltda., *Rio de Janeiro*

CONTENTS

CHAPTER 2. PROBLEM SOLVING AND DESIGNING IN ENGINEERING AND PLANNING

CHAPTER 3. BASIC ENGINEERING ECONOMICS & EVALUATION

CHAPTER 5.   PRINCIPLES OF PROBABILITY: PART I— REVIEW OF PROBABILITY THEORY

CHAPTER 6.   PRINCIPLES OF PROBABILITY: PART II— RANDOM VARIABLES AND PROBABILITY DISTRIBUTIONS

CHAPTER 7.   PRINCIPLES OF PROBABILITY: PART III— JOINT PROBABILITY FUNCTIONS AND CORRELATED VARIABLES

CHAPTER 8. PRINCIPLES OF STATISTICS: PART I— ESTIMATION OF STATISTICAL PARAMETERS AND TESTING VALIDITY OF DISTRIBUTION FUNCTIONS

CHAPTER 9.   PRINCIPLES OF STATISTICS: PART II— HYPOTHESIS TESTING, ANALYSIS OF VARIANCE, REGRESSION AND CORRELATION ANALYSIS

CHAPTER 10. *BASIC HARD SYSTEMS ENGINEERING— PART I*

CHAPTER 11.   BASIC HARD SYSTEMS ENGINEERING— PART II

PREFACE

Society depends to a large extent on socio-political and managerial decisions made that rely, directly or indirectly, on the advice of engineers. In fact, the planning, design, construction, operation, and maintenance of engineering facilities, in the public and private sector, represents the expenditure of billions of dollars every year, and yet many engineers who are responsible for this massive expenditure have little or no formal training in the fundamentals of economics or systems analysis—both being essential for dealing with these kinds of decisions. With the revision of curricula for professional schools of engineering all over North America and abroad, however, this picture is rapidly changing.

The main objective of this book is to present the fundamental principles of economics, probability, statistics, and systems analysis to engineering sophomore, junior, or senior students. While there are scores of excellent textbooks dealing with all four components individually, there are comparatively few textbooks covering these areas in a single volume. Our experience has been that engineering students need to be exposed to these fundamental tools early on in their undergraduate training, so that they can apply the knowledge covered in each of these areas when they take advanced courses toward their bachelor's degree, or in some cases toward their master's degree. This textbook attempts to integrate the power of quantitative analysis with the conceptual richness of capital budgeting and microeconomics into the elements of systems engineering. It provides the reader with the basic concepts and tools that have proven most useful in engineering problem solving.

Some of the special features of the book need to be highlighted. First, a wide range of topics is covered, all drawn from the "systems approach" standpoint. Second, the emphasis is on presenting the fundamental concepts and their practical engineering applications, unobscured by complicated mathematics. Third, realizing that our best practice is far from perfect and our theories incomplete, we have included many open-ended, value-laden, real-world problems, at the end of every chapter. Fourth, although the conventional practice is for engineers to normally deal with natural and physical systems, we have included a chapter on "Soft Systems Thinking and Analysis." This inclusion was in response to the emergence of a range of formal methodologies, which aim not just to produce "optimal" solutions but to facilitate an enriched decision-making process, most suitable for application in an uncertain world. To our knowledge, this is the first attempt at including such material in an undergraduate textbook.

Material included in this book is organized as follows: Chapters 1 and 2 are introductory in nature, focussing on the natural, physical, and human systems and describing the nature of problems likely to be encountered in engineering practice. Chapters 3 and 4 cover the basic topics on engineering economics and the fundamental tools of microeconomics, respectively. The principles of probability are taken up next in Chapters 5, 6, and 7. Each of these chapters covers one of several basic topics in the theory of probability, while Chapters 8 and 9 deal with the principles of applied statistics. The application of probability and statistics in engineering is in such areas as decision-making, design under uncertainty, data analysis and interpretation, and system safety analysis. In this respect, we assume that engineering problem-solving practice, to a large extent, depends on engineering knowledge and the ability to interpret data. As such, the theory of probability and statistics plays an essential role in the decision-making process. Chapters 8 and 9 focus on applied statistics and discuss such topics as the analysis of engineering data, empirical estimation of statistical parameters, hypothesis testing, and correlation analysis. Even though courses in probability and statistics (usually offered by departments of mathematics/statistics) are included in engineering curricula, our experience has been that students taking such courses invariably end up having great difficulty in applying their knowledge to engineering problems. One objective in including chapters on probability and statistics is to emphasize the practical applications and relevance of the basic concepts in these two areas to engineering design.

Chapters 10 and 11 serve as introductory chapters on Hard Systems Engineering, while Chapter 12 deals with Soft Systems Thinking. As is well known, systems thinking developed out of wartime military operations planning, and has been the dominant traditional approach underlying systems engineering, systems analysis, and operations research for the last 50 years (Jackson, 1991). Soft systems thinking, on the other hand, is a more recent development, and in contrast to hard systems thinking, admits that there are multiple perceptions of reality, and of "solving" wicked, messy, complex, and ill-structured problems, characteristics of most contemporary engineering problems, particularly where the socio-economic and political ramifications are predominant.

We have presented the material through plenty of illustrative engineering and managerial worked examples. This will surely motivate practicing engineers and students to grasp the essential concepts for analysis and design. In view of the major worldwide thrust on distance learning and self-study by individuals who need a self-contained textbook dealing with the fundamentals of systems engineering with economics, probability and statistics, we are confident that this textbook will be ideal.

There are a number of audiences for this book. It is quite possible that students could complete the major topics included in this book in two-3 credit semester courses. Instructors in Architecture, Construction Management, Chemical, Electrical, Mechanical, Industrial Engineering, as well as in Urban Planning, in addition to Civil Engineering could formulate basic one- or two-semester course(s) to meet their own specific requirements. This textbook could very effective be used in graduate courses too, particularly in construction management and transportation engineering programs. A solutions manual is available.

Many people warrant acknowledgement, individually or jointly from the authors, and for personal or work-related reasons. We wish to thank our colleagues and students in the Department of Civil and Architectural Engineering, Illinois Institute of Technology (IIT), Chicago, for their help and advice. For the first author, this book began as a set of notes as early as 1978 when he was a faculty member at Washington State University (WSU), Pullman, WA. Many batches of graduate and undergraduate students at WSU and IIT have contributed in one form or another in the development of this book. In more recent years, four of my former students, Dr. P. S. Sriraj, Cemal Ayvalik, Turan Arslan, Raymond Tellis, and Sagar Sonar, helped this author to put the book together. My sincere thanks go to them. The second author expresses his gratitude to his colleagues, Dr. Anatol Longinow of Wiss, Janney, Elstner Associates of Northbrook, Illinois, and Joseph F. Braun of Systems & Electronics, Inc., of Elk Grove, Illinois, for providing an opportunity and reposing their trust in him to apply many of the statistical methods in Chapters 8 and 9 in realworld engineering data analysis problems. Finally, this book would not have taken shape without the admirable help, support, and advice provided by Laura Curless, Scott Disanno and their staff at Prentice Hall.

As with any textbook containing a vast amount of numerical work together with scores of examples and exercises, we would appreciate it very much if errors and inconsistencies are brought to our notice.

C. Jotin Khisty

Jamshid Mohammadi

1

Mapping the Terrain
of the Systems Approach

1.1 INTRODUCTION

In essence, this book is about using the systems approach to make decisions. It answers the basic question: How can we choose the best course of action, taking into account the goals we are trying to achieve and the constraints that limit our action, by such factors as time, labor, money, and the policies set by government or by a private organization? Our main purpose is to give the widest possible overview of systems engineering to a beginning engineering student, and to explain how a combination of the principles of probability and statistics, economics, and systems analysis can be used for solving engineering problems related to planning, design, and management.

This first chapter maps out the terrain of what will be covered in succeeding chapters and also describes some preliminary definitions connected with science and systems engineering. How would an engineer minimize the capital and maintenance cost of a long-span bridge? How could an engineer advise his client on how to maximize (or optimize) the total income from a high-rise building? What would be the best way to maximize the safety of the railroad system running through your city? Should the government subsidize persons buying an electric car to boost the "economy of scale" of electric car manufacturers? Should the city extend the light-rail system in San Diego, and what would be the implications and consequences attached to this decision? These are the kinds of questions you, as an engineer, planner, or manager will have to face when you take up a responsible position with a public or private under-taking. To tackle such questions, you will need a basic knowledge of economics (both capital budgeting and micro economics), the principles of probability and statistics, and a working knowledge of systems engineering. All of these topics are covered in this book.

A professional engineer must understand and apply the basic laws of mathematics, physics, chemistry, and economics, for planning, designing, managing, and operationalizing engineering works. With hundreds of different recognized engineering specialties, a simple yet comprehensive definition of engineering is as follows: Engineering is the profession in which knowledge of the mathematical and physical sciences gained by study, experience, and practice is applied with judgement to develop ways to utilize economically, the materials and forces of nature for the progressive well being of society (Crandall and Seabloom, 1970).

It is the concern with economics that distinguishes engineering from pure science. While economic considerations may be of little or no concern to the pure scientist, the function of the engineer is to utilize the principles of economics to achieve a more efficient and economical end product, such as a highway, a building, a water-supply system and so on. And, it is the evolution of this end product from its conception to its final production, using the creative processes, that is known as engineering design. Design is both an art and a science, in that it is a creative problem-solving process in which the engineer works within the bounds of a limited monetary budget, a prescribed time line, and specific laws and regulations to convert data, information, technical know-how, combined with his/her ideas into an accepted product. When an engineering design is finally approved by those authorized to do so, the finished design can then be implemented (Crandall and Seabloom, 1970).

1.2 THE NATURE OF SCIENCE

All engineers invariably take several courses in mathematics and science, because these courses form the backbone of engineering science. In a broad sense, science is a way of acquiring testable knowledge about the world. It is now acknowledged that the knowledge we gain from the scientific approach is provisional and probabalistic, because it is possible that additional experiments carried out by scientists may alter what we already know. Naturally all theories and laws that we currently know are really approximations of the truth, within a certain domain of validity.

Some important characteristics of the scientific method are:

Hypothesis Setting and Testing. Scientists make propositions or suppositions for reasoning, investigation, or experimentation, for a very small limited number of variables. Then, experiments are conducted to test the hypothesis, holding all other variables constant. If the hypothesis turns out to be correct, it adds to our current knowledge base. If not, the results are rejected.

Replicability. Scientific knowledge must be as objective as possible, which means that a number of observers performing the same experiment, independent of one another, under the same conditions and assumption, should be able to replicate results and verify the observations. This is the scientist's way of verifying (or validating) or falsifying (or rejecting) a proposed hypothesis.

Refutability. While it is impossible for scientists to conduct all possible experiments on a particular topic, due to lack of time, it is important to perform good experiments using appropriate scientific techniques to decide between competing hypotheses. Although many scientists tend to have their theories corroborated by good scientific techniques, it is quite possible that these theories could be refuted through a series of additional experiments.

Reductionism. The real world under study is so complex and messy that scientists can only perform simple experiments to capture and comprehend it. As a result, scientists experiment with small units or entities of the real world that can explain cause and effect in a linear way. This style of thinking and experimentation, called reductionism, consists in isolating the phenomenon under investigation from its environment, which eventually produces a "mechanistic" view of the world (Checkland, 1981; Flood and Carson, 1993).

According to the scientific method, all genuine inquiry and knowledge should be based on hard facts, experimentation, and explanation. It goes further in believing that the methods of science are applicable to all enquiry, especially the human and social sciences. This traditional scientific approach (also referred to as "logical positivism") has been debated and attacked by many scientists and philosophers, and we will take up this debate while considering soft systems thinking in Chapter 12.

1.3 ENGINEERING PLANNING, DESIGN, AND MANAGEMENT

The planning and designing of a product are basic tasks undertaken by engineers to produce an end product. Planning is the arrangement of specific steps for the attainment of an objective. It is a future-oriented and prescriptive process because it assumes our ability to control our own destiny, at least within certain limits. In the context of engineering, planning generally involves the arrangement of spatial patterns over time. However, it must be remembered that it is not the spatial patterns which are planning: they are just the objects of a process. Management on the other hand is the skillful use of means (e.g., technology) to accomplish certain ends (e.g., objectives). Designing, as defined by the Accreditation Board for Engineering and Technology (ABET, 1988) is:

> The process of devising a system, component, or process to meet desired needs. It is a decision making process (often iterative), in which the basic sciences, mathematics, and

engineering sciences are applied to convert resources optimally to meet a stated objective. Among the fundamental elements of the design process are the establishment of objectives and criteria, analysis, synthesis, testing, and evaluation.

1.4 THE SYSTEMS APPROACH

With the rapid technological advances made in every sphere of inquiry, engineers, planners, managers, decision makers, and even the pure scientists realized that the complexity of real-world problems could not be handled by just applying the traditional scientific method, which had its limitations, particularly when dealing with social systems or engineering problems with a social or human component. Indeed, if you look around for an engineering problem without the human factor, you would be hard pressed to find one. So then, where do we start? Or, better still: where should we begin? We will begin with a simple basic definition of the systems approach.

The systems approach represents a broad-based, systematic approach to problems that involve a system. It is particularly geared for solving complex problems (Meredith et al., 1985). A system is a set of interrelated parts, called components, that perform a number of functions in order to achieve common goals. Systems analysis is the application of the scientific method, modified to capture the "holistic" nature of the real world, to solve complex problems. In fact, the systems approach ought to be called the "systemic approach," systemic in the sense that it offers systemic (holistic rather than piecemeal) as well as systematic (step-by-step rather than intuitive) guidelines for engineers to follow (Flood and Carson, 1993).

Goals are desired end states, and operational statements of goals are called objectives which should be measurable, where possible, and attainable. Feedback and control are essential to the effective performance of a system. The development of objectives may in itself involve an iterative process. Objectives will generally suggest their own appropriate measures of effectiveness (MOEs). A MOE is a measurement of the degree to which each alternative action satisfies the objective. Measures of the benefits foregone or the opportunities lost for each of the alternatives are called measures of costs (MOC). MOCs are the consequences of decisions. A criterion relates the MOE to the MOC by stating a decision rule for selecting among several alternative actions whose costs and effectiveness have been determined. One particular type of criterion, a standard, is a fixed objective: the lowest (or highest) level of performance acceptable. In other words, a standard represents a cut off point beyond which performance is rejected (Cornell, 1980; Khisty and Lall, 1998). The following example will help you to understand the basic concepts.

Example 1.1

A medium-sized city with a population of 250,000 plans to investigate the implementation of a public transport system. This is a first-cut preliminary look to be accomplished in, say, a couple of days. Your task is to provide a sample set of goals, objectives, alternatives, measures of cost, and measures of effectiveness, to demonstrate to citizens in your neighborhood how one could begin thinking about these issues.

Solution:

A sample set of goals, objectives, alternatives, and MOEs could be framed with the help of citizen groups, as follows:

Goal:	To provide a quick and economical transport system
Objectives:	1. To carry people at a minimum operating speed of 25 mph during peak hours.
	2. To have fares that would compete with the cost of operating a private car.
Alternatives:	A. Regular bus system (RB)
	B. Street car system (SC)
	C. Light-rail system (LR)
MOEs:	1. Cost to ride: In cents/ride
	2. Punctuality: Delay should be less than ± 5 min.
	3. About the same speed as the private car (25 mph).
	4. Area-wide coverage: Service should be about 10 min. walking distance from residence.
MOCs:	Capital and maintenance cost of providing the service in relative dollar terms is:

$$RB = 20x; SC = 40x; LR = 60x, \text{ where x is in millions.}$$

Assessment: Set up a matrix as shown below and assign scores between 1 and 5, representing poor to excellent values, respectively.

Alternatives	MOEs	1	2	3	4	Total Effectiveness
A		4	3	3	5	= 15
B		3	3	2	3	= 11
C		4	5	5	2	= 16

The matrix indicates that the light-rail system is the best out of the 3 systems considered, but when we compare the scores along with the costs, we find that the Cost/unit of effectiveness is:

For A $= 20x/15 = 1.33x$; B $= 40x/11 = 3.64x$; and for
C $= 60x/16 = 3.75x$. This indicates that the bus system is the best.

Conclusion:

The best alternative based on the cost per unit effectiveness is alternative A, which is the lowest of the three.

Discussion:

This assessment has been done merely to demonstrate how a first-cut assessment could be done. Further data gathering and calculations would be needed to make an accurate judgement regarding which alternative would be best for the city. Input from citizens who would use the system would also be of importance.

1.5 STEPS IN SYSTEMS ANALYSIS

Some of the basic steps recommended for performing an analysis are:

1. Recognizing community problems and values.
2. Establishing goals and defining the objectives.
3. Establishing criteria.
4. Designing alternative actions to achieve step 2.
5. Evaluating the alternative actions in terms of effectiveness and costs.
6. Selecting an alternative action in keeping with the goals and objectives, criteria, standards, and value sets established, through iteration, until a satisfactory solution is reached.

A simplified analysis process is shown in Figure 1.1, and the hierarchical interrelationships among values, goals, objectives, and criteria are shown in Figure 1.2.

1.6 CLASSIFICATION OF SYSTEMS

There is no standard classification scheme for systems. Boulding's (1956) hierarchy was one of the first attempts at classification, ranked in increasing order of complexity. Each level is said to include in some way the lower levels, but to have its own emergent

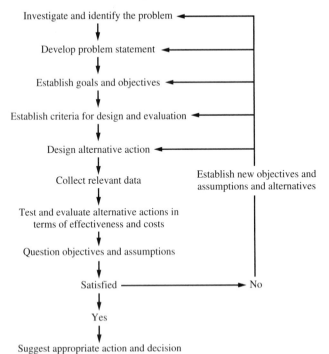

Figure 1.1   Flow chart of system analysis process.

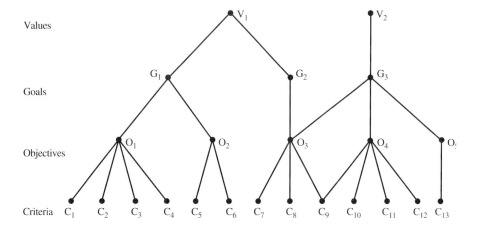

Values

Goals

Objectives

Criteria

Figure 1.2   Hierarchical Interrelations among Values, Goals, Objectives, and Criteria.

properties, although there is no "scale of complexity" attached to this hierarchy. The most important distinction is between living and non-living systems and the different types of relationship in the organizational connections involved within each hierarchy, as well as with lower hierarchies. Table 1.1 displays Boulding's hierarchy.

Boulding says, "One advantage of exhibiting a hierarchy of systems in this way is that it gives us some idea of the present gaps in both theoretical and empirical

TABLE 1.1   BOULDING'S HIERARCHY OF SYSTEMS

Level	Description	Characteristic	Example
1.	Structures	Static, spatial frameworks	Atom, crystal, bridge
2.	Clockworks	Predetermined motion	Solar system, clocks machines
3.	Control	Closed-loop control mechanisms	Thermostats
4.	Open systems	Structurally self-maintaining	Cells
5.	Genetic systems	Society of cells	Plants
6.	Animals	Nervous system, self-awareness	Birds and beasts
7.	Humans	Self-consciousness, knowledge, language	Human beings
8.	Socio-cultural systems	Roles, values, communication	Family, community, society
9.	Transcendental systems	Beyond our knowledge	Religion

knowledge. Adequate theoretical models extend up to about the fourth level, and not much beyond." Since Boulding's remarks in 1956, much progress has taken place in understanding systems, almost at all the levels, and new typologies have been published, in part based on Boulding's hierarchy.

1.7 SYSTEMS CHARACTERISTICS

During the last forty years, several authors have suggested basic considerations concerning systems thinking. Of all the proponents of systems, C. West Churchman (1968) has given us perhaps one of the simplest and yet the most understandable expositions of the subject. He outlines five basic considerations:

1. Objectives of the total system and specifically the measure of performance of the system itself;
2. The system environment;
3. The resources of the system;
4. The components of the system; and
5. The management of the system.

These five considerations are not meant to be all-inclusive, but they capture most of the properties that engineers generally encounter in their practice. A brief explanation will now be given of each of the five points.

1. *The Objectives:* are those goals or ends which the system is working toward. Hence goal-seeking (or teleology) is a characteristic of systems. While the determination of objectives for mechanical systems is comparatively easy, those for human activity systems can be considerably more difficult. One must be cautious to distinguish between stated objectives and the real objectives of the system. For example, a student may say that her objective is to gain knowledge in order to master the subject being studied, while in fact her real objective may be to just obtain good grades. In real life, objectives need to be operationalized, and to do this properly, they need to be quantifiable, in some way or another, in order to measure the performance of the system. Quantification helps us to measure to what degree the system's objectives are being realized.
2. *The Environment:* constitutes all that is "outside" the system. First, the environment includes all that lies outside the system's control. Second, the environment also includes all that determines, in part at least, the manner of the system's performance.
3. *The Resources:* are all the means available to the system for the execution of the activities necessary for goal realization. Resources include all the things that the system can change and use to its own advantage. In human systems, one can also include the opportunities that are available to the system, besides human labor, money, and materials.

4. *The Components:* consist of the missions, jobs, or activities that the system has to perform to realize its objectives.

5. *The Management:* includes two basic functions. First, planning the system which involves all aspects of systems previously encountered, i.e., its goals, environment, utilization of resources, and components and activities. Second, controlling the system which involves both examination of the execution of plans as well as planning for change. Plans must be subject to periodic review and re-evaluation, because no plan can remain static throughout the life of a project. Associated with the planning and control function is the notion of information flow and feedback, often characteristic of cybernetic systems.

1.8 SYSTEMS ANALYSIS AND DECISION-MAKING

We have described Churchman's systems approach for dealing with problems. You may notice that in contrast to the methods used in the pure sciences, the objectives of the systems approach is to recommend a course of action to the decision-maker in addition to merely understanding the problem. Systems analysis is truly a continuous cycle of defining objectives, designing alternative systems to achieve those objectives, evaluating the alternatives in terms of their effectiveness and cost, questioning the objectives and other assumptions underlying the analysis, seeking new alternatives and establishing new objectives, and the iteration goes on indefinitely. This cyclical process bears out the idea of the rational methodology to problems of choice.

As all of us know, we are asked to make decisions on a daily basis, not only for ourselves but for others too. Professionals in all walks of life have to make hard decisions and even harder predictions, and everybody expects them to make the very best decisions. But are we able to make the best decisions under such constraints as time limitations, funding restrictions, lack of resources, and political pressures? In situations of certainty, the decision-maker is supposed to have complete knowledge of everything needed to make a decision. In other words, he has complete knowledge of the value of the outcomes and the occurrence of the states of nature. In situations of risk, he knows the value of the outcomes and the relative probabilities of the states of nature. Under uncertainty, the values of the outcomes may possibly be known, but no information is available on the probability of the events.

1.9 MODELS AND MODEL-BUILDING

In its simplest sense, a model is a representation of reality. The model is arrived at through the process of abstracting from reality those aspects with which one is concerned. For example, a map of Chicago, showing the street system, the locations of schools, hospitals, and major places of interest, including the suburbs, all drawn to scale, is a model of the City of Chicago. This map can be put to use to solve any number of problems an engineer (or a lay person) may have. A model is useful in a practical sense when it accurately duplicates the behavior of the real world system.

One thing to remember is that models are neither true or false; their value is judged by the contribution they make to our understanding of the systems they represent. Also, a model cannot represent every aspect of reality, because the model is at best an approximation of the real object or situation.

Models may be classified by their correspondence to the system being modeled. For example, physical models retain some of the characteristics of the system they represent. A model of a house could, for instance, be made of plywood, scaled down, that might almost look like the house you may want to build. Photographs and blueprints are further examples of this category, and are referred to as Iconic models. Models constructed from a set of physical objects not found in the real system are called physical analogues. For example, an electrical system may be constructed to behave like a water distribution system for a city. Schematic or analogue models, in the shape of flow charts or organizational charts are frequently employed by engineers, using lines and symbols which are mere abstractions of the physical world. Mathematical models of systems consist of sets of equations whose solutions explain or predict changes in the state of the system. Our primary interest is in mathematical models.

We will have an opportunity to examine various types of models in succeeding chapters but it may be helpful to keep in mind that models are capable of portraying infinitely complex problems arising in engineering, in the form of charts, graphs, equations, and symbolic representation, representing a system of inputs, processing and transforming system, and outputs as indicated in Figure 1.3. Here, a system can be observed as one containing a "black box," connecting an input to an output. If the output is simply related to the input and not affected by any kind of feedback to the input, it is said to be a feed-forward system. If, on the other hand, a part of the output is fed back to the input, it is referred to as a feed-back system, as shown in Figure 1.3.

Further insight into the modeling process is shown in Figure 1.4. Starting with data and information regarding a system under investigation, an engineer can use these inputs to harness a variety of tools, such as graphs and flowcharts, through mathematical equations to economic analysis, to perform an analysis.

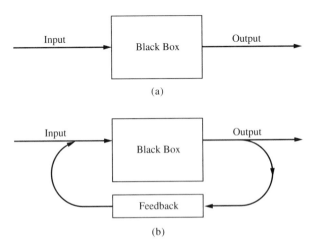

(a)

(b)

Figure 1.3 Black box or transfer function model. (a) Without feedback; (b) with feedback.

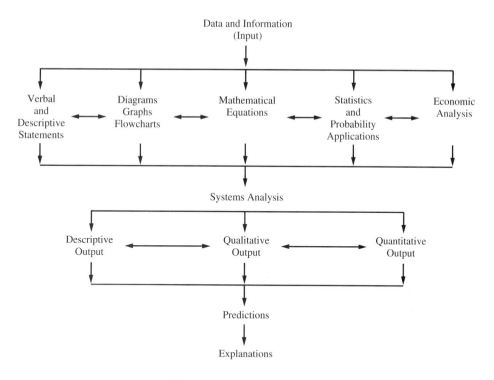

Figure 1.4 The modeling picture.

Proper interpretation of this analysis can result in predictions and explanations of the system under consideration. In the chapters that follow we will have the opportunity to revisit these tools.

SUMMARY

The engineer has professional obligations to society, and therefore has to exercise judgement, make decisions, and accept responsibility for his actions. Society has also become aware of the consequential impacts of engineering work. This requires that engineers realize the nature of social goals and objectives, and appreciate the value of the systems approach.

This chapter has introduced the student to the general nature of science, and the differences between engineering and science. The systems approach was explained and the various steps in systems analysis were outlined. Because systems occurring in engineering are so varied, the nature of iconic, analogue, and mathematical models were described. A short description of models and model-building was also introduced just enough to set the ball rolling to deal with the next chapter on problem-solving.

In summary, systems thinking is a useful framework to keep in mind when dealing with complex problems in a holistic way. Systems thinking promotes systems

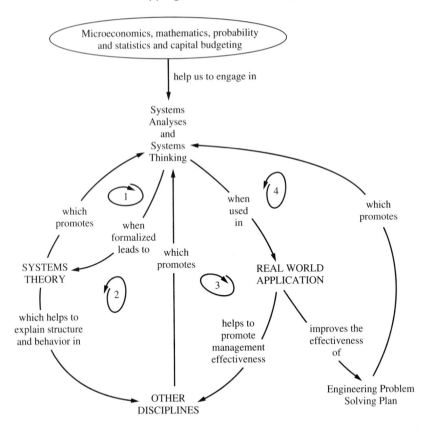

Figure 1.5 Systems thinking's development. (Adapted from Flood and Carson, 1993, p.4.)

theory, enables us to practice good management, provides us with the insight to plan for the future, and helps us to understand the structure and behavior of systems. The interlinked cycles of systems thinking, systems theory, and systems applications are shown in Figure 1.5.

REFERENCES

Accreditation Board for Engineering Technology Report, 1988. Washington, DC.

BOULDING, K. E. (1956). "General Systems Theory—The Skeleton of Science," *Management Science* 2, 197–208.

CHECKLAND, P. (1981). *Systems Thinking, Systems Practice,* John Wiley & Sons, Chichester, UK.

CHURCHMAN, C. W. (1968). *The Systems Approach,* Dell Press, New York, NY.

CORNELL, A. H. (1980). *The Decision-Maker's Handbook,* Prentice-Hall, Englewood Cliffs, NJ.

CRANDALL, K. C., and R. W. SEABLOOM (1970). *Engineering Fundamentals,* McGraw-Hill Inc., New York, NY.

FLOOD, R. L., and E. R. CARSON (1993). *Dealing with Complexity,* 2nd edn., Plenum Press, New York, NY.

KHISTY, C. J., and B. K. LALL (1998). *Transportation Engineering: An Introduction,* Prentice Hall, Upper Saddle River, NJ.

MEREDITH, D. D., K. W. WONG, R. W. WOODHEAD, and R. H. WORTMAN (1985). *Design and Planning of Engineering Systems,* 2nd edn., Prentice Hall, Englewood Cliffs, NJ.

EXERCISES

1. Suppose you were discussing the flooding of a part of your neighborhood with a scientist. How would you convince him/her that the systems approach was more practical to use as opposed to the scientific method?

2. A major road underpass near your neighborhood suffers from occasional floods all year round, blocking traffic. Set up sample goals, objectives, alternatives, measures of effectiveness, and measures of cost, and then draw up conclusions as to what should be done to alleviate the problem.

3. The intersection of Pine Street and Oak Street is currently controlled by stop signs. Unfortunately, it has a high accident rate (2 fatalities/year and 5 minor accidents/month). Due to the high flow of traffic there is considerable delay during the morning and evening peak-hours. How would you go about examining this intersection from a systems point of view?

4. By now, you have probably taken several courses in mathematics, science, and engineering in your university. Pick a course of your choice, and set it into the five components suggested by Churchman. Ask questions such as: what were the goals and objectives of the course, what was the major activity in the class, what did you accomplish, what was the overall outcome and so on.

5. Suppose you have taken up a good summer job in a large-sized city and have rented an apartment 10 miles from downtown where your office is located. If you have the following options: to drive your own car, car-pool with a friend, take the local bus, ride the subway, or take the light-rail system each day, how would you rationalize your choice so as to minimize your expenses and maximize your utility, using the systems approach?

6. Consider the following systems: (a) a hospital; (b) a truck; (c) a domestic washer and drier. In each case indicate the inputs and outputs associated with each of these systems.

7. A brand new hybrid "electric" car, capable of running on gasoline and electric batteries, is being exhibited in a showroom. At any one time, several hundreds of spectators are critically looking at this car, and these include prospective car-owners, car salesmen, car mechanics, gasoline station owners, environmentalists, transport engineers, and city planners. How will each of these people view the car from their point-of-view, with regards to (a) complexity; (b) sales; (c) saving the planet from pollution and (d) profit-making.

8. Draw an organizational chart of the university you are currently attending, indicating the hierarchy and control of the various components, such as the president, deans, professors, office staff, etc. Do you think this is a feed-forward or feed-back system, or is it a combination of both?

9. Which of the following systems appear to you to be feed-forward or feed-back systems? Some may be combinations of both. Sketch diagrams of these systems showing the inputs, outputs, and feed-back: (a) a saving-bank account; (b) stock-market prices; (c) your decision to buy a bicycle; (d) to live on a budget fixed by your parents.

10. In what ways do you expect systems thinking will help you to manage your own life? Draw a sketch of this expectation, making use of ideas taken from Figure 1.5.

2
Problem Solving and Designing in Engineering and Planning

2.1 INTRODUCTION

The last chapter sketched a broad-brush picture of the general nature of systems engineering. In this chapter, we continue to elaborate and expand on some of the topics we introduced. First, we want to find out the nature of the problems encountered in engineering and the various styles that engineers use to tackle them. Next, we critically examine the nature of measurement and data that ultimately affects the models we put to use. This is followed by examining the modeling procedures widely employed by engineers in designing their products. As with any discipline there are a lot of basic definitions that have evolved during the course of the development of systems engineering, and these are explained as the chapter progresses. Keep in mind that we will be coming back to this chapter as we work through the rest of this book.

2.2 PROBLEM SOLVING AND DESIGNING

We confront problems almost every day of our lives, some trivial, others a little more complicated, and a few that are truly formidable. But, what do all problems have in common? Krick (1969) says that a *problem* arises from the desire to achieve a transformation from one state to another. Thorndike's (1931) definition is in some ways quite similar. He says that a problem exists if a system wants something but the actions or solutions necessary to obtain it are not immediately obvious. The task is to *define the problem* and, once this is done, the next step naturally is to solve the problem. *Problem solving* is often described as a search through a vast maze that describes the environment of possibilities. Successful problem solving involves searching the maze selectively and reducing it to manageable proportions (Simon, 1981). For example, if we were given a comparatively simple puzzle as shown below, and asked to find out the numerical values of the letters, to satisfy the addition of "cross" and "roads" given just one single clue that S = 3, how would we go about solving this "alphametic"?

$$+ \text{CROSS}$$
$$+\text{ROADS}$$
$$\text{DANGER}$$

By trial and error we will find that the puzzle works out to be

$$96233$$
$$+ \ 62513$$
$$158746$$

where $A = 5, C = 9, D = 1, E = 4, G = 7, N = 8, O = 2$, and $R = 6$.

What we did in solving this alphametic problem was to conduct a *search* to explore a space of potential and partial solutions. Crossword puzzles are very similar. Exploring a maze, for example, is also a process of problem solving; there is a starting point and a destination (or goal) in mind, while the intersections of passages are solution options or states. Some rational process is needed to get to the goal.

How do we solve such problems? How much time does it take to do it? What are the alternative ways of representing the environment and conducting the search? Does the solution represent the final solution or could there be other possibilities? There are no definite answers to these questions because the knowledge base and experience of each individual problem-solver is so different, and our rationalities and capabilities to solve problems are so limited. Attention has been drawn to our short-term memories by George Miller's (1956) celebrated paper on "The Magical Number Seven, Plus or Minus Two" (*Psychological Review*, 63: 81–97). The facts that emerge from a series of experiments conducted by psychologists is that our short-term memory only permits us to remember about seven bits of information at a time. For example, if we are not interrupted in any way, most of us can possibly remember a string of about seven random numbers (and at the most nine) from a directory to the time we ring up a telephone!

Problem solving implies a concerted effort at searching for a solution. *Designing* on the other hand is concerned with *how things ought to be*—how they ought to be in order to attain goals, and to function efficiently. In other words, designing is considered as a problem-solving process of searching through a state space, where the states represent design solutions (Simon, 1981). This state space may be highly complex and huge; complex in that there may be many intricate relationships between the states, and huge in the sense that there may be a plethora of states, far beyond our comprehension. Problem solving is an *analytical* activity connected with science; *designing* is a *synthetic* skill directly connected with engineering and the artificial (or man-made) world. Remember that natural science is concerned solely with how things are, and is therefore *descriptive*, while engineering by and large is *normative*, connected with goals and *"what ought to be."*

Designing is a fundamental, purposeful human activity, and designers who work on designs are the *change agents* within society whose overall goal is to improve the human condition through physical, economic, and social change. More specifically, the design process can be described as a goal-directed activity that involves the making of decisions by satisfying a set of performance requirements and constraints. For example, if an engineer is asked to design a crane that has the capacity to lift 20 tons of load, and with a budget not to exceed $50,000, she would have to utilize her knowledge of mathematics, engineering, economics, and systems to design this lifting device (Coyne et al., 1990).

Numerous models of the design process have evolved in the past fifty years, but the one that has had general acceptance is one suggested by Asimow (1962), consisting of three phases: *analysis, synthesis,* and *evaluation,* as shown in Figure 2.1.

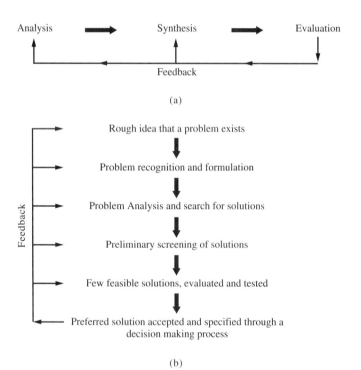

Figure 2.1   Staged process of problem solving and design.

The first phase is one of understanding the problem and of setting goals and objectives. More specifically, the tasks in this phase would be to diagnose, define, and prepare all the preliminaries to really understand the problem and match them with goals. The second phase consists of finding a variety of possible solutions that are acceptable in light of the goals set forth in phase one. The third phase consists of evaluating the validity of each of the solutions proposed in phase two, and selecting an alternative solution (or a combination of solutions, if that is feasible) that satisfies the goals proposed in phase one. This procedure is reiterated as many times as necessary to revise and improve the analysis and synthesis phases, through a feedback process, and represents the basis of a framework for understanding, formulating, analyzing, searching, designing, synthesizing, comparing, selecting, evaluating, and finally deciding on a course of action, subject to budget restraints, political acceptance, social conditions, or other conditions set forth by the decision maker, who may or may not be the design engineer or the chief executive officer.

The systems approach, as we have seen before, is a decision-making process for designing systems. Because we have many alternatives to choose from, decision making is the act of deliberately choosing a course of action for making a choice. Generally, the act of decision making is an iterative process which is characteristic in problem solving, and this is obvious if we examine Figure 1.1 in Chapter 1.

2.3 HIERARCHY: PROBLEM-SPACE, TREES, AND SEMI-LATTICES

As we have repeatedly said, engineering systems are generally highly complex and it is customary that they are broken down into smaller sub-systems to understand them. The nesting of systems and their sub-systems is referred to as hierarchy (Schoderbeck, 1971). But, hierarchy is much more than a concept. It implies a framework that permits complex systems to be built from simpler ones, or for complex systems to be broken down into their component parts. Hierarchy helps us to organize, understand, communicate, and learn about the system and its sub-systems. Given a hierarchy of systems, it is possible to sort out and arrange their corresponding goals and objectives, in which case a system of priorities (or a weighted function) of high- or low-level objectives could be established (van Gigch, 1974).

For example, if we wanted to examine the choices we have in travelling from our home to downtown, we could sketch a diagram drawn in the shape of a tree, indicating the time, the mode of travel, and the routes that are open for us to travel (Rowe, 1987). In fact, this diagram (see Figure 2.2) is a kind of decision tree, which we could possibly use in choosing the way we would like to travel. This tree diagram indicates a problem space. It is an abstract domain containing elements that represent knowledge states to the problem under consideration. It is represented by nodes for decision points and branches for courses of action. In the case of our decision tree, we have decided to go to work during the peak-period driving our car along route 2, although we have many other options to choose from. This choice is indicated by the double lines on Figure 2.2.

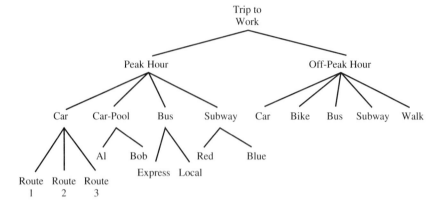

Figure 2.2 A decision tree of travel choices.

However, our traditional emphasis of depicting our ideas and choices in the form of trees is not always realistic. When there are overlaps in choices, the use of semi-lattices becomes necessary. The reality of the social structure of cities, for instance, is replete with overlaps. Take for example, the conflict between vehicles and pedestrian movement in any busy downtown. You have cars, buses, trucks, and delivery vans competing with pedestrians and bicyclists for movement and parking. Notice the interaction between taxis and pedestrians and between parking and motor vehicles, shown in Figure 2.3.

Even a system of friends and acquaintances can be represented by a semi-lattice as shown in Figure 2.4. Consider six persons, Al, Bob, Chris, Dave, Ed, and Fred, represented by the letters A, B, C, D, E, and F. Their relationships are as follows: C and D are regular chess partners, D and E play tennis together on weekends, A, B, and C ski together during the winter months, B, C, and D regularly jog every morning during the summers, A, B, C, D, and E sing in a choir during the Christmas season, and all six belong to the same country club. These relations are shown in Figure 2.4, in the form of a semi-lattice. In the corresponding Venn diagram, each set chosen to be a unit has a line drawn round it. One can see right away how much more complex a semi-lattice can be as compared to a tree. Alexander (1966) says that a tree based on twenty

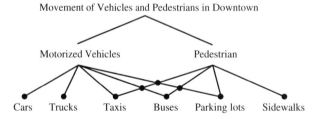

Figure 2.3 Pedestrian/vehicle movement overlap.

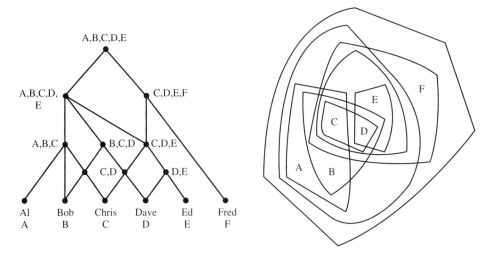

Figure 2.4   (a) Semi-lattice structure of six friends. (b) Venn diagram.

elements can contain at most nineteen further subsets of the twenty, while a semi-lattice based on the same twenty elements can contain more than a million different subsets!

Hierarchical systems and their organizations reveal an important phenomenon that can be summarized in a nutshell: *the whole is greater than the sum of its parts.* What this means is that systems have *emergent* properties. For example, a human being is not the sum of his bodily parts; neither is a society a sum of its groups members. Engineers with their mathematical training tend to believe in mathematical rigor and are reluctant to readily believe in this property, but we all know that the chemical combination of hydrogen and oxygen (which are gases) produces water which is a liquid, having no correspondence with the elements that go to form it. Emergent characteristics of organizations have provided us with the term *synergy* to describe the emergence of unexpected benefits to management through group work. These benefits are not always assured; sometimes there might be disbenefits attached to well-intentioned emergence.

This is a good place to look at the meaning of system complexity. One of the simplest ways of understanding complexity is to study the number of elements and the number of relationships between the elements. When the number of parts and their possible relationships grow the effect can be devastating as shown in the Figure 2.5. Here, "e" represents the number of elements, "r" their relationships, and "s" the states (Flood and Carson, 1993). Using the formula 2^e, s grows rapidly as e increases.

2.4 PROBLEM SOLVING STYLES

Problem-solving styles can be conveniently divided into three categories: trial-and-error, generate-and-test, and means-ends analysis. The *trial-and-error procedure* involves finding a solution to a problem in a random manner, although in most

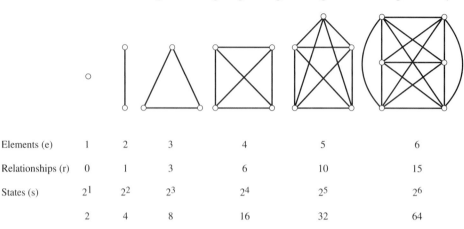

Elements (e)	1	2	3	4	5	6
Relationships (r)	0	1	3	6	10	15
States (s)	2^1	2^2	2^3	2^4	2^5	2^6
	2	4	8	16	32	64

Figure 2.5   Elements, relationships, and states as a measure of complexity.

instances there is some sort of bounding or narrowing down of the strategies that are being examined by the problem-solver. Naturally, some tacit methods (involving intuition) may be used to evaluate solutions, but successive trials are made more or less independently of the results of intermediate tests. Notice that feedback is at best minimal. An example of the trial-and-error style of problem solving is playing with a jigsaw puzzle, without knowing what the true picture looks like. Another example is the exercise of arranging two dozen pieces of furniture in a house with a floor area of 2000 sq.ft., to satisfy some general criteria. In both these cases, one could generate hundreds of candidate solutions by arranging and rearranging the pieces of the puzzle in a fashion that approximates the criteria prescribed, until some acceptable arrangement emerges. This approach is often referred to as the black box approach to which we have referred to in Chapter 1 (Meredith et al., 1985).

The *generate-and-test approach* is not enormously elaborate compared to the trial-and-error procedure. However, its distinguishing feature is that it makes use of information regarding prior trials as the basis for directing further searches for an acceptable solution. This exercise of incrementally moving from worse to better solutions could be conceived as "hill climbing," where the top of the hill is considered as the "best" solution (Rowe, 1987). Figure 2.6 shows how the feedback mechanism operates in the case of the generate-and-test procedure (van Gigch, 1974). In order for a designer to determine if an error exists between what she is doing and what is needed to meet the goal, she must monitor her own activities by feeding back a portion of her designed output for comparison with her input. If the feedback tends to reduce error, rather than aggravate it, the feedback is called *"negative feedback"*—negative because it tends to oppose what the designer is doing.

Figure 2.6 shows two methods: (a) an open-loop control, and (b) a closed-loop control, where the output O(t) is a function of the input I(t), and the value of the multiplier K depends on the system's characteristics. Thus, K = O(t)/I(t). In an

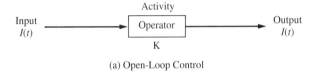

(a) Open-Loop Control

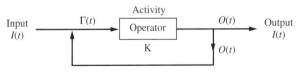

Figure 2.6   Open-loop and Closed-loop
Control.

(b) Closed-Loop Control and Feed back

open-loop system, with a positive multiplier K, the output increases in relation to the input, but there is no possibility for the system to correct itself. Naturally, such systems have to be very carefully designed to start with. With a closed-loop control one can attain much greater reliability because the feedback serves as a self-correcting mechanism. Here $I'(t) = I(t) - O(t)$ and $K' = K/(1 + K)$. When $K' < 1$, we define this condition as negative feedback, which makes $O(t) < I(t)$, and this means the output decreases with an increase in $I(t)$, thus providing the necessary self-correction. With positive feedback, $K' > 1$, which makes $O(t) > I(t)$, and this causes $I(t)$ to increase progressively with each iteration, leading eventually to instability. In actual practice the feedback is achieved by using only a small fraction of the output Δt or using the difference between the standard desired $S(t)$ and the output $O(t)$ as the feedback, $\Delta t = S(t) - O(t)$ (van Gigch, 1974).

Means-ends analysis is, in a way, an extension of the generate-and-test procedure, particularly for examining alternative decision rules for different problem-solving situations. Remember that the "means" of achieving an "end" is really the technology or mechanism of attaining a goal. The question, then, is how do we utilize the means to achieve the goal? There are three essential components associated with this analysis: a prescribed set of actions (means or technology), a prescribed set of goals (or ends), and a set of decision rules (Rowe, 1987). In the case of a reasonably well-defined problem where the goals and the technology are known and proven, means-ends analysis is most effective, particularly when an organizing principle is selected and applied under conditions of constancy. For instance, if an engineer wants to replace a stop sign at a busy intersection with a signaling device, all he has to do is determine the traffic volumes on the approaches, together with the nature and frequency of the accidents at this intersection, and if these records indicate that they exceed those prescribed by law or warrant, he can without much further investigation go ahead and make the necessary changes. Notice that he has a goal, and the necessary technology, together with the prescribed law to implement the change. This is a typical case of a *"tame problem"*, because it is simple and there is hardly any ambiguity attached to the problem or its solution. However, few, if any, engineering problems are as tidy

Ends Means	Goals and Objectives	
	Certain	Uncertain
Certain	A Computation	C Compromise
Uncertain	B Judgement	D Chaos or "Inspiration"

Figure 2.7   Means/Ends Configuration.

and simple as this one. Indeed, most engineering and planning problems would fall into categories where the means as well as the ends are nebulous and fuzzy, in which case the engineer will have to resort to judgement, negotiation, and compromise, as shown in Figure 2.7. The problems encountered in cells B, C, and D of this matrix fall under the category of *"wicked problems"* which will be described a little later in this chapter. Dealing with situations located in cell D is particularly problematic, and these will be examined in subsequent chapters, particularly under soft systems analysis in Chapter 12 (Khisty, 1992).

Heuristic reasoning is often used in *generate-and-test* as well as in *means-ends analysis*. Basically, a *heuristic* is any principle, procedure, or other device that contributes to reduction in the search for a satisfactory solution. It could be considered as a "rule-of-thumb" that often helps in solving a certain class of problems, but does not guarantee a solution. Consequently, heuristic reasoning involves a decision-making process in which we do not know whether we actually have a solution until the line of reasoning is completed, or all the steps are carried out (Rowe, 1987).

Ackoff (1986) suggests that there are at least four ways of treating problems that we encounter on a day-to-day basis. We can "absolve" a problem by simply ignoring that it exists or by imagining (and probably believing) that it will eventually disappear. People suffering from minor illnesses usually believe that eventually the problem will disappear. We can also "resolve" a problem by taking appropriate action, based on our experience and common sense, combined with our quantitative and qualitative expertise. Such a resolution results in the removal or suppression of the problem. Another way of tackling a problem is to work out an outcome that will "optimize" the result, through experimentation or through analytical means. Quite another way of dealing with a problem is by "dissolving" it. One way of doing this is by redesigning the system containing the problem.

Consider the following situation as an example of tackling problems using Ackoff's thinking: A small taxi company rented out its vehicles to drivers on a daily basis but found that the vehicles were abused and misused, resulting in heavy losses to the company. In the early months of running the system, the managers ignored the losses, thinking that in due course the situation would improve. Unfortunately, the damage to the vehicles steadily increased. As a first step, management tried to resolve the problem by asking drivers to pay for all the damages they incurred. But this resulted in the company losing money because drivers were reluctant to rent vehicles from the company. Management tried to solve the problem by asking drivers to share the "damage expenses" on a 50/50 basis. While this strategy worked for some time, it eventually got out of hand with the company over-estimating the share from the drivers (because the recovery included depreciation of the vehicles). Drivers stopped renting and management lost money. Finally, the company and the drivers came to an agreement that saved the situation. The company redesigned the rental system. Instead of renting cars on a daily basis, the company rented their vehicles on a monthly or 3-monthly basis, with the agreement that damages to the vehicles would be assessed by an independent party. Thus, the problem was eventually dissolved.

2.5 WICKED PROBLEMS

Attention has been drawn to wicked problems in the previous section. Most engineering and planning problems are really wicked problems as opposed to tame problems, where the ends or goals are already prescribed and apparent. A common example of a tame problem is the solution of a quadratic equation. The solution requires application of the rules of algebra to the specific structure that is given. In the case of wicked problems, both the ends and the means of solution are unknown at the outset of the problem solving exercise. Rittel and Weber (1993) have characterized wicked problems as follows: 1) There is typically no definite formulation of a wicked problem; additional questions can always be asked, leading to continual reformulation; 2) wicked problems have no stopping rule, and one usually ends up by saying, "That's good enough"; 3) solutions to wicked problems are neither true or false, but just good or bad. For example, there is no such thing as a true or false plan of a house, just good or bad; 4) the solution to a wicked problem has no immediate or ultimate test; 5) every wicked problem is a "one-shot" operation; 6) wicked problems do not have an exhaustive set of potential solutions; 7) every wicked problem is essentially unique; and 8) every wicked problem can be considered a symptom of another wicked problem.

The problem of uncertainty is embedded in all wicked problems along with the problem of human rationality. More than forty years ago Simon (1957) developed the theory of *"bounded rationality and unbounded uncertainty"* to describe rational choice of alternatives, taking into account the cognitive limits of the designer and the decision maker. This means that, while the choices are technically rational, they are nevertheless bounded by practical circumstances. In contrast to "maximizing" behavior, Simon proposed the concept of "satisficing" behavior, because the human mind does not have the capability of choosing from hundreds of alternatives that might be placed in front of him. Problems connected with rationality and uncertainty seem to enter the designing and planning process at every turn in the means-ends configuration.

2.6 MEASUREMENT AND SCALING

2.6.1 Sources of Data

Before we can even make a preliminary examination of a problem situation, we need to have some basic data. Sources of data can generally be classified as obtrusive or unobtrusive. Obtrusive data-collection methods refer to procedures in which data are collected through some form of direct solicitation in which the researcher is directly or indirectly involved, such as face-to-face interviews, questionnaires, and many forms of observations. Unobtrusive methods of data collection are procedures that remove the investigator from the phenomenon being researched, such as through newspaper accounts, minutes of a meeting, and data banks. Huge data banks have been set up by the government and industries devoted to the collections of information for quantifying basic social indicators, such as population, economic status of various sectors of society, and so on (Tarrants, 1980).

2.6.2 Measurement

Ultimately, all data must be subjected to some form of analysis. One way of doing this is through measurement. Measuring is a process that involves the assignment of numerals to objects or events according to rules, or the assignment of numerals to properties. Measurements can serve as models of events and relationships existing in the real world. The purpose of measurement is to represent the characteristics of observations by symbols that are related to each other in the same way that observed objects, events, or properties are related. However, it is important to remember that the real world is never exactly described by any mathematical measurement or model. All such descriptions are only approximations. Measurement is essentially required for control and prediction and is primarily a descriptive process. It allows one to qualify, order, and quantify certain events and ultimately use the results as a basis for control and prediction of actual performance.

While measurement in the scientific arena has progressed much further than one encounters in the behavioral sciences, there is a wide range in the degree of accuracy possible in both fields. Measurement in any case is subject to error, and an estimate of the magnitude of this error is necessary in order to determine whether or not the measurements obtained are usable in a practical situation. There are several possible sources of error in measurement, and these are through: 1) the observer, 2) the instrument used for measurement, 3) the environment, and 4) the object or situation being measured. Accuracy is the measure of the degree to which a given measurement may deviate from what really exists. In our study of measurements, we strive to observe data by means of refined techniques and to employ careful analysis so that we may be reasonably assured a degree of accuracy in our results. The principles underlying our methods are part of the study of mathematical probability and statistics, described in Chapters 5 through 9.

Almost without exception, we need to have solid and reliable data to work with. Fortunately, we appear to have an abundance of data, so much so that we are literally drowning in an overload of information. But data and information do not by themselves provide us with greater insight. Data really provides us with facts of the real world, which in turn must be sorted out to give us focused data for specific problems. Information is needed for problem solving. Our knowledge-base built on our experience and technical know-how is what is ultimately needed for making rational judgements and decisions. Coupled with our knowledge-base we need to have intelligence, which is the ability to deal with novel situations arising in our day-to-day engineering practice (Khisty and Khisty, 1998).

2.6.3 Scales of Measurement

Scales of measurement are used practically on a daily basis by distinguishing among objects and responding appropriately to them. In engineering, it is desirable to make distinctions of degree rather than quality. Four types of measurement scales are in general use: Nominal, ordinal, interval, and ratio, and these are described below (Patton and Sawicki, 1995).

1. *Nominal Data:* is data classified into exhaustive, mutually exclusive, but not into ordered categories. Individual items like football players or car models are placed in a number of categories. For example, we can describe football players as # 29, 45, 63 ... , or car models as Fords, Toyotas, or Buicks. Or we can sort things by means of symbols; by assigning numbers it is possible to classify a given population into males and females, with 1 = males and 2 = females. This scale contains the least information since it concerns only the allocation of a label or name. A special kind of nominal scale is the binary scale, which can express a partial order, such as yes/no. Also, if items or objects are compared pair-wise, a binary scale can be used to denote whether an item is better/worse or larger/smaller than other items.

2. *Ordinal Data:* is data classified into exhaustive, mutually exclusive, and ordered categories. Although it is qualitative, the ordinal scale contains the most information since the numbers in this scale give a rank order. For example, ranking of students can be done in many ways, but one particular example would be as shown below:

```
Students        A   B   C   D   E   F
Rank in Math    4   3   1   6   2   5
```

3. *Interval Data:* is data classified on a scale, which permits them to be measured exactly, using generally accepted units of measurements. This is truly a quantitative scale, but the origin is neither known nor defined, but the intervals are the same. Some statistical tests, such as an F-test or t-test (described in later chapters) can be applied. For example:

```
Room Temperature (degrees F)    30    40    50    60
```

Properties such as height, temperature, time, income, intelligence quotient, and air pollution are measured with the help of interval scales. Again, thermal measurement is a good example. Here the choice of zero is arbitrary; and the equally spaced intervals do not have comparable magnitude (e.g., 30 degrees Fahrenheit is not twice as hot as 15 degree Fahrenheit).

4. *Ratio Data:* is data classified on a scale that permits them to be measured exactly using generally accepted units of measurements, and which includes a non-arbitrary zero point. In this scale, the origin (for example "zero") in a temperature scale is known or defined.

```
Temperature (degrees C)    −40    −20    0    20    40    60
```

5. *Comparative Data:* is commonly used in evaluation forms, for example on test scores:

```
Top 1%    5%    10%    25%    of the class
```

6. *Attitude Data.* There are several standardized techniques commonly used to develop scales or indices. Lickert scales provide a selection of five categories of response for each item: strongly approve, approve, undecided, disapprove, and strongly disapprove. These are ranked from 1 to 5, respectively, and the ranked items are then summed to obtain an individual score for each item. Although Lickert scales are generally used for measuring attitudes, variations of the technique may be applied to behavioral measurement, such as regularly, frequently, sometimes, rarely, or never (Dickey and Watts, 1978). Semantic differential scaling technique is another method used in attitude surveys. It consists of two polar adjectives, such as good-bad, and positive-negative, with ratings depending on the breadth of response desired, but usually 0 to 5 or 7 or 10. The respondent's score is calculated by summing the ratings of all evaluated items.

We can demonstrate how these different scales are used through a simple example. Let us consider three cities A, B, and C, with populations of 50, 25, and 90 thousand respectively. Table 2.1 below indicates how the scales are used, while Table 2.2 provides some of their more important characteristics.

TABLE 2.1   EXAMPLES OF VARIOUS SCALES AND THEIR APPLICATIONS

Scale			Example	Comments
Nominal	A	B	C	Cities
Ratio	50K	25K	90K	Population on 1/1/99
Binary	1	0	1	$0 = \; < 40K \; 1 = \; > 40K$
Ordinal	2	1	3	Rank by population
Interval		$A - B = 25K$	$A - C = 40K$	Differences in population

TABLE 2.2   SCALES OF MEASUREMENT (ADAPTED FROM CHURCHILL, G. A., MARKETING RESEARCH, DRYDEN PRESS, HINSDALE, IL, 1979)

Scale	Comparisons	Typical Example	Measure	Tests
Nominal	Identity	Male-female, Black-white	Mode	Chi-square
Ordinal space or Order	Order	Social class, Graded quality	Median	Rank-order
Interval	Comparison of intervals	Temperature scale, Grade-point-average	Mean	t-test ANOVA
Ratio	Comparison of absolute magnitudes	Units sold, Number of buyers	Geometric or harmonic mean	same as interval

In summary, a nominal scale provides a set of names, categories, classes, groups, qualities, and general responses. An ordinal scale consists of objects in particular order or rank. An interval scale is a set of numbers having a given, fixed interval size, but no absolute zero point. Lastly, a ratio scale consists of a set of numbers having a given, fixed interval size and an absolute zero point.

We will be returning to the subject of measurement when we work on topics dealing with Probability and Statistics, and these are covered in Chapters 5 through 9 of this text.

2.7 SYSTEM MODEL TYPES AND MODEL-BUILDING

This section describes system models in general and provides some clues regarding how they are used in everyday applications. Some of the more familiar models used in engineering are taken up first and then the modeling approaches that we will study in future chapters are described.

2.7.1 Model Types

There are so many varieties of models used in engineering and planning that any kind of description would always leave out some that should have been included. We will start with the simplest and then proceed toward the more sophisticated ones (Krick, 1969).

Descriptive Models.   These models are used to present detailed specifications of what needs to be accomplished for a project, plan, or design. It is a concise description of a problem situation, which provides the framework for problem solution.

Iconic, Graphic, and Diagrammatic Models.   We have all played at some time in our lives with toy trains, airplanes, dolls, teddy-bears, and other three-dimensional representations of physical objects. These are Iconic models. Even photographs, graphs, maps, pictures, blue-prints, and diagrams, which are in some cases two-dimensional representations of three-dimensional objects, fall under the category of Iconic models. In more recent years the use of "rich pictures" has become quite common. They help to capture subjective interpretation of messy, complicated situations. Rich pictures represent and summarize findings and ideas, mostly in pictures and in words. They have been very successful in representing ideas and processes in soft system methodology. An example of a rich picture is shown in Chapter 12.

Analogue Models.   These models represent a set of relationships through a different, but analogous, medium. A car's speedometer, for example, represents speed by analogous displacement of a gauge. Hydraulic engineers have used an analogue computer to represent the behavior of a water distribution system for a city with great success.

Mathematical or Symbolic Models.   We have all used mathematical models without knowing what they are. When we write down the equation of a straight line as $Y = AX + B$, we are making use of a mathematical model. Mathematical equations provide a repertory of ready-made representations. These representations are an effective means for predicting, communicating, reasoning, describing, and explaining our understanding of all kinds of relationships in concise language.

Decision Models.   Many of the mathematical and symbolic models described above are used to achieve a particular objective or purpose. For instance, if we want to fly from New York to Istanbul, we can choose from at least fifteen options of reliable airlines that offer such service, with about thirty different departure and arrival times between these two cities, coupled with offers of stop-overs in London or Frankfurt or Paris. But one of our main considerations is to get the lowest fare, with the best service. There are of course other considerations, such as, which airline offers the best frequent mileage option. How will we come to a decision about the choice of an airline? This book emphasizes decision models and other models that are needed to help unravel the mysteries of decision models. An important role in such model building is to specify how the decision variables will affect the measures of effectiveness and the measures of cost. In my problem of choosing the "best" airline, I could specify my decision variables and match them with my decision objectives.

In addition to classifying models as we have done above, there is another way of slicing the cake. This classification is through considering models as deterministic or probabilistic. Deterministic models are those where all of the relevant data are assumed to be known with certainty. For instance, if we wanted to build a house and were provided with the construction schedule for each of the twenty-five major tasks needed to complete the house, along with the manpower and budget ahead of time, we would be able to tell with some degree of certainty when the house would be complete. This type of deterministic model is widely used adopting the Critical Path Method (CPM) described in Chapter 10, along with other models belonging to this category, such as the use of linear programming. Many of them are optimization models that help us to figure out how we could possibly minimize the cost or maximize the output.

Probabilistic (or stochastic) models on the other hand assume that the decision maker will not know the values of some of the variables with any degree of certainty. For instance, if we did not know with any precision the exact time needed to complete some or all the twenty-five tasks that went into constructing the house we want to build, we would have to modify the CPM model and resort to a somewhat more sophisticated method called Program Evaluation and Review Technique (PERT) to assess the probable time of completion. PERT takes into consideration the probability of completing each task in a specified time by specifying limits on the time needed for each task. These limitations modify the original CPM into a more realistic model of the real world. Notice that the degree of certainty/uncertainty is crucial in working with probabilistic decision making. Models under this general category are widely used in engineering and planning, and can be further classified according to: 1) decisions under risk, where each state of nature has a known objective probability; 2) decision under uncertainty, where each action can result in two or more outcomes, but the probabilities of the states of nature are unknown; and 3) decision under conflict, where courses of action are taken against an opponent who is trying to maximize his/her goal. Decisions made under conflict fall under the area of inquiry called "game theory."

2.7.2 Models Used in Planning and Engineering

We have already noticed that there are differences between models in science and models in planning and engineering. We also noted that the models we encounter in science are closely connected with the natural world, while those we deal with in engineering are with the artificial (or man-made) world. Besides these two major distinctions there is yet a third difference, in that science tends to generate models to

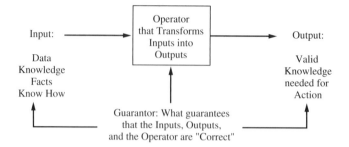

Figure 2.8   An Inquiry System. (Adapted from Mitroff and Linstone, 1993.)

understand the world *as it is,* whereas the goal of engineering is to construct models that will help us to deal with situations *as they ought to be.* This preoccupation of engineering with what ought to be is achieved through the process of analysis, synthesis, and evaluation.

To put in perspective what we have learned so far, let us take up the basic input/output model connected by means of a "black-box." A simple depiction of this system, termed as an Inquiry System (IS) is shown in Figure 2.8. An IS is a system of interrelated components for producing knowledge on a problem or issue (Mitroff and Linstone, 1993). The inputs are the basic entities that come into a system from the real world in the form of data and information and form the valid starting point of the inquiry. Next, the IS employs different kinds of operators (or models). These operators use the basic inputs to transform them into the final output of the system. One can use any number of operators to churn out the output, ranging from heuristic methods to highly sophisticated mathematics, to produce the output or result. But the most important component of this system is the guarantor—the component guaranteeing the operation of the entire system. It literally influences everything that goes on in the model.

Let us take up a very simple problem: A clever community fund-raiser collects donations on the basis that each successive contributor will contribute 1/20 of the total sum already collected to date. The fund-raiser herself makes the first contribution of $100. How many contributors does she need to cross the $1 million target? This is a bounded and well-structured problem, without any ambiguity. We can consult a standard textbook on capital budgeting (or look up Chapter 3 of this book) giving a formula for compound interest calculations, giving an output of $n = 189$. It is easy to see what the input is, and what is in the black box and how we can be assured that the answer is right. The guarantor is the formula given in the textbook on capital budgeting. We are assured that the answer is right by working the problem backward from the output to the input, via the black box. Not all problems are this simple. For example, if we were asked to define and solve the crime problem of downtown Chicago, we would have to get experts in a score of disciplines just to identify the problem, let alone solve it!

2.8 PROBLEM-SOLVING THROUGH GROUP OR COMMITTEE ACTION

Engineers are often confronted with a complex problem where you can safely say that two heads or more are better than one. In such cases, there are many advantages of using individual experts and consultants, and groups of individuals that can work on a wide variety of problem situations using their collective store of information, intelligence, and wisdom. As we have seen before, the emergent properties of group decisions can result in spectacular outcomes. Two such methods are described here, "brainstorming" and the "Delphi" method.

Brainstorming.   It has been realized that ideas and inventions have often started from different points and yet reached similar results. While chance and accident often seem to have played an important part in discovery, so too have brilliant and disciplined thinking and a persistence amounting to obsession. There is a school of thought that believes that a vast accumulation of imperfect ideas and information is always lying dormant, lacking only some element to bring them to life. The advantage of collaborations of scientists, engineers, and lay people sitting together for creative thinking or for a "brainstorming session" was soon realized and has been used quite extensively all over the world.

Usually a group gathers together, examines a problem, and "fires off" the first ideas that come to mind. All criticism, both by word or implication, is ruled out. The wilder the ideas that emerge, the better, the aim being to get as many varied ideas as possible, and to build upon and improve the responses. The result of the session is a mass of ideas, most of them admittedly quite impractical, but a few worthy of closer attention. It is these few ideas that are likely to produce a "bunch of keys" for solving the problem that would not have been achieved by the exclusive use of conventional methods. There are no standard practices prescribed, but experience has indicated that great attention has to be paid to the selection and composition of the team, the presentation of the problem, an atmosphere of openness without the least hint of criticism, the recording process, which needs to be as unobtrusive as possible, and finally the assessment of ideas (Khisty, 1968).

The "Delphi" Method.   It is claimed that the Greek Oracle of Delphi was capable of coming up with forecasts of important future events based on the analysis of such things as the entrails of birds and animals. Of course, such forecasts could be interpreted in several different ways, some of them quite ridiculous and contradictory. But only the "experts" (who were gifted with special powers) were able to come to any kind of agreement about the interpretations.

While there are several advantages of several people from various disciplines sitting together in a brainstorming session trying to tackle a problem, the founders of the "Delphi" method at the Rand Corporation felt that a dynamic procedure for coming to a consensus regarding a problem solution through the use of questionnaires given to experts in the area of inquiry would be fruitful. The use of Delphi is not limited to consensus building, but rather on seeking relevant parameters for models of reality (what is) as well as on "what ought to be" or "what is possible." In some ways, the Delphi resembles a jury system with several characteristics worth noting. First, during a Delphi sequence there is total anonymity, and responses are handled through well-worded questionnaires. Second, the committee chairperson extracts from the responses only that information relevant to the issue and presents them to the committee. Third, a collective statistical summary is refed to the experts for another round of responses, and such feedback and further responses continue for as many rounds as it takes to reach some kind of consensus.

When viewed as a communication process for problem solving, there are few areas of human endeavor that do not qualify as candidates for the application of Delphi. For example, apart from the usual forecasting applications, Delphi has been widely used for evaluating budget allocation for projects, exploring various urban and regional planning options, putting together the structure of a complicated economic model, exploring social and economic goals and prioritizing them, and the list goes on (Dickey and Watts, 1978). We will examine the Delphi process through a simple real-world example.

Example 2.1

Four construction management experts were asked to estimate the duration for completing a complex reconstruction repair to a hydroelectric plant. Their responses (after thorough detailed calculations) are provided below. Each expert was provided with the same information and data. Their individual responses were confidential. The only feedback provided after each round was the mean and standard deviation.

		Rounds		
Experts	I	II	III	IV
A	12	11	9	9
B	8	8	9	9
C	7	9	10	9
D	5	7	8	9
Mean	8.00	8.75	9.00	9.00
Standard Deviation	2.55	1.48	0.71	0.00

In four rounds the convergence of the responses from the four experts boiled down to nine months. It was theoretically not necessary that we wanted perfect conformity of answers from these experts. For example, had the committee chairperson specified that the convergence would be acceptable with a standard deviation of 1.00 and the mean was between 8 and 10, then it is possible that the exercise could have ended with just the third round. It is the decision maker who specifies whether the collective result is acceptable or not, and under what conditions.

SUMMARY

This chapter provides an overview of the problem-solving and design process, with special emphasis on their role as tools for engineers and managers. One has to be equiped to deal with "tame" problems and "wicked" problems on a day-to-day basis, and for this reason the need to classify models and what they are capable of doing is all important. This chapter has also dealt with data and information and ways to handle them in a preliminary way. Lastly, a brief description of problem-solving using collective thinking has been included which will prove useful in tackling complex problems needing group opinion.

REFERENCES

ACKOFF, R. (1999). *Ackoff's Best: His Classic Writings on Management,* John Wiley & Sons, Inc., New York, NY. 115 – 6.

ALEXANDER, C. (1966). "A City is not a Tree," *Ekistics* 139, 344 – 348.

CHURCHILL, G. A. (1979). *Marketing Research,* 2nd edn., Dryden Press, Hinsdale, IL.

COYNE, R. D. ET. AL., (1990). *Knowledge-Based Design Systems,* Addison Wesley Publishing Co. New York, NY.

DICKEY, J. W., and T. M. WATTS (1978). *Analytical Techniques in Urban and Regional Planning,* McGraw-Hill Book Co. New York, NY.

FLOOD, R. L., and E. R. CARSON (1993). *Dealing with Complexity,* 2nd edn., Plenum Press, New York, NY.

KHISTY, C. J. (1968). "Brainstorming: A New Technique in solving Problems in Industry," *Engineering News* 16:2, 677 – 679.

KHISTY, C. J. (1993). "Citizen Participation Using a Soft Systems Perspective," in *Transportation Research Record 1400,* National Academy of Science, Washington, DC, 53 – 57.

KHISTY, C. J. and L. L. KHISTY (1998). "Using Information Systems for Mathematical Problem-solving: A New Philosophical Perspective," in *Proceedings of the Psychology of Mathematics Education,* University of Stellenbosch, Stelenbosch, South Africa, 104 – 111.

KRICK, E. V. (1978). *An Introduction to Engineering and Engineering Design,* 2nd edn., John Wiley and Sons, New York, NY.

MERIDITH, D. D. ET. AL., (1985). *Design and Planning of Engineering Systems,* 2nd edn., Prentice Hall, Englewood Cliffs, NJ.

MILLER, G. A. (1956). "The Magic Number Seven, Plus or Minus Two: Some Limits on our Capacity for Processing Information," *Psychological Review* 63:2, 81 – 97.

MITROFF, I. I., and H. A. LINSTONE (1993). *Unbounded Mind,* Oxford University Press, New York, NY.

PATTON, C. V. and D. S. SAWICKI (1993). *Basic Methods of Policy Analysis and Planning,* 2nd edn., Prentice Hall, Englewood Cliffs, NJ.

Rittel, H., and M. Weber (1973). "Dilemmas in General Theory of Planning," *Policy Science,* 4, 155 – 169.

Rowe, P. (1987). *Design Thinking,* MIT Press, Cambridge, MA.

RUBINSTEIN, M. F., and I. R. FIRSTENBERG (1995). *Patterns of Problem Solving,* 2nd edn., Prentice Hall, Englewood Cliffs, NJ.

SCHODERBECK, P. P. (1971). *Management Systems,* 2nd edn., John Wiley, New York, NY.

SIMON, H. A. (1981). *The Sciences of the Artificial,* 2nd edn., MIT Press, Cambridge, MA.

TARRANTS, W. E. (1980). *The Measurement of Safety Performance,* Garland STPM Press, New York, NY.

THORNDIKE, E. L. (1931). *Human Learning,* MIT Press, Cambridge, MA.

VAN GIGCH, J. P. (1974). *Applied General Systems Theory,* Harper Row Publishers, New York, NY.

EXERCISES

1. What is your understanding of the relationship between information, data, models, and design? Illustrate this with the help of a rich picture.

2. Set up a 3 × 3 "magic square," and fill the nine cells with numbers 1 through 9 (without repeating them), such that the rows, columns and diagonals of the matrix add to 15.

3. Recall the names of your friends and set up a semi-lattice diagram of their activities, not forgetting to add yourself to the number, similar to the example illustrated in the text. Draw a Venn diagram to represent the semi-lattice.

4. If you wanted to choose between three or four summer jobs you were offered, indicate by way of a tree or semi-lattice how you would make a final decision?

5. Using the feedback form of a control system, identify the appropriate parts of the following systems:
   (a) driving an automobile along a freeway, adhering to a speed limit of 65 mph;
   (b) controlling an angry mob that is almost going out of control;
   (c) washing clothes in an automatic washing machine.

5. Classify following problem situations according to the means/ends matrix:
   (a) fixing a flat tire on the freeway;
   (b) sitting in a committee meeting where one of the topics on the agenda is to debate the distribution of money for various social activities in your neighborhood;
   (c) sitting in a large committee of experts dealing with the problem of the homeless in downtown.

6. How would you categorize the following situation according to the various measurement scales mentioned in the text:
   (a) technical and economic factors of a city;
   (b) political and social factors of a city;
   (c) the area of land in each square mile of a city having a slope of greater than 20 degrees;
   (d) the number of vehicle-miles of travel performed in a Chicago in 1998;
   (e) military ranks in the army, navy, and airforce;
   (f) ratings of cars in terms of gasoline consumption;
   (g) number of people using the park by day of the week;
   (h) the popularity of the mayor of your city;
   (i) the dollar amount by which the five bids for 10 miles of a highway exceed the estimated amounts.

7. Think of a truly "wicked" problem you have encountered or have read about in the newspapers. Briefly describe the gist of the problem and then apply Rittel and Weber's characteristics to check whether this is truly a wicked problem. (Hint: the crime problem in the inner city could be an example, but there may be better examples that you probably know about.)

8. Suppose your city's bus service has just received funding for expanding the bus lines by 25%. How would you set up a simple optimization model to help the planners to

choose the new routes and/or to modify existing routes? What minimum data would be needed right up front to set the priorities?

9. Suppose you are the student representative serving on the university parking committee with the task of finding the parking demand for students, staff, and faculty for the Year 2015. How would you organize a (a) brainstorming session to resolve this issue; (b) Delphi exercise using four to five experts?

10. Think of a problem you were confronted with and analyze it to demonstrate whether you absolved, or solved, or resolved, or dissolved it. If you went through more than one strategy, give reasons why you did so.

11. A student in an undergraduate engineering program discovers that she is weak in mathematics. Initially, she ignores the poor mid-term grade she gets in math. Two weeks later she decides to attend a crash refresher course to remedy the weakness, but notices that the extra time she is spending with this course is hurting her ability to do well in other courses. Finally, she consults her academic adviser who suggests she reschedule her time to optimize her ability to gain good grades in all her courses. She eventually does much better in the following semester. Analyze and comment on her strategies.

12. In the last decade hospitals have become more automated, employing modern instrumentation and computers to do most of the mechanical and tedious work. What are the advantages and disadvantages of this new trend? Are there obvious dangers of depending too much on modern technology? How would you eliminate these dangers?

3

Basic Engineering Economics and Evaluation

3.1 INTRODUCTION

This chapter is divided into two parts. The first part (Sections 1 through 8) introduces the basic concepts of engineering economics. This consists of a standard set of procedures for determining the relative economic value of alternative capital investments. The second part (Sections 9 through 19) extends these basic concepts and shows how engineers choose the best alternative from a set of several feasible alternatives.

Engineering economics is a branch of economics used by engineers to evaluate their design and construction projects. Project appraisal and cost-benefit analysis require a knowledge of engineering economics. Engineers and planners are concerned with money whether its use or exchange is in the private or public sector. In the language of economics, articles produced, sold, or exchanged are known as goods. At least four sectors of production are necessary to produce a good: labor, land, capital, and enterprise. Capital includes the money, machinery, tools, and materials required to produce a good. The opportunity cost of capital is measured by the interest rate, and the interest on capital is the premium paid or received for the use of money. Here, opportunity cost represents the cost of an opportunity that is foregone because resources are used for a selected alternative and, therefore, cannot be used for other purposes. The interest rate that relates a sum of money at some date to its equivalent today is called the discount rate.

3.2 NOTATION

The following symbols and definitions are used unless otherwise stated.

P = principal, a sum of money invested in the initial year, or a present sum of money.

i = interest rate per unit of time expressed as a decimal.

n = time, the number of units of time over which interest accumulates.

I = simple interest; the total sum of money paid for the use of the money at simple interest.

F = compound amount; a sum of money at the end of n units of time at interest i, made up of the principal plus the interest payable.

A = uniform series end-of-period payment or receipt that extends for n periods.

S = salvage or resale value at the end of n years.

3.3 SIMPLE INTEREST

When one invests money at a simple interest rate of i for a period of n years, the simple interest bears the following relationship:

$$\text{Simple interest } (I) = Pin \qquad\qquad (3.1)$$

The sum, I, will be added on to the original sum at the end of the specified period, but will remain constant each period, unless the interest changes.

Example 3.1

An amount of $2500 is deposited in a bank offering 5% simple interest per annum. What is the interest at the end of the first year and subsequent years?

Solution:

$$I = (2500)(0.05)(1) = \$125$$

The interest for the second and subsequent years will also be $125. In other words, at the end of the first year, the amount will be $2625; for the second, it will be $2750.

3.4 COMPOUND INTEREST

However, when interest is paid on the original investment as well on the interest earned, the process is known as *compound interest.* If an initial sum, P, is invested at an interest rate, i, over a period of n years,

$$F = P(1 + i)^n \qquad\qquad (3.2)$$

or

$$P = F/(1 + i)^n$$

If interest i is compounded m times per period n,

$$F = P(1 + i/m)^{nm} \tag{3.3}$$

As m approaches infinity (∞), Eq. 3.3 can be written as

$$F = Pe^{in} \tag{3.4}$$

or

$$P = Fe^{-in} \tag{3.5}$$

Equations 3.4 and 3.5 are used when resorting to "continuous compounding," a method frequently used in practice. Factors $(1 + i)^n$ and e^{in} are called compound amount factors, and $(1 + i)^{-n}$ and e^{-in} are called present worth factors for a single payment.

Example 3.2

What is the amount of $1000 compounded (a) at 6% per annum, (b) at 6% per every quarter, (c) at 6% per annum compounded continuously for 10 years?

Solution:

(a) Here, $i = 0.06$, $n = 10$, and $m = 1$. Equation 3.2 becomes

$$F = 1000(1 + 0.06)^{10} = (1000)(1.79084) = \$1790.85$$

(b) Here, $i = 0.06$, $n = 10$, and $m = 4$. Equation 3.3 becomes

$$F = 1000[1 + (0.06/4)]^{40} = (1000)(1.81402) = \$1814.02$$

(c) Here, $i = 0.06$ and $n = 10$. Equation 3.4 becomes

$$F = 1000e^{(0.06)(10)} = (1000)(1.82212) = \$1822.12$$

Example 3.3

What is the *effective* interest rate when a sum of money is invested at a *nominal* interest rate of 10% per annum, compounded annually, semiannually, quarterly, monthly, daily, and continuously?

Solution:

Assume the sum to be $1 for a period of 1 year. Then the sum at the end of 1 year compounded:

Annually	$= 1(1 + 0.1)^{(1)(1)}$	$= 1.10$ therefore, the interest rate	$= 10\%$
Semiannually	$= 1(1 + 0.1/2)^{(1)(2)}$	$= 1.1025$ and the interest rate	$= 10.25\%$
Quarterly	$= 1(1 + 0.1/4)^{(1)(4)}$	$= 1.10381$ and the interest rate	$= 10.381\%$
Monthly	$= 1(1 + 0.1/12)^{(1)(12)}$	$= 1.10471$ and the interest rate	$= 10.471\%$
Daily	$= 1(1 + 0.1/365)^{(1)(365)}$	$= 1.10516$ and the interest rate	$= 10.516\%$
Continuously	$= 1[e^{(0.1)(1)}]$	$= 1.10517$ and the interest rate	$= 10.517\%$

Discussion:

The comparison illustrates the difference between nominal and effective interest rates. Say, for example, the amount obtained adding interest quarterly is equal to $1.1038. Therefore, $1 + i = 1.10381$, and, $i = 0.10381$, or 10.381%.

3.5 UNIFORM SERIES OF PAYMENTS

If instead of a single amount there is a uniform cash flow of costs or revenue at a constant rate, the following uniform series of payment formulas are commonly used in practice.

3.5.1 Compound Amount Factor (CAF)

The use of the Compound Amount Factor (CAF) helps to answer the question: What future sum (F) will accumulate assuming a given annual amount of money (A) is invested at an interest i *for* n years?

$$F = A\left[\frac{(1 + i)^n - 1}{i}\right] = A\left(\frac{x - 1}{i}\right) \qquad (3.6)$$

where $[(x - 1)/i]$ is the uniform series compound amount factor.

3.5.2 Sinking Fund Factor (SFF)

The Sinking Fund Factor (SFF) indicates how much money (A) should be invested at the end of each year at interest rate i for n years to accumulate a stipulated future sum of money (F). The SFF is the reciprocal of the CAF.

$$A = F\left[\frac{i}{(1 + i)^n - 1}\right] = F\left(\frac{i}{x - 1}\right) \qquad (3.7)$$

where $[i/(x - 1)]$ is the uniform series sinking fund factor.

3.5.3 Present Worth Factor (PWF)

The Present Worth Factor (PWF) tells us what amount P should be invested today at interest i to recover a sum of A at the end of each year for n years.

$$P = A\left[\frac{(1 + i)^n - 1}{(1 + i)^n i}\right] = A\left(\frac{x - 1}{xi}\right) \qquad (3.8)$$

where $[(x - 1)/(xi)]$ is the uniform series present worth factor.

3.5.4 Capital Recovery Factor (CRF)

The Capital Recovery Factor (CRF) answers the question: If an amount of money (P) is invested today at an interest i, what sum (A) can be secured at the end of each year for n years, such that the initial investment (P) is just depleted?

$$A = P\left[\frac{i(1 + i)^n}{(1 + i)^n - 1}\right] = P\left(\frac{xi}{x - 1}\right) \qquad (3.9)$$

CRF is the reciprocal of PWF. Another way of considering CRF is: If a sum of *P* is borrowed today at interest rate i, how much A must be paid at the end of each period to retire the loan in n periods?

Example 3.4

If the interest rate is 5% per annum, what sum would accumulate after 6 years if $1000 were invested at the end of each year for 6 years?

Solution:

$$F = A\left[\frac{(1 + i)^n - 1}{i}\right] = 1000(6.80191) = \$6801.91$$

Example 3.5

A realtor buys a house for $200,000 and spends $1000 per year on maintenance for the next 8 years. For how much should she sell the property to make a profit of $40,000? Assume $i = 12\%$ per annum.

Solution:

Future value of $200,000 in 8 years:

$$F = P(1 + i)^n = 200,000(2.475963) = \$495,192.63$$

Future value of annual maintenance:

$$F = A\left[\frac{(1 + i)^n - 1}{i}\right] = 1000(12,299.69) = \$12,299.69$$

Minimum selling price after 8 years, with a profit of $40,000

$$= 495,192.63 + 12,299.69 + 40,000$$
$$= \$547,492.32$$

Example 3.6

The city transit system needs to set up a sinking fund for 10 buses, each costing $100,000, for timely replacements. The life of the buses is 7 years and the interest rate is 6% per annum.

Solution:

$$A = F\left[\frac{i}{(1 + i)^n - 1}\right] = (100,000)(10)[0.119135018]$$
$$= \$119,135.02 \text{ per year}$$

Example 3.7

A contractor wants to set up a uniform end-of-period payment to repay a debt of $1,000,000 in 3 years, making payments every month. Interest rate $= 12\%$ per annum. What is the CRF?

Solution:

$$i = 0.12/12 = 0.01 \qquad n = 3 \times 12 = 36$$

$$A = P\left[\frac{i(1 + i)^n}{(1 + i)^n - 1}\right] = 1,000,000[0.033214309] = \$33,214.31$$

3.6 UNIFORM GRADIENT SERIES

When a uniform series of a number of payments are increasing each year by a similar amount, it is possible to convert them to an equivalent uniform gradient. If the uniform increment at the end of each year is G, then all the compound amounts can be totaled to F.

$$F = \frac{G}{i}\left[\frac{(1 + i)^n - 1}{i}\right] - \frac{nG}{i} \tag{3.10}$$

In order to convert this sum into an equivalent uniform period payment over n periods, it is necessary to substitute the sum for F in the SFF, giving

$$A = \frac{G}{i} - \frac{nG}{i}\left[\frac{i}{(1 + i)^n - 1}\right] \tag{3.11}$$

Example 3.8

The maintenance on a transit bus system amounts to $20,000 by the end of the first year, increasing $5000/year for the subsequent 5 years. What is the equivalent uniform series cost each year, with interest at 5% per annum?

Solution:

$$A = \frac{G}{i} - \frac{nG}{i}\left[\frac{i}{(1 + i)^n - 1}\right] = \frac{5000}{0.05} - \frac{(5)(5000)}{0.05}(0.1809748)$$

$$= 100,000 - 90,487.4 = \$9512.60$$

Therefore, the uniform series equivalent annual cost

$$= 20,000 + 9512.60 = \$29,512.60 \text{ for each of the 5 years}$$

3.7 DISCRETE COMPOUND INTEREST FACTORS

The various factors are summarized in Table 3.1 and their relationships are shown in Figure 3.1.

TABLE 3.1   SUMMARY OF FACTORS

Symbol	Factor	Equation	Symbolic form	Find	Given
A	Single payment:				
	1. Compound amount	$F = P[x]$	F/P,i,n	F	P
	2. Present worth	$P = F/[x]$	P/F,i,n	P	F
B	Uniform series:				
	3. Compound amount	$F = A[(x - 1)/i]$	F/A,i,n	F	A
	4. Sinking fund	$A = F[i/(x - 1)]$	A/F,i,n	A	F
	5. Present worth	$P = A[(x - 1)/ix]$	P/A,i,n	P	A
	6. Capital recovery	$A = P[ix/(x - 1)]$	A/P,i,n	A	P
C	Arithmetic gradient:				
	7. Uniform series equivalent	$A = G\{1/i - (n/i)[i/(x - 1)]\}$	A/G,i,N	A	G

Notes: The factor $(1 + i)^n$ is known as the single payment compound amount factor, and is equal to x. In a similar manner, the expression in each equation within square brackets is the factor corresponding to the description, for example, $[ix/(x - 1)]$ = capital recovery factor (CRF).

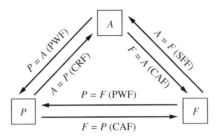

$P = F$ (CAF)

Figure 3.1   Relationships among factors.

3.8 UNIFORM CONTINUOUS CASH FLOW AND CAPITALIZED COST

The present worth of a uniform continuous cash flow is the amount P, invested at an interest rate i that will produce a cash flow of *a* per period for n periods. Consider a small time interval from t to t + δt, during which the flow will be a (δt), and the present worth of this element is (a) (δt)(e^{-it}). The present worth of the entire flow is

$$P = \int ae^{-it}dt = -\frac{a}{i}(e^{-it}) = a\frac{1 - e^{-it}}{i}$$

$$= an\left(\frac{1 - e^{-it}}{in}\right) = anf_w$$

The term $f_w = (1 - e^{-it})/in$ is the present worth factor for uniform flow; it is useful in making comparisons of equipment and services with different service lives, by reducing them to their present values.

Capitalized Cost.   Capitalized Cost (CC) is the present value of a series of services or equipment scheduled to be repeated every n periods to perpetuity. If P is the amount that must be paid every n periods, where n is the life of the equipment, then the CC is

$$K = P + Pe^{-in} + Pe^{-2in} + \text{---} +$$

Summing this geometric series gives

$$K = P\left(\frac{1}{P - e^{-in}}\right) = P\left(\frac{e^{in}}{e^{in} - 1}\right) = P\left(\frac{1}{inf_w}\right)$$

Example 3.9

The Department of Transportation is faced with a problem. Should it rent trucks for $480 a month each or buy for $33,000 each, assuming the useful life of a truck is 10 years and i = 14%?

Solution:

Present value of rented truck = an $(1 - e^{-in})/in$

$$a = 480 \times 12 = \$5760/yr$$

Therefore,

$$P = (5760)(10)(1 - e^{-0.14 \times 10})/(0.14)(10) = (5760)(10)(0.538145) =$$
$$\$30,997.15 < \$33,000$$

Therefore, it is more advantageous to rent trucks.

Example 3.10

A comparison between two types of bridges has to be made using the following details.

Type	Steel	Wood
Initial cost	$400,000	$250,000
Paint and maintenance	$400,000/10yr	$25,000/2yr
Life	40yr	20yr
Interest rate	9%	9%

In the long run, which type of bridge is cheaper?

Solution:

Solution	Steel bridge	Wooden bridge
First cost	$K_1 = P[1/(1 - e^{-in})]$ $= 400,000[1/(1 - e^{-0.09 \times 40})]$ $= 400,000(1.028091)$ $= 411,236.51$	$K_1 = 250,000[1/(1 - e^{-0.09 \times 40})]$ $= 250,000(1.19803)$ $= 299,508.41$
Paint and maintenance	$K_2 = 40,000[1/(1 - e^{-0.09 \times 10})]$ $= 67,404.71$	$K_2 = 12,500[1/(1 - e^{-0.09 \times 2})]$ $= 12,500(6.070547)$ $= 75,881.84$
Total	$478,641	$375,390

Based on the calculations shown above the wooden bridge is cheaper.

3.9 EVALUATION

The term *evaluation* is used in planning and engineering to refer to the merits of alternative proposals. The essence of evaluation is the assessments of the comparative merits of different courses of action. One of these actions may include the "do nothing" alternative (Lichfield et al., 1975).

Engineering and planning alternatives are concerned with problems of choice between mutually exclusive plans or projects (e.g., the examination of alternative investment proposals to alleviate severe traffic congestion in the city center). Evaluation methods may be applied to the problem of choice between sets of independent plans or projects as well as mutually exclusive ones (Mitchell, 1980).

In general, engineering projects in the private sector are built for motives of profit, while in the public sector the motive is, ultimately, the raising of living standards and for social benefit, or for profit, or possibly for political motives. Political motives are not amenable to economic analysis or justification. A value can, however, be put on social benefits and losses (Mitchell, 1980). Even if a decision maker determines as accurately as possible what consequences will flow from each alternative action, preferences still need to be formulated, particularly when a variety of objectives are involved. In such a case, the crux of the problem is that it is impossible to optimize in all directions at the same time. It is this ubiquitous problem, called the *multiattribute problem*, that makes it tough to determine preferences among outcomes (Stokey and Zeckhauser, 1978).

The bottom line seems to be that whereas the basic concepts of evaluation are relatively simple, the actual process of evaluating projects or plans is complex and riddled with controversy. Although engineers and planners try to clarify difficult issues that should be considered by decision makers, it is not uncommon for decision makers to override the results of the analysis. It therefore should be clearly borne in mind that analysis and evaluation are primarily performed by engineers, economists, and planners, whereas the choice of an alternative is done by decision makers (Manheim et al., 1975).

3.10 FEASIBILITY ISSUES

The solution to a problem should invariably be checked to see whether it is suitable for the situation, acceptable to the decision makers and the public, and one that can be eventually implemented, given the investment. Naturally, at some stage or another, a proposed improvement will be required to satisfy engineering, economic, financial, political, environmental, and social feasibility. For this kind of comprehensive investigation, it is necessary, in complex situations, to obtain the services of economists and sociologists to do justice to the analysis.

Engineers and planners are familiar with the large assortment of analytical tools used in evaluating alternatives. However, in most cases, decision makers demand far more information and justification on the consequences of different alternatives than what is contained in the analysis developed by technicians. Much of this additional information may be qualitative rather than quantitative (Mishan, 1976; Meyer and Miller, 1984).

3.11 EVALUATION ISSUES

Most evaluation methodologies utilize some form of rating system. Evaluators calculate an index or score, indicating how the welfare of society (or the quality of life) would be affected if a particular alternative were implemented. In effect, they convert all impacts into commensurate units so that they can be added and compared.

Cost-benefit analysis was one of the first evaluation methods, used extensively, that included a systematic rating procedure and has in the last 25 years been used widely to evaluate all types of public actions. Its rating procedure, although complex, follows the simple arithmetic of placing a monetary value on each impact. The monetary ratings are then aggregated to determine whether benefits exceed costs.

The fact that the cost-benefit method has a number of weaknesses led to the development of several other evaluation techniques.

Some evaluation methodologies have established complex procedures for quantifying social welfare ratings. Most of them appear scientific and objective. It does not really matter how sophisticated these methodologies are, because ultimately, the ratings constitute value judgments. Each method has its own weakness. Indeed, each method could possibly lead to a different conclusion (McAllister, 1982).

Several questions naturally stem from this broad description of evaluation methodologies:

- How should evaluation techniques be selected?
- Are economic values sufficient for weighing the costs and benefits of a contemplated public action?
- How are intangible impacts quantified?
- How can equity issues be considered in evaluation?
- How should the concept of time be treated in evaluations?
- How can discount rates be estimated?

Some of these issues are discussed in this chapter.

3.12 THE EVALUATION PROCESS

The scope of the evaluation process is outlined in Figure 3.2. The evaluation process focuses on the development and selection among several alternatives, and is done in three parts:

1. An evaluation work plan.

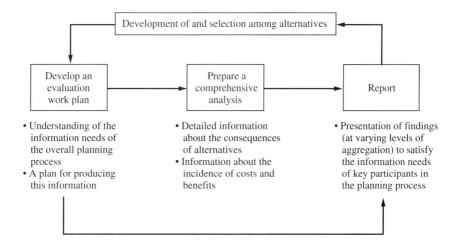

Figure 3.2   Scope of the evaluation process.

2. A comprehensive analysis.
3. A report containing the results of this analysis.

The level of detail and rigor associated with each of these activities will naturally vary from project to project. Figure 3.3 shows a conceptual framework for evaluation of transportation improvements. It identifies the key inputs to the evaluation process, the potential impacts associated with transportation improvements, and the considerations in evaluating the overall merit of improvements. Figure 3.3 also illustrates the interrelationships among the activities constituting the evaluation process, including the iterative nature of evaluation associated with large-scale improvements that often require successive revision and refinement as more critical information is forthcoming about their potential impacts and feasibility.

The economic and financial evaluation process of engineering improvements reflected in this section has three major components: 1) the establishment of evaluation criteria; 2) the estimation of costs, impacts, and performance levels; and 3) the overall evaluation of alternative improvements using cost-efficiency and cost-effectiveness techniques as described later in this chapter.

This process is based on the following principles, which underlie good practice in evaluation (Meyer and Miller, 1984):

1. It should be based on a careful examination of the range of decisions to be made and the issues or important considerations in making these decisions.

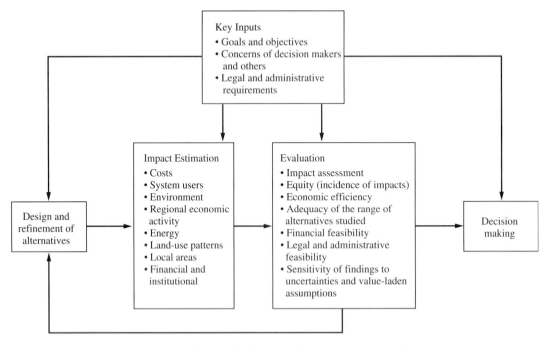

Figure 3.3   Conceptual framework for evaluation.

2. It should guide the generation and refinement of alternatives, as well as the choice of a course of action.

3. Both qualitative as well as quantitative information should be used.

4. Uncertainties or value-laden assumptions should be addressed and explained.

5. All the important consequences of choosing a course of action should be included.

6. Evaluation should relate the consequences of alternatives to goals and objectives established.

7. The impact of each alternative on each interest group should be clearly spelled out.

8. Evaluation should be sensitive to the time frame in which project impacts are likely to occur.

9. The implementation requirements of each alternative should be carefully documented to eliminate the chance of including a "fatal fault" alternative.

10. Decision makers should be provided with information in a readily understandable and useful form.

3.13 VALUES, GOALS, OBJECTIVES, CRITERIA, AND STANDARDS

The evaluation process involves making a judgment about the worth of the consequences of alternative plans. For example, a large number of metropolitan planning organizations have expressed the view that the planning and development of engineering facilities must be directed toward raising urban standards and enhancing the aggregate quality of life of their communities.

It may be appropriate, at this stage, to present a brief description of values, goals, objectives, criteria, and standards. A clear statement of their meaning follows. A set of irreducibles forming the basic desires and drives that govern human behavior are called values. Because values are commonly shared by groups of people, it is possible to speak of societal or cultural values. Four of the basic values of society are, for example, the desire to survive, the need to belong, the need for order, and the need for security.

A *goal* is an idealized end state; and although they may not be specific enough to be truly attainable, goals provide the directions in which society may like to move. An *objective* is a specific statement that is an outgrowth of a goal. Objectives are generally attainable and are stated so that it is possible to measure the extent to which they have been attained.

Criteria result directly from the fact that the levels of attainment of objectives are measurable. In a sense, criteria are the working or operational definitions attached to objectives. They are measures, tests, or indicators of the degree to which objectives are attained. Criteria affect the quantitative characteristics of objectives and add the precision to objectives that differentiate them from goals. One particular type of criterion is a *standard*—a fixed objective [e.g., the lowest (or highest) level of performance acceptable].

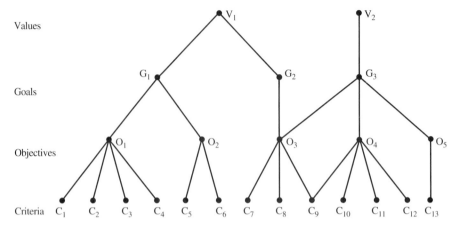

Figure 3.4 Hierarchical interrelationships among values, goals, objectives, and criteria.

The preceding chain is shown in Figure 3.4. A complex structure connects societal values to particular criteria and standards. It may be noted that there may be a high score connected with one criterion as compared to another, in which case trade-offs between criteria may be considered. Of course, decision-makers will find it comparatively easy to deal with goals and objectives with a minimum amount of internal conflicts between themselves (Thomas and Schofer, 1970).

3.14 ESTIMATION OF COSTS, IMPACTS, AND PERFORMANCE LEVELS

3.14.1 Capital, Operating, and Maintenance Costs

Costs play a central role in economic and financial evaluation. When combined with other dollar-valued impacts and compared to other effects, they are helpful in assessing the economic efficiency (i.e., investment worthiness) of the improvement. Detailed knowledge of these costs over the life of the improvement helps to identify and to assign funding sources, thus ensuring that sufficient financial resources are available to implement the improvement.

Existing procedures for estimating costs range from the application of relatively gross average cost measures (e.g., cost per route-mile for two-lane highways) to procedures that use detailed, site-specific information. Achieving a high degree of precision in estimating costs for evaluation of alternatives is important only when similar alternatives are being compared. In such cases, a more detailed cost accounting framework might be required to determine differences between alternatives.

Conversely, when alternatives differ substantially in scale or character, it is more important to establish credible upper and lower limits for the cost of each than to make precise cost estimates based on a single set of detailed assumptions for each alternative (FHWA, 1983).

3.14.2 User Costs

Engineering system user costs include, for example, changes in travel-time savings, vehicle operating costs, safety, and qualitative changes in the level of service provided by the improvement.

Travel-time savings will accrue from most improvements as congestion is decreased, speed limits increased, or as more convenient routes are provided. Travel-time savings for travelers who take advantage of the improvement and receive the benefit are usually expressed in person-hours of time savings and can be converted to a dollar value using an average value of travel-time (i.e., dollars per person-hour).

Vehicle operating cost impacts can accrue if shorter, more direct routes are provided, congestion is decreased, speed limits increased, or if the highway condition improves. Motor vehicle operating costs are usually calculated for the "do-nothing" alternative and each of the improvement alternatives, by estimating the unit cost of the vehicle operation (i.e., cents per vehicle-mile) and the total vehicle miles of travel. The product of these two is the total motor vehicle operating cost.

Safety cost impacts can occur from many types of improvements and can be estimated by applying appropriate "before" and "after" accident rates (e.g., accidents per million vehicle-miles) to the volume of traffic expected to use the proposed improvement. Separate estimates may be developed for fatal injury, non-fatal injury, and property-damage-only accidents if the potential impact is expected to be large or if the project's safety impact is controversial. Unit costs (e.g., dollars per accident) can then be applied to derive dollar values for accident costs.

Qualitative improvements in the level of service provided can reflect any number of types of effects, including better ride quality from improved pavements, improved transit reliability, or impacts that are difficult to quantify or to assign dollar costs (FHWA, 1983).

3.14.3 Impacts

A wide range of possible impacts are associated with engineering improvements. These impacts include environmental as well as economic impacts, and are more often described in qualitative or non-monetary terms rather than in terms of dollars. Such impacts might include air-pollutant emissions from automobiles, noise impacts, water quality impacts, energy consumption, effects on accessibility or land-use patterns, and construction disruption (i.e., for projects that entail substantial amounts of construction activity). To the extent that these impacts represent a significant effect of the improvement, they must be identified and accounted for in the evaluation and factored into the overall assessment (FHWA, 1983).

3.14.4 Performance Levels

In many cases, formally established criteria for expected economic and financial accomplishments can serve as a valuable evaluation tool. For example, performance levels are often incorporated in the stated goals and objectives for a specific facility to narrow the scope of evaluation and set limits on expected results. Such criteria are also used to monitor implementation, establish budgets, and reallocate financial resources on a periodic basis.

3.15 EVALUATION OF ALTERNATIVES

The evaluation of alternatives is related to the size, complexity, and number of alternative improvements to be considered. However, answers to the following types of questions, relying on the techniques described in this chapter, should be sought for any evaluation effort:

- Are there other feasible improvements that are not considered and that might compare favorably to those alternatives that were formally evaluated?
- What alternatives were examined and eliminated in the earlier stages of the planning process?

Impact Assessment

- Have all important differences among alternatives been identified and considered?
- What are the important trade-offs in choosing among alternatives?

Equity

- What is the distribution of benefits and costs (i.e., among highway users, nearby residents, etc.)?
- Do any groups pay shares of the costs that are disproportionate to the benefits they receive?

Economic Efficiency

- Does an alternative provide sufficient benefits to justify the required expenditure? In comparison with less costly alternatives, does an alternative provide additional benefits to justify the additional funds required?
- In comparison with more costly alternatives, has sufficient weight been given to the benefits that would be forgone in the event that additional expenditure of funds is not justified?
- How do non-monetary costs and benefits affect conclusions about economic efficiency?

Financial Feasibility

- Will sufficient funds be available to implement alternatives on schedule? From what sources?
- What is the margin of safety for financial feasibility?
- What adjustments will be necessary if this margin of safety is exceeded?

Legal and Administrative Feasibility

- Is the implementation of an alternative feasible within existing laws and administrative guidelines? If not, what adjustments might be necessary?
- What approaches will be required in later stages of the planning process? Are problems anticipated in obtaining these approvals? If these problems do materialize, can minor modifications or refinements to alternatives overcome them?

Sensitivity of Findings to Uncertainties and Value-Laden Assumptions

- Are there uncertainties or value-laden assumptions that might affect the information assembled to help decision makers answer the earlier questions?
- How much would assumptions have to be changed to suggest different answers to these questions?
- How reasonable are these changes?

The answer to the many questions listed are subjective in nature; it is quite possible that reasonable individuals might answer them differently even when given the same information.

In a comprehensive evaluation, detailed information about alternatives and their impacts should be summarized in the evaluation report. This report should document the major impacts of the performance of the alternatives analyzed and emphasize the difference in the performance of alternatives with respect to the key impact measures (FHWA, 1983).

3.16 ECONOMIC AND FINANCIAL CONCEPTS

In determining the economic and financial implications of an engineering improvement, a clear understanding of several basic concepts is essential. These concepts include monetary impacts such as the cost of time, money, equipment, maintenance, and user benefits, as well as non-monetary costs such as safety, environmental impacts, and effects on the local economy. Each of these concepts is described briefly in what follows. When applied as part of one of the analysis techniques presented in Section 3.17, they can assist planners in determining the overall economic efficiency and effectiveness of an improvement (FHWA, 1983).

Time Value of Money.   Benefits and costs will occur at different times during the life of an improvement. However, a cost incurred today cannot be compared directly with the benefits that it will provide in some future year. The funding for an improvement should be considered as an investment that is expected to generate a return. Consequently, the costs and benefits of an improvement must be compared in equivalent terms that account for their timing. These benefits and costs can be either described in equivalent terms by calculating their "present worth" (for the current year or recent year for which data is available) or for an average year over the life of the improvement. Any future cost or benefit expressed in future dollars is properly converted to its corresponding present value by two factors: an inflation rate and a discount rate.

Discount Rate.   The appropriate discount rate is an estimate of the average rate of return that is expected on private investment before taxes and after inflation. This interpretation is based on the concept that the alternative to the capital investment by government is to leave the capital in the private sector.

Inflation Rate.   Inflation can be ignored in performing most aspects of the basic economic evaluation if the evaluation is prepared in present value terms, since inflation has no effect on present values. However, if the costs used are 2 or 3 years out of date, they should be adjusted to a more current year.

The only time when it might be appropriate to project future inflation in evaluating alternative improvements is when there is reasonable evidence that differential future rates of inflation might apply to important components of the evaluation. However, independent of the evaluation of alternative improvements, projections of inflation must be made for a financial feasibility analysis and development of a capital improvement program (FHWA, 1983).

3.17 ANALYSIS TECHNIQUES

The objective of economic evaluation analysis techniques is to provide sufficient summary information to decision makers and interest groups to do the following:

1. Determine whether the costs of improvements are justified by the anticipated benefits (i.e., whether a proposed improvement is superior to doing nothing).
2. Make comparative overall assessments of different alternative improvements with each other.

In complex situations involving large-scale, costly improvements, it may also be necessary to assess the distribution of benefits and costs among those affected by the improvement, such as user cost, operator cost, and societal cost.

Techniques that support the first purpose come under the category of economic efficiency analysis, or merely *efficiency analysis,* also often called *investment appraisal methods.* These include benefit-cost ratio, present worth, rate of return, equivalent uniform annual value, and other variations of these methods. All involve the translation of impacts (i.e., costs and benefits) into monetary terms. Techniques that support the second purpose come under the category of cost-effectiveness analysis. These include the use of non-monetary effectiveness measures either to assess the relative impacts of all alternative improvements in the same terms or to hold constant the requirements that no alternatives must meet. Effectiveness measures are also used in combination with cost values in the form of ratios (FHWA, 1983).

3.17.1 Economic Evaluation Methods (Efficiency Analysis)

There are four common methods of evaluating engineering projects: 1) net present worth (NPW); 2) equivalent uniform annual cost (EUAC); 3) internal rate of return (ROR); and 4) benefit-cost (B/C) analysis. The bottom line in the evaluation of individual projects is: Which project is the most productive? Or which project produces the highest return? Essentially, there are two indices of economic merit that can help answer these questions. The first is the benefit-cost criterion, and the second is the internal rate of return. A brief explanation of each method follows.

By using the concept of equivalence connected with compound interest, the present worth of a single payment (PWSP) F, n years from now, with a discount rate of i is:

$$PWSP = \frac{F}{(1 + i)^n} \tag{3.12}$$

The present worth of uniform series (PWUS) of equal annual payments is the sum of the present worth of each cost:

$$PWUS = A\left[\frac{(1 + i)^n - 1}{i(1 + i)^n}\right] \tag{3.13}$$

Here, A is the EUAC. The term in brackets is known as the present worth uniform series (PWUS) factor. Its value has been tabulated for various combinations of i and n. Also,

$$A = EUAC = PWUS\left[\frac{i(1 + i)^n}{(1 + i)^n - 1}\right] \tag{3.14}$$

The term in brackets is called the CRF (see Section 3.5.4). For example, if a person borrows $10,000 from a bank and intends to repay the amount in equal yearly installments over an 8-year period at 5% per annum, the EUAC would amount to

$$EUAC = 10,000\left[\frac{0.05(1 + 0.05)^8}{(1 + 0.05)^8 - 1}\right]$$
$$= 10,000 \times 0.154722$$
$$= \$1547.22$$

The internal rate of return method has been proposed as an index of the desirability of projects. Naturally, the higher the rate, the better the project. By definition, it is the discount rate at which the net present value of benefits equals the net present value of costs.

There are many situations where the rate of return needs to be calculated for several alternatives. In such cases the incremental rate of return on the cash flow representing the differences between alternatives is computed. If the incremental rate of return is greater than or equal to the predetermined Minimum Alternative Rate of Return (MARR), choose the higher cost alternative; otherwise, choose the lower-cost alternative.

Benefit-cost analysis is generally applied to engineering projects to ascertain the extent to which an investment will be beneficial to society. This analysis can be quite elaborate, and more will be said about this method of analysis in another section. Suffice it to say here that a project that costs less than the benefits derived from the project would be eligible for consideration of being implemented (B/C $\geq$ 1).

Example 3.11

Three alternatives are being considered for improving a street intersection. The annual dollar savings on account of the improvement is shown. Assume that the intersection will last for 25 years and the interest rate is 5%. It is assumed that each of the three improvements is mutually exclusive but provides similar benefits.

Alternative	Total Cost	Annual Benefits
A	$10,000	$800
B	12,000	1,000
C	19,000	1,400

Solution:

NPW method: Use the present worth factor for uniform series.

$$NPW(A) = -10,000 + (800 \times 14.094) = \$1275.2$$
$$NPW(B) = -12,000 + (1000 \times 14.094) = \$2094.0$$
$$NPW(C) = -19,000 + (1400 \times 14.094) = \$731.6$$

Therefore, select alternative B with the highest net present worth.
EUAC method: Use the capital recovery factor (CRF).

$$EUAC(A) = -(10,000 \times 0.07095) + 800 = 90.50$$
$$EUAC(B) = -(12,000 \times 0.07095) + 1000 = 148.60$$
$$EUAC(C) = -(19,000 \times 0.07095) + 1400 = 51.95$$

Alternative B has the highest EUAC and should be selected.
ROR method: Compare the ROR figure with the "do-nothing" alternative.

$$NPW\ (A) = -10,000 + (800)\ (P/A, i, 25\ yr.) = 0$$
$$(P/A, i, 25\ yr.) = 10,000/800 = 12.5 = > i = 6.25\%$$
$$NPW\ (B) = -12,000 + (1000)\ (P/A, 1, 25\ yr.) = 0$$
$$(P/A, i, 25\ yr.) = 12,000/1000 = 12 = > i = 6.7\%$$
$$NPW(C) = 19,000 + (1400)\ (P/A, i, 25\ yr.) = 0$$
$$(P/A, i, 25\ yr.) = 19,000/1400 = 13.57 = > i = 5.77\%$$

Alternative B is the least of the three because the rate of return is the highest (and, of course, higher than 5%, so better than the "do-nothing" alternative).

Example 3.12

Consider two alternatives X and Y for repairs to a pumping set (in $100).

Year	X	Y
0	−20	−13.10
1	+7.76	+4.81
2	+7.76	+4.81
3	+7.76	+4.81

If the MARR is 11%, which alternative would you recommend?

Solution:

Take the higher initial-cost alternative (X) minus the lower-cost alternative (Y).

Year	X	Y	(X − Y)
0	−20.00	−13.10	−6.90
1	+7.76	4.81	+2.95
2	+7.76	4.81	+2.95
3	+7.76	4.81	+2.95

Solve for the incremental rate of return.

$$\text{PW of cost} = \text{PW of benefits}$$
$$6.90 = 2.95(P/A,i,3)$$
$$(P/A,i,3) = 6.90/2.95 = 2.339$$

From compound interest tables or by direct calculations ROR works out to be between 12 and 15%, which is higher than 11% (MARR). Hence, select A, which is again the one with the higher initial cost.

While present worth analysis is the preferred technique, the annual worth (or annualized benefit, cost, and net benefit) is often used in engineering work. In these two cases the choice of the best project is made using the maximization of net benefits. In the public sector the dominant method is to calculate the benefit-cost ratio (B/C).

$$B/C = \frac{\text{Present worth of benefits}}{\text{Present worth of costs}} = \frac{\text{Eq. uniform annual benefits}}{\text{Eq. uniform annual costs}}$$

For a given interest rate a B/C ≥ 1 reflects an acceptable project.

However, it must be emphasized that the maximization of the B/C ratio is <u>not</u> really the proper economic criterion; it is the maximization of net benefits that is the ultimate goal and the incremental B/C analysis is useful in achieving this goal. The following two cases are considered for incremental analysis:

1. When several alternatives are feasible either with the same benefit or cost, choose the alternative with the largest B/C ratio, subject to the ratio being

greater than or equal to one. If no such alternative exists, choose the "do nothing" alternative.

2. When neither the benefit nor the cost is the same for the feasible alternative, perform an incremental B/C analysis and go through the following steps:

   a) Rank-order the feasible alternatives from the lowest cost to the highest cost and number the projects 1, 2, ... , n.

   b) For projects 1 and 2 compute

   $$\Delta B/\Delta C = (PWB_2 - PWB_1)/(PWC_2 - PWC_1)$$

   or $$\Delta B/\Delta C = (EUAB_2 - EUAB_1)/(EUAC_2 - EUAC_1)$$

   If $\Delta B/\Delta C \geq 1.0$ select project 2 till this stage of analysis.
   If $\Delta B/\Delta C < 1.0$ select project 1 till this stage of analysis.

   c) Compute $\Delta B/\Delta C$ between the best project, till this stage of analysis, and the next most costly project not yet tested.
   If $\Delta B/\Delta C \geq 1.0$, select the most costly project as best till this stage of analysis.
   If $\Delta B/\Delta C < 1.0$, retain the lesser costly project as best till this stage of analysis.

   d) Repeat step (c) till all projects have been tested. The surviving project is the best.

Example 3.13

Six mutually exclusive alternative projects need to be assessed for final selection. They have been ordered from lowest cost to highest cost. Recommend which project should be selected.

Alternatives	1	2	3	4	5	6
Benefits	120	130	195	210	250	300
Costs	75	110	140	175	240	320
B/C Ratio	1.60	1.18	1.39	1.20	1.04	0.94

Compute $\Delta B/\Delta C$ (which is essentially the slope of the line).

Solution:

$$\text{from \#1to\#2} \quad \frac{130 - 120}{110 - 75} = \frac{10}{35} = 0.28 < 1.0 \qquad \therefore \text{ retain \#1}$$

$$\text{\#1to\#3} \quad \frac{195 - 120}{140 - 75} = \frac{75}{65} = 1.15 > 1.0 \qquad \therefore \text{ select \#3}$$

$$\text{\#3to\#4} \quad \frac{210 - 195}{175 - 140} = \frac{15}{35} = 0.243 < 1.0 \qquad \therefore \text{ retain \#3}$$

$$\text{\#3to\#5} \quad \frac{250 - 195}{240 - 140} = \frac{55}{100} = 0.55 < 1.0 \qquad \therefore \text{ retain \#3}$$

Project 3 is the best with $B/C = 1.39$ and present worth of net benefit $= \$55$, although project #1 has a higher B/C ratio.

The steps applied in this example can be shown graphically also.

3.17.2 Cost-Effectiveness Analysis

Cost-effectiveness is a strategy for making decisions rather than establishing a decision rule. This approach provides a general and flexible framework for providing information to aid in the selection of alternative plans. Many of the consequences of proposed engineering plans are difficult to measure, if not intangible. Planners resorting to the benefit-cost method place dollar values on benefits and costs, with the motive of being as objective as they can be and in this process oversimplify the complexity of the problem.

Cost-effectiveness overcomes some of these snags. Cost-effective analysis is essentially an information framework. The characteristics of each alternative are separated into two categories: 1) costs and 2) measures of effectiveness. The choice between alternatives is made on the basis of these two classes of information, eliminating the need to reduce the attributes or consequences of different alternatives to a single scalar dimension. Costs are defined in terms of all the resources necessary for the design, construction, operation, and maintenance of the alternative. Costs can be considered in dollars or in other units. Effectiveness is the degree to which an alternative achieves its objective. Decision makers can then make subjective judgments that seem best to them.

Cost-effective analysis arose out of a recognition that it is frequently difficult to transform all major impact measures into monetary terms in a credible manner, and that important evaluation factors can often be stated in more meaningful measures than dollar costs. Basically, the method should be used when preestablished requirements exist regarding the improvement. Usually, these requirements seek to establish the minimum investment (input) required for the maximum performance (output) among several alternative improvements.

One of the common general engineering performance measures that is used in cost-effective analysis is *level of service.* In practice, it is generally desirable to pre-pare estimates for several cost-effective measures rather than a single measure, because no single criterion satisfactorily summarizes the relative cost-effectiveness of different alternatives. Table 3.2 lists cost-effectiveness indices that might be used for highway and transit evaluation. Many or all of these could be used in a particular cost-effective analysis. Several additional measures could be added, depending on local goals and objectives (Thomas and Schofer, 1970).

Example 3.14

Citizens (particularly children) need a transportation facility to connect their community across a six-lane freeway by means of a footbridge over the freeway or a tunnel under the freeway. The objectives of the project are 1) to provide a safe and efficient system for crossing the freeway, and 2) to maintain and improve (if possible) the visual environment of the neighborhood. The table gives the construction and operating costs of the two alternatives. Annual costs are computed using a twenty-five-year service life and an 8% interest rate. It is anticipated that about 5000 pedestrians will use either of the two facilities per day.

TABLE 3.2 LIST OF TYPICAL COST-EFFECTIVE MEASURES FOR EVALUATION

Highway

Increase in average vehicle speed per dollar of capital investment
Decrease in total vehicle delay time due to congestion per dollar of capital investment
Increase in highway network accessibility to jobs per dollar of capital investment
Decrease in accidents, injuries, and fatalities per dollar of capital investment
Change in air-pollutant emissions per dollar of capital investment
Total capital and operating cost per passenger-mile served

Transit

Increase in the proportion of the population served at a given level of service (in terms of proximity
  of service and frequency) per dollar of total additional cost
Increase in transit accessibility to jobs, human services, and economic centers per dollar of total
  additional cost
Increase in ridership per dollar of capital investment
Increase in ridership per dollar of additional operating cost
Total capital and operating cost per transit rider
Total capital and operating cost per seat-mile and per passenger-mile served
Decrease in average transit trip time (including wait time) per dollar of total additional cost

Alternative	Total Cost	Annual Cost	Annual Operating Cost	Total Annual Cost
Footbridge	$100,000	$9368	$100	$9468
Tunnel	$200,000	$18,736	$350	$19,086

The annual difference in cost is $9618. The average cost per pedestrian per trip using
the bridge is

$$\frac{9468}{5000 \times 365} = 0.52 \text{ cent}$$

and using the tunnel it is

$$\frac{19,086}{5000 \times 365} = 1.05 \text{ cents}$$

The performance of the two alternatives may be summarized as follows:

1. The tunnel would need long, steep grades and may cause inconvenience to the
   elderly and handicapped. On the other hand, the bridge will be provided with stairs
   at either end, and this will eliminate its use by the elderly and handicapped. If ramps
   are to be provided, long steep grades would have to be provided at three times the
   cost of the bridge with stairs.
2. The tunnel is safer than the footbridge during the long winter months.

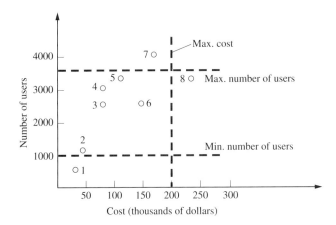

Figure 3.5   Cost-effective analysis: Cost versus Users.

3. From the point of view of aesthetics, the tunnel is preferred to the footbridge.
4. It is possible to predict that the tunnel would be safer than the bridge.

Another way to look at cost-effective analysis is to consider it as a way of maximizing the returns (in terms of effectiveness) of expenditures. Consider the following example: A city is considering eight different minibus network configurations, which are mutually exclusive. The only objective is to adopt a configuration that will maximize the number of potential riders in that sector of the city. The city has established the minimum number of potential riders that the alternative will serve and also maximize the amount of money it is willing to spend. Figure 3.5 shows the results of the analysis.

Notice that alternatives 1, 7, and 8 do not qualify under the criteria set. Alternative 5 would be the one that serves the maximum number of users. This problem could get somewhat complicated if an additional criterion were introduced (e.g., number of hours of operation).

3.17.3 Multicriteria Evaluation Method

The examples that have been given in this chapter so far fall under the general category of single-criterion evaluation methods, because all the benefits and costs have been reduced to monetary terms. The present worth, annual cost, benefit-cost, and rate-of-return methods all fall into this category, because the maximization of net benefits is the single objective the analyst has in mind. However, in the transportation planning process, one usually is dealing with many objectives (or criteria) that reflect the interests of the community. To incorporate several, often conflicting, objectives (or criteria) systematically, planners have developed methods to tackle this situation. One of these methods is generally called the *multicriteria evaluation method.* The steps in applying this method are best illustrated by working through an example.

Example 3.15

A large city is considering the improvement of its transportation system by adopting the following mutually exclusive alternatives: 1) a bus-only system, 2) a light-rail system,

(LRS), 3) a bus + heavy rail system (B + HR), and 4) a subway system (SWS). The city (elected officials and citizens) has recently identified and adopted the following goals and objectives for this improvement project:

1. The alternatives must reduce congestion in the city by capturing the maximum number of commuters in the peak hour.
2. The air-pollution and noise level should be reduced to tolerable acceptance levels through this improvement.
3. The total net revenue to the city should be maximized by adopting one of the alternatives.
4. The rate of deaths and injuries due to accidents should be reduced by at least 50% by adopting one of the alternatives.
5. The alternative chosen should cover the maximum area of the city and should be equitable to all patrons.

The alternatives prepared by consultants to the city are acceptable in principle. However, they all differ in quality, cost, alignment, coverage, and so on. City planners have formulated the following measures of effectiveness for each objective:

Objective 1: percentage reduction of motor vehicles on main arterials and corridors of the city
Objective 2: percentage reduction of pollution
Objective 3: net annual revenue/annual capital cost
Objective 4: probable accident rate/million trips
Objective 5: square miles covered by the proposed network (1 mile on either side of 4 line).

Solution:

		Alternatives		
Objective and MOE	Bus	LRS	B + HR	SWS
1. Congestion reduction	20	(27)	25	15
2. Pollution reduction	15	30	22	(35)
3. Revenue	(25)	20	15	10
4. Accidents reduction	15	20	23	(27)
5. Coverage	30	25	(40)	22

Note that each alternative has been assigned a figure representing a particular measure of effectiveness. Also, certain alternatives rank higher than others in a particular measure; for example, the light-rail system reduces congestion the most, by scoring the highest of the row values, 27; and the bus and heavy-rail alternative score 40 points (the highest) in the row representing "coverage." If these highest scores are matched to the corresponding relative weighting factor, one can erect another matrix, as shown. Here the highest score for MOE 1, 27, is assigned 20 as the relative weighting factor for the light-rail system; 17 is assigned to the

bus + heavy-rail alternative for MOE 5; and so on. By the same token, the other figures are calculated proportionally. The weights (out of 10) and the relative weighting
factors are determined from the table given below. The city's elected officials (through
brainstorming methods and Delphi techniques) have allocated weights on a 10-point
scale to each objective as indicated:

Objective	Weight (out of 10)	Relative weighting factor (%)
1	7	20
2	5	14
3	9	26
4	8	23
5	6	17
Total	35	100

This assignment of weights is subjective, but it is one way of assessing the collective opinion of a large group of people who are affected positively (or negatively) by
the proposed implementation of the chosen alternative.

Next, planners, engineers, sociologists, economists, and estimators set about
collecting data and costs for assigning values to each alternative, as shown in the following matrix. This step is most crucial and involves a lot of work in gathering appropriate data.

Objective and MOE	Alternatives			
	Bus	LRS	B+HR	SWS
1. Congestion Reduction	15	(20)	19	11
2. Pollution Reduction	6	12	9	(14)
3. Revenue	(26)	21	16	10
4. Accidents Reduction	13	17	20	(23)
5. Coverage	13	11	(17)	9
Total	73	81	81	67

It is obvious from the column totals that the light-rail system and the
bus + heavy-rail system each score 81 points and can be declared as winners in comparison to the other two alternatives. It is natural that these two alternatives will be
subjected to further scrutiny and analysis before a final winner is declared.

If, for example, these two top-ranking alternatives are examined by an investigating team who perform an environmental impact study, it is quite possible that a
more calculated decision can be taken. This example illustrates the difficulty in considering situations involving multicriteria application, because the outcome is sensitive to
the weights assigned to the criteria.

TABLE 3.3   CAPITAL COST AND EXPECTED BENEFITS

(1) Alternative	(2) Miles	(3) Capital cost	(4) User savings	(5) Savings − cost	(6) Δ(savings) − Δ(cost)
1	5	80	220	140	
2	10	100	300	200	60
3	15	130	340	210	10
4	20	180	370	190	−20
5	25	270	390	120	−70
6	30	380	425	45	−75

3.17.4 Benefit-Cost Analysis

This section is an extension of economic evaluation dealt with in Section 17.1. Public expenditure decisions are generally evaluated using benefit-cost analysis. A simple example of this type of evaluation is demonstrated here. Table 3.3 gives information on the capital cost and expected potential benefits by constructing from 5 to 30 miles of a light-rail line between downtown and the outskirts of a large city. Column one shows the six alternatives, and column two indicates the length of each of these six alternatives. The capital cost (in units of millions of dollars per year) is shown in column three. The present value of user benefits is indicated and this has been derived assuming a money stream for 20 years at 10% per annum in units of millions of dollars. Column five is column four minus column three. The last column indicates marginal benefits minus marginal cost. The benefits and costs of the six light-rail systems are plotted in Figure 3.6. The abscissa denotes the length of the light-rail system. The marginal benefits and marginal costs are plotted directly below.

It is obvious, by sheer inspection, that as the light-rail system is extended farther out in the suburbs of the city, the revenues (benefits) from the system become less and less attractive. The question now is: What criteria should be used in evaluating these six alternatives? Because of the nature of the data presented, the economic criterion is used to identify the best course of action.

The figures shown in Table 3.3 are for discrete lengths of the light-rail system. If the cost-benefit relations shown in Figure 3.6 were continuous, the optimum length of light-rail would be one where the marginal benefit curve cuts the marginal cost curve. This intersection of curves occurs at 17 miles from the city center. The alternative closest to this intersection is alternative 3 (15 miles).

Applications of Benefit-Cost Analysis.   It is best at this stage to understand the applications of benefit-cost analysis through practical examples. Take the case of a decision maker who is confronted with five projects whose details are provided in Table 3.4.

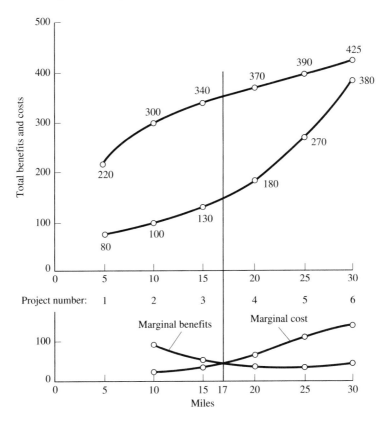

Figure 3.6   Total and marginal benefit-cost analysis.

TABLE 3.4   COST-BENEFIT AND COST OF PROJECTS

Project	Benefits B	Costs C	Ratio B/C	Net benefits B - C	Cumulative initial cost
A	32	4	8	28	4
B	60	10	6	50	14
C	120	40	3	80	54
D	300	150	2	150	204
E	500	450	1.11	50	654

Case 1.   Assume that the projects are mutually exclusive, but there is no funding constraint. In the absence of a budgetary constraint, it would be clearly advantageous to build project D, which would yield a net benefit of 150.

Case 2.   Now assume that the projects are no longer mutually exclusive and that a number of projects of the same category (A through E) up to the limit of the budget can be implemented. For example, A through E are alternative forms of bridges. If the budget constraint in this case were 160, then 40 bridges of type A could be built for 160, providing 1280 as benefits and 1120 as net benefits. Similarly, 16 bridges of type B could be built, providing $(960 - 160) = 800$ as net benefits. Or, four bridges of type C: could be undertaken, resulting in 320 as net benefits. Even one bridge of type D could be considered for 150, but this would give only a 150 net benefit. Obviously, the best solution here would be to adopt 40 versions of project A. Ratios are therefore applicable when dealing with a budget constraint.

Case 3.   Assume that the budget is only 10, in which case only projects A and B are eligible. But here again one runs into the problems of indivisibilities, and therefore the only choice is project B.

Case 4.   Assume that a new project C' is added to the list, as follows:

C': Benefit $= 192$, Cost $= 96$, B/C $= 2$, B $-$ C $= 96$, cumulative cost 150

Also, assume that the budget constraint is 204 and that the projects are not mutually exclusive. Therefore, selecting projects from the top of the list and also taking into account project C', one should undertake A + B + C + C' $= 150$. The question that comes up here is: Which is better—choosing A + B + C + C' or choosing just D, as the choice in case 1, both choices aggregating 150?

Net benefit when A + B + C + C' are considered $= 28 + 50 + 80 + 96 = 254 > 150$ (if D is considered). This exercise indicates rather clearly how limitations of the budget changes the outcome.

Example 3.16

An existing highway is 20 miles long connecting two small cities. It is proposed to improve the alignment by constructing a highway 15 miles long costing $500,000 per mile. Maintenance costs are likely to be $10,000 per mile per annum. Land acquisition costs run $75,000 per mile. It is proposed to abandon the old road and sell the land for $10,000 per mile. Money can be borrowed at 8% per annum. It has been estimated that passenger vehicles travel at 35 mph at a cost of 20 cents per mile with a car occupancy of 1.5 persons per car. What should be the traffic demand for this new road to make this project feasible if the cost of the time of the car's occupants is assessed at $10.00 per hour?

Solution:

Basic costs:

Construction 15 miles at $500,000	=	$7,500,000
Land acquisition 15 miles at $75,000	=	$900,000
		$8,400,000

Deduct sale of land (old alignment)		
20 × 10,000	=	−$200,000
		$8,200,000

It is assumed that the new road will last indefinitely. Therefore, the investment need not be repaid, only the interest.

Annual cost of initial investment:

$$8\% \text{ of } \$8,200,000 \qquad = \qquad \$656,000$$

Net annual income: Assume that N vehicles per annum use the road, 5 miles saved at 20 cents per mile.

$$N\left(\frac{5 \times 20}{100}\right) = \$N$$

Time saved per vehicle/trip:

5 miles at 35 mph = 5/35 = 0.143 hour
Car occupancy = 1.5 persons/car
Value of time = $10 per hour
Therefore,
Cost saving in time at $10/hour = $0.143 \times 1.5 \times N \times 10 = 2.14N$
Maintenance savings = 5 miles × $10,000 = $50,000
Total savings = $50,000 + $N + 2.14N = 50,000 + 3.14N$

Benefit-cost ratio: In order that the project could be justified, the BIC ratio must be equal to or greater than 1. Because the project is assumed to have an infinite life,

$$B/C = \frac{\text{annual benefits}}{\text{annual costs}}$$

or

$$50,000 + 3.14N = 656,000$$

$$N = 192,994 \text{ per annum or about 528 vehicles/day}$$

The project, therefore, would be justified if about 528 vehicles used the new road on a daily basis.

Discussion:

The following points should be noted regarding this problem.

1. The social costs of land use have not been considered. For example, the land on either side of the old road would decrease in value, whereas the land adjacent to the new route would increase in value. The net result would raise the value of *N*.

2. When one works out the B/C ratio, it is generally advisable to use total benefits and total costs. In this problem, B/C was assumed to be 1 and is therefore permissible.

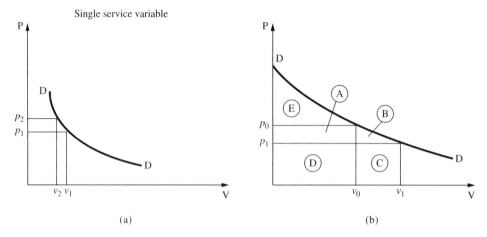

Figure 3.7   Willingness to pay.

3.17.5 The Willingness-to-Pay Concept

The willingness-to-pay concept is useful in visualizing the viewpoint of users of a system, such as a bridge or a toll road. In the case of a single-service variable, as shown in Figure 3.7a (Manheim et al., 1975), if DD is the demand and the price (p) changes from p_1 to p_2, there will be a corresponding change in volume (v) from v_1 to v_2. The $(v_1 - v_2)$ users who abandoned the system are those who got just enough benefit from the system at price p_1 to use it.

If we consider Figure 3.7b using the same argument, reducing the price from p_0 to p_1 increases the number of users from v_0 to v_1. There are three alternatives views on the method of measuring the amount of benefit to users.

1. Gross-benefit view:
   Total benefit to users = (E) + (A) + (D), when volume = v_0.
   Total benefit to users = (E) + (A) + (D) + (B) + (C), for v_1
   Difference between the two actions = (B) + (C)
2. Consumer surplus view: the amount of benefit received by users beyond what they actually pay = (A) + (B)
3. User-cost view = (A) − (C)

Approximation:
$$\text{Gross benefit } B + C = (1/2) (p_0 + p_1) (v_1 - v_0)$$
$$\text{Consumer surplus } A + B = (1/2) (p_0 - p_1) (v_1 + v_0)$$
$$\text{User cost } A - C = v_0 p_0 - v_1 p_1$$
An examination of these three views indicates how different the results can be.

Example 3.17

A section of a busy road, 1 mile long, has a very high pedestrian accident rate. It is proposed to construct a pedestrian bridge over the road for $18 million and increase the existing speed limit on the road. Details of the existing and proposed conditions are as follows:

Details	Existing	Proposed
Vehicle operating speed	25 mph	35 mph
Peak-hour flow	3000 veh/hr	4000 veh/hr
Length of section	1 mile	1 mile
Accident rate/year	450	25 (estimated)
Cost of driving (veh-mi)	$0.35	$0.20
Cost/accident	3000	3000
Peak hours affected	4 hr	4 hr

Determine the feasibility of this project, if the interest rate is 6% per annum and the design life of the pedestrian bridge is 30 years.

Solution:

The direct benefits derived from the construction of the pedestrian bridge can be determined by applying the concepts of consumer's surplus. The following analysis shows the gain in consumer's surplus.

$$\text{Existing price} = \$0.35/\text{veh-mi} \times 1 \text{ mile} = \$0.35/\text{veh}$$
$$\text{Proposed price} = \$0.20/\text{veh-mi} \times 1 \text{ mile} = \$0.20/\text{veh}$$

Annual number of users.
Existing: 3000 veh/hr × 4 hr/day × 365 days = 4.38 million veh/yr.
Proposed: 4000 veh/hr × 4 hr/day × 365 days = 5.84 million veh/yr.
Consumer's surplus as annual
savings = 0.5 (0.35 − 0.20) (4.38 + 5.84) million = $0.7665 million/yr.
Annual savings from accident reduction = 3000 (450 − 25) = $1.275 million/yr.
Total benefits = $2.0415 million/yr.
NPW factor @6% for 30 years = 13.7649
NPW = ($2.0415 million × 13.7649) − 18 = $10.1041 million
Because the NPW of this project is greater than zero, the pedestrian project is sound.

3.18 DEPRECIATION AND TAXES

In day-to-day practice, economic decisions have to consider such items as depreciation, inflation, and taxes, and these are briefly dealt within this section.

Depreciation.   Depreciation, in the accounting sense, is the loss in value of a piece of equipment over time, generally caused by wear and tear, deterioration, obsolescence, or all of the above. One can prepare a graph of the market value of the equipment with time. There are three methods of calculating depreciation:

1. Straight-line;
2. Sum of the years, and;
3. Double declining balance.

Let

P = cost of equipment
n = depreciable life in years
S = salvage value

and

D = depreciation charge per period of time

Then, according to the straight-line method $D = (P - S)/n$
and by the sum-of-years method

$$D = \frac{\text{Remaining life at the beginning of year}}{\text{Sum of years digits for total useful life}}(P - S)$$

where sum of years digits $= 1 + 2 + 3 + \ \dots \ \dots \ + n = \frac{n}{2}(n + 1)$

And, by the double declining balance

$$D = \frac{2}{n}(P - \text{Depreciation charges to date})$$

Example 3.18

An electric motor and pump costing $10,000 has an anticipated salvage value of $2000 at the end of its 4-year depreciable life. Compute the depreciation schedule by the three methods.

Solution:

a) Straight-line depreciation

$$D = \frac{(P - S)}{n} = (10,000 - 2,000)/4 = 2,000/\text{year}$$

b) Sum-of-years digits depreciation

$$\text{sum-of-years-digits} = \frac{n}{2}(n + 1) = \frac{4}{2}(5) = 10$$

$$1^{\text{st}} \text{ year depreciation} = \frac{4}{10}(8,000) = 3,200$$

$$2^{\text{nd}} \text{ year depreciation} = \frac{3}{10}(8,000) = 2,400$$

$$3^{rd} \text{ year depreciation} = \frac{2}{10}(8,000) = 1,600$$

$$4^{th} \text{ year depreciation} = \frac{1}{10}(8,000) = 800$$

c) Double declining balance depreciation

$$1^{st} \text{ year depreciation} = \frac{2}{4}(10,000 - 0) = 5,000$$

$$2^{nd} \text{ year depreciation} = \frac{2}{4}(10,000 - 5,000) = 2,500$$

$$3^{rd} \text{ year depreciation} = \frac{2}{4}(10,000 - 7,500) = 1,250$$

$$4^{th} \text{ year depreciation} = \frac{2}{4}(10,000 - 8,750) = 625$$

Because we have been given that there is a salvage value of $2000, we cannot exceed a total depreciation of more than $10,000 − 2000 = $8000 using the double declining. Therefore, the schedule is as follows:

Year	Straight line	Sum of digits	Double declining
1	2,000	3,200	5,000
2	2,000	2,400	2,500
3	2,000	1,600	500
4	2,000	800	0
	8,000	8,000	8,000

Taxes.   Income tax has to be considered as part of an economic analysis. One generally starts by computing before-tax cash flow, and for this three types of entries are considered.

a) Payment of money to purchase capital assets for which there is no direct tax imposition;
b) Periodic receipts and/or disbursements of the firm for which there is tax liability, and;
c) Receipts of money from the sale of capital assets for which the tax depends on the book value (e.g., cost minus depreciation taken) of the asset. If the salvage value is greater than the book value there is capital gain and taxes have to be paid. On the other hand, if salvage value is less than the book value, there is capital loss.

The best way to determine after-tax cash flow is to tabulate the figures as shown in the example below.

Example 3.19

A company expects to receive $30,000 each year for 20 years from the sale of machines. There is an initial investment of $120,000. Manufacture and sale expenses will be $4,000 per year. Determine the project after-tax ROR. (Assume straight-line depreciation, with no salvage value). Use 30% income tax rate.

Solution:

$$\text{Straight-line depreciation} = \frac{(P - S)}{n} = \frac{120{,}000 - 0}{20} = \$6{,}000/\text{year}$$

Year	Before-tax cash flow	Depreciation	Taxable income	Income tax 30%	After-tax cash flow
0	$-120{,}000$				$-120{,}000$
1	$(30{,}000 - 4{,}000)$ $= 26{,}000$	6,000	20,000	6,000	14,000
2	26,000	6,000	20,000	6,000	14,000
–					
–					
30	26,000	6,000	20,000	6,000	14,000

Now, take the after tax cash flow and compute the ROR at which the present worth of cost equals the present worth of benefits

$$120{,}000 = 14{,}000(P/A,i,20)$$

$$(P/A,i,20) = 120{,}000/14{,}000 = 8.5714$$

From compound interest tables, i = 9.9%

3.19 REPORTING RESULTS

A well-organized summary report can significantly influence the outcome of an economic evaluation effort. In this section, we describe the preparation of a summary report and related materials for use by decision-makers.

The objective of good reporting is to satisfy the information needs of decision makers and other people with a wide range of perspectives, technical understanding, and constituents. Properly conceived and executed, written reports and oral presentations should enable decision makers to select, narrow, or reconfigure the alternative improvements, and generally facilitate, rather than complicate, the decision-making process.

A common format for summarizing key evaluation findings has measures or impact categories listed down the left-hand side of a table and alternatives listed across the top, with entries in the table indicating the status of each alternative with respect to each evaluation measure. For those measures that are in common units (e.g., dollars),

TABLE 3.5 ILLUSTRATIVE SUMMARY FORMAT FOR PRESENTATION OF EVALUATION RESULTS

		Alternative		
	0. "Do nothing"	1. TSM program	2. Arterial improvement	3. Bus improvement program
Mobility	Severe congestion, level of service F by 1986; transit ridership −10%	Reduced congestion, level of service C maintained; transit ridership −10%	Postponed congestion, level of service F by 1998; transit ridership −10%	Reduced congestion, level of service C maintained; transit ridership +80%
Social	Traffic will harm neighborhood	Slightly less traffic disruption	Will make pedestrian movements more difficult	Will strengthen community
Air quality	(percent reduction in pollutant concentration from 1978 levels)			
	No sites in any alternative are expected to violate 1- or 8-hour national ambient air quality standards			
	Total daily corridor emissions (1995)			
	CO −60%	CO −65%	CO −65%	CO −70%
	HC −55%	HC −55%	HC −55%	HC −60%
	NO_x −40%	NO_x −40%	NO_x −40%	NO_x −40%
Noise	Areas with potential for significant noise impact (80 db or more)			
	4 areas	4 areas	6 areas	5 areas
Disruption during construction	—	Minor	2 years of modest construction	1 years of modest construction

TABLE 3.5 ILLUSTRATIVE SUMMARY FORMAT FOR PRESENTATION OF EVALUATION RESULTS (CONTINUED)

Monetary evaluation	(All dollar values are present values in thousands of 1978 dollars based on a discount rate of 10%)			
Time	$1550	$850	$1200	$700
Vehicle operating	$400	$250	$350	$200
Accidents	$300	$150	$200	$100
User subtotal	$2250	$1250	$1750	$1000
Transit operating	$650	$750	$750	$500
O & M subtotal	$1450	$1650	$1600	$1050
Capital	$50	$100	$150	$200
Total transportation costs	$3750	$3000	$3500	$2250
Net benefits	—	$750	$250	$1500
Cost effectiveness	(All dollar values are present values in thousands of 1978 dollars based on a discount rate of 10%)			
Capital, O & M costs per daily person miles of travel	$87.7	$101.7	$101.7	$71.4
Capital costs per hour of daily time savings compared to "do nothing"	—	$230	$320	$210
Additional jobs accessible within 30 minutes/$1000				
Via auto	—	200	230	20
Via transit	—	250	90	460
Total both modes	—	450	320	480

TABLE 3.6 TYPICAL OUTLINE OF EVALUATION SUMMARY REPORT

Cover: should effectively communicate the following:
   What is being studied
   Location: what part of which area
   What decision is about to be made
   Who is involved: jurisdiction and/or agencies

Abstract: about two or three pages elaborating on the foregoing items, making clear choices and the major issues

Map: showing the configuration of the alternatives evaluated

Summary of arguments pro and con for each alternative: a single table highlighting the reasons for selection or rejection of each base on the evaluation findings

Purpose of report: should identify the problem to be addressed by the proposed improvement

The alternatives:
   How they were identified or arrived at?
   One-page summary of each, including a more detailed description, benefits and issues
   More detailed map of each

Evaluation:
   A summary table showing the major differences among options
   More detailed tabular evaluations with text as necessary
   Elaboration on the differences among options
   Explanations for the lack of differences where ones may be expected
   Discussion and clarification of the arguments that may have been advanced by various interests or advocates

Appendix:
   Summary of methodology
   Annotated bibliography of available technical references
   Summary explanation of relevant government regulations and programs

---

subtotals can be provided. The normal bias toward quantitative measures can be avoided by including rows summarizing the key difference among alternatives that can only be characterized by a brief phrase. Table 3.5 provides an illustrative example of such a table.

Table 3.6 shows an outline of a typical summary report. The cover, abstract, map, and summary arguments table could be made into a small brochure of about six single-page sheets. A slightly longer version might include one-page summaries of each alternative.

SUMMARY

Evaluation of engineering works improvement can have different meanings and concerns for different people, depending on the project under investigation. Twenty-five years ago, for instance, projects were evaluated by just taking into account the economics of benefits and costs to the potential user on an aggregate basis. Today, most evaluation exercises take into consideration the environmental, social, economic, and disaggregate effects of improvements.

There are at least three basic points to be kept in mind in deciding on, and later working with, a particular analysis technique, and these are 1) the evaluator should be fully aware of the goals and objectives of the proposed improvements, and their corresponding measures of effectiveness; 2) the evaluation method adopted must be clear and transparent, even to the layperson; and 3) the evaluation procedure should assist the decision maker to come to a rational determination of what is best for the community or city.

Economic evaluation methods are the most common procedures used in most engineering contexts. However, their use entails the conversion of measures of effectiveness to dollar units, and this occasionally poses problems. Planners have therefore evolved several other procedures to obviate this problem.

The evaluation of improvements is considered as one of the more difficult tasks in the field of engineering economics. Not only do the principles of capital budgeting need to be understood and applied, but the evaluator needs to have a basic knowledge of microeconomics and equity (Bauer and Gergen, 1968; de Neufville, 1971; Quade, 1975). More recent references on this subject are texts by Rigg and West (1986) and Schofield (1989).

REFERENCES

BAUER, R. A., and K. J. GERGEN (eds.) (1968). *The Study of Policy Analysis,* W. W. Norton, New York.

DE NEUFVILLE, RICHARD, and J. H. STAFFORD (1971). *Systems Analysis for Engineers and Managers,* McGraw-Hill, New York.

FEDERAL HIGHWAY ADMINISTRATION (FHWA) (1983). Transportation Planning and Problem Solving for Rural Areas and Small Towns, Student Manual, U.S. Department of Transportation, Washington, DC.

JEWEL, T. K. (1980). *A Systems Approach to Civil Engineering, Planning and Design,* Harper & Row, New York.

JOHNSON, R. E. (1990). *The Economics of Building,* John Wiley, New York.

LICHFIELD, N., et al., (1975). *Evaluation in the Planning Process,* Pergamon Press, Oxford.

MANHEIM, M. L., et al, (1975). *Transportation Decision-Making. A Guide to Social and Environmental Consideration,* NCHRP Report 156, Transportation Research Board, National Research Council, Washington, DC.

MCALLISTER, D. M. (1982). *The Evaluation in Environmental Planning,* The MIT Press, Cambridge, MA.

MEYER, M. D, and E. J. MILLER (1984). *Urban Transportation Planning,* McGraw-Hill, New York.

MISHAN, E. T. (1976). *Cost-Benefit Analysis,* Praeger, New York.

MITCHELL, ROBERT L. (1980). *Engineering Economics,* John Wiley, New York.

PILCHER, R. (1992). *Principles of Construction Management,* 3rd edn., McGraw-Hill, London.

QUADE, E. S. (1975). *Analysis for Public Decisions,* Elsevier North-Holland, New York.

RIGGS, J. L., and T. M. WEST (1986). *Engineering Economics,* McGraw-Hill, New York.

SCHOFIELD, J. A. (1989). *Cost-Benefit Analysis in Urban and Regional Planning,* Unwin Hyman, London, UK.

STOKEY, E., and RICHARD ZECKHAUSER (1978). *A Primer for Policy Analysis*, W. W. Norton, New York.

THOMAS, F. N., and J. L. SCHOFER (1970). *Strategies for the Evaluation of Alternative Transportation Plans*, NCHRP Report 96, Highway Research Board, National Research Council, Washington, DC.

EXERCISES

1. What is the present worth of a future sum of $3500 in 10 years with interest at 10%?

2. A man deposits $1200, $2000, and $4000 at the end of 1, 2, and 3 years, respectively, at 10% interest per annum. What will be the accumulation at the end of 6 years?

3. A client wants to finance the purchase of a house costing $50,000 over a period of 10 years. If the interest is 10% per annum, what will be a) the annual payment and b) the monthly payment?

4. A bank offers the following interest rates: a) 6% compounded annually; b) 5.9% compounded semiannually; c) 5.8% compounded quarterly; d) 5.5 % compounded monthly; e) 5.45 % compounded continuously. Which rate would you select to provide the highest return?

5. We want to double a large sum of inherited money. Our bank offers two interest rates: a) 9% compounded annually; and b) 8.70% compounded continuously. Which one should we select and why?

6. A person buys an automobile, promising to pay $300 per month for 5 years, but after 2 years, when the 24th payment is due, she decides to make a lump sum payment to settle the account. If the interest rate is 10%, what amount will she have to pay?

7. The maintenance for a bus, whose life is 10 years, is $1500 per year starting the fourth year, increasing by $200 for each successive year. What is the present worth of maintenance cost?

8. A businessman asks you for a loan of money and offers to pay $20,000 at the end of 5 years. How much should you loan him now if you expect 15% interest per year on your loan.

9. Tom is thinking of buying a used car. The price is $8000 with $1000 as a down payment and the balance in 60 equal installments, with interest at 3% per month. If payments are due at the end of each month, what is the monthly installment?

10. A wealthy businessman wants to establish a fund at his favorite university to help needy students. If he assigns that $20,000 be raised through this trust account earning 10% interest, how much money should he set aside in his trust?

11. Two alternatives for an improvement to a house have the following cash flows:

	Alternatives	
Year	X	Y
0	−40,000	−56,000
1	+16,000	+22,000
2	+16,000	+22,000
3	+16,000	+22,000

At 6% interest rate which alternative is superior:
Using present worth analysis
Using future worth analysis

12. A small project having a useful life of 5 years has five mutually exclusive alternatives. Based on an interest rate of 6%, which alternative should be selected?

	Alternatives				
	I	II	III	IV	V
Initial cost	800	200	400	1000	300
Uniform annual benefit	210	60	90	250	60

13. Six different alternatives have been proposed for improving the water supply for a city, but only one option can be implemented. Each option has a lifetime of eight years and the MARR set is 5%. All figures are in millions of dollars.

	P	Q	R	S	T	U
Capital cost	27	4	17	1	10	5
Annual cost	1	2.5	1.4	1.4	3	2.3
Annual benefit	9	3	8	8	5	2.5

a) Solve by present worth analysis.

b) Solve by annual cash flow analysis.

c) Solve by incremental B/C ratio analysis.

d) Solve by incremental rate of return analysis.

14. A clever community fund-raiser collects funds on the basis that each successive contributor will contribute 1120 of the total collected to date. The collector makes the first contribution of $100.

(a) What is expected from the 150th contributor?

(b) How many contributors does she need to cross the $1 million target?

15. What is the rate of return if $2000 is invested to bring in a net profit of $450 for each of the six succeeding years?

16. A person invests $3000 anticipating a net profit of $200 by the end of the first year, and this profit increases by 25% for each of the next 6 years. What is the rate of return?

17. A transit system is estimated to cost $2,000,000 with operating and maintenance costs of $28,000 per year after the first year, and 10% incremental increases over the next 12 years. At the end of the sixth year, it is anticipated that new equipment and buses will be needed at a total cost of $3,000,000. Calculate the present worth of costs for this system if the rate of return is $9\frac{1}{2}\%$.

18. Estimate the total present sum of money needed to finance and maintain a small transit system, given the following details: initial cost of buses, $2,150,000; annual maintenance cost of buses, $80,000; initial cost of shelters, workshops, etc., $1,500,000; annual maintenance cost of shelters, $40,000; initial cost of equipment, $38,000; annual upkeep of equipment, $13,000; estimated life of buses, 7 years; estimated life of shelters 10 years; estimated life of equipment 5 years; interest rate 10%.

19. A small section of a highway can be dealt with in three different ways: 1) it can be left as it is (do nothing); 2) an embankment-bridge combination can be used; or 3) a cutting tunnel combination can be provided. Using whatever method is suitable, determine which alternative has the best financial advantage.

Alternative	Life	Initial cost	Maintenance
1. As is (do nothing)	Perpetual	—	$35,000
2. Embankment bridge	Perpetual 50 years	$170,000 $200,000	$1000/year $2000/year
3. Cutting tunnel	Perpetual 50 years	$75,000 $300,000	$700/year $2000/year

20. In Example 3.15, objectives 1 through 5 have certain weights assigned. Suppose that these weights were reassigned as follows:

   Objective 1: weight 9 out of 10
   Objective 2: weight 8 out of 10
   Objective 3: weight 7 out of 10
   Objective 4: weight 6 out of 10
   Objective 5: weight 5 out of 10
   What would be the result of your analysis?

21. An old hill road (A) is used by vehicles and the current cost of vehicle and social costs amount to $3.00 million per year. The maintenance cost runs $20,000 per year. Two alternative routes (B and C) are now proposed and their details are given in the table. Discuss which alternative should be adopted, including the one using the old hill road.

Alternative	A	B	C
Interest on construction	—	450	900
Purchase land	—	200	180
Vehicle and social	3000	1500	900
Maintenance	20	10	15

22. Different configuration of a highway network for a new town have been proposed. The capital cost and user savings are as shown in the following table. Which configuration would be most economical?

Alternative	Length (mi)	Capital cost (millions of dollars)	User savings (millions of dollars)
A	32	120	130
B	40	121	170
C	45	125	185
D	49	132	195
E	54	140	198
F	59	150	210
G	66	160	212
H	70	172	220

23. A small city has four transportation alternatives for a bus depot based on three criteria: architectural worth, cost, and public opinion. The architectural features have been assessed by a set of 10 architects and urban planners. The cost has been assessed by an independent firm of construction specialists. Public opinion has been obtained through the elected officials of the city council. The results are as follows. The serviceable life of the depot is 40 years.

Alternative	Initial cost (millions of dollars)	Maintenance per year (thousands of dollars)	Architects in favor (out of 10)	Elected officials in favor (out of 25)
A	2.0	9.2	9	18
B	2.8	8.3	7	14
C	2.9	7.8	6	20
D	3.4	6.3	6	17

Provide an analysis for the decision maker to come to a rational decision and discuss your results.

24. A bus company serves passenger transport between two cities having a demand function $p = 1200 - 7q$, where p is the price in dollars/trip and q is the riders/day. Currently, the fare is $30/trip. The company is planning to buy new buses for a total of $1 million and reduce the fare to $25/trip.

(a) What is the current and anticipated daily and annual ridership?

(b) What would be the change in consumer's surplus?

(c) If the design life of the new buses is 7 years and annual interest rate is 8%, what is the feasibility of this investment?

25. The local public works department has six mutually exclusive proposals for consideration. Their expected life is 30 years at an annual interest rate of 8%. Details follow:

Project	1	2	3	4	5
Cost (millions of $)	980	2450	6900	750	4750
Annual maintenance cost (millions of $)	50	70	250	30	180
Annual benefit	150	50	120	95	85

(a) Rank-order the proposals based on increasing first cost, considering mainte-
    nance as a cost.
(b) Knowing that the budget of the department is limited, which project would you select?
(c) If the largest net benefit is the criterion, which project would you select?

26. Two highway routes having the following characteristics are being considered for
construction:

Routes	A	B
Length (miles)	32	22
Initial cost (millions of $)	15	20
Maintenance cost (millions of $)/yr.	0.16	0.18
Vehicular traffic/day	10,000	15,000
Speed (mph)	40	30
Value of time (dollar/hr)	10	10
Operating cost of veh/mi (cents)	30	40

Compare the two alternative routes and recommend which one should be implemented.

4

Basic Microeconomics for Engineers and Planners

4.1 THE SCOPE OF ECONOMICS AND MICROECONOMICS

"Economics is the study of how people and society end up choosing, with or without the use of money, to employ scarce productive resources that could have alternative uses to produce various commodities and distribute them for consumption, now and in the future, among various persons and groups in society. It analyzes the costs and benefits of improving patterns of resource allocation" (Samuelson, 1976).

Economists conveniently divide the broad area of economics into two main streams. *Microeconomics* is concerned with the study of economic laws that affect a firm on a small scale. It deals with the economic behavior of individual units such as consumers, firms, and resource owners. Microeconomics studies the factors that determine the relative prices of goods and inputs. This chapter describes how economists measure the response of output to changes in prices and income. *Macroeconomics* is the study, on the national and international scale, of the wealth of society. It deals with the behavior of economic aggregates such as gross national product and the level of employment (Mitchell, 1980).

Planning, designing, constructing, operating, and maintaining engineering facilities represent annual commitments of hundreds of billions of dollars, yet engineers, planners, and policy analysts who are responsible for such work often have little or no formal training or education in economics (Wohl and Hendrickson, 1984).

The area covered by microeconomics is very large, and therefore the reader is urged to refer to standard books on this and applied subjects for an in-depth understanding. The topics covered in this chapter are selective and have been included to provide readers with an introduction.

Included in this chapter are the basic concepts of demand and supply functions that are fundamental to understanding, designing, and managing engineering systems. Much of the work conducted in engineering is devoted to specifying and estimating performance function (e.g., demand and supply).

4.2 SOME BASIC ISSUES OF ECONOMICS

Before we get into the details of microeconomics it may be useful to examine a few basic concepts of economics. Scarcity, for example, is considered to be one of the problems that economists study, since all resources are limited in their availability and our desires are unlimited. There is always the fundamental set of questions: what to produce, how to produce, how much, and for whom? In fact, the price system has come about because of scarcity, and consumers must bid on what they are prepared to pay for goods they desire. Economic goods are scarce and limited, while free goods are available at no price, such as free air. Also, there is a difference between consumer goods and capital goods. The former directly satisfies the demands of the consumer, while the latter indirectly satisfy consumer demands, for example real capital.

Another important concept is opportunity cost. This concept is connected to scarcity, because scarcity forces people to make choices and make trade-offs. Getting more of one thing implies getting less of another. Also, when the units of a good are interchangeable, each good should be valued by the goods marginal value—the value of the use that would be forgone if there were one less unit of the good.

The demand curve shows the relationship between the price of a good and the quantity of the good purchased. In Figure 4.1, the demand for bicycles shows that an increase in the price of bicycles from $200 to $250 decreases the demand from 300 per week to 200. According to the law of demand, an increase in price decreases the quantity demanded while everything else remains the same, and as such, most demand curves are negatively sloped.

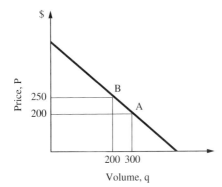

Figure 4.1 Demand for bicycles.

4.3 DEMAND FOR GOODS AND SERVICES

In general, a firm is an enterprise or company that produces a commodity or service for profit. If the total revenue, the product of the unit selling price times the number of items sold, is greater than the cost to produce them, the firm makes a profit; if not, it suffers a loss. Therefore, the efficiency of a firm manufacturing a commodity is an important consideration for its success. A firm's selling price of a good is equally important because it has a direct bearing on the level of production and its ability to gain a profit.

The demand for goods and services, in general, depends largely on consumers' income and the price of the particular good or service relative to other prices. For example, the demand for automobiles depends on the income of the buyers. The demand curve shows the relationship between the price of a good and the quantity of good purchased.

A demand function for a particular product represents the willingness of con- sumers to purchase the product at alternative prices. An example of a linear demand function for scooters is shown in Figure 4.2(a). Such a demand function is useful for predicting prices over a wide range of conditions. This demand function assumes a particular level and distribution of income, population, and socioeconomic charac- teristic. Note that it is an aggregate demand curve, representing the number of scooters demanded at different prices by different people. Functionally,

$$q = \alpha - \beta p \tag{4.1}$$

where q is the quantity of scooters demanded, and α and β are constant demand parameters. The demand function is drawn with a negative slope expressing a famil- iar situation where a decrease in perceived price usually results in an increase in the quantity demanded, although this is not always true.

Figure 4.2(b) shows a series of shifted demand curves, representing changes in the quantity of scooters demanded due to variables other than the perceived price. Naturally, at a price p_0 one could expect different quantities q_1, q_2, and q_3 to be demanded, as the demand curve changes from D_1 to D_2 and D_3. If the curve shifts upward (from D_1 to D_3), it probably indicates an increase in income of people buying scooters.

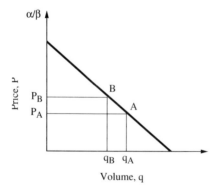

Figure 4.2   (a) Typical demand function.

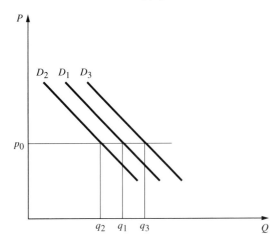

Figure 4.2   (b) Shifted demand curves.

It is important to distinguish short-run changes in quantity due to price changes represented by movement along a single demand curve, as shown in Figure 4.2 *a* from long-run changes due to activity or behavioral variables, represented by shifts in demand functions (as shown in Figure 4.2 *b*).

4.4 DEMAND, SUPPLY, AND EQUILIBRIUM

We have seen that the demand function is a relationship between the quantity demanded of a good and its price. In a similar manner, the supply function (or service function) represents the quantity of goods a producer is willing to offer at a given price, for example, bus seats at a given price, or tons of wheat at a given price. If the demand and supply function for a particular good is known, then it is possible to deal with the concept of equilibrium.

Equilibrium is said to be attained when factors that affect the quantity demanded and those that determine the quantity supplied result in being statically equal (or converging toward equilibrium). According to the law of supply, an increase in the price increases the quantity supplied, while everything else remains the same. The supply curve could shift towards the right because of changes in price or production technology. Simple examples will serve to illustrate equilibrium between demand and supply.

Example 4.1

An airline company has determined the price of a seat on a particular route to be $p = 200 + 0.02n$. The demand for this route by air has been found to be $n = 5000 - 20p$, where p is the price in dollars, and n is the number of seats sold per day. Determine the equilibrium price charged and the number of seats sold per day.

Solution:

$$p = 200 + 0.02n$$
$$n = 5000 - 20p$$

These two equations yield $p = \$214.28$ and $n = 714$ seats.

Discussion:

The logic of the two equations appears reasonable. If the price of an airline ticket rises, the demand would naturally fall. Plotting the two equations to scale may help to visualize the equilibrium price.

Example 4.2

The travel time on a stretch of a highway lane connecting two activity centers has been observed to follow the equation representing the service function.

$$t = 15 + 0.02v$$

where t and v are measured in minutes and vehicles per hour, respectively. The demand function for travel connecting the two activity centers is $v = 4000 - 120t$.

(a) Sketch these two equations and determine the equilibrium time and speed of travel.
(b) If the length of the highway lane is 20 miles, what is the average speed of vehicles traversing this length?

Solution:

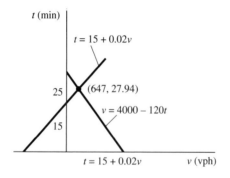

Figure E4.2   Static equilibrium of demand and supply.

$$t = 15 + 0.02v$$
$$v = 4000 - 120t$$

Therefore,

$$v = 647 \text{ vehicles/hour}$$
$$t = 27.94 \text{ minutes}$$
$$\text{Speed} = (20 \times 60)/27.94 = 42.95 \text{ mph}$$

Discussion:

It is customary to plot price, time, or price units on the vertical axis and quantity units on the horizontal axis.

If the price of a good is less than the equilibrium price, there will be a shortage of that good. Let us look at Figure 4.3, showing the number of bicycles sold per week. At a price of $300, which is the equilibrium price, the number of bicycles supplied equals the quantity demanded, so there is neither a shortage nor a surplus of bicycles. However, if the price is less than the equilibrium price, there will be a shortage of bicycles. For example, if the price is at $200, the market will be at point C on the demand curve, and consumers would like to buy 2600 bicycles, and producers are willing to sell only 1000 bicycles (at Point D), resulting in a shortage of 1600 bicycles.

By the same token, if the initial price exceeds the equilibrium price, there will be a surplus of bicycles. For example, if the price of a bicycle is fixed at $400 the market will be at point J on the demand curve and consumers would like to buy 1400 bicycles. However, at point K on the supply curve, producers are willing to sell 3000 bicycles, in which case there is a surplus of 1600 bicycles. Because producers want to sell more bicycles than consumers are willing to buy, one would expect the price of bicycles to decrease over time.

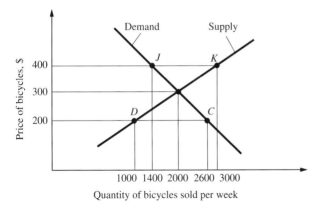

Quantity of bicycles sold per week

Figure 4.3   Quantity of bicycles sold per week.

4.5 SENSITIVITY OF DEMAND

Knowledge of the functional form of demand can be used to forecast changes in the quantity caused by specified changes in the short run. A useful descriptor for explaining the degree of sensitivity to a change in price (or some other factor) is the elasticity of demand (ep).

If $q = \alpha - \beta p$ (see Eq. 1), and e_p = percentage change in quantity demanded that accompanies a 1 percent change in price

then
$$e_p = \frac{\delta q/q}{\delta p/p} = \frac{\delta q}{\delta p} \times \frac{p}{q} \qquad (4.2)$$

where δq is the change in quantity that accompanies δp, the change in price.

$$\text{Arc price elasticity} = \frac{\delta q}{\delta p} \times \frac{p}{q} = \frac{Q_1 - Q_0}{P_1 - P_0} \times \frac{(P_1 + P_0)/2}{(Q_1 + Q_0)/2} \qquad (4.3)$$

where Q_0 and Q_1, represent the quantity demanded corresponding to prices P_0 and P_1, respectively.

For a linear demand function, we can determine the elasticity with respect to price by taking the derivative

$$e_p = \frac{\delta q}{\delta p} \times \frac{p}{q} = \frac{-\beta p}{q} \qquad (4.4)$$

or after substitution for p, using the equation

$$e_p = 1 - \frac{\alpha}{q} \qquad (4.5)$$

Example 4.3

An aggregate demand function is represented by the equation

$$q = 200 - 10p$$

where q is the quantity of a good, and p is the price per unit. Find the price elasticity of demand when

$$q = 0, q = 50, q = 100, q = 150, q = 200 \text{ units}$$

corresponding to

$$p = 20, p = 15, p = 10, p = 5, p = 0 \text{ cents}$$

Solution:

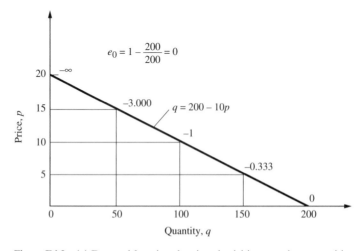

Figure E4.3   (a) Demand function showing elasticities at various quantities.

$$e_p = 1 - \frac{\alpha}{q} \quad \text{where } \alpha = 200$$

$$e_5 = 1 - \frac{200}{150} = -0.333$$

$$e_{10} = 1 - \frac{200}{100} = -1$$

$$e_{15} = 1 - \frac{200}{50} = -3$$

$$e_{20} = 1 - \frac{200}{0} = -\infty$$

When the elasticity is less than -1 (i.e., more negative than -1), the demand is described as being elastic, meaning that the resulting percentage change in quantity will be larger than the percentage change in price. In this case, demand is relatively sensitive to price change. However, when the elasticity is between 0 and -1, the demand is described as being inelastic or relatively insensitive. These ranges are shown in Figure E4.3(b).

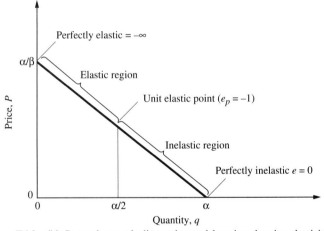

Figure E4.3   (b) General case of a linear demand function showing elasticities.

Discussion:
From Figure E4.3(a), it is obvious that when the price per unit is 20 cents, no units are bought. Also, when nothing is charged per unit, 200 units are bought. Notice that the price elasticity for this system varies from 0 to $-\infty$, with unit elasticity when p $=$ 10.

A linear demand curve has several interesting properties. Notice, as one moves down the demand curve, the price elasticity of demand becomes smaller (i.e., more inelastic). In fact, the elasticity at a given point equals the length of the demand line segment below the point divided by the length of the line segment above it. Another point to note is that the slope of the line is constant, but the *elasticity changes* from ∞ at the top, where the demand line intersects the vertical axis, to zero, where the demand line intersects the horizontal axis. Because elasticity changes along the demand curve, it is essential to specify over what range of prices or quantity the elasticity is measured.

Example 4.4

When the admission rate to an amusement park was $5 per visit, the average number of visits per person was 20 per year. Since the rate has risen to $6, the demand has fallen to 16 per year. What is the elasticity of demand over this range of prices?

Solution:

Arc price elasticity,
$$e_p = -\frac{\Delta Q(P_1 - P_0)/2}{\Delta P(Q_1 + Q_0)/2} = \frac{4 \cdot (5.5)}{(1)(18)} = -1.22$$

Therefore, elastic.

Discussion:

Note that there are problems connected with arc price elasticity because it will differ from point elasticity, the difference increasing as ΔP or ΔQ increase. Also note that elasticity is a unit-free measure of the percent change in quantity demanded (or supplied) for a 1 percent change in price.

4.6 FACTORS AFFECTING ELASTICITIES

4.6.1 Income Elasticities

Income elasticities have a special significance in engineering and are denoted by
$$e_i = \frac{\%\ change\ in\ quantity\ of\ good\ demanded}{\%\ change\ in\ income} \tag{4.6}$$

A good is considered to be *normal* if the demand for the good goes up when a consumer's income increases ($e_i > 0$). Most goods are normal. A good is a *superior* good if it goes up in demand when a consumer's income increases and its share in income also goes up ($e_i > 1$). On the other hand, a good is inferior if the demand for the good goes down when a consumer's income goes up. In North America, an automobile is considered as a superior good, whereas spending money on traveling by mass transit is often considered as an inferior good. Gourmet food is a superior good while cheap beer is an inferior good.

4.6.2 Price Elasticities

In general, consumers buy more of a good than usual when the price goes down and buy less than usual when the price goes up. Some factors that affect price elasticity are:

1. If a consumer spends a substantial percentage of income on, say, transportation, the more willing will he or she be to search hard for a substitute if the price of transportation goes up.
2. The narrower the definition of a good, the more substitutes the good is likely to have, and thus the more elastic its demand will be. For example, the demand for Toyotas is more elastic than the demand for automobiles and the demand for automobiles is more elastic than the demand for transportation.

3. If consumers find out that the price and availability of substitutes are easy, the more elastic the demand will be. Advertising plays an important role in making available substitutes to consumers. In the same context, the more time consumers have to find substitutes, the more elastic demand becomes.
4. Those goods that consumers consider to be "necessities" usually have inelastic demands, whereas goods considered by consumers to be "luxuries" usually have elastic demands. For instance, eyeglasses for a consumer are a necessary good, with few substitutes, whereas a vacation trip to Europe is a luxury good with several substitutes.

4.6.3 Elasticity and Total Revenue

It is possible to tell what the total revenue (price multiplied by output) of a firm is likely to be if the price of a unit changes. Here,

$$e_i = \frac{\% \ change \ in \ quantity \ of \ units \ demanded}{\% \ change \ in \ price} \tag{4.7}$$

If e > 1, price and total revenue are *negatively* related (or demand is elastic); therefore, an increase in price will reduce total revenue, but a decrease in price will increase total revenue.

If e < 1, price and total revenue are *positively* related (or demand is inelastic), in which case, an increase in price will increase total revenue, and a decrease in price will decrease total revenue.

If e = 1, total revenue will remain the same whether the price goes up or down.

Example 4.5

A bus company's linear demand curve is $P = 10 - 0.05Q$, where P is the price of a one-way ticket, and Q is the number of tickets sold per hour. Determine the total revenue along the curve.

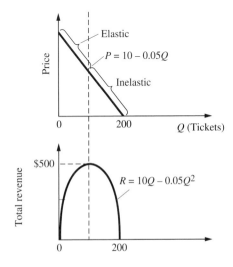

Figure E4.5   Total revenue curve.

Solution:

$$P = 10 - 0.05Q$$
$$R = Q(10 - 0.05Q) \text{ where } R = \text{total revenue}$$
$$R = 10Q - 0.05Q^2$$
$$dR/dQ = 10 - (0.05 \times 2)Q$$

and this is equal to zero when R is maximum.
Therefore, $Q = 100$ when R is 500 (maximum).

Discussion:

Starting from a price of \$10 when hardly any tickets are sold and decreasing the price eventually to half (\$5), the revenue steadily increases to a maximum of \$500/hour (over the elastic portion). After that, the revenue decreases as the price further decreases and finally approaches near zero, when the demand approaches 200 (over the inelastic portion).

4.6.4 Price Elasticity of Supply

Just like we have calculated price elasticity of demand, we can calculate the price elasticity of supply. It is the percentage change in the quantity supplied of a product for a 1 percent change in price. While the formulas for price elasticity of supply are identical to those for the price elasticity of demand, care has to be taken to measure quantity and price changes along its own specific curve or schedule.

4.7 KRAFT DEMAND MODEL

We occasionally come across a demand function where the elasticity of demand for a good with respect to its price is essentially constant. The demand function for such a situation corresponds to the equation:

$$Q = \alpha(P)^\beta \tag{4.8}$$

where α and β are constant parameters of the demand function. To prove that this function has a constant elasticity, we differentiate this function with respect to price:

$$\frac{dQ}{dP} = \alpha\beta P^{\beta-1}$$

and substitute the result into the standard elasticity equation (Eq. 2).

$$
\begin{aligned}
e_p &= \frac{dQ}{dP} \cdot \frac{P}{Q} \\
&= \alpha\beta P^{\beta-1}\frac{P}{Q} \\
&= \alpha\beta P^{\beta-1}PQ^{-1} \quad \text{(Substituting Q from Eq. 4.8)} \\
&= \beta
\end{aligned}
$$

Thus, β, the exponent of price, is the price elasticity.

Example 4.6

The elasticity of transit demand with respect to price has been found to be equal to -2.75, which means that a 1 percent increase in transit fare will result in a 2.75 decrease in the number of passengers using the system. A transit line on this system carries 12,500 passengers per day, charging 50 cents per ride. The management wants to raise the fare to 70 cents per ride. What advice would you offer to management?

Solution:

$$Q = \alpha P^\beta \qquad\qquad (4.8)$$
$$12,500 = \alpha(50)^{-2.75}$$
$$\alpha = 12,500 \times 50^{2.75}$$
$$= 5.876 \times 10^8$$
$$Q = 5.876 \times 10^8 \times (70)^{-2.75}$$
$$= 4955$$

Therefore, the increase in fare from 50 to 70 cents (a 40 percent increase) is likely to reduce the patronage on this line from 12,500 passengers per day to 4955 (a 60.36 percent decrease). In terms of revenue, the results are as follows:

$$50 \text{ cents/rider} \times 12,500 \text{ passengers} = \$6250$$
$$70 \text{ cents/rider} \times 4955 \text{ passengers} = \$3468.50$$
$$\text{Loss in revenue} = \$3406$$

Advice to management would be not to increase the fare.

Discussion:

In general, it has been observed that when the price is elastic (e.g., -2.75), raising the unit price will result in total loss, but lowering price will result in total gain. The converse is also true; if the price is inelastic, raising the unit price will result in total gain, whereas lowering the unit price will result in total loss. Students may like to graph these cases to discover why this is so.

Example 4.7

The demand function for transportation from the suburbs to downtown in a large city is as follows:

$$Q = T^{-0.3}C^{-0.2}A^{0.1}I^{-0.25}$$

where

Q = number of transit trips
T = travel time on transit (hours)
C = fare on transit (dollars)
A = cost of automobile trip (dollars)
I = average income (dollars)

(a) There are currently 10,000 persons per hour riding the transit system, at a flat fare of $1 per ride. What would be the change in ridership with a 90-cent fare? What would the company gain per hour?

(b) By auto, the trip costs $3 (including parking). If the parking charge were raised by 30 cents, how would it affect the transit ridership?

(c) The average income of auto riders is $15,000 per year. What raise in salary will riders require to cover their costs in view of the change in parking charge noted in part (b)?

Solution:

(a) This is essentially a Kraft model. The price elasticity of demand for transit trips is

$$\frac{\delta Q/Q}{\delta C/C} = -0.2$$

This means that a 1 percent reduction in fare would lead to a 0.2 percent increase in transit patronage. Because the fare reduction is $(100 - 90)/100 = 10$ percent, one would expect an increase of 2 percent in patronage. Patronage would now be $10,000 + (10,000 \times 0.02) = 10,200$.

$$10,000 \text{ passengers at } \$1.00/\text{ride} = 10,000$$

$$10,200 \text{ passengers at } \$0.90/\text{ride} = 9,180$$

The company will lose $820 per hour.

(b) The automobile price cross elasticity of demand is 0.1, or

$$\frac{\delta Q/Q}{\delta A/A} = 0.1$$

This means that a 1 percent rise in auto costs (including parking) will lead to a 0.1 percent rise in transit trips. A $0.30 rise is 10 percent of $3. Therefore, a 10 percent rise in auto cost would raise the transit patronage by 1 percent, from 10,000 to 10,100 riders.

(c) The income elasticity should be looked at first:

$$\frac{\delta Q/Q}{\delta I/I} = -0.25$$

which means that an income raise of 1 percent will result in a 0.25 percent decrease in transit patronage, or $\delta Q/Q = 1$ percent, from part (b). Therefore,

$$\frac{1\%}{\delta I/I} = -0.25 \text{ and } \frac{\delta I}{I} = \frac{1\%}{-0.25} = 0.04 = 4\%$$

So a 4 percent increase in income would cover a 30-cent increase (or 10 percent increase) in auto cost. If the average income were $15,000, a $600 raise in salary would change the minds of those auto drivers who were planning to ride the transit system.

4.8 DIRECT AND CROSS ELASTICITIES

The effect of change in the price of a good on the demand for the *same* good is referred to as *direct* elasticity. However, the measure of responsiveness of the demand for a good to the price of another good is referred to as *cross* elasticity.

When consumers buy more of good A when good B's price goes up, we say that good A is a substitute for good B (and good B is a substitute for good A). For example, when the price of gasoline goes up, travelers tend to use more transit. On the other hand, when consumers buy less of good A when good B's price goes up, we say that good A is a complement to good B. In general, complementary goods are ones that are used together. Thus, for example, when the price of downtown parking goes up, the demand for driving a car downtown goes down (and the demand for an equivalent trip by transit or by taxi to downtown goes up).

Goods are substitutes when their cross elasticities are positive, and goods are complements when their cross elasticities of demand are negative.

Example 4.8

A 15 percent increase in gasoline costs has resulted in a 7 percent increase in bus patronage and a 9 percent decrease in gasoline consumption in a midsized city. Calculate the implied direct and cross elasticities of demand.

Solution:

Let

P_0 = price of gas before
P_1 = price of gas after
Q_0 = quantity of gas consumed before
Q_1 = quantity of gas consumed after

Then for *direct elasticity:*

Q_0 (gas) $\times$ 0.91 = Q_1 (gas)
P_0 (gas) $\times$ 1.15 = P_1 (gas)

$$e = \frac{(\Delta Q/Q)}{(\Delta P/P)} = \left[\frac{-0.09/(1 + 0.91)}{0.15/(1 + 1.15)} \right] = -0.361$$

Therefore, the change in gasoline consumption with respect to gasoline cost is inelastic.

B_0 = bus patronage before
B_1 = bus patronage after

Then for *cross elasticity:*

B_0 (bus) $\times$ 1.07 = B_1 (bus)
P_0 (gas) $\times$ 1.15 = P_1 (gas)

$$e = \frac{(\Delta B/B)}{(\Delta P/P)} = \left[\frac{0.07/(1 + 1.07)}{0.15/(1 + 1.15)} \right] = + 0.48$$

Discussion:

In the case of direct elasticity we are calculating the percent change in gasoline consumption due to a 1 percent change in the price of gasoline, while in the case of cross elasticity we are calculating the percent change in bus patronage due to a 1 percent change in gasoline price.

4.9 CONSUMER SURPLUS

Consumer surplus is a measure of the monetary value made available to consumers by the existence of a facility. It is defined as the difference between what consumers might be willing to pay for a service and what they actually pay. A patron of a bus service pays a fare of, say, 50 cents per trip but would be willing to pay up to as much as 75 cents per trip, in which case, his surplus is 25 cents.

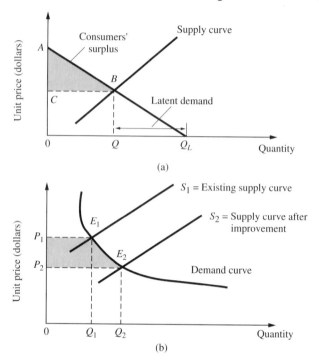

Figure 4.4 (a) Consumer surplus concept, (b) change in consumers surplus.

The demand curve can be considered as an indicator of the utility of the service in terms of price. The consumer surplus concept is shown in Figure 4.4(a). The area ABC represents the total consumer surplus. Maximization of consumer surplus is indeed the maximization of the economic utility of the consumer. In project evaluation, the use of this concept is common, for example for transit systems and irrigation projects.

In general, an improvement of a facility can be measured in terms of the change in consumer surplus. Figure 4.4(b) indicates the case of a street having a traffic supply curve S_1, intersecting a demand curve at E_1. An additional lane has been added, shifting the supply curve to S_2 and therefore intersecting the demand curve at E_2. The change in consumer surplus can be quantified as the area of trapezoid $P_1P_2E_2E_1$, or $(P_1 - P_2)(Q_1 + Q_2)/2$. The consumer surplus is normally defined as the difference between the maximum amount that consumers are willing to pay for a specified quantity of a good rather than going without it. In general, $AOQB$ is equal to the total community benefit, $BCOQ$ is equal to the market value, and ACB is equal to the consumer surplus or net community benefit.

Figure 4.4(a) illustrates an additional concept that is useful to engineers: *latent demand.* Note that travelers between Q and the point of intersection of the demand function and the abscissa do not currently make trips, but would do so if the price per trip were lower than the equilibrium price. The number of such potential travelers is popularly called latent demand. The concept can be used in several ways; for instance, a transit operator hoping to increase transit patronage by introducing a discount rate valid for non peak hours may like to investigate latent demand. Indeed, the quantity of trips demanded, if the price of a trip were zero (free transit), would be $Q_L - Q$, as indicated in Figure 4.4(a).

Example 4.9

A bus company with an existing fleet of one hundred 40-seater buses increases its fleet size by 20 percent and reduces its fare of $1 to 90 cents per ride. Calculate the change in consumer surplus and the price elasticity of demand. Assume that the existing buses had a load factor of 90 percent and it is anticipated that the improvement will result in a 95 percent load factor. Does the company lose money? Assume that all the buses in the fleet are being used during the peak hours. (*Note:* the vehicle load factor is a measure of seat availability, and a load factor of 1.0 means that every seat is occupied.)

Solution:

With the existing situation:

$$100 \text{ buses} \times 40 \text{ seats} \times 0.90 \text{ (load factor)} = 3600 \text{ persons/hr}$$

$$\text{Revenue: } 3600 \times 1.00 = \$3600/hr$$

With the improved situation:

$$120 \text{ buses} \times 40 \text{ seats} \times 0.95 = 4560 \text{ persons/hr}$$

$$\text{Revenue: } 4560 \times 0.90 = \$4104/hr$$

The company gains $4104 - $3600 = $504/hr.
Change in consumer surplus = $(1.00 - 0.90)(3600 + 4560)/2 = \$408/hr$
Price elasticity of demand

$$= \frac{(Q_1 - Q_2)}{(P_1 - P_0)/2} \cdot \frac{(P_1 + P_0)/2}{(Q_1 + Q_0)/2}$$

$$= -\frac{960}{0.10} \cdot \left(\frac{0.95}{4080}\right) = -2.235$$

Discussion:
This is an interesting situation. Even if the number of buses was not increased and the prices were lowered as indicated, resulting in an increase in the load factor, there would be an increase in total revenue by $200 because the price elasticity is elastic (-2.235). Naturally, with more buses being deployed the situation is even better. Consumer surplus is a good way to compare two alternatives.

Example 4.10

Bob is willing to pay up to $10 to travel by bus once every month to visit his family, $8 to travel twice, and $6 to travel three times for the same purpose. (a) If the price of a bus ticket to visit his family is $7, what is Bob's consumer surplus? (b) If the bus company offers three tickets per month for a flat price of $19, will Bob accept the deal? (c) What is the maximum the bus company should charge for Bob to take the three-ticket offer?

Solution:

(a) Bob's individual consumer surplus is $4. For the first trip, Bob's consumer surplus is $10 - 7 = $3 and for the second trip it is $1, which adds up to $4. [He will not go for the third trip.]

(b) Yes, because for three tickets, his consumer surplus is ($10 + 8 + 6 = 24 - 19) = $5, which is better than buying the tickets individually.

(c) At best, Bob will pay $20 for the three-ticket offer, which is the amount that would be the same consumer surplus ($4) as the option of buying the tickets separately ($24 - $20 = $4).

Discussion:

Note that the bus company makes more money from Bob with the package deal. Also, note that in this problem we are calculating an individual's consumer surplus, and not an aggregate (or total) consumer surplus, as in Example 9.

4.10 COSTS

It is essential to have a knowledge of costs or the value of a product or service. To establish the true cost of a product, the analyst must determine, for example, where delivery takes place, who pays for transportation, and who pays for insurance and storage.

Before finding average costs, it is convenient to break down costs into fixed costs, variable costs, and total costs. Fixed costs are inescapable costs and do not change with use. If a plant is producing 500 trucks per day and the plant costs $1 million to run whether one truck is produced or a hundred, the fixed cost is $1 million. Naturally, the fixed cost per truck produced will be reduced with increasing production, even though the fixed cost itself remains unchanged. Variable costs, on the other hand, increase with output or production. If, for example, the labor cost for assembling one truck is $1000, it is likely that this labor cost for assembling two trucks is $1900. The total costs of production is the sum of fixed and variable costs and will increase with production. For any particular level of production, the average cost of a single unit (one truck) can be found by dividing the total cost by the number of units corresponding to the total cost.

4.10.1 Laws Related to Costs

Two concepts related to costs are of importance in engineering. The first, the *law of diminishing returns* states that although an increase in input of one factor of production may cause an increase in output, eventually a point will be reached beyond which increasing units of input will cause progressively less increase in output. The second, the *law of increasing returns to scale* states that in practice, the production of units is often likely to increase at a faster rate than the increase of factors of production. This phenomenon may be due to any number of factors, such as technological features or the effects of specialization.

4.10.2 Average Cost

The mathematical relationship connecting the total cost (C) of a product to the unit cost (c) and magnitude of the output (q) can be written as:

$$C = cq = \alpha + \beta(q)$$

where parameter α equals the fixed cost of production, and the function $\beta(q)$ equals the variable cost of production.

The average cost ($\bar{c}$) of each item produced is equal to:

$$\bar{c} = \frac{C}{q} = \frac{cq}{q} = \frac{\alpha + \beta(q)}{q} = \frac{\alpha}{q} + \frac{\beta(q)}{q} \qquad (4.9)$$

The relationships of the total and average cost functions are shown in Figure 4.5. Notice that in this particular case, as output q increases, the average cost of production decreases, and then increases at higher levels of production. When the production level reaches q', the average cost is a minimum ($\bar{c}$). *Economy of scale* is defined as a decrease in average cost as output increases. There is an economy of scale for production levels between 0 and q'; beyond q', there is no economy of scale, because the average cost rises. This concept is useful to engineers in deciding whether additional capacity (or production) or growth would result in higher profits.

4.10.3 Marginal Cost

The marginal cost of a product is the additional cost associated with the production of an additional unit of output. This is an important concept used in engineering in several ways. An example will clarify this term. The cost of running a train system

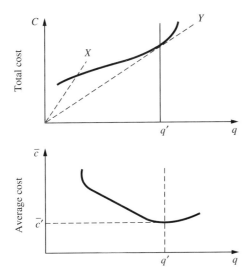

Figure 4.5   Total and average cost.

TABLE 4.1   COSTS ASSOCIATED WITH WAGONS PER TRAIN

(1)	(2)	(3)	(4)	(5)	(6)
Number of wagons/train	Fixed cost, FC	Variable cost, VC	Total cost, TC	Average cost, AC	Marginal cost/unit, MC
1	55	30	85	85.0	
2	55	55	110	55.0	25
3	55	75	130	43.3	20
4	55	105	160	40.0	30
5	55	155	210	42.0	50
6	55	225	280	46.7	70
7	55	315	370	52.9	90
8	55	425	480	60.0	110
9	55	555	610	67.8	130
10	55	705	760	76.0	150

with variable number of wagons is given in Table 4.1. From this table of costs all other costs can be computed. Column (5) is obtained by dividing the total cost given in column (4) by the number of wagons per train shown in column (1). The marginal cost is calculated by subtraction of adjacent rows of total cost (Morlock, 1978).

The figures in column 1 to 4 of Table 4.1 are plotted in Figure 4.6a. Similarly, the figures from column 5 and 6 are plotted in Figure 4.6b. Note that the point of minimum cost ($40) occurs at the intersection of the average cost (AC) and marginal cost (MC) curves. Also, the projection of this point to Figure 4.6a corresponds to the point where the gradient of the tangent drawn from the origin has the minimum slope.

In general, we can summarize what has been demonstrated in our exercise in the train problem:

$$\text{Total cost} = TC(x) = FC = VC(x) \tag{4.10}$$

$$\text{Average cost} = AC(x) = \frac{TC(x)}{x} = \frac{FC}{x} + \frac{VC(x)}{x} \tag{4.11}$$

$$\text{Marginal cost} = MC(x) = TC(x) - TC(x-1) \tag{4.12}$$

where

TC = total cost
FC = fixed cost
VC = variable cost
MC = marginal cost
AC = average cost

When the output is a continuous function, the differential form of the marginal cost is used, in which the marginal cost is the rate of change of total cost with respect to a change in output. In this form, the equation is

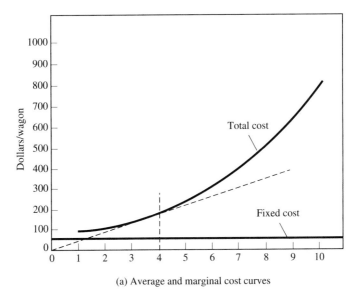

(a) Average and marginal cost curves

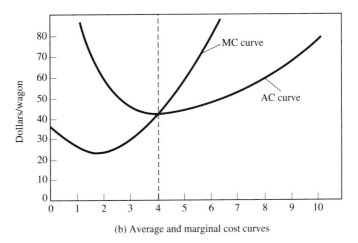

(b) Average and marginal cost curves

Figure 4.6   Total cost, average cost, and marginal cost.

$$MC(x) = \frac{dTC(x)}{dx} = \frac{dVC(x)}{dx} \tag{4.13}$$

From the geometry of the AC and MC curves, it may also be noted that the average cost is proportional to the slope of a line connecting the origin of the total cost curve with a point on that curve corresponding to the total output. In our example, the slope of such a line begins at infinity at zero output and then decreases to its lowest point, when $x = 4$. Beyond this point of $x = 4$, the slope increases again. On the other hand, the marginal cost curve is the slope of the tangent drawn at any point on the total cost curve.

Cost and Production.   In general, a private company or firm will continue to produce and market a product or good as long as it is making a profit. The net profit (P) is equal to the total revenue (R) minus the total cost (C).

$$P = R - C = pq - cq$$

where p is the selling price of one unit of product q, and c is the production cost of one unit.

To maximize net profits of a firm, the necessary condition is

$$\frac{dP}{dq} = \frac{dR}{dq} - \frac{dC}{dq} = 0$$

or

$$\frac{dP}{dq} = \frac{d(pq)}{dq} - \frac{d(cq)}{dq} = 0$$

Thus,

$$\frac{d(pq)}{dq} = \frac{d(cq)}{dq}$$

Let

$$MR = \text{marginal revenue} = \frac{dR}{dq} = \frac{d(pq)}{dq}$$

$$MC = \text{marginal cost} = \frac{dC}{dq} = \frac{d(cq)}{dq}$$

Therefore,

$$MR = MC \qquad\qquad (4.14)$$

This equation says that to achieve the goal of maximizing profits, the firm should produce where marginal revenue equals marginal cost.

Example 4.11

A transport company hauling goods by truck has a cost function, $C = 15q^{1.25}$, where C is the total cost of supply q.

(a) Determine the average cost and the marginal cost.

(b) Prove that the cost elasticity is 1.25.

(c) Is there an economy of scale?

Solution:

(a) $\bar{c} = \dfrac{C}{q} = \dfrac{15q^{1.25}}{q} = 15q^{0.25}$ which is the average cost

$MC = \dfrac{dC}{dq} = (15 \times 1.25)q^{0.25} = 18.75q^{0.25}$

(b) $e = \dfrac{MC}{AC} = \dfrac{18.75q^{0.25}}{15q^{0.25}} = 1.25$ (See Eq. 4.15 below)

(c) Economy of scale does not exist because the average cost increases with increased q.

Cost Elasticity.   The cost elasticity e, is defined as the ratio of percentage change in cost C to the percentage change in supply q.

$$e_c = \frac{\% \, \Delta \text{in cost}}{\% \, \Delta \text{in supply}} = \frac{(\Delta C/C) \cdot 100}{(\Delta q/q) \cdot 100} = \frac{q}{C} \cdot \frac{\Delta C}{q}$$

In the limit when $\Delta q = 0$, $e = (q/C)(dC/dq)$. Rearranging terms,

$$e = \frac{dC/dq}{C/q} = \frac{MC}{AC} \tag{4.15}$$

4.11 CONSUMER CHOICE

A consumer who is operating on a fixed budget must decide how to allocate it among a large number of goods, for example food, clothing, rent, transportation, etc. His problem is to find the affordable consumption bundle that maximizes his utility. In such a situation, a consumer subjectively makes use of indifference curves and a budget line. The indifference curve summarizes the consumer's subjective preferences about alternative consumer goods, while the budget line shows the limits (or constraints) imposed on the consumer.

Suppose a person gets satisfaction or utility from consuming just two goods, A and B as shown in Fig. 4.7. To construct an indifference curve we can pick a series of points 1, 2, 3, 4 and 5 that generate the same level of satisfaction or utility to this person and join these points by a smooth line. What about points 6, 7, 8 and 9, shown on this figure? All combinations above the indifference curve generate more satisfaction than those located on the curve, while those combinations below the curve generate less satisfaction. The shapes of indifference curves vary from one consumer to another.

The slope of the indifference curve is the marginal rate of substitution (MRS) between the two goods and indicates the rate at which this person is willing to substitute one good for another. Notice that the MRS changes as one goes down the curve.

An indifference map is a set of indifference curves. In general, a persons utility increases as he moves in the north easterly direction to higher indifference curves as shown in Figure 4.7.

A person's budget set includes all combinations of goods that he can afford given his income and the price of commodities (or goods). Considering only two goods, the budget line shows all combinations that can exhaust his budget. The slope of the budget line is the market trade-off between two goods. The consumer's objective is to maximize utility subject to the budget constraint. In graphical terms a

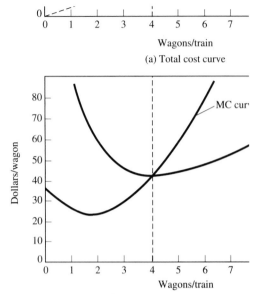

(a) Total cost curve

(b) Average and marginal cost cur   **Figure 4.7** Indifference curves.

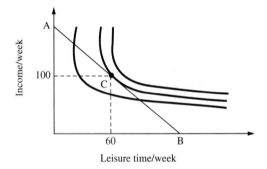

Leisure time/week

Figure 4.8 Budget line and indifference curves.

person will choose a point on the highest feasible indifference curve, as shown in Figure 4.8.

In this figure the indifference curve can be used to find out a worker's choice between leisure time and labor time (or earning time). The budget line AB shows the rate at which he can trade leisure time for income. The slope of the budget line is the wage. (A one-hour decrease in leisure time increases income by the hourly wage.) This worker whose budget line and indifference map are shown, will maximize utility at point C because it is the combination of leisure and income that lies on the highest feasible indifference curve.

Example 4.12

Given a weekly budget of $200 for goods X and Y of $20 and $10 respectively, what is the equation of the budget line?

Solution:

The budget line, AB, includes baskets of X and Y that together are equal to $2000.

Let I = consumer income

Then, $I = XP_x + YP_y$

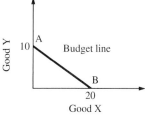

Figure E4.12 Budget line.

Or,

$$Y = \frac{I - XP_x}{P_y} = \frac{I}{P_y} - \left(\frac{P_x}{P_y}\right) \cdot X$$

$$Y = \frac{200}{20} - \left(\frac{10}{20}\right) \cdot X = 10 - \left(\frac{1}{2}\right) \cdot X$$

Example 4.13

The figure below shows a budget line drawn along an indifference curve for a consumer who is primarily interested in two goods X and Y. If the price of good X is $50/unit, (i) what is the consumer's income? (ii) what is the price of good Y? (iii) what is the equation of the budget line? And (iv) find the MRS at equilibrium.

Solution:

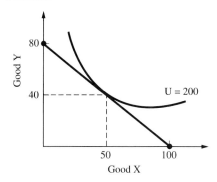

Figure E4.13 Budget and indifference curve.

(i) The consumer's income (or budget) for these two goods must be $(100 \times 50) = \$5000$, because he/she can afford to buy 100 units @ $50/unit of good X if she does not choose to buy any units of good Y.

(ii) The price of good Y per unit must be $5000/80 = \$62.50$

(iii) The equation for the budget line

$(P_x)(X) + (P_y)(Y) = I$, where I = income for the two goods.

$(50)(X) + (62.5)(Y) = 5000$

(iv) At equilibrium, MRS $= P_x/P_y = 50/62.5 = 0.8$

SUMMARY

Economics is the study of how people choose to allocate their scarce resources. Microeconomics is the branch of economics that studies the behavior of individual firms and applies it to business decision making. Terms such as demand, supply, elasticity, consumers' surplus, and latent demand are briefly described.

REFERENCES

DE NEUFVILLE, R., and J. H. STAFFORD (1971). *Systems Analysis for Engineers and Managers,* McGraw-Hill, New York.

MANSFIELD, EDWIN (1975). *Microeconomics: Theory and Applications,* 2nd edn., W. W. Norton, New York.

MITCHELL, ROBERT L. (1980). *Engineering Economics,* John Wiley, New York.

MORLOCK, E. K. (1978). *Introduction to Transportation Engineering and Planning,* McGraw-Hill, New York.

SAMUELSON, PAUL A. (1976). *Economics,* 10th edn., McGraw-Hill, New York.

STUBBS, P. C., W. J. TYSON, and M. Q. DALVI (1980). *Transportation Economics,* Allen & Unwin, London.

WOHL, MARTIN, and CHRIS HENDRICKSON (1984). *Transportation Investment and Pricing Principles,* John Wiley, New York.

EXERCISES

1. What do you consider to be the universal basic economic problem? Suppose you won a national lottery that paid you $1 million per year for life, would you still be subject to economic scarcity?

2. What is microeconomics and how is it different from macroeconomics?

3. The demand and supply for a product are found to be:

$$Q_D = 10,000 - 7500P; \text{ and}$$
$$Q_S = 15,000P + 500$$

   (a) What is the equilibrium price per unit and the quantity?
   (b) If the supply changes to $Q_S = 15,000P$, how would this affect the equilibrium price and quantity?

4. The performance function for a highway connecting a suburb with the business district can be represented by a straight line of the form $t = a + bq$, where t is the travel time in minutes, q is the traffic flow in vehicles per hour, and a and b are constants equal to 10 minutes and 0.01 minute/vehicle-hour, respectively. The demand function, also represented by a straight line, is $q = c + dt$, where c and d are constants equal to 5000 vehicles/hr and -100 vehicles/hour/minute, respectively.

   (a) Find the equilibrium flow (q') and the corresponding equilibrium time (t') algebraically, and sketch the functions.
   (b) If the length of this highway is 22.5 miles, what is the average speed of vehicles along this highway?
   (c) It is proposed to improve this highway such that constant b is now 0.005. What would be the new values of t' and q' and what would be the average speed on this highway?

5. The population growth and added commercial activity have affected the highway link described in Example 4.2 and improvements planned for this highway are reflected by equations representing the new conditions. The new equations are:

$$t_1 = 15 + 0.004v_1$$
$$v_1 = 4333 - 130t_1$$

(a) Sketch the existing and proposed service and demand functions.

(b) What are your estimates of the equilibrium time and vehicle flow on the proposed link?

(c) If the length of this link is 20 miles, what is the average speed over the link?

6. The demand for travel over a stretch of highway is given by the function

$$q = 2000/(t + 1)$$

where q is the travel flow, and t is the travel time (minutes). Plot this demand function and calculate the change in vehicle-hours of travel when travel time increases from 10 to 15 minutes due to road congestion.

7. The demand function for a transit system can be represented by a straight line connecting fare per person and ridership. Observations made on this system resulted in the following: When the fare was $1.50 per ride, the ridership per hour was 2000; when the fare was raised to $2 per ride, the ridership dropped to 1000. What is the equation of the demand function? What would be the patronage if the fare was (a) 50 cents per ride; (b) zero?

8. A bus company is charging a flat rate of 50 cents per ride to any part of the city and has a patronage of 500,000 per day. They have decided to raise the fare to 60 cents per ride and it is estimated that 470,000 people will ride the buses. Calculate (a) the arc-price elasticity; (b) the possible total gain or loss in total revenue per day.

9. Within certain limits, a bus company has a demand function connecting patronage (Q) and price per ride (P) as follows:

$$Q = 2125 - 1000P$$

where Q is person-trips/day, and P is the price (dollars/ride). The manager has the following options to increase the total revenue: (1) attracting additional riders by rescheduling and rerouting the service and thus changing the demand function to $Q = 2150 - 1000P$ or (2) encouraging more riders onto the system by reducing the fare from $1.30 to $1. Which option would you advise the manager to adopt, and give good reasons for doing so.

10. (a) A bus company found that the price elasticity of demand for bus trips during peak hours is -0.40 for small price changes. Management would like to increase the current fare but fears (1) that this action would lead to a reduction in patronage, and (2) that this action would also result in a loss of revenue for the company. Are these fears justified? Discuss your assessment.

(b) If the same situation were to occur in another city where the price elasticity is -1.3, would the fears still be justified?

11. An airline company currently sells a package deal for a $100 return ticket and sells 5000 tickets per week. Because of the high demand, the company raises its fare to $120 per ticket hoping to raise its revenue. If the price elasticity of demand is currently -1.2, what will be the sale of tickets per week and how will this affect total revenue? What conclusions do you draw from this exercise?

12. When the supply of motor scooters falls by 10 percent, the price of scooters goes up 40 percent. What is the price elasticity of demand of scooters? What would happen if scooter-sellers raise prices of scooters by 50 percent because of this reduction of supply?

13. Which of the following pairs of products can be considered as complements and which as substitutes?

    Group A: car batteries and automobiles
    Group B: car tires and automobiles
    Group C: bus travel and airplane travel
    Group D: hot dogs and hamburgers
    Group E: horses and carriages
    Group F: hot dogs and buns

14. Refer to Example 4.6 in the text. If all the conditions remain the same, but the elasticity is -0.75, what would be the advice you would offer to the management of this transit company?

15. The demand function for automobile travel along a major corridor in a medium-sized city is estimated to be

$$Q = aA^{-2.2}B^{0.13}C^{-0.4}D^{0.75}$$

where

    Q = automobile trips per hour (peak-hour)
    a = constant
    A = travel time by automobile in minutes
    B = travel time by bus in minutes
    C = average cost by automobile
    D = average cost by bus

(a) Justify the signs ($+$ or $-$) of the exponents of parameters A, B, C, and D.

(b) Because of congestion likely to occur on this corridor, the travel times of automobiles would increase by 20 percent, and travel times of buses would increase 10 percent. At the same time, auto travel costs rise 5 percent and bus costs decrease 15 percent. What will be the percentage change in auto traffic?

(c) If the average cost of travel by bus increases by 10 percent, but the travel time by bus decreases by 10 percent, what would be the overall percentage increase or decrease in auto travel?

16. A transit company estimates that the cross elasticity of demand between its fast express bus and its ordinary bus is 2. Calculate the effect on the revenue received from the express service if the price of the ordinary bus service is reduced from $75 to $50 while the price of the express bus service remains the same.

17. Latent demand for highway travel is defined as the difference between the maximum number of trips that could be made and the number of trips that are actually made. Given a demand function $q = 1800 - 150t$, what is the time elasticity of demand when $t = 2$ minutes? What is the latent demand at this travel time?

18. A toll bridge is constructed but for the time being it is cost free. If the demand for using it is $P = 120 - 2Q$, where P is the price in $, and Q is the number of vehicles using the bridge per hour.

(a) Sketch the demand curve for bridge crossings.

(b) If the crossings are free, how many vehicles are likely to cross the bridge?

(c) If a toll of $20 is charged per crossing, how many will use the bridge per hour and what will be the loss in consumer's surplus?

19. A transit authority wants to improve one segment of a light-rail system by increasing the peak-hour seating by 20 percent and also by repricing the fare to achieve full utilization. The existing capacity is 2000 seats/hour at $1/seat, and the price elasticity is −0.75. What additional consumer surplus would be generated by this action? Would the transit authority gain from this action?

20. A bus system consisting of 50 buses (55-seaters) charges $1 per ride. It has been decided to put 10 percent more buses into service. What should be the new fare per ride in order to achieve full utilization of capacity if the price elasticity of demand for ridership is −0.3? What will be the additional consumer surplus generated by this action?

21. The ferry service from a city to a recreational island is currently served by regular ferries and a luxury boat. Five thousand passengers per day use the regular ferries and 7000 use the luxury boat. Travel times (min) and fares ($) are

	TRAVEL TIME (MIN)	FARE ($)
Regular	45	1
Luxury	30	2

The linear arc-time and arc-price elasticities of demand are as follows:

		REGULAR		LUXURY
	TIME	FARE	TIME	FARE
Regular	−0.03	−0.04	+0.02	+0.05
Luxury	+0.05	+0.02	−0.07	−0.20

(a) If the fare on the luxury boat is raised to $2.50, what will be the effect on ridership?
(b) If the travel time on the luxury boat is reduced to 25 min, what will be the effect on ridership?
(c) If the regular ferries increase their travel time to 50 min, what will be the effect on ridership?
(d) How will the total revenue of the service be affected by parts (a), (b), and (c)?

22. A survey of college students revealed that, in general, they value one train trip a month to a resort at $40, the second the same month at $30, the third at $20, a fourth at $15, and a fifth at $5. The survey found that students would not take more than five trips even if they were free.
(a) If the train tickets cost $25 a trip, how many trips, on average, will a typical student take?
(b) A travel club, charging monthly dues, allows students to travel free. How much, at most, would a student be willing to pay per month as monthly dues?

23. A rapid transit system has estimated the following costs of operation for one of its routes, making a variety of combinations of cars per train:

Number of Cars	Fixed Cost ($/mi)	Variable Cost ($/mi)
1	45	30
2	45	54
3	45	76
4	45	102
5	45	150
6	45	225
7	45	310

Plot the information for each combination, including the total cost, the average cost, and the marginal cost of operating the system. What is the optimum number of cars per train that should be operated?

24. A concrete-mix plant needs to hire a few men at either $5/hour (if semi-skilled) or $3.50 per hour (if non-skilled). The following data are available for making a decision:

Number of workers	2	3	4	5	6	7	8
Hours of output (yd³)	56	120	180	200	210	218	224

Additional fixed costs are $50/hour when semiskilled labor is used and $60/hour when nonskilled labor is used. Determine the number of workers to be hired to minimize production costs. What is the corresponding cost per cubic yard?

25. A small bus company has a cost function of $C = 5 + 7q$, where q is the number of buses, and C is the cost in 1000's.
(a) Determine the average and marginal cost function.
(b) Determine the elasticity function.
(c) Does an economy of scale exist?
(d) Would you recommend providing additional bus capacity based on (c)?

26. Refer to Exercise 25. A similar bus company in a city has a cost function of $C = 7q$. Answer parts (a) through (d) for this city.

27. An orange-juice manufacturer noted that as the price of fresh oranges decreased from $1 to $0.85 per basket, the number of cans of orange-juice purchased per day increased from 70 to 100. Compute the cross elasticity of demand.

28. Draw a set of indifference curves that display the properties described below:
(a) A person likes one fried egg served on an English muffin, and no other way.
(b) Given two brands of wine X and Y, a person likes each one of them equally well.
(c) A person likes a spoon of jam on any kind of bread.

29. The number of leather shoes demanded and supplied by a company per month are as follows:

Price ($)	Demanded (1000s)	Supplied (1000s)
60	22	14
80	20	16
100	18	18
120	16	20

(a) Graph these values and find the equilibrium price and quantity.

(b) What is the price elasticity of demand when the price is $80?

(c) What is the price elasticity of supply when the price is $80?

(d) If the shoe manufacturers association sets a price ceiling of $80, will there be a surplus or shortage of these shoes and what will be its magnitude?

30. The demand for two-bedroom apartments in a city is $Q = 100 - 5P$, where Q is the number of 2-bedroom apartments in thousands and P is the monthly rent in 100s of dollars. The supply of these apartments is $Q = 50 + 5P$.

(a) What is the equilibrium rent?

(b) If the city rent control department sets a maximum monthly rent of $400, what would be the result?

(c) If it were decided to have a fixed monthly rent of $900, what would happen?

31. The price of magazines is $8/each, while the price of paperbacks is $10/each. A student with a monthly budget of $80 has already spent his money on four magazines, which leaves him with $48 to spend on more magazines and paperbacks. Draw his budget line. If his remaining budget is spent on 1 magazine and 4 paperbacks, show his indifference curve on his budget line.

32. A woman considers movies and musical concerts as perfect substitutes.

(a) Draw a set of indifference curves showing her preference for movies and concerts.

(b) If movies cost $6 and concerts cost $12, which combination will she choose and show this on your graph, assuming her budget is $40.

PART I

5

Review of Probability Theory

5.1 INTRODUCTION

Probability plays an essential role in the evaluation and analysis of data. Almost any set of data, whether collected in the field, compiled in a laboratory or acquired through an expert opinion survey is subject to variability. The existence of variability in a data set collected for a quantity imposes certain degrees of randomness in it. As a result, the prediction of specific limits or values for the quantity will involve uncertainty. Because of this uncertainty, the theory of probability and various methods of statistical analyses are useful in evaluating the data, identifying specific functions, and estimating parameters that can be used to properly define the quantity for which the data has been collected for. Furthermore, the theory of probability can become a useful tool in treating design and decision making problems that involve uncertainties. As an example, suppose an engineer is planning to improve an intersection for a more efficient handling of the traffic. The engineer can utilize two different designs. One involves adding left-turn pockets at the intersection and utilizing left-turn traffic lights. The second method simply involves using a four-way stop sign system. It is obvious that the latter is less costly and can be implemented in a relatively short time. However, this method may involve a larger number of traffic accidents than the method utilizing the traffic lights. As a requirement for each design, the number of accidents per unit time (say a year) for the intersection must be limited to a predetermined maximum value. Because the future accidents for both designs are uncertain, the engineer may wish to utilize a probabilistic formulation in predicting the probability that the number of accidents at the intersection will be limited to the selected maximum value. This probability is then computed for both design options. If the probability associated with the stop-sign design is very high, the engineer may wish to recommend the stop-light design alternative even though it involves a higher cost. The theory of probability may prove to be useful in many such problems where design and decision making are made under an uncertain condition. This chapter reviews the basic elements of the theory of probability and is intended to provide the background needed for understanding the statistical methods that are presented in the subsequent chapters of this book. The chapter also provides several example problems as a means of introducing the role of probability in formulating an engineering problem where analysis, design, and decision making require the treatment of uncertainties and estimation of outcomes of uncertain events.

Generally, a probabilistic problem in engineering is composed of two parts. These are: (1) the theory and model formulation; and (2) the data or knowledge compilation. The theory requires an understanding of the theory of probability and events. The data and knowledge compilation part requires an understanding of statistical methods that can be used in analyzing and treating the collected data for use in the theory and model formulation. We begin the discussion with the review of the theory of probability in this chapter. The subsequent chapters continue with the theory of probability and then extend the discussion into topics in statistics and data analyses. Throughout the review of the probability theory, we present examples that may refer to the model formation and/or the data compilation part.

5.2 EVENTS

To present a simplified description of an event and probability, we refer to a quantity for which certain type of data (in laboratory or field) have been compiled. If n samples are collected for a quantity X, then these n values are expected to differ from one another due to a variety of reasons. The quantity X may simply have different outcomes at different times. For example, if X represents the stress at a critical location in a bridge girder, it is obvious that because of the variation in the intensity of the vehicle load applied on the bridge, the stress will have different values at different times. There are, however, many other reasons for X to have different outcomes. Even if all conditions influencing the variation in X are identical, the error in measuring X may impose a variation in it. The n samples compiled for X actually only represent a small portion of a much larger set of possibilities for the quantity X. By definition, a sample space S for X is a set that contains all possible values of X. A specific outcome (i.e., value) for X is only one possibility and is referred to as a *sample point* (or an *element*). An *event* is defined as a sub-domain or subset of the sample space S. This means that if we identify and single out a group of values in S, we have just made an event which is specific to the quantity X. The sample space S is written in the following form:

$$S:\{x_1, x_2, \dots \} \tag{5.1}$$

which means S contains all possible values of X as described by $x_1, x_2, \dots$ An event such as A is a subset of S and contains a portion of the sample points in S. Thus it can be said that event A *belongs* to S. This can be shown as follows:

$$A \subset S \tag{5.2}$$

thus subsets $A_1:\{x_1\}$ and $A_2:\{x_1, x_2\}$ are two events that belong to S. Note that in a special case an event can contain all the sample points in S. Such an event is the sample space itself and is referred to as one that is *certain* or *sure*. In contrary to this, an event may have none of the sample points of S. Such an event is an *empty* subset of S and is referred to as an *impossible* event. An impossible event is often shown with the symbol ϕ.

In terms of the elementary set theory, an event (which is a subset of S) can be shown with the Venn diagram representation as shown in Figure 5.1. We observe that theoretically, many events can be defined in a sample space. Again, from the set theory, one can refer to definitions described in the following sections.

5.2.1 Complementary Event

The complementary event of A is an event $\overline{A}$ that contains those sample points, of the space S, that do not belong to A. Thus if the space S contains n sample points designated by x_i ($i = 1, 2, \dots, n$), and event A within S contains only x_1 and x_2 then $\overline{A}$ will contain all x_i with the exception of x_1 and x_2. This can be described with the following series of expressions:

$$S:\{x_i; i = 1, 2, \dots, n\}; A \subset S; A:\{x_1, x_2\}; \overline{A}:\{x_3, x_4, \dots, x_n\} \tag{5.3}$$

5.2.2 Combination of Events

Union of Two Events.   The union of events A and B is an event C which contains those sample points that are in A or in B. The symbol $\cup$ is used to describe the union. Note that union is actually an operation conducted on two events. The union can also be conducted on several events. Considering the two events A and B, one can write:

$$C = A \cup B \tag{5.4}$$

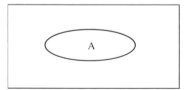

Figure 5.1   Presentation of an event using the Venn diagram.

When the union of n events E_i $(i = 1, 2, \ldots, n)$ is desired, the operation can be written as:

$$C = E_1 \cup E_2 \cup \ldots \cup E_n \qquad (5.5)$$

or in a more condensed form as:

$$C = \bigcup_{i=1}^{n} E_i \qquad (5.6)$$

For example if $A:\{x_1, x_2, x_3\}$ and $B:\{x_1, x_2, x_4, x_6\}$, then event C, which is the union of A and B will be $C:\{x_1, x_2, x_3, x_4, x_6\}$.

Intersection of Events.   For two events (such as A and B), the intersection is an event D such that it contains those sample points that are both in A and B. The symbol $\cap$ is used to describe the intersection. The intersection is another operation on events. It can also be applied to several events. Thus for two events A and B,

$$D = A \cap B \qquad (5.7)$$

and for n events,

$$D = E_1 \cap E_2 \cap \ldots \cap E_n \qquad (5.8)$$

or in a more condensed form,

$$D = \bigcap_{i=1}^{n} E_i \qquad (5.9)$$

Again, considering $A:\{x_1, x_2, x_3\}$ and $B:\{x_1, x_2, x_4, x_6\}$, then the event D, which is the intersection of A and B, will be $D:\{x_1, x_2\}$.

Figure 5.2 shows the union and intersection with the help of the Venn diagram. Notice that events C and D both belong to the sample space S.

5.2.3 Mutually Exclusive and Collectively Exhaustive Events

Mutually Exclusive Events.   If events A and B have no common sample points, their intersection will be an impossible event (ϕ). In this case A and B are said to be *mutually exclusive.* As seen in Figure 5.3, two mutually exclusive events, as

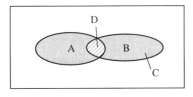

Figure 5.2   Union and intersection of events.

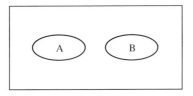

Figure 5.3   Mutually exclusive events.

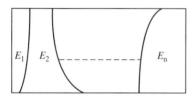

Figure 5.4   Mutually exclusive and collectively exhaustive events.

represented by the Venn diagram, have no common area. Also notice that an event and its complementary event are mutually exclusive.

Collectively Exhaustive Events.   Two or more mutually exclusive events that make up the entire sample space are said to be *collectively exhaustive* (see Figure 5.4). With this definition, we observe that if n events E_i $(i = 1, 2, \ldots, n)$ are mutually exclusive and collectively exhaustive, then:

$$S = E_1 \cup E_2 \cup \ldots \cup E_n \tag{5.10}$$

Furthermore, notice that an event A and its complementary event $\overline{A}$ are also collectively exhaustive. Thus:

$$S = A \cup \overline{A} \tag{5.11}$$

It is important to recognize the mutually exclusive events that make up the entire sample space and are thus considered collectively exhaustive. The identification of these events depends on the sample space and how it is defined in a given problem. Although the Venn diagram may be helpful in recognizing these properties among events, in certain problems, the diagram may not be shown in a simple straightforward manner. As it is later discussed in the section on probability, one way of recognizing whether events are mutually exclusive and collectively exhaustive is through their occurrences within the sample space. If n events are mutually exclusive and collectively exhaustive within S, then the occurrence of one of these events will exclude the occurrence of the other $n - 1$ events. For example, a vehicle that is approaching an intersection will either go straight (event E_1), or make a right turn (event E_2) or a left turn (event E_3). These three events are mutually exclusive. If the sample space concerns the three events only, then they are also collectively exhaustive. This means once it is certain, for example, that the vehicle will go straight (i.e., event E_1 occurs), the other two possibilities are out.

Example 5.1

In a series of field data observations on the type of heavy vehicles on a bridge, vehicle types are divided into seven categories as summarized in Table E5.1.

Establish events describing these categories and identify mutually exclusive events and combination of events within the sample space.

Solution:

Using the designation letters described in Table E5.1, we define an event V_i to represent the event that a vehicle belongs to category i (where $i = 1$ to 7). The sample space will then describe the type of vehicles using the bridge. For a heavy vehicle approaching the bridge, the event of being one of the seven types will belong to the sample space. The events V_i are mutually exclusive. Thus once it is certain that the approaching vehicle is for example a 3-axle truck, then event V_3 will be certain. This means all other events will be out. The combination of the events V_i are only possible through the

TABLE E5.1   CATEGORIES FOR VEHICLE TYPES

Category	Type of Vehicle	Designation
1	Buses	V_1
2	2-axle trucks	V_2
3	3-axle trucks	V_3
4	4-axle trucks	V_4
5	5-axle trucks	V_5
6	6-axle trucks	V_6
7	Trucks with 7 or more axles	V_7

union rule. We can describe a new category that combines two or more of these events. For example, we introduce event W which concerns trucks with less than 5 axles. In this case $W = V_1 \cup V_2 \cup V_3 \cup V_4$. The intersection of two or more events is an impossible events since they are mutually exclusive.

Example 5.2

A construction company is currently bidding for two jobs. Considering a sample space (S) containing the outcome of winning or losing these jobs,

(a) Identify all sample points in S.
(b) Identify the sample points in the following events:
   A = the event that the company will win only one job;
   B = the event that the company will win no jobs; and,
   C = the event that the company will win at least one job.
(c) Identify sample points in the $A \cap B$ and $A \cup B$.

Solution:
(a) Let W represent winning a job; and L losing a job. Thus WW means winning both jobs; WL means winning the first and losing the second job, etc. The sample points in S will then be

$$S: \{WW, WL, LW, LL\}$$

(b) Event A will contain two sample points as follows:

$$A: \{WL, LW\}$$

furthermore, $B: \{LL\}$ and $C: \{LW, WL, WW\}$

(c) The intersection of A and B is an impossible event; since A and B have no sample points in common. Thus $A \cap B = \phi$. The union of A and B contains three sample points as given below:

$$A \cup B: \{WL, LW, LL\}$$

Since events and the sample space follow the principles of the set theory, they are subject to rules governing sets. The following equations present these rules.

$$A \cup B = B \cup A \tag{5.12}$$

$$A \cap B = B \cap A \tag{5.13}$$

$$A \cup (B \cap C) = (A \cup B) \cap (A \cup C) \tag{5.14}$$

$$A \cap (B \cup C) = (A \cap B) \cup (A \cap C) \tag{5.15}$$

5.3 PROBABILITY

We recall that within the sample space S, an event A is a set among several other sets that belong to S. The possibility for A to occur is defined by a numerical value called *probability*. We refer to this possibility as the *probability of A, or P(A)*. This numerical value describes the likelihood that A will occur among all other events that can be identified within S. Mathematically speaking, $P(A)$ is bounded by 0 and 1. We also observe the following:

$$P(\phi) = 0 \tag{5.16}$$
$$P(S) = 1 \tag{5.17}$$

indicating that the probability of an impossible event is zero; whereas, a sure event has a probability of 1. A logical definition for Eq. 5.17 is that since S contains all possible events within the sample space, thus the probability of occurrence of any one event (without being specific as to which one) within S will be unity. For example, in the case of a car approaching an intersection, $P(S)$ simply means the probability that the car will either make a left turn, or a right turn or will go straight. Obviously the probability for this will be unity.

Example 5.3

Assume that Table E5.3 summarizes data gathered on the number per day of each vehicle type listed in Table E5.1 as discussed in Example 5.1. The total number of data points is 192. Assuming that all data points have the same weight among the total of 192, compute the probability of individual events V_i.

Solution:

Since all data points have the same weight, the probability of an individual events V_i will depend on the ratio of the number of data points for the specific vehicle type to the total number of data points. Thus:

$P(V_1)$ = Probability that the vehicle type will be the "buses" type = $5/192$ = 0.026;
$P(V_2)$ = Probability that the vehicle type will be the "2-axle trucks" type = $15/192$ = 0.078;

TABLE E5.3

Vehicle type	Number of vehicle/day
Buses	5
2-axle trucks	15
3-axle trucks	25
4-axle trucks	30
5-axle trucks	105
6-axle trucks	6
Trucks with 7 or more axles	6
Total	192

$P(V_3)$ = Probability that the vehicle type will be the "3-axle trucks" type = 25/192 = 0.130;

$P(V_4)$ = Probability that the vehicle type will be the "4-axle trucks" type = 30/192 = 0.156;

$P(V_5)$ = Probability that the vehicle type will be the "5-axle trucks" type = 105/192 = 0.547;

$P(V_6)$ = Probability that the vehicle type will be the "6-axle trucks" type = 6/192 = 0.031; and,

$P(V_7)$ = Probability that the vehicle type will be the "trucks with 7 or more axles" type = 6/192 = 0.031.

Since the events V_i are mutually exclusive and collectively exhaustive, the sum of the probabilities of the seven events V_1 through V_7 will be equal to 1 because the union of the seven events makes the entire sample space S; i.e., $P(V_1 \cup V_2 \cup \ldots \cup V_7) = P(S) = 1$.

Knowing that an event A and its complementary $\overline{A}$ are mutually exclusive and collectively exhaustive, as described by Eq. 5.11, it can be shown that the probability of $\overline{A}$ is one minus probability of A.

$$P(A \cup \overline{A}) = P(S) = 1 \tag{5.18}$$

Thus

$$P(A) + P(\overline{A}) = 1 \tag{5.19}$$

or

$$P(\overline{A}) = 1 - P(A) \tag{5.20}$$

5.3.1 Probability of the Union of Events

In Example 5.2, the probability of union of events can simply be written as the sum of individual probabilities because the corresponding events are mutually exclusive. However, in general, computing the probability of the union of two or more events is not as simple. Consider first the union of two events A and B. From Figure 5.2, it is obvious that if we simply add the probability of A to that of B, the result will be the probability of union of A and B plus the probability of the intersection of the two events, i.e.:

$$P(A) + P(B) = P(A \cup B) + P(A \cap B) \tag{5.21}$$

Thus from Eq. 5.21, we obtain

$$P(A \cup B) = P(A) + P(B) - P(A \cap B) \tag{5.22}$$

Equation 5.22 can be used to show that the probability of the union of three events A, B, and C, is

$$P(A \cup B \cup C) = P(A) + P(B) + P(C) - P(A \cap B) - P(A \cap C) - P(B \cap C) + P(A \cap B \cap C) \tag{5.23}$$

An expression for the probability of the union of four or more events can also be obtained similarly. However, the expression will involve many terms. In such cases, it may be simpler if the probability of the union of several events be written in terms of the intersection of the complementary of the events following the *deMorgan* rule as described later.

5.3.2 Conditional Probability and Probability of Intersection of Events

In order to derive relations describing the probability of intersection of events, we first introduce the concept of *conditional probability*. If an event A depends on another event B, the occurrence of A within the domain of B is shown with $A|B$ and defined as the event of A given B. The corresponding probability is therefore $P(A|B)$ and is defined as the conditional probability of A given B. Within this definition, A depends on the occurrence of B. Thus the conditional probability $P(A|B)$ assumes that B occurs; and, as such, B becomes a sure event. The conditional probability $P(A|B)$ can then be defined as the portion of event A which is within B. As seen in Figure 5.2, this portion is the intersection of the two events. Since in reality, the event B itself has a probability of occurrence, i.e. $P(B)$, thus the conditional probability $P(A|B)$ will be

$$P(A|B) = \frac{P(A \cap B)}{P(B)} \tag{5.24}$$

Similarly,

$$P(B|A) = \frac{P(B \cap A)}{P(A)} \tag{5.25}$$

From these equations, the following equations for the probability of the intersection of two events can be written as

$$P(A \cap B) = P(A|B)P(B) \tag{5.26}$$

and

$$P(B \cap A) = P(B|A)P(A) \tag{5.27}$$

Of course, the left sides of Eqs. 5.26 and 5.27 are equal. As it is explained later, this will result in Bayes' theorem which can be used to relate $P(A|B)$ to $P(B|A)$ and vice versa.

Equations 5.26 and 5.27 can be generalized to derive equations for the probability of intersection of three or more events. For example, the intersection of the three events A, B, and C can be written as

$$P(A \cap B \cap C) = P(A|B \cap C)P(B \cap C) = P(A|B \cap C)P(B|C)P(C) \tag{5.28}$$

Example 5.4

Figure E5.4 shows a pipeline system made up of two links A and B. The system is used to deliver water between the two points 1 and 2. The probability that during any given month any of the two links fails is 0.03. If link A fails for any reason (say severe freez-

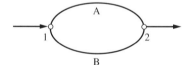

B   **Figure E5.4**   Links in parallel.

ing conditions in winter months), there is 0.1 probability that link B will also fail. Com-pute the probability that there will be no water delivered between the two points 1 and 2 during a given month.

Solution:

Let

$P(A)$ = probability of failure of link A;
$P(B)$ = probability of failure of link B; and,
$P(C)$ = probability that there will be no water delivered to point 2 from point 1.
Since both link A *and* B must fail so that the deliver of water stops, event C will be the intersection of the two events A and B. According to the problem, $P(A) = P(B) = 0.03$. Also $P(B|A) = 0.1$. Thus

$$P(B \cap A) = P(B|A)P(A) = 0.1 \times 0.03 = 0.003.$$

Example 5.5

In Example 5.4, assume links A and B are connected in series as shown in Figure E5.5. With the same information for the probabilities, indicated in Example 5.4, for the fail-ure of individual links, compute the probability that no water is delivered to point 2 from point 1.

Solution:

In this case, if any of the two links or both fail, water delivery at point 2 will be dis-rupted. Denoting C as this event $C = A \cup B$, and

$$P(C) = P(A \cup B) = P(A) + P(B) - P(A \cap B) = 0.03 + 0.03 - 0.003 = 0.057.$$

Note that the probability of the intersection of two events can only be found when the information on the conditional probability of the occurrence of one on the other is known. If the two events are independent of each other, then the occurrence of one will not depend on the other. In this situation, one can write:

$$P(A|B) = P(A) \tag{5.29}$$

and, as such, Eq. 5.26 will be:

$$P(A \cap B) = P(A)P(B) \tag{5.30}$$

The two events A and B that are governed by Eqs. 5.29 and 5.30 are said to be *statisti-cally independent.* In many engineering problems, and within certain approximations, statistical independence between two events may be assumed as a means to simplify the computation of the probability of the intersection of events. For example, in a trans-portation engineering problem, the occurrence of accidents in two intersections that are not directly linked together may be assumed to be independent. It is also important to distinguish the difference between statistical independence and mutually exclusiveness. Note that if the two events A and B are mutually exclusive, the occurrence of one auto-matically excludes the other. This means that the intersection of A and B will be an impossible event. On the other hand, if A and B are statistically independent, occurrence of one does not exclude the other. Although the two events are not related, yet their intersection exists and has a non-zero probability. This simply explains that the proba-bility of the occurrence of A and B does exist and can be computed through Eq. 5.30.

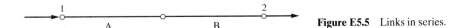

Figure E5.5   Links in series.

Example 5.6

A motorist is driving at the posted speed along a roadway. He has two intersections ahead. The probability of encountering a red light at any of the two intersections is 0.30. Assume the event of encountering a red light at any one intersection is independent of the same event at the other intersection.

(a) Compute the probability that the motorist will encounter at least one red light.
(b) Compute the probability that the motorist will encounter red lights at both intersections.

Solution:

Let A be the event of encountering a red light at the first intersection; and B the same event at the second intersection.

(a) In this part, the probability of encountering at least one red light means encountering a red light at either intersections or at both. Thus the union of the two events A and B is desired. Defining this union as C, $P(C) = P(A) + P(B) - P(A \cap B)$. Since the two events A and B are independent, then $P(C) = P(A) + P(B) - P(A)P(B) = 0.30 + 0.30 - 0.30 \times 0.30 = 0.51$.

(b) If D is defined as the event of concern in this part, then $D = A \cap B$. Thus $P(D) = P(A)P(B) = 0.09$.

In regard to conditional probability, we further observe that the probability of the complementary event of A is written as:

$$P(\overline{A}|B) = 1 - P(A|B) \qquad (5.31)$$

Note that the "given" event, i.e., B, does not change on both sides of the equation. This is to say that $P(\overline{A}|\overline{B}) \neq 1 - P(A|B)$; but $P(\overline{A}|\overline{B}) = 1 - P(A|\overline{B})$.

5.3.3 Bayes' Theorem

In light of Eqs. 5.26 and 5.27, one can write:

$$P(A|B) = \frac{P(B|A)P(A)}{P(B)} \qquad (5.32)$$

This relation is known as *Bayes' theorem.* In many engineering problems, Eq. 5.32 may be useful as a means to compute a desired conditional probability.

Example 5.7

The probability of a traffic congestion in the northbound lanes of a freeway during the morning rush-hours in any working day is estimated as 0.02. The probability of a traffic congestion during the same time period in the southbound lanes is only 0.005. There is a dependence between the traffic congestion in the southbound and the northbound lanes during rush-hours. If a congestion in the northbound lanes occurs, there will be 0.17 probability that the southbound will also experience congestion.

(a) Compute the probability that during the morning rush-hours, there will be congestions in both the northbound and the southbound lanes.
(b) Compute the probability that there will be a congestion in the freeway during the morning rush-hours.
(c) If there is a congestion in the southbound lanes, what will the probability that the northbound lanes has also experienced a congestion be?

Solution:

For simplicity, let:

A = event of a traffic congestion in the northbound lanes; and B = event of traffic congestion in the southbound lanes. Then the following information is known from the problem.

$P(A) = 0.02$; and $P(B) = 0.005$. Furthermore, notice that if A occurs, there is 0.17 probability that B will also occur. Thus $P(B|A) = 0.17$.

(a) In this part, since the occurrence of both A and B is desired, the intersection of the two events must be formed. Calling this event as C, we can write:

$$P(C) = P(A\cap B) = P(B|A)P(A) = 0.17 \times 0.02 = 0.0034$$

(b) In this part, since no specific reference to the direction of the lanes has been made, the event of concern is the union of A and B. In fact, we are looking for the probability that there will be a traffic congestion in either the northbound (Event A) or in the southbound lanes (Event B) or in both. Calling the event of concern as D, we can write:

$$P(D) = P(A\cup B) = P(A) + P(B) - P(A\cap B) = 0.02 + 0.005 - 0.0034 = 0.0216$$

(c) In this part $P(A|B)$ is desired. Bayes' theorem (Eq. 5.32) can be used for this purpose.

$$P(A|B) = P(B|A)P(A)/P(B) = 0.17 \times 0.02/0.005 = 0.68.$$

Example 5.8

Derive an expression for $P(\overline{A}|\overline{B})$ in terms of $P(A|B)$, $P(A)$ and $P(B)$.

Solution:

Equations 5.31 and 5.32 can be used for this purpose. The following shows the sequence of operations.

$$P(\overline{A}|\overline{B}) = 1 - P(A|\overline{B}) = 1 - \frac{P(\overline{B}|A)P(A)}{P(\overline{B})} = 1 - \frac{[1 - P(B|A)]P(A)}{1 - P(B)}$$

or

$$P(\overline{A}|\overline{B}) = 1 - \frac{\left[1 - \dfrac{P(A|B)P(B)}{P(A)}\right]P(A)}{1 - P(B)} = 1 - \frac{P(A) - P(A|B)P(B)}{1 - P(B)}$$

Using the numerical values in Example 5.7,

$$P(\overline{A}|\overline{B}) = 1 - (0.02 - 0.68 \times 0.005)/(1 - 0.005) = 0.9833.$$

This means that if there is no traffic congestion in the southbound lanes, there will be 0.9833 probability that the northbound lanes do not have any congestion either. We emphasize that other methods (including the use of the Venn diagram) can also be employed in deriving an expression for $P(\overline{A}|\overline{B})$.

5.3.4 deMorgan's Rule

deMorgan's rule applied to two events A and B is defined via the following two equations:

$$P(\overline{A\cup B}) = P(\overline{A}\cap\overline{B}) \tag{5.33}$$

$$P(\overline{A\cap B}) = P(\overline{A}\cup\overline{B}) \tag{5.34}$$

To prove these equations, the Venn diagram can be used. However, they can also be proved via equations governing the combination of events and probabilities. Considering the expression found for $P(\overline{A}|B)$ in Example 5.8, we can write:

$$P(\overline{A}|\overline{B})[1 - P(B)] = 1 - P(B) - P(A) + P(A|B)P(B)$$

or

$$P(\overline{A}|\overline{B})P(\overline{B}) = 1 - P(A \cup B)$$

The left side of the equation is $P(\overline{A} \cap \overline{B})$; while the right side is $P(\overline{A \cup B})$. Thus, Eq. 5.33 is proved. Considering again the expression found in Example 5.8, we can also write:

$$P(A|B) = 1 - \frac{[P(\overline{A}) - P(\overline{A}|\overline{B})P(\overline{B})]}{1 - P(\overline{B})}$$

or

$$P(A|B)[1 - P(\overline{B})] = 1 - P(\overline{B}) - [P(\overline{A}) - P(\overline{A}|\overline{B})P(\overline{B})]$$

or

$$P(A \cap B) = 1 - P(\overline{B}) - P(\overline{A}) + P(\overline{A} \cap \overline{B}) = 1 - P(\overline{A} \cup \overline{B})$$

or

$$1 - P(A \cap B) = P(\overline{A} \cup \overline{B})$$

The left side of this equation is $P(\overline{A \cap B})$. Thus, Eq. 5.34 is proved.

It can easily be shown that in general forms, deMorgan's rule can be defined via the following equations:

$$P(\overline{E_1 \cup E_2 \cup E_3 \cup \ldots \cup E_n}) = P(\overline{E_1} \cap \overline{E_2} \cap \overline{E_3} \cap \ldots \cap \overline{E_n}) \tag{5.35}$$

$$P(\overline{E_1 \cap E_2 \cap E_3 \cap \ldots \cap E_n}) = P(\overline{E_1} \cup \overline{E_2} \cup \overline{E_3} \cup \ldots \cup \overline{E_n}) \tag{5.36}$$

The following example shows an application of deMorgan's rule and the proof of these equations through a practical engineering problem.

Example 5.9

A large engineering system is made up of 15 components. A failure in any component will result in a system malfunction. In a series of laboratory tests, the probability of failure of any one component has been estimated to be 0.0025. Assuming that the conditions between failure of individual components are statistically independent, compute the probability of malfunction of the system.

Solutions:

In general, for a system made up of n components, the probability of malfunction (failure), p_F, can be written via the union rule as follows:

$$p_F = P(E_1 \cup E_2 \cup E_3 \cup \ldots \cup E_n)$$

in which E_i = event of failure in component i. The probability of no malfunction in the system p_S is equal to $(1 - p_F)$ and can be written as:

$$p_S = 1 - p_F = 1 - P(E_1 \cup E_2 \cup E_3 \cup \ldots \cup E_n) = P(\overline{E_1 \cup E_2 \cup E_3 \cup \ldots \cup E_n})$$

The probability p_S can also be obtained independently considering the probabilities of no failure (i.e., survival) of individual components. The system will have no malfunction if all components survive. This means that the event of no malfunction in the system is

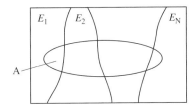

Figure 5.5 The Venn diagram presentation of total probability theorem.

the intersection of the complementary events of E_i. Introducing $\overline{E}_i$ as the complementary of E_i (i.e., the survival of element i), then p_S can be formulated as follows:

$$p_S = P(\overline{E}_1 \cap \overline{E}_2 \cap \overline{E}_3 \cap \ldots \cap \overline{E}_n)$$

which proves deMorgan's rule. In this example problem, the Events E_i are statistically independent. This means that their complimentary events are also independent. Accordingly, the probability of no malfunction will be:

$$\begin{aligned}
p_S &= P(\overline{E}_1)P(\overline{E}_2)P(\overline{E}_3) \ldots P(\overline{E}_n) \\
&= [1 - P(E_1)][1 - P(E_2)][1 - P(E_3)] \ldots [1 - P(E_n)] \\
&= (1 - 0.0025)^{15} = 0.9631
\end{aligned}$$

and the probability of malfunction is:

$$p_F = 1 - 0.9631 = 0.0369.$$

5.3.5 Total Probability Theorem

If an event A depends on n mutually exclusive and collectively exhaustive events such as $E_1, E_2, E_3, \ldots, E_n$, then the probability of A is obtained from the *total probability theorem*. As seen in Figure 5.5, the intersection of the event A and any of the n events E_i is an event $A \cap E_i$. Since the events $A \cap E_i$ are mutually exclusive, then the probability of A can be written as:

$$P(A) = P(A \cap E_1) + P(A \cap E_2) + \ldots + P(A \cap E_n) \tag{5.37}$$

or

$$P(A) = P(A|E_1)P(E_1) + P(A|E_2)P(E_2) + \ldots + P(A|E_n)P(E_n)$$

$$= \sum_{i=1}^{n} P(A|E_i)P(E_i) \tag{5.38}$$

In light of Eqs. 5.32 and 5.38, a generalized equation for Bayes' theorem can be written as follows:

$$P(E_i|A) = \frac{P(A|E_i)P(E_i)}{P(A)} = \frac{P(A|E_i)P(E_i)}{\sum_{i=1}^{n} P(A)|E_i)P(E_i)} \tag{5.39}$$

Example 5.10

The probability of failure of a cable used in a suspension bridge depends on the tension load transferred to the cable. For simplicity, the load in the cable is divided into three groups, namely, light, moderately heavy, and heavy with relative probabilities of 3 to 2 to 1, respectively. A structural analysis of the cable shows that if the load is light, the probability of failure of the cable is only 0.0001. However, if the load is moderately heavy, the failure probability is 0.005. For a heavy load, the failure probability is 0.2.

(a) Compute the probability of failure of the cable.

(b) If the cable fails, what is the probability that the failure is caused by a light load?

Solutions:

In this problem, let A be the event of failure of the cable for any type of load; and E_i the events representing the types of loading in the cable. Thus,

$E_1 =$ event that the load will be light;

$E_2 =$ event that the load will be moderately heavy; and

$E_3 =$ event that the load will be heavy.

Since the loading can only be one of these three conditions, then the three events E_1, E_2, and E_3 are mutually exclusive and collectively exhaustive. Based on the information given in the problem, the following probabilities are computed for these three events:

$P(E_1) = 3/(3 + 2 + 1) = 0.500$

$P(E_2) = 2/(3 + 2 + 1) = 0.333$

$P(E_3) = 1/(3 + 2 + 1) = 0.167$

Note that the sum of these three probabilities must be equal to 1. The information on the failure probability of the cable is in the form of conditional probabilities given the three loading types. This information can be written as follows:

$P(A|E_1) = 0.0001$

$P(A|E_2) = 0.005$

$P(A|E_3) = 0.2$

(a) From Eq. 5.38, using the total probability theorem

$$P(A) = 0.0001 \times 0.500 + 0.005 \times 0.333 + 0.2 \times 0.167 = 0.0351$$

(b) In this part, the probability of concern can be computed using Bayes' theorem (Eq. 5.39). The required probability is $P(E_1|A)$. From Eq. 5.39:

$$P(E_1|A) = 0.0001 \times 0.500/0.0351 = 0.0014.$$

Example 5.11

Accidents in a roadway junction depend on the volume V of traffic (in number of cars/minute) approaching the junction; and the average speed S (in km/h) of the approaching cars. For simplicity, only two possibilities for each of these factors are considered. Table E5.11 presents the probability of a traffic accident at the junction during any minute time period for various combination of these two factors.

TABLE E5.11 PROBABILITY OF ACCIDENTS IN TERMS OF TRAFFIC VOLUME (V) AND AVERAGE SPEED (S)

	$V \leq 10$	$V > 10$
$S \leq 50$	0.01	0.12
$S > 50$	0.18	0.32

During any minute time period, there is a 50 percent chance that the average speed is less than or greater than 50 km/h. Also the traffic can be less than or greater than 10 cars/min with a 50 percent chance. Assume V and S are statistically independent.

(a) Compute the probability of accidents during any minute time period at the junction.

(b) If there are 8 identical such junctions in a row along a portion of the roadway, compute the probability that none of the junctions will experience accidents during any minute time period. Assume conditions between these junctions are statistically independent.

Solution:

Considering the possibilities listed in Table E5.11, there are four combinations of S and V. These combinations make four mutually exclusive and collectively exhaustive events as describe below:

E_1 = event of $V \leq 10$ and $S \leq 50$; $P(E_1) = 0.5 \times 0.5 = 0.25$
E_2 = event of $V > 10$ and $S \leq 50$; $P(E_2) = 0.5 \times 0.5 = 0.25$
E_3 = event of $V \leq 10$ and $S > 50$; $P(E_3) = 0.5 \times 0.5 = 0.25$
E_4 = event of $V > 10$ and $S > 50$; $P(E_4) = 0.5 \times 0.5 = 0.25$

(a) From the total probability theorem, if A is the event of accidents in the junction, then $P(A)$ can be computed as follows:

$$P(A) = P(A|E_1)P(E_1) + P(A|E_2)P(E_2) + P(A|E_3)P(E_3) + P(A|E_4)P(E_4)$$

$$P(A) = 0.01 \times 0.25 + 0.18 \times 0.25 + 0.12 \times 0.25 + 0.32 \times 0.25 = 0.1575$$

(b) The intersection rule is used in this part. If A_i is the event of accidents for junction i, the event of no accidents for the eight junctions (say event $\bar{B}$) will be

$$\bar{B} = \bar{A_1} \cap \bar{A_2} \cap \bar{A_3} \cap \ldots \cap \bar{A_8}$$

and $P(\bar{B}) = (1 - 0.1575)^8 = 0.254$.

Example 5.12

Life cycle analysis of bridge structures often calls for a planning study to optimize the cost associated with bridge maintenance. Maintenance includes a host of activities ranging from a minor repair to total replacement. Often the decision to repair versus to replace requires a careful evaluation and analysis on the part of the engineer. For simplicity, assume there are only three options considered for a bridge. These are repair, rehabilitation, and replacement. Repair involves any type of work to keep the bridge in operation. Rehabilitation involves major repair along with an upgrade on the bridge condition such that an improvement in the service is achieved. Replacement means complete removal of the structure and replacement with a new structure.

An engineer is planning for the next year budget for the maintenance of the bridge that will include only one of the three options (i.e., repair, rehabilitation, and replacement). From past experience, the engineer estimates that the odds for similar bridges to require repair, rehabilitation, or replacement, respectively, are 1 to 2 to 3. The budget allotted to this bridge is a fixed amount. If the decision is to only repair the bridge, the probability that the cost will be within the budget will be 1. If the decision is to rehabilitate, the probability that the cost will be within the budget will be 0.99. However, if the decision is to replace the bridge, the probability that the cost will be within the budget will be 0.03. The engineer is not sure what decision will finally be selected.

(a) Compute the probability that the cost associated with maintenance (that includes any of the three options) will be within the allotted budget.

(b) If there is a cost over-run (i.e., the allotted budget is exceeded by the cost), compute the probability that the decision is for the rehabilitation option.

Solution:

The three options are mutually exclusive and collectively exhaustive. Let:

E_1 = event that the decision will be in favor of repair
E_2 = event that the decision will be in favor of rehabilitation
E_3 = event that the decision will be in favor of replacement
A = event that the cost of maintenance will be within the allotted budget

From the information given in the problem,

$P(E_1) = 1/(1 + 2 + 3) = 0.167$
$P(E_2) = 2/(1 + 2 + 3) = 0.333$
$P(E_3) = 3/(1 + 2 + 3) = 0.500$

(a) Since it is not certain which option will be selected, then $P(A)$ can be formulated using the total probability theorem considering all possible options. From information provided by the problem,

$$P(A|E_1) = 1.0; \; P(A|E_2) = 0.99; \; P(A|E_3) = 0.03$$

$$P(A) = P(A|E_1)P(E_1) + P(A|E_2)P(E_2) + P(A|E_3)P(E_3)$$
$$= 1.0 \times 0.167 + 0.99 \times 0.333 + 0.03 \times 0.500 = 0.512.$$

(b) This part is an application of Bayes' theorem. Note that the event of over-run is the complementary event of A. Thus the required probability is $P(E_2|\overline{A})$ and can be computed as follows:

$$P(E_2|\overline{A}) = P(\overline{A}|E_2)P(E_2)/P(\overline{A}) = [1 - P(A|E_2)]P(E_2)/[1 - P(A)]$$
$$= (1 - 0.99) \times 0.333/(1 - 0.512) = 0.007.$$

SUMMARY

In this chapter, the basic rules governing events and equations related to probabilities were reviewed. Probability is a numerical measure that describes the chance of occurrence of a specific event among a number of possibilities. The need to use probability stems from the fact that there is an element of uncertainty involved in any engineering decision making process, and in any engineering analysis and design procedure. Essentially, the purpose of analysis and evaluation of engineering data is to provide information for a meaningful estimation of parameters that influence decision making, and system analysis and design. The basic elements of the theory of probability are especially important in understanding the underlying concepts in evaluation of data and estimation of statistical values of parameters that are involved in engineering problems.

The review of events and probability provided in this chapter is brief. Nevertheless, the chapter provides nearly all essential equations needed to proceed with solving a given engineering problem. Several examples were provided to better acquaint the reader to the types of problems that an engineer may be facing to. For a more complete treatment of the theory of probability as applied to engineering problems, the reader is referred to the list of references at the end of this chapter. These suggested references provide the reader with an ample number of illustrative examples that are useful for better understanding the application of the theory of probability to engineering problems.

REFERENCES

ANG, A. H.-S. and W. H. TANG (1975). Chapter 2 in *Probability Concept in Engineering Planning and Design, Volume I-Basic Principles,* John Wiley & Sons.

BENJAMIN, J., and C. A. CORNELL (1970). *Probability, Statistics and Decision-Making for Civil Engineers,* McGraw-Hill Book Company, New York, NY.

MILTON, J. S., and J. C. ARNOLD (1986). Chapter 2 in *Probability and Statistics in the Engineering and Computer Sciences,* McGraw-Hill Book Company, New York, NY.

WALPOLE, R. E., R. H. MYERS, and S. L. MYERS (1998). Chapter 2 in *Probability and Statistics for Engineers and Scientists,* Sixth Edition, Prentice Hall.

EXERCISES

1. Two events A and B are defined with their sample points as follows:

$$A:\{a, b, c, d, e, f\} \qquad B:\{a, c, g, h\}$$

Determine the sample points that belong to:

(a) Event C which is the union of A and B.

(b) Event D which is the intersection of A and B.

2. In designing a runway for a small airport, the wind velocity and wind direction are important factors. Assume the direction makes an angle θ with respect to north. The possible values for θ range from 0 to 180 degrees. The wind velocity V ranges between 0 to 140 km/h.

(a) Show possible values of θ and V in the form of a Venn Diagram.

(b) Identify and show the following events on the diagram.

$$E_1: 20 < V \le 140 \text{ and } 0 < \theta \le 45$$

$$E_2: 50 < V \le 100 \text{ and } 0 < \theta \le 90$$

(c) Define and show $E_1 \cup E_2$ and $E_1 \cap E_2$.

3. Events A and B given below contain possible values for the soil bearing capacities (kN/m^2) of three adjacent sites.

$A = \{100,120,150,170\}$
$B = \{120,130,140\}$
$C = \{130,135\}$

(a) Determine the sample points in the intersection of A and B and in the union of A and B.

(b) Determine the sample points in the intersection of B and C and in the union of B and C.

(c) Among the events A, B, and C, which two are mutually exclusive?

(d) Determine the sample points in the union of A, B, and C.

4. The duration of a construction project ranges between 121 to 160 days. There is an equal chance for the duration to be equal to any number of days between 121 and 160. Currently the project is scheduled to be finished in less than or equal to 130 days.

(a) Compute the probability that the project will be finished on time.

(b) Compute the probability that the project will be delayed.

5. A water pipeline system is made up of three links in series. The probability of failure in each link (i.e., the probability that the pipeline link will not be able to deliver water) is 0.01 in any given year. The condition between the links is statistically independent. Compute the probability of failure of the pipeline system.

6. Repeat Exercise 5, however assume that the three links are parallel to each other.

7. Delay in a construction project depends mainly on either the material shortage or bad weather conditions. From past performance data, the following are known:

   • In any given season, the probability of shortage of material is 0.01; the probability of experiencing a bad weather condition is 0.05. Assume these two events are statistically independent.

   • If only one of these factors occurs, the probability of delay in the project is 0.10; whereas, if both factors apply, the probability of project delay is 0.60.

   (a) Compute the probability of delay in the project.

   (b) If delay is certain, what is the probability that shortage of material is causing it? Hint: Use the total probability theorem and Bayes' theorem.

8. The water for a small town is provided from two sources A and B. In any given dry season, there is 0.01 probability that source A will not be able to provide the expected amount of water needed. The corresponding probability for source B is 0.02. If source A is not able to meet the demand, there is 0.3 probability that B will not be either. On the other hand, if only one source cannot meet the demand, the probability of water shortage in town will be 0.40; whereas, if both sources cannot meet the demand, the probability of water shortage in the town will be 0.90.

   (a) Compute the probability of water shortage in the town in the next season.

   (b) If there is a shortage, what is the probability that *only* source A is causing it?

9. Of every 100 cars approaching an interstate junction, 60 will go straight, 15 will make a left turn and the rest will make a right turn.

   (a) What is the probability that a car approaching the junction will make a turn?

   (b) It is certain that an approaching car will make a turn, what is the probability that it will be a right turn?

10. Prove that Eq. 5.23 for the union of three events is valid. Derive a similar expression for the union of four events.

11. A construction company is currently bidding on a job overseas in country X. The chance of winning the job depends on the upcoming election results in X. If party A wins the election, the chance of the company winning the job is 60 percent; otherwise there is only a 20 percent chance that the company will win the job. On the other hand from poll data, the probability that the party A will win the election is 0.85. Compute the probability of the company's success in winning the job.

12. A roof system is made up of 15 parallel wood trusses. Proof load testing has shown that the probability of failure of any such roof truss is 0.02 if the total applied load exceeds 20 kN. If during a snow storm, the total load transmitted to each truss exceeds 20 kN,

what will the probability of the failure of the roof system be? Assume the conditions between trusses are statistically independent.

13. The on-time completion of an activity A in a construction project depends on the on-time completion of two prior activities B and C. If both B and C are completed on time, A will for sure be completed on time. If only one of the two activities B and C are completed on time, A will have 50 percent probability that will be completed on time. If none of the activities B and C are completed on time, A will only have 10 percent probability that will be completed on time. From past experience, we know that the activities B and C each have 80 percent probability to be completed on time. Events B and C are independent.

(a) Compute the probability that the activity A will be completed on time.

(b) If we allow a delay in the completion of A, what is the probability that *only* activity B is not completed on time?

14. The probability of weather-related traffic accidents in winter months in an intersection depends on the road conditions. For simplicity assume there are three possibilities for the road conditions. These are: (1) dry; (2) wet; and (3) icy conditions. If during the traffic rush-hours, the roads are dry, the probability of one or more accidents at the intersection is 0.001. The corresponding probabilities for the wet and icy conditions are 0.10 and 0.30 respectively. The probability of roads being dry at any time during the winter month is 0.80. The probability for the wet condition is 0.15.

(a) Compute the probability that the intersection will experience any number of accidents during the traffic rush-hours in winter months.

(b) Compute the probability that three such intersections located along a road will have no accidents during the traffic rush-hours in winter months. Assume statistical independence between the intersections.

15. Three construction companies (designated as A, B, and C) are bidding on a job. These companies have equal chances to win the job. From past performance records, if either company A or B wins the job, there is 0.80 probability that the job will be completed on time. The corresponding probability for company C is 0.90.

(a) Compute the probability that the job will be completed as scheduled.

(c) If we allow the completion time to be delayed, compute the probability that A wins the job.

(d) Repeat part (c) for companies B and C.

16. A motorist is driving at the posted maximum speed along a roadway. If he encounters a red traffic light at an intersection, the probability that he will encounter a red light at the next intersection is 0.60. However, if he does not encounter a red light in the first intersection, there is still 0.10 probability that he will encounter a red light at the next intersection.

(a) The motorist has two consecutive intersections ahead. The probability of encountering a red light at the first intersection is 0.3. What is the probability that he will not encounter any red lights passing the two intersections?

(b) Based on the information given, compute the probability of encountering a red light in the second intersection.

17. A company is currently bidding on three jobs. The odds of winning any job is 0.50. The winning of a job is independent of winning the other two.

(a) Compute the probability that the company will win all three jobs.

(b) Compute the probability that the company will win any two jobs.

18. A gas distribution pipeline network consists of 24 links distributing gas to houses in a subdivision. The probability that a link will develop a leak in any given year is 0.003. Assuming the conditions between the links are statistically independent:

(a) Compute the probability that the entire system will not develop any leak in any given year.

(b) In light of the result obtained in part (a), compute the probability that the system will not develop any leak ten years in a row.

19. A highway bridge is currently scheduled to be inspected once every two years. There is 3 percent probability that during an inspection, a major defect will be found. Compute the probability that in the next 12 years, no defects will be found in the bridge. Assume statistical independence concerning finding defects in different inspections.

20. In Exercise 16, assume the motorist has three intersections ahead. These intersections are labeled as A, B, and C. The motorist will reach A first, then B, and finally C. The probability that he will encounter a red light at B depends on whether or not he encountered a red light at A. The probability that he will encounter a red light at C depends on whether or not he encountered a red light at the previous intersection (i.e., B) only. As described in Exercise 16, if he encounters a red light at A, there is 0.60 probability that he will also encounter a red light at B. If he does not encounter a red light at A, there is still 0.10 probability that he will encounter a red light at B. Similarly, given a red light encounter at B, the probability that the motorist will encounter a red light at C is also 0.60. However, if no red light is encountered at B, there is still 0.10 probability that he will encounter a red light at C. There is 0.30 probability that he will encounter a red light at the first intersection, i.e., A.

(a) Compute the probability that the motorist will not encounter any red light passing through the three intersections.

(b) Compute the probability that the motorist will encounter a red light at B.

(c) Repeat part (b) but for intersection C.

21. In an improvement design for an intersection, two alternatives are suggested by a traffic engineer. These are: (Alternative A) use a traffic light system; and (Alternative B) use a 4-way stop sign system. The maximum number of accidents allowed for the intersection is 20 per year. If the design alternative A is selected, there is 0.10 probability that there will be more than the allowable 20 accidents/year. However, if the design alternative B is selected, this probability will be 0.45. The odds that the design alternative B is selected over A is 3 to 1.

(a) Compute the probability that once an improvement is completed, the intersection will have less than the allowable number of accidents/year.

(b) We wish to investigate the effect of the design alternative A on the safety of the intersection. Assuming the accidents will exceed the allowable number after the improvement plan is implemented, compute the probability that the design alternative A is the choice for the improvement plan.

22. Possible values for the resistance of a type of cable used as a tension member are 70, 80, and 90 kN, respectively. These possibilities are equally likely to occur. There are also three equal possibilities for the applied load. These are 65, 75, and 85 kN, respectively.

(a) What is the probability that the resistance of such a cable selected at random will be at least equal to 80 kN?

(b) What is the possibility that the load will be at most equal to 75 kN?

(c) What is the probability of failure of the cable?

6
Random Variables and Probability Distributions

6.1 RANDOM VARIABLES

Nearly all events can be defined by *random variables.* Likewise any variable, a random variable such as X can accept different values; however, these values follow an uncertain or random pattern. If specific values or ranges are assigned to a random variable, then events are formed. Thus a random variable offers a mathematical tool that can be used to introduce events within a defined sample space. The sample space is simply defined by a lower bound and an upper bound that specify the range of all possible values that the random variable can accept. If no lower and upper bounds are specified, then the range for the random variable is within $\pm\infty$. For example, if X is used to define the vertical acceleration in an aircraft during a flight, the ranges are within a negative acceleration (e.g., $-3g$, where g is the gravity acceleration) to a maximum positive acceleration (e.g., $+5g$). Any specific range assigned to X will define an event. For example, the expression $-2g < X \le 2g$ indicates the event that the acceleration at any given time period will be within $\pm 2g$. In this example, $-3g < X \le 5g$ covers the entire sample space and, as such, defines a sure event. Note that within this range many events are possible and can be defined as either a one-sided or two-sided inequality.

6.1.1 Discrete Random Variables

In many engineering problems, the possibilities within the lower and upper bound of a random variable are countable. Such a random variable is *discrete*. Problems dealing with a specific number of occurrences of a quantity are often defined with discrete random variables. For example, the number of defective products in any given day in the production line of a manufacturing firm can be defined as a discrete random variable. The possibilities are countable. If X is used to define the number of defective products, then possibilities are $X = 0$, $X = 1, \ldots, X = x$. Note that each possibility is an event and that these individual events are mutually exclusive. Furthermore, events can also be formed by assigning a range for X. For example, $2 < X \leq 6$ defines an event that the number of defective units will be less than or equal to 6 and larger than 2. This event contains four sample points, i.e., $X = 3$, $X = 4$, $X = 5$, and $X = 6$.

Several other examples of quantities that can be defined by discrete random variables are as follows:

- Number of projects a construction firm wins in a given year.
- Occurrences of natural hazards such as earthquakes, tornadoes, etc. The number of such events in any given time period can be defined via discrete random variables.
- Number of component failures in a multi-component engineering system.
- Number of accidents in a given time period at a busy intersection.
- Number of airplanes taking off and landing during a given time period in an airport.
- Number of cars approaching a toll booth in a tollway during any given hour.

6.1.2 Continuous Random Variables

If the number of possibilities defined by a random variable is infinite, then the variable is said to be *continuous*. For example, the strength of a given material can be considered to be a continuous random variable. Theoretically, the strength can be any positive value. Denoting this random variable as X, events can be formed via specific ranges assigned to X. These ranges are defined using inequality expressions. An inequality expression such as $a < X \leq b$ describes the event that X will be within the two limits a and b; whereas, an inequality $X > c$, for example, describes the event that X will be within c and infinity (∞). With continuous random variables, the events are always defined with ranges; even if these ranges are infinitesimally small. Thus although $X = x$ is practically meaningful, theoretically, it can define an event only if it is shown with the inequality expression $x < X \leq x + dx$; in which dx is an infinitesimally small range of X.

The following is an example of several other engineering quantities that are defined via continuous random variables:

- The magnitude of load applied on a structural system;
- Duration of a construction project;
- The length of a crack in metals;
- The time intervals between subsequent breakdowns of a mechanical system;
- The amount of a certain raw material available in a manufacturing unit;
- The amount of rainfall (using mm) during a future rainstorm.

It is noted that the above quantities can also be defined via discrete random variables. This will be possible only if a series of definite discrete ranges are assigned to each quantity as demonstrated in Example 6.1.

Example 6.1

The stress data for a main girder in a timber bridge have been compiled as shown in Table E6.1. The stress has been defined via 6 ranges in the megapascal (MPa) unit. Each range is a discrete possibility within the total of 6 possibilities. The random variable describing these possibilities is X. There are no occurrences for stresses larger than 6 MPa.

    (a) Compute the probability of each of the six events described by values of X.

    (b) Compute the probability of $X \leq 2$.

    (c) Compute the probability of $1 < X \leq 5$.

Solution:

    (a) The six possibilities make up the entire sample space; they are mutually exclusive and collectively exhaustive. Thus for the discrete random variable X, the probabilities are the relative frequencies computed and shown in Table E6.1., i.e.

$$P(X = 0) = 0;$$
$$P(X = 1) = 0.603;$$
$$P(X = 2) = 0.204;$$
$$P(X = 3) = 0.121;$$
$$P(X = 4) = 0.059;$$
$$P(X = 5) = 0.012;$$
$$P(X = 6) = 0.001; \text{ and,}$$

TABLE E6.1   STRESS RANGE DATA

Values of X	Stress range (MPa)	Number of occurrences/day	Relative frequency
1	0.00 to 1.00	4,234	$4{,}234/7{,}017 = 0.603$
2	1.01 to 2.00	1,432	$1{,}432/7{,}017 = 0.204$
3	2.01 to 3.00	850	$850/7{,}017 = 0.121$
4	3.01 to 4.00	411	$411/7{,}017 = 0.059$
5	4.01 to 5.00	85	$85/7{,}017 = 0.012$
6	5.01 to 6.00	5	$5/7{,}017 = 0.001$
		Total = 7,017	1.000

$$P(X > 6) = 0.$$

(b) From the results in (a):

$$P(X \leq 2) = P(X = 1) + P(X = 2) = 0.807.$$

(c) Again from results in (a):

$$P(1 < X \leq 5) = P(X = 2) + P(X = 3) + P(X = 4) + P(X = 5) = 0.396.$$

Note that if no discrete ranges are specified in Example 6.1 and that the strain can accept any value within 0 to 6 MPa, then the random variable describing the strain will be a continuous one.

Example 6.2

The error associated with the outcome of a laboratory measurement device is a continuous random variable, X, and ranges uniformly between -6 percent to $+6$ percent.

(a) Compute the probability that the error will be between -2 percent and $+2$ percent.

(b) Compute the probability that the error will be a positive value.

(c) Compute the probability that the random variable X will be within a small range dx.

Solution:

(a) Since the random variable ranges uniformly between -6 and $+6$, the probability that the variable is between a given range will be the ratio of the range to the overall range of the random variable. The overall range of the variable is $6 - (-6) = 12$. Thus,

$$P(-2 < X \leq +2) = 4/12 = 0.333.$$

(b) In this part, the probability of the event $X > 0$ is required. Thus,

$$P(X > 0) = 6/12 = 0.500.$$

(c) In this part, the probability of the event $x < X \leq x + dx$ is desired. Since the range for X is dx,

$$P(X < X \leq x + dx) = dx/12.$$

6.2 PROBABILITY FUNCTIONS

Probability functions are used to define probabilities of events associated with a random variable. Most such functions are in mathematical forms. However, there may be cases in which a probability function is given in a tabular or graphical format. Probabilities of events defined by a discrete random variable are described by means of a *probability mass function* and a *cumulative distribution function*. For a continuous random variable, the corresponding functions are the *probability density function* and *probability distribution function*.

6.2.1 Probability Mass Function and Cumulative Distribution Function

The probability mass function of a discrete random variable X is defined with a function $p(x)$. Notice that p is written as a function of x (and not X). This is because x shows the specific values that X can take; i.e., $x \subset X$. Furthermore, $p(x)$ describes the probability of $X = x$. Thus,

$$p(x) = P(X = x) \tag{6.1}$$

Note that since X is a discrete random variable, the values of x can only be whole integer numbers such as $0, \pm 1, \pm 2, \ldots$ Furthermore, note that the function $p(x)$ is also discrete. The cumulative distribution function is shown as $F(x)$ and describes the probability of the event $X \leq x$. Since the events $X = x$ are mutually exclusive, then $F(x)$ can be written as follows:

$$F(x) = P(X \leq x) = \sum_{all\ x_i \leq x} p(x_i) \tag{6.2}$$

Note that in Eq. 6.2, the summation is over all $x_i \leq x$. The function $F(x)$ appears in the form of a step function. Since this function defines a probability, it is then bounded by 0 and 1, i.e.,

$$F(-\infty) = P(X \leq -\infty) = 0 \tag{6.3}$$

and

$$F(+\infty) = P(X \leq +\infty) = 1 \tag{6.4}$$

The latter equation covers the entire sample space. Thus Eq. 6.4 can also be written as follows.

$$F(+\infty) = \sum_{all\ x_i} p(x_i) = 1 \tag{6.5}$$

Note that in Eq. 6.5, the summation covers all values of the random variable X. One can also write the following equations.

$$P(X > x) = 1 - P(X \leq x) = 1 - F(x) \tag{6.6}$$

$$P(a < X \leq b) = F(b) - F(a) = \sum_{all\ x_i} p(x_i) \quad \text{for } a < x_i \leq b \tag{6.7}$$

Figure 6.1 shows a typical probability mass function and the corresponding cumulative distribution function.

6.2.2 Probability Density Function and Probability Distribution Function

These are specific to continuous random variables. The probability density function is defined by $f(x)$, where

$$f(x) = P(x < X \leq x + dx)/dx \tag{6.8}$$

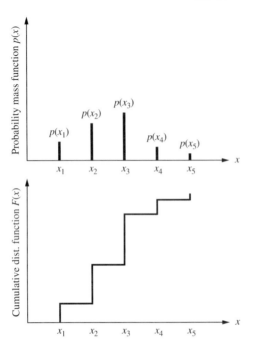

Figure 6.1 Probability mass function $p(x)$ and cumulative distribution function $F(x)$.

or

$$P(x < X \leq x + dx) = f(x)dx \qquad (6.9)$$

Again notice that f is written as a function of x (and not X). As seen in Figure 6.2, $P(x < X \leq x + dx)$ is the small shaded area, i.e., $f(x)dx$, under the probability density function curve in the x, $x + dx$ region. Thus the probability of the event $P(-\infty < X \leq x)$ is sum of infinite number of small areas between $-\infty$ and x. This means that:

$$P(-\infty < X \leq x) = P(X \leq x) = \int_{-\infty}^{x} f(x)dx \qquad (6.10)$$

The probability distribution function is shown with $F(x)$ and is defined as follows:

$$F(x) = P(X \leq x) \qquad (6.11)$$

In light of Eqs. 6.10 and 6.11, one can write:

$$F(x) = \int_{-\infty}^{x} f(x)dx \qquad (6.12)$$

or

$$f(x) = dF(x)/dx \qquad (6.13)$$

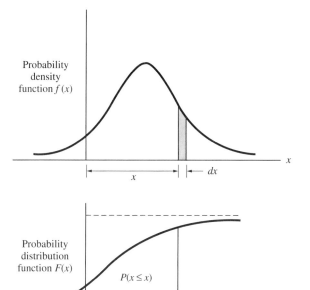

Probability
density
function $f(x)$

dx

Probability
distribution
function $F(x)$

$P(x \le x)$

Figure 6.2   Probability density and
distribution functions.

Equation 6.12 implies that the probability distribution function is the area under
the density function curve (see Figure 6.2). Furthermore, one can write the following equations:

$$P(a < X \le b) = \int_a^b f(x)dx = F(b) - F(a) \tag{6.14}$$

$$F(-\infty) = 0 \tag{6.15}$$

and

$$F(\infty) = 1 \tag{6.16}$$

The latter equation also indicates that,

$$\int_{-\infty}^{\infty} f(x)dx = 1 \tag{6.17}$$

This simply means that the area under the entire probability density function is
equal to 1.

In real situations, engineering data are compiled in discrete form and presented in discrete form. A desired parameter, e.g., strain in a critical component of a
structure, is measured using a specific sampling rate. If n samples, i.e., $x_1, x_2, \ldots x_n$,
are collected, the data compiled represent a small sub-domain of all possible values
of the random variable describing the parameter. Furthermore, it is noted that due

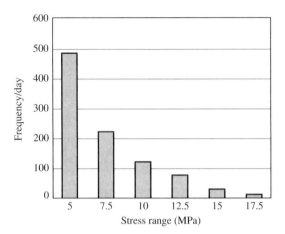

Figure 6.3   Discrete plot of stress range data.

to the discrete nature of the n samples, the values between any two consecutive values (say x_i, and x_{i+1}) are not known (it is often assumed that the parameter is either constant or varies linearly between x_i, and x_{i+1}). Thus the representation of the random variable as a continuous one will only be an approximation. However, in most applications, this approximation is acceptable if additional analyses are conducted to support the validity of the probability distribution model selected to represent the random variable. Figure 6.3 shows a discrete plot of the stress data compiled in the main girder of several bridges. It is obvious that the random variable describing stress is continuous. As seen in Figure 6.3, there is a trend in the stress data in the form of a probability density function. Once the type of distribution model that can be used to represent the data is selected, statistical tests can be performed to support the validity of the model. This subject is described in subsequent chapters.

6.3 DESCRIBING PARAMETERS OF A RANDOM VARIABLE

The probability functions described in Section 6.2 provide a complete description on random variables. In addition, there are also several parameters that are considered as *descriptors* of a random variable. The descriptors are parameters that can be found using the probability mass or density functions. These parameters are discussed in this section.

6.3.1 Mathematical Expectation

By definition, the mathematical expectation of any function $g(X)$ of the random variable X is shown as $E[g(X)]$ and is mathematically described by:

$$E[g(X)] = \sum_{all\ x_i} g(x_i)p(x_i) \tag{6.18}$$

for discrete random variables, where the summation covers all x_i; and,

$$E[g(X)] = \int_{-\infty}^{\infty} g(x)f(x)dx \tag{6.19}$$

for continuous random variables. The mathematical expectation is a deterministic parameter and is in fact a weighed average. Considering a discrete random variable X, the average value of all $g(x_i)$ values using $p(x_i)$ as the weights can be written as $\Sigma g(x_i)p(x_i)/\Sigma p(x_i)$, in which the summations are for all values of x_i. Since $\Sigma p(x_i) = 1$, then the average so obtained is $E[g(X)]$. A similar logic can also be stated for a continuous random variable.

In a special case where the function $g(X)$ is simply X, the mathematical expectation, i.e., $E(X)$, is called the *expected value* of X, or the *mean value* of X (as described later). If the function $g(X)$ is equal to X^2, the mathematical expectation, i.e., $E(X^2)$ is called *the mean square* of X.

6.3.2 Mean or Expected Value

The mean value μ of the random variable X is the mathematical expectation of X. Thus,

$$\mu = E(X) = \sum_{all\ x_i} x_i p(x_i) \tag{6.20}$$

for a discrete random variable; and,

$$\mu = E(X) = \int_{-\infty}^{\infty} xf(x)dx \tag{6.21}$$

for a continuous random variable. Note that the mean value is simply a weighed average of all values of the random variable X.

6.3.3 The Variance and Standard Deviation

The variance is the mathematical expectation of the function $(X - \mu)^2$. Thus if function $g(X)$ is taken equal to $(X - \mu)^2$, then,

$$E[(X - \mu)^2] = \sum_{all\ x_i} (x_i - \mu)^2 p(x_i) \tag{6.22}$$

for the case where X is discrete; and,

$$E[(X - \mu)^2] = \int_{-\infty}^{\infty} (x - \mu)^2 f(x)dx \tag{6.23}$$

for the case where X is continuous. In an alternative form the variance can be written in terms of the mean square, i.e., $E(X^2)$, as demonstrated below.

$$E[(X - \mu)^2] = E[X^2 - 2\mu X - \mu^2] = E(X^2) - 2\mu E(X) + \mu^2 = E(X^2) - \mu^2 \tag{6.24}$$

Equation 6.24, can also be proven by expanding the right-hand side of either Eq. 6.22 or Eq. 6.23.

The square root of the variance is the *standard deviation* and is shown with σ, i.e.,

$$\sigma = [E(X - \mu)^2]^{1/2} \tag{6.25}$$

From Eq. 6.24, it can be shown that:

$$E(X^2) = \sigma^2 + \mu^2 \qquad (6.26)$$

Note that σ and μ have the same unit as the random variable. The mean may be a positive, negative, or zero value. However, the standard deviation is always a non-zero positive value. In the case the standard deviation is zero, the variable will not be random. Dividing the standard deviation by the mean value results in a dimensionless quantity called the *coefficient of variation* (COV). The COV is shown with δ and describes the standard deviation as a fraction of the mean value. The COV is then computed as follows:

$$\delta = \sigma/\mu \qquad (6.27)$$

The COV can also be presented as a percentage.

6.3.4 Median and Mode

The median is a specific value of the random variable X at which the 50 percentile probability is obtained. The median x_m is obtained from the following equation:

$$P(X > x_m) = 0.50 \qquad (6.28)$$

The mode of a random variable is a specific value of the variable at which the density function has its peak.

6.3.5 Moments of a Random Variable

The moments of a random variable are mathematical expectation of X^n and $(X - \mu)^n$, in which n is a numerical value. According to this definition, the mean value is the first moment (since $n = 1$); whereas, the variance is a second moment. The third moment is used to describe the skewness in the probability density (or mass) function. The skewness factor, θ, is defined as follows:

$$\theta = E[(X - \mu)^3]/\sigma^3 \qquad (6.29)$$

If the density (or mass) function is symmetric, then $\theta = 0$.

Example 6.3

The tensile strength of a cable (X) is defined as a random variable following a triangular probability density function as shown in Figure E6.3.

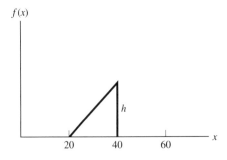

Figure E6.3   Triangular probability density function.

(a) Compute h and write an equation for the probability density function of X.

(b) Compute the mean and standard deviation of X.

(c) If the load applied to the cable is 25 kN, compute the probability of failure of the cable.

Solution:

(a) In light of Eq. 6.17, $h \times (40 - 20)/2 = 1$. Thus $h = 1/10$. The equation for $f(x)$ is written as follows:

$$f(x) = (x - 20)/200 \qquad \text{for } 20 \le x \le 40$$
$$f(x) = 0 \qquad\qquad\quad \text{elsewhere}$$

(b) In this part we use Eqs. 6.21 and 6.23.

$$\mu = \int_{20}^{40} [x(x - 20)/200]dx = 33.3$$

$$\sigma^2 = \int_{20}^{40} [(\mu - x)^2(x - 20)/200]dx = 22.2 \text{ and } \sigma = 4.71.$$

(c) The probability of failure is defined by event $X \le 25$; because the failure occurs when the load exceeds the resistance of the cable. To compute this probability we can utilize Eq. 6.14. Alternatively, the area under the $f(x)$ between $x = 20$ and 25 can be computed as the probability of concern. Using Eq. 6.14,

$$P(\text{cable failure}) = P(x \le 25) = \int_{20}^{25} [(x - 20)/200]dx = 0.063$$

Example 6.4

The number of trucks leaving a concrete manufacturing plant in any hour is defined with a random variable X. The probability mass function of X is proposed as

$$p(x) = \frac{c}{x^2 + 1} \qquad \text{for } x = 0, 1, 2, 3 \text{ and } 4.$$
$$p(x) = 0 \qquad\qquad \text{elsewhere.}$$

(a) Compute the constant c.

(b) Compute the mean and standard deviation of X.

(c) Compute the probability that the number of trucks leaving the plant in any hour is less than or equal to 2.

Solution:

(a) From Eq. 6.5,

$$c\left[\frac{1}{x_1^2 + 1} + \frac{1}{x_2^2 + 1} + \ \cdots\ \right] = c\left[\frac{1}{0 + 1} + \frac{1}{1 + 1} + \frac{1}{4 + 1} + \frac{1}{9 + 1} + \frac{1}{16 + 1}\right] = 1$$

This results in $c = 0.538$.

(b) The mean and standard deviation are computed from Eqs. 6.20 and 6.22.

$$\mu = c\left[x_1\frac{1}{x_1^2 + 1} + x_2\frac{1}{x_2^2 + 1} + \ldots \right]$$

$$= c\left[0 \times \frac{1}{0 + 1} + 1 \times \frac{1}{1 + 1} + 2 \times \frac{1}{4 + 1} + 3 \times \frac{1}{9 + 1} + 4 \times \frac{1}{16 + 1} \right] = 0.772$$

and

$$\sigma^2 = c\left[(\mu - x_1)^2\frac{1}{x_1^2 + 1} + (\mu - x_2)^2\frac{1}{x_1^2 + 1} + \ldots \right]$$

$$= c\left[(0.772 - 0)^2 \times \frac{1}{0 + 1} + (0.772 - 1)^2 \times \frac{1}{1 + 1} + \ldots \right] = 1.094$$

This results in $\sigma = 1.05$. Of course, the mean value in this case is a symbolic measure, since the number of trucks can only be a whole number.

(c) In this case $P(X \le 2)$ is desired. This probability from Eq. 6.2 is:

$$P(X \le 2) = P(X = 0) + P(X = 1) + P(X = 2) = c\left[\frac{1}{x_1^2 + 1} + \frac{1}{x_2^2 + 1} + \frac{1}{x_3^2 + 1} \right]$$

$$= c\left[\frac{1}{0 + 1} + \frac{1}{1 + 1} + \frac{1}{4 + 1} \right] = 0.915.$$

6.4 SEVERAL PROBABILITY FUNCTIONS

In this section, several probability functions are described. Additional functions are introduced throughout the book whenever a particular discussion necessitates the introduction of a specific type of distribution model.

6.4.1 Normal (Gaussian) Function

The normal probability density function is widely used as a function to describe continuous random variables. The normal probability density function is written as:

$$f(x) = \frac{1}{\sigma\sqrt{2\pi}} \exp\left[-\frac{1}{2}\left(\frac{x - \mu}{\sigma}\right)^2 \right] \qquad -\infty \le x \le \infty \qquad (6.30)$$

where σ and μ are the parameters of the distribution. It can be shown that the expected value of X using Eq. 6.30 will result in the parameter μ; whereas the variance will be the square of the parameter σ (i.e., the standard deviation). The normal function has the familiar bell shape. It is symmetric with respect to the mean value. As shown in Figure 6.4, the standard deviation determines the shape of the curve. A large standard deviation indicates that the random variable contains values that are scattered with less concentration of values around the mean. A small standard deviation, on the other hand, indicates that values of the random variable are mainly concentrated around the mean.

A special form of the normal probability density function has a zero mean and a standard deviation equal to unity (i.e., $\sigma = 1$). This is called the *standard normal*

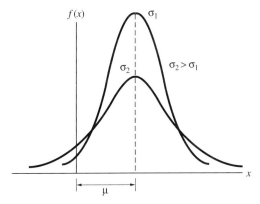

Figure 6.4 Normal probability density function.

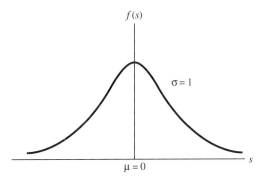

Figure 6.5 Standard normal probability density function.

density function. Using S as the random variable represented by the standard normal function, $f(s)$ can be written as:

$$f(s) = \frac{1}{\sqrt{2\pi}}\exp\left[-\frac{1}{2}s^2\right] \qquad -\infty \leq s \leq \infty \qquad (6.31)$$

The standard normal function is shown in Figure 6.5. The probability distribution function of the standard normal random variable S is the integral of Eq. 6.31. Rather than the usual form $F(s)$, the standard normal probability distribution function is shown with $\Phi(s)$; i.e.,

$$\Phi(s) = P(S \leq s) = \frac{1}{\sqrt{2\pi}}\int_{-\infty}^{s}\exp\left[-\frac{1}{2}s^2\right]ds \qquad (6.32)$$

The function $\Phi(s)$ cannot be obtained in closed form. It can be computed numerically for various values of s. Table A.1 in Appendix A presents the values of $\Phi(s)$. Since the standard normal function is symmetric with respect to $s = 0$ (i.e., the mean), the following relations can be written as:

$$\Phi(0) = 0.5 \qquad (6.33)$$

$$\Phi(-s) = 1 - \Phi(s) \qquad (6.34)$$

A linear transformation can be used to convert any normal function into the standard normal form. This can be proved using the following sequence of computations.

Let $S = (X - \mu)/\sigma$ or $X = \mu + S\sigma$. If s and x are specific values of the random variables S and X, respectively, then, $x = \mu + s\sigma$, or $dx = \sigma ds$. Now recall that the probability distribution function of X is the integral of $f(x)$. Thus,

$$F(x) = \frac{1}{\sigma\sqrt{2\pi}} \int_{-\infty}^{x} \exp\left[-\frac{1}{2}\left(\frac{x-\mu}{\sigma}\right)^2\right] dx \qquad (6.35)$$

Since $dx = \sigma ds$ and $s = (x - \mu)/\sigma$, then,

$$F(x) = P(X \le x) = \frac{1}{2\pi} \int_{-\infty}^{\frac{x-\mu}{\sigma}} \exp\left[-\frac{s^2}{2}\right] ds \qquad (6.36)$$

This equation is identical to the standard normal function (Eq. 6.32) with the only difference being the upper limit of the integral. Thus,

$$F(x) = P(X \le x) = \Phi\left(\frac{x-\mu}{\sigma}\right) \qquad (6.37)$$

In light of Eqs. 6.14, 6.36, and 6.37, one can also write

$$P(a < X \le b) = P(X \le b) - P(X \le a) = \Phi\left(\frac{b-\mu}{\sigma}\right) - \Phi\left(\frac{a-\mu}{\sigma}\right) \qquad (6.38)$$

Example 6.5

The target time for the completion of a project is 120 days. The project duration is a normal random variable X with a mean of 115 and standard deviation of 20 days.

(a) Compute the probability of project delay (i.e. the project will not be finished within the target time).

(b) If a probability of delay equal to 0.10 is accepted for the project, compute the target time that corresponds to this probability.

Solution:

(a) In this part, $P(X > 120)$ is desired. This is computed using Eq. 6.37 as follows
$$P(X > 120) = 1 - P(X \le 120) = 1 - \Phi[(120 - 115)/20] = 1 - \Phi(0.25)$$
From the table of normal probability values in the Appendix, $\Phi(0.25) = 0.5987$, thus
$$P(X > 120) = 1 - 0.5987 = 0.4013.$$

(b) In this part, the target time is to be determined. Taking the target time as t, we can write $P(X > t) = 0.10$; or $P(X \le t) = 0.90$; or $\Phi[(t - 115)/20] = 0.90$. From the normal probability table $\Phi(1.28) \approx 0.90$, thus
$$(t - 115)/20 = 1.28, \text{ or } t = 141 \text{ days.}$$

Example 6.6

In Example 6.5, part (a), assume that rather than 120 days, there is an uncertainty involved in the target time. In fact, there is 80 percent probability that the target time $t = 120$ days. There is 20 percent probability that the target time will be 100 days. These are the only two possibilities for the target time. Now recompute the probability of the project delay.

Solution:

The sample space for the target time has the only two possibilities, i.e., $t = 120$ days and $t = 100$ days. These are mutually exclusive and collectively exhaustive. Thus the total probability theorem can be used as follows:

$$P(X > t) = P(X > t | t = 120)P(t = 120) + P(X > t | t = 100)P(t = 100)$$

The individual terms in the above equation are computed as follows:

$$P(X > t | t = 120) = 1 - P(X \le t | t = 120) = 1 - \Phi[(120 - 115)/20]$$
$$= 1 - \Phi(0.25) = 1 - 0.5987 = 0.4013;$$

$$P(X > t | t = 100) = 1 - P(X \le t | t = 100) = 1 - \Phi[(100 - 115)/20]$$
$$= 1 - \Phi(-0.75) = \Phi(0.75) = 0.7734;$$

$$P(t = 120) = 0.80 \text{ (given by the problem); and,}$$

$$P(t = 100) = 0.20 \text{ (given by the problem).}$$

Thus

$$P(X > t) = 0.4013 \times 0.80 + 0.7734 \times 0.20 = 0.4757.$$

Example 6.7

In Example 6.5, Part (a), assume the target time is 120 days only and that the standard deviation for the duration of the project is 10 days rather than 20 days. This simply means that there is now less uncertainty regarding the duration of the project. Compute the probability of delay.

Solution:

$$P(X > 120) = 1 - P(X \le 120) = 1 - \Phi[(120 - 115)/10]$$
$$= 1 - \Phi(0.5) = 1 - 0.6915 = 0.3085.$$

Notice that in Example 6.5, the mean duration time was shorter than the target time. Nevertheless there was a probability that a delay would take place. This is because of the randomness in the project duration time (i.e., uncertainty in the duration time). In Example 6.6, there was also an uncertainty in the target time. Because of this uncertainty, a larger probability of delay than that in Example 6.5 was obtained. Example 6.7 had a smaller standard deviation (i.e., less uncertainty) for the project duration. This resulted in a smaller probability of delay than that in Example 6.5.

In Examples 6.5–6.7, the project duration time was assumed to be a normal random variable. Theoretically, this random variable can range between $-\infty$ to $+\infty$. However, it is obvious that the duration time cannot accept negative values. To overcome this difficulty, a different distribution such as *logarithmic normal* (or *lognormal*) or *Rayleigh* can be used. Both of these models only accept positive values and are more suitable to model variables that are always positive. Ang and Tang, 1975 provide information and application problem on Rayleigh distribution. The logarithmic normal distribution is explained in the next section.

6.4.2 Logarithmic Normal

The logarithmic density function is:

$$f(x) = \frac{1}{\sqrt{2\pi} \, \nu \, x} \exp\left[-\frac{1}{2}\left(\frac{\ell n \, x - \lambda}{\nu}\right)^2\right] \qquad 0 < x < \infty \qquad (6.39)$$

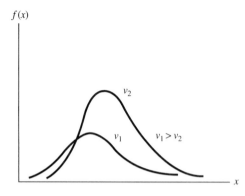

Figure 6.6 Lognormal probability density function.

in which λ and ν are the parameters of the logarithmic distribution and are the mean and standard deviation of $\ell n(X)$, respectively. These parameters are written as:

$$\lambda = E(\ell n X)$$

and

$$\nu = \sqrt{Var(\ell n X)}$$

Figure 6.6 shows the logarithmic normal probability density function. As seen in this figure, smaller values of the parameter ν result in a more condensed variation. This indicates less variability in the random variable. The logarithmic normal distribution is related to the normal distribution. It can be shown that any probability associated with the logarithmic normal distribution can easily be computed from the standard normal probability distribution function Φ using the following equation:

$$P(a < X \le b) = \Phi\left(\frac{\ell n\, b - \lambda}{\nu}\right) - \Phi\left(\frac{\ell n\, a - \lambda}{\nu}\right) \tag{6.40}$$

Furthermore, it can be shown that:

$$\nu^2 = \ell n(1 + \sigma^2/\mu^2) \tag{6.41}$$

and

$$\lambda = \ell n\mu - \nu^2/2 \tag{6.42}$$

The proof of Eqs. 6.40–6.42 is left to the reader as an exercise problem.

Example 6.8

The resistance of a tension member used in a truss is a logarithmic normal random variable with a mean value of 60 kN and a standard deviation of 15 kN.

(a) Compute the probability that the resistance at any given time will be between 40 and 70 kN.

(b) If a load equal to 30 kN is transferred to this member, compute the probability of failure of the member.

Solution:

(a) In this part we are interested in $P(40 < X \le 70)$. Using Eq. 6.40,

$$P(40 < X \le 70) = \Phi\left(\frac{\ell n 70 - \lambda}{\nu}\right) - \Phi\left(\frac{\ell n 40 - \lambda}{\nu}\right)$$

The parameters λ and ν are computed from Eqs. 6.41 and 6.42:

$$\nu^2 = \ell n(1 + 225/3600) = 0.06 \text{ and } \nu = 0.25$$

and

$$\lambda = \ell n 60 - (0.25)^2/2 = 4.06$$

Thus,

$$P(40 < X \le 70) = \Phi(0.75) - \Phi(-1.48) = 0.704.$$

(b) In this part, we observe that the failure will occur when the resistance X will be less than the applied load. Thus we are interested in $P(X \le 30)$. Although the mean value of the resistance is much larger than the load, there still exists a chance for failure.

$$P(X \le 30) = \Phi\left(\frac{\ell n 30 - \lambda}{\nu}\right) = \Phi(-2.64) = 0.004.$$

6.4.3 The *t*-Distribution

The *t*-distribution (also called the student *t*-distribution) is also used for continuous random variables and is similar to the standard normal in shape. The difference is that it is only defined with one parameter called the degree of freedom (ν). The density function is symmetric with respect to 0. Using T as the random variable described by the *t*-distribution, the density function, $f(t)$, is written as:

$$f(t) = \frac{\Gamma(\frac{\nu + 1}{2})}{\Gamma(\nu/2)\sqrt{\pi\nu}}(1 + t^2/\nu)^{-(\nu+1)/2} \qquad -\infty < t < \infty \qquad (6.43)$$

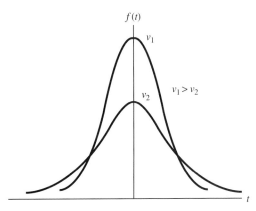

Figure 6.7   *t*-distribution.

in which $\Gamma(.)$ is the *gamma* function described with the following integral:

$$\Gamma(\alpha) = \int_0^\infty z^{\alpha-1}e^{-z}dz \qquad \alpha > 0 \tag{6.44}$$

and with the following properties:

$$\Gamma(\alpha) = (\alpha - 1)\Gamma(\alpha - 1) \tag{6.45}$$

$$\Gamma(1) = 1 \tag{6.46}$$

The degree of freedom (ν) is a positive integer value. It is taken as $n - 1$, in which n is the number of sample data points collected in a data acquisition process for a variable. The parameter ν is in fact a shape parameter. As the value of ν increases, the variance of the random variable T decreases. This means that larger ν values are associated with more compact density functions (see Figure 6.7). The t-distribution density function approaches the standard normal function as ν approaches ∞. The t-distribution tables are summarized for different t values for various probability levels and degrees of freedom (see Appendix A). For example, at $\nu = 10$ and 0.95 probability, $t = 1.812$. This means that with a degree of freedom equal to 10, $P(T \leq 1.812) = 0.95$. At $\nu = \infty$, and 0.95 probability, $t = 1.645$. This value is identical with the corresponding value from the normal probability table, i.e., $P(T \leq 1.645) = 0.95$ both from the t-distribution table and the normal probability table. The application of the t-distribution is mainly in establishing confidence intervals for a mean value that is obtained from data and also in the analysis of variance when means from two data sets (two populations) are compared as discussed in subsequent chapters.

6.4.4 Binomial Distribution

The binomial distribution (also known as the Bernoulli sequence) is used for discrete random variables. The function is suitable in modeling random variables that concern the occurrence of x trials among a total of n trials. The basic assumptions in the binomial distribution are that: (1) each trial has only two outcomes, namely, either occurrence or non-occurrence; (2) the probability of occurrence of any one trial is p which is the same for all trials; and (3) the trials are statistically independent. A classics example of binomial distribution in engineering is the problem of a system that is made up of n identical components. Assuming that the probability of failure of any one component is p, then the binomial distribution can be used to estimate the probability that $X = x$ component failures (out of a total of n) will occur. For example if $n = 3$ and the probability of exactly two component failures $(X = 2)$ is desired, this probability can be computed by considering all possible cases that two trials (out of three) will take place. It is obvious that there will be three possibilities for two component failures (and one no-failure). Thus $P(X = 2) = 3p^2(1 - p)$. Notice that each possibility, i.e., $p^2(1 - p)$, is obtained as the intersection of two occurrence events and one non-occurrence event. The intersection is simply written as the product of the three probabilities $p, p,$ and $(1 - p)$ because the respective events are statistically independent of one another. In a general case, when x trials among a total number of n are desired, the number of possibilities n_x can be computed by considering all possible combination of x trials in the set of n total trials. Thus,

$$P(X = x) = n_x p^x (1 - p)^{n-x} \qquad x = 0, 1, 2, \ldots, n \qquad (6.47)$$

in which

$$n_x = \frac{n!}{x!(n - x)!} \qquad (6.48)$$

Notice that Eq. 6.47 describes the probability mass function for the discrete random variable X and that p is the parameter of the function.

Example 6.9

An engineering system is made up of 11 components each with a probability of failure $p = 0.0004$. Compute the probability of failure of the system. Component failures are independent of one another.

Solutions: Assuming that any component failure will result in the system failure, the binomial distribution can be used to compute the system failure probability. In this case a trial is the failure of any one component. This failure may or may not occur.

$$P(\text{system failure}) = P(X \geq 1) = 1 - P(X = 0)$$
$$n_x = 11!/(0! \times 11!) = 1$$
$$P(\text{system failure}) = 1 - 1 \times (0.0004)^0 (1 - 0.0004)^{11-0} = 1 - 0.9956 = 0.0044.$$

The binomial distribution can easily be applied to time-dependent problems. In such a case, time is first divided into identical intervals; and second, it is assumed that within each interval only one occurrence of the event of concern is possible. In electronic systems a time unit equal to one hour is often used. The component probabilities are then defined via a *failure rate* which is the probability of failure per hour. The probability that the failure will happen after t time intervals can also be obtained from the binomial distribution. However, in such a case the distribution is called the *geometric distribution*. In a more general case, the probability that the failure occurs after t intervals for the nth time can also be computed. The corresponding distribution is then referred to as the *hypergeometric distribution*. The reader is referred to references at the end of this chapter for more information on these distributions. Considering the failure rate of electronic components, using the geometric and hypergeometric distributions, it can be shown that the average time between failures is equal to $1/p$. The average time between failures is often used as a measure of the reliability of a system.

Example 6.10

A flight data recorder is made up of 267 electronic components. The reliability of each component is 0.999999 per hour. Assuming that failures among components are independent and that the component failure rates are identical:

(a) Compute the failure rate and average time between failure of any given component.

(b) Compute the failure rate of the recorder per hour.

(c) Compute the reliability of the recorder and its average time between failures.

Solution:

(a) The failure rate is the probability of failure per hour (p) which is:

$$p = 1 - 0.999999 = 10^{-6} \text{ per hour}$$

The average time between failures for any one component is $1/10^{-6} = 1,000,000$ hours.

(b) The failure rate (failure probability) of the recorder is obtained using the binomial distribution. The assumption is that the failure in any one component causes the failure of the recorder.

$$P(\text{system failure}) = P(X > 0) = 1 - P(X = 0)$$
$$= 1 - (1 - p)^{267} = 1 - (1 - 0.000001)^{267} = 0.000267 \text{ per hour.}$$

(c) The reliability of the recorder $= 1 - 0.000267 = 0.999733$; and the average time between failure is $1/0.000267 = 3{,}745$ hours.

6.4.5 Poisson Distribution

The Poisson distribution is often used in time or space-related problems. It is suitable for discrete random variables and defines the probability of occurrence of a desired number of identical events in a desired time or space interval. Several examples of events used in conjunction with the Poisson distribution are provided below:

- Occurrence of at least one traffic accident in a week in an intersection;
- Occurrence of no accidents in a construction site during the next thirty months;
- Occurrence of any number of earthquakes (i.e., at least one earthquake) in a certain county in central United States in the next 25 years;
- The occurrence that exactly five airplanes will arrive at an airport in the next 20 minutes;
- The occurrence that within a two-meter length of an aluminum structural component, there will be at least two cracks.

The latter example deals with space; whereas all the others deal with time.

The key parameter in the Poisson distribution is λ, which is called the *occurrence rate* or the *activity rate*. The parameter λ is the average number of occurrences of the event of concern in unit time or unit space. Obviously the information on λ must be compiled from past occurrences, or test data depending on the type of problem. The probability mass function of a discrete random variable X, that follows the Poisson distribution, is defined as:

$$P(X = x) = \left(\frac{r^x}{x!}\right)e^{-r} \qquad x = 0, 1, 2, \ldots \qquad (6.49)$$

in which, $r = \lambda t$. Also note that $X = x$ is the event of x occurrences within time t. Equation 6.49 can be found directly or from the binomial distribution. In the latter form, it can be shown that in a time-related problem, for example, when the number of time intervals approaches infinity, the binomial distribution approaches the Poisson. This can be shown with the aid of the *Maclaurin* series defined as follows:

$$e^r = 1 + r + r^2/2! + r^3/3! + r^4/4! + \ldots \qquad (6.50)$$

The proof is beyond the scope of this book and is left to the reader as an exercise (see Ang and Tang, 1975 for a complete discussion).

As in the binomial distribution, the individual events associated with the Poisson distribution are assumed to be independent. However, the Poisson distribution offers several advantages over the binomial distribution when time-related problems are involved. In the Poisson distribution, there is no need to divide the time into intervals. Furthermore, any number of occurrences within the unit time is possible. As you recall, in the binomial distribution a basic assumption was that within each interval only one occurrence is possible.

Example 6.11

The data compiled at an intersection indicate that in the past 3 years 9 major traffic accidents have occurred at the intersection. Compute the following:

(a) the probability that next month the intersection will be accident free;

(b) the probability that in the next three months exactly two such accidents will occur at the intersection; and,

(c) the probability that the intersection will have at most two such accidents in the next three months.

Solutions:

The Poisson distribution will be used to model the number of accidents. The parameter λ is estimated from the available data. A time unit equal to one month will be considered. Thus,

$$\lambda = 9/36 = 0.25 \text{ accidents/month}$$

Note that theoretically the parameter λ can accept a value as a fraction of 1.

(a) In this part $t = 1$ month and $r = \lambda t = 0.25 \times 1 = 0.25$. The desired probability is $P(X = 0)$. Thus,

$$P(X = 0) = (0.25^0/0!)e^{-0.25} = 0.779$$

(b) In this case $r = 0.25 \times 3 = 0.75$ and the desired probability is $P(X = 2)$. Thus,

$$P(X = 2) = (0.75^2/2!)e^{-0.75} = 0.133$$

(c) In this case $r = 0.75$; however, the desired probability is $P(X \leq 2)$.

$$P(X \leq 2) = P(X = 0) + P(X = 1) + P(X = 2)$$
$$= (0.75^0/0!)e^{-0.75} + (0.75^1/1!)e^{-0.75} + (0.75^2/2!)e^{-0.75} = 0.472 + 0.354 + 0.133 = 0.959.$$

For a series of events that follow the Poisson distribution, we introduce the random variable T as the time until the first occurrence of such events. The probability $P(T > t)$ can be obtained from Eq. 6.49. Note that the first occurrence is after t, thus during the time interval 0 to t there is no occurrence of the event. Thus

$$P(T > t) = P(X = 0) = (r^0/0!)e^{-r} = e^{-\lambda t} \tag{6.51}$$

Introducing the probability distribution function of T as $F(t)$, then

$$F(t) = P(T \leq t) = 1 - P(T > t) = 1 - e^{-\lambda t} \tag{6.52}$$

and the probability density function of T is

$$f(t) = dF/dt = \lambda e^{-\lambda t} \tag{6.53}$$

The density function described by Eq. 6.53 is called the *exponential distribution*. Although it is used in conjunction with the Poisson distribution, it can also be used independently. The function is suitable for modeling the useful life (life to failure) of many engineering systems. In such a case, the random variable T will be the system useful life. Using Eq. 6.53, the expected value of T can be shown to be:

$$E(T) = 1/\lambda \tag{6.54}$$

This is the mean time between failures, or simply the average life of a system, and is also called the *return period*.

For events modeled with the Poisson distribution, it is also possible to compute the probabilities associated with a time after which an event of concern will occur for the second, third or nth time. The corresponding distribution function is called gamma distribution. The discussion on this distribution is provided in Ang and Tang (1975).

Example 6.12

An electronic device has an average useful life of 1,000 operating hours. Compute the probability that the device will fail in the first 500 hours of its operation.

Solution:

From Eq. 6.54, the average failure rate of the device $\lambda = 1/1,000 = 0.001$. Using Eq. 6.52, we find

$$P(T \leq 500) = 1 - e^{-0.001 \times 500} = 1 - e^{-0.5} = 0.393.$$

Of course, this probability could have been directly found from Eq. 6.51 by computing $P(X > 0)$ for $t = 500$ hours.

SUMMARY

In this chapter, the definition of a random variable and distribution functions used for computing various events associated with the variable were provided. Furthermore, mathematical parameters known as descriptors of a random variable were introduced; and expressions for computing them were presented. Several probability distribution functions were described to familiarize the reader with the underlying concept in using such functions in computing the probability of a desired event. Additional probability functions are introduced in subsequent chapters wherever there is a need to use a specific type of the probability distribution function. Several additional topics related to random variables are also important in the application of the theory of probability. Among these are: (1) the joint probability distribution functions; and (2) the mathematical expressions as functions of one or more random variables. The joint probability distribution functions are used wherever an event must be defined with two (or more) random variables that are correlated. This subject is important in understanding the statistical correlation between two (or more) variables and is discussed in subsequent chapters. The functions of random variables are mathematical expressions that are written in terms of one or more random variables. These functions are used in a variety of engineering problems when the formulation of an event of concern involves a relation between several random variables. Computation of the probability of the event would then require information on the individual random variable probability distribution functions and their respective joint distributions. This subject is discussed in Chapter 7.

REFERENCES

Ang, A. H.-S. and W. H. Tang (1975). Chapters 3 and 4 in *Probability Concept in Engineering Planning and Design, Volume I-Basic Principles,* John Wiley & Sons.

BENJAMIN, J. and C. A. CORNELL (1970). *Probability, Statistics and Decision-Making for Civil Engineers,* McGraw-Hill Book Company, New York, NY.

MILTON, J. S. and J. C. ARNOLD (1986). Chapters 3–5 in *Probability and Statistics in the Engineering and Computer Sciences,* McGraw-Hill Book Company, New York, NY.

EXERCISES

1. The maximum tensile force in a cable follows a normal probability density function with a mean = 55 kN and a coefficient of variation (COV) = 0.25. The resistance of the cable is 75 kN (the resistance is not a random variable).
   (a) Compute the probability of failure of the cable.
   (b) Two such cables are used in parallel in carrying the load of an elevator. Assuming the conditions between the cables are statistically independent, compute the probability of failure of the two-cable system.
   (c) Considering one cable again, if the desired probability of failure is 0.01, determine what the resistance should be.

2. The waiting time (T) for a car before it can make a left turn at an intersection is modeled with the following probability density function:
$$f(t) = h(2 - t/30) \qquad \text{for } 30 \le T \le 60 \text{ seconds}$$
$$= 0 \qquad \text{elsewhere}$$
   (a) If h is constant, compute h.
   (b) Draw this probability density function: and show (on the graph) what portion of the area under the curve represents the probability that the waiting time is less than 45 seconds. Compute this probability.
   (c) Compute the mean and standard deviation of T.

3. Leaks in a 2-mile gas delivery pipeline occur randomly. In the past 36 months there were 5 leaks reported along the pipeline.
   (a) What type of distribution is suitable to represent the number of leaks at any time period along the pipeline?
   (b) Compute the probability that in the next 6 months there will be no leak occurred along the pipeline.
   (c) If a leak occurs, there is 0.15 probability that the gas delivery will be disrupted so that a repair can be done. What is the probability that there will be no disruption in gas delivery due to probable leaks in the next 6 months.

4. The maximum bending moment in a beam is a normal random variable with a mean = 50,000 N.m and a coefficient of variation (COV) = 0.3. The resistance of the beam is 85,000 N.m (the resistance is not a random variable).
   (a) Compute the probability of failure of the beam due to bending.
   (b) Twelve such beams are used in a roof system. The failure of the roof system requires that at least two beams in the roof system fail. If conditions between beams are statistically independent, compute the failure probability of the roof system.

5. Accidents in a construction site occur following a Poisson distribution. Data from similar sites indicate that on the average 2 accidents occur every year.
   (a) If the duration of the construction project is expected to be 36 months, estimate the probability that the site will be accident free for the entire duration of the project.
   (b) Compute the probability that exactly two accidents will occur during the 36-month period.

6. A motorist drives at the posted speed on a roadway. The motorist will pass seven inter-sections in a 6-km stretch. The probability that the motorist will encounter a red light at an intersection is 0.3. This probability is constant for all seven intersections. Assume that the event of encountering a red light at an intersection is independent of the same event for all the other intersections.

(a) Compute the probability that the motorist will not encounter any red light for all the seven intersections.

(b) Compute the probability that the motorist will only encounter one red light within the 6-km of travel.

7. Derive Eqs. 6.40–6.42.

8. Repeat Exercise 4 but use a logarithmic normal distribution function instead of normal.

9. Repeat Exercise 1 but use a logarithmic normal distribution function instead of normal.

10. The useful life of an electrical component used in a flight data recorder follows an expo-nential probability density function. The mean useful time is specified as 20,000 hours by the manufacturer.

(a) Using T as the random variable describing the useful life of the component, establish the equation for the probability density function of T.

(b) If a target useful time is specified as 1,000 hours, compute the probability that the component will actually surpass this target time.

(c) The flight data recorder is made up of 20 such components. Compute the probability that the recorder will survive the first 1,000 hours of operation. Assume the condi-tions between the components are independent. Furthermore, assume that the failure in any one component will cause the failure of the recorder.

(d) Assume a specification requires 0.8 probability of survival for the recorder for the first 1,000 hours of operation. Compute the desired mean useful life for the electri-cal component.

11. The occurrences of strong motion earthquakes in an area are modeled using a Poisson probability mass function. The historical data shows that in the past 40 years there were 2 such earthquakes that occurred in the area.

(a) Compute the probability that there will be no such earthquakes in the area in the next 10 years.

(b) Compute the probability that such an earthquake may occur next year.

(c) If a strong motion earthquake occurs in the area, there is 0.01 probability that a dam located in the area will suffer damage. Compute the probability of damage to the dam in the next 10 years due to earthquakes.

12. In studying the possibility of foundation settlement (using mm as the unit) in piers sup-porting a highway bridge, the data from similar bridges indicate the following probabil-ity values:

$$P(X = 0) = 0.20$$
$$P(X = 5) = 0.30$$
$$P(X = 10) = 0.20$$
$$P(X = 15) = 0.15$$
$$P(X = 20) = 0.10$$
$$P(X = 25) = 0.05$$

In which X is a discrete random variable describing the foundation settlement in mm. The data given constitute the only possibilities for X.
(a) Plot the probability mass function of the foundation settlement.
(b) Compute the mean and standard deviation of the foundation settlement.
(c) Compute the probability that the foundation settlement will exceed 15 mm.

13. The duration of a construction project is modeled as a normal random variable. The mean duration is 90 days and the corresponding coefficient of variation 0.25.
(a) Compute the probability that the project will be delayed, if the target time for the completion of the project is 100 days.
(b) With improved workmanship, the coefficient of variation can be reduced to 0.15. With the same duration, compute the target time, if the accepted probability of delay is 0.10.

14. On the average, an intersection experiences five major accidents per year. If an accident occurs, there is 0.02 probability that the traffic will need to be rerouted to avoid the accident site.
(a) What is the probability that there will be no accidents in the next 3 months?
(b) What is the probability that no traffic needs to be rerouted due to potential accidents in the next 3 months?

15. Cars approach a toll bridge according to a Poisson process. Currently, according to design specifications, the bridge can handle 2 cars per minute with 0.20 probability of delay every minute (delay means traffic exceeding this capacity). If the bridge is improved, the capacity can be increased to 5 cars per minute. Estimate the probability of delay when the bridge is improved.

16. In design of a dam, the occurrence of floods is modeled with a Poisson process. The occurrence rate for the floods is mentioned as 0.01. However, further investigations show that the occurrence rate may be as high as 0.02. Since there are merits with both estimates, we decide that the two occurrence rates are both likely with 50–50 chances.
(a) Compute the probability that the dam will not experience any floods in the next 10 years.
(b) Compute the probability that the dam will experience no more than 2 floods in the next 10 years.

17. Within the past 20 years, a construction company has been consistently bidding on five jobs every year. The company's performance shows that it was successful to win 29 jobs in the 20-year period.
(a) Based on data provided, what is the probability of winning any job per year?
(b) The company is bidding on five jobs this year; what is the probability that it will win all five jobs?
(c) Repeat part (b) but compute the probability that the company will only win one job.

18. Two different sources publish two different values for the rate of tornado activities in a certain county in the Midwest. Source A indicates 0.2 tornadoes per year; whereas, source B has indicated a value equal to 0.4 per year. To utilize both sources, we assume they are both credible and the activity rate may be either one value with 50–50 chances.
(a) Based on data given, estimate the probability that next year, there will be no tornado in the county.
(b) Estimate the probability that there will be exactly one tornado in the county next year.

19. The past performance of a construction company indicates the following probabilities of success in winning jobs every year (X = number of jobs won):

$P(X = 0) = 0.15$

$P(X = 1) = 0.40$

$P(X = 2) = 0.20$

$P(X = 3) = 0.20$

$P(X = 4) = 0.05$

(a) Plot the probability mass function of X.

(b) Compute the mean and standard deviation of X.

(c) Compute the probability that the company will win at least 2 jobs this year.

20. The resistance of a cable follows a lognormal distribution. The cable has a 90 percent chance of survival carrying a 50 kN load. If the coefficient of variation of the cable resistance is 0.15, estimate the probability that the cable will survive a 70-kN load.

21. In Exercise 12, provide an estimate for the median deflection.

7

Joint Probability Functions and Correlated Variables

7.1 INTRODUCTION

In Chapters 5 and 6 the basic concepts underlying the theory of probability and probability distribution functions were presented. The discussion focused on a single random variable. Many engineering problems, however, may involve two or more random variables that can be correlated with one another via a mathematical function. For example the amount of toll collected on any given day at a toll booth depends on the number of vehicles approaching the booth in a day. Assume Y describes the amount of toll collected in a day and X_i ($i = 1, 2, \ldots, n$) presents the random variable describing the number of vehicles of type i that approach the booth. With n different types of vehicles identified, Y (*dependent variable*) will be a function of n random variables $X_1, X_2, \ldots, X_n$ (*independent variables*). In this example, the relationship between Y and X_i ($i = 1, 2, \ldots, n$) is obtained by observation using collected data. However, there are other examples in engineering in which the relationship between the dependent variable and independent variables can be established through basic principles governing engineering problems. For example, consider the stress at a location in a girder used in a bridge. The stress (dependent variable) is theoretically related to the applied load and the cross-sectional properties of the girder. No matter what the base of the relationship between Y and X_i

$(i = 1, 2, \ldots, n)$ is (whether theoretical or empirical), the relationship can be written in a general form as:

$$Y = g(X_1, X_2, \ldots, X_n) \tag{7.1}$$

in which g is the function describing the relationship between Y and X_1, $X_2, \ldots, X_n$. In a typical probabilistic problem, we will be interested in the expected value and the variance of Y and probabilities associated with Y. These can be computed based on either the expected values and variances of X_1, $X_2, \ldots, X_n$ or the probability distribution functions describing them. In this chapter we will focus on probability concepts governing functions between two or more random variables. We start out with the basic assumption that the function g is known and the dependent variable can be written in the form of Eq. 7.1. We will then treat the problem of correlation between two random variables for which joint probability functions governing probability values associated with the combined effects of the random variables are known. This is followed by a discussion on methods used for approximate estimation of the expected value, variance, and probabilities associated with a dependent variable (such as Y in Eq. 7.1).

7.2 JOINT PROBABILITY FUNCTIONS

In many engineering problems, an event of concern depends on a combination of two or more other events. In such problems, more than one random variable will be needed to formulate the event of concern. If these random variables are correlated among themselves, then a new set of probability functions (e.g., probability mass function or probability density function) need to be defined to describe the combined or joint occurrence of events represented by these individual random variables. An example will clarify this problem. Suppose a traffic engineer is interested in knowing the probability that the rush-hour traffic volumes in the northbound and southbound directions of an urban tollway each are less than a certain value (say x_1 and x_2). Using X_1 and X_2 as random variables describing the rush-hour traffic volumes in the northbound and southbound directions, respectively, the event of concern can be described with the combined events of $X_1 \leq x_1$ and $X_2 \leq x_2$. The corresponding probability will be $P(X_1 \leq x_1 \cap X_2 \leq x_2)$ or simply $P(X_1 \leq x_1; X_2 \leq x_2)$. If the two events $X_1 \leq x_1$ and $X_2 \leq x_2$ are independent, the probability can simply be written as $P(X_1 \leq x_1) \cdot P(X_2 \leq x_2)$. These individual probabilities can be computed knowing the probability density functions of X_1 and X_2. However, if X_1 and X_2 are correlated, the probability $P(X_1 \leq x_1; X_2 \leq x_2)$ can only be computed if a probability function describing the combined or joint occurrences of $X_1 \leq x_1$ and $X_2 \leq x_2$ is known. A probability density function (or a mass function if random variables are discrete) corresponding to such a probability function is called a *combined* or *joint* probability density (or mass) function.

7.2.1 Joint Probability Mass Function

If X_1 and X_2 are two correlated random variables, their joint probability mass function, $p_{1,2}(x_1, x_2)$ is defined as:

$$p_{1,2}(x_1, x_2) = P(X_1 = x_1; X_2 = x_2) \tag{7.2}$$

The joint cumulative probability function $F_{1,2}(x_1, x_2)$ is defined as:

$$F_{1,2}(x_1, x_2) = P(X_1 \le x_1 \ ; \ X_2 \le x_2) = \sum_i \sum_j p_{1,2}(x_{1i}, x_{2j}) \tag{7.3}$$

in which x_{1i} $(i = 1, 2, 3, \ldots)$ are values of the random variable X_1 and x_{2j} $(j = 1, 2, 3, \ldots)$ are values of the random variable X_2. The double summation in Eq. 7.3 is for all $x_{1i} \le x_1$ and all $x_{2j} \le x_2$. Notice that:

$$F_{1,2}(-\infty, +\infty) = 1 \tag{7.4}$$

In light of Eq. 7.2, we can also write

$$p_{1,2}(x_1, x_2) = P(X_1 = x_1 \mid X_2 = x_2) \, P(X_2 = x_2) \tag{7.5}$$

Denoting the conditional probability of x_1 given x_2 as $p_{1|2}$, we have:

$$p_{1|2}(x_1|x_2) = P(X_1 = x_1 \mid X_2 = x_2) \tag{7.6}$$

Combining eqs. 7.5 and 7.6 will result in:

$$p_{1,2}(x_1, x_2) = p_{1|2}(x_1|x_2) p_2(x_2) \tag{7.7}$$

The function $p_{1|2}(x_1|x_2)$ is referred to as the *conditional probability mass function* of x_1 given x_2; whereas $p_2(x_2)$ is the *marginal probability mass function* of x_2. Notice that $p_{1|2}(x_1|x_2)$ describes the conditional probability of $X_1 = x_1$ given $X_2 = x_2$. From Eq. 7.7,

$$p_{1|2}(x_1|x_2) = \frac{p_{1,2}(x_1, x_2)}{p_2(x_2)} \tag{7.8}$$

Equation 7.3 can also be written as:

$$F_{1,2}(x_1, x_2) = \sum_i \sum_j p_{1,2}(x_{1i} \mid x_{2j}) p_2(x_{2j}) \tag{7.9}$$

If $x_1 = +\infty$, then,

$$F_{1,2}(+\infty, x_2) = \sum_j p_2(x_{2j}) \tag{7.10}$$

which indicates that

$$\sum_j p_2(x_{2j}) = \sum_i \sum_j p_{1,2}(x_{1i}, x_{2j}) \text{ for all } x_{1i} \tag{7.11}$$

or simply

$$p_2(x_2) = \sum_i p_{1,2}(x_{1i}, x_2) \text{ for all } x_{1i} \tag{7.12}$$

This indicates that the marginal probability mass function of the random variable X_2 can be found by the summation of the values of the joint probability mass function for all values of x_1. Similarly,

$$p_1(x_1) = \sum_j p_{1,2}(x_1, x_{2j}) \text{ for all } x_{2j} \tag{7.13}$$

If X_1 and X_2 are statistically independent of one another, then

$$p_{1,2}(x_1, x_2) = P(X_1 = x_1). P(X_2 = x_2) = p_1(x_1).p_1(x_2) \tag{7.14}$$

and as such $p_{1|2}(x_1|x_2) = p_1(x_1)$ and $p_{2|1}(x_2|x_1) = p_2(x_2)$.

Example 7.1

Two random variables X_1 and X_2, respectively, define the number of trucks entering and leaving a concrete mixing plant every hour. The joint probability mass function of X_1 and X_2 is assumed to be:

$$p_{1,2}(x_1, x_2) = \frac{c}{1 + x_1 + x_2} \text{ for } x_1 = 0, 1 \text{ and } 2 \text{ and } x_2 = 0, 1 \text{ and } 2$$

$$p_{1,2}(x_1, x_2) = 0 \text{ elsewhere}$$

(a) Compute c.
(b) Compute the probability that the number of trucks entering the plant every hour is less than 2 and no truck is leaving the plant during the same hour.
(c) Compute the marginal probability mass functions $p_1(x_1)$ and $p_2(x_2)$.
(d) Compute the conditional probability mass functions $p_{1|2}(x_1|x_2)$ and $p_{2|1}(x_2|x_1)$.

Solution:

(a) From Eq. 7.4

$$\sum_{i=1}^{3} \sum_{j=1}^{3} p_{1,2}(x_{1i}, x_{2j}) = 1.0$$

Thus,

$$c\left[\frac{1}{1 + x_{11} + x_{21}} + \frac{1}{1 + x_{11} + x_{22}} + \frac{1}{1 + x_{11} + x_{23}} \right.$$

$$\left. + \frac{1}{1 + x_{12} + x_{21}} + \frac{1}{1 + x_{12} + x_{22}} \ldots \right] = 1.0$$

in which x_{11}, x_{12}, and x_{13} are values of X_1 and are equal to 0, 1, and 2, respectively. Similarly, x_{21}, x_{22}, and x_{23} are values of X_2 and are also equal to 0, 1, and 2, respectively. Using these values, $3.7c = 1.0$. This results in $c = 0.27$.

(b) In this part $P(X_1 < 2; X_2 = 0)$ is desired.

$$P(X_1 < 2; X_2 = 0) = P(X_1 \le 1; X_2 = 0)$$
$$= p_{1,2}(0,0) + p_{1,2}(1,0) = 0.27/(1 + 0 + 0) + 0.27/(1 + 1 + 0) = 0.405.$$

(c) From Eq. 7.13

$$p_1(x_1) = \frac{0.27}{1 + x_1 + 0} + \frac{0.27}{1 + x_1 + 1} + \frac{0.27}{1 + x_1 + 2}$$

The values of $p_1(x_1)$ are $p_1(0) = 0.495$, $p_1(1) = 0.293$ and $p_1(2) = 0.212$. Similarly,

$$p_2(x_2) = \frac{0.27}{1 + 0 + x_2} + \frac{0.27}{1 + 1 + x_2} + \frac{0.27}{1 + 2 + x_2}$$

(d) From Eq. 7.8

$$p_{1|2}(x_1|x_2) = \frac{\dfrac{0.27}{1 + x_1 + x_2}}{\dfrac{0.27}{1 + x_2} + \dfrac{0.27}{2 + x_2} + \dfrac{0.27}{3 + x_2}} = \frac{1}{(1 + x_1 + x_2)\left(\dfrac{1}{1 + x_2} + \dfrac{1}{2 + x_2} + \dfrac{1}{3 + x_2}\right)}$$

For example given $x_2 = 0$, the values of the conditional probability mass function $p_{1|2}$ are $p_{1|2}(0|0) = 0.5455$, $p_{1|2}(1|0) = 0.2727$, and $p_{1|2}(2|0) = 0.1818$. Since the function $p_{1,2}(x_1, x_2)$ is symmetric with respect to x_1 and x_2, the function $p_{2|1}(x_2|x_1)$ can be obtained from $p_{1|2}(x_1|x_2)$ by changing x_1 to x_2 and x_2 to x_1.

Example 7.2

Assume X_1 and X_2 are discrete random variables describing, respectively, the number of accidents per hour in the northbound and the southbound lanes of an urban freeway during rush-hours. Assume hypothetically that the joint probability mass function of X_1 and X_2 are available by the values in Table E7.2 for $0 \le x_1 \le 3$ and $0 \le x_2 \le 3$. For any other x_1 and x_2, the values of the joint probability mass function are zero.

(a) Verify the validity of the values given in Table E7.2 as joint probability mass function values.
(b) Compute the probability that the number of accidents in the northbound lanes and the southbound lanes each is less than 2.
(c) Compute and tabulate the values of marginal probability functions $p_1(x_1)$ and $p_2(x_2)$.
(d) Compute and tabulate the values of the conditional probability mass function $p_{1|2}$ $(x_1|x_2)$ and $p_{2|1}$ $(x_2|x_1)$.

Solution:

(a) From Eq. 7.4

$$\sum_{i=0}^{3} \sum_{j=0}^{3} p_{1,2}(x_{1i}, x_{2j}) = 0.16 + 0.14 + 0.08 + 0.06 + 0.014 + \ \ldots \ = 1.0$$

Thus the values listed in Table E7.2 are the values of the joint probability mass function within the limits listed for the two random variables X_1 and X_2.

TABLE E7.2   VALUES OF $p_{1,2}$ (x_1, x_2)

	$x_1 = 0$	$x_1 = 1$	$x_1 = 2$	$x_1 = 3$
$x_2 = 0$	0.16	0.14	0.08	0.06
$x_2 = 1$	0.14	0.07	0.05	0.03
$x_2 = 2$	0.08	0.05	0.03	0.01
$x_2 = 3$	0.06	0.03	0.01	0

(b) In this part $P(X_1 < 2; X_2 < 2)$ is desired. This probability can be computed from Eq. 7.3 as follows

$$P(X_1 \leq 1; X_2 \leq 1) = 0.16 + 0.14 + 0.14 + 0.07 = 0.51.$$

(c) From Eq. 7.13, the values of the marginal probability mass function $p_1 (x_1)$ can be obtained by summation of the values of $p_{1,2} (x_1, x_2)$ in individual columns of Table E7.2. Thus,

$p_1 (0) = 0.16 + 0.14 + 0.08 + 0.06 = 0.44$
$p_1 (1) = 0.14 + 0.07 + 0.05 + 0.03 = 0.29$
$p_1 (2) = 0.08 + 0.05 + 0.03 + 0.01 = 0.17$
$p_1 (3) = 0.06 + 0.03 + 0.01 + 0 = 0.10$

Similarly, from Eq. 7.12, the values of $p_2(x_2)$ are obtained by summation of the values of $p_{1,2} (x_1, x_2)$ in individual rows of Table E7.2. Thus,

$p_2 (0) = 0.16 + 0.14 + 0.08 + 0.06 = 0.44$
$p_2 (1) = 0.29$
$p_2 (2) = 0.17$
$p_2 (3) = 0.10.$

(d) In this part, for example, given $x_2 = 0$, the values of the conditional probability mass function $p_{1|2} (x_1|x_2)$ can be computed as follows:

$p_{1|2} (0|0) = p_{1,2} (0, 0)/p_2 (0) = 0.16/0.44 = 0.36$
$p_{1|2} (1|0) = p_{1,2} (1, 0)/p_2 (0) = 0.14/0.44 = 0.32$
$p_{1|2} (2|0) = p_{1,2} (2, 0)/p_2 (0) = 0.08/0.44 = 0.18$
$p_{1|2} (3|0) = p_{1,2} (3, 0)/p_2 (0) = 0.06/0.44 = 0.14.$

Identical results are also found for $p_{2|1}$ values.

7.2.2 Joint Probability Density Function

The probabilities of combined events of two or more continuous random variables are obtained through joint probability density functions. If only two random variables are involved, a joint probability density function is shown with $f_{1,2} (x_1, x_2)$ and is described via the following equation:

$$P(x_1 < X_1 \leq x_1 + dx_1 \cap x_2 < X_2 \leq x_2 + dx_2) = f_{1,2}(x_1, x_2)\, dx_1\, dx_2 \quad (7.15)$$

Using Eq. 7.15, the joint distribution function $F_{1,2}(x_1, x_2)$ of random variables X_1 and X_2 is

$$F_{1,2}(x_1,x_2) = \int_{-\infty}^{x_1}\int_{-\infty}^{x_2} f_{1,2}(x_1,x_2)dx_1dx_2 = P(X_1 \leq x_1 \; ; \; X_2 \leq x_2) \quad (7.16)$$

and as such,

$$F_{1,2}(-\infty,+\infty) = 1.0 \quad (7.17)$$

Introducing $f_{1|2} (x_1|x_2)$ and $f_{2|1} (x_2|x_1)$ as conditional probability density functions and $f_1(x_1)$ and $f_2 (x_2)$ as the marginal probability density functions, we can write:

$$P(X_1 \le x_1 \; ; \; X_2 \le x_2) = \int_{-\infty}^{x_2} P(X_1 \le x_1 | x_2 < X_2 \le x_2 + dx_2) f_2(x_2) dx_2$$

$$= \int_{-\infty}^{x_1} \int_{-\infty}^{x_2} f_{1|2}(x_1|x_2) f_2(x_2) dx_1 dx_2 \qquad (7.18)$$

Comparing Eqs. 7.16 and 7.18,

$$f_{1,2}(x_1, x_2) = f_{1|2}(x_1 | x_2) f_2(x_2) \qquad (7.19)$$

Similarly,

$$f_{1,2}(x_1, x_2) = f_{2|1}(x_2 | x_1) f_1(x_1) \qquad (7.20)$$

From Eqs. 7.19 and 7.20

$$f_{1|2}(x_1 | x_2) = \frac{f_{1,2}(x_1, x_2)}{f_2(x_2)} \qquad (7.21)$$

and

$$f_{2|1}(x_2 | x_1) = \frac{f_{1,2}(x_1, x_2)}{f_1(x_1)} \qquad (7.22)$$

When $x_1 = +\infty$

$$P(X_1 \le x_1 \; ; \; X_2 \le x_2) = \int_{-\infty}^{x_2} \left[\int_{-\infty}^{+\infty} f_{1,2}(x_1, x_2) dx_1 \right] dx_2$$

$$= \int_{-\infty}^{x_2} \left[\int_{-\infty}^{+\infty} f_{1|2}(x_1 | x_2) dx_1 \right] f_2(x_2) dx_2 = \int_{-\infty}^{x_2} f_2(x_2) dx_2 \qquad (7.23)$$

Notice that in Eq. 7.23, the integral inside the bracket is equal to 1. Thus,

$$f_2(x_2) = \int_{-\infty}^{+\infty} f_{1,2}(x_1, x_2) dx_1 \qquad (7.24)$$

and similarly,

$$f_1(x_1) = \int_{-\infty}^{+\infty} f_{1,2}(x_1, x_2) dx_2 \qquad (7.25)$$

In a special case where the random variables X_1 and X_2 are statistically independent

$$f_{1|2}(x_1 | x_2) = f_1(x_1) \text{ and } f_{2|1}(x_2 | x_1) = f_2(x_2) \qquad (7.26)$$

and

$$P(X_1 \le x_1 \; ; \; X_2 \le x_2) = \int_{-\infty}^{x_1} f_1(x_1) dx_1 \int_{-\infty}^{x_2} f_2(x_2) dx_2 \qquad (7.27)$$

Example 7.3

The live loads on any two floors in an office building are correlated. Assume for simplicity that the live loads on two given floors are random variables X_1 and X_2 which are defined by the following joint probability density functions:

$$f_{1,2}(x_1, x_2) = c(e^{-x_1} + e^{-x_2}) \qquad \text{for } 0 \le (x_1 \text{ and } x_2) \le 2{,}400 \text{ N/m}^2$$

$$= 0 \qquad \text{elsewhere}$$

(a) Compute c.
(b) Compute the probability that both X_1 and X_2 are not more than 1,000 N/m^2.
(c) Derive expressions for the marginal probability density functions of X_1 and X_2.
(d) Derive expressions for the conditional probability density functions $f_{1|2}(x_1|x_2)$ and $f_{2|1}(x_2|x_1)$.

Solution:

(a) From Eq. 7.17

$$\int_0^{2400}\int_0^{2400} c(e^{-x_1} + e^{-x_2})dx_1 dx_2 = 1.0$$

This result in $c = 1/4800$.

(b) In this part $P(X_1 \leq 1,000; X_2 \leq 1,000)$ is desired. Using 7.16,

$$P(X_1 \leq 1000 \; ; \; X_2 \leq 1000) = \frac{1}{4800}\int_0^{1000}\int_0^{1000}(e^{-x_1} + e^{-x_2})dx_1 dx_2 = 0.417.$$

(c) In this part, we apply Eq. 7.25:

$$f_1(x_1) = \int_0^{2400} f_{1,2}(x_1,x_2)dx_2 = \frac{e^{-x_1}}{2} + \frac{1}{4800} \qquad \text{for } 0 \leq x_1 \leq 2,400$$

$$= 0 \qquad \text{elsewhere}$$

Similarly, using Eq. 7.24:

$$f_2(x_2) = \int_0^{2400} f_{1,2}(x_1,x_2)dx_1 = \frac{e^{-x_2}}{2} + \frac{1}{4800} \qquad \text{for } 0 \leq x_2 \leq 2,400$$

$$= 0 \qquad \text{elsewhere.}$$

(d) From Eq. 7.21

$$f_{1|2}(x_1|x_2) = \frac{e^{-x_1} + e^{-x_2}}{2400e^{-x_2} + 1}$$

Again, the function is valid for x_1 and x_2 between 0 and 2400. Similarly,

$$f_{2|1}(x_2|x_1) = \frac{e^{-x_1} + e^{-x_2}}{2400e^{-x_1} + 1}$$

Notice that the joint probability density function forms a surface in the three-dimensional space. Any probability value represented by Eq. 7.16 will be a portion of the volume under this surface. The total volume under the surface will be equal to unity. Figure 7.1 shows a joint probability density function represented by the joint normal probability density function (bivariate normal) which is described in Section 7.3.3.

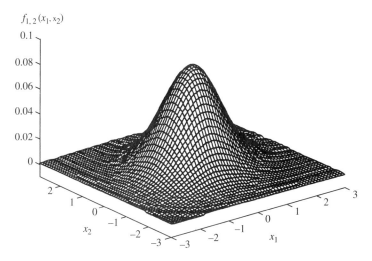

$f_{1,2}(x_1, x_2)$

Figure 7.1   Joint probability density function.

7.3 COVARIANCE AND CORRELATION

7.3.1 Covariance

As discussed in Chapter 6, the moments (or mathematical expectation) of a random variable can be computed using the generalized relationship of Eqs. 6.18 and 6.19. The same concept can also be applied to two random variables that are defined with a joint probability density function or a joint probability mass function. By definition, the mathematical expectation of a function $g(x_1, x_2)$ is computed using the following expression:

$$E[g(X_1 X_2)] = \sum_i \sum_j g(x_{1i}, x_{2j}) p_{1,2}(x_{1i}, x_{2j}) \tag{7.28}$$

for discrete random variables; and

$$E[g(X_1, X_2)] = \int_{-\infty}^{+\infty} \int_{-\infty}^{+\infty} g(x_1, x_2) f_{1,2}(x_1, x_2) dx_1 dx_2 \tag{7.29}$$

for continuous random variables. In Eq. 7.28, the double summation is for all values of the random variable X_1 (i.e., $x_{11}, x_{12}, x_{13}, \dots$), and all values of the random variable X_2 (i.e., $x_{21}, x_{22}, x_{23}, \dots$). In a special case where function $g = (X_1 - \mu_1)(X_2 - \mu_2)$, with μ_1 and μ_2 being the mean values of the random variables X_1 and X_2, respectively, the mathematical expectation is called the *covariance* of X_1 and X_2 and is identified with $Cov(X_1, X_2)$. Using Eqs. 7.28 and 7.29, the covariance of X_1 and X_2 is:

$$Cov(X_1, X_2) = E[(X_1 - \mu_1)(X_2 - \mu_2)]$$

$$= \sum_i \sum_j (x_{1i} - \mu_1)(x_{2j} - \mu_2) p_{1,2}(x_{1i}, x_{2j}) \tag{7.30}$$

for discrete random variables; and

$$Cov(X_1,X_2) = \int_{-\infty}^{+\infty} \int_{-\infty}^{+\infty} (x_1 - \mu_1)(x_2 - \mu_2) f_{1,2}(x_1,x_2) dx_1 dx_2 \qquad (7.31)$$

for continuous random variables. Another form for $Cov(X_1, X_2)$ can be written as:

$$Cov(X_1, X_2) = E[(X_1 - \mu_1)(X_2 - \mu_2)] = E(X_1 X_2) - \mu_1 \mu_2 \qquad (7.32)$$

in which (by virtue of Eqs. 7.28 and 7.29)

$$E(X_1 X_2) = \sum_i \sum_j x_{1i} \, x_{2j} \, p_{1,2}(x_{1i}, x_{2j}) \qquad (7.33)$$

for discrete random variables; and

$$E(X_1,X_2) = \int_{-\infty}^{+\infty} \int_{-\infty}^{+\infty} x_1 x_2 \, f_{1,2}(x_1,x_2) dx_1 dx_2 \qquad (7.34)$$

for continuous random variables. Notice that if $X_1 = X_2$, the covariance of X_1, X_2 will be the same as the variance of X_1. This means that the covariance of a random variable with itself is the same as the variance of that random variable. In a special case where X_1 and X_2 are statistically independent of each other, $Cov(X_1, X_2) = 0$. This can easily be proved by virtue of the fact that for two random variables that are statistically independent of each other, $p_{1,2}(x_1, x_2) = p_1(x_1) p_2(x_2)$, and $f_{1,2}(x_1,x_2) = f_1(x_1) f_2(x_2)$. For example for two continuous random variables from Eq. 7.34

$$E(X_1,X_2) = \int_{-\infty}^{+\infty} \int_{-\infty}^{+\infty} x_1 x_2 \, f_1(x_1) f_2(x_2) dx_1 dx_2 = \mu_1 \mu_2 \qquad (7.35)$$

Substituting Eq. 7.35 in Eq. 7.32 will result in $Cov(X_1, X_2) = 0$.

Example 7.4

In Example 7.1, compute $E(X_1 X_2)$ and $Cov(X_1, X_2)$.

Solution:

From Eq. 7.33

$$E(X_1 X_2) = c\left[\frac{x_{11}x_{21}}{1 + x_{11} + x_{21}} + \frac{x_{11}x_{22}}{1 + x_{11} + x_{22}} + \frac{x_{11}x_{23}}{1 + x_{11} + x_{23}} \right.$$

$$\left. + \frac{x_{12}x_{21}}{1 + x_{12} + x_{21}} \quad \cdots \quad \right] = 2.13c = 0.576.$$

The mean values of X_1 and X_2 can be computed from $p_1(x_1)$ and $p_2(x_2)$, respectively.

$$\mu_1 = \sum_i x_{1i} p_1(x_{1i}) \quad \text{and} \quad \mu_2 = \sum_j x_{2j} \, p_2(x_{2j})$$

For example since

$$p_1(x_1) = 0.27\left(\frac{1}{1 + x_1} + \frac{1}{2 + x_1} + \frac{1}{3 + x_1} \right),$$

$\mu_1 = 0.716$. Similarly, $\mu_2 = 0.716$. Thus,

$$Cov(X_1, X_2) = 0.576 - 0.716 \times 0.716 = 0.064.$$

7.3.2 Correlation Coefficient

By definition, the correlation coefficient (ρ) of two random variables X_1 and X_2 is computed by dividing the covariance of X_1 and X_2 by their respective standard deviations. This means that

$$\rho = \frac{Cov(X_1, X_2)}{\sigma_1 \sigma_2} = \frac{E(X_1 X_2) - \mu_1 \mu_2}{\sigma_1 \sigma_2} \qquad (7.36)$$

in which σ_1 and σ_2 are the standard deviations of X_1 and X_2, respectively. Notice that if the two random variables X_1 and X_2 are statistically independent, $\rho = 0$. On the other hand if X_1 and X_2 are perfectly correlated, and the relationship between X_1 and X_2 is linear, one of the two random variables, say X_2, can be fully represented by the other, i.e., X_1. This means that $\sigma_1 = \sigma_2$, and also $E(X_1 X_2) = E(X_1^2)$ and $\mu_1 = \mu_2$, and as such $\rho = 1$. It is noted that ρ may be negative. In such a case a perfect *negative* correlation will be represented by $\rho = -1$. It is also noted that ρ is a measure of a linear correlation between X_1 and X_2. Thus, if a non-linear correlation between X_1 and X_2 exists, Eq. 7.36 will result in $|\rho| < 1$. Figure 7.2 illustrates a few examples of values of ρ for several types of relationship between X_1 and X_2. In Figures 7.2a and 7.2b, the correlation is perfect (linear relationship). Figures 7.2c and 7.2d show no correlation. In these cases, changes in one variable will not affect the other. In Figures 7.2e and 7.2f, although in each case a relationship between X_1 and X_2 exists, $|\rho|$ will not be equal to unity because these relationships are not linear. It can be said that in these cases, the linear correlation between X_1 and X_2 is only partial. To further clarify on cases where two random variables may only be partially correlated, consider the following example:

Let's define X_1 and X_2 as the volume of concrete and reinforcing steel, respectively, delivered to a construction site each day. The delivery of the two materials to the site will depend on several factors such as the means of transportation, source of each material, delays in roadways, shortage of raw materials in the market, etc. If steel and concrete are provided through two different sources, factors that affect one variable may not necessarily affect the other. However, at any given time, there may be several other factors that would affect both variables, i.e., X_1 and X_2. Figure 7.3 presents three different cases for values of X_1 and X_2 in a five-day period. If in a special case, both materials are supplied through the same source; and exactly the same factors are affecting X_1 and X_2, the two variables are likely to be perfectly correlated. Figure 7.3a is an example of this case. This means that if there is any reduction or increase in the value of X_1, it is very likely that X_2 will also experience the same changes and will follow X_1. In Figure 7.1a, notice that the ratio of the volume of steel to that of concrete delivered daily to the site for the five day period was constant. Furthermore, in this case, the plot of X_1 versus X_2 shows a perfect linear relationship. Now assume only some of the factors are commonly affecting X_1 and X_2. In this case, the correlation between the two random variables will be only partial. This means that if there are, for example, reductions in X_1, there will be reductions in X_2 only on some days; while on other days there are no changes or there may even be increases in X_2. Figure 7.3b depicts this case. Notice that when X_1 versus X_2 is plot-

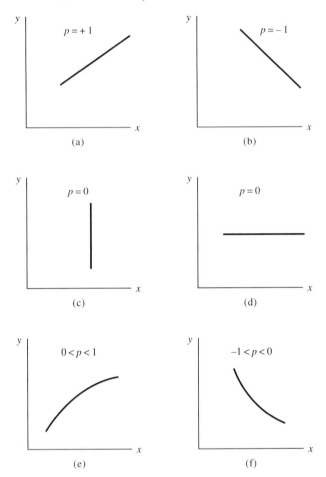

Figure 7.2   Values of correlation coefficient for several cases of y vs. x.

ted, there is some scatter in the data indicating a partial correlation between X_1 and X_2. Now consider a case where factors affecting X_1 are totally different from those affecting X_2. In this case, any reduction or increase in X_1 will not be followed by X_2. This case is represented by Figure 7.3c. Notice that the values for X_2 are unchanged, while X_1 values are changing daily. This is a case of no correlation. Notice that the plot of X_1 versus X_2 in this case results in a vertical line indicating no correlation.

Example 7.5

In Example 7.4, compute the correlation coefficient.

Solution:

The correlation coefficient is computed from Eq. 7.36. The standard deviations of the two random variables are computed knowing their probability mass functions. For example for X_1

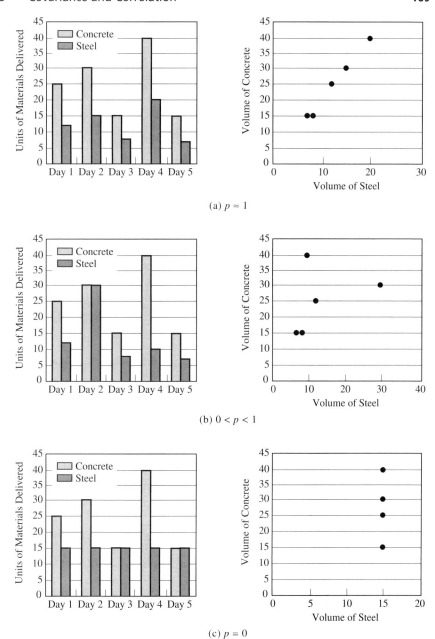

Figure 7.3   Examples of correlation coefficient in an engineering problem.

$$p_1(x_1) = 0.27\left(\frac{1}{1+x_1} + \frac{1}{2+x_1} + \frac{1}{3+x_1}\right),$$

and the standard deviation σ_1 is computed from $\sigma_1^2 = E[(X_1 - \mu_1)^2] = \Sigma(x_{1i} - \mu_1)^2 p_i (x_{1i})$ in which the mean value $\mu_1 = 0.716$ and the summation covers all values of the random variable X_1 (which are $x_{11} = 0, x_{12} = 1,$ and $x_{13} = 2$). The computation is as follows:

$$\sigma_1^2 = (0.27)\left[(0 - 0.716)^2\left(\frac{1}{1+0} + \frac{1}{2+0} + \frac{1}{3+0}\right)\right.$$

$$+ (1 - 0.716)^2\left(\frac{1}{1+1} + \frac{1}{2+1} + \frac{1}{3+1}\right)$$

$$\left. + (2 - 0.716)^2\left(\frac{1}{1+2} + \frac{1}{2+2} + \frac{1}{3+2}\right)\right]$$

or $\sigma_1 = 0.791$. Similarly $\sigma_2 = 0.791$ and $\rho = 0.064/(0.791 \times 0.791) = 0.102$. This indicates that the linear correlation between the two random variables X_1 and X_2 is weak.

Example 7.6

Figure E7.6 shows a beam that provides a support for a crane system. At any given time, the magnitude of the load Q and its location X from the left support are random variables. Random variable Q follows a uniform distribution ranging between 0 and 160 KN. Random variable X also follows a uniform distribution ranging between 0 and 12 meters.

(a) At the location of the load, compute shear V (immediately to the left of the load) and bending moment M.

(b) Compute the mean and standard deviation of Q and X.

(c) Compute the mean value of V and M, and $E(VM)$.

(d) Compute the correlation coefficient between V and M.

Solution:

(a) The shear and moment at the location of the load are

$$V = (1 - X/12)Q \qquad \text{and} \qquad M = X(1 - X/12)Q$$

(b) The uniform probability density function for a random variable X ranging between a and b is defined as

$$f(x) = 1/(b - a) \qquad a \le x \le b$$
$$= 0 \qquad\qquad \text{elsewhere}$$

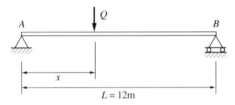

Figure E 7.6 Simply-supported beam with random load location.

This results in a mean value $\mu_X = (a + b)/2$ and standard deviation

$$\sigma_X = \frac{b - a}{2\sqrt{3}}.$$

Applying these equations to the two random variables Q and X,

$$\mu_Q = 80 \text{ KN}, \sigma_Q = 46.2 \text{ KN, and } \mu_X = 6 \text{ m}, \sigma_X = 3.46 \text{ m}.$$

(c) Since the two random variables Q and X are independent, their joint probability density function is the product of their individual probability density functions. This means:

$$f_{Q,X}(q,x) = f_Q(q)f_X(x) = (1/160)(1/12) = (1/1920)$$
$$\text{for } 0 \le q \le 160 \quad \text{and} \quad 0 \le x \le 12$$

The mean value of V is computed as follows:

$$\mu_V = E(V) = E[(1 - X/12)Q] \text{ or}$$

$$\mu_V = \int_0^{160} \int_0^{12} (1 - x/12)q \ f_{Q,X}(q,x)dq \ dx = 40.$$

And,

$$\sigma_V^2 = E(V^2) - \mu_V^2 = E[(1 - X/12)^2 Q^2] - (40)^2$$

$$= \int_0^{160} \int_0^{12} (1 - x/12)^2 q^2 f_{Q,X}(x,q)dq \ dx - (40)^2$$

$$= \int_0^{160} \int_0^{12} (1 - x/12)^2 q^2 \frac{1}{1920} dq \ dx - (40)^2$$

which results in $\sigma_V = 35.3$. Similarly, the mean and standard deviation of M can be computed.

$$\mu_M = E[(1 - X/12)XQ] = \int_0^{160} \int_0^{12} (1 - x/12)xq \ f_{Q,X}(q,x)dq \ dx = 160,$$

and

$$\sigma_M^2 = E(M^2) - \mu_m^2 = \int_0^{160} \int_0^{12} (1 - x/12)^2 x^2 q^2 \ f_{Q,M}(q,x)dq \ dx - (160)^2 = 15360,$$

which results in $\sigma_M = 123.9$. In order to compute the correlation coefficient, we also need to compute $E(VM)$. This is computed as follows:

$$E(VM) = E[(1 - x/12)q(1 - x/12)xq]$$

$$= \int_0^{160} \int_0^{160} (1 - x/12)^2 xq^2 f_{Q,X}(q,x)dq \ dx = 8533.$$

Using Eq. 7.36, the correlation coefficient of V and M will be

$$\rho = (8533. - 40 \times 160)/(35.3 \times 123.9) = 0.49.$$

Notice that although Q and X are independent, there still exists some correlation between V and M. This is because the equations for V and M depend on the same random variables.

In cases where n random variables $X_1, X_2, \ldots, X_n$ are involved, the expected value of any two variables (say X_i and X_j) are

$$E(X_iX_j) = \int_{-\infty}^{+\infty}\int_{-\infty}^{+\infty} x_ix_j\, f_{i,j}dx_idx_j \qquad \text{If } i \neq j \qquad (7.37)$$

and

$$E(X_iX_j) = E(X_i^2) = \mu_{X_i}^2 + \sigma_{X_i}^2 \qquad \text{If } i = j \qquad (7.38)$$

These expected values are arranged in a symmetric matrix such as

$$\begin{bmatrix} E(X_1^2) & E(X_1X_2) & \cdots & E(X_1X_n) \\ E(X_2X_1) & E(X_2^2) & \cdots & E(X_2X_n) \\ \cdots & & & \\ E(X_nX_1) & E(X_nX_2) & \cdots & E(X_n^2) \end{bmatrix} \qquad (7.39)$$

and in terms of correlation coefficient as

$$\begin{bmatrix} 1 & \rho_{1,2} & \cdots & \rho_{1,n} \\ \rho_{2,1} & 1 & \cdots & \rho_{2,n} \\ \cdots & & & \\ \rho_{n,1} & \rho_{n,2} & \cdots & 1 \end{bmatrix} \qquad (7.40)$$

Notice that the principal diagonal elements of matrix in Eq. 7.40 are all equal to one. This is because the correlation coefficient of a random variable with itself is equal to unity.

In practice, the correlation coefficient is rarely computed from Eq. 7.36. Instead, an estimate of ρ is computed from data obtained for X_1 and X_2. This subject is discussed in Chapter 9.

7.3.3 Bivariate Normal Distribution

The joint probability density function of two normally distributed random variables X and Y with a correlation coefficient ρ is defined by the bivariate normal function

$$f_{X,Y}(x,y) = \frac{1}{2\pi\sigma_X\sigma_Y\sqrt{1-\rho^2}} \exp\left\{ -\frac{1}{2(1-\rho^2)}\left[\left(\frac{x-\mu_X}{\sigma_X}\right)^2 \right.\right.$$
$$\left.\left. - 2\rho\left(\frac{x-\mu_X}{\sigma_X}\right)\left(\frac{y-\mu_Y}{\sigma_Y}\right) + \left(\frac{y-\mu_Y}{\sigma_Y}\right)^2\right]\right\} \qquad (7.41)$$

for $-\infty < x$ and $y < +\infty$.

In Eq. 7.41, if the correlation coefficient is zero (i.e., the random variables are statistically independent), the joint density function $f_{X,Y}$ will become the product of the individual probability density functions f_X and f_Y. Equation 7.41 is plotted as shown in Figure 7.1. It appears in the shape of a bell in a three-dimensional space.

7.4 FUNCTIONS OF A SINGLE RANDOM VARIABLE

As discussed in Section 7.1, a quantity may be related to a random variable through a definite function. Defining this function as g, a quantity Y can be written in terms of a random variable X as follows:

$$Y = g(X) \tag{7.42}$$

This is a simple form of Eq. 7.1. The dependent variable Y follows the independent random variable X within the rule governed by the function g. If the probability function (i.e., probability mass function or density function) of X is available, any probability associated with the random variable Y can be computed by virtue of the fact that for any given value of X, such as x, there is a value for Y, such as y. The relation between y and x is

$$y = g(x) \tag{7.43}$$

Furthermore, moments of Y (e.g., the mean and variance) can also be computed if the probability function of X is available.

7.4.1 Discrete Random Variable Case

When random variables X and Y are discrete, any probability associated with Y can be written as:

$$P(Y = y) = P(X = x) = p_X(x) \tag{7.44}$$

in which $p_X(x)$ is the probability mass function of X. Equation 7.44 can be evaluated only if x can be solved in terms of y from Eq. 7.43. Solving for x from Eq. 7.43

$$x = g^{-1}(y) \tag{7.45}$$

where g^{-1} is the inverse function of g. Furthermore, we can write:

$$P(Y \leq y) = P(X \leq x) = \Sigma p_X(x_i) \tag{7.46}$$

in which the summation includes all $x_i \leq x$ or all $x_i \leq g^{-1}(y)$. The expected value and variance of Y can also be computed in terms of $p_X(x)$ as follows:

$$E(Y) = \mu_Y = E[g(X)] = \Sigma g(x_i) p_X(x_i) \tag{7.47}$$

$$\text{Var}(Y) = E(Y^2) - (\mu_Y)^2 = \Sigma g^2(x_i) p_X(x_i) - (\mu_Y)^2 \tag{7.48}$$

In both Eqs. 7.47 and 7.48, the summation includes all x_i.

Example 7.7

Figure E7.7 shows a cantilever beam with a uniformly distributed load q acting over the length X. Length X is a discrete random variable. Possible values for X are $L, 3L/4$, $L/2$, and $L/4$. The probability mass function of X is defined as

$$p_X(x) = cx/L \qquad x = L/4, L/2, 3L/4 \text{ and } L$$
$$p_X(x) = 0 \qquad \text{elsewhere}$$

Assume q and L are deterministic.

(a) Compute constant c, mean, and standard deviation of X.

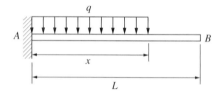

Figure E 7.7 Cantilever beam with random load area.

(b) Write an expression for moment M_A at A in terms of X.
(c) Compute the mean and standard deviation of M_A.
(d) Compute the probability that M_A will be less than or equal to $qL^2/8$.

Solution:

(a) Since $\Sigma\, p_X(x_i) = 1$, using $x_1 = L/4$, $x_2 = L/2$, $x_3 = 3L/4$, and $x_4 = L$ will result in $c = 0.4$.
(b) The moment at A is $M_A = qX^2/2$.
(c) From Eq. 7.47

$E(M_A) = E(qX^2/2) = \Sigma(qx_i^2/2)p_X(x_i)$ for all x_i. Since q is deterministic, $E(M_A) = q\Sigma(x_i^2/2)p_X(x_i)$. Thus, using $x_1 = L/4$, $x_2 = L/2$, $x_3 = 3L/4$, and $x_4 = L$ will result in $E(M_A) = 5qL^2/16$. The variance and standard deviation are computed from Eq. 7.48.

$$\mathrm{Var}(M_A) = E[(M_A)^2] - (5qL^2/16)^2 = \Sigma(qx_i^2/2)^2\, p_X(x_i) - (5qL^2/16)^2.$$

The summation is for all x_i. This will result in $\mathrm{Var}(M_A) = 15q^2L^4/512$, or a standard deviation equal to $0.17qL^2$.

(d) In this part, $P(M_A \le qL^2/8)$ is desired. Substituting for M_A, this probability will be equal to $P(X \le L/2)$, which is the sum of $P(X = L/4)$ and $P(X = L/2)$. Using $c = 0.4$ and the probability mass function given, $P(M_A \le qL^2/8)$ will be equal to 0.3.

7.4.2 Continuous Random Variable Case

In this case, the probability density function of the independent random variable X is defined by $f_X(x)$. Again, the dependent random variable Y is related to X through Eq. 7.42. Furthermore, in light of Eq. 7.43, for any given value of X, such as x, there exists a value for Y (such as y). It is assumed that an expression for x can be obtained by solving Eq. 7.45. The expected value and variance of Y can be computed as follows:

$$\mu_Y = E(Y) = E[g(X)] = \int_{-\infty}^{+\infty} g(x)f_X(x)dx \qquad (7.49)$$

$$\mathrm{Var}(Y) = E(Y^2) - \mu_Y^2 = \int_{-\infty}^{+\infty} g^2(x)f_X(x)dx - \mu_Y^2 \qquad (7.50)$$

In addition, any probability associated with the random variable Y can be computed in terms of $f_X(x)$:

$$P(Y \le y) = P(X \le x) = \int_{-\infty}^{x} f_X(x)dx = \int_{-\infty}^{g^{-1}(y)} f_X(x)dx \qquad (7.51)$$

In light of Eq. 7.51, it can be shown that the probability density function of Y is:

$$f_Y(y) = f_X(g^{-1}) \left| \frac{dg^{-1}}{dy} \right| \qquad (7.52)$$

The proof of this equation is left to the reader (the absolute value used in the equation is because the function $f_Y(y)$ is positive for all values of y). Usually there is no need to use Eq. 7.52 in computing the probabilities associated with the random variable Y since these probabilities can readily be computed from Eq. 7.51.

Example 7.8

In a special case of Eq. 7.42, Y is a linear function of X in the form of $Y = a + bX$, in which a and b are constants and X is a continuous random variable following a normal probability density function.

(a) Compute the mean and standard deviation of Y in terms of the mean and standard deviation of X.

(b) Show that Y will also be a normally-distributed random variable.

Solution:

(a) From Eqs. 7.49 and 7.50:

$$\mu_Y = \int_{-\infty}^{+\infty} (a + bx)f_X(x)dx = a \int_{-\infty}^{+\infty} f_X(x)dx + b \int_{-\infty}^{+\infty} xf_X(x)dx = a + b\mu_X$$

and

$$Var(Y) = E(Y^2) - \mu_Y^2 = \int_{-\infty}^{+\infty} (a + bx)^2 f_X(x)dx - \mu_Y^2$$

$$= \int_{-\infty}^{+\infty} (a^2 + 2bx + b^2x^2)f_X(x)dx - (a + b\mu_X)^2$$

$$= a^2 + 2b\mu_X + b^2 E(X^2) - a^2 - 2b\mu_X - b^2\mu_X^2$$

$$= b^2[E(X^2) - \mu_X^2] = b^2\sigma_X^2$$

Thus the standard deviation of Y, $\sigma_Y = |b\sigma_X|$. Notice that even if b is negative, σ_Y will always be positive.

(b) In this part, we start out by computing $P(Y \le y)$. Since $y = a + bx$, $g^{-1}(y) = (y - a)/b$. Then from Eq. 7.51,

$$P(Y \le y) = P(X \le x) = P\left(X \le \frac{y - a}{b}\right) = \Phi\left(\frac{\dfrac{y - a}{b} - \mu_X}{\sigma_X} \right)$$

$$= \Phi\left[\frac{y - (a + b\mu_X)}{b\sigma_X} \right] = \Phi\left(\frac{y - \mu_Y}{\sigma_Y} \right)$$

This result indicates that Y is a normally-distributed random variable with a mean equal to $a + b\mu_X$ and a standard deviation $b\sigma_X$. Alternatively, Eq. 7.52 can be used to prove that Y is a normally-distributed random variable.

Example 7.9

In Example 7.7, assume X is a continuous random variable with the following probability density function

$$f_X(x) = c\left(1 - e^{-\frac{x}{L}}\right) 0 \le x \le L$$

$$= 0 \qquad \text{elsewhere}$$

(a) Compute c.
(b) Compute the mean and standard deviation of X.
(c) Compute the expected value, variance and standard deviation of M_A, the moment at A.
(d) Compute $P(M_A \le qL^2/8)$.

Solution:

(a) Since the integral of the probability density function for the entire range of the random variable X is equal to one, we can write,

$$c\int_0^L \left(1 - e^{-\frac{x}{L}}\right) = 1$$

This will result in $c = 2.718/L$.

(b) The mean and standard deviation of X are computed as follows:

$$\mu_X = \int_0^L x f_X(x)dx = \frac{2.718}{L}\int_0^L x\left(1 - e^{-\frac{x}{L}}\right)dx = 0.641\,L$$

$$\sigma_X^2 = E(X^2) - \mu_X^2 = \frac{2.718}{L}\int_0^L x^2\left(1 - e^{-\frac{x}{L}}\right)dx - (0.641\,L)^2 = 0.0586\,L^2$$

or $\sigma_X = 0.242L$.

(c) The moment at A is defined as $M_A = qX^2/2$. The expected value and variance of M_A are computed using Eqs. 7.49 and 7.50.

$$E(M_A) = \frac{q}{2}E(X^2) = \frac{q}{2}\int_0^L x^2 f_X(x)dx = 0.235\,qL^2$$

$$Var(M_A) = E(M_A^2) - \mu_{M_A}^2 = E\left(\frac{q^2 X^4}{4}\right) - (0.235\,qL^2)^2$$

$$= \frac{q^2}{4}\int_0^L x^4 f_X(x)dx - (0.235\,qL^2)^2 = 0.021\,q^2L^4$$

This results in a standard deviation equal to $0.145qL^2$.

(d) In this part, we observe that the event $M_A \le qL^2/8$ is identical with the event $X \le L/2$. Thus,

$$P(M_A \le qL^2/8) = P(X \le L/2) = \int_0^{L/2} f_X(x)dx = 0.29.$$

7.5 FUNCTIONS OF MULTIPLE RANDOM VARIABLES

In certain engineering problems, the dependent variable Y is a function of two or more random variables $X_1, X_2, \ldots, X_n$, i.e.,

$$Y = g(X_1, X_2, \ldots, X_n) \qquad (7.53)$$

In a special case where Y is a function of two discrete random variables (say X_1 and X_2), the expected value and variance of Y can be computed once the joint probability mass function of X_1 and X_2 is available as given below.

$$E(Y) = \mu_Y = E[g(X_1,X_2)] = \sum_i \sum_j g(x_{1i},x_{2j})p_{1,2}(x_{1i},x_{2j}) \qquad (7.54)$$

$$Var(Y) = E(Y^2) - \mu_Y^2 = E[g^2(X_1,X_2)] - \mu_Y^2$$

$$= \sum_i \sum_j g^2(x_{1i},x_{2j})p_{1,2}(x_{1i},x_{2j}) - \mu_Y^2 \qquad (7.55)$$

In this case x_{1i} ($i = 1,2, \ldots$) are all values belonging to the random variable X_1, and x_{2j} ($j = 1,2, \ldots$) are all values belonging to the random variable X_2. The double summation is for all x_{1i} ($i = 1,2, \ldots$) and all x_{2j} ($j = 1,2, \ldots$). Furthermore, any probability associated with Y, such as $P(Y = y)$ will be:

$$P(Y = y) = P[g(X_1,X_2) = y] \qquad (7.56)$$

Since for any given x_1 and x_2 there is a y which satisfies Eq. 7.53, solving x_1 in terms of y and x_2 will result in

$$x_1 = g^{-1}(y, x_2) \qquad (7.57)$$

and Eq. 7.56 becomes

$$P(Y = y) = P(X_1 = x_1) = p_1(x_1) = \sum_{all \ x_{2j}} p_{1,2}(g^{-1},x_{2j}) \qquad (7.58)$$

in which $g^{-1} = g^{-1}(y, x_{2j})$. The problem becomes more complicated when Y is a function of three or more discrete random variables. However if $X_1, X_2, \ldots, X_n$ are independent of each other, the computation of the expected value and variance of Y and probabilities associated with Y becomes simpler since the joint probability mass function can be written as s product of the individual probability mass functions of $X_1, X_2, \ldots, X_n$.

Example 7.10

In Example 7.7, assume the load is also a discrete random variable Q that is statistically independent of X. There are only two possible values for Q; namely $0.5\,\bar{q}$ and $\bar{q}$. The probability mass function of Q is defined as

$$p_Q(q) = c_1 q/\bar{q} \qquad \text{for } q = 0.5\,\bar{q} \text{ and } \bar{q}$$

$$= 0 \qquad \text{elsewhere.}$$

The parameter $\bar{q}$ is a constant.
(a) Compute $E(M_A)$ and $Var(M_A)$.
(b) Compute $P(M_A \le \bar{q}L^2/8)$.

Solution:

(a) We first compute the constant c_1.

$$c_1(0.5\bar{q})/\bar{q} + c_1(\bar{q})/\bar{q} = 1.$$

This results in $c_1 = 2/3$. Since Q and X are independent

$$p_{Q,X}(q,x) = p_Q(q)\,p_X(x) = [(2/3)q/\bar{q}][0.4x/L] = 4qx/(15\,\bar{q}\,L).$$

From Eq. 7.54

$$E(M_A) = \mu_{M_A} = \sum_{all\ q_i}\sum_{all\ x_j} g(q_i,x_j)p_{Q,X}(q_i,x_i) = \sum_{all\ q_i}\sum_{all\ x_j} \frac{q_i x_j^2}{2}\,\frac{4q_i x_j}{15\bar{q}L} = \frac{25\bar{q}L^2}{96}$$

The variance is

$$Var\,(M_A) = E(M_A^2) - \mu_{M_A}^2 = \sum\sum g^2(q_i,x_j)p_{Q,X}(q_i,x_i) - \mu_{M_A}^2$$

$$= \sum_{all\ q_i}\sum_{all\ x_j} \left(\frac{q_i x_j^2}{2}\right)^2 \frac{4q_i x_j}{15\bar{q}L} - \left(\frac{25\bar{q}L^2}{96}\right)^2 = 0.0274\,\bar{q}^2 L^4.$$

The standard deviation of M_A is $0.17\,\bar{q}L^2$.

(b) In this part, we first identify all possible values for the random variable M_A. These are $\bar{q}L^2/64$, $2\bar{q}L^2/64$, $4\bar{q}L^2/64$, $8\bar{q}L^2/64$, $9\bar{q}L^2/64$, $18\bar{q}L^2/64$, $16\bar{q}L^2/64$, and $32\bar{q}L^2/64$. The probabilities associated with these possibilities are computed from the probability mass functions of Q and X. These probabilities are, respectively, 1/30, 2/30, 2/30, 4/30, 3/30, 6/30, 4/30, and 8/30. For example $P(M_A = \bar{q}L^2/64) = P(Q = 0.5\bar{q})P(X = L/4) = [(2/3) \times 0.5] \times [0.4 \times (L/4)/L] = 1/30$, and so on. The probability of $M_A \le \bar{q}L^2/8$ will then be

$$1/30 + 2/30 + 2/30 + 4/30 = 9/30 = 0.30.$$

If the n random variables $X_1, X_2, \ldots, X_n$ are continuous, $E(Y)$, $Var(Y)$, and any desired probability associated with the dependent variable Y can be computed using the joint probability density function of $X_1, X_2, \ldots, X_n$.

$$E(Y) = E[g(X_1,X_2,\ldots,X_n)] = \int_n g(x_1,x_2,\ldots,x_n)\,f_n(x_1,x_2,\ldots,x_n)dx_1 dx_2 \ldots dx_n \qquad (7.59)$$

$$Var(Y) = E(Y^2) - \mu_Y^2 = E[g^2(X_1,X_2,\ldots,X_n)] - \mu_Y^2$$

$$= \int_n g^2(x_1,x_2,\ldots,x_n)\,f_n(x_1,x_2,\ldots,x_n)dx_1 dx_2 \ldots dx_n \quad - \quad \mu_Y^2 \qquad (7.60)$$

$$P(Y \le y) = \int_{n,\ g\le y} g(x_1,x_2,\ldots,x_n)\,f_n(x_1,x_2,\ldots,x_n)dx_1 dx_2 \ldots dx_n \qquad (7.61)$$

in which $\int_n$ is an n-fold integral with $\pm\infty$ limits, $\int_{n,\ g\le y}$ is an n-fold integral computed over the region specified by the inequality $g(x_1, x_2, \ldots, x_n) \le y$ in the n-dimensional space, and f_n is the joint probability density function of the random variables $X_1, X_2, \ldots, X_n$. If the random variables $X_1, X_2, \ldots, X_n$ are statistically independent, the joint probability density function f_n will simply be equal to the product of the individual probability density functions of $X_1, X_2, \ldots, X_n$. The computation of $E(Y)$, $Var(Y)$, and $P(Y \le y)$ from Eqs. 7.59–7.61 is complicated. In general, in many real application problems, the joint density function f_n is not known; and at best, only the individual density functions for $X_1, X_2, \ldots, X_n$, are available. In such a case, one may have to assume that $X_1, X_2, \ldots, X_n$ are independent so that the computation of $E(Y)$, $Var(Y)$, and $P(Y \le y)$ may become simpler.

Example 7.11

In Example 7.7, assume X and Q are independent continuous random variables with the density functions given below

$$f_X(x) = c\left(1 - e^{-\frac{x}{L}}\right) \qquad\qquad 0 \le x \le L$$

$$= 0 \qquad\qquad\qquad \text{elsewhere}$$

$$f_Q(q) = c_1\frac{q}{\bar{q}} \qquad\qquad\qquad 0 \le q \le \bar{q}$$

$$= 0 \qquad\qquad\qquad \text{elsewhere}$$

In which $\bar{q}$, c and c_1 are constants.

(a) Compute c_1.
(b) Compute the mean and standard deviation of the moment at A (i.e., M_A).
(c) Compute the probability that M_A is less than or equal to $\bar{q}L^2/8$.

Solution:

(a)

$$\int_0^{\bar{q}} f_Q(q)dq = 1, \quad c_1 = \frac{2}{\bar{q}}$$

(b) Since Q and X are independent, the joint probability density function of them is simply written as the product of their respective probability density functions, i.e.,

$$f_{Q,X}(q,x) = f_Q(q)f_X(x) = \left[\frac{2}{\bar{q}}q\right]\left[\frac{2.718}{L}\left(1 - e^{-\frac{x}{L}}\right)\right]$$

The moment at A is $M_A = QX^2/2$, thus,

$$E(M_A) = \int_0^{\bar{q}}\int_0^L \left(\frac{qx^2}{2}\right)f_{Q,X}(q,x)dqdx = 0.156\,\bar{q}L^2.$$

Also

$$Var(M_A) = E(M_A^2) - \mu_{M_A}^2 = \int_0^{\bar{q}}\int_0^L \left(\frac{qx^2}{2}\right)^2 f_{Q,X}(q,x)dqdx - (0.156\bar{q}L^2)^2$$

$$= 0.0137(\bar{q}L^2\,)^2.$$

This results in a standard deviation equal to $0.117\,\bar{q}L^2$.

(c) Let $m = \bar{q}L^2/8$, then, the desired probability is $P(M_A \le m)$. Since $M_A = g(Q,X) = QX^2/2$, the domain of integration in Eq. 7.61 is $qx^2/2 \le m$. Solving for x, $x \le (2m/q)^{1/2}$, and

$$P(M_A \le m) = \int_{q=0}^{q=\bar{q}}\int_{x=0}^{x=\sqrt{\frac{2m}{q}}} f_{QX}(q,x)dqdx = 0.516.$$

In solving this integral, we set $\bar{q}$ and L each equal to 1 and use a commercial math solver software.

7.5.1 Special Case: Linear Functions of Independent Normal Random Variables

In a special case where Y in Eq. 7.53 is a linear combination of n independent normally distributed random variables, Y will also be a normal random variable. This is presented without proof in this book. The reader is referred to the references cited at the end of this chapter for the proof. In the special case,

$$Y = a_1 X_1 + a_2 X_2 + \ \ldots \ + a_n X_n \tag{7.62}$$

$a_1, a_2, \ldots,$ and a_n are constants and $X_1, X_2, \ldots, X_n$ are statistically independent random variables. The mean and standard deviation of Y are:

$$\mu_Y = a_1 \mu_1 + a_2 \mu_2 + \ \ldots \ + a_n \mu_n \tag{7.63}$$

$$\sigma_Y = \sqrt{a_1^2 \sigma_1^2 + a_2^2 \sigma_2^2 + \ \ldots \ + a_n^2 \sigma_n^2} \tag{7.64}$$

where μ_i and σ_i $(i = 1, 2, \ldots, n)$ are the mean and standard deviation of the random variable X_i, respectively.

7.5.2 Special Case: The Product (or Quotient) of Independent Log-Normal Random Variables

In this special case, Y in Eq. 7.53 is written as:

$$Y = X_1 . X_2 \ldots X_n \tag{7.65}$$

or, for example,

$$Y = X_1 . X_2 / X_3 \tag{7.66}$$

If the random variables X_i $(i = 1, 2, \ldots, n)$ are independent log-normal random variables, then the random variable Y will also be a log-normal with parameters λ and ν. In Eq. 7.65 these parameters are:

$$\lambda_Y = \lambda_1 + \lambda_2 + \ \ldots \ + \lambda_n \tag{7.67}$$

and

$$\nu_Y = \sqrt{\nu_1^2 + \nu_2^2 + \ \ldots \ + \nu_n^2} \tag{7.68}$$

In Eq. 7.66 they are:

$$\lambda_Y = \lambda_1 + \lambda_2 - \lambda_3 \tag{7.69}$$

and

$$\nu_Y = \sqrt{\nu_1^2 + \nu_2^2 + \nu_3^2} \tag{7.70}$$

Again, the above equations are presented without proof. The reader is referred to the references cited at the end of this chapter for the proof.

Example 7.12

An elevator cable is subject to a random load (Q) with a mean and standard deviation of 12,000 and 750 N, respectively. The ultimate strength of the cable (R) is also a random variable with a mean and standard deviation of 16,000 and 1,500 N, respectively.

  (a) Assume Q and R are independent normal variables and compute the probability of failure of the cable.

PDF

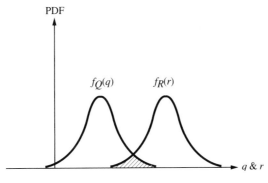

$f_Q(q)$ $f_R(r)$

Figure E7.12   Presentation of failure probability of a cable in tension (shaded area = probability of failure).

$q \& r$

(b) Assume Q and R are independent log-normal random variables. Re-compute the probability of failure of the cable.

Solution:

(a) In this part, we observe that failure will occur if $Q > R$. Although the mean of Q is less than the mean of R, there is a chance that Q may actually be larger than R. This is shown in Fig. E7.12. The shaded area represents the region where $Q > R$ and thus is equal to the probability of failure. A simple method for solving for the probability of failure is by using Eqs. 7.63 and 7.64. Let $Y = R - Q$, thus the failure probability will be defined via the event $Y \leq 0$. Because R and Q are independent normal variables, Y will also by a normal random variable with a mean μ_Y and σ_Y which are:

$$\mu_Y = \mu_R - \mu_Q = 16{,}000 - 12{,}000 = 4{,}000 \text{ N} \qquad \sigma_Y = [\sigma_R^2 + \sigma_Q^2]^{1/2} = 1{,}677 \text{ N}.$$

Probability of failure $= p_F = P(Y \leq 0) = \Phi(-4{,}000/1{,}677) = 0.0084$.

(b) In this part, because Q and R are independent log-normal random variables, we use $Y = R/Q$. Thus, $p_F = P(Y \leq 1)$. Based on the data given in the problem, $\delta_R = 1{,}500/16{,}000 = 0.094$ and $\delta_Q = 750/12{,}000 = 0.063$ since $v_R^2 = \ell n(1 + \delta_R^2)$, $v_R = 0.094$. Similarly, $v_Q = 0.063$. Also $\lambda_R = \ell n(\mu_R) - v_R^2/2 = 9.68$. Similarly, $\lambda_Q = 9.39$. Now applying Eqs.7.69 and 7.70, we get:

$$\lambda_Y = \lambda_{R-} \lambda_Q = 9.68 - 9.39 = 0.29 \qquad \text{and} \qquad v_Y = [v_R^2 + v_Q^2]^{1/2} = 0.11.$$

Probability of failure $= p_F = P(Y \leq 1) = \Phi(-0.29/0.11) = 0.0041$.

7.6. APPROXIMATE METHODS FOR COMPUTING MEAN, VARIANCE AND PROBABILITY

As it is evident in Examples 7.10 and 7.11, computing the expected value, variance and probabilities associated with the random variable Y in Eq. 7.53 can become complicated when more than two random variables are involved. Frequently, we encounter problems in engineering in which Eq. 7.53 forms a non-linear function of two or more random variables that some of which may be inter-related. Consider the following examples.

In materials engineering, a mode of metal failure is fatigue. Fatigue is a sudden failure resulting from rupture in the material. The failure occurs when the material is subject to a cyclical stress application over an extended period of time. The relationship between the number of cycles of stress until failure to occur and the intensity of stress range (stress range is the rise and fall of stress in one cycle of load application) is empirically obtained in the following form:

$$N = C/S^M \tag{7.71}$$

in which N = number of cycles of stress range S to failure and C and M are constants that depend on the type of material. Clearly N (which plays the same role as Y in Eq. 7.53) is a non-linear function of three random variables C, S and M (these are similar to X_1, X_2, and X_3 in Eq. 7.53). In Eq. 7.71, we are often interested in computing the expected value and variance of N. If C and M are assumed to be deterministic, knowing the probability density function of S, $E(N)$ and $Var(N)$ can easily be computed from Eqs. 7.49 and 7.50. However if C and M are treated as random variables (which may also be inter-correlated), computation of $E(N)$ and $Var(N)$ may become very complicated.

In strength of materials, the relationship between bending stress (S) and bending moments M_X and M_Y (acting in two perpendicular directions on the cross section of a beam) is defined as:

$$S = \frac{M_X C_Y}{I_X} + \frac{M_Y C_X}{I_Y} \tag{7.72}$$

in which I_X and I_Y are the moments of inertia of the beam cross section with respect to x and y axes of the cross section, respectively. C_Y is the distance of the extreme top (or bottom) fiber of the cross section from the x axis and C_X is the distance of the extreme right (or left) fiber of the cross section from the y axis. In Eq. 7.72, S is the dependent variable. If all independent variables are considered random, there will be at least six variables involved. In this case, the computation of the mean and variance of S will be very complicated.

In transportation planning, when dealing with the life-cycle cost of a facility (such as a highway bridge), the cost (C) of action items such as repair, rehabilitation, or reconstruction is written in terms of several variables as follows:

$$C = a_1 C_1 + a_2 C_2 + \ldots + a_n C_n + C_I \tag{7.73}$$

in which C_i ($i = 1, 2, \ldots, n$) = cost of action item i in one life cycle, C_I = initial cost or users' cost, and a_i ($i = 1, 2, \ldots, n$) are factors that depend on the structural condition of the facility. There are often uncertainties involved in all variables in Eq. 7.73; and as such, they are, more appropriately, treated as random variables. The uncertainties arise from the fact that generally the capital budget available for repair, rehabilitation, or reconstruction of a given facility is not known. Furthermore, when planning for future years is being considered, it is not known, exactly what action items should best suit the facility. Accordingly, the dependent variable C will be a function of several random variables that may be inter-correlated. The computation of the expected value and variance of C will then become complicated.

In each of the examples cited above, approximate methods are used in computing the expected value and the variance of, and any probabilities associated with, the dependent random variable. There are two approximate methods via which these quantities can be computed: (1) the simulation method; and (2) the method based on the first or second-order approximation of function g in Eq. 7.53.

7.6.1 Simulation Method

The simulation method is generally used for estimating the probabilities associated with a dependent variable Y. However, the method can also be used if estimates for the expected value and the variance of Y are desired. The procedure can be conducted in a variety of ways. A necessity in conducting simulation is a means by which random numbers can be generated, because the method is based on artificially generated values that belong to a specific random variable such as X_i. The method becomes quite efficient when the probability density functions of individual independent random variables X_i in Eq. 7.53 are available and can be used for generating values that belong to the random variable X. To clarify this method, assume we have a means available that can be used to generate values belonging to random variables $X_1, X_2, \dots, X_n$. We start the process by generating a random value for each of the n random variables $X_1, X_2, \dots, X_n$. Assume these values are, respectively, x_{11}, $x_{21}, \dots, x_{n1}$. Notice that the first subscript identifies the random variable; whereas, the second subscript indicates the first round of generating random values. The random values in the second round will be $x_{12}, x_{22}, \dots, x_{n2}$; and in general, in the round k they are $x_{1k}, x_{2k}, \dots, x_{nk}$. Upon generating random values in each round, we substitute them in Eq. 7.53 and compute *one* value for the dependent variable Y. Thus if the simulation process is conducted in k rounds, there will be k values for Y. These will be $y_1, y_2, \dots$, and y_k. We can state that:

$$y_1, y_2, \dots, \text{ and } y_k \subset Y.$$

Now any probability associated with the random variable Y can be computed if k is sufficiently large. Suppose we are interested in estimating the probability $P(Y \le y)$. Furthermore, suppose that among those k values obtained for Y, a total of k' of them are less than or equal to y. The probability of concern is then approximated as:

$$P(Y \le y) \approx k'/k.$$

Although this process seems to be rather simple, it can effectively be used to arrive at a reasonable estimate for $P(Y \le y)$. In practice, a computer program with capabilities to generate random numbers is needed to conduct the process. Usually a very large k (i.e., a large number of simulations or trials) is required to come up with a reasonable estimate of the probability of concern. This is especially true if the probability of concern is very small. The simulation process can also be conducted in several batches. Say for example, the simulation is conducted in 15 batches and each batch includes 10,000 trials. Each batch of random numbers will result in a different estimate for $P(Y \le y)$. This means there will be 15 different estimates for this probability. The average of these estimates is then used to represent a single value for $P(Y \le y)$. The details of the simulation process can be found in Ang and Tang (1984).

As it was discussed earlier, the simulation process can also be used to arrive at estimates for $E(Y)$ and $Var(Y)$. This can simply be achieved by treating $y_1, y_2, \dots,$

and y_k as any other observed set of data collected for Y and use the statistical methods of estimating mean and variance as explained in Chapter 8.

The process of generating random values for a random variable X_i starts by generating a random number between 0 and 1. If we call this random number u, as it is described in Ang and Tang (1984), a random value for a variable X is computed as follows:

$$x_i = F^{-1}(u) \tag{7.74}$$

in which F^{-1} is the inverse of the probability distribution function $F(x)$ of the random variable X. As an example assume using a random number generator, u becomes equal to 0.61. If X follows a standard normal probability distribution function, then a random value for X (i.e., x_i) can be obtained from the table of standard normal probability values. This means:

$$x_i = \Phi^{-1}(0.61) = 0.28.$$

If the random variable X is a normal variable with a mean value equal to μ and standard deviation equal to σ, with $u = 0.61$, the random value x_i will be

$$(x_i - \mu)/\sigma = \Phi^{-1}(0.61) = 0.28 \qquad \text{or} \qquad x_i = \mu + 0.28\sigma.$$

As it is evident, generating random numbers using Eq. 7.74 is often complicated since the computation of the inverse of the function $F(x)$ will be required for each round of simulation. If the random variable X is normal or log-normal, a simpler method to generate x_i is available. If u_1 and u_2 are a pair of random numbers between 0 and 1, then the following are two *independent* standard normal random values:

$$s_1 = (-2\ell n \ u_1)^{1/2} \cos(2\pi \ u_2) \tag{7.75}$$
$$s_2 = (-2\ell n \ u_1)^{1/2} \sin(2\pi \ u_2) \tag{7.76}$$

In which s_1 and s_2 are two random values that belong to independent standard normal variables S_1 and S_2, respectively. The proof of this theorem can be found in Ang and Tang (1984) and Au et al. (1972). Notice that if X_1 and X_2 are two independent normal random variables, random values that belong to these two random variables can be generated using Eqs. 7.75 and 7.76 in terms of the means and standard deviations of X_1 and X_2. If these random values are designated with x_1 and x_2, then,

$$x_1 = \mu_1 + \sigma_1.s_1 \tag{7.77}$$
$$x_2 = \mu_2 + \sigma_2.s_2 \tag{7.78}$$

in which μ_1 and σ_1 are the mean and standard deviation of the random variable X_1, respectively; and μ_2 and σ_2 are those of the random variable X_2. Similarly if X_1 and X_2 are independent log-normal, random values belonging to these two random variables can be computed as follows:

$$x_1 = Exp(\lambda_1 + s_1\nu_1) \tag{7.79}$$
$$x_2 = Exp(\lambda_2 + s_2\nu_2) \tag{7.80}$$

in which λ_1 and ν_1 are the parameters of the random variable X_1; and λ_2 and ν_2 are the parameters of the random variable X_2, respectively.

Example 7.13

In a simplified version of Eq. 7.72, when only one bending moment component exists, $S = M_X C_Y / I_X$. Assume we are computing the bending stress in a timber beam. Due to the uncertainties in the cross-sectional properties of a timber beam, I_X is treated as a random variable. For a given beam, this random variable is uniformly distributed between the two values 10.5×10^8 and 12.2×10^8 mm^4. Furthermore, assume also that both M_X and C_Y are uniform random variables. M_X varies between 110 and 135 KN · m; and C_Y between 190 to 210 mm.

(a) Using a simulation method, compute the probability of failure of the beam. Failure happens when stress S exceeds the beam resistance which is 23 MPa. Use 20 samples in the simulation process.

(b) In this part, assume the resistance is also a uniform random variable ranging between 18 and 28 MPa. Repeat Part (a) and compute the probability of failure using 20 samples in the simulation process.

Solution:

(a) We will use a scientific calculator to generate random numbers. Most such calculators have a built-in function that can be used to generate a random number between 0 and 1. If this random number is u, then from Eq. 7.74, a random value x_i that belongs to the uniform random variable X is

$$x_i = a + (b - a) u$$

in which a and b are the limits of the uniform random variable X. For example for M_X, $a = 110$ and $b = 135$. Using this equation, twenty random values for each of the three random variables M_X, C_Y, and I_X are generated as shown in Table E7.13A. The reader is reminded that depending on the calculator, the sequence of random numbers will be different from those listed in Table E7.13A. However, the final outcome of the simulation process will be close to that presented here. For each set of simulated values for M_X, C_Y, and I_X, a value for S is computed. If this value of S is larger than 23, a Y (Y = Yes) is entered in the table; otherwise an N (N = No) is listed. The probability of failure is then estimated as the ratio of the total number of Y's to the total number of trials (i.e., 20 in this example). Since there are only five cases where $S > 23$, the probability of failure $\approx 5/20 = 0.25$.

Notice that with a limited 20 trials we are only able to obtain an estimate of the probability with a limited accuracy. More number of trials will result in a more refined estimate of the probability.

(b) The event of failure in this case is represented by $S > R$, where R is the resistance which is also a uniform random variable. We randomly generate 20 values for R within the specified range for R. Then we count the number of times $S > R$. As seen in Table E7.13B, this occurs 9 times. Thus, the probability of failure $\approx 9/20 = 0.45$.

Again, the answer is approximate based on the 20 trials used. If the probability of failure is expected to be very small, then more trials will be needed. For example if the probability of failure is expected to be about 0.001, then at least 1000 trials will be needed, since in every 1000 trials on the average only once S will be larger than R. Of course, the trials can be conducted in batches and these results can be averaged to obtain an estimate for the probability of concern as described earlier.

TABLE E7.13A

Trial number	M_X (KN.m)	C_Y (mm)	I_X (mm^4)	S (Mpa)	Is $S > 23$?, Y or N
1	121.6	203.3	11.10	22.3	N
2	125.8	200.8	11.21	22.5	N
3	112.9	202.5	11.18	20.5	N
4	124.4	194.6	11.08	21.8	N
5	133.1	195.5	11.11	23.4	Y
6	110.4	196.5	11.39	19.0	N
7	131.3	202.3	10.76	24.7	Y
8	134.0	191.3	11.32	22.6	N
9	132.4	201.6	11.07	24.1	Y
10	120.6	204.1	10.92	22.5	N
11	118.8	192.3	11.62	19.7	N
12	118.4	205.0	10.96	22.1	N
13	113.2	208.1	11.89	19.8	N
14	123.1	190.1	10.75	23.4	Y
15	126.1	206.2	11.62	22.4	N
16	114.3	209.1	12.10	19.8	N
17	130.9	194.0	11.59	21.9	N
18	122.5	200.3	12.01	20.4	N
19	120.6	204.4	11.36	21.7	N
20	132.5	203.2	10.88	24.8	Y

7.6.2 Approximate First and Second Order Estimates for the Mean and Variance

In this method, Eq. 7.53 is expanded into a polynomial using the Taylor series. The expansion is carried around the mean values of the random variables X_i. In the first-order approximation, only the linear terms in the Taylor series are selected; whereas, in the second-order approximation both the linear and parabolic terms are selected. To describe this method further, consider the Taylor expansion of Eq. 7.53:

$$Y = g(\mu_1, \mu_2, \ldots, \mu_n) + \sum_{i=1}^{n} (X_i - \mu_i) \frac{\partial g}{\partial X_i}$$

$$+ \frac{1}{2!} \sum_{i=1}^{n} \sum_{j=1}^{n} (X_i - \mu_i)(X_j - \mu_j) \frac{\partial^2 g}{\partial X_i \partial X_j} + \ldots \qquad (7.81)$$

in which μ_i is the mean value of X_i, and all partial differential terms are evaluated at mean values μ_i and μ_j. This means they are all constants. Adapting the first-order approximation and taking $c_i = \partial g / \partial X_i$

$$Y \approx g(\mu_1, \mu_2, \ldots, \mu_n) + \sum_{i=1}^{n} (X_i - \mu_i) c_i \qquad (7.82)$$

The expected value and variance of Y can easily be computed from the linear Eq. 7.82:

TABLE E7.13B

S (Mpa)	R (Mpa)	Is S > R? Y or N
22.3	21.0	Y
22.5	18.9	Y
20.5	19.1	Y
21.8	22.1	N
23.4	23.8	N
19.0	21.9	N
24.7	25.2	N
22.6	22.4	Y
24.1	19.3	Y
22.5	23.8	N
19.7	26.1	N
22.1	19.8	Y
19.8	19.9	N
23.4	18.1	Y
22.4	23.3	N
19.8	19.0	Y
21.9	25.1	N
20.4	21.3	N
21.7	20.7	Y
24.8	25.4	N

$$EY \approx g(\mu_1,\mu_2,\dots,\mu_n) \tag{7.83}$$

$$Var(Y) = E(Y^2) - \mu_Y^2 = E\left[g^2(\mu_1,\mu_2,\dots,\mu_n) + \sum_{i=1}^{n}(X_i - \mu_i)^2 c_i^2 \right.$$
$$\left. + \sum_{i \neq j}^{n}\sum^{n}(X_i - \mu_i)(X_j - \mu_j)c_ic_j \right] - \mu_Y^2$$

or

$$Var(Y) = \sum_{i=1}^{n} c_i^2\sigma_i^2 + \sum_{i \neq j}^{n}\sum^{n} c_ic_j Cov\,(X_i,X_j) \tag{7.84}$$

or in terms of ρ_{ij}, i.e., the correlation coefficient between the two random variable X_i and X_j,

$$Var(Y) = \sum_{i=1}^{n} c_i^2\sigma_i^2 + \sum_{i \neq j}^{n}\sum^{n} c_ic_j\sigma_i\sigma_j\rho_{ij} \tag{7.85}$$

Notice that in these equations the double summation excludes all terms where $i = j$. Since the correlation coefficient of a random variable with itself is equal to 1, Eq. 7.85 can be written in a more condensed form such as:

$$Var(Y) = \sum_{i=1}^{n}\sum_{j=1}^{n} c_ic_j\sigma_i\sigma_j\rho_{ij} \tag{7.86}$$

In this form, the double summation includes terms with $i = j$; however, notice that when $i = j$, the respective correlation coefficient is equal to 1.

The first-order approximation works well when the coefficients of variation (δ_i) of the random variables X_i are small. The approximate expected value and variance of Y can be improved by using both the linear and parabolic terms in the Taylor series of Eq. 7.81. In this case, the computation becomes more involved and includes higher moments of the random variables X_i. For example if Y is only a function of one random variable X, the approximate expected value and variance of Y can be shown to be (see Ang and Tang, 1975):

$$E(Y) \approx g(\mu_X) + \frac{1}{2}\sigma_X^2 \frac{d^2g}{dX^2} \tag{7.87}$$

and

$$Var(Y) \approx \sigma_X^2\left(\frac{dg}{dX}\right)^2 - \frac{1}{4}\sigma_X^4\left(\frac{d^2g}{dX^2}\right)^2 + E(X - \mu_X)^3\frac{dg}{dX}\frac{d^2g}{dX^2}$$

$$+ \frac{1}{4}E(X - \mu_X)^4\left(\frac{d^2g}{dX^2}\right)^2 \tag{7.88}$$

Again, the derivatives are all evaluated at the mean values.

Example 7.14

In Example 7.13, use the first-order approximation and compute the mean and standard deviation of the dependent variable S.

Solution:

Notice that the probability density functions for the three random variables M_X, C_Y, and I_X are uniform. For a random variable with uniform distribution bounded by limits a and b, the mean and variance are $(a + b)/2$ and $(b - a)^2/12$, respectively. Using the information given in Example 7.13 for the three independent random variables, we obtain the following mean and standard deviations:

Random Variable	Mean	Standard Deviation
M_X	$\mu_M = 122.5$	$\sigma_M = 7.22$ KN.m
C_Y	$\mu_C = 200$	$\sigma_C = 5.77$ mm
I_X	$\mu_I = 11.35 \times 10^8$	$\sigma_I = 0.49 \times 10^8$ mm^4

Using Eq. 7.83, the mean of S is

$$\mu_S = E(S) = \mu_M\mu_Y/\mu_I = (122.5 \times 10^6)(200)/(11.35 \times 10^8) = 21.6 \text{ MPa}$$

Now using Eq. 7.85, since the three independent variables are not inter-correlated, all ρ values are zero. Thus,

$$Var(S) = \sum_{i=1}^{n} c_i^2\sigma_i^2 = c_M^2\sigma_M^2 + c_C^2\sigma_C^2 + c_I^2\sigma_I^2$$

in which

$$c_M = \frac{\partial S}{\partial M_X} = \left.\frac{C_Y}{I_X}\right|_{At\ mean\ values} = \frac{\mu_C}{\mu_I}$$

or $c_M = 200 \ 10^6/11.35 \times 10^8 = 17.62 \times 10^{-2}$. Similarly,

$$c_C = \frac{\partial S}{\partial C_Y} = \frac{\mu_M}{\mu_I}$$

and

$$c_I = \frac{\partial S}{\partial I_X} = -\frac{\mu_M \mu_C}{\mu_I^2}$$

which means $c_C = (122.5 \times 10^6)/11.35 \times 10^8 = 0.108$, and $c_I = -(122.5 \times 10^6)$ $(200)/(11.35 \times 10^8)^2 = -190.2 \times 10^{-10}$. Substituting these in the equation given above for the $Var(S)$

$$Var(S) = 2.87 \text{ and } \sigma_S = 1.69 \text{ MPa.}$$

SUMMARY

In this chapter, functions of random variables, probability functions for multiple random variables and correlated random variables were discussed. In particular, the procedure for computing important parameters (e.g., mean and variance) of a dependent variable in terms of the means and variances of independent variables was described. We noticed that in many practical problems, it is difficult to use the mathematical formulations presented in this chapter in computing the probabilities associated with a dependent variable. Certain approximations may result in simplifications of these mathematical expressions. One of these approximations was to assume that the independent random variables are statistically independent of one another. This assumption may be helpful in cases where the inter-correlation among independent variables is rather weak. Other approximations included the use of the first-order simplification in computing the mean and variance of the dependent variable and simulation for estimating probabilities. The first-order simplification works relatively well where the variances of the independent variables are small. The simulation is simple, but its accuracy depends on the magnitude of the probability value that is being estimated. If the probability of concern is expected to be very small, a very large number of trials may be necessary to arrive at a reasonable estimate of the probability. Usually simulations are conducted via a computer program using a random number generator.

REFERENCES

ANG, A. H.-S. and W. H. TANG (1975). Chapter 4 in *Probability Concept in Engineering Planning and Design, Volume I-Basic Principles,* John Wiley & Sons, New York, N.Y.

ANG, A. H.-S. and W. H. TANG (1984). Chapter 6 in *Probability Concept in Engineering Planning and Design, Volume II,* John Wiley & Sons, New York, N.Y.

AU, T., R. M. SHANG, and L. A. HOEL (1972). Chapters 3 and 10 in *Fundamentals of System Engineering, Probabilistic Models,* Addison-Wesley Publishing Company, Reading, Massachusetts.

WALPOLE, R. E., R. H. MYERS, and S. L. MYERS (1998). Chapter 7 in *Probability and Statistics for Engineers and Scientists,* Sixth Edition, Prentice Hall, Upper Saddle River, NJ.

EXERCISES

1. Figure P7.1 shows a simply supported beam with a load q applied along the length X. The length X is a discrete random variable with possible values equal to $0.2L, 0.4L, 0.6L, 0.8L$ and L, respectively. The probability mass function of X is defined as:

$$p(x) = cx/L$$

   in which c is a constant.
   (a) Write an expression for the moment at the midspan of the beam.
   (b) Compute the constant c.
   (c) Compute $E(X)$ and $Var(X)$.
   (d) Compute the expected value and the variance of the moment at the midspan.
   (e) Compute the probability that the moment at the midspan will be less than $qL^2/8$.

2. Loads X_1 and X_2 are independent random variables applying on a cantilever beam as shown in Fig. P7.2. The probability density function for these random variables are f_1 and f_2, respectively, and described as follows:

$$f_1(x_1) = c_1 x_1/70 \qquad 0 \le x_1 \le 70 \text{ KN}$$
$$f_2(x_2) = c_2 x_2/90 \qquad 0 \le x_1 \le 90 \text{ KN}$$

   in which c_1 and c_2 are constants.
   (a) Compute the constants c_1 and c_2.
   (b) Form the joint probability density function of X_1 and X_2, and compute the mean and standard deviation of the moment at the fixed end of the cantilever beam.
   (c) Compute the probability that the moment at the fixed end of the beam exceeds the beam resistance which is 350 KN. Use $a_1 = 4$ m and $a_2 = 2$ m.

3. The axial load in an interior column in a two-story building is a random variable Y described as the sum of the floor loads X_1 and X_2. The floor load each is a normally-distributed random variable with a mean value of 90 KN.m and a coefficient of variation of 0.20. The random variables X_1 and X_2 are independent.

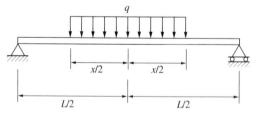

Figure P7.1   Simply-supported beam with random load area.

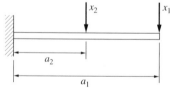

Figure P7.2   Cantilever beam with random loads.

(a) Compute the mean and standard deviation of Y.

(b) If the resistance of the column (R) is a normal random variate with a mean of 270 KN and a coefficient of variation of 0.20, compute the probability of failure of the column assuming that Y and R are statistically independent.

4. In Exercise 3, part b, compute the probability of failure using the simulation process. Use five rounds of 100 samples in each round. Then average the results computed for the five rounds.

5. In Example 7.2:

(a) Compute $E(X_1 X_2)$

(b) Compute $Cov(X_1 X_2)$

(c) Compute the correlation coefficient between X and Y.

6. The modulus of elasticity of concrete E depends on the density W and the compressive strength of concrete f. The relationship is written as:

$$E = 0.043\ W^{1.5} f^{1/2}$$

in which E and f are in MPa and W is in kg/m³. Assume W and f are random variables with mean values equal to 2350 kg/m³ and 28 MPa, respectively. The coefficient of variation for these random variables each is equal to 0.20.

(a) Using the first-order approximation compute the mean value and standard deviation of E assuming W and f are statistically independent.

(b) Repeat part a assuming f and W are correlated with a correlation coefficient ρ. Take ρ equal to several values and plot the coefficient of variation of E versus ρ.

7. The stability of an earth dam is being investigated. One mode of failure is the dam overturning about the toe (Point A in Fig. P7.7). Force P is due to the hydrostatic pressure and is applied at a distance X from the base as shown. Because of the variation in water depth, both P and X change with time; and as such, they are considered random variables. There is also a small variation in the weight W of the dam. Random variables P and X are correlated with a correlation coefficient $\rho = 0.8$; whereas, there is no correlation between P and W nor between W and X. The means and standard deviations for the three random variables are summarized below:

Variable P: Mean = 450; Standard deviation = 67 KN

Variable W: Mean = 1125; Standard deviation = 36 KN

Variable X: Mean = 4.5; Standard deviation = 0.9 meters

(a) Write a function (Z) describing the overturning mode of failure of the dam (Z = resisting moment-overturning moment). Compute the mean and standard deviation of Z assuming the first order approximation.

(b) If Z is assumed to be normal, compute the failure probability of the dam because of overturning.

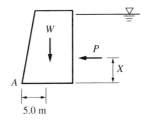

5.0 m

Figure P7.7   Loads applied on an earth dam.

8. Using the probability of the dependent random variable Y given in Eq. 7.43, prove that the probability density function of Y can be computed from Eq. 7.52.

9. Prove that the random values described by Eqs. 7.75 and 7.76 belong to two independent standard normal random variables (such as S_1 and S_2).

10. In Eq. 7.71, assume that C and M are deterministic and that S is the only random variable. If S is a normally-distributed random variable with a mean and standard deviation equal to μ and σ, respectively, derive an expression for the probability density function of N.

11. In a simple form, the productivity in a construction project is modeled in terms of the volume of work scheduled to be completed in a day (X_1) and the work-shift hours per day (X_2). In a particular project, the possible values for X_1 are 1, 2 and 3 units; and the possible values for X_2 are 8, 9 and 10. Furthermore, in this project, the productivity Y is defined as the ratio of work completed to the work planned to be completed. Assume the following relationship is given for Y:

$$Y = 0.2/X_1 + 6.0/X_2.$$

Furthermore, the values of the probability mass function of X_1 are:

$$p_1(1) = P(X_1 = 1) = 0.60; \qquad p_1(2) = P(X_1 = 2) = 0.30; \text{ and}$$
$$p_1(3) = P(X_1 = 3) = 0.10.$$

Also, the values of the probability mass function of X_2 are:

$$p_2(8) = P(X_2 = 8) = 0.50; \qquad p_2(9) = P(X_2 = 9) = 025; \text{ and}$$
$$p_2(10) = P(X_2 = 10) = 0.25.$$

(a) Assuming X_1 and X_2 are statistically independent, compute the expected value and the standard deviation of Y.

(b) Compute the probability that the productivity will be greater than 0.8.

12. Using Eq. 7.72, the maximum stress in a beam under a biaxial moment action is computed. In a particular beam, the following information for the mean and standard deviation of the six independent variables in Eq. 7.72 is available:

Random Variable	Mean	Standard Deviation
M_X	150	7.00 KN.m
C_Y	180	7.00 mm
I_X	11.35×10^8	0.50×10^8 mm^4
M_Y	50	3.00 KN.m
C_X	80	2.00 mm
I_Y	2.5×10^8	0.24×10^8 mm^4

Using the first-order approximation, compute the expected value and the standard deviation of the stress S.

13. In a simple model, there are only three cost items involved in Eq. 7.73. The factors a_i and the initial cost C_I are taken as deterministic values. The total cost in $1,000 is written as:

$$C = a_1 C_1 + a_2 C_2 + a_3 C_3 + 300$$

in which $a_1 = a_2 = a_3 = 1$. Furthermore, the three costs C_1, C_2, and C_3 are all normal random variables with the following mean and standard deviation values:

C_1: Mean = 300, Standard deviation = 15;

C_2: Mean = 550, Standard deviation = 27; and,

C_3: Mean = 700, Standard deviation = 37.

(a) Compute the mean and standard deviation of the total cost C.

(b) Compute the probability that the total cost will be less than $1.5 million.

14. The deflection Y of a cantilever beam of span L carrying a load P at its free end is

$$Y = PL^3/EI$$

in which E = modulus of elasticity and I = moment of inertia. If P, E, and I are independent random variables, derive expressions for the mean and coefficient of variation of Y in terms of the mean values and coefficients of variations of P, E and I.

15. In Exercise 14, the beam cross section is rectangular with a width equal to B and depth equal to D. The mean and standard deviation of B are 120 and 12 mm, respectively. The mean and standard deviation of D are 240 mm and 24 mm, respectively.

(a) Compute the mean and standard deviation of I, assuming D and B are independent.

(b) Repeat part a but assume B and D are correlated with a correlation coefficient equal to 0.7.

(c) Discuss why B and D can be correlated.

16. In Exercise 14, L = 1.8 m; and the following values are available for the means and coefficients of variation of the three random variables P, E, and I.

Random Variable	Mean	Coefficient of Variation
P	12 kN	0.15
E	2.0E04 Mpa	0.10
I	1.4E08 mm	0.20

(a) Compute the mean and coefficient of variation of the deflection Y.

(b) If for any deflection more than 40 mm, the beam is considered failed, estimate the probability of failure of the beam, assuming Y is a lognormal distribution function.

17. The duration of a construction project is treated as a random variable with a mean of 120 days and a standard deviation of 12 days. The target time for the completion of the project is uncertain. It is assumed to have a mean of 130 days with a standard deviation equal to 15 days.

(a) Assume both the completion and target time follow normal distribution and compute the probability of delay in the project.

(b) Repeat part a but use lognormal distributions.

18. A study concerns the combined effect of duration of the yellow light (random variable X) and the traffic flow average speed (random variable Y) on accidents during rush hours in an intersection. Three possibilities for the duration of the yellow light and speed each are considered. Table P7.18 summarizes the possible values of X and Y and the corresponding probability of accidents $p(x,y)$ at the intersection.

(a) Verify the validity of values given in Table P7.18 as joint probability mass function values.

(b) Compute the probability of accidents for duration of yellow light less than or equal to 7 seconds and the speed less than or equal to 50 km/h.

TABLE P7.18

Speed (km/h)	Yellow Light Duration (seconds)		
	$X = 4$	$X = 7$	$X = 10$
$Y = 40$	0.10	0.07	0.09
$Y = 50$	0.14	0.10	0.05
$Y = 55$	0.21	0.16	0.08

(c) Compute and tabulate the values of the marginal probability functions $p_X(x)$ and $p_Y(y)$.

(d) Compute and tabulate the values of the conditional probability mass function $p_{X|y}(x|y)$ and $p_{Y|x}(y|x)$

19. Figure P7.19 shows an activity network for a construction project. The four activity durations X_1, X_2, X_3, and X_4 are independent normal random variables with their respective mean and standard deviation values as indicated in the figure.

(a) Compute the mean and standard deviation for each of the two paths ABCD and ABE.

(b) Compute the probability that each path will be completed within 65 days.

20. In Exercise 19 compute the correlation coefficient between the paths ABCD and ABE.

21. In Exercise 19, the target time for the completion of activity AB is 25 days. If the target time for the entire network shown in Fig. P7.19 is 65 days, compute the probability that the project will be completed on time.

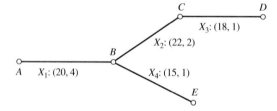

Figure P7.19   A small activity network.

8
Estimation of Statistical Parameters and Testing Validity of Distribution Functions

8.1 INTRODUCTION

In Chapters 6 and 7, the basic theories of random variables, probability, and probability distribution functions were presented. In nearly all example problems cited in those chapters, the basic assumption was that the distribution model describing a random variable is known. However, in real world problems, such information is not available. In fact, the available information comprises a set of data samples compiled through experiments, field investigations, or subjective judgment. Before one can apply theoretical distribution models to an engineering decision-making problem, a determination of the type of distribution model that can best describe the data must be made. Figure 8.1 shows the flow of activities in conducting an engineering design and decision-making under uncertainties using the theory of probability. We observe that the link between engineering knowledge and the theoretical probability modeling is statistical analyses of data. This link is crucial in providing the necessary information as to what type of distribution model should be used and what parameters describe the distribution model. A wide variety of statistical analyses are available, many of which are specifically useful in engineering problems. A simple statistical data analysis consists of estimating such parameters as the mean and standard deviation and/or arranging the data in the form of a bar chart. More advanced analyses may include establishing confidence intervals for the mean, con-

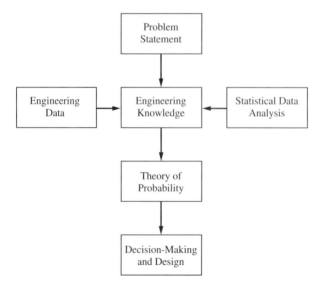

Figure 8.1 Flow of activities in an engineering decision-making and design problem under uncertainties.

ducting a test for the validity of a distribution model to represent the data, testing hypotheses, estimating correlation between two sets of data, and conducting regression analyses. In Chapters 8 and 9, we present several common statistical methods that are especially useful in the analysis of engineering data. Chapter 8 concentrates primarily on the estimation of statistical parameters, confidence intervals, and statistical tests for normality and for the validity of other distribution models. Chapter 9 discusses the analysis of variance (ANOVA), comparison between two or more populations, regression analysis, and correlation. Hypothesis testing is also discussed in Chapter 9.

8.2 DATA COMPRESSION

One of the first steps in analyzing and processing data is *data compression*. Data compression simply means to filter, arrange, and summarize data in a form that can readily be used for the intended engineering decision-making, analysis, and design. A simple data compression scheme is to arrange the data in the form of a frequency-of-occurrence diagram or a bar chart. Time-dependent data may be compressed into *exceedance* curves or into a frequency-domain graph. More advanced data compression methods may involve derivation of distribution models suitable to represent the data, and use of data to establish an empirical relationship between two or more variables. Depending on the type of data compiled, one or more of these methods may be used for data compression. Laboratory and field data often consist of a series of sample values for a quantity. Data compression for this type of data is generally composed of establishing frequency diagrams, generating exceedance rates, or a plot of maximum and minimum values. An exceedance rate simply presents the number of times the sample values compiled for the quantity was larger than (i.e., exceeded) certain pre-determined thresholds. Subjective data is compiled through interviews or by conducting a questionnaire survey among experts. Depending on the type of problem, the outcome of the subjective data collection process may be a set of numerical values obtained for a quantity. In such a case, the data is treated similar to the laboratory or field data. In certain cases, the outcome of the data collection process may be in linguistic terms. For example, the outcome may be expressed in the form of a series of *yes* and *no* answers. In such a case the data compression may simply involve the development of percentages describing the relative ratio of the *yes* responses to the *no* responses. In a more elaborate process, non-parametric statistical methods may be used to identify any correlation between different groups of data and to establish cause-and-effect relationships.

The objective of this section is to present several simple methods that can be helpful in compression of most engineering data.

8.2.1 Processing Data into Occurrence Frequencies

This method is very popular and results in a table or graph demonstrating the frequency of occurrence of data within various ranges. These ranges are selected *a priori* and cover all possible values obtained for the quantity for which the data has been compiled. The data compressed in this form is considered to be a first step in developing additional information on its trends and the estimates for key statistical parameters of its distribution and probability values. The frequency-of-occurrence graphs are usually used for cases where the sample values need not be presented in a time-dependent fashion. For example, in conducting laboratory investigations for the compressive strength of a batch of concrete, each sample value represents a compressive strength. Such data is arranged using frequency-of-occurrence diagrams without any specific reference to time because all samples tested for strength have the same age. In another example, when the change in the strength of concrete over, for example, a 28-day period is desired, the sample values are time-dependent. A simple frequency-of-occurrence diagram may not offer a suitable technique for data compression and processing in this case. Rather, the data is displayed in the form of a graph showing the strength as a percentage of the maximum strength versus curing time.

The procedure in developing frequency-of-occurrence diagrams involves the following steps:

1. Select a definite number of ranges within the compiled data.
2. Count the number of times (i.e., the frequency of occurrence) that the sample values fall within these individual ranges.
3. Plot the results in step 2 versus the ranges; or alternatively, divide the frequencies by the total sample size and then plot the results versus the ranges.

The following examples illustrate this method.

Example 8.1

Twenty measurements of the monthly maximum wind velocity at a station near the airport of a major city have been made. The sample data is provided below using km/h as the unit.

22, 35, 48, 17, 42, 19, 52, 33, 8, 38, 24, 28, 40, 14, 9, 27, 33, 36, 18, 37

(a) Arrange the data in the form of occurrence frequencies. Plot the results.

(b) Using the relative frequencies (i.e., the frequencies divided by the sample size), estimate the probability that the maximum monthly wind velocity will be less than 30 km/h.

Solution:

(a) We select 6 ranges as 0–9, 10–19, 20–29, 30–39, 40–49, and 50–59. Notice that these ranges cover all possible values collected for the wind velocity. Within 0–9, there are only two values recorded; whereas within 10–19, there are 4 values recorded. For the entire data, Table E8.1 is obtained.

A plot of the compressed data is provided in Fig. E8.1. Notice that the relative frequencies add up to 1.00. Also within the collected data, the probability that maximum monthly wind velocity is within the limits of a specific range is equal to the relative frequency for that range. For example, the probability that the maximum monthly wind velocity is within 10 to 19 km/h is 0.20.

TABLE E8.1

Range (km/h)	Frequency of Occurrence	Relative Frequency
0–9	2	2/20 = 0.10
10–19	4	4/20 = 0.20
20–29	4	4/20 = 0.20
30–39	6	6/20 = 0.30
40–49	3	3/20 = 0.15
50–59	1	1/20 = 0.05
Sum	20	1.00

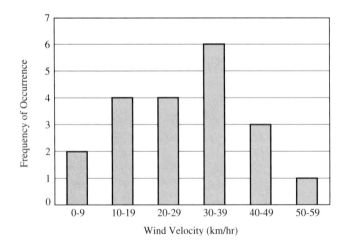

Figure E8.1   Frequency of occurrences of wind velocity in an area.

(b) In this part, using X as the maximum monthly wind velocity, we will get
$P(X < 30) = 0.10 + 0.20 + 0.20 = 0.50$.

Example 8.2

Twenty-five specimens taken from freshly-made batches of a type of concrete were tested for the 28-day compressive strength. The results are in MPa as listed below:
22.75, 21.70, 23.80, 23.45, 21.74, 25.20, 22.61, 24.15, 24.92, 21.00, 25.00, 25.70, 20.75, 23.85, 23.95, 22.43, 27.56, 21.33, 22.19, 24.00, 23.75, 26.75, 20.40, 22.80, 23.42
(a) Compress the data into the occurrence frequency format.
(b) Plot the results.

Solution:

(a) The selected ranges, the frequency of occurrence for each range and relative frequencies are summarized in Table E8.2.
(b) The plot is presented in Fig. E8.2.

TABLE E8.2

Range (MPa)	Frequency of Occurrence	Relative Frequency
20.00–20.99	2	2/25 = 0.08
21.00–21.99	4	4/25 = 0.16
22.00–22.99	5	5/25 = 0.20
23.00–23.99	6	6/25 = 0.24
24.00–24.99	3	3/25 = 0.12
25.00–25.99	3	3/25 = 0.12
26.00–26.99	1	1/25 = 0.04
27.00–27.99	1	1/25 = 0.04
Sum	25	1.00

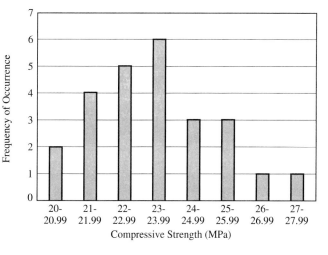

Figure E8.2 Frequency of occurrence of compressive strength in a sample of concrete.

8.2.2 Processing Time-Dependent Data

Time-dependent data is sometimes shown in the form of a time-history graph. This is simply a graph of a quantity versus time. Such graphs often contain many peaks and valleys and may not be readily used due to the large amount of information they display. Instead of the time-history graphs, data can be compressed into a more manageable form. Two common types of data processing for time-dependent quantities are:

- Conversion of data into a frequency-dependent function by conducting a Fourier transform.
- Conversion of data into exceedance graphs using a *cycle counting* method.

These two methods are explained in this section.

Frequency-Dependent Function. A typical sample of data for this type of data processing is the vibration of a mechanical or structural system. Ground vibration during an earthquake is another example of this kind of data. Such data is often compiled in the form of ground accelerations versus time. Figure 8.2 shows a record complied in 1941 during the El Centro, a California earthquake. The curve has been simplified for clarity. As seen in the record, the entire period of vibration is only about 30 seconds. The sample data is compiled at very short time intervals; and as such, it may not immediately provide detailed informtion on the vibrational characteristics of the earthquake. Since the vibration is not steady, it is a mixture of many vibration frequencies. Figure 8.3 shows the vibrational characteristics similar to that generated by the operation of an engine. The accelerations generated are rather small in magnitude and are relatively constant for the entire vibration period. The period of vibration (T) is constant and the frequency of vibration is $\mathcal{F} = 1/T$ (the angular frequency $\omega = 2\pi\mathcal{F}$). The difference between the record in Fig. 8.3 and the one in Fig. 8.2 is the *frequency contents*. While the record in Fig. 8.2. is a mixture of many frequencies; the one in Fig. 8.3 is primarily composed of one frequency (i.e., $\mathcal{F}$).

To convert the vibration data into a frequency-domain graph, the Fourier transformation is used. We first present the theoretical equations governing the Fourier transformation. Numerical equations suitable for use for a sample size of n compiled through laboratory or field observations are then presented. Considering a time-dependent function such as $g(t)$, the frequency-domain function $S(\omega)$ is

$$S(\omega) = \frac{1}{2\pi} \int_{0}^{+\infty} g(t)e^{-i\omega t}dt \tag{8.1}$$

in which $i = \sqrt{-1}$. In Eq. 8.1, we consider the fact that $t \geq 0$; and as such, the lower limit of the integral starts at zero rather than $-\infty$. According to the Fourier transformation, we can also write,

$$g(t) = \int_{0}^{+\infty} S(\omega)e^{i\omega t}d\omega \tag{8.2}$$

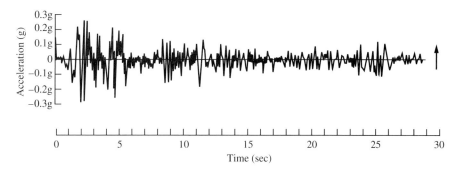

Figure 8.2 A sample of vibrations of ground from an earthquake.

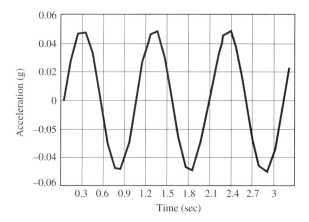

Figure 8.3 An example of vibrations generated by a machine.

which means $g(t)$ can be obtained if $S(\omega)$ is known through Eq. 8.2. Equations 8.1 and 8.2 are the Fourier transform functions. In practice, rather than a definite form for $g(t)$, only a set of sample values, compiled in an experiment or field investigation, is available. In such cases, a discrete form of Eq. 8.1 is used. One form which is used in commercial software (e.g., in Mathcad as cited in the list of references at the end of this chapter) is as follows:

$$S_j = \frac{1}{\sqrt{n}} \sum_k g_k \exp\left[i\left(2\pi \frac{j}{n}\right) k \right] \qquad (8.3)$$

in which $g_k = k^{th}$ value compiled (in the set of sample values); $S_j =$ the value of the frequency-domain function for the jth frequency and $n =$ total number of sample values. In Eq. 8.3, all g_k are compiled at equal time intervals. Furthermore, Eq. 8.3 requires n to be in the form of 2^m, in which m is a non-zero integer number. Also notice that instead of the angular frequency ω, the frequency term $j = \omega/2\pi$ is used. Using Eq. 8.3, 2^{m-1} sample values for S_j at equal frequencies are obtained. Equation 8.3 does not give values in terms of the actual frequencies of the original time-dependent data set g_k. To obtain the actual frequencies, the following equation is used:

$$\mathcal{F}_j = (j/n)\mathcal{F}_S \qquad (8.4)$$

in which $\mathcal{F}_j$ = the jth frequency and $\mathcal{F}_S$ = the *sampling* frequency of the compiled data g_k. For example, if $n = 64$, and there are five samples per second compiled to obtain g_k, then $\mathcal{F}_S = 5$. This means that the total time period used in compiling the data was $t = 64/5 = 12.8$ seconds. Also notice that $n = 64 = 2^6$. Thus the total number of samples computed for S_j will be $2^{6-1} = 32$. If the S_j results, for example, show a peak at $j = 3$, it means a dominant frequency of the compiled data was $\mathcal{F}_3 = (3/64) \times 5 = 0.23$ hertz (from Eq. 8.4).

According to Eq. 8.4, it will be impossible to detect any frequency of the compiled data that is above the sampling frequency $\mathcal{F}_S$. Thus in order to be able to detect all frequencies of the compiled data, the sampling frequency must be sufficiently large enough so a reasonable estimate of the frequency contents of the data is obtained.

As it is evident from Eq. 8.3, the values obtained for S_j are complex numbers:

$$S_j = Re(S_j) + i\, Im(S_j) \qquad (8.5)$$

in which $Re(S_j)$ = real part of S_j and $Im(S_j)$ = imaginary part of S_j. Usually, to plot or present the frequency-domain values (i.e., S_j), we use $|S_j|$ which is:

$$|S_j| = \sqrt{[Re(S_j)]^2 + [Im(S_j)]^2} \qquad (8.6)$$

Example 8.3

Table E8.3 summarizes a set of 32 sample values compiled for the accelerations at the base of a shaking table subject to a sudden shock. The entire record was for 3.1 seconds, and the samples were compiled at a rate of ten per second (sampling frequency = 10).

TABLE E8.3

Time (Sec)	Acceleration (g)	Time (Sec)	Acceleration (g)
0	0	1.6	0.221
0.1	0.471	1.7	0.170
0.2	0.709	1.8	0.080
0.3	0.754	1.9	0.015
0.4	0.374	2.0	−0.061
0.5	0.361	2.1	−0.091
0.6	0.073	2.2	−0.107
0.7	−0.175	2.3	−0.053
0.8	−0.313	2.4	−0.014
0.9	−0.324	2.5	0.036
1.0	−0.324	2.6	0.060
1.1	−0.180	2.7	0.074
1.2	−0.031	2.8	0.099
1.3	0.088	2.9	0.072
1.4	0.189	3.0	0.038
1.5	0.239	3.1	0.006

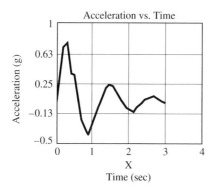

Figure E8.3a Time history plot of acceleration of a shaking table.

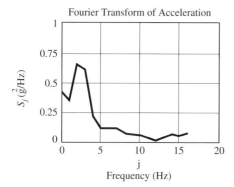

Figure E8.3b Frequency graph of the acceleration of a shaking table.

(a) Plot the data (g_k) in terms of time.
(b) Using Eq. 8.4, compute S_j for $j = 1$ to 32 and plot S_j.
(c) Identify the dominant frequency content of the compiled data.

Solution:

(a) Figure E8.3a shows the plot of g_k versus time. As is evident from this graph, there is a mix of several frequencies inherent in the record. In this form, it is difficult to identify the dominant frequency.

(b) Using commercial software (e.g., Mathcad or Microsoft Excel) we compute S_j. Alternatively, Eq. 8.4 can be solved numerically using a spreadsheet or a simple computer program for numerical integration. The plot of $|S_j|$ appears in Figure E8.3b.

(c) Clearly, the dominant frequency is between $j = 2$ and $j = 3$. Since the sampling frequency $\mathcal{F}_S = 10$, then from Eq. 8.4:

$$\mathcal{F}_2 = (2/32) \times 10 = 0.625 \text{ hertz; and}$$

$$\mathcal{F}_3 = (3/32) \times 10 = 0.938 \text{ hertz.}$$

The average gives a frequency of 0.78 hertz.

Example 8.4

Apply a Fourier transformation to the vibration depicted in Figure 8.3.

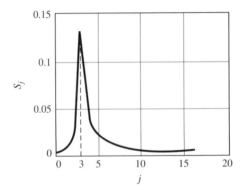

Figure E8.4 Fourier transformation of vibrations with a constant frequency.

Solution:

Clearly, there is only one frequency in this record. Using 32 samples from the data, $|S_j|$ is obtained and plotted in Fig. E8.4. Since the dominant frequency is at $j = 3$, then the actual frequency with the sampling frequency of $\mathcal{F}_S = 10$ is

$$\mathcal{F}_j = (3/32) \times 10 \approx 1 \text{ Hz.}$$

Cycle Counting Process. In some engineering applications, the time-dependent data shows a cyclic fluctuation. In such cases, each cycle of the quantity can be described as a rise to a peak value followed by a fall (or inversely a fall to a valley followed by a rise). The change in the value of the parameter can be considered to be the complete rise from a valley to a peak or vice versa in one cycle of the data. The data compiled for the quantity may be compressed to show the number of times the change in the quantity is equal to a pre-determined specific value. Various rules can be set up to count the number of cycles. For example, as a simple rule, any rise in a certain stress value above a specific stress (i.e., S_0) in a structural component can be counted as one cycle. Other rules may also be established for cycle counting. The most popular method, however, is called the *rainflow* method as described by the American Society for Testing and Materials (ASTM).

According to the rainflow method, a quantity (i.e., stress) starting from a reference level (i.e., zero) and rising to a peak should return back to the reference level before a cycle can be counted. A secondary fluctuation of the quantity within a major cycle will also be counted if a rise followed by a fall (or inversely, a fall followed by a rise) equal to at least a pre-determined minimum value of the quantity occurs. For example, if the quantity is the stress at a location in a mechanical or structural component, this minimum value will be taken equal to the smallest stress value that will be significant to the component. In metal fatigue problems, this minimum level is defined as the smallest stress range that can cause fatigue damage. In fatigue analysis, this stress range level is referred to as the *endurance limit* or *fatigue limit.*

The following example illustrates the rainflow method (see Fig. 8.4) applied to stress range at a location which is considered to be critical for potential fatigue damage. The minimum stress range selected is ΔS. Thus any stress range greater than or equal to ΔS will be counted. Major cycles are ABC and

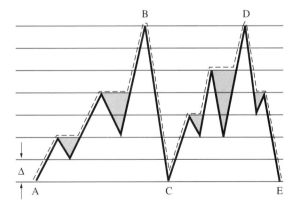

Figure 8.4   Cycle-counting using rainflow.

CDE, which both have a rise and fall of $7\Delta S$. Secondary cycles formed within the major cycles are those in the shaded areas in Fig. 8.4. For example, as the stress rises from point A to B, a $1\Delta S$ and a $2\Delta S$ are counted. When the stress drops from D to E, there occurs a $1\Delta S$ stress range count. Using this method, for the stress variation shown in Fig. 8.4, the rainflow stress range counts are summarized for all ranges in Table 8.1. A detailed description of the method is provided by the ASTM. The cycle counting method can be easily programmed into the data acquisition system used in the field or laboratory. As a result, compressed data in a form similar to those in Table 8.1 can be obtained as the data are being compiled.

8.3 ESTIMATION OF MEAN AND VARIANCE

As discussed in Chapter 6, the mean and variance are two important parameters describing a random variable. The exact values for these parameters

TABLE 8.1 RAINFLOW STRESS
RANGE CYCLES FOR STRESS DATA
IN FIGURE 8.4

Street Range Level	Cycle Count
$7\Delta S$	2
$6\Delta S$	0
$5\Delta S$	0
$4\Delta S$	0
$3\Delta S$	1
$2\Delta S$	1
$1\Delta S$	3

require the knowledge of the probability mass function or the probability density function (depending on whether the random variable is discrete or continuous). Since any set of data essentially can be considered as a population belonging to a random variable, it will be possible to arrive at estimates for the mean and variance by making certain assumptions on the distribution model of the random variable. Methods that are used to estimate the mean and variance are either based on the *point estimation* or *interval estimation* techniques. In conducting the point estimation, one can assume that the distribution model is either uniform, or it follows a frequency-of-occurrence diagram (such as the one shown in Fig. E8.1). In such cases, the point estimation is said to be based on *the method of moments*. In another point estimation process, one may use a distribution model along with the compiled data to come up with estimates for the parameters of the distribution function directly through maximization of the likelihood that the function will be able to represent the compiled data. The point estimation based on this technique is called *the method of maximum likelihood*. Of course, once the parameters of the distribution functions are estimated, the estimates can be used to compute the mean and variance. These methods are presented in this section. The interval estimation is discussed in Section 8.4.

Suppose n sample values for a quantity have been compiled as described by $x_1, x_2, \ldots, x_n$. If the sample size n is relatively small, we can assume x_i ($i = 1$ to n) belong to a discrete random variable X with a uniform probability mass function, i.e.,

$$P(X = x_i) = p(x_i) = c \qquad \text{for all } x_i \tag{8.7}$$

in which c is a constant and $p(x)$ is the probability mass function of the random variable X. Assuming that the n sample values make up the entire sample space, then

$$p(x_1) + p(x_2) + \ldots + p(x_n) = 1 \tag{8.8}$$

or

$$n\,p(x_i) = nc = 1 \tag{8.9}$$

This will result in $c = 1/n$. By applying Eqs. 6.20 and 6.22, the mean and variance of X can be obtained. However, since this will only be an estimate for the actual mean, we use m to define the mean.

$$m = \sum_{i=1}^{n} x_i\, p(x_i) = \frac{1}{n} \sum_{i=1}^{n} x_i = \frac{1}{n}(x_1 + x_2 + \cdots + x_n) \tag{8.10}$$

This equation is the one most often used in computing the average of n values. As is evident, the estimate for the mean is based on the fact that all x_i have the same weight. Using Eq. 6.22, the variance can also be estimated. We use s^2 to describe the estimate for the variance (i.e., s is the estimate for the standard deviation).

$$s^2 = \sum_{i=1}^{n} (x_i - m)^2 p(x_i) = \frac{1}{n} \sum_{i=1}^{n} (x_i - m)^2 \tag{8.11}$$

According to Fruend (1962), this is only a biased estimate of the variance; an unbiased estimate can be obtained when $n - 1$ rather than n is used. In such a case,

$$s^2 = \frac{1}{n-1} \sum_{i=1}^{n} (x_i - m)^2 \tag{8.12}$$

If n is very large, it may be more appropriate to compress the data in the form of the frequency-of-occurrence diagram (histogram); and then use the graph as an approximation for the probability mass function of X. By applying Eqs. 6.20 and 6.22, the effect of the weight of an individual sample value such as x_i in the population will then be considered. Usually, when the data is compressed in the form of a histogram, the frequency-of-occurrence is given for all different ranges of x_i. For example, a frequency-of-occurrence f_i represents the number of times the value of the compiled data was between x_i and x_{i+1}. If f_i is the relative frequency (i.e., the frequency divided by the sample size n), then we can write:

$$f_i \approx P(x_i < X \le x_{i+1}) \tag{8.13}$$

We can simply assume that $f_i \approx p(x_i)$, if x_i and x_{i+1} are very close to each other; or otherwise assume $f_i \approx p(x_{im})$, in which $x_{im} = (x_i + x_{i+1})/2$. Then the estimates for the mean and variance will be:

$$m = \sum_{i=1}^{n} x_{im} p(x_{im}) = \sum_{i=1}^{n} f_i x_{im} \tag{8.14}$$

$$s^2 = \sum_{i=1}^{n} (x_{im} - m)^2 p(x_{im}) = \sum_{i=1}^{n} f_i(x_{im} - m)^2 \tag{8.15}$$

Notice that the relative frequencies f_i satisfy the following equation:

$$f_1 + f_2 + \ldots + f_n = 1$$

Example 8.5

In Example 8.1:
(a) Compute the sample data mean and standard deviation assuming all measured velocities have the same weight.
(b) Recompute the sample data mean and standard deviation considering the relative frequencies obtained for the data.

Solution:

(a) In this part, Eqs. 8.10 and 8.12 are used.

$$m = (22 + 35 + 48 + \ldots)/20 = 29 \text{ km/h}$$
$$s^2 = [(22 - 29)^2 + (35 - 29)^2 + (48 - 29)^2 + \ldots]/19 = 155.4$$

and $s = 12.46$ km/h.

(b) In Example 8.1, six ranges were used and relative frequencies were obtained. We will use Eqs. 8.14 and 8.15 to compute the mean and standard deviation. Table E8.5 summarizes the ranges, x_{im} for each range and the relative frequencies f_i.

TABLE E8.5

Range	x_{im}	Relative Frequency, f_i
0–9	4.5	0.10
10–19	14.5	0.20
20–29	24.5	0.20
30–39	34.5	0.30
40–49	44.5	0.15
50–59	54.5	0.05

From Eq. 8.14

$$m = 0.10 \times 4.5 + 0.20 \times 14.5 + 0.20 \times 24.5$$
$$+ 0.30 \times 34.5 + 0.15 \times 44.5 + 0.05 \times 54.5 = 28 \text{ km/h}$$

and from Eq. 8.15

$$s^2 = 0.1(4.5 - 28)^2 + 0.2(14.5 - 28)^2 + 0.20(24.5 - 28)^2$$
$$+ 0.3(34.5 - 28)^2 + 0.15(44.5 - 28)^2 + 0.05(54.5 - 28)^2 = 182.75$$

or $s = 13.52$ km/h.

As it is evident from Example 8.5, the estimates for the mean and variance from Eqs. 8.14 and 8.15 will depend on the ranges selected to establish the frequency-of-occurrence diagram. The use of these equations over Eqs. 8.10 and 8.12 is preferred in cases where the sample size is large enough so that many narrow ranges can be selected. With a large sample size (i.e., $n \geq 50$), the frequency-of-occurrence diagram will better represent the distribution inherent in the data; and as such, Eqs. 8.14 and 8.15 may result in more accurate estimates for the mean and variance.

8.4 CONFIDENCE INTERVALS FOR STATISTICAL PARAMETERS

8.4.1 Confidence Intervals for the Mean

The mean and variance computed from the compiled data are considered to be estimates only. If additional data becomes available, the values obtained for m and s^2 will change. This simply means that the exact mean and variance are not known. However, it is possible to establish confidence intervals for the estimated mean, the standard deviation, and for other statistical parameters. For example, the confidence intervals for the mean simply indicate how good our estimate for it is. Usually, confidence intervals provide us with an upper and a lower bound value for the mean. The confidence level associated with these bounds is the probability that the actual mean will be within these bounds. This method of establishing bounds for the mean is called the *interval estimation* method.

Consider again the n sample values $x_1, x_2, \ldots, x_n$ compiled in a data acquisition session. We can assume that each sample value x_i belongs to an independent random variable X_i. The n independent random variables $X_1, X_2, \ldots, X_n$ will have a mean value M which is:

$$M = (X_1 + X_2 + \ ... \ X_n)/n \tag{8.16}$$

Notice that the estimate for the sample mean (m) belongs to the random variable M. The expected value of the random variable M is:

$$E(M) = [E(X_1) + E(X_2) + \ ... \ + E(X_n)]/n \tag{8.17}$$

Assuming that all X_i are identically distributed each with a mean value μ and standard deviation σ, Eq. 8.17 becomes:

$$E(M) = (n\mu)/n = \mu \tag{8.18}$$

This indicates that the expected value of the random variable M is equal to the actual mean value of the sample data. Furthermore, the variance of M will be:

$$Var(M) = [Var(X_1) + Var(X_2) + \ ... \ + Var(X_n)]/n^2 \tag{8.19}$$

Since $Var(X_1) = Var(X_2) = \ ... \ = Var(X_n) = \sigma^2$, then:

$$Var(M) = (n\sigma^2)/n^2 = \sigma^2/n \tag{8.20}$$

This implies that the random variable M has a mean value equal to μ and a standard deviation equal to $\sigma/\sqrt{n}$.

The term $\sigma/\sqrt{n}$ is also known as the *standard error of the mean*. Notice that when n approaches infinity, $\sigma/\sqrt{n}$ will approach zero; and as such, M will become a deterministic (non-random) value. In such a case, the estimate of the mean (i.e., m) will be the exact mean. In practice, $\sigma/\sqrt{n}$ will always be associated with the random variable M and indicate the error corresponding to the estimate of the mean (i.e., m).

When n is sufficiently large, based on the *central limit theorem* (Ang and Tang, 1975), we can assume that M will be a normal random variable with a mean equal to μ and a standard deviation $\sigma/\sqrt{n}$. The random variable $\dfrac{M - \mu}{\sigma/\sqrt{n}}$ will then follow the standard normal probability density function.

Considering a specific probability value such as $1 - \alpha$, we can select the two values $k_{\alpha/2}$ and $-k_{\alpha/2}$ such that the probability of $\dfrac{M - \mu}{\sigma/\sqrt{n}}$ being between $k_{\alpha/2}$ and $-k_{\alpha/2}$ will be equal to $1 - \alpha$. As seen in Figure 8.5:

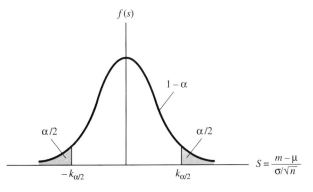

Figure 8.5   Confidence intervals.

$$P\left(-k_{\alpha/2} < \frac{M - \mu}{\sigma/\sqrt{n}} \leq k_{\alpha/2}\right) = 1 - \alpha \tag{8.21}$$

This probability is the area under the standard normal probability density function bounded by $\pm k_{\alpha/2}$. Notice that the area before $-k_{\alpha/2}$ and after $k_{\alpha/2}$ each is equal to $\alpha/2$. This means that:

$$k_{\alpha/2} = \Phi^{-1}(1 - \alpha/2) \tag{8.22}$$

This value is referred to as the *critical value* at α. Based on $1 - \alpha$ probability, and for a sample size equal to n, from Eq. 8.21, the upper and lower bounds for the actual mean μ can be established as follows:

$$m - \sigma.k_{\alpha/2}/\sqrt{n} \leq \mu \leq m + \sigma.k_{\alpha/2}/\sqrt{n} \tag{8.23}$$

Equation 8.23 presents an interval estimation for the mean. The interval is said to be based on a $(1 - \alpha)$ confidence level. Sometimes the estimated interval for the mean is said to be based on α. This means that the confidence level used to establish the interval is $(1 - \alpha)$.

The interval established for the actual mean is based on the assumption that the sample size is large and that the estimated standard deviation s is equal to the exact standard deviation σ. If the sample size is small, the t-distribution (as described in Chapter 6) is used. The t-distribution depends on the sample size n. As $n \rightarrow \infty$, the t-distribution will approach the normal distribution. Using the t-distribution, and considering the estimated standard deviation s, the interval for the mean μ will be:

$$m - s.t_{\alpha/2}/\sqrt{n} \leq \mu \leq m + s.t_{\alpha/2}/\sqrt{n} \tag{8.24}$$

in which

$$t_{\alpha/2} = T_\nu^{-1}(1 - \alpha/2) \tag{8.25}$$

In Eq. 8.25, T_ν plays the same role as Φ function and is the standard t-probability distribution function. This is to say that the random variable $\dfrac{M - \mu}{s/\sqrt{n}}$ follows the standard t-distribution function.

The parameter ν appearing as a subscript in T_ν is called the degree of freedom and is taken as $n - 1$. Values of $t_{\alpha/2}$ can be obtained from Table A.2 of Appendix A for various degrees of freedom.

Example 8.6

In Example 8.5, assume the standard deviation is known and is equal to the estimated value s.

(a) Using a confidence level equal to 99%, establish confidence intervals for the mean.

(b) Repeat part (a) but use a 95% confidence level.

Solution:

(a) Since $1 - \alpha = 0.99$, $\alpha = 0.01$ and $\alpha/2 = 0.005$. From tables of normal probability values

$k_{\alpha/2} = \Phi^{-1}(1 - \alpha/2) = \Phi^{-1}(0.995) = 2.57$, and
$m + \sigma k_{\alpha/2}/\sqrt{n} = 29 + 12.46 \times 2.57/\sqrt{20} = 36.16$
$m - \sigma k_{\alpha/2}/\sqrt{n} = 29 - 12.46 \times 2.57/\sqrt{20} = 21.84$

Thus $21.84 \leq \mu \leq 36.16$ for 99% confidence (or at $\alpha = 0.01$).

(b) In this part since $1 - \alpha = 0.95$, $\alpha = 0.05$ and $\alpha/2 = 0.025$. From tables of normal probability values

$k_{\alpha/2} = \Phi^{-1}(1 - \alpha/2) = \Phi^{-1}(0.975) = 1.96$, and
$m + \sigma k_{\alpha/2}/\sqrt{n} = 29 + 12.46 \times 1.96/\sqrt{20} = 34.46$
$m - \sigma k_{\alpha/2}/\sqrt{n} = 29 - 12.46 \times 1.96/\sqrt{20} = 23.54$

Thus $23.54 \leq \mu \leq 34.46$ for 95% confidence (or at $\alpha = 0.05$).

Notice that in Example 8.6, when the confidence level was reduced, the bounds for the mean became closer. This indicates that although the intervals estimated for the mean are narrower, we have less confidence in the intervals established.

Example 8.7

Repeat Example 8.6 but use t-distribution. This means we assume the standard deviation is not known and we only have an estimate for it.

Solution:

(a) For $(1 - \alpha) = 0.99$; $\alpha = 0.01$ and $\alpha/2 = 0.005$. This is the value we use to compute $T_\nu^{-1}(1 - \alpha/2)$ from Table A.2 of Appendix A. Thus, the critical value of t-distribution for a degree of freedom $\nu = 20 - 1 = 19$ is $t_{\alpha/2} = T_\nu^{-1}(0.995) = 2.861$. The lower and upper bounds for the mean are:

$m - s t_{\alpha/2}/\sqrt{n} = 29 - 12.46 \times 2.861/\sqrt{20} = 21.03$
$m + s t_{\alpha/2}/\sqrt{n} = 29 + 12.46 \times 2.861/\sqrt{20} = 36.97$
and $21.03 \leq \mu \leq 36.97$ at $\alpha = 0.01$.

(b) For $(1 - \alpha) = 0.95$, $\alpha = 0.05$, $\alpha/2 = 0.025$ and $(1 - \alpha/2) = 0.975$. Thus for $\nu = 19$, $t_{\alpha/2} = T_\nu^{-1}(0.975) = 2.093$. In this case, the lower and upper bounds for the mean are:

$m - s t_{\alpha/2}/\sqrt{n} = 29 - 12.46 \times 2.093/\sqrt{20} = 23.17$
$m + s t_{\alpha/2}/\sqrt{n} = 29 + 12.46 \times 2.093/\sqrt{20} = 34.83$
and $23.17 \leq \mu \leq 34.83$ at $\alpha = 0.05$.

As the degree of freedom increases, the critical values of the t-distribution become nearly equal to those of the normal distribution for the same α.

8.4.2 One-Sided Confidence Limits

In many engineering applications, it may be desirable to establish one-sided confidence limits for the mean. Depending on the type of problem, either a lower or upper confidence limit can be established. Using the normal probability distribution

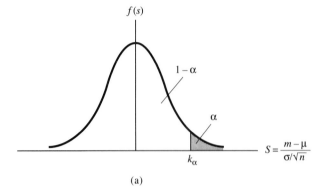

(a)

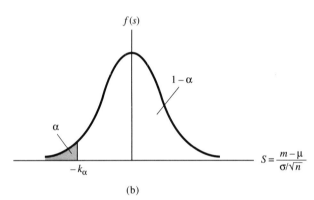

(b)

Figure 8.6 One-sided confidence limits (a = lower limit; b = upper limit).

function, with $(1 - \alpha)$ confidence level, the critical value k_α is established as shown in Fig. 8.6. Notice that

$$k_\alpha = \Phi^{-1}(1 - \alpha) \tag{8.26}$$

In Fig. 8.6a,

$$P\left(\frac{M - \mu}{\sigma/\sqrt{n}} \le k_\alpha\right) = 1 - \alpha \tag{8.27}$$

This results in the following inequality which describes a one-sided confidence level for the mean:

$$\mu \ge m - k_\alpha \sigma/\sqrt{n} \tag{8.28}$$

This is a lower confidence limit for the mean. Eq. 8.28 implies that there is $(1 - \alpha)$ probability that the mean value will be at least equal to $(m - k_\alpha \sigma/\sqrt{n})$ based on a sample size n.

To establish an upper confidence limit, from Fig. 8.6b, we observe:

$$P\left(\frac{M - \mu}{\sigma/\sqrt{n}} \ge -k_\alpha\right) = 1 - \alpha \tag{8.29}$$

This results in

$$\mu \le m + k_\alpha \sigma/\sqrt{n} \tag{8.30}$$

In this case, there is $(1 - \alpha)$ probability that the mean will be at most equal to $(m + k_\alpha \sigma / \sqrt{n})$ based on a sample size n.

Again, for a small sample size and the case where only the estimate for the standard deviation is known, t-distribution will be used. In this case,

$$t_\alpha = T_\nu^{-1}(1 - \alpha) \tag{8.31}$$

and

$$\mu \geq m - t_\alpha s / \sqrt{n} \tag{8.32}$$

for the lower confidence limit; and

$$\mu \leq m + t_\alpha s / \sqrt{n} \tag{8.33}$$

for the upper confidence limit.

In engineering, quantities that describe a system's capacity or *supply* are usually treated with the lower confidence limits. Examples of such quantities include the strength of a material, capacity of a highway in terms of hourly traffic, capacity of a data acquisition system in storing incoming data, the output power of a machine or other mechanical systems, etc. In these examples, we would like to establish a confidence level that the quantity will not be less than the limit set by Eqs. 8.28 or 8.32. On the other hand, quantities that represent *demand* are treated with the upper confidence limits. Examples of such quantities are the applied load on a structure, the actual flow of traffic in a highway, the actual flow of data entering a data acquisition system, etc. In these examples, we would like to establish a confidence level that the demand will not exceed the upper limit set by Eqs. 8.30 or 8.33.

Example 8.8

In measuring the maximum seasonal snow load in an area, the records from the past fifteen years are available. These records (using N/m^2) are:

833, 604, 432, 970, 1043, 777, 890, 345, 432, 991, 895, 1300, 1105, 704, 832

(a) Compute the mean and standard deviation for the maximum seasonal snow load.
(b) Establish a 95% upper confidence limit for the snow load assuming the standard deviation is known.
(c) Repeat part b but assume that only an estimate for the standard deviation is known.

Solution:

(a) The estimated mean and standard deviation using the point estimation method are:

$$m = 810.2 \text{ N/m}^2 \quad \text{and} \quad s = 268.7 \text{ N/m}^2$$

(b) Assuming $\sigma = s = 268.7$, at 0.95 confidence, $\alpha = 0.05$ and $k_\alpha = \Phi^{-1}(0.95) = 1.64$; and $(m + k_\alpha \sigma / \sqrt{n}) = 810.2 + 268.7 \times 1.64 / \sqrt{15} = 924.0$. Thus, we can say with 95% confidence that the mean snow load will not exceed 924.0 N/m².
(c) In this part with $\nu = 15 - 1 = 14$ and with $(1 - \alpha) = 0.95$ confidence, from Table A.2, $t_\alpha = 1.761$ and $(m + t_\alpha s / \sqrt{n}) = 932.4 \text{ N/m}^2$. Thus the mean snow load will not exceed 932.4 N/m² at $\alpha = 0.05$ (which is at 95% confidence).

Example 8.9

In conducting a study of the traffic flow capacity of the northbound lanes in an urban highway, several observations during the peak traffic hours were made at various locations. In each observation a measure of traffic/hour causing a traffic congestion was made.

After 41 such measurements, the estimated mean value for the traffic/hour causing congestion was obtained as 8044 vehicles/hour. It was decided that this value can be used as the mean flow capacity. The corresponding standard deviation was 710. Establish a 95% lower confidence level for the mean value of the flow capacity using the t-distribution.

Solution:

With a degree of freedom equal to $\nu = 41 - 1 = 40$ and $(1 - \alpha) = 0.95$ confidence, $t_\alpha = 1.684$ and $(m - t_\alpha s/\sqrt{n}) = 7858$. Thus the traffic flow capacity of the northbound lanes of this highway will be at least equal to 7858 vehicles/hour based on $\alpha = 0.05$.

8.4.3 Determination of the Sample Size in an Experiment

An application of the interval estimation is in the determination of the sample size in a laboratory or field experiment. Considering the bounds established for the mean (Eq. 8.23), the term $\pm \sigma k_{\alpha/2}/\sqrt{n}$ indicates an error term. Dividing this by the mean value μ, the error term will be:

$$\Delta = \frac{\left(\dfrac{\sigma}{\mu}\right) k_{\alpha/2}}{\sqrt{n}} = \frac{\delta k_{\alpha/2}}{\sqrt{n}} \tag{8.34}$$

in which δ is the coefficient of variation. Solving Eq. 8.34 for n,

$$n = \left(\delta \frac{k_{\alpha/2}}{\Delta}\right)^2 \tag{8.35}$$

Thus by knowing an approximate value for δ, we can decide on the error Δ (above and below the mean) and a confidence level $(1 - \alpha)$ and then estimate the sample size n. If a confidence level equal to 99.75% is selected, then $\alpha = 0.0025$ and $k_{\alpha/2} = \Phi^{-1}(0.99875) \approx 3.0$. This results in $n = 9(\delta/\Delta)^2$. This equation has been commonly reported as a quick estimate for the sample size in design of an experiment.

Example 8.10

In estimating the mean compressive strength of a concrete mix, an engineer is interested in knowing the desired sample size for testing. The coefficient of variation is estimated to be 0.15.

(a) Compute the sample size based on 99.75% confidence and an accepted $\pm 10\%$ error for the mean compressive strength.

(b) If after 17 tests it is determined that the coefficient of variation is 0.20, determine how many additional tests need to be performed.

Solution:

(a) With $(1 - \alpha) = 99.75\%$ and $\Delta = 0.10$, $k_{\alpha/2} \approx 3.0$. Thus $n = 9(\delta/\Delta)^2 = 9(0.15/0.10)^2 = 21$.

(b) Using $\delta = 0.20$, $n = 9(0.20/0.10)^2 = 36$. Thus $36 - 17 = 19$ additional tests must be conducted.

8.4.4 Confidence Intervals for Other Statistical Parameters

Using a method similar to that for the mean value, confidence intervals for the variance can also be established. The use of confidence intervals for the variance is limited and for this reason, the discussion is not presented in this book. The reader is referred to Ang and Tang (1975) for a detailed description and equations for establishing confidence intervals for the variance.

One statistical parameter for which confidence intervals are often established is the *proportion*. We saw in Chapter 6 that for those engineering applications where the probability of occurrence of a sequence of events is required, the binomial distribution is used. The parameter p of the distribution represents the probability of occurrence for one *trial*. For example, considering the past performance of a construction company in winning jobs, p represents the probability of winning a job. Recall that this probability is constant for all trials (in this case winning individual jobs). The parameter p is estimated by proportion. The process of establishing confidence intervals for p is explained in this section.

The compiled data in this case constitutes a sample size of n. The n sample values are either 1 or 0, where 1 indicates success and 0 indicates failure. For example, the past record of a construction company shows that it bid for n jobs. If the company won the first job, then $x_1 = 1$; whereas if the company lost the bid on the second job, then $x_2 = 0$; and so on. This type of data is compiled by either reviewing historical records, past occurrences, or simply by observations. For example, we observe and record truck overload cases at a weigh station. If there is an overload, the sample value will be 1; otherwise 0. The parameter p can simply be obtained as the sum of the $x_1, x_2, \ldots, x_n$ divided by n (note that the x_i are either 1 or 0). Since the occurrence or non-occurrence of the event of concern is independent of subsequent events in the sequence, we can assume that each sample value x_i belongs to an independent random variable X_i. A random variable P is described as:

$$P = \frac{1}{n} \sum_{i=1}^{n} X_i \tag{8.36}$$

This represents the proportion of successful occurrences of the event of concern in n trials. Since P is a random variable, we can compute its expected value as follows:

$$E(P) = E\left(\frac{1}{n} \sum_{i=1}^{n} X_i\right) = \frac{1}{n} \sum_{i=1}^{n} E(X_i) \tag{8.37}$$

If the exact parameter of the binomial distribution is p, and since the possible values for X_i are either 1 or 0, we can write:

$$E(X_i) = 1(p) + 0(1 - p) = p \tag{8.38}$$

and

$$Var(X_i) = (1 - p)^2 p + (0 - p)^2 (1 - p) = p(1 - p) \tag{8.39}$$

Thus,

$$E(P) = (np)/n = p \tag{8.40}$$

Equation 8.40 indicates that the expected value of P is equal to the exact p. Furthermore, the variance of P is:

$$Var(P) = \frac{1}{n^2} \sum_{i=1}^{n} Var(X_i) = \frac{1}{n^2}\left[\sum_{i=1}^{n} E(X_i^2) - E^2(X_i)\right] \tag{8.41}$$

Since $Var(X_i) = p(1 - p)$, then:

$$Var(P) = \frac{1}{n^2}[n(p - p^2)] = \frac{p(1 - p)}{n} \tag{8.42}$$

This indicates that the random variable P has a variance that will approach zero at large n. For large n, P can be assumed to follow a normal distribution based on the central limit theorem. This assumption can be used to establish confidence intervals for the exact parameter of the binomial distribution p. If the estimate for p is available and is denoted as $\bar{p}$, then we can assume that the mean and standard deviation of P are approximately equal to $\bar{p}$ and $\sqrt{\bar{p}(1 - \bar{p})/n}$, respectively. Hence with $(1 - \alpha)$ confidence level,

$$P\left(-k_{\alpha/2} < \frac{\bar{p} - p}{\sqrt{\bar{p}(1 - \bar{p})/n}} \leq k_{\alpha/2}\right) = 1 - \alpha \tag{8.43}$$

From Eq. 8.43, confidence intervals (at α) are established for the parameter p as follows:

$$\bar{p} - k_{\alpha/2}\sqrt{\bar{p}(1 - \bar{p})/n} \leq p \leq \bar{p} + k_{\alpha/2}\sqrt{\bar{p}(1 - \bar{p})/n} \tag{8.44}$$

Notice that for very large n, $p \approx \bar{p}$.

Example 8.11

A small company manufactures pre-stressed pre-fabricated floor joists. For quality control purposes, samples of manufactured joists are selected randomly and tested for the desired load capacity of 45 kN. The past data on 120 beams tested thus far indicated a failure in 9 beams. Failure means a beam not meeting the desired capacity.

(a) Assuming the binomial distribution represents the failure among joists, estimate the parameter p of the distribution.

(b) Establish 95% confidence intervals for p.

Solution:

(a) From the data provided,

$$\bar{p} = 9/120 = 0.075.$$

(b) At 95% confidence, $\alpha = 0.05$ and $k_{\alpha/2} = 1.96$. Furthermore, $\sqrt{\bar{p}(1 - \bar{p})/n} = \sqrt{0.075(1 - .075)/120} = 0.024$. Thus,

$$\bar{p} - k_{\alpha/2}\sqrt{\bar{p}(1 - \bar{p})/n} = 0.075 - 1.96 \times 0.024 = 0.028$$

and

$$\bar{p} + k_{\alpha/2}\sqrt{\bar{p}(1 - \bar{p})/n} = 0.075 + 1.96 \times 0.024 = 0.122$$

Hence, $0.028 \leq p \leq 0.122$ based on $\alpha = 0.05$ (i.e., 95% confidence).

8.4.5 Determination of Sample Size for Estimating Proportions

In Section 8.4.3, we discussed a method for estimating the number of sample values that need to be obtained in an experiment. In field observations and surveys where proportions are desired, we can select a limited sample size for estimating a proportion. However, the selected sample size must be capable of statistically representing the entire data population. As an example, consider a situation where the proportion of overloaded trucks on a highway is desired. We can keep track of all overloaded trucks on a continuous basis and update the proportion of overloaded trucks periodically. This method will be costly and may be unnecessary, however. Instead, we can randomly select a limited sample size and arrive at an estimate for the proportion within certain accepted marginal error and based on a desired confidence level. For this purpose we will utilize Eq. 8.44, which was found for establishing bounds for the proportion p. Notice that in Eq. 8.44, the term $k_{\alpha/2}\sqrt{\bar{p}(1-\bar{p})/n}$ is an indication of the difference between $\bar{p}$ and the actual p. Dividing this term by $\bar{p}$ and introducing the result by Δ we obtain the following:

$$\Delta = k_{\alpha/2}\sqrt{\frac{\bar{p}(1-\bar{p})}{\bar{p}^2 n}} \tag{8.45}$$

which means the ratio $p/\bar{p}$ differs by at most Δ. Solving Eq. 8.45 for n results in

$$n = \frac{1-\bar{p}}{\bar{p}}\left(\frac{k_{\alpha/2}}{\Delta}\right)^2 \tag{8.46}$$

As is evident, this equation depends on $\bar{p}$. Thus, it is applicable only if prior knowledge on the value of $\bar{p}$ is available. In many situations, $\bar{p}$ is not known. In these cases n can be determined by using certain assumptions. Recall that the term $\bar{p}(1-\bar{p})$ is the variance associated with the proportion. The maximum possible value for this term is 0.25 which corresponds to a $\bar{p}$ value equal to 0.5. Using this $\bar{p}$ value in Eq. 8.46 will result in

$$n = \left(\frac{k_{\alpha/2}}{\Delta}\right)^2 \tag{8.47}$$

This equation is, of course, an approximation. If no prior knowledge on $\bar{p}$ is available, one may wish to use Eq. 8.47 for estimating n. After compiling a reasonable amount of data, $\bar{p}$ can be computed and used along with Eq. 8.46 for computing a revised value for n.

As indicated earlier, the term $\bar{p}(1-\bar{p})$ is the variance associated with the proportion. The standard error of the proportion $\bar{p}$ or the *sampling error* will then be:

$$Sampling\ Error = \sqrt{\bar{p}(1-\bar{p})/n} \tag{8.48}$$

This is similar to the standard error of the mean discussed in Section 8.4.1. As $n \to \infty$, the sampling error approaches zero and the estimate for the proportion becomes equal to the actual proportion.

Example 8.12

In selecting the sample size for the overloaded trucks along a highway, we wish to limit the error for the proportion p to $\pm 10\%$ (i.e., $\Delta = 0.10$). From previous data we know that the estimate for the proportion of the overloaded truck for this highway is 0.10 (i.e., $\bar{p} = 0.1$). Estimate the sample size n for a 99.75% confidence.

Solution:

For $1 - \alpha = 0.9975$, $\alpha = 0.0025$ and $k_{\alpha/2} \approx 3$. Thus From Eq. 8.46,

$$n = \frac{1 - 0.10}{0.10}(3.0/0.10)^2 = 8100.$$

Example 8.13

In conducting a survey of the proportion of commercial motor vehicles (CMVs) involved in traffic violations, a statistical sample size is desired.

(a) If no prior knowledge on $\bar{p}$ is available, estimate the sample size n for a 90% confidence and $\pm 5\%$ limit on the error for the actual proportion of CMVs involved in traffic violations.

(b) If after 400 samples selected at random it is determined that $\bar{p} = 0.25$, compute the sampling error.

(c) If after 400 samples selected at random it is determined that $\bar{p} = 0.25$, recompute n for the same requirements in part a.

Solution:

(a) In this part, we use Eq. 8.47 since no prior information on $\bar{p}$ is available. For a 90% confidence, $\alpha = 0.1$ and $k_{\alpha/2} \approx 1.65$. Thus,

$$n = (1.65/0.05)^2 = 1089.$$

(b) With $n = 400$, and $\bar{p} = 0.25$ the sampling error is:

$$\text{Sampling error} = \sqrt{\frac{0.25(1 - 0.25)}{400}} = 0.022$$

(c) In this part, since now a prior knowledge on $\bar{p}$ is available, we use Eq. 8.46.

$$n = \frac{1 - 0.25}{0.25}(1.65/0.05)^2 = 3267.$$

Thus additional samples needed will be $3267 - 400 = 2867$.

8.5 ESTIMATION OF STATISTICAL PARAMETERS USING THE METHOD OF MAXIMUM LIKELIHOOD

This method is used for estimating the parameters of a desired distribution model. The collected data are used to maximize the likelihood that the data will be represented by the distribution model. Once the parameters are estimated, Eqs. 6.20–6.23 may be used to estimate the mean and variance of the sample population.

Suppose $x_1, x_2, \ldots, x_n$ are n values compiled for a quantity. The data can be represented by a probability density function in the form of $f(x, \theta_1, \theta_2, \ldots, \theta_m)$ in which θ_i ($i = 1$ to m) are m parameters of the density function. A *likelihood* function L is then defined as:

$$L = f(x_1, \theta_1, \theta_2, \ldots, \theta_m)f(x_2, \theta_1, \theta_2, \ldots, \theta_m) \ldots f(x_n, \theta_1, \theta_2, \ldots, \theta_m) \quad (8.49)$$

The function L is maximized for parameters θ_i ($i = 1$ to m). This can be done by using the following set of equations:

$$\partial L/\partial \theta_i = 0 \quad (i = 1, 2, \ldots, m) \quad (8.50)$$

For certain functions, it may be easier to use $\ell n(L)$ as the maximization function. Equation 8.49 assumes that x_i values belong to independent random variables taken from the probability density function f. The probability that $X_1 = x_1, X_2 = x_2, \ldots,$

and $X_n = x_n$ is proportional to the product L. Thus Eqs. 8.50 will result in the optimization of this probability.

Example 8.14

The vehicle waiting time at a railroad crossing is being investigated. This is the time (in seconds) that vehicles have to wait before the crossing is clear and safe to pass. Twelve observations at several crossings are made and the waiting time is recorded. The results are as follows:

25, 60, 73, 55, 62, 75, 33, 27, 58, 43, 62, 54.

(a) Using the method of maximum likelihood and assuming a log-normal probability density function, estimate the parameters λ and ν of the distribution model.

(b) Using the results in part a, compute the mean and standard deviation of the data and compare them with those from the point estimation method.

Solution:

(a) In this problem, $m = 2$ (i.e., $\theta_1 = \lambda$, and $\theta_2 = \nu$). The function L will be:

$$L = \prod_{i=1}^{n} \frac{1}{2\pi\nu x_i} \exp\left[-\frac{1}{2}\left(\frac{\ell n\, x_i - \lambda}{\nu}\right)^2 \right]$$

$$= (2\pi\nu)^{-n} \frac{1}{x_1 x_2 \ldots x_n} \exp\left\{ -\frac{1}{2}\left[\left(\frac{\ell n\, x_1 - \lambda}{\nu}\right)^2 + \left(\frac{\ell n\, x_2 - \lambda}{\nu}\right)^2 + \ldots \right] \right\}$$

Using $\ell n(L)$, we have:

$$\ell n(L) = \ell n(2\pi\nu)^{-n} + \ell n\left(\frac{1}{x_1 x_2 \ldots x_n}\right) - \frac{1}{2}\left[\left(\frac{\ell n\, x_1 - \lambda}{\nu}\right)^2 + \left(\frac{\ell n\, x_2 - \lambda}{\nu}\right)^2 + \ldots \right]$$

Conducting the maximization

$$\partial \ell n(L)/\partial \lambda = 0 \quad \text{and} \quad \partial \ell n(L)/\partial \nu = 0.$$

These equations will result in the following equations for λ and ν.

$$\lambda = \sum_{i=1}^{n} \frac{\ell n\,(x_i)}{n}$$

and

$$\nu^2 = \frac{\sum_{i=1}^{n} (\ell n x_i - \lambda)^2}{n}$$

In this problem, $n = 12$. Now using the twelve sample values,

$$\lambda = (\ell n\, 25 + \ell n\, 60 + \ell n\, 73 \ldots)/12 = 3.90$$

$$\nu^2 = [(\ell n\, 25 - 3.90)^2 + (\ell n\, 60 - 3.90)^2$$
$$+ (\ell n\, 73 - 3.90)^2 + \ldots]/12 = 0.127 \text{ or } \nu = 0.356.$$

(b) The relationship between the mean (μ) and the coefficient of variation (δ) and λ and ν is:

$$\lambda = \ell n\, \mu - \nu^2/2 \quad \text{and} \quad \nu^2 = \ell n(1 + \delta^2)$$

Using these equations will result in $\mu = 52.9$, $\delta = 0.368$ and standard deviation $\sigma = 19.5$. Using the method of moments, the estimates for the mean and standard deviation are $m = 52.25$ and $s = 16.73$ (from Eqs. 8.10 and 8.12). Notice that the latter values correspond to assume a uniform distribution for the sample data.

8.6 TESTING DATA FOR A DESIRED DISTRIBUTION MODEL

As discussed in Section 8.5, the knowledge of the type of the distribution model that can best represent the data will be needed before one can estimate the parameters describing the model. Often, we can use simple methods in arriving at a quick esti-mate as to what type of probability distribution functions may be suitable to repre-sent the data. More elaborate methods may then be employed for testing these models to determine the one that best represents the data. As is evident, the process of estimating the parameters of a distribution model is done simultaneously to the process of determining the type of model. In this section, several methods for iden-tifying and testing the validity of probability distribution models are presented. We begin by introducing simple methods and conclude the section with the description and application of more elaborate methods that are used for testing the validity of a desired distribution model.

8.6.1 Branch-and-Leaves Method

The branch-and-leaves is a quick method at guessing what the shape of the distrib-ution may be. No prior arrangement of the data will be necessary. For simplicity, all data values may be multiplied by a common factor. The data values can also be rounded up to the nearest whole number. To apply this method, a two-column table is formed. In the first table the *branches* are listed; the second column con-tains the *leaves* corresponding to the individual branches. The leaves are the digits to the right of the individual data values; the branches are the remaining digits. The leaves for a given branch are listed in the second column in a row (without any space or other separators between them). When the entire data is processed, the cluster of leaves will form the shape of a distribution model. Example 8.15 illus-trates this method.

Example 8.15

Use the data in Example 8.2 and apply the branch-and-leaves method.

Solution:

To apply this method, we first round up sample values to form the following data set:
22.8, 21.7, 23.8, 23.5, 21.7, 25.2, 22.6, 24.2, 24.9, 21.0, 25.0, 25.7, 20.8, 23.9, 24.0, 22.4, 27.6, 21.3, 22.2, 24.0, 23.8, 26.8, 20.4, 22.8, 23.4.
Since the smallest sample value is 20.4 and the largest 27.6, the branches are:
20, 21, 22, 23, 24, 25, 26 and 27.

Considering 20 as a branch, the only leaves are 4 and 8; considering 21, the leaves are 7, 7, 0 and 3, respectively. We then arrange all branches and leaves as listed below:

Branches	Leaves
20	48
21	7703
22	86428
23	85984
24	2900
25	207
26	8
27	6

The cluster of leaves shows a non-symmetric distribution. A log-normal or Rayleigh distribution as described in Ang and Tang (1975) is perhaps suitable for this set of data. Notice the resemblance of the distribution to the graph shown in Fig. E8.2. Further testing of a log-normal or Rayleigh distribution will be required to determine the validity of either distribution model to represent the data.

8.6.2 Determination of the Shape of Distribution from Frequency-of-Occurrence Diagram

In this method, the data needs to be sorted and plotted in the form of a frequency-of-occurrence diagram. The frequency bars serve to point to the shape of a suitable diagram. In Example 8.2, it is evident that a log-normal or Rayleigh distribution may be suitable for representing the data.

8.6.3 Probability-Scaled Plotting

In this method, a cumulative distribution of the collected data is developed by sorting the data in ascending order. This cumulative distribution is then plotted against the cumulative values from a theoretical distribution model that is being considered. A straight line is an indication that the distribution model selected is suitable to represent the data. The cumulative values from the theoretical distribution can be used to actually construct a probability-scaled coordinate system as a tool for hand-plotting the data. This type of plotting system is referred to as the *probability paper*. The plotting positions are obtained through the following model which is based on a step-wise cumulative probability function (note that the data values are first arranged in ascending order, i.e., $x_1 < x_2 < x_3 < \ldots < x_n$).

$$
\begin{aligned}
p_i &= 0 & x_i &< x_1 \\
p_i &= \frac{i}{n+1} & x_1 &\leq x_i \leq x_n \\
p_i &= 1 & x_i &> x_n
\end{aligned}
\tag{8.51}
$$

The x_i values are then plotted against the x_i' values which are obtained from the following equation:

$$P(X \le x_i') = p_i \tag{8.52}$$

If the standard form of the theoretical probability distribution function that is being considered is $F_S(x)$, the x_i' values are:

$$x_i' = F_S^{-1}(p_i) \tag{8.53}$$

For example, if the normal probability function is being considered, then

$$x_i' = \Phi^{-1}(p_i) \tag{8.54}$$

Example 8.16

Use the data in Example 8.15 and prepare a probability-scaled plot to determine whether the normal distribution will be suitable to represent the data.

Solution:

We must first rearrange the data in ascending order. This means $x_1 = 20.4$, $x_2 = 20.8$, $x_3 = 21.0, \ldots$, and $x_n = 27.6$, in which $n = 25$. From Eq. 8.51, $p_1 = 1/26$, $p_2 = 2/26$, $p_3 = 3/26, \ldots$, and $p_n = 25/26$. Furthermore, from Eq. 8.54,

$$x_1' = \phi^{-1}(1/26) = -1.77$$

$$x_2' = \phi^{-1}(2/26) = -1.43$$

$$\vdots$$

$$x_n' = \Phi^{-1}(25/26) = 1.77.$$

A summary of the values for the sample data x_i, p_i, and x_i' are provided in Table E8.16. Figure E8.16 presents a plot of x_i versus x_i' values. As seen in the figure, a straight line can be used to approximately pass through the data points. This indicates that perhaps the normal probability density function may be used to represent the data.

Notice that for the normal probability density function, $P(X \le \mu) = 0.5$. This probability value corresponds to $x_i' = 0$. This indicates that the mean value of the sample data can be obtained by finding the value of x_i (i.e., from the ordinate of the probability-scaled plot) that corresponds to $x_i' = 0$. In Fig. E8.16, the estimated mean $m = 23.5$. If the plot is represented by a straight line, the mean value can be estimated by plotting a vertical line at $x_i' = 0$ and reading the ordinate at the intersection of the vertical line and the straight line representing the $x_i - x_i'$ relation. Furthermore, the ordinate corresponding to $x_i' = 1$ can be used to estimate the standard deviation of the sample data. Denoting this ordinate as x_s, the slope of the straight line representing the plot will be equal to

$$\text{Slope} = (x_s - m)/(1 - 0) = x_s - m.$$

If the standard deviation is denoted as s, then

$$P(X \le x_s) = \Phi\left(\frac{x_s - m}{s}\right) = \Phi(1).$$

TABLE E8.16

x_i	Rank	p_i	$x'_i = \Phi^{-1}(p_i)$
20.4	1	1/26 = 0.038	−1.77
20.8	2	2/26 = 0.077	−1.43
21.0	3	3/26 = 0.115	−1.20
21.3	4	0.153	−1.03
21.7	5	0.192	−0.87
21.7	6	0.231	−0.74
22.2	7	0.269	−0.62
22.4	8	0.308	−0.50
22.6	9	0.346	−0.40
22.8	10	0.385	−0.29
22.8	11	0.423	−0.19
23.4	12	0.462	−0.10
23.5	13	0.500	0
23.8	14	0.538	0.10
23.8	15	0.577	0.19
23.9	16	0.615	0.29
24.0	17	0.654	0.40
24.0	18	0.692	0.50
24.2	19	0.731	0.62
24.9	20	0.769	0.74
25.0	21	0.808	0.87
25.2	22	0.846	1.03
25.7	23	0.885	1.20
26.8	24	0.923	1.43
27.6	25	0.962	1.77

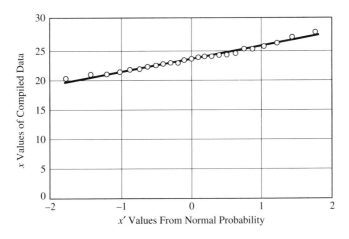

Figure E8.16 Probability-scaled plotting.

This indicates that $s = x_s - m$. Thus, the slope of the line representing the plot is equal to the standard deviation. In Fig. E8.16, a vertical line drawn at $x_i' = 1$, intersects the graph at 25.2. Thus the standard deviation $s = 25.2 - 23.3 = 1.7$.

A similar technique can also be used to plot the data against the values from log-normal probability distribution function. In this case, rather than plotting x_i versus x_i', the logarithm of x_i is plotted against x_i'. If the plot shows a straight line, the data can be represented with a log-normal probability density function. It can be shown that in this case, the ordinate of the straight line plot at $x_i' = 0$ corresponds to the sample data median, and the slope of the line corresponds to the parameter ν of the log-normal distribution. More discussion on this subject can be found in Ang and Tang (1975) under the subject of probability papers.

8.6.4 Chi-Square Goodness-of-Fit Test for Testing Validity of a Distribution Model

The techniques presented in Sections 8.6.1 to 8.6.3 are primarily intended as quick methods of arriving at a first estimate for the type of distribution model that may be suitable for a set of data. In this section, the Chi-Square goodness-of-fit test is explained. This is a statistical test that is conducted on the data against a desired theoretical distribution model. The differences between the *observed* frequencies (computed from the data) and the *theoretical* frequencies (computed from the theoretical distribution model) are calculated. These difference are then combined and represented as a single value. This value is then compared with a critical value to determine whether the test passes. The critical value is based on a predetermined *significance level*. To apply this method, the data is arranged in the form of occurrence frequencies as described in Section 8.2.1. For each range such as i, the theoretical distribution (that is being tested) is used to compute a theoretical frequency e_i as follows:

$$e_i = n P (x_{i-1} < X \leq x_i) \tag{8.55}$$

in which $x_{i-1} < X \leq x_i$ shows the limits of range i, and n is the sample size. The observed frequency for this range is n_i and is simply the number of sample values of the data set that are within the $x_{i-1} < X \leq x_i$ limits. The differences between the theoretical frequencies and the observed frequencies are obtained for all the ranges and combined to form a value c according to the following equation:

$$c = \sum_{i=1}^{k} \frac{(n_i - e_i)^2}{e_i} \tag{8.56}$$

in which k is the total number of ranges. This value c belongs to a random variable C that follows a Chi-Square distribution. The Chi-Square probability density function is a one-tailed function that depends on the sample size. The density function is:

$$f(c) = \frac{1}{2^{\nu/2}\Gamma(\nu/2)}c^{\nu/2-1}e^{-c/2} \qquad \text{for } c > 0 \tag{8.57}$$

$$= 0 \qquad\qquad\qquad \text{elsewhere}$$

in which v is an integer describing the degrees of freedom and Γ is the gamma function. Using Eq. 8.57, a critical value for a predetermined probability level (i.e., $1 - \alpha$) can be established. This critical value is said to be based on α significance. The degree of freedom used in Eq. 8.57, when used for testing the validity of a distribution model, is taken as $v = k - 1$, if the parameters of the distribution (that is being tested) are known. However, if only the estimates for the parameters are available, $v = k - 1 - r$, in which r is the number of parameters in the distribution model (for example $r = 1$ for the Poisson distribution; $r = 2$ for the normal and log-normal distribution). Notice that in computing v, the number of ranges k is used. The ranges are selected in such a way that they cover all possible values of the random variable in the theoretical distribution model. For example, if the normal distribution is being tested against a set of data, ranges covered are between $\pm\infty$. The ranges do not need to be at equal intervals. The minimum number of ranges suggested is 5.

The critical value at α significance is $C_{1-\alpha,v}$ and satisfies the following equation:

$$P(C \leq C_{1-\alpha,v}) = 1 - \alpha \qquad (8.58)$$

Thus if the computed c is less than $C_{1-\alpha,v}$, the value of c is too small to happen by chance; and as such, the test passes. This means that the theoretical distribution is suitable for representing the data. The Chi-Square critical values ($C_{1-\alpha,v}$) are provided in Table A.3 in Appendix A.

Example 8.17

In an investigation of productivity in a construction project, the completion times for twelve identical projects were evaluated. The data given below shows the completion times for the twelve projects in days:

141, 137, 124, 121, 132, 136, 139, 141, 144, 152, 161, 118

Conduct a Chi-Square test to determine if the normal distribution is suitable for the data at $\alpha = 0.05$ significance.

Solution:

Using the point estimation method, the estimates for the mean and standard deviation (i.e., the parameters of the normal distribution function) are $m = 137.2$ and $s = 12.4$ days, respectively. Since these are estimates, the actual parameters of the distribution are considered to be unknown. Next, we use five ranges ($k = 5$). These ranges, the corresponding observed and theoretical frequencies and the term $(n_i - e_i)^2/e_i$ are listed in Table E8.17.

The critical value of Chi-Square at $\alpha = 0.05$ and $v = 5 - 1 - 2 = 2$ degrees of freedom is 5.99 (from Table A.3 in Appendix A). Since $c = 0.1027 < 5.99$, the test passes.

8.6.5 Kolmogorov-Smirnov Test

The Kolmogorov-Smirnov (KS) test can also be used to test the validity of a distribution model. This test is preferred over the Chi-Square test because it is simpler and does not require the data be arranged in ranges. In this method, the cumulative distribution values $S_n(x_i)$ for the test data are computed using a simple step-wise model. Furthermore, using the theoretical distribution model $F(x_i)$, that is being

TABLE E8.17

Range	Observed Frequency (n_i)	Theoretical Frequency $(e_i)*$	$(n_i - e_i)^2/e_i$
$X \le 120$	1	0.99	0.0001
$120 < X \le 130$	2	2.38	0.0610
$130 < X \le 140$	4	3.72	0.0210
$140 < X \le 150$	3	3.09	0.0026
$X > 150$	2	1.82	0.0180
SUM			0.1027

*The theoretical frequencies are computed as follows:

$$e_1 = 12P(X \le 120) = 12\Phi\left(\frac{120 - 137.2}{12.4}\right) = 12 \times 0.0823 = 0.99$$

$$e_2 = 12P(120 < X \le 130) = 12\left[\Phi\left(\frac{130 - 137.2}{12.4}\right) - \left(\frac{120 - 137.2}{12.4}\right)\right]$$

$$= 12 \times (0.2810 - 0.0823) = 2.38$$

And so on.

tested, the cumulative probability values for all x_i are also computed. For a given sample value such as x_i, the difference (D_i) between the cumulative values from the observed data and from the theoretical distribution model is computed as follows:

$$D_i = |S_n(x_i) - F(x_i)| \tag{8.59}$$

Considering all sample values, $x_1, x_2, \ldots, x_n$, the respective differences will be D_1, $D_2, \ldots, D_n$. The maximum among these n values D_{max} is a random variable that follows the KS distribution. The critical value from the KS distribution is obtained based on a significance level α and the sample size n. This critical value is denoted as $D_{\alpha,n}$. If D_{max} is less than this critical value, the KS test passes because D_{max} is to small to occur by chance. This implies that

$$P(D_{max} \le D_{\alpha,n}) = 1 - \alpha \tag{8.60}$$

which means there is $1 - \alpha$ probability that the maximum difference will be less than the critical value. If the test passes at α significance, we can decide that the theoretical distribution model is appropriate to represent the sample data. The values of $D_{\alpha,n}$ are provided in Table A.4 in Appendix A. To obtain the cumulative values for the observed data, first the sample data is arranged in ascending order that $x_1 < x_2 < \ldots < x_n$. The cumulative values are then computed using the following step-wise function:

$$S_n(x) = 0 \qquad x < x_1 \tag{8.61a}$$

$$S_n(x) = \frac{i}{n} \qquad x_i \le x < x_{i+1} \tag{8.61b}$$

$$S_n(x) = 1 \qquad x > x_n \tag{8.61c}$$

Example 8.18

Seventeen samples of a new stainless steel wire were tested for tensile strength in kN. The following results were obtained:

153.0, 95.0, 123.0, 122.0, 108.4, 131.0, 138.1, 131.5, 107.0, 117.0, 126.0, 125.8, 112.3, 129.1, 124.8, 110.3, 140.0

(a) Estimate the mean and standard deviation of the tensile strength of the wire.
(b) Estimate the parameters λ and ν from the results in part a if we assume a log-normal distribution will represent the data.
(c) Conduct a Kolmogorov-Smirnov test to determine if the log-normal distribution will pass at $\alpha = 0.05$ significance.

Solution:

(a) Using the point estimation method, the mean (m) and the standard deviation (s) are respectively

$$m = 123.2 \text{ kN}, \quad \text{and} \quad s = 14.1 \text{ kN}.$$

(b) The relationship between the log-normal distribution parameters, the mean (μ), and the coefficient of variation (δ) are

$$\lambda = \ell n(\mu) - \nu^2/2 \quad \text{and} \quad \nu^2 = \ell n(1 + \delta^2).$$

Using the estimates for the mean and standard deviation, $\delta = 14.1/123.2 = 0.114$. Thus

$$\lambda = \ell n(123.2) - (0.114)^2/2 = 4.807 \quad \nu^2 = \ell n[1 + (0.114)^2] = 0.0129 \quad \nu = 0.114.$$

(c) In this part we rearrange the data in ascending order; then we compute the cumulative values from the data using Eqs. 8.61 and from the log-normal distribution. For example, since $x_1 = 95.0$, then $S_n(x_1) = 1/17 = 0.0588$ and

$$F(x_1) = P(x \le 95.0) = \Phi\left(\frac{\ell n 95 - \lambda}{\nu}\right) = 1 - \Phi(2.22) = 1 - 0.9868 = 0.0132.$$

Thus $D_1 = |0.0588 - 0.0132| = 0.0456$. Table E8.18 summarizes the cumulative values and the computed differences for all sample values.

As seen in Table E8.18, the maximum difference $D_{max} = 0.0878$. The critical KS value at $\alpha = 0.05$ and $n = 17$ is taken from Appendix A, i.e, $D_{0.05,17} = 0.32$. Since $D_{max} = 0.0878 < D_{0.05,17} = 0.32$, we conclude that the test passes. This means that the log-normal distribution will be appropriate to represent the data.

SUMMARY

In this chapter, several basic topics in statistics were discussed. The main objective of the chapter was to describe methods that are commonly used to analyze a set of data compiled through experimental investigations, field testing, or interviews with experts. The methods by which the data is compressed into more meaningful results were presented. The estimation of statistical parameters describing the sample data was also discussed. Point estimation and interval estimation methods for the mean and other statistical parameters were presented. The analyses presented in

TABLE E8.18

Sample Data	$S_n(x)$	$F(x)$	$D_i = \lvert S_n(x) - F(x) \rvert$
$x_1 = 95.0$	$1/17 = 0.0588$	0.0132	0.0456
$x_2 = 107.0$	$2/17 = 0.1176$	0.1190	0.0014
$x_3 = 108.4$	$3/17 = 0.1765$	0.1446	0.0319
$x_4 = 110.3$	$4/17 = 0.2353$	0.1814	0.0539
$x_5 = 112.3$	$5/17 = 0.2941$	0.2266	0.0675
$x_6 = 117.0$	$6/17 = 0.3529$	0.3483	0.0046
$x_7 = 122.0$	$7/17 = 0.4118$	0.3974	0.0144
$x_8 = 123.0$	$8/17 = 0.4706$	0.5199	0.0493
$x_9 = 124.8$	$9/17 = 0.5294$	0.5675	0.0381
$x_{10} = 125.8$	$10/17 = 0.5882$	0.5948	0.0066
$x_{11} = 126.0$	$11/17 = 0.6470$	0.6026	0.0444
$x_{12} = 129.1$	$12/17 = 0.7059$	0.6808	0.0251
$x_{13} = 131.0$	$13/17 = 0.7647$	0.7257	0.0390
$x_{14} = 131.5$	$14/17 = 0.8235$	0.7357	0.0878
$x_{15} = 138.1$	$15/17 = 0.8824$	0.8554	0.0270
$x_{16} = 140.0$	$16/17 = 0.9412$	0.8810	0.0602
$x_{17} = 153.0$	$17/17 = 1.000$	0.9750	0.0250

this chapter are especially important in decision making and design in engineering problems. Data compiled for various engineering parameters is essential and supplementary to the modeling inherent in engineering decision making and design. Through the compiled data and relevant statistical analyses, an engineer is able to provide the supporting elements needed to arrive at meaningful conclusions that bear the uncertainty inherent in the data. The materials presented in this chapter also provide the background needed for determining the type of probability distribution model and the estimate for key statistical parameters that make up the theories in Chapters 5, 6, and 7.

REFERENCES

ANG, A. H.-S. and W.H. TANG (1975). Chapters 5 and 6 in *Probability Concepts in Engineering Planning and Design, Volume I-Basic Principles,* John Wiley & Sons, New York, N.Y.

FOWLER, JR., F.J. (1993). Pages 26–31 of *Survey Research Methods,* Second Edition, Applied Social Research Methods Series, Volume 1, SAGE Publications, Thousand Oaks, CA.

FREUND, J.E. (1962). Mathematical Statistics, Prentice Hall, Englewood Cliffs, NJ.

MATHCAD (1998). Reference Manual, MathSoft, Inc., Cambridge, MA.

WALPOLE, R.E., R.H. MYERS, and S.L. MYERS (1998). Chapters 8 and 9 in *Probability and Statistics for Engineers and Scientists,* 6th Edition, Prentice Hall, Upper Saddle River, NJ.

EXERCISES

1. A concrete manufacturing plant received an order to make concrete with a mean strength in excess of 42 MPa. For quality control purposes, 14 cylinders were prepared and tested. The following values were obtained for the strength:
   42.4   56.7   44.1   35.7   43.8   63.4   34.3   51.1   40.6   44.8   58.1   45.9   50.8   52.5
   (a) Develop a frequency-of-occurrence graph. Select ranges as 32.6–35.0, 35.1–37.5, 37.6–40.0, etc. Plot the graph.
   (b) Based on results in part a, estimate the probability that the compressive strength of concrete will be at least equal to the desired 42.0 MPa.

2. In evaluating the quality of construction work conducted by a contractor, a group of fifteen experts were invited to rank the quality on a scale of 1 to 7, where 1 means totally unsatisfied with the quality while 7 means total satisfaction with quality. The results of the survey are as follows:
   5, 1, 6, 6, 5, 4, 3, 4, 4, 5, 2, 7, 5, 5, 3 .
   As is evident, the random variable describing quality, referred to as the *quality index*, is discrete. Thus, in this problem, instead of using ranges for the data simply use the numerical values 1, 2, 3, ... 7 and construct a frequency-of-occurrence graph for the quality of construction work.

3. For the data in Exercise 1:
   (a) Using the method of moments, estimate the mean and standard deviation for the strength.
   (b) Establish 95% confidence intervals for the mean assuming the standard deviation is known.
   (c) Repeat part b but assume that only an estimate for the standard deviation is known.

4. For the data in Exercise 2:
   (a) Compute the estimate for the mean and standard deviation assuming all sample values have the same weight.
   (b) Repeat part a but use the frequency-of-occurrence results obtained in Exercise 2 as the probability mass function for the construction quality index.

5. In a study of accidents involving commercial motor vehicles on interstate highways, accident data for fifteen four-lane rural highways in several states was complied. The sample values are adjusted to present the annual number of accidents per kilometer of highway. The following results are obtained:
   0.15, 0.50, 0.25, 1.18, 0.37, 0.23, 0.65, 0.84, 0.33, 0.90, 0.25, 0.43, 0.55, 0.47, 0.71.
   (a) Plot the data in the form of a frequency-of-occurrence graph using ranges such as 0–0.19, 0.2–0.39, etc.
   (b) Compute the mean and standard deviation using the results in part a.

6. In Exercise 5:
   (a) Use the method of maximum likelihood along with the log-normal distribution and estimate the distribution parameters λ and ν.
   (b) Based on the results in part a, compute the mean and standard deviation.

7. Repeat Exercise 6 but use the Rayleigh distribution with the following probability density function (notice that this distribution has only one parameter a).

$$f(x) = \frac{x}{a^2}\exp\left[-\frac{1}{2}\left(\frac{x}{a}\right)^2\right] \qquad x \geq 0$$

8. In compiling data for the failure rates among components in an electronic measurement equipment when exposed to harsh environments, 150 components were tested and only 4 failed.
   (a) Assuming failure among components follow a binomial distribution, estimate the parameter p of the distribution.
   (b) Establish 95% confidence intervals for p.
   (c) If the electronic equipment system is made up of 25 components, compute the probability of failure of the equipment when exposed to harsh environments.

9. In Exercise 5, use the Kolmogorov-Smirnov method to test the validity of the lognormal distribution to represent the data. Use the λ and ν parameters you computed in Exercise 6. Use $\alpha = 0.05$.

10. Soil samples from nine locations in a site are taken to determine the bearing capacity in kN/m^2. The results are summarized below:
    23.1, 42.4, 30.3, 31.0, 28.4, 39.3, 32.4, 27.4, 38.0
    (a) Estimate the mean, standard deviation, and coefficient of variation of the data.
    (b) Compute the standard error of the mean.
    (c) Establish 95% confidence intervals for the mean.
    (d) Using the coefficient of variation from part a, how many samples must be tested to have $\pm 10\%$ error for the mean at 95% confidence?

11. In Exercise 5:
    (a) Use the probability-scaled plotting and comment whether the normal distribution will be suitable to represent the data.
    (b) Use the results in part a and estimate the sample mean and standard deviation.

12. In Exercise 5, conduct a Chi-square test at $\alpha = 0.01$ to test the validity of the normal distribution in representing the data.

13. An engineer is hired to inspect the condition of terra cotta blocks used in the facade of a building. The engineer examined a random sample of 52 terra cotta blocks and found that 6 had loose connections. These were considered failures.
    (a) Based on the information found by the engineer and assuming the binomial distribution represents the failure among terra cotta blocks, estimate the parameter p.
    (b) Establish 95% confidence for p.
    (c) If the same bounds found for p in part b must be maintained but at 99% confidence, how many additional terra cotta blocks the engineer must examine?

14. An engineer is planning to test the reliability of a small aluminum bracket which supports an automated control device in a brand of passenger cars. A mode of failure for the bracket is fatigue that is initiated from steady vibrations. Fifty brackets were tested by simulating a designated level of vibration on a shaking table for a specific period of time. One bracket failed.
    (a) If the conditions among brackets are assumed independent, estimate the failure probability for any given bracket.
    (b) Establish 95% confidence intervals for the failure probability in part a.

15. In order to study the misalignment in rotating blades of a turbine, vibration data at or around the hub was compiled. The sample of acceleration data composed of 32 sample values are given below (the acceleration unit is g):
    0.01, 0.08, 0.12, 0.07, 0, -0.08, -0.15, -0.04, 0.08, 0.09, 0.15, 0.07, 0, -0.04, -0.16, -0.21, -0.14, -0.01, 0.04, 0.08, 0.12, 0.07, -0.04, -0.10, -0.15, -0.08, 0.08, 0.10, 0.12, 0.18, 0.04, 0.
    These values were compiled at every 0.5 seconds.
    (a) Plot the acceleration data versus time.

(b) Use a commercial software and obtain the Fourier transform of the data.

(c) Estimate the dominant frequency of the vibration data.

16. A small manufacturing facility specializes in making pre-stressed, pre-cast joists of various span lengths. With each production batch, a joist is selected at random and tested under the application of a load R applied at the midspan. The strength of a joist is taken equal to the load R (using kN unit) causing failure. The data provided in Table P8.16 shows the strength values for 103 samples of $L = 6$ m span length.

TABLE P8.16

Values of P (kN)	Number of Samples
$0 < R \le 5$	0
$5 < R \le 10$	1
$10 < R \le 15$	2
$15 < R \le 20$	4
$20 < R \le 25$	8
$25 < R \le 30$	12
$30 < R \le 35$	18
$35 < R \le 40$	32
$40 < R \le 45$	17
$45 < R \le 50$	6
$50 < R \le 55$	2
$55 < R \le 60$	1
$60 < R$	0

(a) Estimate the mean and standard deviation of R.

(b) Establish a one-sided lower confidence level at $\alpha = 0.05$. Use the t-distribution.

(c) Using the results in part a, estimate the parameters of the log-normal distribution; then conduct a Chi-Square test for the log-normal distribution at $\alpha = 0.10$.

17. A new composite material was tested for strength evaluation purposes. Ten samples were tested and the following results were obtained for the compressive strength in MPa. 79, 81, 84, 86, 90, 91, 78, 69, 73, 80.

(a) Use the branch-and-leaves method and show if the normal distribution is suitable to represent the data.

(b) Estimate the mean and standard deviation of the data.

(c) Establish a one-sided lower confidence level at $\alpha = 0.05$ for the compressive strength.

(d) How many more samples should be tested to obtain the same confidence level in part c but at $\alpha = 0.01$? Use the same standard deviation as the one in part c.

18. Within the past 20 years, a construction company has been bidding on five jobs every year. Based on the company's past record, the following data is compiled for the number of jobs won each year by this company.

(a) Estimate the parameter p for use in the binomial distribution modeling the number of wins in a total of five bids per year.

(b) Test whether the binomial distribution will be suitable for modeling the number of wins in a total of five bids per year. Use $\alpha = 0.05$.

TABLE P8.18

Number of Years	Jobs Won out of 5 Bids per Year
4	0
7	1
6	2
2	3
1	4
0	5

19. The number of airplanes approaching a medium-sized airport in any hour is a random variable X. Seventy observations were made for X; and the results are summarized in Table P8.19.

TABLE P8.19

Number of Airplanes/Hr	Observed Frequency
0	3
1	10
2	15
3	16
4	12
5	8
6	4
7	2
8 or more	0

(a) Assuming the Poisson distribution for X, estimate the parameter λ of the distribution.

(b) Conduct a Chi-Square test to determine whether the Poisson distribution passes at $\alpha = 0.01$.

20. A survey was conducted among a group of 18 experts for compiling data on the failure rate of fittings used in extension gas pipes attached to home gas appliances. Failure was defined as a leak initiated at a fitting. The experts were asked the following question: "In your opinion, how many fittings in extension pipes attached to home appliances will develop gas leaks in a 10-year period? Please provide your estimates based on 1000 cases." The following responses were received:
0, 3, 1, 5, 2, 4, 7, 6, 4, 2, 8, 3, 5, 2, 4, 6, 3, 3.

(a) Plot the data in the form of a frequency of occurrence diagram.

(b) Estimate the mean and standard deviation and the standard error of the mean using the method of moments.

(c) At $\alpha = 0.05$, what will the one-sided upper confidence level for the failure rate be?

21. In a survey of the number of vehicles that make a left turn at an intersection, 300 samples were selected at random. Fifteen of these vehicles made a left turn.

   (a) Estimate the proportion of the vehicles making the left turn for this intersection.

   (b) Compute the sampling error associated with the estimated proportion.

   (c) Establish a 95% confidence interval for the actual proportion p.

   (d) If the same interval in part c is desired but with 99% confidence, how many more samples must be selected. Use the same estimated proportion as in part a.

22. An engineer is conducting a survey among medium-sized construction companies to determine the proportion of companies that use a certain software for construction management (CM) purposes.

   (a) If no prior knowledge on the proportion of companies that use the software for the CM purposes exists, determine the sample size for a $\pm 10\%$ error for the actual proportion (i.e., $\Delta = 0.10$) and a 90% confidence level.

   (b) Before proceeding with the survey, the engineer comes across a research paper that indicates about 20% of medium size companies use the software for CM purposes. To comply with the requirements in part a, what sample size should the engineer select?

PART II

Principles of Statistics

9

Hypothesis Testing, Analysis of Variance, Regression, and Correlation Analysis

9.1 INTRODUCTION

In Chapter 8, we introduced several basic methods of statistics. Although these methods are adequate for treating engineering data, they may not be sufficient to provide for a more comprehensive evaluation and analysis of data. In this chapter we introduce several additional topics in statistics that are useful in the design of an experiment or a field data collection session, comparing two or more sets of data compiled from similar sources, identifying correlation between two sets of data, and establishing a regression between two parameters for which data has been compiled. The methods presented in this chapter include *hypotheses testing* of the statistical parameters (for example the mean value) of a population, *analysis of variance* (ANOVA), *multiple range test* for comparing the mean values from two or more populations, and correlation and regression analyses.

Hypothesis testing for the mean or other parameters of a population is conducted to support or reject a notion that a desired parameter will have a predetermined limit. For example, in determining the applied snow load on a building, a design engineer believes that the maximum snow load will be less than 950N/m^2. The engineer compiles historical snow load data for the region where the building will be located at. The data is then used to test whether the mean snow load will be less than 950N/m^2 based on a prescribed confidence level.

In certain applications, we may wish to compare the mean values from two populations. As an example, consider a project dealing with measuring strain in a structural component in an airframe system. To measure the strain, two different methods may be used. One method is to employ a common type of strain gage which is made up of an electric circuit of resistors. The gage is mounted on the component. When the structural component experiences deformation and strain, changes in electric resistance will occur in the sensor. These changes are used to determine the strain induced in the component. A newer device for strain measurement is the optical fiber. The fiber is mounted on the component. A light source emits light that passes through the fiber from one end and is sensed on the other end. Any deformity or strain will cause a change in the amount of light received at the exiting end. This change is used to determine strain. Suppose we compile 100 sample values for the strain. However, 50 sample values are obtained using strain gages, while the other 50 are obtained using optical fibers. We wish to test the hypothesis that the mean value of strain from measurements made by using optical fibers is the same as the mean value of strain from measurements made by strain gages. Depending on whether the two populations have equal variances, different statistical methods are used for comparing the population means. These methods, which may involve either pooling or pairing data, are discussed in this chapter.

The ANOVA is an analytic procedure by which a population is divided into several subgroups. Each subgroup contains data obtained for a common parameter. However, different methods or systems are used in data compilation within each group. The variation in the measured parameter within each subgroup (also called a *treatment*) is then associated with an identified source and used to test a hypothesis on the equality of group means.

In connection with ANOVA, sometimes we wish to conduct further analyses to test whether the mean values computed for two or more sets of data are statistically different. We use a multiple range test for this purpose. To clarify on situations where this method may be used, consider again the strain data for a component in the airframe system. However, we use the same type of gage on several similar aircraft. Suppose the ANOVA results in the rejection of the hypothesis that the population means are identical. We would like to investigate the data sets further to identify where the difference between the means lies.

In conducting hypothesis and multiple range tests, critical values that determine whether or not a hypothesis is supported are obtained from the standard normal probability distribution function (when the sample size is large), or from the *t*-distribution (when sample size is small). Thus it is imperative that the data follows the normal or *t*-distribution functions. Accordingly, we often conduct a test of normality to determine whether the normal distribution is valid. If the data does not follow any distribution, then distribution-free methods must be used in testing hypotheses or when comparing two sample populations. These methods are also explained in this chapter.

The correlation analysis was discussed in theory in Chapter 7. In this chapter we present statistical methods that can be used to determine the correlation between two sets of data. The regression analysis is conducted to arrive at a suitable relationship that describes the expected value of a dependent variable in terms of one or more independent variables. Although the correlation and regression analyses are two different methods with different objectives, they are related to each other. When the compiled data for two random variables are ranked, the usual methods of correlation analysis may not be suitable. In this case we can use a *rank correlation analysis*. For data presented in linguistic terms, or in cases where one believes a correlation exists between two measured parameters yet the usual statistical methods do not result in an acceptable level of correlation, methods based on *fuzzy logic* may be used. Another method that can be used to determine correlation and establish the relation between a dependent variable and a series of independent variables is based on *artificial neural network* (ANN) systems. These systems require the use and programming of ANN software to recognize the relation between the dependent variable and the independent variables. These topics are not covered in detail in this chapter. However, pertinent references are provided at the end of this chapter for additional reading, (see Klir, et al., 1997; Nelson and Illingworth, 1990; Vanluchene and Roufei, 1990; and Yao, 1985).

9.2 HYPOTHESES TESTING

In Chapter 8, our discussion of data analysis focused on using data for computing estimates for parameters that describe a random variable. This was achieved by analyzing a set of data for estimating the mean, variance, or establishing confidence intervals for these parameters. However, the analysis was done without any prior information on the typical ranges or limits for these parameters. If there is a perceived notion that the value of an estimator, such as θ, will be within a limit, a statistical analysis can be conducted to determine whether this notion is supported. This type of analysis falls under the general subject of *hypotheses testing*. To further clarify this type of problem, consider an example involving the investigation of the rate of accidents by commercial motor vehicles (CMVs) operating along an interstate highway. Based on the engineer's previous experience, it is believed that on the average more than 20 percent of CMVs involved in accidents have a type of equipment safety problem. With sufficient data and a statistical analysis, it can be stated whether the engineer's notion can be supported or else rejected. Upon collection of data, of course, simple statistical analyses (such as those discussed in Chapter 8) can be used to arrive at an estimate for the mean value of the percentage of CMVs with safety problems that are involved in accidents. Notice that if the mean value is greater than 20 percent, we still need to provide statistical proof that this did not occur by chance. In this problem, the hypothesis is that the mean percentage of CMVs with safety violations that are involved in accidents is greater than 20 percent. Statistical tests can then be conducted to support or reject the hypothesis.

In another example, a production engineer, working in a concrete manufacturing plant, believes that a new batch of concrete produced in the plant will have a mean strength of at least 28 MPa. Suppose, upon collection of data on the strength of this batch of concrete, the mean value of the strength is found to be equal to 31 MPa. Although numerically this value is larger than 28 MPa, statistical tests can be conducted to prove that with a certain confidence level the mean strength value is too large to occur by chance. As a result, the hypothesis that the mean strength is at least equal to 28 MPa is supported.

In both these examples, a value has been assigned to a parameter that imposes a prior knowledge, belief, or simply a subjective estimate on the statistical parameter. This value (designated by θ_0) is referred to as the *null value*. The engineer's perceived notion on the statistical parameter is referred to as the *alternate* or *research hypothesis*, and is often shown with the symbol H_1. Whereas, the negation of this theory or hypothesis is called the *null hypothesis* and is described with H_0. Usually, inequality expressions describe H_0 and H_1. However, there may be applications where a specific value (presented by a statement of equality) is assigned to H_0. The objective of hypothesis testing is to support H_1 and to reject H_0. In any problem where hypothesis testing is desired, it is important to identify H_0 and H_1, and θ_0 before one can start compiling data to determine whether H_0 can be rejected in support of H_1. In identifying and formulating a hypothesis problem, it is noted that:

1. The H_0 and H_1 identities are complementary of each other and often described by two inequalities in terms of the null value θ_0. The statement of equality is included in H_0.
2. The objective of the analysis is to compile data and to determine whether H_0 can be rejected in support of H_1.
3. The data compiled for hypothesis testing follows the normal distribution.

The following examples are intended to demonstrate H_0 and H_1 and the null value θ_0 in several hypothesis-testing problems.

Example 9.1

In the problem dealing with the accident rates of commercial motor vehicles (CMVs), the traffic engineer believes that the rate of CMVs, with safety violations, which are involved in accidents is greater than 20%. Identify the null value, the null hypothesis and the alternate or research hypothesis.

Solution:

Let:

μ = mean percentage of CMVs involved in accidents and with safety violation records.
    Then
μ_0 = null value = 0.20;
$H_0: \mu \le \mu_0$ Null hypothesis
$H_1: \mu > \mu_0$ Alternate or research hypothesis.

Notice that the statement of equality is included in H_0.

Example 9.2

In the example of the strength of the new batch of concrete, the engineer's perceived notion is that the mean strength is greater than 28 MPa. Identify the null value, the null hypothesis and the alternate or research hypothesis.

Solution:

Let:

μ = mean strength. Then
μ_0 = null value = 28;
$H_0: \mu \leq \mu_0$ Null hypothesis
$H_1: \mu > \mu_0$ Alternate or research hypothesis.

Example 9.3

The design snow load in an area is not listed in the design code. An engineer believes that the mean snow load applied on the roof of a building is less than $950\,\text{N/m}^2$. Identify the null value, the null hypothesis and the alternate or research hypothesis.

Solution:

Let:

μ = mean strength. Then
μ_0 = null value = 950;
$H_0: \mu \geq \mu_0$ Null hypothesis
$H_1: \mu < \mu_0$ Alternate or research hypothesis.

To support H_1, sufficient data must be compiled and used in the analysis.

In conducting the hypothesis testing, the outcome will be one of the following:

1. The analysis shows that H_0 is rejected and H_1 is supported. This means that a correct decision was made when the null value and the hypotheses were established.

2. The analysis shows that we fail to reject H_0 and thus H_1 is not supported. In this case, the decision making based on the H_1 hypothesis results in an error. This is referred to as a Type I error. Thus Type I results in the rejection of H_0 when it is true?

3. The analysis shows that H_1 is supported and H_0 is rejected. In most cases, this is identical to 1 above and will result in a correct decision.

4. The analysis shows that H_1 cannot be supported and thus H_0 cannot be rejected. The error associated with the decision-making process in this case is referred to as a Type II error. In other words, Type II results in the acceptance of H_0 when it is not true.

Table 9.1 presents a summary of the above four outcomes.

TABLE 9.1   OUTCOMES IN HYPOTHESES TESTING

	Situation	
Hypothesis	Rejected	Fail to Reject
H_0	Correct decision	Type I error
H_1	Type II error	Correct decision

9.2.1 Hypothesis and Significance Testing of a Population Mean

Many engineering problems involve estimation of the mean of a sample population. Various design and decision-making strategies can be made by knowing the mean value. For this reason, the hypothesis and significance testing for the mean of a population constitutes an important part of an engineering decision-making process. Recall from Example 9.3 that the design engineer believed the mean snow load was going to be less than 950 N/m². The design snow load value D is computed in terms of the mean μ and standard deviation σ as follows:

$$D = \mu + \beta\sigma \qquad (9.1)$$

in which the parameter β is larger than 1 and is related to the probability that the load will be greater than the design value D (see Figure 9.1). As is evident from Eq. 9.1, the design load is directly related to the mean load. After compiling data for the snow load, if the null hypothesis in this problem (i.e., H_0: $\mu \geq 950$) cannot be rejected, then the engineer's notion on the load cannot be supported; as such, a change in the design may have to be made.

In this section, the procedure for hypothesis and significance testing for the mean is presented along with several example problems.

Depending on the type of problem, and the statement leading to the formation of H_0 and H_1, the hypothesis testing problem can be classified as: (a) the right-tailed; (b) the left-tailed; and (c) the two-tailed significance problem. These are described below:

Right-Tailed Significance Problems.   This type of problem is defined by the following expressions:

$$H_0: \mu \leq \mu_0$$
$$H_1: \mu > \mu_0$$

Examples 9.1 and 9.2 represent a right-tailed significance problem. We recall from Chapter 8 that Eqs. 8.10 and 8.14 can only provide an estimate μ for the mean. The mean from a sample population is a random variable with an expected value equal

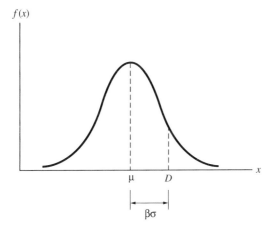

$f(x)$

μ D

$\beta\sigma$

Figure 9.1   Design value D vs. mean value.

to the actual mean and a standard deviation equal to $\sigma/\sqrt{n}$. From the central limit theorem, the probability density function of the mean will be normal when $n \to \infty$. With a sufficiently large n, and assuming the sample standard deviation is known, the random variable $\frac{\mu - m}{\sigma/\sqrt{n}}$ will then follow the standard normal probability density function.

In a right-tailed significance problem, a significance level (such as α) is selected and the corresponding critical value k_α is obtained from the tables of standard normal probability distribution function. As shown in Figure 9.2, the probability associated with H_1 can be formulated as follows:

$$P(\mu > \mu_0) = 1 - P(\mu \le \mu_0) = 1 - \Phi\left(\frac{\mu_0 - m}{\sigma/\sqrt{n}}\right) = \Phi\left(\frac{m - \mu_0}{\sigma/\sqrt{n}}\right)$$

Notice that when $\frac{m - \mu_0}{\sigma/\sqrt{n}} = k_\alpha$, then $P(\mu > \mu_0) = 1 - \alpha$. However, when $\frac{m - \mu_0}{\sigma/\sqrt{n}} > k_\alpha$ the corresponding probability $P(\mu > \mu_0)$ will be larger $(1 - \alpha)$. Or, in other words, $P(\mu > \mu_0)$ will be at least equal to the confidence level $(1 - \alpha)$. This means that in order to reject H_0 in favor of H_1 at α significance, we must have $\frac{m - \mu_0}{\sigma/\sqrt{n}} > k_\alpha$.

If the standard deviation is not known, the random variable $\frac{\mu - m}{\sigma/\sqrt{n}}$ follows a standard t-distribution with $\nu = n - 1$ degrees of freedom. Again with α significance, the corresponding critical value of the t-distribution will be t_α. In this case, H_0 is rejected in favor of H_1 when $\frac{m - \mu_0}{s/\sqrt{n}} > t_\alpha$, in which s is the estimate for the population standard deviation.

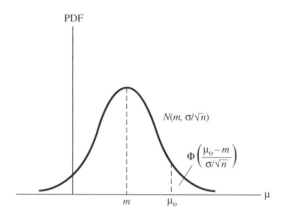

Figure 9.2   Probability density function of the mean μ.

Left-Tailed Significance Problems.   In this case, the null and alternate hypotheses are presented as follows:

$$H_0: \mu \geq \mu_0$$
$$H_1: \mu < \mu_0.$$

If the standard deviation is known, then

$$P(\mu < \mu_0) = \Phi\left(\frac{\mu_0 - m}{\sigma/\sqrt{n}}\right).$$

If $\frac{\mu_0 - m}{\sigma/\sqrt{n}} = k_\alpha$, then $P(\mu < \mu_0) = 1 - \alpha$. However, when $\frac{\mu_0 - m}{\sigma/\sqrt{n}} > +k_\alpha$, then $P(\mu < \mu_0)$ will be at least equal to $1 - \alpha$. Thus, in order to reject H_0, we must have $\frac{\mu_0 - m}{\sigma/\sqrt{n}} > k_\alpha$. Or,

$$\frac{m - \mu_0}{\sigma/\sqrt{n}} < -k_\alpha.$$

If σ is not known, a t-distribution with $\nu = n - 1$ degrees of freedom is used, and H_0 is rejected when

$$\frac{m - \mu_0}{\sigma/\sqrt{n}} < -t_\alpha.$$

Two-Tailed Significance Problems.   In this case, the objective is to support the notion that μ will not be equal to μ_0. The null and alternate hypotheses are as follows:

$$H_0: \mu = \mu_0$$
$$H_1: \mu \neq \mu_0.$$

The two-sided significance involves the critical values $\pm k_{\alpha/2}$ as shown in Fig. 9.3. If μ is not equal to μ_0, then it must be either less than or greater than μ_0. This implies that either

$$\frac{\mu_0 - m}{\sigma/\sqrt{n}} < -k_{\alpha/2} \text{ or } \frac{\mu_0 - m}{\sigma/\sqrt{n}} > k_{\alpha/2}.$$

Rearranging these inequalities, H_0 will be rejected if

$$\frac{m - \mu_0}{\sigma/\sqrt{n}} > k_{\alpha/2} \text{ or } \frac{m - \mu_0}{\sigma/\sqrt{n}} < -k_{\alpha/2}.$$

Again, if σ is not known, the estimate for the standard deviation (i.e., s) is used along with a t-distribution with $\nu = n - 1$ degrees of freedom. The critical values of the t-distribution will be $\pm t_{\alpha/2}$; and the null hypothesis H_0 is rejected when

$$\frac{m - \mu_0}{s/\sqrt{n}} > t_{\alpha/2} \text{ or } \frac{m - \mu_0}{s/\sqrt{n}} < -t_{\alpha/2}.$$

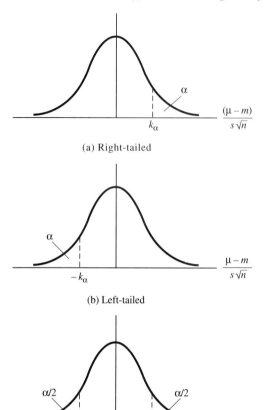

(a) Right-tailed

(b) Left-tailed

(c) Two-tailed

Figure 9.3 (a) Right tailed; (b) left tailed; (c) two tailed.

Example 9.4

In Example 9.1, suppose that the traffic engineer conducts a summary of 17 highways and finds out that the fraction (p) of CMVs involved in accidents with safety violations has an estimated mean of 0.25 and standard deviation of $s = 0.08$, respectively. Determine whether the engineer's notion of $p > 0.2$ is supported at $\alpha = 0.05$ significance. If $p > 0.2$, then the engineer will propose a more stringent regulation for safety inspection of CMVs.

Solution:

This is a right-tailed significance problem. Using the t-distribution, the critical value at $\alpha = 0.05$ (or at $1 - \alpha = 0.95$ probability) and $\nu = 17 - 1 = 16$ degrees of freedom is

$$t_\alpha = 1.746.$$

Based on $\mu_0 = 0.2$ and mean $m = 0.25$, $\dfrac{m - \mu_0}{s/\sqrt{n}} = \dfrac{0.25 - 0.20}{0.08/\sqrt{16}} = 2.5.$

This value exceeds $t_\alpha = 1.746$; as such the null hypothesis is rejected at $\alpha = 0.05$ in support of the engineer's notion that the mean fraction of the number of CMVs involved in accidents and with safety violations is greater than 0.20. In this problem, the engineer's decision to suggest a more stringent regulation for safety inspection of CMVs is a correct one. Notice that the standard deviation was considered to be unknown; and as such, the t-distribution was used.

Example 9.5

In Example 9.2, to support the belief that the concrete mean strength is greater than 28 MPa, the engineer conducts a laboratory test on 50 samples. The estimates for the mean and standard deviation are 29.75 and 2.8 MPa, respectively. Determine whether the engineer's notion is supported. Use $\alpha = 0.05$ significance.

Solution:

Again, this is a right-tailed problem. Since n is relatively large, we can use the normal distribution. The critical value of normal distribution at $\alpha = 0.05$ (i.e., 0.95 probability) is $k_\alpha = 1.65$.

Notice that if we use the t-distribution, at $\alpha = 0.05$ significance and with $v = 50 - 1 = 49$ degrees of freedom, the critical value of the t-distribution is $t_\alpha = 1.67$, which is only marginally larger than k_α.

Based on $\mu_0 = 28$ and mean $m = 29.75$, $\dfrac{m - \mu_0}{s/\sqrt{n}} = \dfrac{29.75 - 28.00}{2.8/\sqrt{50}} = 4.42$ which is larger than the critical value.

This means that the null hypothesis $H_0: \mu \leq \mu_0$ is rejected in favor of the alternate hypothesis ($H_1: \mu > \mu_0$). The decision by the engineer to use at least 28 MPa strength is correct.

Example 9.6

In Example 9.3, the design engineer plans to use a mean snow load of at most $950\,N/m^2$. To support this, the records of the past 15 seasons are reviewed and used in the analysis. The mean maximum seasonal snow load is estimated to be equal to $m = 1{,}140\,N/m^2$ and an estimated standard deviation of $s = 380\,N/m^2$. Determine whether the engineer's decision is correct. Use $\alpha = 0.01$.

Solution:

This is a left-tailed significance problem since the alternate hypothesis is presented by $\mu < 950$ based on the engineer's belief. At $\alpha = 0.01$ significance and using the t-distribution with a degree of freedom equal to $15 - 1 = 14$, the critical value of the t-distribution is $-t_\alpha$ where $t_\alpha = 2.62$. Based on $\mu_0 = 950$ and mean $m = 1{,}140$

$$\frac{m - \mu_0}{s/\sqrt{n}} = \frac{1140 - 950}{380/\sqrt{15}} = 1.94$$

Certainly this is not smaller than the critical value which is -2.62. This means that the null hypothesis $H_0: \mu > \mu_0$ cannot be rejected. Thus, the engineer has made an error in deciding on the mean snow load.

9.2.2 Hypothesis Testing of a Proportion

Hypothesis testing can also be applied to proportion p. Recall that p is the probability of occurrence for any one trial in the binomial distribution. The hypothesized value for p is p_0, which is usually defined as a prior knowledge or belief by an engineer. As in the case of the mean value, the three types of tests are:

$$H_0: p \leq p_0 \qquad H_0: p \geq p_0 \qquad H_0: p = p_0$$
$$H_1: p > p_0 \qquad H_0: p < p_0 \qquad H_0: p \neq p_0$$
Right-tailed test   Left-tailed test   Two-tailed test

The test statistic for p is based on the random variable selected for establishing the confidence intervals for p as discussed earlier. Denoting this test statistic as z, we can write

$$z = \frac{p - p_0}{\sqrt{p_0(1 - p_0)/n}} \qquad (9.2)$$

in which $p = x/n$ represents the proportion of the number of times (x) the event of concern occurred to the total number of trials (n) used in estimating the proportion. Using an α significance, the critical value from the normal distribution is k_α. In a right-tailed test, if z is less than this critical value, then the null hypothesis cannot be rejected. In a left-tailed test, if z is less than $-k_\alpha$, then the null hypothesis *is* rejected. In a two-tailed test, the critical values of the normal distribution at α are $\pm k_{\alpha/2}$. In this case, the null hypothesis cannot be rejected if z is within the two limits.

Example 9.7

A small manufacturing plant produces pre-fabricated joists for use in the construction of floors in residential buildings. The joists are rated for a total load of 45 kN. On rare occasions, the applied load may exceed this value and reach 90 kN. Under this heavy load, the production engineer believes that the probability of failure will be less than 0.20. To further support this notion, the engineer tests $n = 15$ beams; 4 fail. At $\alpha = 0.10$, determine whether there is enough statistical evidence to support the engineer's belief.

Solution:

The null and alternate hypotheses follow those in the left-tailed test. We wish to test the alternate hypothesis $H_1: p < p_0$. Based on the data, the estimate for the proportion p is computed as $4/15 = 0.27$. The test statistic is:

$$z = \frac{0.27 - 0.20}{\sqrt{0.20(1 - 0.20)/15}} = 0.67.$$

The critical value for the normal distribution at $\alpha = 0.10$ is described as $-k_\alpha$, where

$$k_\alpha = \Phi^{-1}(1 - \alpha) = \Phi^{-1}(0.90) = 1.28.$$

Since z is larger than the critical value (i.e., -1.28), the null hypothesis cannot be rejected. Thus the engineer's belief is not supported statistically.

9.3 COMPARING TWO POPULATION MEANS

In certain problems it is often necessary to make a judgment on whether the mean values from two populations (data sets) are statistically different from one another. As an example, consider data compiled on stress values at the midspan locations of certain girders from two highway bridges with similar structural conditions. The stress values are generated as a result of the passage of trucks on these bridges. A bridge engineer is interested in knowing whether there is enough statistical evidence to believe that the mean stress values from the two bridges are different. In another example, consider data compiled on the vertical accelerations of two identical aircraft. Upon compiling the data, an engineer is interested in knowing whether the mean vertical accelerations from the two aircraft are statistically identical (i.e. no significant difference exists between the two mean values). In each of these examples, the random samples from two populations can be assumed to be independent. If the variances of the two populations are identical, a *pooled* sample variance will be used in comparing the mean values. However, if the variances are not identical, pooling the variances cannot be used. In certain problems, the sample populations are not independent. Consider the rate of accidents at several intersections before and after an improvement plan is implemented on the intersections. Sample population I constitutes the number of accidents per year before implementing the plan. Sample population II consists of the number of accidents per year after the improvement plan is implemented. The accident rates before and after the implementation of the plan may be related. In this case a *paired* sample population is used for comparing the mean values.

In this section, comparing means for three situations is described. These are: (a) independent populations with equal variances; (b) independent populations with unequal variances; and (c) dependent populations. In cases where the sample populations are independent, we need to know whether the variances of the two populations are equal. The method for comparing two variances is explained below.

9.3.1 Testing of Equality of Two Variances

To decide whether two variances are identical, we need to provide a statistical evidence that the difference between the two variances is not significant. We cannot make a judgment on the equality of the two variances by simply computing the difference between the two and expressing an opinion based on the fact that the difference appears to be small. A random variable that can be used to establish a *test statistic* for testing a hypothesis on the equality of the variances must be defined. To establish the test statistic, the ratio of the two variances (rather than the difference between them) is used as a random variable for hypothesis testing. Since the ratio is used as a random variable here, the probability distribution used will be of those with one infinite end. The F distribution is used for this purpose as described later.

The two population variances are σ_1^2 and σ_2^2. The idea is to provide enough statistical evidence that the ratio σ_1^2/σ_2^2 is close to 1. If the ratio is too small to reasonably occur by chance, then the observed σ_1^2/σ_2^2 is close to zero. On the other hand, if the ratio is too large to reasonably occur by chance, then it is much larger than 1. In both these cases, $\sigma_1^2 \neq \sigma_2^2$. In conducting the test of equality of the two variances, however, we use the estimates for the variances, since the exact variances are not known. The estimates are S_1^2 and S_2^2, and the ratio $\theta = S_1^2/S_2^2$. Note that we use capital letters (S) to define variances, because they are taken as random variables. The hypothesis testing for the equality of the variances is a two-tailed one and is defined by the following null hypothesis H_0 and alternative hypothesis H_1:

$$H_0: \theta = 1$$
$$H_1: \theta \neq 1$$

As described earlier, the F distribution is used for θ in testing the H_0 and H_1 hypotheses. The F distribution is obtained as the ratio of two Chi-square distributions. The numerator has $\nu_1 = n_1 - 1$ degrees of freedom describing S_1^2; whereas the denominator has $\nu_2 = n_2 - 1$ degrees of freedom describing S_2^2. Note that n_1 and n_2 are the sample sizes for the two distributions. The F distribution is always described with the degrees of freedom ν_1 and ν_2. As shown in Figure 9.4 the critical values of the F distribution based on $\alpha/2$ can be obtained such that:

$$P(f_{1-\alpha/2} < F \leq f_{\alpha/2}) = 1 - \alpha \tag{9.3}$$

The critical values of the F distribution for various combinations of the degrees of freedom ν_1 and ν_2 are provided in Table A.5 of Appendix A. Note that as usual $\alpha/2$ represents the probability that the random variable F will be greater than $f_{\alpha/2}$; i.e.,

$$P(F > f_{\alpha/2}) = \alpha/2 \tag{9.4}$$

and

$$P(F \leq f_{\alpha/2}) = 1 - \alpha/2 \tag{9.5}$$

Furthermore, the following relationship holds between the critical values of the F distribution:

$$f_{1-\alpha/2}(\nu_1, \nu_2) = \frac{1}{f_{\alpha/2}(\nu_2,\nu_1)} \tag{9.6}$$

For example, for $\alpha = 0.05$, $\nu_1 = 10$ and $\nu_2 = 15$

$$f_{\alpha/2} = f_{0.025}(10,15) = 3.06.$$

This indicates that

$$P(F > 3.06) = 0.025, \text{ and } P(F \leq 3.06) = 1 - 0.025 = 0.975.$$

To obtain $f_{1-\alpha/2} = f_{0.975}$ for $\nu_1 = 10$ and $\nu_2 = 15$, we will need $f_{0.025}(15,10)$ which is 3.52. Thus, in light of Eq. 9.6

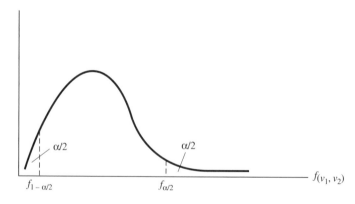

Figure 9.4   Probability density function for F-distribution.

$$f_{0.975}(10,15) = \frac{1}{f_{0.025}(15,10)} = \frac{1}{3.52} = 0.28.$$

We then use the critical values of the F distribution to test whether the null hypothesis H_0 cannot be rejected. If the null hypothesis cannot be rejected, then we have enough evidence to support the equality of the two population variances.

Example 9.8

Samples of soils from two nearby sites with similar characteristics were taken and tested for bearing capacity. The following results provide the summary of the findings:

Site I:	Site II:
$n_1 = 10$ samples	$n_2 = 13$ samples
$m_1 = 182\,kN/m^2$	$m_2 = 171\,kN/m^2$
$S_1 = 15.2\,kN/m^2$	$S_2 = 13.8\,kN/m^2$

Determine whether the variances from these populations are identical at $\alpha = 0.05$ significance.

Solution:

We wish to test the null hypothesis H_0. Since $S_1^2 = 231.04$ and $S_2^2 = 190.44$, then $\theta = 231.04/190.44 = 1.21$. The critical values of the F distribution at $\nu_1 = 10 - 1 = 9$ and $\nu_2 = 13 - 1 = 12$ are:

$$f_{\alpha/2} = f_{0.025}(9,12) = 3.44$$
$$f_{1-\alpha/2} = f_{0.975}(9,12) = 1/f_{0.025}(12,9) = 1/3.87 = 0.26.$$

Since $\theta = 1.21$ is within $f_{1-\alpha/2} = 0.26$ and $f_{\alpha/2} = 3.44$, the null hypothesis cannot be rejected; as such, the variances from the two populations are identical at $\alpha = 0.05$.

9.3.2 Comparing Mean Values from Independent Populations with Identical Variances (Pooled t)

When variances S_1^2 and S_2^2 are identical, the standard t random variable used in hypothesis is:

$$t = \frac{(M_1 - M_2) - (\mu_1 - \mu_2)}{\sqrt{\sigma^2(1/n_1 + 1/n_2)}} \qquad (9.7a)$$

in which $(M_1 - M_2)$ is the point estimation of the difference in the two population means (a random variable); μ_1 and μ_2 are the population means, and σ^2 is the common variance of the two populations. Since this variance is not known, an unbiased estimate for σ^2 is computed as follows based on S_1^2 and S_2^2:

$$S_p^2 = \frac{(n_1 - 1)S_1^2 + (n_2 - 1)S_2^2}{n_1 + n_2 - 2} \qquad (9.8)$$

S_p^2 is a *pooled* variance. The hypotheses to be tested are defined below:

$H_0\colon \mu_1 \leq \mu_2$	$H_0\colon \mu_1 \geq \mu_2$	$H_0\colon \mu_1 = \mu_2$
$H_1\colon \mu_1 > \mu_2$	$H_1\colon \mu_1 < \mu_2$	$H_1\colon \mu_1 \neq \mu_2$
Right-tailed	Left-tailed	Two-tailed

Substituting S_p for σ in Eq. 9.7a, the standard t variable can be written as

$$t = \frac{(M_1 - M_2) - (\mu_1 - \mu_2)}{\sqrt{S_p^2(1/n_1 + 1/n_2)}} \qquad (9.7b)$$

When the objective is to determine whether the difference between the two mean values is statistically insignificant (i.e., the means are statistically identical), the null and alternative hypothesis may be written as a two-tailed problem as follows:

$$H_0: D = 0$$
$$H_1: D \neq 0$$

in which the test statistic, D, is written as

$$D = \frac{(m_1 - m_2) - d_0}{\sqrt{S_p^2(1/n_1 + 1/n_2)}} \qquad (9.9)$$

and m_1 and m_2 are the estimates for the two population means. The parameter d_0 is the hypothesized difference in the two population means. In most applications, $d_0 = 0$. At α significance, the critical values of the t-distribution are $\pm t_{\alpha/2}$ with $\nu = (n_1 + n_2 - 2)$ degrees of freedom. If $-t_{\alpha/2} < D < +t_{\alpha/2}$, the null hypothesis H_0 cannot be rejected; as such, the difference between the means is not significant.

It is emphasized that the above procedure is valid when the two populations follow the normal distribution. The test of normality for these populations may be conducted using the methods described in Section 8.6.4 and 8.6.5.

Example 9.9

In Example 9.8, since the variances are statistically identical, determine whether the difference between the two population means is significant at $\alpha = 0.05$.

Solution:

The pooled variance S_p^2 is computed using Eq. 9.8.

$$S_p^2 = (9 \times 231.04 + 12 \times 190.44)/(10 + 13 - 2) = 207.84.$$

Using $d_0 = 0$, the test statistics D for the difference between the two means is

$$D = \frac{182 - 171}{\sqrt{(207.84)^2(1/10 + 1/13)}} = 1.81.$$

The critical value of the t-distribution at $\alpha = 0.05$ and $\nu = (10 + 13 - 2) = 21$ degrees of freedom is

$$t_{\alpha/2} = T_\nu^{-1}(1 - \alpha/2) = 2.08.$$

Since $-2.08 < D < +2.08$, the difference between the two means is not significant at $\alpha = 0.05$.

Example 9.10

Flight data for two identical aircraft was complied for several hours of test flight. The data compiled was the number of cases where the aircraft vertical acceleration exceeded 3.0g, where g is the gravity acceleration. Aircraft I had $n_1 = 11$ cases of vertical acceleration exceeding 3.0g with a mean vertical acceleration equal to 3.6g and a corresponding standard deviation equal to 0.40g. The data for Aircraft II showed

$n_2 = 16$ cases of the vertical acceleration exceeding 3.0g with a mean value of 3.2g and corresponding standard deviation equal to 0.36g.

(a) Show that the variances corresponding to accelerations (exceeding 3.0g) from the two aircraft are identical at $\alpha = 0.10$ significance.

(b) Given the results in part a, determine whether the difference between the two means is statistically significant at $\alpha = 0.10$. Assume the two populations have been tested for and passed the normal distribution function.

Solution:

(a) The variances for the two populations are:

$$S_1^2 = 0.16g^2 \text{ and } S_2^2 = 0.13g^2 \text{ thus } \theta = S_1^2/S_2^2 = 1.23.$$

At $\alpha = 0.10$ and degrees of freedom $\nu_1 = 11 - 1 = 10$ and $\nu_2 = 16 - 1 = 15$

$$f_{\alpha/2} = f_{0.05}(10,15) = 2.54$$

and

$$f_{1-\alpha/2} = f_{0.95} = 1/f_{0.05}(15,10) = 1/2.85 = 0.35.$$

Since the test statistic $\theta = 1.23$ is between the critical values 0.35 and 2.54, the two variances are statistically identical at $\alpha = 0.10$.

(b) The pooled variance S_p^2 is

$$S_p^2 = (10 \times 0.16g^2 + 15 \times 0.13g^2)/(11 + 16 - 2) = 0.142g^2.$$

Using the hypothesized difference $d_0 = 0$, the test statistic D is:

$$D = \frac{(3.6g - 3.2g) - 0}{\sqrt{(0.142g^2)(1/11 + 1/16)}} = 2.71.$$

The critical values of the t-distribution at $\alpha = 0.10$ for $\nu = 11 + 16 - 2 = 25$ degrees of freedom are $\pm t_{\alpha/2}$ where $t_{\alpha/2} = 1.708$. Since $D > 1.708$, the difference between the two population means is statistically significant.

9.3.3 Comparing Means from Independent Populations with Unequal Variances

In those cases where variances are statistically unequal, they cannot be combined by pooling. Instead, a combined variance in the form of

$$\sigma^2 = \sigma_1^2/n_1 + \sigma_2^2/n_2 \tag{9.10}$$

must be used, where σ_1^2 and σ_2^2 are the variances of the two populations. The standard t variable describing the difference between the two means μ_1 and μ_2 will be:

$$t = \frac{(M_1 - M_2) - (\mu_1 - \mu_2)}{\sqrt{S_1^2/n_1 + S_2^2/n_2}} \tag{9.11}$$

in which S_1 and S_2 are the estimates for σ_1 and σ_2, respectively. The number of degrees of freedom is obtained from the data. Different methods are suggested for computing the degrees of freedom ν. The Smith-Satterthwaite procedure (Milton and Tsokos, 1983) is used in this book. The degree of freedom is:

$$\nu = \frac{(S_1^2/n_1 + S_2^2/n_2)^2}{\dfrac{(S_1^2/n_1)^2}{n_1 - 1} + \dfrac{(S_2^2/n_2)^2}{n_2 - 1}} \tag{9.12}$$

The value obtained for ν from Eq. 9.12 is rounded down to the nearest integer for use in the t-distribution table. Again, we must first perform a normality test for the two populations before testing a hypothesis in this case. The three hypothesis problems are similar to those in Section 9.3.2. In particular, if the desired test is meant to investigate whether the difference between the two population means is significant, the hypothesis is written as a two-tailed problem in the following form:

$$H_0: D = 0$$
$$H_1: D \neq 0$$

in which

$$D = \frac{m_1 - m_2 - d_0}{\sqrt{S_1^2/n_1 + S_2^2/n_2}} \tag{9.13}$$

Again the hypothesized difference d_0 is often taken as zero.

Example 9.11

In order to compare two brands of a piece of construction equipment, the data on the operation time until the first breakdown in each brand is studied. The operation time until the first breakdown is measured in hours. For the two brands, the following statistics are obtained:

Brand I	Brand II
$m_1 = 1253$ hours	$m_2 = 1433$ hours
$S_1 = 125$ hours	$S_2 = 208$ hours
$n_1 = 25$	$n_2 = 16$

Assume the operation time follows a normal distribution.
(a) Determine whether the variances from the two populations are equal at $\alpha = 0.10$.
(b) Determine whether the two mean values are significantly different.

Solution:

(a) To compare the variances, we establish $\theta = S_1^2/S_2^2 = 0.36$. At $\alpha = 0.10$ and degrees of freedom $\nu_1 = 25 - 1 = 24$ and $\nu_2 = 16 - 1 = 15$,

$$f_{\alpha/2} = f_{0.05}(24,15) = 2.29$$
$$f_{1-\alpha/2} = f_{0.95}(24,15) = 1/f_{0.05}(15,24) = 1/2.11 = 0.47.$$

Since $\theta = 0.36 < 0.47$, the two variances are statistically unequal.
(b) Given the results in part a, to compare the means we can use the procedure in Section 9.3.3 for unequal variances. Using $d_0 = 0$ in Eq. 9.13

$$D = \frac{(1253 - 1433) - 0}{\sqrt{(125)^2/25 + (208)^2/16}} = -3.12$$

The degree of freedom ν is:

$$\nu = \frac{[(125)^2/25 + (208)^2/16]^2}{\dfrac{[(125)^2/25]^2}{24} + \dfrac{[(208)^2/16]^2}{15}} = 22$$

The critical values of the t-distribution at $\alpha = 0.10$ and $\nu = 22$ are $\pm t_{\alpha/2}$ where

$$t_{\alpha/2} = T_\nu^{-1}(1 - \alpha/2) = 1.717.$$

Since $D = -3.12 < -1.717$, the difference between the two means is statistically significant.

9.3.4 Comparing Means from Dependent Populations (Paired t)

In certain problems the two random samples are not independent. This usually occurs when the sample data represents the same variable under two different conditions or environments. As an example, consider the rate of accidents in a series of intersections along a 10-km roadway before and after implementation of a traffic signal coordination. The traffic signal coordination is achieved by synchronizing the duration of red lights at intersections so that a motorist travelling at the posted maximum speed will encounter the smallest number of red lights. As another example, suppose a safety regulation is imposed on construction companies in an area to enhance the safety of construction workers. The two populations in this case may be (1) the number of yearly accidents on the sites before the implementation of the safety regulation; and (2) the number of yearly accidents on the same sites after the implementation of the safety regulation. In these examples, the observed data sets are *paired* because of their dependence. If X_i and Y_i are the ith observed values from the two populations X and Y, respectively, the difference between the two values X_i and Y_i (i.e., d_i) belongs to a random variable $D = X - Y$. Estimates for the mean and standard deviation of D can be obtained using the point estimation method. Since the sample size for both populations is n, then

$$m_D = \frac{1}{n}\sum_{t-1}^{n} d_i \tag{9.14}$$

$$S_D^2 = \frac{1}{n-1}\sum_{i-1}^{n}(d_i - m_D)^2 \tag{9.15}$$

The hypotheses for testing whether the difference between the two population means is significant in a two-tailed problem are as follows:

$$H_0: \overline{D} = 0$$

$$H_1: \overline{D} \neq 0$$

where

$$\overline{D} = \frac{m_D - 0}{S_D/\sqrt{n}} \tag{9.16}$$

The difference between the two means is significant when $\overline{D} < -t_{\alpha/2}$ or $\overline{D} > t_{\alpha/2}$ in which $\pm t_{\alpha/2}$ are the critical values of the t-distribution at α significance and $\nu = n - 1$ degrees of freedom.

Example 9.12

In the problem of the traffic signal coordination, 15 intersections along a roadway were studied before and after implementation of a synchronized red light system. The results in Table E9.12 present the number of accidents in these intersections.

TABLE E9.12

Intersection	Accidents/year Before Signal Coordination (X)	Accident/year After Signal Coordination (Y)	$D = X - Y$
1	3	2	1
2	9	8	1
3	3	5	-2
4	0	1	-1
5	0	2	-2
6	3	3	0
7	4	5	-1
8	0	0	0
9	2	1	1
10	7	8	-1
11	7	9	-2
12	2	2	0
13	0	1	-1
14	5	4	1
15	2	6	-4

Determine whether the mean number of accidents before and after signal coordination are statistically significant.

Solution:

The values for the random variable D are listed in Table E9.12. The mean value and standard deviation of D are computed from Eqs. 9.14 and 9.15.

$$m_D = -0.67, S_D^2 = 2.095, S_D = 1.447$$

Clearly, the signal coordination has increased the mean number of accidents; but we need to conduct a test to determine whether the difference is significant. At $\alpha = 0.05$, the critical values of t-distribution are $\pm t_\alpha/2$ where $t_{\alpha/2} = 2.145$ for a degree of freedom $\nu = 15 - 1 = 14$. The test statistic $\overline{D}$ is:

$$\overline{D} = \frac{-0.67 - 0}{1.447/\sqrt{15}} = -1.79$$

Since $-2.145 < \overline{D} = -1.79 < 2.145$, there is not enough evidence to prove the difference between the mean number of accidents before and after the implementation of the signal coordination is significant at $\alpha = 0.05$.

9.4 ANALYSIS OF VARIANCE

In Section 9.3, we discussed methods for comparing the means and variances from two populations. In this section, we extend these methods to include more than two populations. These methods are referred to as the analysis of variance (ANOVA). The purpose of ANOVA is to conduct hypothesis testings among the mean values of several data sets. In order to perform testing, the total variation in the compiled data is divided into segments. Once the source of variations in each segment is known, the hypothesis testing on the differences between the population means can be performed. Consider as an example the vertical accelerations compiled for a fleet of five identical airplanes. Each data set contains measurements made for the accelerations of one of the five aircraft. No other variables are considered in the data sets. Upon conducting the normality test on the data sets, ANOVA can be used to test whether the differences between means are significant. This type of comparison is referred to as *the one-way classification, completely random design with fixed effect.*

9.4.1 One-Way Classification, Completely Random Design with Fixed Effect

This method is called one-way because only one parameter is under study. For example, in the flight data acquisition problem, we are only interested in the vertical acceleration without any other difference between the aircraft (such as their age in service, history of flight, etc.) being considered. The data sets are independent of each other; for this reason, the method is considered completely random. Fixed effect refers to the fact that the data is compiled from specific sources. In the flight data acquisition problem, the data is compiled from five specific aircraft rather than from a random group of aircraft.

In this method, we observe the following two general problems:

1. A total of N samples are going to be studied using k different treatments. The N samples are randomly divided into k groups of sizes $n_1, n_2, \ldots, n_k$. Each group will be subject to a different treatment. As an example of this type, assume three methods are suggested for enforcing the speed limits in N roadways. These methods are: method A, which involves using flashing lights along the roadway; method B, which involves using electronic boards that display the speed of an approaching motorist; and method C, which involves having a continuous patrol present along the roadway. We randomly assign n_1 roadways to receive method A; n_2 roadways to receive method B; and n_3 roadways to receive method C. Note that $n_1 + n_2 + n_3 = N$. We monitor the number of speed violations in these roadways for a year. Now we wish to compare the mean number of speed violations for the three groups of roadways that received the three different methods (treatments).

2. There are k populations of sizes $n_1, n_2, \ldots, n_k$. All populations are subject to the same treatment. As an example, consider four groups of construction companies from different states. A new safety regulation is being implemented on the groups. We want to compare the mean number of accidents per year for each group after the implementation of the safety regulation. In this case, only differences in the results are attributed to the basic differences among the k population, and not to the type of treatment.

The two problems cited above are different. However, in both these problems we wish to determine whether the mean values from the k populations are statistically identical. The hypotheses to be tested are:

$$H_0: \mu_1 = \mu_2 = \ldots = \mu_k$$
$$H_1: \mu_i \neq \mu_j \text{ For some } i \text{ and } j$$

The null hypothesis states that there is no difference between the mean values; the alternative hypothesis states that at least one mean value is different from the others.

Recall that group i has n_i sample values. We introduce X_{ij} as the jth sample value in group i (also known as the *factor level*), where $i = 1, 2, \ldots, k$ and $j = 1, 2, \ldots, n_i$. For example, the sample values in group 1 will be $X_{11}, X_{12}, X_{13}, \ldots, X_{1n_1}$ whereas, the sample values in group 2 will be $X_{21}, X_{22}, X_{23}, \ldots, X_{2n_2}$ and so on. We further introduce the following parameters:

$$T_i = \sum_{j=1}^{n_i} X_{ij} = \text{Sum of sample values in group } i \tag{9.17}$$

$$M_i = \frac{T_i}{n_i} = \text{Sample mean for group } i. \tag{9.18}$$

$$T = \sum_{i=1}^{k} T_i = \sum_{i=1}^{k} \sum_{j=1}^{n_i} X_{ij} = \text{Sum of all sample values from all groups} \tag{9.19}$$

$$M = \frac{T}{N} = \text{Sample mean for all groups (grand mean)} \tag{9.20}$$

$$\sum_{i=1}^{k} \sum_{j=1}^{n_i} X_{ij}^2 = \text{Sum of squares of all sample values for all groups} \tag{9.21}$$

Notice that μ_i ($i = 1, 2, \ldots, k$) are the theoretical mean values for the k populations. If μ represents the theoretical mean for all data combined, we can then introduce a model for hypothesis testing. Furthermore, notice that μ ignores the group effect (factor level effect) on the outcome. If various groups have no effect on the outcome, then all μ_i will be the same and equal to μ. However, the factor levels will usually affect the outcome; and as such $\mu_i - \mu$ will represent the effect of the group (or factor level) i. As it is expected due to the variations in the data, within each group there will also be certain levels of variability associated with the population means. The difference between a specific sample value X_{ij} and the group mean μ_i (i.e., $X_{ij} - \mu_i$) is referred to as the *random error*. The term $\mu_i - \mu$ on the other hand represents the error in μ_i due to the differences between methods (or treatments) applied to various groups. A model for hypothesis testing can be developed as follows:

$$X_{ij} = \mu + (\mu_i - \mu) + (X_{ij} - \mu_i) \tag{9.22}$$

for

$$i = 1, 2, \ldots, k$$
$$j = 1, 2, \ldots, n_i$$

The model represented by Eq. 9.22 simply indicates that the outcome for the sample value X_{ij} is written as the overall mean plus two error terms; one from the fact that group i received a different treatment; and the other due to the variations within the group. If groups are not receiving different treatments, most of the errors will be due to the variations within the group. It is emphasized that the basic assumptions underlying the model of Eq. 9.22 are that: (a) the k populations are independent; (b) each population follows a normal distribution; and (c) each sample population has the same variance σ^2. Furthermore, since μ_i and μ are not known, their estimates are used in the model of Eq. 9.22. Thus;

$$X_{ij} = M + (M_i - M) + (X_{ij} - M_i) \tag{9.23}$$

or

$$(X_{ij} - M) = (M_i - M) + (X_{ij} - M_i) \tag{9.24}$$

where M_i and M are estimates for μ_i and μ, respectively. In Eqs. 9.23 and 9.24, capital M is used to define means as random variables. If each side of Eq. 9.24 is squared and summed over all possible values of i and j, the following equation is obtained. This is called the *sum of square identity*.

$$\sum_{i=1}^{k} \sum_{j=1}^{n_i} (X_{ij} - M)^2 = \sum_{i=1}^{k} n_i(M_i - M)^2 + \sum_{i=1}^{k} \sum_{j-1}^{n_i} (X_{ij} - M_i)^2 \tag{9.25}$$

In this identity, let

$$SS_T = \sum_{i=1}^{k} \sum_{j=1}^{n_i} (X_{ij} - M)^2 = \sum_{i=1}^{k} \sum_{j=1}^{n_i} X_{ij}^2 - \frac{T^2}{N} \tag{9.26}$$

$$SS_M = \sum_{i=1}^{k} n_i(M_i - M)^2 = \sum_{i=1}^{k} \left(\frac{T_i}{n_i}\right)^2 - \frac{T^2}{N} \tag{9.27}$$

$$SS_E = \sum_{i=1}^{k} \sum_{j=1}^{n_i} (X_{ij} - M_i)^2 \tag{9.28}$$

where

SS_T = the sum of squares of deviations of sample values from the grand mean. This is a measure of total variability in the data;

SS_M = the weighed sum of squares of deviations of group means from the grand mean. This is a measure of variability in different groups due to different methods or treatment applied to them; and

SS_E = the sum of squares of deviations of sample values from the group mean. This is a measure of variability within each group and is called *error* (or *residual*) sum of squares.

In light of the identity represented by Equations 9.25–9.28,

$$SS_T = SS_M + SS_E \tag{9.29}$$

To test the null hypothesis on the equality of the group means, we define two statistics as functions of SS_M and SS_E. These are referred to as the *treatment mean square* (MS_M) which is found by dividing SS_M by $(k - 1)$; and the *error mean square* (MS_E) which is found by dividing SS_E by the value $(N - k)$. Thus

TABLE 9.2 ANOVA: ONE-WAY CLASSIFICATION, COMPLETELY RANDOM DESIGN WITH FIXED EFFECT

Source of Variation	Degrees of Freedom	SS	MS	E(MS)	F
Treatment	$k-1$	SS_M	$\dfrac{SS_M}{k-1}$	$\sigma^2 + \displaystyle\sum_{i=1}^{k} \dfrac{n_i(\mu_i - \mu)^2}{k-1}$	MS_M/MS_E
Error	$N-k$	SS_E	$\dfrac{SS_E}{n-k}$	σ^2	
Total	$N-1$	SS_T			

$$MS_M = \frac{SS_M}{k-1} = \text{treatment mean square} \qquad (9.30)$$

$$MS_E = \frac{SS_E}{N-k} = \text{error mean square} \qquad (9.31)$$

Both MS_M and MS_E are random variables that follow some type of a distribution model. The expected values of MS_M and MS_E (presented here without proofs) are:

$$E(MS_M) = \sigma^2 + \sum_{i=1}^{k} \frac{n_i(\mu_i - \mu)^2}{k-1} \qquad (9.32)$$

$$E(MS_E) = \sigma^2 \qquad (9.33)$$

in which σ^2 is the population common variance. To test the null hypothesis (H_0), we need to provide statistical evidence that $\mu_1 = \mu_2 = \ldots = \mu_k = \mu$. This means that the second term in Eq. 9.32 must be zero. This also implies that if H_0 is true, then MS_M and MS_E will be close in value and the ratio MS_M/MS_E will be close to unity. This ratio can be used as a test statistic. The ratio follows an F distribution with $\nu_1 = (k-1)$ and $\nu_2 = (N-k)$ degrees of freedom. The null hypothesis is rejected when the ratio is larger than the critical value of the F distribution at α significance and with ν_1 and ν_2 degrees of freedom. The test is always a right-tailed one. In practice, the ANOVA process is usually shown in tabular form as in Table 9.2. Furthermore, SS_T can easily be computed. Having computed SS_M, the value of SS_E can be computed as $SS_T - SS_M$.

Example 9.13

In the example of speed control methods for roadways, suppose we wish to determine whether there is enough evidence to show that the three methods (identified as Methods A, B, and C) result in an identical number of speed violations. Upon implementation of the three methods, the data on speed violations for the three groups of roadways is obtained and summarized in Table E9.13A.

Test the hypothesis that the mean values of the number of speed violations/month for the three methods are identical at $\alpha = 0.05$. Assume that the data in each group follows the normal distribution.

TABLE E9.13A   NUMBER OF SPEED VIOLATIONS/MONTH

Method A (flashing lights)	Method B (electronic board displaying motorist speed)	Method C (continuous patrol present)
6	3	8
3	4	9
7	3	2
6	8	4
10	2	3
11	10	3
4	9	3
0	4	6
3	6	1
7	8	3
2	6	
	3	
	0	
	1	
$n_1 = 11$	$n_2 = 14$	$n_3 = 10$
Total = 11 + 14 + 10 = 35		

Solution:

Based on the data presented in Table E9.13A

$M_1 = (6 + 3 + 7 + \ldots)/11 = 5.36$

$M_2 = (3 + 4 + 3 + \ldots)/14 = 4.79$
$M_3 = (8 + 9 + 2 + \ldots)/10 = 4.20$

Furthermore

$T_1 = 59$, $T_2 = 67$ $T_3 = 42$, and $T = 168$. The grand mean M is

$M = (6 + 3 + 7 + \ldots + 3 + 4 + 3 + \ldots + 8 + 9 + 2 + \ldots)/35 = 4.80$.

and

$$SS_T = \sum_{i=1}^{3}\sum_{j=1}^{n_i} X_{ij}^2 - \frac{T^2}{N} = 1112 - (168)^2/35 = 305.60$$

$$SS_M = \sum_{i=1}^{3}\left(\frac{T_i}{n_i}\right)^2 - \frac{T^2}{N} = (59)^2/11 + (67)^2/14 + (42)^2/10 - (168)^2/35 = 7.10$$

$SS_E = SS_T - SS_M = 305.60 - 7.10 = 298.50$

$MS_M = SS_M/(k - 1) = 7.10/(3 - 1) = 3.55$

$MS_E = SS_E/(N - k) = 298.50/(35 - 3) = 9.33$

The test statistics $F_{2,32} = MS_M/MS_E = 3.55/9.33 = 0.38$.

TABLE E9.13B   ANOVA SUMMARY

Variation Source	DF	SS	MS	F	f_α
Method (Treatment)	2	7.10	3.55	0.38	3.30
Error	32	298.50	9.33		
Total	34	305.60			

With the degrees of freedom $\nu_1 = 3 - 1 = 2$ and $\nu_2 = 35 - 3 = 32$, the critical value of the F distribution at $\alpha = 0.05$ is $f_\alpha = f_{0.05}(2,32) = 3.30$ (using interpolation). Since $F_{2,32} = 0.38 < f_\alpha = 3.30$, the null hypothesis H_0 cannot be rejected. Thus, the three methods result in a statistically identical number of speed violations. The results are summarized in Table E9.13B.

We emphasize that for ANOVA, the populations must follow the normal distribution. Thus the test of normality must be conducted before ANOVA. Furthermore, we need to test whether the population variances are statistically identical. The reader is referred to Bartlett's or Cochran's test for this purpose (see Guttman, et al., 1982; Milton and Tsokos, 1983).

9.4.2 Multiple Range Test

In conducting ANOVA for one-way classification, completely random design with fixed effect, we often need to conduct further analyses for the population means. This will be the case where the null hypothesis is rejected and there is evidence that the means are statistically different. Occasionally, the ANOVA results in a very small significance (small α) for the equality of the population means. For example, we find the test statistic F to be smaller than $f_{0.025}$ but larger than $f_{0.05}$. This indicates that the probability that the critical value becomes larger than F is small. In this situation, we may wish to further investigate the data to analyze where the differences between the two populations lie. A method used for this purpose (when H_0 in ANOVA is rejected) is called the *multiple range test*. The test was originally designed by D. B. Duncan for equal sample sizes, and later extended by C. Y. Kramer for different sample sizes.

Multiple Range Test for Equal Sample Sizes.   In this method, the population means are arranged in ascending order that $\mu_1 < \mu_2 < \ldots < \mu_k$. Considering any two population means such as μ_i and μ_j, where $j > i$, the corresponding difference $(\mu_j - \mu_i)$ is significant if it is larger than a value called the *shortest significant range*, R_p. The value of R_p is computed from the following equation:

$$R_p = r_p \sqrt{\frac{MS_E}{n}} \tag{9.34}$$

The subscript p identifies the sample means that are being compared. For example, if μ_i and μ_j are compared, $p = j - i + 1$. Furthermore, $n =$ common sample size for each population, and MS_E is the error mean square from ANOVA. The values of

TABLE E9.14A   BRIDGE RATINGS

Bridge Number	Engineer 1	Engineer 2	Engineer 3	Engineer 4
1	5	6	5	3
2	3	6	4	3
3	7	6	8	5
4	4	6	6	3
5	6	8	6	5
6	6	7	8	5
7	6	3	7	4
8	3	4	7	4
9	8	7	8	6
10	3	6	4	4
11	7	6	6	5
12	4	5	6	3
Total	12	12	12	12

r_p for a degree of freedom $\nu = N - k$ (the degree of freedom associated with MS_E) are provided in Table A.6 of Appendix A.

Example 9.14

In conducting an inspection of conditions of single span steel girder bridges, bridge engineers use a rating scale ranging from 0 to 9. A rating of 0 indicates the bridge is in a critical situation requiring an immediate attention; a rating of 9 means the bridge is in perfect condition. To investigate the differences in subjective ratings, four bridge engineers were invited to independently rate twelve bridges. The results are summarized in Table E9.14A. Assume that appropriate tests have been conducted and passed for the normality of the populations and the equality of variances.

(a) Conduct a one-way classification completely random design ANOVA with fixed effect to test the equality of the population means at $\alpha = 0.05$.

(b) Given the results in part a, conduct a multiple range test at $\alpha = 0.05$ to determine whether differences among means are statistically significant.

Solution:

Based on the data given in Table E9.14A;

$$T_1 = 62, T_2 = 70, T_3 = 75, \text{ and } T_4 = 50, \text{ and}$$
$$T = 257.$$

Also,

$$\sum_{i=1}^{4} \sum_{j=1}^{12} X_{ij}^2 = 1493$$

(a) The population means are: $62/12 = 5.17$, $70/12 = 5.83$, $75/12 = 6.25$, and $50/12 = 4.17$. Furthermore,

TABLE E9.14B   ANOVA SUMMARY

Variation Source	DF	SS	MS	F	f_α
Method (Treatment)	3	29.73	9.91	5.01	2.83
Error	44	87.25	1.98		
Total	47	116.98			

$$SS_M = \sum_{i=1}^{4} \frac{T_i^2}{n_i} - \frac{T^2}{N} = (62)^2/12 + (70)^2/12 + (75)^2/12 + (50)^2/12 - (257)^2/48 = 29.73$$

$$SS_T = \sum_{i=1}^{4} \sum_{j=1}^{12} X_{ij}^2 - \frac{T^2}{N} = 1493 - (257)^2/48 = 116.98$$

$$SS_E = SS_T - SS_M = 116.98 - 29.73 = 87.25.$$

With $\nu_1 = 4 - 1 = 3$, and $\nu_2 = 48 - 4 = 44$,

$$MS_M = SS_M/3 = 29.73/3 = 9.91$$
$$MS_E = SS_E/44 = 87.25/44 = 1.98$$
$$F_{3,44} = MS_M/MS_E = 9.91/1.98 = 5.01$$
At $\alpha = 0.05$, $f_\alpha(3,44) = 2.83$.

As is evident, since $F_{3,44} > f_\alpha$, the null hypothesis is rejected. This means there is not enough evidence to prove that the means are identical. The results of ANOVA is provided in Table E9.14B.

(b) To further investigate the source of variation, we must conduct a multiple range test. We first rearrange means in ascending order. Thus,

$$m_1 = 4.17 \qquad m_2 = 5.17 \qquad m_3 = 5.83 \qquad m_4 = 6.25$$

(Engineer 4)   (Engineer 1)   (Engineer 2)   (Engineer 3)

Comparing m_2 and m_1, $(m_2 - m_1) = 5.17 - 4.17 = 1.0$. At $\alpha = 0.05$, $r_p = r_2 \approx 2.85$ (by interpolation) for $\nu = 44$. Also $r_3 = 3.00$ and $r_4 = 3.096$ (for $\nu = 44$). The corresponding R_p values are:

$$R_p = r_p \sqrt{\frac{MS_E}{n}}$$

$$R_2 = 2.85 \sqrt{\frac{1.98}{12}} = 1.16$$

$$R_3 = 3.00 \sqrt{\frac{1.98}{12}} = 1.22$$

$$R_4 = 3.096 \sqrt{\frac{1.98}{12}} = 1.26$$

Comparing m_1 and m_2, $(m_2 - m_1) = 1.0 < 1.16$. Thus the difference is not significant. Comparing m_1 and m_3, $(m_3 - m_1) = 1.66 > 1.22$. Thus the difference *is* significant.

TABLE E9.14C   MULTIPLE RANGE TEST SUMMARY

Test Group	Difference (d)	p	R_p	Is $d > R_p$ (?)	Summary
I	$(m_2 - m_1) = 1.0$	2	1.16	No	
	$(m_3 - m_1) = 1.66$	3	1.22	Yes[*]	$\underline{m_1\ m_2\ m_3\ m_4}$
II	$(m_3 - m_2) = 0.66$	2	1.16	No	
	$(m_4 - m_2) = 1.08$	3	1.22	No	$\underline{m_2\ m_3\ m_4}$
III	$(m_4 - m_3) = 0.42$	2	1.16	No	$\underline{m_3\ m_4}$

[*]Difference is significant.

Comparing m_2 and m_3, $(m_3 - m_2) = 0.66 < 1.16$. Thus the difference is not significant.

Comparing m_2 and m_4, $(m_4 - m_2) = 1.08 < 1.22$. Thus the difference is not significant.

Comparing m_3 and m_4, $(m_4 - m_3) = 0.42 < 1.16$. Thus the difference is not significant.

The results are summarized in Table E9.14C. As shown in the table, if differences are not significant, an underline is used to connect the means.

Note that in group I, no comparison between m_1 and m_4 is made. This is because m_3 and m_1 showed a significant difference; and since $m_3 < m_4$, the difference between m_4 and m_1 will be significant. As shown in Table E9.14C, the difference between m_1 and m_4 and between m_1 and m_3 are significant. This means $m_1 \neq m_4$, and $m_1 \neq m_3$. No other differences have been detected. The significance level ($\alpha = 0.05$) indicates there is 0.05 probability that at least one of these conclusions is incorrect.

Multiple Range Test for Unequal Sample Sizes.   Duncan's method was extended by C. Y. Kramer in 1956 for cases with unequal sample sizes. In this modified method, the shortest significant range is adjusted as follows:

$$R'_p = \sqrt{MS_E}r_p \tag{9.35}$$

The test statistic is also modified as follows:

$$d' = (m_j - m_i)\sqrt{\frac{2n_in_j}{n_i + n_j}} \tag{9.36}$$

in which n_i and n_j are the sample size for the data sets i and j, respectively. Again, the means are arranged in ascending order; thus $m_j > m_i$. The significant studentized range r_p is obtained as before for α significance and a degree of freedom ν, where

$$\nu = \sum_{i=1}^{k} (n_i - 1) \tag{9.37}$$

in which k is the number of populations (data sets). If $d' > R'_p$, the difference between m_j and m_i is significant.

Example 9.15

Fly ash is an additive used in manufacturing high-strength concrete. Suppose three different types of fly ash are tested on several samples of concrete in three batches. Upon testing the materials, the compressive strengths are obtained in a laboratory. All other parameters (i.e., water cement ratio, aggregate type) are identical for all samples. Assume normality and equality of variance tests for the three populations have been conducted and passed. The results obtained for the three batches using ANOVA are:

$$MS_E = 4.10$$

For batch I, number of cylinders tested, $n_1 = 12$, the mean strength $m_1 = 49.5$ MPa.

For batch II, number of cylinders tested, $n_2 = 13$, the mean strength $m_2 = 64.1$ MPa.

For batch III, number of cylinders tested, $n_3 = 11$, the mean strength $m_3 = 68.6$ MPa.

Conduct a multiple range test to further investigate whether the differences among the means are significant at $\alpha = 0.05$.

Solution:

The degree of freedom $\nu = (12 - 1) + (13 - 1) + (11 - 1) = 33$.

At $\alpha = 0.05$ and $\nu = 33$, $r_2 = 2.885$. The corresponding R'_p value is $R'_2 = \sqrt{4.10} \times 2.885 = 5.84$
Comparing m_1 and m_2,

$$d' = (64.1 - 49.5)\sqrt{\tfrac{2 \times 12 \times 13}{12 + 13}} = 51.6 > R'_2 = 5.84 \text{ Difference is significant.}$$

Comparing m_2 and m_3,

$$d' = (68.6 - 64.1)\sqrt{\tfrac{2 \times 13 \times 11}{13 + 11}} = 15.5 > R'_2 = 5.84 \text{ Difference is significant.}$$

The conclusion is that $m_1 \neq m_2 \neq m_3$. The results are shown as:

$$\underline{m_1}\ \underline{m_2}\ \underline{m_3}$$

9.4.3 Random Effect

In certain cases, the k data groups are selected from a larger set of populations. Thus, the procedure will not be one with fixed effect. Rather, it is one with *random effect*. A somewhat different method is then used to investigate whether some variability exists among the data groups within the larger set of population. As an example, consider the statistics on the number of accidents per year in medium-sized construction sites in eight Midwestern states. We randomly select three states for conducting a test on the variability in the number of accidents per year in construction companies in Midwestern states. The procedure to conduct this test can be found in Milton and Tsokos (1983) and Walpole, et al. (1998).

9.5 DISTRIBUTION-FREE METHODS

So far, a basic requirement for statistical procedures which we have discussed is that the sample data must follow a normal distribution. In certain problems, the normality test does not pass; as such, we face the question of whether we can still use these methods. This is especially the case when the sample size is small ($n < 10$). In general, if the normality assumption is not valid, the use of these statistical methods will lead to results that may not be reliable. Distribution-free methods may offer a better solution. These methods generally require ranking the data and deriving the test statistics using simple counting methods. In this section, several such methods are presented for: (a) hypothesis testing; (b) comparing two populations using paired data; and (c) comparing two independent populations. These are parallel to the statistical methods discussed in Section 9.3.

9.5.1 Test of Location for One Sample Data

Recall that when normality assumption is valid, the population mean is the measure of the center of location of the distribution of the random variable. In this case, the mean and median are theoretically at the same location along the x-axis of the distribution function. In distribution-free methods, the center of location is usually the median. In general, the median represents the *50-percentile* value. Denoting the median as M, for a continuous random variable $P(X \leq M) = 1/2$. A more general description of the median is defined by the two following expressions:

$$P(X < M) \leq 1/2 \quad \text{and} \quad P(X \leq M) \geq 1/2$$

The idea of a test location is to test the median of a population against a hypothesized value such as M_0. The hypothesis testing will involve the following:

$H_0: M \leq M_0$	$H_0: M \geq M_0$	$H_0: M = M_0$
$H_1: M > M_0$	$H_1: M < M_0$	$H_1: M \neq M_0$
Right-tailed	Left-tailed	Two-tailed

Several methods are available to test the median hypotheses; one is called *sign test*, which is based on the binomial distribution for the number of sample values that are smaller than M_0; the other is the *Wilcoxon signed-rank test*. The latter is discussed here.

9.5.2 Wilcoxon Signed-Rank Test

The null hypothesis in this test is that the distribution of the data is symmetric about M_0. In a set of data consisting of n sample values $X_1, X_2, \ldots, X_n$, the differences from M_0 are $(X_1 - M_0), (X_2 - M_0), \ldots, (X_n - M_0)$. For the null hypothesis to be true, these differences must be from a random variable that is symmetric about zero. In conducting the test, the absolute values of these differences are ranked in ascending order. The smallest absolute value of the difference receives a rank 1, the largest n. If in conducting the ranking a tie occurs, the average of the ranks will be used for the tied scores. Furthermore, if $X_i - M_0$ is negative, the corresponding rank will be assigned a negative sign. As a result, if we designate the rank for $(X_i - M_0)$ as r_i, some r_i will be negative. All positive ranks are added together to form a value W_+. The absolute value of the sum of negative ranks is also computed and denoted as W_-, i.e.,

$$W_+ = \sum r_i \quad \text{for all positive ranks} \qquad (9.38)$$
$$W_- = |\sum r_i| \quad \text{for all negative ranks} \qquad (9.39)$$

TABLE E9.16

X_i	$(X_i - M_0)$	Rank (r_i)	Sign
4	−2.7	7	−
8	1.3	4.5*	+
8	1.3	4.5*	+
3	−3.7	8	−
5	−1.7	6	−
6	−0.7	2	−
7.5	0.8	3	+
7	0.3	1	+

*Tied scores

If the null hypothesis is true, then W_+ and W_- should be about the same. The test statistic is W which is the smaller of W_+ and W_-, i.e.,

$$W = min(W_+, W_-) \qquad (9.40)$$

This value is then compared against a critical value from the table of values for the Wilcoxon signed-rank test (see Table A.7 in Appendix A). If W is equal to or smaller than the critical Wilcoxon value, then the null hypothesis is rejected.

Example 9.16

In conducting subjective ratings for a steel girder in single span, two-lane bridges, the median rating is believed to be 6.7 (a scale of 0 to 9 is used for bridge rating). Eight such bridges are rated for their steel girders. The results are:

4   8   8   3   5   6   7.5   7

Conduct a Wilcoxon test for the null hypothesis at $\alpha = 0.05$.

Solution:

In this problem $M_0 = 6.7$. Table E9.16 summarizes the data given, X_i, $(X_i - M_0)$, and the ranks. Note that instead of ranks 4 and 5, the average (4.5) is listed because of the two tied scores for $(X_i - M_0) = 1.3$. From Eqs. 9.38 and 9.39,

$$W_+ = 4.5 + 4.5 + 3 + 1 = 13$$
$$W_- = |-7 - 8 - 6 - 2| = 23$$

The smaller of the two is $W = 13$. At $\alpha = 0.05$ (i.e., $p = 0.05$ for one-sided test in Table A.7 of Appendix A) and for $n = 8$, the critical value for the test will be 6. Since $W = 13 > 6$, the null hypothesis cannot be rejected and there is sufficient evidence that the median is equal to 6.7.

9.5.3 Wilcoxon Signed-Rank Test for Paired Data

In this case there are two populations from two continuous random variables with paired sample values (X_1, Y_1), (X_2, Y_2), . . ., (X_n, Y_n). The difference between the paired values (i.e., $X_i - Y_i$ for $i = 1, 2, . . ., n$) is also from a continuous random variable. The null hypothesis in this case is that the differences are symmetric about zero. To conduct this test, the absolute values of the differences are arranged in ascending order. They are ranked from 1 to n. A negative sign is then assigned to the ranks (r_i) that correspond to the differences that are negative. Using Eqs. 9.38 and 9.39, W_+ and W_- are computed. The test statistic W is the smaller of W_+ and W_-. If W is smaller than the critical values from the Wilcoxon table, then the null hypothesis is rejected.

In assigning the ranks, r_i tied differences will receive the average rank for the tied values. If a difference becomes zero, its rank is usually considered to be negative. This will increase the size of W_- and thus make it harder to reject the null hypothesis.

Example 9.17

In the evaluation of construction productivity, an engineer believes that if daily work shift hours are shortened by 0.5 hours, there will be an increase in productivity. Productivity in this example is measured as the ratio of the volume of work completed to the volume of work scheduled to be completed in a given period of time. In a survey, eight construction companies agree to change their daily work shift hours by 0.5 hours. The engineer conducts a research and compiles the data presented in Table E9.17A.

TABLE E9.17A   CONSTRUCTION PRODUCTIVITY (%) BEFORE AND AFTER DAILY WORK SHIFT HOUR MODIFICATION

Case Number	Productivity Before Modification (X_i)	Productivity After Modification (Y_i)	Difference ($X_i - Y_i$)
1	84	73	11
2	80	86	-6
3	78	90	-12
4	85	85	0
5	90	88	2
6	76	71	5
7	85	90	-5
8	78	81	-3

Determine if there is enough evidence to prove that the modification of the daily work shift will improve productivity using the Wilcoxon signed-rank test by pairing data.

Solution:

Table E9.17B summarizes the differences in construction productivity, the ranking and sign used for the ranks.

Notice that for $X_i - X_j = 0$, a negative sign is assigned to the corresponding rank. Furthermore, ranks 4 and 5 are tied; thus the average (4.5) is used for both, although one received a negative sign and one a positive sign. From Table E9.17B:

$$W_+ = \text{sum of all positive ranks} = 7 + 2 + 4.5 = 13.5$$

$$W_- = \text{absolute value of sum of all negative ranks} = |-6 - 8 - 1 - 4.5 - 3| = 22.5$$

Thus $W = 13.5$. Using $\alpha = 0.05$ (i.e., $p = 0.05$) and $n = 8$, the Wilcoxon critical value

TABLE E9.17B

Case Number	Difference $(X_i - X_j)$	Rank r_i	Rank Sign
1	11	7	+
2	-6	6	-
3	-12	8	-
4	0	1	-
5	2	2	+
6	5	4.5	+
7	-5	4.5	-
8	-3	3	-

from Table A.7 of the Appendix A is 6. Since $W = 13.5 > 6$, the null hypothesis cannot be rejected. This means that the reduction in daily work shift hours will not increase the productivity significantly.

9.5.4 Wilcoxon Rank-Sum Test for Unmatched Data

In this case, $X_1, X_2, \ldots, X_m$ and $Y_1, Y_2, \ldots, Y_n$ represent data from two populations with different sample sizes m and n where $m < n$. The null hypothesis is that these populations are identical. If the two populations are different in location, then the null hypothesis is likely to be rejected. The procedure in this case is to pool the populations to form $m + n$ observations. Then the pooled data is arranged in ascending order and ranked from 1 to $m + n$. The test statistic W is the sum of ranks for X_i populations (the smaller-sized population). This decision can well be explained considering the case where X_i is located above or below the location for the Y_i population. If X_i is below, then the X_i values will have smaller ranks. Thus a small value for W will be obtained. On the other hand, if X_i is above Y_i then the X_i values will have larger ranks. This will result in a large W. The null hypothesis is either too small or too large compared to the critical values for this test. Thus, it cannot be rejected if W is within the critical Wilcoxon values based on a two-tailed test. However, if we suspect that the X_i values are above the Y_i values, then the critical Wilcoxon value will be based on a one-sided (right-tailed) test. In this case if W is less than this critical value, then the null hypothesis cannot be rejected. On the other hand, if we suspect that the X_i values are below the Y_i values, then the critical Wilcoxon value will be based on a one-sided (left-tailed) test, and the null hypothesis cannot be rejected if W is larger than this critical value. The critical Wilcoxon values for the rank-sum test are summarized in Table A.8 of Appendix A. Notice that two critical values are listed for each α (or p value, as listed in the table). For example, if $\alpha = 0.05$, $m = 7$ and $n = 10$, the critical right-tailed value is 80; whereas the critical left-tailed value is 46. However, at $\alpha = 0.05$, $m = 7$ and $n = 10$, the two-tailed critical values are 43 and 83.

Example 9.18

In comparing the soil bearing capacities for two adjacent sites, 7 samples from Site 1 and 9 samples from Site 2 are taken and tested. The corresponding capacities in KN/m^2 are summarized in Table E9.18A.

Conduct a Wilcoxon test by pooling the data to test whether the two populations are identical at $\alpha = 0.05$.

TABLE E9.18A
SOIL BEARING
CAPACITY
(KN/m^2)

Site 1	Site 2
190	185
174	147
184	193
136	110
200	90
188	117
153	178
	159
	165
$m = 7$	$n = 9$

TABLE E9.18B   RANKING FOR
SITE 1 AND SITE 2 POOLED DATA

Sample Values	Group	Rank
90	2	1
110	2	2
117	2	3
136	1	4
147	2	5
153	1	6
159	2	7
165	2	8
174	1	9
178	2	10
184	1	11
185	2	12
188	1	13
190	1	14
193	2	15
200	1	16

Solution:

After pooling the data, we arranged them in ascending order and ranked them. The results are summarized in Table E9.18B.

Adding the ranks for Site (Group) 1,

$$W = 4 + 6 + 9 + 11 + 13 + 14 + 16 = 73.$$

From Table A.8 of Appendix A for $m = 7$ and $n = 9$ and at $\alpha = 0.05$, the critical values of the Wilcoxon two-tailed test are 41 and 78. Since $W = 73$ is bounded by 41 and 78, the null hypothesis cannot be rejected. This means the two populations are statistically identical. If we suspect that Site I bearing capacity value tends to be larger than those in Site II, then we use a right-tailed test. In this case for $\alpha = 0.05$, $m = 7$ and $n = 9$, the critical Wilcoxon value is 76. Since $W = 73$ is less than this critical value, then the null hypothesis cannot be rejected; as such, the two populations are identical.

It is noted that the Wilcoxon test is usually applicable when we know populations are symmetric. If we are not sure of this, then other tests of locations, for example the *sign test* (Guttman, et al., 1982; Milton and Tsokos, 1983; and Walpole, et al., 1988) may be used instead of the Wilcoxon test.

9.5.5 Tests for Several Populations

There are other tests available that can be used for comparing k populations. One such test is the Kruskal-Wallis test used for k populations for both matched and unmatched data. The details of these tests can be found in Milton and Tsokos (1983).

9.6 REGRESSION AND CORRELATION ANALYSIS

In Chapter 7 we discussed the dependence of a random variable on another. A correlation coefficient was introduced and described the degree of linear correlation between a dependent variable and independent variable. In many engineering problems, we may have to go beyond simply finding the correlation. In fact, the interest may be in investigating whether a relationship exists that would describe the dependent variable Y in terms of the independent variable X. It is noted that the basis for establishing such a relationship is a set of data compiled for the dependent and independent variables. A *regression analysis* refers to the analysis of data to arrive at this relationship. The correlation and regression analyses are conceptually different. However, they are related. Any established relation between Y and X is within the range of data compiled. The validity of such relation is evaluated through the correlation between Y and X.

In problems where only one independent variable is involved, the regression analysis is called *simple regression*. When several independent variables X_i ($i = 1$ to q) are involved, the regression is said to be *multiple*. Furthermore, recall that the correlation coefficient (ρ) described in Chapter 7 is a measure of linear correlation between X and Y. As a result, if a non-linear relation between Y and X exists, the correlation coefficient will be substantially less than 1 (recall that $|\rho| = 1$ is an indication of a perfect linear correlation between X and Y). In most engineering applications, the regression analysis is primarily conducted to arrive at an empirical equation for the dependent variable. The equation is then adapted for use in design and decision-making problems when the exact relation between Y and X is not known or cannot easily be found through theoretical formulations.

Regression analysis problems can be classified into one of the following cases:

- Linear regression of the dependent variable Y on the independent variable X.
- Linear regression of the dependent variable Y on q independent variables X_i $(i = 1, 2, \ldots, q)$.
- Non-linear regression of Y on X or Y on several independent variables X_i.

In addition, we may be interested in investigating the correlation between Y and X (or between Y and X_i) in these cases. When the data set involves ranks or the sample size is small enough that it can easily be ranked, a measure of linear correlation can also be obtained using the ranks. In any correlation and regression analysis, it is important to note that the statistical samples play a crucial role. A regression equation is only valid within the range of the data collected. As such, one should not extrapolate the regression relationship beyond the boundaries of the compiled data. The correlation coefficient represents a statistical parameter for which confidence levels may be established.

We begin the discussion with simple linear regression analysis. This is followed by the non-linear analysis and a comprehensive discussion on correlation analysis.

9.6.1 Simple Linear Regression Analysis

This problem involves regression analysis of a dependent variable Y on an independent variable X. In theory, we will be interested in finding $E(Y|x)$, which yields the expected value of Y given a specific outcome for X such as x. We can write:

$$E(Y|x) = a + bx \qquad (9.41)$$

in which a and b are constants. The estimates for a and b are found using the *least square* analysis. Suppose in a data acquisition session, we compile n pairs of sample values for Y and X. These pairs will be (x_1,y_1), (x_2,y_2), $\ldots$, (x_n,y_n). Each x_i corresponds to a specific value for Y such as y_i. The pair of values for X and Y are obtained in an experiment, through field data collection, by surveys and so on. A plot of y_i versus x_i often appears in the form of a cluster of points. If a strong linear correlation between X and Y exists, the data will cluster close to each other and show a linear trend. Very weak correlation between X and Y will result in a large scatter in the plotted points and no specific trend between the two. Figure 9.5 shows these two situations. Assuming the exact values for the constants a and b are known, Eq. 9.41 can also be plotted along with the scatter plot of y_i versus x_i. As seen in Figure 9.6, for any given value for X such as x_i, there are two values for Y. These are y_i, which is obtained from the data, and y_i^*, which is from Eq. 9.41. The difference between the two values $\Delta_i = y_i^* - y_i$ is called the *residue*. In conducting the least square method, the sum of square values of the residues is minimized to obtain estimates for a and b. These estimates will represent the *best-fit* equation for the data. Denoting the sum of squares of the residues as SS_E,

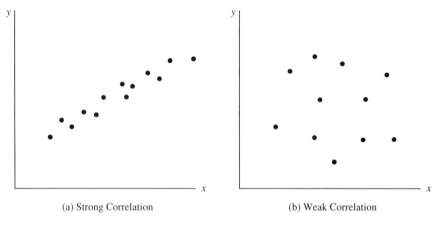

(a) Strong Correlation   (b) Weak Correlation

Figure 9.5   Strong vs. weak condition. (a) Strong correlation; (b) weak correlation.

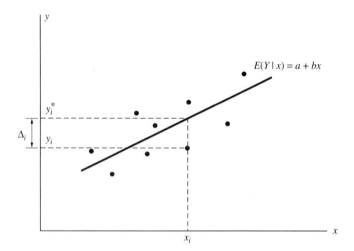

Figure 9.6   Regression line.

$$SS_E = \sum_{i=1}^{n} (y_i^* - y_1)^2 = \sum_{i=1}^{n} (a + bx_i - y_i)^2 \tag{9.42}$$

The minimization involves the following operations:

$$\frac{\partial SS_E}{\partial a} = 0$$

$$\frac{\partial SS_E}{\partial b} = 0$$

These will result in the following two equations for a and b. Note that because the equations provide only the estimates for a and b, the symbols $\hat{a}$ and $\hat{b}$ are used to indicate that these are only estimates.

$$\hat{a} = m_y - \hat{b}m_x \tag{9.43}$$

$$\hat{b} = \frac{n\sum_{i=1}^{n} x_i y_i - \sum_{i=1}^{n} x_i \sum_{i=1}^{n} y_i}{n\sum_{i=1}^{n} x_i^2 - \left(\sum_{i=1}^{n} x_i\right)^2} \tag{9.44}$$

Here, m_x and m_y are estimates of mean values for X and Y, respectively (see Eq. 8.10). Other variations to Eq. 9.44 can also be found. The proof of Eqs. 9.43 and 9.44 are left to the reader as an exercise problem. Notice that $Y|x$ is a random variable whose mean value is $E(Y|x)$. An unbiased estimate for the variance of this random variable is denoted by $S_{Y|x}^2$ and is computed as follows:

$$Var(Y|x) = S_{Y|x}^2 = \frac{1}{n-2}\sum_{i=1}^{n} (y_i^* - y_i)^2 = \frac{1}{n-2}\sum_{i=1}^{n} (a + bx - y_i)^2$$

$$= \frac{SS_E}{n-2} \tag{9.45}$$

The standard deviation of $Y|x$ (i.e., $s_{Y|x}$) is sometimes shown with two parallel lines along with the regression line on the $Y - X$ graph. We must emphasize that this standard deviation is different from s_y, since s_y is the standard deviation of Y without any reference to X. As it is explained in the next section the two standard deviations, i.e. $s_{Y|x}$, and s_y, are related to each other through the correlation coefficient.

9.6.2 Correlation Coefficient

Recall from Section 7.3.2 that the linear correlation coefficient is computed from Eq. 7.36. In theory, Eq. 7.36 requires information on the joint probability density (or mass) function of X and Y. An estimate for ρ can be found using the data compiled for X and Y. Assuming a uniform joint probability distribution for X and Y, the covariance of X and Y can be written as:

$$Cov(X,Y) = E[(X - \mu_X)(Y - \mu_Y)] = \frac{1}{n}\sum_{i=1}^{n} (x_i - m_x)(y_i - m_y) \tag{9.46a}$$

An unbiased estimate for the covariance can be found when $n - 1$ instead of n is used:

$$Cov(X,Y) = \frac{1}{n-1}\sum_{i=1}^{n} (x_i - m_x)(y_i - m_y) \tag{9.46b}$$

Using s_x and s_y, i.e., the estimates for the standard deviation of X and Y, and denoting the correlation coefficient as r as an estimate of ρ, in light of Eq. 7.36:

$$r = \frac{\sum_{i=1}^{n} (x_i - m_x)(y_i - m_y)}{\sqrt{\sum_{i=1}^{n} (x_i - m_x)^2 \sum_{i=1}^{n} (y_i - m_y)^2}} \tag{9.47a}$$

or

$$r = \frac{1}{n-1} \frac{\sum\limits_{i=1}^{n} x_i y_i - n(m_x m_y)}{S_x S_y}$$ (9.47b)

From Eqs. 9.44 and 9.47, it can be shown that:

$$r = \frac{\sum\limits_{i=1}^{n}(x_i - m_x)(y_i - m_y)}{\sum\limits_{i=1}^{n}(x_i - m_x)^2} \frac{S_x}{S_y} = b\frac{S_x}{S_y}$$ (9.47c)

Considering the unbiased estimate for $s_{Y|x}$ (Eq. 9.45), and in light of Eq. 9.47c, it can be shown that:

$$s_{Y|x}^2 = \frac{n-1}{n-2}s_y^2(1 - r^2)$$ (9.48)

Solving this equation for r^2

$$r^2 = 1 - \frac{n-2}{n-1}\frac{S_{Y|x}^2}{S_y^2}$$ (9.47d)

For large values of n, the ratio $(n - 2)/(n - 1) \approx 1$ and

$$r^2 = 1 - \frac{s_{Y|x}^2}{s_y^2}$$ (9.47e)

For a perfect correlation $r = 1$ and $s_{Y|x} = 0$. This means that there will be no scatter about the regression line. However, it is emphasized that this does not mean s_y is zero because s_y is an estimate of the standard deviation of Y without any reference to its relationship to X.

Example 9.19

In studying the productivity in construction sites discussed earlier, we want to establish a linear regression equation between the productivity (dependent variable) and the work shift hours/day (independent variable). The productivity is measured as the percentage of work completed as opposed to the scheduled work *to be* completed within a specific time period. In a survey, nine observations were made and the results in Table E9.19A were obtained.

(a) Establish the regression equation $E(Y|x) = a + bx$.
(b) Estimate the standard deviation of $Y|x$.
(c) Estimate the correlation coefficient.

Solution:

(a) Equations 9.43 and 9.44 are used for estimating a and b. Table E9.19B summarizes the statistical values needed for a and b computation. For simplicity, we use a and b to represent estimates (without the symbol ^).

$$b = \frac{9 \times 5915 - 72.5 \times 745}{9 \times 605.75 - (72.5)^2} = -3.977$$

$$m_x = 72.5/9 = 8.056 \qquad m_y = 745/9 = 82.778$$

$$a = 82.778 + 3.977 \times 8.056 = 114.817$$

TABLE E9.19A PRODUCTIVITY VERSUS WORK SHIFT HOURS/DAY

Productivity (%), Y	Work Shift Hours/Day, X
90	7
85	6.5
75	9.5
83	7
88	7
78	10
90	7.5
87	7
69	11

TABLE E9.19B

x_i	y_i	x_i^2	y_i^2	$x_i \times y_i$
7	90	49	8100	630
6.5	85	42.25	7225	552.5
9.5	75	90.25	5625	712.5
7	83	49	6889	581
7	88	49	7744	616
10	78	100	6084	780
7.5	90	56.25	8100	675
7	87	49	7569	609
11	69	121	4761	759
$\Sigma x_i = 72.5$	$\Sigma y_i = 745$	$\Sigma x_1^2 = 605.75$	$\Sigma y_1^2 = 62097$	$\Sigma x_1 \times y_i = 5915$

$$a = 82.778 + 3.977 \times 8.056 = 114.817$$
$$E(Y|x) = 114.817 - 3.977x.$$

(b) In this part we utilize Eq. 9.45. By expanding this equation we obtain

$$Var(Y|x) = (na^2 + b^2\Sigma x_i^2 + \Sigma y_i^2 + 2ab\Sigma x_i - 2a\Sigma y_i - 2b\Sigma x_i y_i)/(n-2)$$
$$= [9(114.817)^2 + (-3.977)^2(605.75) + (62097) + 2(114.817)(-3.977)(72.5)$$
$$-2 \times (114.817)(745) - 2(-3.977)(5915)]/7 = 84.0/7 = 12.00$$

The standard deviation $s_{Y|x} = 3.46$.

(c) In this part we can either use Eq. 9.47a or 9.47b. We first must compute s_x and s_y.
$s_x^2 = (\Sigma x_i^2 - nm_x^2)/(n-1) = [605.75 - 9(8.056)^2]/8 = 2.707$, and $s_x = 1.645$. Similarly, $s_y^2 = [62097 - 9(82.778)^2]/8 = 53.403$, and $s_y = 7.308$. Thus using Eq. 9.47b
$$r = [(5915 - 9 \times 8.056 \times 82.778)/(1.645 \times 7.308)]/(9-1) = -0.90.$$

Figure E9.19 presents the data and the regression line. Notice that $s_{Y|x} = 3.46$ is shown as two parallel lines above and below the regression line.

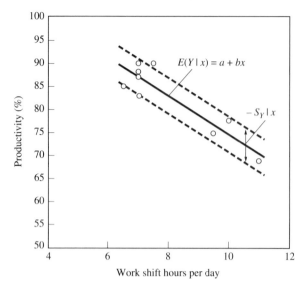

Figure E9.19
Productivity vs. work
shift hours per day.

9.6.3 Strength of Linear Correlation

The least square method used in establishing a straight line fit to the X,Y data is merely a mathematical tool that always results in a linear equation between $E(Y|x)$ and x. However, one must use this equation with caution, since in reality there may be no linear relation between Y and X, or at best the linear relation may be weak. It is therefore necessary to investigate how well the straight line obtained through the least square analysis fits the data. Of course, the correlation coefficient can be used as a measure to determine how well the linear equation fits the data. More elaborate methods are conducted by employing a statistic called the *coefficient of determination* and by using an analysis of variance. Both these methods are explained in this section.

In Section 9.6.2, we established a direct relationship between the estimates of b (i.e., the slope of the regression line) and r (see Eq.9.47c). Equation 9.47c indicates that b and r always have the same algebraic sign. The positive values of r will always be accompanied by a rise in the regression line (positive slope), while the negative r will be accompanied by a negative slope. We further derived an expression between the correlation coefficient r and the random variation in Y about x (as denoted by $s^2_{Y|x}$) and the variation in Y alone (as denoted by s^2_y). The following notations are introduced:

$$S_{xy} = \sum_{i=1}^{n} (x_i - m_x)(y_i - m_y)$$

and

$$S_{xx} = \sum_{i=1}^{n} (x_i - m_x)^2$$

and

$$S_{yy} = \sum_{i=1}^{n} (y_i - m_y)^2$$

and it is known that $SS_E \sim s^2_{Y|x}$ and $S_{yy} \sim s^2_y$, Eq. 9.47e can also be written as

$$r^2 = 1 - \frac{SS_E}{S_{yy}} = \frac{S_{yy} - SS_E}{S_{yy}}. \tag{9.47f}$$

The numerator in this equation is a measure of variability in Y that concerns the linear relationship with X. This is to say that r^2 is the ratio of the measure of variation in linearity of Y to the measure of total variation in Y (without any reference to X). This ratio is called the *coefficient of determination*. The maximum value for this ratio is 1. If r^2 is large (closer to 1), it can be concluded that there is a strong linear relation between X and Y. Smaller r^2 values (i.e., below 0.4) indicate a somewhat weaker linear relation.

The analysis of variance can also be used as a means to test whether the straight line equation obtained for $Y|x$ is associated with statistically significant variation in Y. To conduct ANOVA, we need to identify components such that the sources of the variability can be recognized through these components. Recall from Section 9.6.1 that the sum of squares of the difference between the observed values of Y and those from the linear equation was shown as SS_E, where

$$SS_E = \sum_{i=1}^{n} [y_i - (a + bx_i)]^2$$

It can be shown that

$$SS_E = S_{yy} - bS_{xy}$$

or

$$S_{yy} = bS_{xy} + SS_E$$

Thus the total variation in Y (i.e., S_{yy}) is now written in terms of two components. These are: (1) the variation that is attributed to the linear regression between Y and X (i.e., bS_{xy}); and (2) the *error,* or *residual, sum of squares* (unexplained error). Denoting bS_{xy} as SS_R, we notice that if the relationship between X and Y is very close to linear, then most of the variability in Y will be in SS_R. The relative size of SS_R to SS_E can then be used as a basis for ANOVA.

In order to develop a model to conduct ANOVA, we assume that k specific values of the random variable X are selected. These are $x_1, x_2, \ldots, x_k$. Considering the regression of Y on X, there will be k random variables $Y|x_i$ where $i = 1, 2, \ldots, k$. At this point, we assume that these random variables are independent normal with a common variance σ^2. If the regression of Y on X is linear, then the mean values of these k random variables must be all located on the line represented by the regression equation. The regression line representing the mean values can be expressed with an expression $\mu_{Y|x} = \alpha + \beta x$ as shown in Figure 9.7. We further assume that a random sample of size n_i is selected from each normal distribution describing the random variable $Y|x_i$. If y_{ij} is denoted as the jth element of the random sample i, then it has a mean value equal to $\alpha + \beta x_i$ and a variance equal to σ^2. There will also

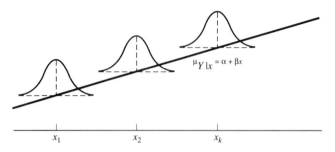

Figure 9.7   Regression line representing the mean value.

be an observed value associated with Y_{ij}; however, this observed value will differ from the mean of Y_{ij} by a random amount Δ_{ij}. Denoting this observed value as Y^*_{ij}, we can write

$$Y^*_{ij} = \alpha + \beta x_i + \Delta_{ij} \tag{9.49}$$

This equation is valid for $i = 1, 2, \ldots, k$ and $j = 1, 2, \ldots, n_i$. Note that if $\beta = 0$, then the variation in Y will not be due to the linear model since all variation in Y will be random. On the other hand, if $\beta \neq 0$, Eq. 9.49 will depend on x_i. This means that a portion of variation in Y will be due to the regression line. The null and alternate hypotheses can then be written as follows:

$$H_0: \beta = 0$$
$$H_1: \beta \neq 0$$

If the null hypothesis cannot be rejected, it indicates a lack of linear regression at the significance level tested. However, if the null hypothesis *is* rejected, then there is enough statistical evidence to suggest that the linear regression is valid.

To establish the test statistics for ANOVA, we utilize SS_R and SS_E, as described earlier, to define: (1) MS_R, which is called the *regression mean square,* and (2) MS_E, which is referred to as the *error mean square.* The degrees of freedom associated with these statistics are 1 and $n - 2$, respectively, where $n = n_1 + n_2 + \ldots n_k$. We can thus write:

$$MS_R = SS_R/1 \quad \text{and} \quad MS_E = SS_E/(n - 2) \tag{9.50}$$

in which $SS_R = bS_{xy}$ and $SS_E = S_{yy} - SS_R$.

Conceivably, if the null hypothesis is true, then the observed value of the ratio MS_R/MS_E will be close to 1. If the null hypothesis is rejected, the ratio is said to be *inflated,* and as such, the regression equation is linear. This ratio will follow an F distribution function with degrees of freedom equal to 1 and $n - 2$. In practice, the necessary calculations for ANOVA are arranged in tabular form as shown in Table 9.3.

Example 9.20

In Example 9.19;
(a) Discuss the strength of the linear regression.
(b) Conduct an ANOVA to further investigate the statistical evidence of the linear relationship between Y and X.

TABLE 9.3   ANOVA FOR LINEAR REGRESSION

Variation Source	Degrees of Freedom	Sum of Squares SS	Mean Square MS	F
Regression	1	$SS_R = bS_{xy}$	$SS_R/1$	MS_R/MS_E
Error	$n - 2$	$SS_E = S_{yy} - bS_{xy}$	$SS_E/(n - 2)$	
Total	$n - 1$	S_{yy}		

TABLE E9.20   ANOVA RESULTS

Variation Source	Degrees of Freedom	SS	MS	F	$f_{0.05}(1,7)$
Regression	1	$SS_R = 344.96$	344.96	29.35	5.59
Error	7	$SS_E = 82.26$	11.75		
Total	8	427.22			

Solution:

(a) In this part, we compute r^2 to equal 0.81. This ratio is large enough to suggest that the linear relationship between X and Y is strong.

(b) To conduct ANOVA we must compute S_{xy} and S_{yy}.

$$S_{xy} = \Sigma(x_i - m_x)(y_i - m_y) = \Sigma x_i y_i - n(m_x m_y)$$
$$= 5915 - 9 \times 8.056 \times 82.778 = -86.74$$

$$S_{yy} = \Sigma(y_i - m_y)^2 = \Sigma y_i^2 - n(m_y)^2 = 62097 - 9(82.778)^2 = 427.22.$$

Based on these, we have

$SS_R = bS_{xy} = -3.977 \times (-86.74) = 344.96$, and
$SS_E = S_{yy} - SS_R = 427.22 - 344.96 = 82.26$. Thus
$MS_R = SS_R/1 = 344.96$, and
$MS_E = SS_E/(n - 2) = 82.26/7 = 11.75$.

The test statistic is

$$F = MS_R/MS_E = 344.96/11.75 = 29.35.$$

The critical value of the F distribution for $\nu_1 = 1$ and $\nu_2 = 9 - 2 = 7$ degrees of freedom is $f_{0.05}(1,7) = 5.59$ at 0.05. Since $F = 29.35$ is larger than the critical value, the ratio F is *inflated;* and as such the null hypothesis is rejected. This means there is enough statistical evidence to have a linear regression of Y on X. The ANOVA results are summarized in Table E9.20.

9.6.4 Multiple Linear Regression

Occasionally, in certain engineering problems, it may be necessary to establish the linear regression between the dependent variable Y and q independent variables X_1, $X_2, \ldots$, and X_q. The regression equation in this case is written as:

$$E(Y|x_1, x_2, \ldots x_q) = a + b_1 x_1 + b_2 x_2 + \ldots + b_q x_q \tag{9.51}$$

The procedure for estimating the constants a and b_j (where $j = 1, 2, \ldots, q$) is the same as that in single linear regression. Upon establishing SS_E, the sum of the square of the difference between the observed values of Y (i.e., y_i) and the theoretical values from Eq. 9.51, SS_E is minimized. This will result in $q + 1$ simultaneous equations that are then solved for a and b_j ($j = 1, 2, \ldots, q$). It can be shown that

$$a = m_y - \sum_{j=1}^{q} b_j m_j \tag{9.52}$$

and that the constants b_j can be obtained from the following q simultaneous equations:

$$b_1 \Sigma(x_{1i} - m_1)(x_{1i} - m_1) + b_2 \Sigma(x_{1i} - m_1)(x_{2i} - m_2) + \ldots$$
$$+ b_q \Sigma(x_{1i} - m_1)(x_{qi} - m_q) = \Sigma(x_{1i} - m_1)(y_i - m_y)$$

$$b_1 \Sigma(x_{2i} - m_2)(x_{1i} - m_1) + b_2 \Sigma(x_{2i} - m_2)(x_{2i} - m_2) + \ldots$$
$$+ b_q \Sigma(x_{2i} - m_2)(x_{qi} - m_q) = \Sigma(x_{2i} - m_2)(y_i - m_y)$$

$$b_1 \Sigma(x_{qi} - m_q)(x_{1i} - m_1) + b_2 \Sigma(x_{qi} - m_q)(x_{2i} - m_2) + \ldots$$
$$+ b_q \Sigma(x_{qi} - m_q)(x_{qi} - m_q) = \Sigma(x_{qi} - m_q)(y_i - m_y) \tag{9.53}$$

in which m_j is the mean value of the variable X_j ($j = 1, 2, \ldots, q$); and m_y is the mean value of Y. Furthermore, in Eqs. 9.53 the summations are from $i = 1$ to n (note that n is the size of each of the variables Y and X_j); and a term such as x_{ji} means the ith element of the variable X_j. For simplicity, in Eqs. 9.52 and 9.53 we have dropped the symbol $\wedge$ which is often used to describe the estimates for a and b_j. The variance of Y in the regression equation can also be obtained as in the case of the single linear correlation, i.e.,

$$Var(Y|x_1, x_2, \ldots x_q) = SS_E/(n - q - 1) \tag{9.54}$$

in which

$$SS_E = \Sigma(y_i - a - b_1 x_{1i} - b_2 x_{2i} - b_3 x_{3i} - \ldots - b_q x_{qi})^2 \tag{9.55}$$

9.6.5 Nonlinear Regression

In many engineering problems, the data set may show a non-linear trend between Y and X. In these problems, it is desirable to establish a non-linear regression between Y and X. Usually the scatter plot of Y data versus X sample values will suggest the type of function that may be suitable for the relation between X and Y. If it is determined that the relation follows a specific type of function, such as $g(x)$, then the regression equation can simply be established by linearization. However, if the type of function cannot be identified, a polynomial may be attempted in order to establish the regression equation. In this case, one may wish to closely examine the scatter plot of Y versus X to decide on the order of polynomials that would best fit the data. In this section these two methods are explained.

   Regression by Using a Pre-Determined Function.   Suppose the scatter plot of Y versus X suggests that the relationship is in the form of a function $g(x)$. For exam ple, this function is exponential or logarithmic (i.e., $g = e^x$ or $g = \ell nx$). The regression of Y on X can then be written as:

$$E(Y|x) = a + bg(x) \tag{9.56a}$$

The linearization is achieved by substituting an auxiliary variable z for $g(x)$. Since $z = g(x)$, then Eq. 9.56a becomes:

$$E(Y|z) = a + bz \tag{9.56b}$$

Constants a and b can now be estimated from Eqs. 9.43 and 9.44. However, in these equations all x_i will be substituted by $z_i = g(x_i)$.

   Nonlinear Regression Using a Polynomial Function.   In this case, the regression equation is written as a polynomial of mth order.

$$E(Y|x) = a_0 + a_1x + a_2x^2 + \ldots + a_mx^m \tag{9.57}$$

Once m is selected, a procedure similar to the linear regression method is used to minimize the sum of squares of the differences between the observed values of Y (i.e., y_i) and the theoretical value from Eq. 9.57. This results in $m + 1$ simultaneous equations for computing the estimates for the constants $a_0, a_1, \ldots, a_m$ in the form of

$$\frac{\partial SS_E}{\partial a_j} = 0 \text{ for } j = 0 \text{ to } m$$

These $m + 1$ equations can be written in matrix as

$$[C]\{a\} = \{R\} \tag{9.58}$$

in which it can be shown that

$$[C] = \begin{Bmatrix} n & \Sigma x_i & \Sigma x_i^2 & \ldots & \Sigma x_i^m \\ \Sigma x_i & \Sigma x_i^2 & \Sigma x_i^3 & \ldots & \Sigma x_i^{m+1} \\ \ldots & & & & \\ \Sigma x_i^m & \Sigma x_i^{m+1} & \Sigma x_i^{m+2} & \ldots & \Sigma x_i^{2m} \end{Bmatrix}$$

and

$$\{R\} = \begin{Bmatrix} \Sigma y_i \\ \Sigma y_ix_i \\ \Sigma y_ix_i^2 \\ \ldots \\ \Sigma y_ix_i^m \end{Bmatrix}$$

and

$$\{a\} = \begin{Bmatrix} a_0 \\ a_1 \\ a_2 \\ \ldots \\ a_m \end{Bmatrix}$$

For more information on regression analysis in general, see Myers (1990).

Example 9.21

Bus fares in suburban communities of a major metropolitan area are a function of rides per bus line per day. In a survey of eight communities, the data in Table E9.21A was gathered on the bus fare in dollars (dependent variable, Y) and number of rides per line per day (independent variable, X).

A regression equation in the form of $Y = a + b\ell n(x)$ has been suggested for the data. Compute the estimates for a and b and discuss the correlation of Y on $\ell n(X)$.

Solution:

We introduce $Z = \ell n(X)$ and establish a linear regression between Y and Z. Table E9.21B summarizes the results.

$$b = \frac{8 \times 43.004 - 57.693 \times 5.95}{8 \times 416.30 - (57.693)^2} = 0.396$$

$$m_z = 57.693/8 = 7.212 \qquad m_y = 5.95/8 = 0.744$$

$$a = 0.744 - 0.396 \times 7.212 = -2.112$$

$$E(Y|z) = -2.112 + 0.396z = -2.112 + 0.396\,\ell n(x).$$

To compute the correlation coefficient between Y and Z, we can either use Eq. 9.47a or 9.47b. We first must compute s_z and s_y.

TABLE E9.21A

Rides/Line/Day	Fare ($)
1050	0.60
1100	0.75
1255	0.70
1270	0.65
1420	0.80
1530	0.75
1625	0.85
1750	0.85

TABLE E9.21B

x_i	$z_i = \ell n(x_i)$	y_i	z_i^2	y_i^2	$z_i y_i$
1050	6.957	0.6	48.40	0.360	4.174
1100	7.003	0.75	49.04	0.563	5.252
1255	7.135	0.70	50.91	0.490	4.995
1270	7.147	0.65	51.08	0.423	4.646
1420	7.258	0.80	52.68	0.64	5.806
1530	7.333	0.75	53.77	0.563	5.500
1625	7.393	0.85	54.66	0.723	6.284
1750	7.467	0.85	55.76	0.723	6.347
Sum	57.693	5.95	416.30	4.485	43.004

$s_z^2 = (\Sigma z_i^2 - nm_z^2)/(n - 1) = [416.30 - 8(7.212)^2]/7 = 0.0281$, and $s_z = 0.168$. Similarly,

$$s_y^2 = [4.485 - 8(0.744)^2]/7 = 0.0081, \text{ and } s_y = 0.09.$$

Thus using Eq. 9.47b

$$r = [(43.004 - 8 \times 7.212 \times 0.744)/(0.168 \times 0.09)]/(8 - 1) = 0.74.$$

The r^2 factor is about 0.6. This indicates a reasonable strength for the relationship.

9.6.6 Spearsman's Rank Correlation Coefficient

In estimating the correlation coefficient between X and Y, we may find out that the data consists of ranks or that the data set is small and it can be ranked readily. In these cases, the Spearsman's rank correlation coefficient is used for measuring the correlation coefficient. Suppose we have compiled n sets of values for X and Y denoted by (x_i, y_i) where $i = 1$ to n. We rank both the X and Y data in ascending order. The ranks for the X values are denoted by r_{xi} and those for Y by r_{yi}. Thus we now have n pairs of ranks such as (r_{xi}, r_{yi}). For tied scores, again we use the average of the ranks for those scores that are tied. Spearsman's rank correlation coefficient r_s is obtained from the following equation

$$r_s = \frac{n\Sigma r_{xi}r_{yi} - \Sigma r_{xi}\Sigma r_{yi}}{\sqrt{[n\Sigma r_{xi}^2 - (\Sigma r_{xi})^2][n\Sigma r_{yi}^2 - (\Sigma r_{yi})^2]}} \tag{9.59}$$

The summations in Eq. 9.59 each is from $i = 1$ to n. The results from this equation are usually slightly different from those from Eqs. 9.47. For large n, the two results are in close agreement with each other. If there are no ties in ranks, the Spearsman's coefficient is given by the following simple equation

$$r_s = 1 - \frac{6\Sigma d_i^2}{n(n^2 - 1)} \tag{9.60}$$

in which $d_i = r_{xi} - r_{yi}$ and again the summation is from $i = 1$ to n. As discussed previously, the values of r_s close to ± 1 indicate a strong correlation between X and Y.

Example 9.22

In Example 9.19, compute the correlation coefficient using Spearsman's equation.

Solution:

We need to rank the values of X and Y in ascending order from 1 to 9. Table E9.22 summarizes the ranks for X (i.e., r_{xi}) and ranks for Y (i.e., r_{yi}), r_{xi}^2, r_{xi}^2 and $r_{xi}r_{yi}$. Note that tied scores receive the average of the ranks in the tied-score group.

Using Eq. 9.59

$$r_s = \frac{9 \times 192.25 - 45 \times 45}{\sqrt{[9 \times 280.00 - (45)^2][9 \times 284.50 - (45)^2]}} = -0.57$$

TABLE E9.22   RANKED DATA

Work shift Hrs/day, X	Ranks r_{xi}	Productivity %, Y	Ranks r_{yi}	r_{xi}^2	r_{yi}^2	$r_{xi}r_{yi}$
7	3.5*	90	8.5**	12.25	72.25	29.75
6.5	1	85	5	1.00	25.00	5.00
9.5	7	75	2	49.00	4.00	14.00
7	3.5*	83	4	12.25	16.00	14.00
7	3.5*	88	7	12.25	49.00	24.50
10	8	78	3	64.00	9.00	24.00
7.5	6	90	8.5**	36.00	72.25	51.00
7	3.5*	87	6	12.25	36.00	21.00
11	9	69	1	81.00	1.00	9.00
Sum	45		45	280.00	284.50	192.25

*This is the average of ranks 2, 3, 4, and 5 that are tied.
**This is the average of ranks 8 and 9 that are tied.

SUMMARY

In this chapter, we reviewed several useful statistical methods for the analysis of engineering data. The focus of the discussion was on hypothesis testing, comparing means from two or more populations, the analysis of variance and correlation and regression analysis. The discussion on these methods is rather comprehensive. We presented only those methods that are commonly used in statistical analysis of data. The applications of these methods in engineering are numerous. One may wish to apply these methods as statistical evidence that the data sets compiled in two groups are either identical or different. Furthermore, an engineer may wish to apply these methods in connection with providing the necessary evidence as to whether a presumed notion is valid. In general, we recommend the use of the methods presented in this chapter for those engineers who are involved in research that require field or laboratory data compilation.

REFERENCES

GUTTMAN, I., S.S. WILKS, and J.S. HUNTER (1982). *Introductory Engineering Statistics*, Third edn., John Wiley & Sons, New York, NY.

KLIR, G.J., U.H. ST.CLAIR, and B. YUAN (1997). *Fuzzy Set Theory, Foundations and Applications*, Prentice Hall PTR, Upper Saddle River, NJ.

MILTON, J.S., and J.O. TSOKOS (1983). *Statistical Methods in the Biological and Health Sciences*, McGraw-Hill Publishing Company, New York, NY.

MYERS, R.H., (1990). *Classical and Modern Regression with Applications*, 2nd edn, Duxbury Press, Boston Massachusetts.

NELSON, M. and W. ILLINGWORTH (1990). *A Practical Guide to Neural Nets*, Addison-Wesley Publishing Company, Inc.

VANLUCHENE, R. and S. ROUFEI (1990). *Neural Networks in Structural Engineering,* Elsevier Science Publishing Co.

WALPOLE, R.E., R.H. MYERS, and S.L. MYERS (1998). *Probability and Statistics for Engineers and Scientists,* Sixth Edn, Prentice Hall, Upper Saddle River, NJ.

YAO, J.T.P. (1985). *Safety and Reliability of Existing Structures,* Pittman Publishing, Marshield, Massachusetts.

EXERCISES

1. In designing the traffic light for an intersection, a traffic engineer believes that the duration of the yellow light is 3.0 seconds on the average. The engineer collects sample data from 10 similar intersections. The results are as follows:

$$2.5, 2.5, 4.0, 3.0, 1.5, 2.0, 1.5, 3.0, 2.0, 3.5$$

   (a) Estimate the mean and standard deviation of the compiled data.
   (b) Conduct a hypothesis test at $\alpha = 0.05$ to determine whether the engineer's belief on the mean duration of yellow light is supported.

   Hint: Use a two-tailed hypothesis testing.

2. Use the least square analysis to derive Eqs. 9.43 and 9.44.

3. In conducting an inspection of the condition of main steel girders in several railroad bridges, an engineer believes that the mean effective cross section area is at least equal to 90% of the original cross-sectional area as indicated on the design drawings. In a survey of some 12 girders, the cross-sectional area was measured as a fraction of the "design cross-sectional area" at the midspan of each girder. The results were

$$0.76, 0.95, 0.73, 0.82, 0.85, 0.85, 0.89, 0.91, 0.78, 0.81, 0.86, 0.87.$$

   (a) Compute the mean and standard deviation of the data given.
   (b) Test the hypothesis that the mean ratio of the cross section area to the design cross-sectional area is larger the 0.90 per engineer's notion.

4. Two groups of structural engineers were invited to rate the condition of several single family unreinforced masonry houses following a moderate earthquake in a seismic area. One group (Group I) consisted of $n_1 = 16$ surveys; the other (Group II) consisted of $n_2 = 13$ surveys. The engineers rated the houses on a scale system of 1-5 These scales are interpreted as follows:

   1 = severe damage to the house, house needs to be demolished;

   2 = major damage including large cracks, some foundation displacements; major repair is needed.

   3 = Moderate damage including some cracks, moderate levels of repair will be needed;

   4 = minor damage to masonry and plaster, some repair will be needed; and,
   5 = no damage occurred to the house.

   Upon the completion of the survey, the scales from each group were analyzed. The mean (m) and standard deviation (s) for each group were then computed as given below:

Group I	Group II
$n_1 = 16$	$n_2 = 13$
$m_1 = 3.6$	$m_2 = 4.0$
$s_1 = 0.70$	$s_2 = 0.95$

(a) Determine whether the variances from the two groups are identical at $\alpha = 0.05$.

(b) Given the result in (a), compare the two mean values at $\alpha = 0.05$ and determine whether the difference between them is significant.

5. In a traffic engineering research, the efficiency of gates at toll booths is being investigated. Two different devices are considered for automatic opening of gates. One uses coins; the other a pre-paid card. The average time to collect the toll for each car and open the gate for the car to pass through is estimated in a random sample of $n_1 = 26$ cars for the coin-collector system; and $n_1 = 31$ for the card system. The results for the mean (m) and standard deviation (s) are summarized below:

Coin System	Card System
$n_1 = 26$	$n_2 = 31$
$m_1 = 6.2$ seconds	$m_2 = 5.0$ seconds
$s_1 = 0.70$	$s_2 = 0.95$

(a) Determine whether the variances from the two populations are identical at $\alpha = 0.05$.

(b) Given the result in (a), compare the two means at $\alpha = 0.05$ and determine whether the difference between them is significant.

6. A concrete manufacturing plant is testing the effectiveness of two types of agents that delay the curing of concrete without compromising the compressive strength and concrete workability. In a series of tests, concrete samples were prepared using the two agents (designated as Agents I and II). The delay time was measured for these samples. The results are summarized below:

Agent I	Agent II
$n_1 = 9$	$n_2 = 9$
$m_1 = 95$ minutes	$m_2 = 106$ minutes
$s_1 = 15$	$s_2 = 12$

(a) Determine whether the variances from the two populations are identical at $\alpha = 0.10$.

(b) Based on the result in (a), compare the two means at $\alpha = 0.10$ and determine whether the difference between them is significant.

7. In Exercise 6, the compressive strength was also computed. The results were

Agent I	Agent II
$n_1 = 9$	$n_2 = 9$
$m_1 = 53.0$ MPa	$m_2 = 49.0$ MPa
$s_1 = 5.0$ MPa	$s_2 = 3.9$ MPa

(a) Determine whether the two variances from these populations are identical at $\alpha = 0.10$.

(b) Based on the finding in (a), compare the two means at $\alpha = 0.10$ and determine whether the difference between them is significant.

8. For quality assurance purposes, an engineer wishes to compare three brands of high strength bolts for their shear capacity in KN. Samples of the three brands were obtained and tested for shear capacity. All test samples had 19 mm diameters. The results for the three brands appear in Table P9.8.

TABLE P9.8 BOLT SHEAR CAPACITY IN KN

Brand I	Brand II	Brand III
81	76	82
75	92	80
83	83	76
86	79	77
78	88	89
85	82	85
90	88	84
	77	80
$n_1 = 7$	90	79
		88
	$n_2 = 9$	86
		$n_3 = 11$

Assume the distribution for each sample is normal.

(a) Compute the mean shear strength in each group and the grand mean for all groups.
(b) Conduct a one-way classification completely random design ANOVA with fixed effect to test the hypothesis that the means are identical at $\alpha = 0.10$ and $\alpha = 0.05$.

9. In Exercise 8, conduct a multiple range test to further compare the means at $\alpha = 0.05$.

10. In Exercise 1, assume the engineer notion is that the median for the yellow light duration is 3 seconds. Furthermore assume that the test of normality does not pass; and as such a distribution-free method is more appropriate. Conduct a Wilcoxon signed-rank test for the null hypothesis that the median yellow light duration is equal to 3 seconds. Note that there are several groups of tied scores in the data given.

11. In Exercise 8, assume the normality test does not pass.

(a) Compare Brands I and II using the Wilcoxon signed-rank test (unmatched data) to determine whether the two populations are identical at $\alpha = 0.10$. (Hint: you need to pool the data)
(b) Repeat part a for comparing Brands I and III.
(c) Repeat part a for comparing Brands II and III.

12. An engineer managing a construction project is developing a scheduling and activity network for use in the critical path method. There is an uncertainty associated with the estimated duration of an activity in the network. The engineer believes that the median duration of this activity is 12 days. To further support this notion, she compiles actual data for the same activity in 9 previous projects. The results in days are

$$10, 8, 8.5, 14, 11, 7, 9.5, 9.5, 7.5$$

Conduct a Wilcoxon signed-rank test for the null hypothesis that the median for the duration of the activity is equal to 12 days at $\alpha = 0.05$.

13. In Exercise 12, assume that the test of normality passes. Furthermore assume that the mean duration for the activity is believed to be equal to 12 days. Use the data given in Exercise 12 and test the null hypothesis that the mean is equal to 12 days at $\alpha = 0.10$.

14. The stress value at a location on the flange of an aluminum front spar in the right wing of a test aircraft is affected by the aircraft's vertical accelerations that exceed 2.0g, where g is the gravity acceleration. In a flight survey, the incidences of acceleration exceeding 2.0g were measured during 300 flight hours. At each occurrence of acceleration exceeding 2.0g, the stress at the aforementioned location was also measured. In total there were 20 such occurrences. The results appear in Table P9.14

TABLE P9.14

Vertical Acceleration in g (Variable X)	Stress in MPa (Variable Y)
3.2	72
3.4	80
2.8	60
3.0	43
3.3	56
3.0	64
3.5	71
2.2	47
2.7	54
3.0	76
2.1	38
2.7	60
3.6	87
2.2	49
2.3	57
2.4	63
2.9	75
3.1	79
2.5	49

(a) Plot the dependent variable Y versus X.
(b) Compute the constants a and b in the regression equation $E(Y|x) = a + bx$.
(c) Compute $Var(Y|x)$.
(d) Compute the correlation coefficient between X and Y.
(e) What will the estimated stress be at an acceleration equal to 3.25g?

15. In Exercise 14
   (a) Discuss the strength of the linear regression between X and Y.
   (b) Conduct ANOVA to further investigate the linear regression of Y on X.

16. The annual growth of the volume of commercial motor vehicles (CMV) for a highway depends on the average daily traffic (ADT) volume along the highway. Assume in a survey of eleven roadways, the average percentage of annual CMV growth over a five-year period versus the ADT volumes was obtained as summarized in Table P9.16.

TABLE P9.16

ADT Volume (Variable X)	CMV Yearly Growth (Variable Y) in %
16,350	3.2
17,690	3.0
18,390	3.6
20,430	3.5
21,740	3.6
22,400	4.0
23,390	3.9
25,630	4.0
26,600	4.1
27,950	4.3
28,840	4.3

   (a) Establish a linear regression of Y on X.
   (b) Compute the correlation coefficient between X and Y.
   (c) Given an ADT volume of 24,500 vehicles, what will the estimate for the CMV growth per year be?

17. In Exercise 16
   (a) Discuss the strength of linear regression.
   (b) Conduct an ANOVA to further discuss the linearity of the regression of Y on X.

18. In Exercise 16, a non-linear regression equation in the form of $E(Y|x) = a + b\ell n(x)$ is suggested. Compute a and b, and estimate the annual CMV growth for an ADT volume of 24,500 vehicles.

19. Two groups of experts were invited to rank the quality of construction conducted by 10 contractors of public works. One group consisted of engineers from the public sector; and the other from private consulting companies. The ranking was done on a scale of 1 to 10; in which a ranking of 10 means excellent quality of work, and 1 means unacceptable qual-

ity. The scales 2–9 are intermediate measures of quality between the two extreme scales. Table P9.19 summarizes the rankings from the two groups of experts.
Compute the correlation coefficient using Spearsman's equation for the opinions expressed by the two groups.

TABLE P9.19

Contractor	Rankings by Group I Experts	Rankings by Group II Experts
A	1	1
B	3	2
C	10	10
D	2	4
E	6	7
F	5	5
G	7	6
H	8	3
I	9	8
J	4	9

20. A company is marketing an additive for gasoline to improve car millage per gallon of gasoline consumed. To conduct test runs, 10 cars were selected. The highway miles per gallon (MPG) for each car before and after using the additive were measured. The results are provided in Table P9.20.

TABLE P9.20

Car Number	MPG Without Additive	MPG With Additive
1	25.5	25.0
2	19.0	20.1
3	18.2	19.2
4	17.5	18.2
5	24.0	24.0
6	21.0	21.5
7	27.5	27.4
8	18.5	20.0
9	19.4	20.1
10	26.0	26.2

(a) Compute the mean MPG before and after using the additive.
(b) Determine whether there is enough statistical evidence that the MPG is improved upon using the additive. Use $\alpha = 0.05$. Hint: compare means using paired t by assuming the data in each group follows the normal distribution.

21. In Exercise 20 use a distribution-free method (Wilcoxon) to compare the two populations.

10

Basic Hard Systems Engineering—Part I

10.1 INTRODUCTION: HARD SYSTEMS ANALYSIS

In Chapter 1 we dealt briefly with the rudiments of the systems approach to problem solving. In this chapter, we will begin by elaborating the meaning of some specific terms associated with the systems approach. This approach offers systemic (holistic rather than piece-meal) and/or systematic (step-by-step rather than intuitive) guidelines to problem solving. Both systemic and systematic methodologies and techniques are used by engineers. Techniques, in general, are precise specific programs of action that will produce a standard result. Methodology, on the other hand, lacks the precision of a technique, but is a firmer guide to action as compared to a philosophy.

Almost all important real-world problems we face on a day-to-day basis are systemic problems, such as sustainability and environmental problems, homelessness and poverty problems, social and economic problems, etc. These complex problems are truly systemic in the sense that they cannot be attacked on a piece-meal basis, partly because of their interconnectedness. From the early 1950s, systems analysis (which is the economic appraisal of different means of meeting a defined end) and systems engineering (which involves the design of complex, technical systems in order to insure that all components operate in an integrated, efficient way) have been widely used in problem solving all over the world. When systems analysis and systems engineering are put to use for solving problems concerning natural and physical systems, we describe this approach as the "hard" systems approach. Essentially, the hard systems approach defines the objectives to be achieved and then "engineers" the system to achieve these objectives. However, when dealing with problems involving human activity systems, one notices that the problem itself is usually ill defined. Such cases are defined as soft systems. In contrast to hard systems engineering, soft systems methodology does not seek to mechanically design a solution as much as it orchestrates a process of learning (Checkland, 1981; Khisty, 1993).

Operations research (OR) and management science can also be classified as a hard systems methodology comprising a range of techniques that are typical of the means-end approach. As has been well recorded, OR emerged as a means of tackling the vast logistical problems that were encountered during World War II. Later, a whole variety of formal quantitative techniques were developed for use in every conceivable area such as manufacturing, production, transportation, and construction management, based on the principles of OR.

This chapter deals with several techniques that form the basis of hard systems methodology. First, we will deal with methods based on calculus. Next, three of the best known methods of network analysis (Critical Path Method [CPM], Program Evaluation and Review Technique [PERT], and Line-of-Balance [LOB]) used extensively in construction management will be presented, followed by three other methods of network analysis; shortest path, minimal spanning tree and maximal flow. Lastly, the basic ideas of linear programming (LP) are described. LP is a quantitative method of analysis used extensively in business and engineering.

10.2 METHODS BASED ON CALCULUS

The classical methods of calculus provide elegant and powerful solutions to a relatively large number of problems encountered in engineering and economics. At the same time, one of the principal assumptions on which it rests is that the variables which describe a problem must be continuous along all points. This assumption limits its use for practical problem solving, i.e., network systems in transportation or choosing between discrete projects in construction management.

Many of the tools described in this chapter are predominantly linear and involve the solution of sets of linear equations. A large number of managerial problems consist of one or more non-linear relationships, where traditional linear solution methods are not applicable. Fortunately, you have already been exposed to the basic principles of microeconomics in Chapter 4, and some of the examples worked out with respect to demand, supply, and elasticity will be revisited in this section.

The optimization of a non-linear objective function may be constrained or unconstrained. The former may be solved by the method of substitution or by the use of Lagrangian multipliers. The best way to get familiar with these techniques is to work through the examples given in this chapter.

10.2.1 Production Function Characteristics

A production function is a basic representation for the conversion of resources to products. A production function could be represented as:

$$Z = k \, (x_1, x_2, \ldots, x_n)$$

For example, Z could be the maximum number of houses provided by a city, where x_1 represented the land provided, x_2 the labor supplied, and so on. The shape of the production function has important implications regarding where to search for an optimum solution. The following example illustrates the use of calculus.

Example 10.1

If the total cost (TC) of providing labor for the repair of motors is given by

$$TC = 40 + 24X - 5.5X^2 + (1/3)X^3$$

where X = number of labor involved in repairs and TC = total cost, find the relative minimum and maximum labor force required for this cost function. What is your recommendation?

Solution:

$$TC = 40 + 24X - 5.5X^2 + (1/3)X^3$$

The necessary and sufficient condition for a maximum or minimum are

$$\frac{d(TC)}{dx} = 24 - 11X + X^2 = 0$$

$$\therefore X = 8 \text{ or } X = 3$$

Taking the second derivative,

$$\frac{d^2(TC)}{dx^2} = -11 + 2X$$

At X = 8, $-11 + (2)(8) = 5 > 0$
At X = 3, $-11 + (2)(3) = -5 < 0$

Thus at X = 8, TC = $40 + 24(8) - 5.5(8)^2 + \frac{1}{3}(8)^3 = \$50.67$ (minimum) and at X = 3, TC = $40 + 24(3) - 5.5(3^2) + \frac{1}{3}(3)^3 = \$71.50$ (maximum).
It is recommended that the labor force be kept at 8 to minimize the cost function.

10.2.2 Relationship Among Total, Marginal, and Average Cost Concepts and Elasticity

You were introduced to the price elasticity and cost functions in Chapter 4. We will make use of these concepts in this section. Remember that the price elasticity (e) of demand is

$$e = \frac{dQ}{dP} \cdot \frac{P}{Q}$$

which is frequently expressed as

$$e = \frac{dQ/dP}{Q/P} = \frac{\text{marginal cost}}{\text{average cost}}$$

The next example makes use of this relationship.

Example 10.2

If the demand for airline travel tickets between two cities is $Q = 800 - 5P - P^2$, where P, the price of the ticket, is $10, and Q is the number of tickets sold. What is the price elasticity of demand?

Solution:

$$Q = 800 - 5P - P^2$$

$$\frac{dQ}{dP} = -5 - 2P$$

Substituting the value of $P = 10$, in the equation:

$$\frac{dQ}{dP} = (-5) - (2)(10) = -25$$

Next, find the number of tickets sold when $P = \$10$

$$Q = 800 - 5(10) - (10)^2 = 650$$

Substituting these values

$$e = \frac{dQ}{dP} \cdot \frac{P}{Q}$$

$$= (-25)\left(\frac{10}{650}\right)$$

$$= -0.3846. \qquad \text{Hence elastic.}$$

Example 10.3

If a company's demand function for machines is $P = 45 - 0.5Q$ and its average cost function is

$$AC = Q^2 - 8Q + 57 + \frac{2}{Q}$$

find the level of output which (a) maximizes total revenue (b) minimizes marginal cost and (c) maximizes profits.

Solution:

(a) Demand function is $P = 45 - 0.5Q$
   Total Revenue (TR) is $(P)(Q) = (4.5 - 0.5Q)Q$

$$= 45Q - 0.5Q^2$$

To maximize Q: $\dfrac{d(TR)}{dQ} = 45 - (0.5)(2)Q$, and equating this to zero

$$Q = 45 \qquad .$$

Testing the 2nd order condition

$$\frac{d^2(TR)}{dQ^2} = -1 < 0$$

$$\therefore \text{ at } Q = 45, \text{ TR is a maximum.}$$

(b) From the average cost function $AC = Q^2 - 8Q + 57 + 2/Q$

$$\text{Total cost, } TC = (AC)(Q) = \left(Q^2 - 8Q + 57 + \frac{2}{Q}\right)Q$$

$$= Q^3 - 8Q^2 + 57Q + 2$$

Marginal cost,

$$MC = \frac{d(TC)}{dQ} = 3Q^2 - 16Q + 57$$

Marginal cost is minimized when

$$\frac{d(MC)}{dQ} = 6Q - 16 = 0, \text{ and } Q = 2\frac{2}{3}$$

Testing the second-order condition $\dfrac{d^2(MC)}{dQ^2} = 6 > 0$

$$\therefore \text{ at } Q = 2\frac{2}{3}, MC \text{ is at maximum}$$

(c) Profit = TR − TC

$$= (45Q - 0.5Q^2) - (Q^3 - 8Q^2 + 57Q + 2)$$
$$= -Q^3 + 7.5Q^2 - 12Q - 2$$

for maximizing profit (Pr).

$$\frac{d(Pr)}{dQ} = -3Q^2 + 15Q - 12 = 0$$

$$\therefore Q = 1 \text{ or } Q = 4$$

testing the second order conditions

$$\frac{d^2(Pr)}{dQ^2} = -6Q + 15$$

At $Q = 1$ this results in $9 > 0$

At $Q = 4$ this results in $-9 < 0$

$$\therefore \text{ Profits are maximized at } Q = 4$$

and Profit $= -(4)^3 + 7.5(4)^2 - 12(4) - 2 = 6$

10.2.3 The Method of Lagrange Multipliers

The method of Lagrange multipliers can be used for solving constrained optimization problems consisting of a non-linear objective function and one or more linear or non-linear constraint equations. The constraints, as multiples of a Lagrange multiplier, λ, are subtracted from the objective function resulting from a unit change in the quantity value of the constraint equation. This characteristic will be obvious when the following example is worked through.

Example 10.4

The cost function of a firm selling two products A and B is $C = 8A^2 - AB + 12B^2$. However, the firm is required by contract to produce a minimum quantity of A and B totaling 42. What are the values of A and B, and what is your interpretation of the value of λ?

Solution:

Set the constraint to 0, multiply it by λ and form the Lagrangian function.

$$C = 8A^2 - AB + 12B^2 + \lambda(A + B - 42)$$

Take the first order partials

$$C_A = 16A - B + \lambda = 0$$
$$C_B = -A + 24B + \lambda = 0$$
$$C_\lambda = A + B - 42 = 0$$

$$\therefore A = 25; B = 17; \text{ and } \lambda = -383$$

which means that a one-unit increase in the production quota will lead to an increase in cost by approximately $383.

10.3 CRITICAL PATH METHOD

One of the popular uses of network analysis is for the planning and monitoring of projects before and during execution. Such analysis is vital in order to finish a project within the budget allotment and prescribed time limit. The Critical Path Method (CPM) and the Program Evaluation and Review Technique (PERT) are the two most popular network analysis techniques used for project planning. Developed in the late 1950s to aid in the planning and scheduling of large projects, today, CPM and PERT are used all over the world.

Both techniques have many characteristics in common, although CPM is deterministic while PERT is probabilistic. Both involve the identification and proper sequencing of specific tasks or activities in order to complete projects in time. Also, the relationship between specific tasks and the logic of precedence is important, as is their duration and quantification. Coupled with these qualities is the classification and number of workers along with their periods of time and wages. The planning of cash flows and financial assistance is also a crucial part of CPM and PERT.

Project planning involves the identification and sequencing of specific tasks, their duration, and their relationships. This process is represented by a network, not necessarily drawn to scale. Two types of networks are currently in use; an Activity-on-Arrow (AOA) and an Activity-on-Node (AON). We will describe only the AOA network.

The AOA network consists of arrows (branches) and nodes. The arrows represent activities (or tasks) while the nodes represent the beginning and the end of activities referred to as events. Since a number of terms are used in CPM, it is best to begin describing them with the help of a typical diagram (see Figure 10.1).

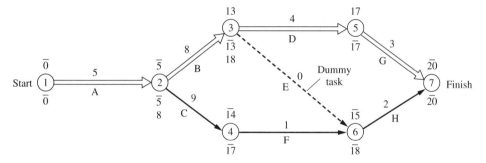

(a) CPM Network showing nodes and arrows

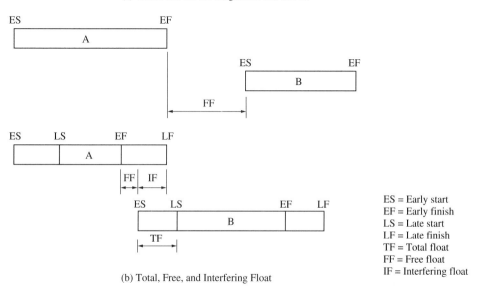

(b) Total, Free, and Interfering Float

ES = Early start
EF = Early finish
LS = Late start
LF = Late finish
TF = Total float
FF = Free float
IF = Interfering float

Figure 10.1   (a) CPM network showing nodes and arrows. (b) Total, free, and interfering float.

10.3.1 Key Concepts

1. **CPM is linear graph consisting of nodes and arrows, as shown in Figure 10.1.**
2. **Two methods of diagramming can be used: Activity On Node (AON), and Activity On Arrow (AOA). We will use the AOA method.**
3. **Dummy activities have zero duration. For example, activity (3–6) is a dummy activity which means that activity (6–7) cannot start before activity (2–3) is completed.**
4. **The forward pass gives the early start (ES) and the early finish (EF) time of an activity. The forward pass establishes for each event the earliest event time.**

5. The backward pass gives the late start (LS) and the late finish (LF) time of an activity. The backward pass is simply a reversal of that for calculating the earliest event time.

6. When ES = LS for an activity, it lies on the critical path.

7. The CP is the set of activities that cannot be delayed if the project is to be completed on time.

8. Total float (TF) is the amount of time that an activity may be delayed without delaying the completion of the project. TF = LF − EF = LS − ES.

Free float (FF) is the time that the finish of an activity can be delayed without delaying the early start time of any following activity.

FF = ES of the following activity minus EF of the activity in question.

9. The CP is the minimum time in which a project can be completed, and is the duration of the longest path through the network.

10.3.2 CPM Scheduling

To keep control over a CPM network while it is being prepared and worked out, the following steps are useful:

(a) List all the activities sequentially and estimate their duration. There may be two or more activities that are done simultaneously.

(b) Pay special attention to which activity precedes (or follows) another activity, so that a proper logic of the project is maintained.

(c) Draw an AOA network with the activities and events properly interconnected. If necessary, introduce dummy activities to maintain the logic and sequencing (in time) of all the activities in question.

(d) Make a forward and backward pass through the network to establish early start (ES), late start (LS), early finish (EF), and late finish (LF) times for all the activities.

(e) Determine the CP and the corresponding critical activities.

(f) Prepare a table with all the details as shown in sample Table 10.1.

Note that the first activity starts at zero and we add the duration to its ES to obtain its EF time. In this manner, you can progress through the network calculating ES and EF times for all activities, always choosing the preceding EF with largest time, at that node. Next, we can work backwards from right to left, which is called the backward pass. On the last activity the EF time becomes the LF time, in order to finish the project as soon as possible. The LF time of the last activity is its LF time minus its duration. Working backward, the LF and LS times for preceding activities can be determined noting always that the smaller value has to be taken into account. The CP is the longest interconnected path through the network. All activities on this path have the same ES and LS times (and similarly they have the same EF and LF times). Note that these activities have no float to their durations. Finally, all values of ES, LS, EF, and LF times are put in a table (see Table 10.1) and the total and free floats are calculated as per definitions given before.

TABLE 10.1.   ACTIVITIES, TIMES, AND FLOATS

Activity	Duration	ES	EF	LS	LF	TF	FF	IF
*A	1–2	5	0	5	0	5	0	0	0
*B	2–3	8	5	13	5	13	0	0	0
C	2–4	9	5	14	8	17	3	0	0
*D	3–5	4	13	17	13	17	0	0	0
E	3–6	0	—	—	—	—	—	—	—
F	4–6	1	14	15	17	18	1	0	0
*G	5–7	3	17	20	17	20	0	0	0
H	6–7	2	15	17	18	20	2	0	0

*Activities on the Critical Path.

10.3.3 The Time-Grid Diagram and Bar Charts

CPM networks are not generally drawn-to-scale and therefore the lengths of the arrows do not represent the duration of tasks. However, the arrows in time-grid diagrams are drawn to scale in the horizontal direction (but not in the vertical scale). Float times are represented by broken horizontal lines whose lengths indicate time. (See Figure E10.5.) Project network activities can also be represented by bar charts (or Gantt charts) as shown in Figure E10.5.

10.3.4 Resource Scheduling

Project managers generally want to proceed with projects under the condition that they will be executed efficiently at scheduled rates. They would like to verify that the resources, in the shape of man-power, cash flows, machinery, and requirements are available to them. It is worthwhile for managers to draw up a resource allocation diagram, say with an early start timing to see whether it could be improved. One can, of course, only tinker with those activities that are not on the critical path. This is exactly what has been done through resource leveling procedure shown in Figure E10.5. Notice how the fluctuations of labor have been leveled off.

Example 10.5

An electric substation is to be installed and the following basic tasks are identified. The site will be cleared and leveled and the necessary materials for preparing the foundations and fencing will be procured and stored at site. Next, the foundation excavation and pouring of concrete will be done, a fence will be constructed, and the site will be cleared up and handed over to the authorities. Draw the activities network, perform the forward and backward passes, complete the activities, times, and floats table, draw the time-grid and Gantt chart, and finally sketch resource allocation diagrams, first with early start times followed by the procedure of leveling the labor resource.

Activity	Task	Duration	Labor	Logic and Sequence
A	Select site	4	3	A is independent
B	Clear site	4	5	B and C can be done simultaneously
C	Procure materials	5	6	C follows A, F can follow C and D
D	Excavate foundation	3	10	
E	Fix fence	6	4	E can be done only after A and B are finished
F	Pour concrete and cure	8	8	F can be done only after D is finished
G	Fix gate to fence	5	2	After E and F are completed
H	Dummy	0	0	Clean up cannot start till gate is fixed
I	Clean up and hand over	2	7	

Solution:

Activity	Event	Duration	ES	EF	LS	LF	TF	FF	IF	
A*	1–2	4	0	4	0	4	0	0	0	
B*	2–3	4	4	8	4	8	0	0	0	
C	2–4	5	4	9	6	11	2	2	0	
D*	3–4	3	8	11	8	11	0	0	0	
E	3–6	6	8	14	13	19	5	5	0	
F*	4–6	8	11	19	11	19	0	0	0	
G	3–5	5	8	13	14	19	6	6	0	
H	5–6	0	19	19	19	19	0	0	0	Dummy
I*	6–7	2	19	21	19	21	0	0	0	

*On the critical path

Figure E10.5 shows (a) the plan of the substation, (b) the activities network, (c) the forward and backward passes, (d) a typical way of showing ES, EF, LS, and LF, (e) the time-grid diagram, (f) the Gantt chart, (g) resource allocation based on early start, and (h) resource leveling.

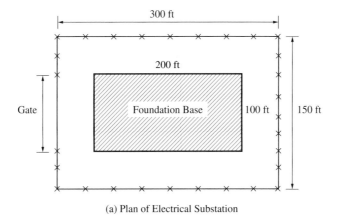

(a) Plan of Electrical Substation

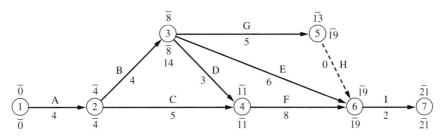

(b) Activities Network

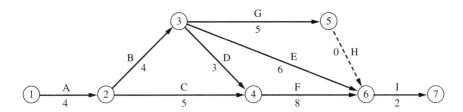

(c) Forward and Backward Pass

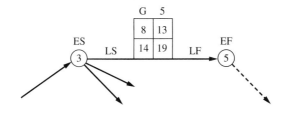

(d) Typical Way of Showing ES, EF, LS, LF on Activities

Figure E10.5   Critical path.

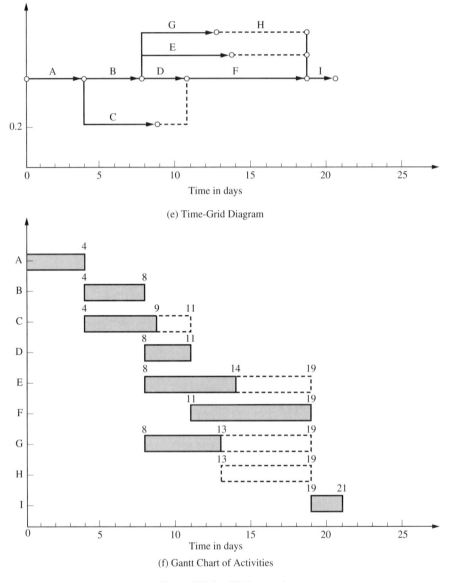

(e) Time-Grid Diagram

(f) Gantt Chart of Activities

Figure E10.5   CPM example.

10.3.5 Time-Cost Optimization

CPM is effective in discovering the possibility of minimizing the cost of the project from its normal duration by reducing (or "crashing") the duration of some of the individual activities in the network that lie on the critical path, by paying a higher cost (or "crash cost"). This extra cost is often offset by savings gained through lower overall indirect cost (or overhead cost). This technique of com-

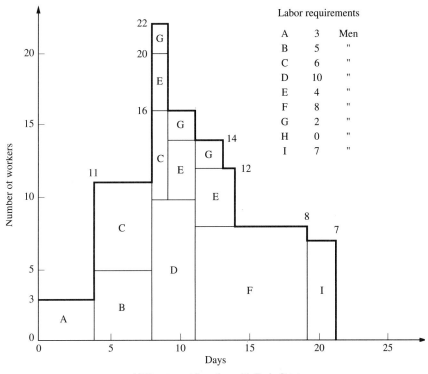

(a) Resource Allocation with Early Start

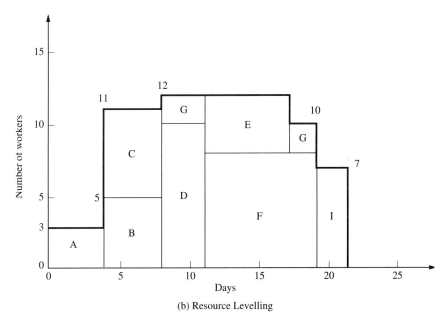

(b) Resource Levelling

Figure E10.5   CPM example.

pressing certain tasks and thereby optimizing a project cost is often called *project crashing.* Typically, the crash cost per unit of time for an activity can be found as follows:

$$\text{Crash cost} = \frac{\text{Crash cost} - \text{Normal cost}}{\text{Normal time} - \text{Crash time}}$$

The first step in crashing a project is to identify the critical activity with the minimum crash cost per unit of time and crash it with the allowable limit, taking into consideration the amount of float available with respect to multiple critical paths. The second step is to revise the network to identify new or multiple critical paths until all of the activities available for crashing have been utilized. Finally, all the crashing steps together with the corresponding cost increases are compared with the savings derived from overhead costs. See the following example for clarification.

Example 10.6

Determine the optimal completion time for a project whose logic is shown in Figure E10.6. Indirect cost is $150 per day. All other details are given in the table.

Activity	Normal Duration T_N	Total Cost (Normal) C_N	Crash Duration T_C	Total Cost (Crash) C_C
A	4 days	600	2 days	$1,000
B	6	800	3	1,400
C	8	500	3	1,200
D	7	600	2	1,200
E	2	500	2	500
F	1	100	1	100

Solution:

The first task is to complete the activities table shown below, after performing the forward and backward passes, as shown in Figure E10.6.

Activity	Duration	ES	EF	LS	LF	TF
A	4	0	4	0	4	0
B	6	0	6	11	17	11
C	8	4	12	4	12	0
D	7	12	19	12	19	0
E	2	6	8	17	19	11
F	1	19	20	19	20	0

The table above is completed followed by working out the time schedules to find the one that is the cheapest. These schedules are graphically shown in Figure E10.6.

Schedule 1: Normal Schedule; Critical Path $1 - 2 - 4 - 5 - 6 = 20$ days

$$\text{Cost} = (600 + 800 + 500 + 600 + 500 + 100) = \$3,100$$

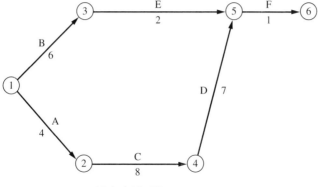

(a) Activities Diagram

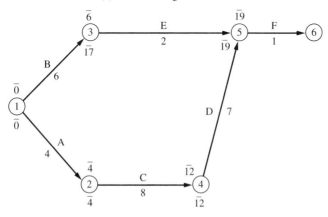

(b) Forward and Backward Passes

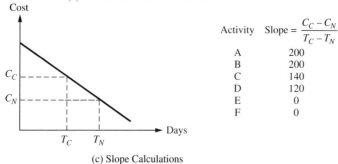

(c) Slope Calculations

Figure E10.6   Activities and activity slopes.

Schedule 2: Select activities on CP; choose D (smallest slope)
          Compress D (limit 5 days; total float 11 days)
          Direct cost $= 3100 + (120 \times 5) = \$3700$; Time : 15 days
          TF: $11 - 5 = 6$, CP : $1 - 2 - 4 - 5 - 6 = 15$ days

Schedule 3: Compress next cheapest activity
          Compress C; TF $= 6$ Crash 5 days @$140/day

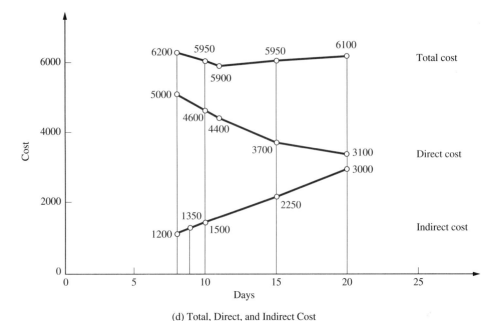

(d) Total, Direct, and Indirect Cost

Figure E10.6 Time-cost optimization.

Direct cost = 3710 + (140 × 5) = $4400
Time 9 days; TF: 6 − 5 = 1 CP: 1 − 2 − 4 − 5 − 6 = 10 days

Schedule 4: Compress next cheapest activity
Compress A; TF = 1 Crash = 2
Compress A for only 1 day @$200/day
Direct cost = $4400 + (200 × 1) = $4600

Time 9 days TF: 1 − 1 = 0 CP: 1 − 2 − 4 − 5 − 6 = 9 days and CP:
1 − 3 − 5 − 6 = 9 days

Schedule 5: Any other compression will affect both CPs.
Also, A can be compressed only 1 more day.
Compress A and B, one day each = $400
Direct cost = $4600 + $400 = $5000
Cost $5000; Time 8 days.

Schedule	5	4	3	2	1
Days	8	9	10	15	20
Direct	5,000	4,600	4,400	3,700	3,100
Indirect	1,200	1,350	1,500	2,250	3,000
Total	6,200	5,950	5,900	5,950	6,100

Schedule 3 is the cheapest at $5900.

10.4 PROGRAM EVALUATION AND REVIEW TECHNIQUE AND THE LINE-OF-BALANCE TECHNIQUE

The Program Evaluation and Review Technique (PERT) and the Line-of-Balance (LOB) technique are both closely associated with CPM. The PERT was developed to analyze projects in an environment of uncertainty, particularly with projects where the specific duration of activities could not be estimated with reliability. PERT uses two probability density functions; the beta (β) distribution for each activity; and the normal distribution for estimating the completion time of the entire project. Other than the use of these probability functions, PERT is similar to CPM. PERT is described first in Section 10.4.1. The LOB technique was developed by the U.S. Navy for controlling and managing production processes. It has since been used in the construction industry. LOB is described in Section 10.4.2.

10.4.1 Key Concepts of PERT (see Figure 10.2)

- PERT introduces the concepts of uncertainty into time estimates as opposed to CPM, which is essentially deterministic.
- PERT uses expected mean time (t_e) with standard deviation σ_{te} or variance ν_{te}.
- The expected mean time (t_e) of an individual task is an estimate having an approximate chance of 50 percent success.
- The value of t_e is calculated from: t_a, the optimistic time of completion of an individual task; t_m, the most likely time; and t_b, the pessimistic time of completion of this task. This forces the planner to take an overall view of each task's duration.
- The beta (β) distribution uses t_a, t_b, and t_m to estimate the expected mean time. The expected mean time t_e is

$$t_e = \frac{t_a + 4t_m + t_b}{6}$$

with a standard deviation, $\sigma_{te} = \dfrac{t_b - t_a}{6}$

and a variance, $\nu_{te} = \sigma_{te}^2 = \left(\dfrac{t_b - t_a}{6}\right)^2$

- t_a and t_b have small probabilities, of the order of 5 to 10 percent.
- Once t_e and ν_{te} are found for each activity, the critical path is found in the same fashion as in CPM.
- Project duration = Expected mean duration T_x^p, which is the expected mean time along the CP.
- Once the expected mean time for an event (T_x) and its standard deviation (σ_{Tx}) are determined, calculate the event schedule time (T_s). This has a normal probability distribution with mean T_x and σ_{Tx}.

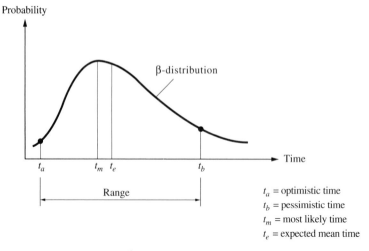

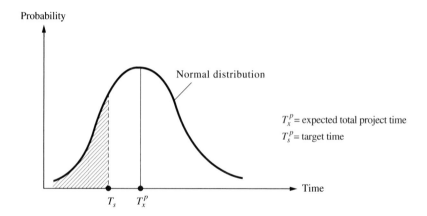

Probability

t_a = optimistic time
t_b = pessimistic time
t_m = most likely time
t_e = expected mean time

(i) Beta (β) Distribution

T_x^p = expected total project time
T_s^p = target time

(ii) Normal Distribution

Figure 10.2   Key concepts (PERT). (i) Beta distribution. (ii) Normal distribution.

- The effect of adding a series of independent β-distribution gives a normal distribution.
- To determine the probability that the expected total project time T_x will exceed some target time T_s, first calculate the value of Z, a dimensionless parameter expressing the horizontal axis of the standardized normal distribution function.

$$\text{where } Z = \frac{(T_s - T_x)}{\sigma_{Tx}}$$

- Refer to Table 10.2 to find the corresponding probability associated with the value of Z.

TABLE 10.2   VALUES OF Z AND PROBABILITY

Z	Probability	Probability	Z
−2.0	.02	.98	+2.0
−1.5	.07	.93	+1.5
−1.3	.10	.90	+1.3
−1.0	.16	.84	+1.0
−0.9	.18	.82	+0.9
−0.8	.21	.79	+0.8
−0.7	.24	.76	+0.7
−0.6	.27	.73	+0.6
−0.5	.31	.69	+0.5
−0.4	.34	.66	+0.4
−0.3	.38	.62	+0.3
−0.2	.42	.58	+0.2
−0.1	.46	.54	+0.1
0	.50	.50	0

Example 10.7

An activity network for a small house is shown in Figure E10.7. The table shows the optimistic, most likely, and pessimistic times for the various activities under column 2, 3, 4. What is the probability of finishing this project in 110, 115, 117, 119, 124 days?

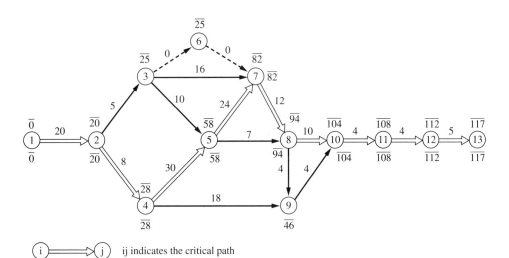

Figure E10.7   PERT network.

Solution:

The expected mean time of all the activities are calculated using the formula $t_e = (t_a + 4t_m + t_b)/6$ and entered in column 5. These values are also shown against each activity on the network. One can now do a forward and backward pass to determine the CP (in a manner similar to what was explained in the section on CPM). Now that the CP is known, one can calculate the standard deviation σ_{te} and variance ν_{te} of the critical activities and enter these in column 6 and 7 respectively. The critical activities are marked with an asterisk and the total project duration works out to be 117 days with a corresponding variance of 74.41 days. Taking the square root of 74.41 days gives a standard deviation of 8.63 days. Notice that we cannot add values under column 6 to get the standard deviation. We add the variance of critical activities and then take the square root of this total to get the standard deviation.

While we have found that the expected mean duration of this project is 117 days with a standard deviation of 8.63 days, one could be asked the probability of finishing the project at a target time of 110, 115, 119, or 124 days. For finding these probabilities we must calculate the corresponding values of Z, as shown under the table. Notice that the probability of completing the project in 117 days is merely 50 percent.

1	2	3	4	5	6	7
Activity	t_a	t_m	t_b	t_e	σ_{te}	ν_{te}
*1–2	18	20	22	20	0.67	0.44
2–3	4	5	6	5		
*2–4	6	7	14	8	1.33	1.77
3–5	8	10	12	10		
3–7	14	16	18	16		
*4–5	20	25	60	30	6.67	44.44
4–9	14	18	22	18		
*5–7	18	20	46	24	4.67	21.77
5–8	6	7	8	7		
*7–8	11	12	13	12	0.33	0.11
8–9	4	10	16	10		
9–10	4	4	4	4		
*8–10	8	8	20	10	2.00	4.00
*10–11	2	3	10	4	1.33	1.77
*11–12	3	4	5	4	0.33	0.11
*12–13	5	5	5	5	0	0
				117	8.63	74.41

*On the critical path. Note that $\sqrt{74.41} = 8.63$.

Expected time T_{xe}	Standard Deviation σ	Target time	$Z = \dfrac{T_s - T_x}{\sigma}$	Probability (%)
117	8.63	110	−0.811	21
		115	−0.231	43
		117	−0	50
		119	+0.231	79
		124	−0.811	57

10.4.2 The LOB Technique

The LOB technique is a management-oriented tool for collecting, measuring, and presenting information relating to the time and accomplishment of repetitive tasks during production. One of the major problems facing managers is obtaining information on the status of various operations soon enough to take effective action. LOB is particularly useful in repetitive construction work such as multi-house projects, road pavement construction, and the manufacturing of repetitive identical units, such as small septic tanks, pylons, and beams.

The LOB technique consists of four elements: (1) the objective chart, (2) the program chart, (3) the progress chart, and (4) the comparison. The objective chart is a graph showing the cumulative end product to be manufactured over a period of time, while the program chart is a flow process diagram showing sequenced tasks and their interrelationship with *lead times.* Lead time is the number of time periods by which each activity must precede the end event in order to meet the objective. The progress chart consists of vertical bars representing the cumulative progress of each monitoring point based on site visits to the production area indicating the actual performance. The comparison activity is derived from the objective, program, and progress charts to draw the LOB. When one draws the LOB on the program chart, it represents the number of completed units that should have passed through each control point at the time of the study in order to deliver the completed units according to the contract schedule.

10.4.3 Progress Charts and Buffers

Suppose a company has been awarded a contract to erect ten steel pylons. The sequential operations involved are A = excavate; B = pour concrete; C = erect pylon as shown in Figure 10.3a.

This sequence needs to be repeated ten times to complete the work. However, to provide for a margin of error in the time taken to complete each operation, a time buffer is provided between two operations, as shown in Figure 10.3b.

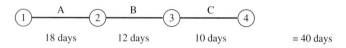

(a) Activities A, B, and C without buffers

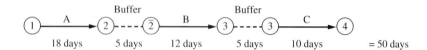

(b) Activities A, B, and C with buffers

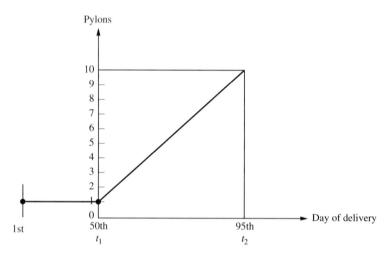

(c) Completion schedule of 10 pylons

Figure 10.3   Line-of-balance. (a) Activities A, B, and C without buffers. (b) Activities A, B, and C with buffers. (c) Completion schedule.

If the 10 pylons take 50 days each, including buffers, they must be ready at a target completion rate of one each week (1 week = 5 days). We can use the straight-line equation $Q = mt + c$ to find the time needed to complete the job. Suppose the first pylon is to be ready on the 50th day; on which day would the tenth pylon be ready? Refer to Figure 10.3c.

$$Q_1 = 1; t_1 = 50; Q_2 = 10; m = 1/5; t_2 = ?$$

$$t_2 = \left(\frac{10 - 1}{1/5}\right) + t_1 = (9 \times 5) + 50 = 95 \text{ days.}$$

On the 95th day, the tenth pylon will be completed. Notice that when we graph this problem, we must be mindful that on the 50th day we are ready to complete the first pylon, with 9 more to go. Also, notice that we must begin work on the first pylon on the first day to get it ready by the 50th day.

We will now consider a simple example to illustrate same basic principles of LOB.

Example 10.8

A septic tank prefabricator has received a contract to supply 1000 septic tanks, and to deliver 40 units each month beginning on the first of the 20th month. The major control points of the production scheme are shown in Figure E10.8a.

An LOB study performed on the first of the 26th month revealed that the number of completed units that actually passed through each control point is as follows:

Control point	Units
A	450
B	520
C	420
D	440
E	400
F	440
G	410
H	285
I	250

Draw the objective chart, the program progress chart and the LOB chart. Determine the deviation of units.

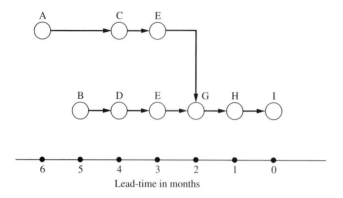

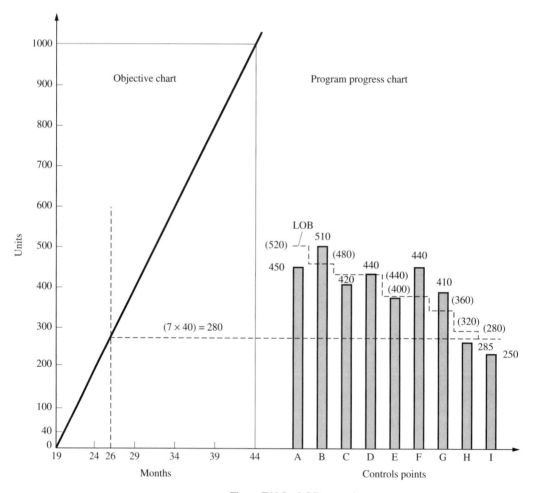

Figure E10.8   LOB example.

Solution:

Control point	Cumulative units to be delivered	Units actually completed	Deviation
A	520	450	−70
B	480	510	+30
C	440	420	−20
D	440	440	0
E	400	380	−20
F	400	440	+40
G	360	410	+50
H	320	285	−35
I	280	250	−30

The table indicates that the performance of control points A, C, E, H, and I are behind schedule, and that corrective action is needed.

10.4.4 Resource and LOB Schedule

Estimation of resources including labor requirements are an important feature of LOB schedules. In general such estimation is best done by: preparing a logic diagram of all the activities and tasks including sequenced and parallel (or simultaneous) activities; estimating the manhours required to complete each task; choosing realistic buffer times that reflect the risk entailed in not completing sequenced activities; calculating the required output target to meet a given project completion date; and finally putting all the information in the form of a convenient table as shown in Table 10.3.

TABLE 10.3   CALCULATION SHEET FOR LOB SCHEDULE

1	2	3	4	5	6	7	8
Activity	Man power per activity	Men per activity	Theoretical gang size	Actual gang size	Actual rate of output	Time in days for 1 activity	Time in days

Explanation of columns:

Column 1: major activities or tasks.
Column 2: estimate of man–hours needed for each activity.
Column 3: the optimum number of labor needed for each task (which is labor in each team).
Column 4: the theoretical gang size needed to maintain the output rate (R)

given by

$$\frac{R \times (\text{column 2})}{\text{number of hours/week}}$$

Column 5: the actual gang size is chosen as a number which is a multiple of men required for one team.

$$\text{Column 6: actual rate of output} = \frac{\text{Actual gang size} \times \text{target rate}}{\text{Theoretical gang size}}$$

Column 7: time taken for one activity =

$$\frac{\text{manhours for activity}}{\text{number of men in one team} \times \text{number of hours in a working day}}$$

Column 8: the time in days from the start of the first section to the start of the last section is:

$$\frac{(\text{Number of sections} - 1) \times \text{number of working days per week}}{\text{Actual rate of build}}$$

Table 10.3 helps us to draw the various activities which show the sections completed against time. Also, the slope of the activities is a function of several factors, such as the total units of time required to complete Q repetitive units; F, the resource unit factor, is the number of units of the resource that are required in order to achieve the rate of working necessary to meet the handover program; d, the activity duration; and m, the rate of handover. The buffer time allowed plays an important role in the entire completion time. Lastly, the actual gang size in relation to the men per activity is important as it determines the slope of the activity as shown in Figure 10.4. If a task takes 7 days, with one team shifting from one unit to the next, it would take 35 days for the completion of 5 units. If the same task is arranged with two teams (a and b), the 5 units would be completed in 21 days.

The following example explains the procedure of LOB.

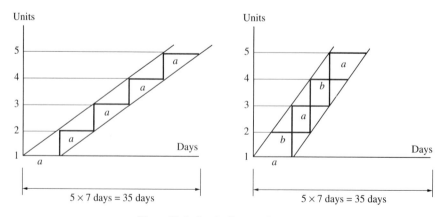

Figure 10.4   Logic diagram for teams.

Example 10.9

A contract has been awarded to erect 15 steel pylons at the rate of three per week, (assuming 5 days of 8 hours each) as per details given below:

	Task	Man hours	Optimum number of men per operation
A	Excavate pit	180	6
B	Concrete pit	320	4
C	Fix pylon	200	4
D	Adjust/finish	60	2

A minimum buffer of 5 days is provided between tasks to take care of delays. Prepare a LOB schedule showing gang sizes and rates of build. Finally, draw a sketch showing the LOB schedule with buffers for all 15 pylons.

Solution:

The calculation of gang sizes and rates of build, with a target rate of three per week is shown in the table on the following page, and the LOB schedule for the four tasks is sketched in Figure E10.9.

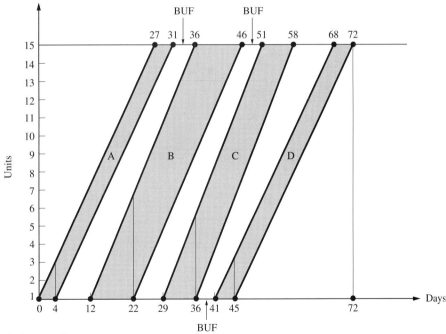

"BUF" indicates buffers necessary

Figure E10.9   LOB schedule showing buffers.

Activity 1	Man power per activity 2	Men per activity 3	Theoretical gang size 4	Actual gang size 5	Actual rate of output 6	Time in days for 1 activity 7	Actual time 4	Time from start on first section to start on last section 8	Actual Time	Buffer
A	180	6	13.50	12	2.67	3.75	4	26.22	27	5
B	320	4	24.00	24	3.00	10.00	10	23.33	24	5
C	200	4	15.0	16	3.20	6.25	7	21.88	22	5
D	60	2	4.5	4	2.67	3.75	4	26.22	27	5

Note: Figures in columns 3 must be multiples of column 5.

	First unit		Last unit		
	Begin	End	Begin	End	Buffer
A	0	4	27	31	5
B	12	22	36	46	5
C	29	36	51	58	5
D	41	45	68	72	5

10.5 NETWORK FLOW ANALYSIS

Everybody is familiar with highway, telephone, and cable networks. They are all arrangements of paths and crossings for facilitating the flow of goods, people, and communication. In this section we will be dealing with three types of network flow problems: the minimum spanning tree, the maximum flow, and the shortest path techniques.

10.5.1 Key Concepts

Graph theory and network theory are branches of mathematics which have grown in the last 75 years. The building of large physical systems such as highways, railroads, and pipe-lines has created wide interest in network theory. We have already seen many problems of sequencing and scheduling such as CPM and PERT that can also be looked upon as problems in graph and network theory.

A graph is formed when a number of points, nodes, or vertices are joined together by one or more lines, arcs, links, branches, or edges. Nodes may be joined by more than one arc and may be oriented by indicating a sense of direction for them, using an arrow. A loop is formed when the extremity nodes of a path through a graph are one and the same node (see Figure 10.5).

A network is a graph through which flows of money, traffic, commodities, etc. may take place, and the direction of the arc represents the direction of flow. In some networks there are distinct nodes from which flows emanate, and there are other nodes to which all flows finally go. These are called sources and sinks respectively (see Figure 10.5).

10.5.2 Minimum Spanning Tree

This type of problem involves finding the least length of links needed for connecting all the nodes in a network. For example, if it is required to find the shortest length of cable needed to connect all the nodes in a city network, this problem would fall under the category of finding the minimum spanning tree.

The procedure for finding the minimum spanning tree of a network is as follows:

1. Select the shortest link in the network.
2. Identify an unconnected node with the shortest distance to the node in Step 1.
3. Connect these two nodes. In case of a tie, select one arbitrarily.
4. Continue connecting one node after another till all nodes are connected.

Example 10.10

A small village needs to be connected by cable to seven main nodes. What is the minimum length of cable needed to connect all the nodes? Distances are marked on the nodes.

Solution:

See Figure E10.10

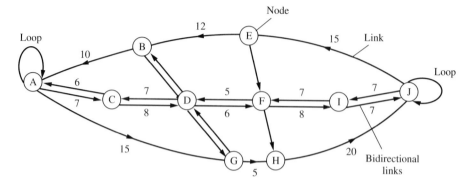

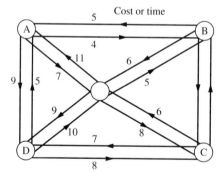

A = Source
B = Sink

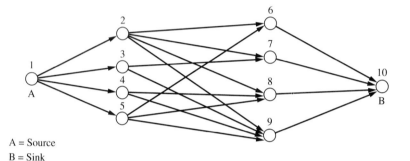

Figure 10.5   Network details.

1. The shortest link in the network is EG = 11.
2. The next shortest link connected to either E or G is GF = 13. Join GF.
3. The next shortest link, either E or F, is ED = 15. Join ED.
4. The next link at D, F or G is DC = 26. Join DC and so on.

The sequence of linking is EG, GF, ED, DC, CB, and BA, totaling 107 units, which is the minimum length of cable needed to join all the nodes in the network.

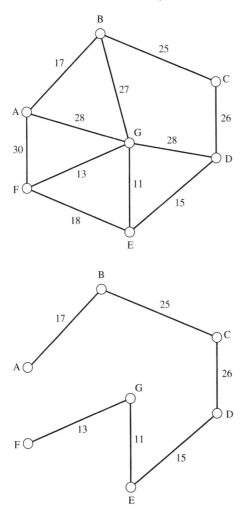

Total length of minimum spanning tree = 107 units   **Figure E10.10**   Minimum spanning free.

10.5.3 The Maximal Flow Problem

There are countless instances in which one would like to know the maximum number of trucks or wagons that can flow in a railroad or highway network from a source (or origin) to a sink (or destination). For example, in a highway network you could have traffic flow on a one-way street or a two-way street, whereas in a pipeline network, oil could flow in both directions.

The procedure for determining the maximum flow in a network is as follows:

1. Identify the source node and the sink node of the network.
2. Determine all the feasible paths from source to sink that would be able to handle the flow.

3. Determine whether there are possibilities of reverse flows, depending on the information supplied.

4. Sum up all the flows through each link of the network.

Example 10.11

A small railroad network with the indicated link flow capacities are shown in the Figure E10.11. Determine the maximum flow from Source node 1 to Sink node 5, and indicate the flow on each link.

Solution:

Source node = 1   Sink node = 5
Feasible paths with flows:
A. Path 1–2–4–5   Flow 2 units
B. Path 1–2–5   Flow 2 units
C. Path 1–3–4–5   Flow 2 units
D. Path 1–3–5   Flow 2 units
E. Path 1–4–2–5   Flow 3 units
                                                     Total 11 units

Links	Flow	
1–2	4	
1–3	4	
1–4	3	
2–4	2	Note that link 2–4 has flow in both directions
2–5	5	
3–4	2	
3–5	2	
4–5	4	
4–2	3	

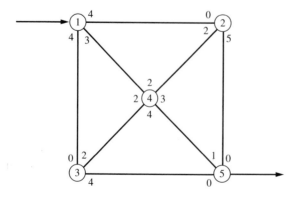

Figure E10.11   Maximal flow problem.

10.5.4 Shortest-Path or Minimum-Path Technique

The shortest-path or minimum-path technique is based on the assumption that travelers want to use the minimum impedance route between two points. Efficient methods of determining minimum paths were developed, because manual determinations would be nearly impossible. In Figure 10.6, 40 different paths must be tested to determine the minimum between A and B. You can imagine the problem of finding the shortest path in a network with thousands of links and nodes.

Work that was undertaken to determine the minimum paths for long-distance telephone calls provided the help that planners needed. Rather than simply testing each path, algorithms allowed planners to find minimum paths to complete networks. The algorithm used most commonly is Moore's algorithm.

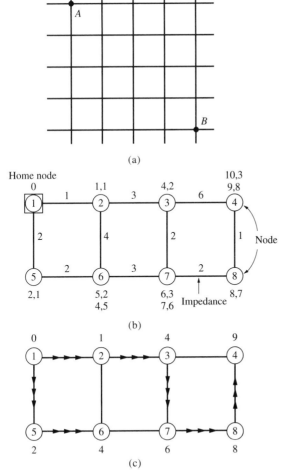

Figure 10.6 Minimum path technique: (a) Small network: 24 links, 16 nodes; (b) minimum path through a network; (c) skim tree from node one to all other nodes.

Using Moore's algorithm, minimum paths are developed by fanning out from their origin to all other nodes. Determining the minimum path from node 1 to each of the other nodes results in a *skimtree* from node 1 to all other nodes, as shown in Figure 10.6.

Moore's algorithm is now applied to Figure 10.6*b*:

1. Start at node 1 (the origin) and determine the shortest time (or distance) to get to a directly connected node. The two nodes directly connected to node 1 are nodes 2 and 5, with the shortest time of 1 and 2, respectively.

2. Since there is no doubt the shortest times to reach nodes 2 and 5 are 1 and 2 respectively, we refer to these nodes as comprising the "permanent set."

3. Repeat the foregoing steps by determining all the nodes directly connected to the nodes in the permanent set (nodes 1, 2, and 5). Now, nodes 3 and 6 are directly connected to nodes 2 and 5.

4. Two paths can be identified connected to node 6 (2–6 and 5–6), with times of 4 and 2 respectively. Also, the path along 1–2–6 takes 5 units of time, while path 1–5–6 takes 4 units. Therefore, the shortest path to node 6 from node 1 is 1–5–6. And, this path is indicated in Figure 10.6*c*.

5. Nodes 1, 2, 5, and 6 are now part of the permanent set, and one can proceed to other nodes repeating the process described in steps 1 through 4.

6. The shortest path from the starting (or home) node to all other nodes can be tabulated as follows:

From	To	Path	Duration
1	2	1–2	1
1	3	1–2–3	4
1	4	1–2–3–7–8–4	9
1	5	1–5	2
1	6	1–5–6	4
1	7	1–2–3–7	6
1	8	1–2–3–7–8	8

Once the minimum paths are found, the trips between the zones are loaded onto the links making up the minimum path. This technique of assigning trips to the network is sometimes referred to as all-or-nothing, because all trips between a given origin and destination are loaded on links comprising the minimum path, and nothing is loaded on the other links. After all possible interchanges are considered, the result is an estimate of the volume on each link in the network.

Moore's algorithm can be stated as follows:

1. Label the start node (or home node) as zero.

2. Calculate working values for each node that is directly connected to the node labeled zero, using working values indicated on the links. Select the minimum

of the labeled values plus the distance from the labeled node. This establishes a "permanent set."

3. Select an unlabeled node with the lowest working value and label it with that value.

4. Repeat Steps 2 and 3 until all nodes have been labeled.

5. Mark all links lying on the shortest path; this is the skim tree rooted in the start (or home) node.

6. Repeat Steps 1 through 5, selecting successive nodes as start nodes.

Example 10.12

A highway network consisting of 4 nodes and 10 links is shown in the Figure E10.12. A trip table showing the number of vehicles wanting to use the network per hour from one node to another is also provided. Assign the trips to the network.

Solution:

Refer to Figure E10.12. The origin-to-destination flows corresponding to each node of the trip table are assigned with the links that make up the minimum. The aggregate flow on each link is then shown.

10.6 LINEAR PROGRAMMING

The objective of linear programming is to determine the optimal allocation of scarce resources among competing products or outputs. In most engineering and economic problems, one is frequently called upon to optimize a function that is subject to several constraints. When a single constraint is involved, the Lagrangian method is used because of its simplicity. However, when more than one constraint is involved, linear programming is usually enacted. However, if the constraints are limited to only two variables (or at most three in some special cases), the graphical approach is the easiest to use. When a problem involves more than two variables, the best way of dealing with it is by using the *simplex* algorithm. We will first deal with the graphical method and then follow up with the simplex.

10.6.1 The Graphical Method

This method is generally used for solving maximization or minimization problems involving two variables. It is best described by means of an example.

Example 10.13

A steel firm produces two products, small beams (X_1) and small poles (X_2). Each beam requires 2.5 hours for cutting and welding, 3 hours for finishing, and 1 hour for checking and testing. Each pole requires 1 hour for cutting and welding, 3 hours for finishing, and 2 hours for checking and testing. The firm is limited to no more than 20 hours for cutting and welding, 30 hours for finishing, and 16 hours for checking and testing. The firm makes a profit of $3 per beam and $4 per pole. How many beams and poles should the firm produce to maximize profit?

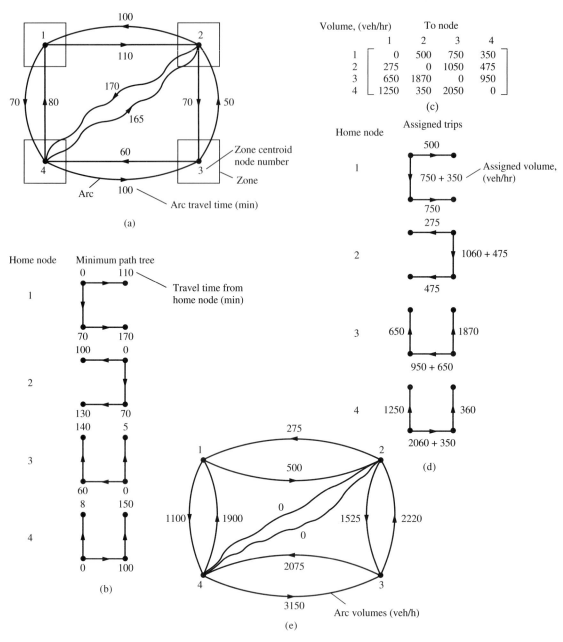

Figure E10.12 Example of all-or-nothing traffic assignment: (a) network; (b) minimum-path trees; (c) origin-destination trip table; (d) assignment of trips to minimum-path trees; (e) assigned traffic volumes (Morlock, 1978).

Solution:

The firm's objective function is to maximize profit, and the total profit is the sum of the individual profit gained from each of the two products. First, express the information given in the form of equations or inequalities. The objective function can be written as:

$$Z = 3\,X_1 + 4\,X_2, \text{ subject to constraints}$$
$$2.5\,X_1 + X_2 \le 20$$
$$3\,X_1 + 3\,X_2 \le 30$$
$$X_1 + 2\,X_2 \le 16$$
$$X_1, X_2 \ge 0$$

The first three inequalities are technical constraints dictated by the availability of time, while the last constraint is imposed on all such problems to avoid negative values from the solution.

The three inequality constraints are treated as follows:

(1) $\quad X_2 = 20 - 2.5\,X_1$
(2) $\quad X_2 = 10 - X_1$
(3) $\quad X_2 = 8 - 0.5\,X_1$

The graph of these three equations is shown in Figure E10.13. The feasibility area satisfying the equations above and the inequalities originally derived are shown by the area included in OABCD.

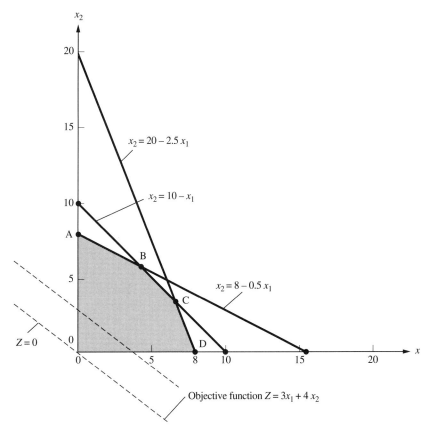

Figure E10.13   Graphical method of L.P (maximization).

To find the optimal solution within the feasible area, graph the objective function.

$$Z = 3 X_1 + 4 X_2, \quad \text{and} \quad \therefore X_2 = (Z/4)) - (3/4) X_1$$

The objective function has a slope of $(-3/4)$. Raising the objective function from its initial position at $(0,0)$ when the profit is zero, and testing it at the four extreme corners of the feasible area (A, B, C, D), one finds that the maximum profit is derived at point B (4, 6). Substituting the values of $X_1 = 4$, and $X_2 = 6$ in the objective function equation gives:

$$Z = 3(4) + 4(6) = 36.$$

As a check, the amount of profit at the other extreme points can also be determined.

At	A $(0, 8)$:	$3(0) + 4(8) = 32$
	B $(4, 6)$:	$3(4) + 4(6) = 36$ (maximum profit)
	C $(7, 3)$:	$3(7) + 4(3) = 33$
	D $(8, 0)$:	$3(8) + 4(0) = 24$

Example 10.14

A nutritionist wants patients in a hospital to receive the minimum requirements of three vitamins in two kinds of diets, as given in the table below. Diet X_1 costs \$1.00/lb, while diet X_2 costs \$2.00/lb. What combination of A and B will produce an adequate diet at a minimum cost?

	Units/lb of diet X_1	Units/lb of diet X_2	Minimum requirement units
Vitamin A	1	3	90
Vitamin B	5	1	100
Vitamin C	3	2	120

Solution:

Note, that this is a minimization problem and therefore one will have to be careful in deciding what the feasible region will be. The constraints are:

Vitamin A:	$X_1 + 3 X_2 \geq 90$
Vitamin B:	$5 X_1 + X_2 \geq 100$
Vitamin C:	$3 X_1 + 2 X_2 \geq 120$

The objective function $Z = 1.0 X_1 + 2.0 X_2$
Therefore, $X_2 = (Z/2) - (1/2) X_1$
Slope of $Z = -1/2$
The feasible area is the shaded area shown to the northeast of the points OPQR in Figure E10.14. When Z is moved up from the origin, the first point to hit is point Q, whose coordinates are (25.8, 21.4). This point gives the minimum cost for the combination of the two diets containing the specified requirements of vitamins A, B, and C.
      The cost of such a diet is $Z = 1(25.8) + 2(21.4) = \$225.80$
Notice that the amount of vitamin B $= 5(25.8) + 1(21.4) = 150.4$ units, which is more than the 100 units prescribed by the nutritionist.

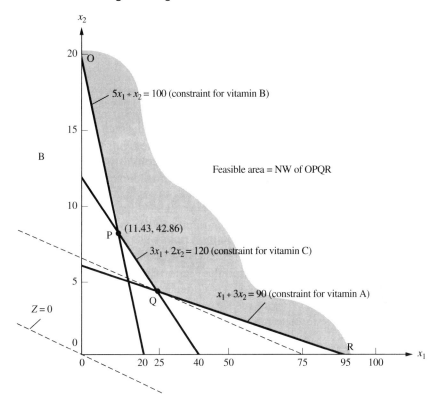

Figure E10.14   Graphical method of L.P (minimization).

10.6.2 Simplex Algorithm

An algorithm is a set of rules or procedures for finding a solution to a problem. The SIMPLEX algorithm first developed by George Dantzig in 1947 is a computational procedure for determining basic feasible solutions to a system of equations and testing the solution for optimality. The algorithm moves from one basic feasible solution to another, always improving upon the previous one, until the optimal solution is reached. The best way to understand this algorithm is through a simple example as described in Example 10.15. The explanation of the simplex tableau is given.

		Solution	C_1	C_2	...	...	...	...	...	...	θ
c_j											
c_b	Basis	'b'	X_1	X_2	...	S_1	S_2	...	A_1	...	
	Z_j										
	$C_j - Z_j$										

c_j = Unit contribution rate for each variable (i.e., unit profit, or unit cost, etc). The row starts with the decision variables followed by the slack (S_i), surplus, and artificial variables (A_i).

c_b = Unit contribution rate for each of the basic variables.

Basis = Basis column where the basic variables for each of the constraints are listed.

Solution = Solution values of the basic variable (b); consisting of constants from the restriction equation.

Z_j = Total value or contribution of the objective function. In each of the variable columns, the Z_j value represents the total profit that needs to be sacrificed to produce one unit of each variable for a maximization problem.

$C_j - Z_j$ = Net increase of profit associated with the production of one unit of each variable in a maximization problem.

θ = Value of b for each row divided by the entry in the pivot column for that row.

To determine the basic variables that have solution values, they must be converted into equalities as follows:

Constraint type	Adjustment required
Less than or equal to, $\leq$	Add a slack variable, S_i
Exactly equal to, $=$	Add an artificial variable, A_i
Greater than or equal to, $\geq$	Subtract a surplus variable and add an artificial variable, $(-S_i + A_i)$

Example 10.15

A manufacturer produces two types of machines from parts X_1 and X_2. The resources needed for producing machines X_1 and X_2 and the corresponding profits are:

Machines	Labor hrs/unit	Capital ($/unit)	Profit $
X_1	10	40	40
X_2	20	30	50

There are 400 hours of labor and $1200 worth of capital available per day for assembling the machines. How many machines, X_1 and X_2, should be produced per day to maximize profit?

Solution:

This problem is first worked out graphically as shown in Figure E10.15.

$$Z = 40\,X_1 + 50\,X_2$$

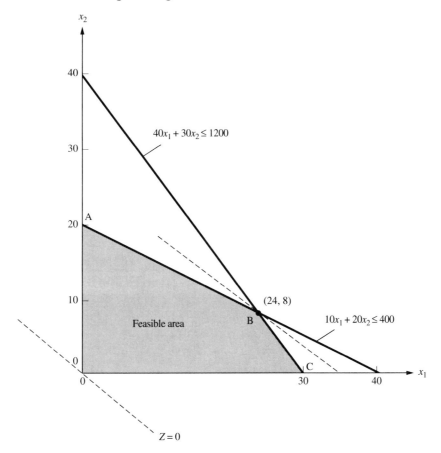

Figure E10.15   Graphical solution to manufacturer producing two types
of machines.

Subject to

$$10\,X_1 + 20\,X_2 \le 400$$
$$40\,X_1 + 30\,X_2 \le 1200$$
$$X_1, X_2 \ge 0$$

$$X_2 = (Z/50) - (40/50)X_1 \text{ with a slope of } -4/5.$$

The feasible area is OABC. Point B gives the maximum profit. Therefore, 8 units of
machine X_1 and 24 units of machine X_2 should be produced to maximize profit. The
profit is worked out as:

$$Z = (40)(24) + (50)(8) = \$1360$$

We will now use the simplex algorithm to maximize profits represented by
$Z = 40\,X_1 + 50\,X_2$, which is the objective function subject to

$$10\,X_1 + 20\,X_2 \le 400$$
$$40\,X_1 + 30\,X_2 \le 1200$$

Step 1: Convert the inequalities to equations by adding slack variables (S)

$$10\,X_1 + 20\,X_2 + S_1 = 400$$
$$40\,X_1 + 30\,X_2 + S_2 = 1200$$

Express the constraint equations in matrix form:

$$\begin{bmatrix} 10 & 20 & 1 & 0 \\ 40 & 30 & 0 & 1 \end{bmatrix} \begin{bmatrix} X_1 \\ X_2 \\ S_1 \\ S_2 \end{bmatrix} = \begin{bmatrix} 400 \\ 1200 \end{bmatrix}$$

Step 2: Set up an initial simplex tableau composed of the coefficient matrix of the constraint equations and the column vector of constants set above in a row of indicators, as shown below:

TABLEAU 1

C_i C_j	Basic variables	Quantity b	40 X_1	50 X_2	0 S_1	0 S_2	θ
0	S_1	400	10	20	1	0	20
0	S_2	1200	40	30	0	1	40
	Z_j	0	0	0	0	0	
	$C_j - Z_j$		40	50	0	0	

The meaning of the last column (θ) will be explained later. The values of the Z_j row are computed by multiplying each C_j column value (on the left side) by each column value under quantities X_1, X_2, S_1, and S_2, and then aggregating each of these sets of values.

Step 3: Start with a feasible initial solution (at the origin), $X_1 = 0$, $X_2 = 0$. The first column C_j gives their C values, which are zero.

Step 4: Compute the row marked $Z_j = \Sigma a_{ij}\, C_i$, where a_{ij} = any cell value.

$Z_j = 400(0) + 1200(0) = 0$ under column "b"

$Z_j = 10(0) + 40(0) = 0$ under column "X_1"

and so on.

Step 5: The $C_j - Z_j$ row shows the profit to be derived from adding a unit of that variable. The best variable to bring in is X_2, because every unit brought in brings $50 to the profit function (i.e., the column with the highest ($C_j - Z_j$)).

Step 6: Determine the row to be removed from the solution (i.e., the row with the lowest contribution). Calculate the θ column: $\theta_1 = 400/20 = 20$; $\theta_2 = 1200/30 = 40$; θ_1 is the lowest value and is therefore the pivot row.

Step 7: Calculate the rows and columns of second tableau.

    (a) New X_2 row replaces S_1 row. Divide each element of the old S_1 row by the pivot element 20. Thus, in the new row the old pivot element is replaced by 1, and the new row values are:

$$X_2 \quad 20 \quad 1/2 \quad 1 \quad 1/20 \quad 0$$

    (b) A new S_2 row is obtained from the old one by deducting from it, element by element, the new S_2 row, multiplied by the pivot element of the old row.

New	-	20	1/2	1	1/20	0
Old S_2		1200	40	30	0	1
-30 (new X_2)		-600	-15	-30	$-3/2$	0
New S_2		600	-25	0	$-3/2$	1

Step 8: Compute the Z_j and $C_j - Z_j$ row values.

$$Z_j = (50)(20) + (0)(60) \qquad = \quad 1000$$
$$X_1: \; Z_1 = (50)(1/2) + (0)(25) \qquad = \quad 25$$
$$X_2: \; Z_2 = (50)(1) + (0)(0) \qquad = \quad 50$$
$$S_1: \; Z_3 = (50)(1/20) + (0)(-3/2) \; = \quad -5/2$$
$$S_2: \; Z_4 = (50)(0) + (0)(1) \qquad = \quad 0$$

The largest value of $C_j - Z_j$ is X_1 which is 15 and therefore the pivot column is X_1. Now, calculate the θ column values: $\theta_1 = 20/(1/2) = 40$; $\theta_2 = 600/25 = 24$. The least value $= 24$, therefore row S_2 goes out.

TABLEAU 2

C_j	Basic Variables	Quantity b	X_1	X_2	S_1	S_2	θ
50	X_2	20	1/2	1	1/20	0	40
0	S_2	600	25	0	$-3/2$	1	24
	Z_j	1000	25	50	$-5/2$	0	
	$C_j - Z_j$		15	0	$-5/2$	0	

Step 9: Repeat Step 7 for the third tableau.

(a) New X_1 replaces old S_2 row by dividing old S_2 by pivot cell (25)

$$X_1 \quad 24 \quad 1 \quad 0 \quad -3/50 \quad 1/25$$

(b) New X_2 row is obtained from old one by deducting from it, element by element, the new X_1 row multiplied by the pivot element of the old row.

Old X_2	20	1/2	1	1/20	0
$-1/2$ (new X_1)	-12	$-1/2$	0	3/100	$-1/50$
New X_2	8	0	1	8/100	$-1/50$

TABLEAU 3

C_j	Basic Variables	b	X_1	X_2	S_1	S_2
50	X_2	8	0	1	8/100	$-1/50$
40	X_1	24	1	0	$-3/50$	1/25
	Z_j		40	50	8/5	3/5
	$C_j - Z_j$		0	0	$-8/5$	$-3/5$

Step 10: Compute the Z_j and $C_j - Z_j$ row values

$$Z_j = (50)(8) + (40)(24) \qquad = \quad 1360 \quad C_j - Z_j$$
$$X_1: \; Z_1 = (50)(0) + (40)(1) \qquad = \quad 40 \qquad 40 - 40 = 0$$
$$X_2: \; Z_2 = (50)(1) + (40)(0) \qquad = \quad 50 \qquad 50 - 50 = 0$$

S_1: $Z_3 = (50)(8/100) + (40)(-3/50)$ $=$ $8/5$ $0 - 8/5 = -8/5$

S_2: $Z_4 = (50)(-1/50) + (40)(1/25)$ $=$ $3/5$ $0 - 3/5 = -3/5$

All $C_j - Z_j$ values are either zero or negative and therefore the solution is optimal.

$$X_1 = 24; X_2 = 8$$

Step 11: Verify the results.

$$Z \quad = \quad 40\,X_1 + 50\,X_2$$

$$Z \quad = \quad (40)(24) + (50)(8) \quad = \quad \$1360 \text{ per day.}$$

This result matches the one derived by the graphical method.

Example 10.16

An oil company produces two products, X_1 and X_2, that bring in profits of $12 and $36 for each gallon respectively. Both products require processing by machines A and B. X_1 requires 12 hours in A and 8 hours in B. Machines A and B have 24 and 32 hours of capacity respectively. (a) How many gallons of each product should be produced to get optimal profit? (b) How would you interpret the optimal solution? (c) Determine the effect of changes in the constraints.

Solution:

(a) The objective function and constraints are:

$$\text{Max. } Z = 12\,X_1 + 36\,X_2$$

Subject to

C_1	$8\,X_1 + 12\,X_2 \le 24$
C_2	$16\,X_1 + 8\,X_2 \le 32$
and	$X_1, X_2 \ge 0$

TABLEAU 0

C_b	Basis	B_i	X_1	X_2	S_1	S_2	θ
0	S_1	24	8	12	1	0	2
0	S_2	32	16	8	0	1	4
	Z_j	0	0	0	0	0	
	$C_j - Z_j$		12	36	0	0	

TABLEAU 1

C_b	Basis	B_i	X_1	X_2	S_1	S_2	θ
36	X_2	2	0.667	1	0.083	0	
0	S_2	16	10.667	0	-0.667	1	
	Z_j	72	24	36	3	0	
	$C_j - Z_j$		-12	0	-3	0	

Final optimal solution: $Z = \$72$; X_1 is not in solution; $X_2 = 2$ gallons.
Before we proceed with the rest of this example, let us obtain the solution graphically, as this will help us to visualize the interpretation through Figure E10.16.

(b) Interpretation of the final tableau:

Variables in solution have ones and zeros. X_2 is in solution with a value of 2 units. S_2 is in solution with a value of 16 units. Remember that each unit of X_2 requires 8 hours of machine B, so 2 units of X_2 require 16 hours of the 32 hours available. This leaves 16 hours of machine B slack, as indicated under the third column for S_2, which is also in solution.

The objective function $Z = \$72$ represents the profit which comes from producing two units of X_2 at \$36 each, plus 16 units of slack at \$0 each. The figures in the $(C_j - Z_j)$ row of the tableau mean the following:

(i) The (-12) to produce one gallon of X_1 would reduce profits by \$12 because it would take time away from machine A from the production of X_2.

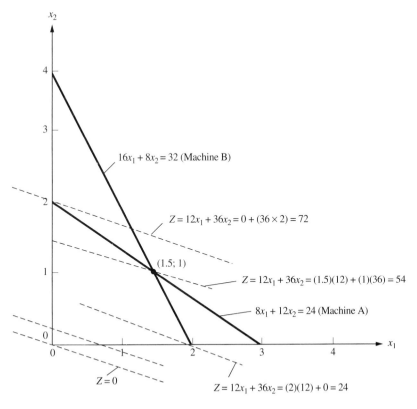

Maximum value of $Z = 72$

Figure E10.16   Graphical solution for interpreting the simplex algorithm results.

The $12 amount is explained by column X_1. Introducing one unit of out of variable X_1 would reduce X_2 by 0.667 units at $36 per unit = $24 reduction; and reduce S_2 by 10.667 units at $0 = $0 reduction, for a total amount of $24 − $0 = $24 cost which is off-set by $12 profit from each unit of X_1. The result is a net loss contribution of $C_j − Z_j = $12 − $24 = −$12.

(ii) The zero under the X_2 column indicates that X_2 is in solution (which means it is being produced).

(iii) The two values (-3.0) and (0) under columns S_1 and S_2 respectively, are referred to as shadow prices. Shadow prices go with constraints and show the amount of change in the objective function that would result from each unit of change in the constraint. They indicate the net effect of increasing (or decreasing) the slack or idle time of machines A and B by one unit.

(iv) Because machine A is fully utilized, to take one hour out of production and acquire one hour of idle time would reduce profit by $3 (Note that the profit from X_2 is $36 for each 12 hours of work on A, that is, a rate of $3 per hour.) Conversely, if another hour could be made available, say, by shifting a current job from A, the time on A could be profitably utilized at a profit of $3 per hour.

(v) The zero corresponding to the constraint of machine B signifies that machine B already has slack time. Increasing B's available time (or decreasing it) by one unit would have no effect on profits.

(c) Determine the effect of changes in the constraints.

Machine A is the only active constraint. The sensitivity ratios for this constraint are:

For X_2:   (Column B)/$(-S_1)$ = $2/(-0.083)$ = -24
For S_2:   (Column B)/$(-S_1)$ = $16/0.667$ = 24

The smallest positive ratio is 24 associated with S_2 which suggests that constraint A may be relaxed by 24 hours before machine B constraint begins to limit the solution.

   If we examine the graphic solution, it is obvious that as the constraint for machine A is relaxed (i.e., more hours are added), the constraint for machine B takes effect at $X_2 = 4$. At that point, the profit would be $Z = 12 X_1 + 36 X_2 = $(12)(0) + $(36)(4) = 144. Also, at $X_2 = 4$, both machines A and B would be fully utilized as shown below.

Old constraint	Revised limit	At $X_1 = 0; X_2 = 4$
Machine A: $8 X_1 + 12 X_2 \le 24$	$8 X_1 + 12 X_2 \le 48$	$(8)(0) + (12)(4) = 48$
Machine B: $16 X_1 + 8 X_2 \le 32$	No change	$(16)(0) + (8)(4) = 32$

10.6.3 Marginal Value or Shadow Pricing

In addition to answering the standard question, How much of each product A, B, and C should be produced in order to maximize profit?, the simplex method allows one to examine how much one would be paying for additional quantities of any resource.

Example 10.17

Consider the following problem. A manufacturer makes two types of chemicals X_1 and X_2 that require three processes A, B, and C to manufacture each chemical.

Hours Needed			
Process	X_1	X_2	Constraint
A	6	2	36
B	5	5	40
C	2	4	28
Profit	$50/unit	$30/unit	

The number of hours needed by the machines for each chemical X_1 and X_2 and the constraint are shown above. The profit from each chemical per pound is also indicated. How much of each chemical should be produced to maximize profit?

Solution:

The objective function Z = $50X_1 + 30X_2$
Subject to $6X_1 + 2X_2 \leq 36$

$$5X_1 + 5X_2 \leq 40$$
$$2X_1 + 4X_2 \leq 28$$
$$2X_1 + 4X_2 \leq 20$$
$$X_1, X_2 \geq 0$$

The final tableau is shown below:

C_b	C_j Basis	B_i	5 X_1	3 X_2	0 S_1	0 S_2	0 S_3
50	X_1	5	1	0	0.25	−0.10	0
30	X_2	3	0	1	−0.25	0.30	0
0	S_3	6	0	0	0.50	−1	1
	Z_j	340	50	30	5	4	0
	$C_j - Z_j$		0	0	−5	−4	0

The value under each slack variable in the final tableau express the marginal value or shadow price of the input associated with the variable. In other words, how much would the objective function change as a result of a one-unit increase in the input? For example, profit would increase by $5 for a one-unit change in the constant value of constraint 1; by $4 for a one-unit increase in the constant value of constraint 2; and by $0 for a one-unit increase in value in constraint 3. Since constraint 3 has a positive slack variable, it is not fully utilized in the optimal solution and its marginal value is zero, which means that an addition of yet another unit would add nothing to the profit function, the optimum value of the objective function will always equal the sum of the marginal value of each input times the amount available of each input. If A, B, and C symbolize the constants in constraints 1, 2, and 3 respectively:

$$\text{Profit} = 50X_1 + 30X_2 = (50 \times 5) + (30 \times 3) = \$340$$
$$A: 6X_1 + 2X_3 + S_1 = (6 \times 5) + (2 \times 3) + 0 = 36$$
$$B: 5X_1 + 5X_2 + S_2 = (5 \times 5) + (5 \times 3) + 0 = 40$$
$$C: 2X_1 + 4X_2 + S_3 = (2 \times 5) + (4 \times 3) + 6 = 28$$
$$\text{Profit} = MP_A(A) + MP_B(B) + MP_C(C)$$
$$= 5(36) + 4(40) + 0(28)$$
$$= 180 + 160 + 0$$
$$= \$340$$

10.6.4 Primal and Dual Problem Formulation Characteristics and Interpretation

Every maximization problem in linear programming has a corresponding minimization problem, and vice versa. If the original problem is called the primal, the corresponding problem is called the dual. The relationship between the two can best be expressed through the use of the parameters they share in common. An example will help to show the connection.

Example 10.18

Consider a small toy company making two kinds of toys X_1 and X_2 on an hourly basis. Toy X_1 produces a profit of $5 while X_2 produces $3 in profit. The resources for producing the toys are as follows:

Resources	X_1	X_2	Total available/hour
Labor (hr)	6	2	36
Parts	5	5	40
Packing material	2	4	28
Profit	$5	$3	

The company wants to know the number of toys of type X_1 and X_2 that should be produced per hour to maximize profit. The model can be formulated as follows:

Solution:

Maximize

$$Z = 5 X_1 + 3 X_2$$

Subject to

$$6 X_1 + 2 X_2 \leq 36$$
$$5 X_1 + 5 X_2 \leq 40$$
$$2 X_1 + 4 X_2 \leq 28$$
$$X_1, X_2 \geq 0$$

This is the primal form representing a maximization model. The dual form is the minimization model as shown below:

Minimize

$$Z = 36 Y_1 + 40 Y_2 + 28 Y_3$$

Subject

$$6 Y_1 + 5 Y_2 + 2 Y_3 \geq 5$$
$$2 Y_1 + 5 Y_2 + 4 Y_3 \geq 3$$
$$Y_1, Y_2, Y_3 \geq 0$$

(a) We have used the coefficients along the vertical lines and interchanged $\geq$ for $\leq$.

(b) The dual variables Y_1, Y_2, Y_3 correspond to the model constraints in the primal.

(c) The quantity values 36, 40, and 28 in the primal form the objective function $Z = 36 Y_1 + 40 Y_2 + 28 Y_3$ in the dual.

Let us interpret the primal simplex solution.

			5	3	0	0	0
C_j	Basic	Quantity	X_1	X_2	S_1	S_2	S_3
5	X_1	5	1	0	0.25	−0.10	0
3	X_2	3	0	1	−0.25	0.30	0
0	S_3	6	0	0	0.50	−1.0	1.0
	Z_j	34	5	3	0.50	0.40	0
	$C_j - Z_j$		0	0	−0.50	−0.40	0

Toy $X_1 = 5$; Toy $X_2 = 3$; $S_3 = 6$ (Packing); $Z = \$34.00$. this primal simplex tableau also contains information about the dual. In the $C_j - Z_j$ row, the negative values of −0.5 and −0.4 under the S_1 and S_2 columns indicate that if one unit of either S_1 or S_2 were entered into the solution, the profit would decrease by 50 cents and 40 cents, respectively. Also note that S_1 represents unused labor and S_2 represents unused parts. In this example they are not basic variables and are both equal to zero, which means that they are fully utilized (or that there is no slack). The values 50 cents and 40 cents are the "marginal" values of labor (S_1) and parts (S_2) respectively. These values are also referred to as "shadow" prices, since they reflect the maximum "price" one would be willing to pay to obtain one more unit of the resource. However, the $C_j - Z_j$ value for S_3 representing packaging is zero, which indicates that the marginal value of S_3 is zero, or that we would be unwilling to pay anything for one unit of packaging. In fact, there is a surplus of 6 units of packaging, left unused after the two types of toys were produced, as shown in the row marked S_3.

Example 10.19

A farmer has three resources to produce two types of wheat A and B as shown below.

Resources	Requirement for Wheat A	Requirement for Wheat B	Total available
Water/unit	10	15	300
Fertilizer/unit	5	9	100
Labor/unit	3	6	120
Profit	$110	$180	

(a) Write the primal linear program model.

(b) Write the dual model.

(c) Explain the units of the dual model.

Solution:

(a) The primal model is

$$\text{Maximize } Z \quad = \quad 110\,A + 180\,B$$
$$\text{Subject to} \qquad 10\,A + 15\,B \le 300$$
$$5\,A + 9\,B \le 100$$
$$3\,A + 6\,B \le 120$$
$$A, B \ge 0$$

(b) In the primal model there are 2 primal variables and 3 constraints, while the dual model has 3 variables and 2 constraints, as follows:

$$\text{Minimize:} \quad Z = 300\,C + 100\,D + 120\,E$$
$$\text{Subject to} \quad 10\,C + 5\,D + 3\,E \ge 110$$
$$15\,C + 9\,D + 6\,E \ge 180$$
$$C, D, E \ge 0$$

(c) The units of the dual model are:

C = the dollar value of a unit of water

D = the dollar value of a unit of fertilizer

E = the dollar value of a unit of labor

Z = the cost function which is being minimized

10.6.5 Solving Minimization Problems with Simplex

When minimization problems need to be solved using the simplex, several adjustments must be made. First, constraints in the form of $\ge$ are converted to equalities by subtracting the surplus or slack amounts. Second, to get an initial solution to the problem, an artificial variable is added to the constraint, because merely introducing a slack variable is insufficient. Third, the cost of a surplus variable is $0, while the cost of an artificial variable is M, a very large positive number that will prevent the artificial variable from having a non-zero value. Fourth, because the objective is to minimize, we will be computing $Z_j - C_j$ in the bottom row of the simplex tableau, instead of $C_j - Z_j$.

Example 10.20

A farmer feeds his cattle with nutrients X_1 and X_2 made up of two basic ingredients, carbohydrates (C) and protein (P). The details of the nutrients and their costs per pound are given below.

Ingredients	Nutrients		Minimum requirements (units)
	X_1	X_2	
Carbohydrates (C)	1	2	80
Protein (P)	3	1	75
Cost in $/lb.	4	6	

What combination of C and P should be provided as an adequate diet at minimum cost?

Solution:

Minimize $Z = 4 X_1 + 6 X_2$

Subject to $X_1 + 2 X_2 \geq 80$

$3 X_1 + X_2 \geq 75$

$X_1, X_2 \geq 0$

Convert the inequalities to equations by subtracting a slack variable(s) and adding artificial variables (A). Thus,

$$X_1 + 2 X_2 - S_1 + A_1 = 80$$
$$3 X_1 + X_2 - S_2 + A_2 = 75$$

where As must not appear in the final solution and therefore must be of high value $= M$.

Simplex Tableau: 0

C_j			4	6	0	0	M	M	θ
C_b	Basis	B_i	X_1	X_2	S_1	S_2	A_1	A_2	
M	A_1	80	1	2	-1	0	1	0	80
M	A_2	75	3	1	0	-1	0	1	25 (out)
	Z_j	155 M	4 M	3 M	$-M$	$-M$	M	M	
	$C_j - Z_j$		4–4 M	6–3 M	M	M	0	0	
			(IN)						

Simplex Tableau: 1

C_b	Basis	B_i	4 X_1	6 X_2	0 S_1	0 S_2	M A_1	M A_2	θ
M	A_1	55	0	1.667	-1	0.333	1	-0.333	33 (out)
4	X_1	25	1	0.333	0	-0.333	0	0.333	75
	Z_j	10099	4	M	$-M$	$-M$	M	$-M$	
	$C_j - Z_j$		0	M	M	M	0	$-M$	
				(IN)					

Simplex Tableau: 2

C_j C_b Basis	B_i	4 X_1	6 X_2	0 S_1	0 S_2	M A_1	M A_2
6 X_2	33	0	1	-0.6	0.2	0.6	-0.2
4 X_1	14	1	0	0.2	-0.4	-0.2	0.4
Z_j	254	4	6	-2.8	-0.4	2.797	0.406
$C_j - Z_j$		0	0	-2.8	-0.4	$-M$	$-M$

Final Optimal Solution = 254

An alternative method of solving the minimization problem concerning the farmer's feed for his cattle can be done by converting this primal problem into its dual, which will be a maximization problem. Recall that we had the following equations representing the primal:

Minimize

$$Z = 4\,X_1 + 6\,X_2$$

Subject to

$$X_1 + 2\,X_2 \geq 80 \dots\dots\dots\dots\dots\dots\dots Y_1$$
$$3\,X_1 + X_2 \geq 75 \dots\dots\dots\dots\dots\dots\dots Y_2$$
$$X_1, X_2 \geq 0$$

Rewriting, the dual (maximization) form

$$Y_1 + 3\,Y_2 \leq 4$$
$$2\,Y_1 + Y_2 \leq 6$$

Maximize

$$Z = 80\,Y_1 + 75\,Y_2$$

Notice that the dual variables Y_1 and Y_2 correspond to the model constraints in the primal, and the quantity values 80 and 75 in the primal form, are the coefficients in the objective function of the dual.

Example 10.21

Rework the previous examples using the simplex method, using the Dual form.

Solution:

Maximize

$$Z = 80\,Y_1 + 75\,Y_2$$

Subject to

$$Y_1 + 3\,Y_2 \leq 4$$

$$2\,Y_1 + Y_2 \leq 6$$

Simplex Tableau: 0

C_j C_b	Basis	B_i	80 Y_1	75 Y_2	0 S_1	0 S_2
0	S_1	4	1	3	1	0
0	S_2	6	2	1	0	1
	Z_j	0	0	0	0	0
	$C_j - Z_j$		80	75	0	0

Simplex Tableau: 1

C_j C_b	Basis	B_i	80 Y_1	75 Y_2	0 S_1	0 S_2
0	S_1	1	0	2.5	1	−0.5
80	Y_1	3	1	0.5	0	0.5
	Z_j	240	80	40	0	40
	$C_j - Z_j$		0	35	0	−40

Simplex Tableau: 2

C_j C_b	Basis	B_i	80 Y_1	75 Y_2	0 S_1	0 S_2
75	Y_2	0.4	0	1	0.4	−0.2
80	Y_1	2.8	1	0	−0.2	0.6
	Z_j	254	80	75	14	33
	$C_j - Z_j$		0	0	−14	−33

Final Optimal Solution $Z = 254$

10.6.6 Interpretation of the Primal and Dual Models

Let us interpret the final tableau of the primal model given in Example 10.20. We observe that for minimizing the total cost, nutrient $X_1 = 14$ units and nutrient $X_2 = 33$ units, which works out to $254. This primal tableau also contains information under the S_1 and S_2 columns indicating that if one unit of either S_1 or S_2 were entered into the solution, the cost would increase by $2.8 and $0.4 respectively, remembering that S_1 represents unused carbohydrates (C) and S_2 represents unused protein (P). This means that all of the C and P are being used for producing X_1 and X_2, and that there is no slack left over. In fact, the negative $C_j - Z_j$ row values of 2.8 and 0.4 units are the marginal values of C and P respectively. These dual values are also referred to as shadow prices. Note that the minimum cost is $254. Now, let us

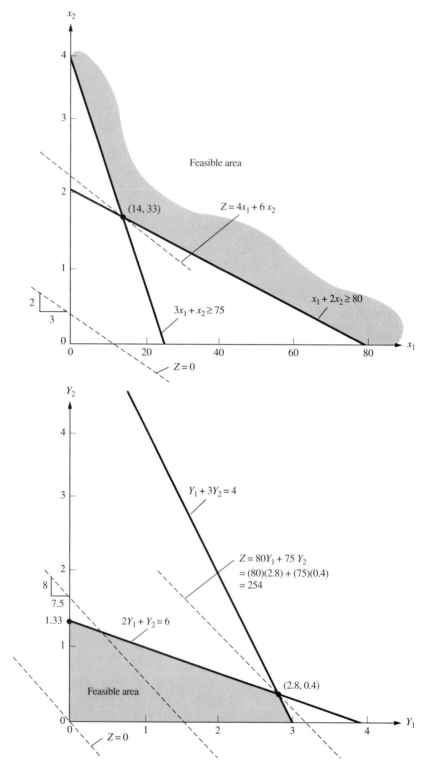

Figure E10.21 Primal and dual solutions.

look at the final tableau of the dual model (the maximization model). Here, we must understand the meaning of Y_1 and Y_2 as well as S_1 and S_2. The interpretation is as follows:

Y_1 = marginal value of one unit of carbohydrate (C)

Y_2 = marginal value of one unit of protein (P)

S_1 = value of a unit of nutrient X_1

S_2 = value of a unit of nutrient X_2

The cost of this optimum combination is $254.

The graphical solution to the primal and dual problems are shown in Figure E10.21. The economic significance of Y_1 is that it is worth it to the producer to provide one unit of carbohydrate C; Y_2 is the worth per unit of protein P. The objective function $Z = 80Y_1 + 75Y_2$, and represents the worth to the producer of meeting the needs. Its optimal value must be identical to the original (least-cost) optimum.

The simplex solution to the dual is shown in the first tableau of example 10.20. The solution is for optimal values of Y_1 and Y_2, but actually the optimal values of X_1 and X_2 appear as the $(C_j - Z_j)$ entries for S_1 and S_2 respectively. The converse is also true; $Y_1 = 2.8$ and $Y_2 = 0.4$ appear as $C_j - Z_j$ entries for S_1 and S_2 respectively. Notice that $Z = \$254$ is the same in both cases.

Check:

$$
\begin{aligned}
\text{Optimal } Z \quad &= \quad 80\,Y_1 + 75\,Y_2 \\
&= \quad (80)(2.8) + (75)(0.4) \\
&= \quad 224 + 30 \qquad\qquad\qquad = \quad \$254 \\
\text{or,} \quad Y_1 + 3\,Y_2 + S_1 \quad &= \quad 2.8 + 3(0.4) + 0 \quad = \quad 4 \ldots\ldots\text{(A)} \\
2\,Y_1 + Y_1 + S_1 \quad &= \quad 2(2.8) + (0.4) + 0 \quad = \quad 6 \ldots\ldots\text{(B)} \\
\text{Therefore, Optimal } Z \quad &= \quad mP(A) + mP(B) \\
&= \quad (4)(14) + (6)(33) \quad = \quad \$254
\end{aligned}
$$

EXERCISES

1. A metal box company is designing hundreds of steel container boxes per day with the following specifications: the box must have a square base with an open top, and a volume of 64 cubic feet internal. It must use a minimum of sheet metal. What should the optimum dimensions of the box be?

2. Calculate the output of computer parts per day that should be produced in order to earn the maximum possible profit, remembering that for profit maximizing the marginal revenue should be equal to marginal cost. The cost and revenue functions are:

   Total cost $= 0.016Q^3 - 6Q^2 + 800Q + 60$

   Total revenue $= 50Q$, where Q represents the number of parts.

3. A shopping center expert has observed that the number of customers visiting the center depends on the number of parking spaces provided. The estimate is given by the equation $Q = Kx^a$, where Q is the number of customers visiting the center and K and a are constants. What should the optimal number of parking spaces provided be?

4. If the total revenue of a company is TR, (a) derive an expression for the marginal revenue in terms of the elasticity of demand and the price; and (b) show that an increase in quantity sold results in an increase in revenue if the elasticity is greater than 1? (c) What would you advise a bicycle manufacturer, if the elasticity of demand is 0.9, and he wants to increase the unit price of bicycles? Set up a sample case to prove your advice is correct.

5. A cloth manufacturer produces two types of cloth, A and B. His profit function is:

   Profit $= 128A - 4A^2 + 8AB + 64B - 28$

   What should be the level of output of A and B to maximize profit?

6. The cloth manufacturer in Exercise 5 is faced with a constraint. He can only manufacture a total of 50 units of cloth A and B together. What should be his level of production to maximize profit?

7. A company has the following production function:

   $Q = 20L^{0.5}K^{0.5}$, where Q = quantity of output produced per hour, L = amount of labor, and K = capital expended. The company's total cost function is $TC = 10L + 40K$. In order to meet customer demand, the firm needs to produce 100 units of the product per day at the minimum cost. How many units of labor and capital are needed to meet these conditions?

8. Solve Exercise 7 using Lagrangian multiplier.

9. The network shown below indicates the activity times in weeks for completing a small culvert construction. Complete a table of ES, EF, LS, LF, and TF times and indicate the critical path and project duration.

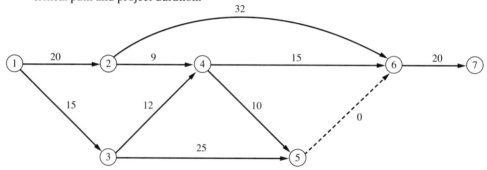

Problem 9

10. The network represents the activities for constructing a culvert. Set up the ES, EF, LS, LF, TF, FF, and interfering float (IF) table and indicate the critical path. Draw a time-grid diagram and a manpower resource schedule.

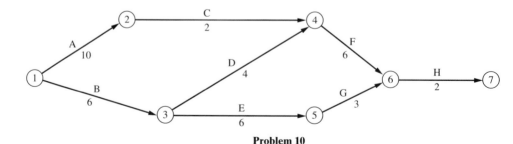

Problem 10

	Manpower required
A	5 men
B	7 men
C	8 men
D	9 men
E	6 men
F	10 men
G	4 men
H	8 men

11. An engineer draws up an activity network of 8 activities, assigning the most likely time in weeks for finishing each task, as shown below:

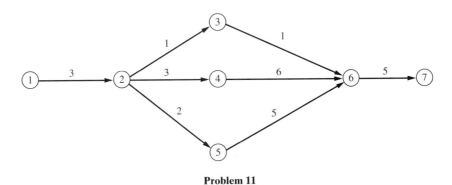

Problem 11

(a) Compute the ES, EF, LS, LF, and TF times for the various tasks.
(b) What is the critical path and the most likely time the project will be completed?

12. In Exercise 11, the engineer solicits the ideas of an architect to estimate the time required for each task. The table below shows the optimistic, most likely, and pessimistic times for each task. (a) What is the estimated completion time for this project? (b) If it is desired to finish the project with a probability of 90 percent, what is the probability of finishing this project?

Task	a-m-b
1–2	2–3–8
2–3	1–1–3
2–4	2–3–5
2–5	1–2–4
3–6	1–1–1
4–6	5–6–8
5–6	2–5–7
6–7	4–5–6

13. An engineer has estimated the duration of each activity under normal and crash conditions for constructing an office extension. The cost of crashing each task in $/day is also given.
    (a) What would be the normal time of completion of this project?
    (b) By how many days can the project be compressed?
    (c) If the overhead charges are $50/day, what crash schedule would be optimal?

| | Time (days) | | Cost of crashing |
Activity	Normal	Crash	in $/day
1–2	9	6	20
1–3	8	5	25
1–4	15	10	30
2–4	5	3	10
3–4	10	6	15
4–5	2	1	40

14. A shelter is planned for construction consisting of five major activities as shown in the figure below:

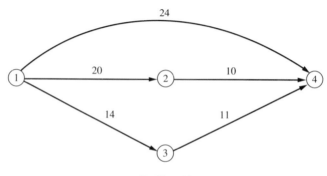

Problem 14

Details of the normal and crash times in weeks along with the corresponding costs in hundreds of dollars are indicated below.

Activity	$i - j$	Time in weeks Normal	Crash	Cost in hundreds of $/week Normal	Crash
1	1–2	20	8	10.00	14.80
2	1–4	24	20	12.00	14.00
3	1–3	14	7	7.00	11.90
4	2–4	10	6	5.00	8.20
5	3–4	11	5	5.50	7.30

(a) How much can the project time be compressed?
(b) Compute the normal and crash costs of the project.
(c) If the overhead cost of construction is $10,000 per week, what would be an optimum crashing schedule?

15. A garage is planned to be an extension to a house with the following activities shown in the table below:
(a) Determine the critical path and the project duration.
(b) If the project target time of completion is 25 days, what is the probability of completion?

Activity	$i - j$	a	Time m	b	
0	0–1	4	4	4	
1	1–2	1	3	5	
2	1–4	2	3	5	
3	1–5	2	4	7	
4	2–3	1	3	4	
5	3–4	2	5	8	
	4–5	0	0	0	Dummy
6	4–6	1	2	2	
7	5–7	3	6	8	
8	6–8	2	4	5	
9	7–8	3	4	6	
10	8–9	1	2	4	
11	9–10	1	1	1	

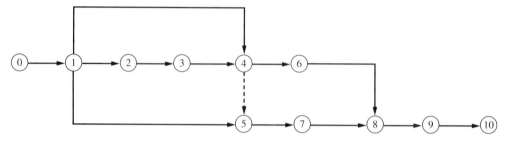

Problem 15

16. An architect lists 15 tasks for constructing a house. The logic and duration of the activities and the labor needed for completing the house are shown below. Determine the ES, EF, LS, LF, TF and IF times for the activities shown in the table. How would you allocate the labor so that there would be more or less equal manpower requirements throughout the duration of the project? (Draw a time-grid diagram to help you out.) All times are in weeks.

#	Task	Predecessor activity	Time	Labor
1	1–2	—	1	1
2	2–3	1–2	2	1
3	2–5	1–2	3	1
4	3–4	2–3	4	1
5	4–5	3–4	16	2
6	4–6	3–4	14	1
7	4–7	3–4	14	2
8	5–8	(4–5), (2–5)	12	2
9	5–9	(4–5), (2–5)	14	3
10	5–10	(4–5), (2–5)	10	1
11	6–11	(4–6) (Dummy)	0	0
12	7–11	(4–7) (Dummy)	0	0
13	8–11	(5–8)	5	1
14	9–11	(5–9)	4	2
15	10–11	(5–10)	6	1
16	11–12	(6–11), (7–11), (8–11), (9–11), (10–11)	3	2
17	12–13	(11–12)	6	1

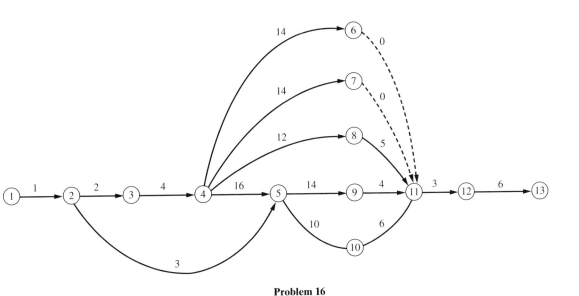

Problem 16

17. Refer to Exercise 16. The architect feels that the time of the tasks on the critical path could be easily revised as follows. (2–3) 1 week, (3–4) 3 weeks, (4–5) 15 weeks, (5–9) 13 weeks, (9–11) 3 weeks, (11–12) 2 weeks, and (12–13) 5 weeks. What is the new critical path and what is the duration of the project?

18. Refer to Exercise 16. The architect consults his colleagues about the activity time (in weeks) which he has allocated to each activity and is advised to adopt a PERT type network with optimistic, most likely, and pessimistic times as indicated below.

#	Activity	a	m	b	
			Time		
1	1–2	1	1	3	
2	2–3	1	2	3	
3	2–5	2	3	5	
4	3–4	2	4	6	
5	4–5	14	16	25	
6	4–6	13	14	20	
7	4–7	12	14	19	
8	4–8	10	13	18	
9	5–9	12	14	15	
10	5–10	8	10	14	
11	6–11	0	0	0	Dummy
12	7–11	0	0	0	Dummy
13	8–11	4	5	6	
14	9–11	2	4	5	
15	10–11	5	6	8	
16	11–12	3	3	5	
17	12–13	5	6	7	

(a) What is the expected time of completion of the project?

(b) What is the critical path?

(c) If the architect wants to be assured that the project be completed with 90 percent confidence, what is the time-line?

19. A manager notes that one of his electricians takes anywhere between 30 minutes to 1 hour to do motor repairs. However, 40 minutes is the most frequent duration. If this electrician's task were on a PERT project;

(a) What would be the expected duration of a repair job?

(b) What is the variance and standard deviation?

(c) If he performs 8 such repairs per day with a 10 minute break between two repairs, what would be the expected time he spends on repairs per day?

(d) What is the variance and standard deviation of his working day?

(e) What is the probability he spends (i) 6.5 hours (ii) 6.75 hours (iii) 7 hours at work per day (including breaks)?

20. The project network for a repair job is shown below.

Activity	Link	t_a	Time t_m	t_b
A	1–2	4	5	6
B	1–3	9	12	15
C	2–4	2	2	2
D	3–4	8	10	18
E	3–5	2	4	12
F	5–6	1	2	3
G	4–6	4	6	8

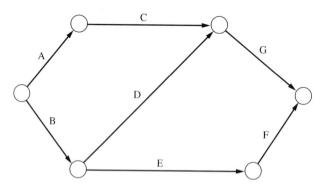

Problem 20

(a) Find the expected duration and variation of each activity.

(b) What is the expected project length and its variance and standard deviation?

(c) What is the probability that the project will be completed (a) at least 2 days earlier than expected (b) no more than 2 days later than expected?

(d) If the project due date is 30 days, what is the probability of lateness?

(e) What due date has about 98 percent chance of being met?

21. Refer to Example 10.8, worked out in this chapter. The prefabricator has now agreed to deliver 50 units of septic tanks each month beginning with the 30th month. All other conditions remain the same. If an LOB study is to be conducted in the 40th month, what would an inspector expect to find with respect to each control point?

22. A pre-cast concrete beam fabricator is awarded a contract to produce 10,000 beams to be delivered as per schedule shown. The production schedule consists of 6 distinct stages and one supply stage as shown. No buffer is provided. An LOB study was done on the twelfth day after production started, and the report indicated that the actual cumulative number in hundreds of beams in stages 1 through 7 were as shown below:

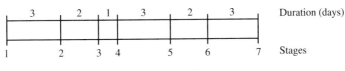

Problem 22

Stage				1	2	3	4	5	6	7
Cummulative (100s) found on 12th day				88	85	83	81	76	70	30

Delivery Schedule:

Day	1	2	3	4	5	6	7	8	9	10
Quantity (100s)	2	1	2	2	1	2	2	2	2	2

Day	11	12	13	14	15	16	17	18	19	20
Quantity (100s)	2	7	8	9	8	9	7	9	8	2

Day	21	22	23	24	25	26	27	28
Quantity (100s)	1	2	1	1	2	2	2	2

Draw the LOB chart and indicate the deviations between the ideal and actual production of beams at various stages.

23. A concrete road is being planned for repetitive stretches of 30 sections each. The sequence of activities is: (a) prepare foundation, (b) pour concrete, and (c) grade and finish. The man hours and teams sizes are shown below:

Task	A	B	C
Man hours/section	240	580	300
Men/team	6	12	8

(a) Assuming there is no buffer between operations, and there are 5 days of work per week at 8 hours per day, prepare a LOB for 4 units per week.
(b) If a buffer of 5 days is provided between operations, and everything else remains the same, prepare a revised LOB for 4 units/week.

24. A small city wants to develop a bikeway plan connecting 9 major attractions. The existing street plan shows distance units. What is the minimal spanning tree?

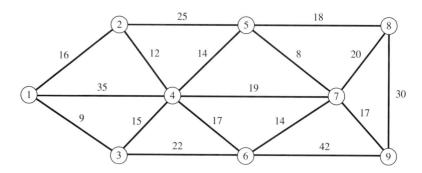

Problem 24

25. A street plan of a historic city is shown below, showing 16 nodes that have ancient artifacts. A bikeway plan connecting all 16 nodes is planned. What is the minimal spanning tree for this city?

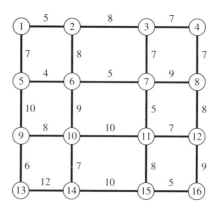

Problem 25   A street plan of a historic city.

26. An amusement park with 10 attractions needs to be connected with the minimum length of paths. How would you plan it?

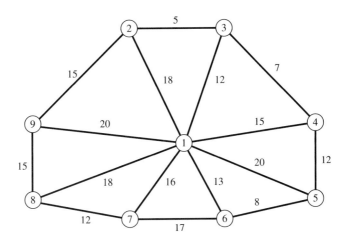

Problem 26   An amusement park having 10 attractions.

27. A new stadium is under construction at node 1 of the street network shown, along with one-way capacities of individual links. What is the total capacity of the network for vehicles to travel from the stadium to the nearest freeway on-ramp located at node 6? What is the individual flow on each link? All streets can handle two-way flow.

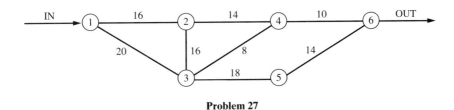

Problem 27

28. The network shown below carries trucks at a construction site which has link capacities in hundreds as shown. What is the possible flow of trucks from node 1 to node 6? How many trucks do individual links carry? [Link Capacities: $1 - 2 = 32$; $1 - 3 = 24$; $2 - 4 = 16$; $2 - 5 = 28$; $3 - 5 = 12$; $3 - 6 = 8$; $4 - 5 = 10$; $4 - 7 = 20$; $5 - 6 = 6$; $5 - 7 = 12$; $6 - 7 = 14$.]

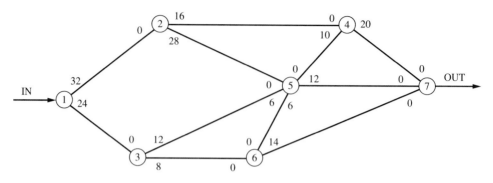

Problem 28

29. An oil pipe-line system carries oil from node 1 to node 9 through individual pipes as shown below. What is the capacity of the system and how much does each link carry? All pipes can handle flow in both directions.

		Flow	Inverse Flow
Link	1–2 = 14		0
Link	1–3 = 8		0
Link	1–4 = 12		0
Link	2–3 = 4		6
Link	2–5 = 8		0
Link	3–4 = 2		10
Link	3–5 = 4		0
Link	3–6 = 4		0
Link	4–6 = 8		4
Link	5–6 = 6		10
Link	5–7 = 14		0
Link	6–8 = 12		0
Link	7–8 = 16		0
Link	7–9 = 16		0
Link	8–9 = 12		0

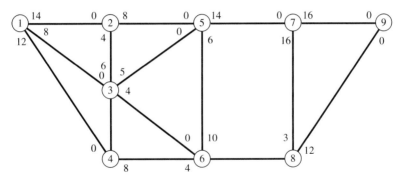

Problem 29

30. A highway network consisting of five nodes and eight links is shown below. The cost of transportation is also shown. A trip table shows the numbers of vehicles per hour wanting to go from one node to another. Assign the trips to the network.

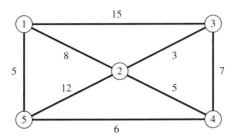

Problem 30

To From	1	2	3	4	5	
1	0	50	60	70	30	210
2	40	0	30	60	80	210
3	90	40	0	20	50	200
4	80	70	90	0	30	270
5	30	40	50	60	0	180
	240	200	230	210	190	1070

31. A simple network shown in the figure has two-way links. The time cost is also shown. Find the shortest path from nodes A, B, C, and D to all other nodes and intersections.

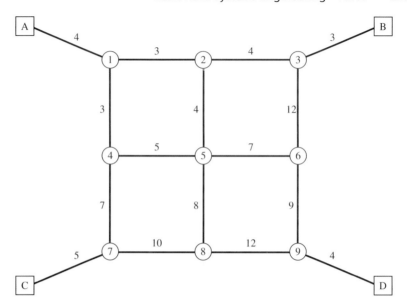

Problem 31

32. A trip table (veh/hr) needs to be loaded on the network shown for Exercise 31. Find the total volume on each link, assuming an all-or-nothing assignment.

	To			
From	A	B	C	D
A	0	50	40	20
B	30	0	80	10
C	90	80	0	20
D	60	70	50	0

33. A network connected to four centroids is loaded with trips as shown in the figure. Assign the trips (using the all-or-nothing technique) assuming the following: figures on links indicate travel cost; a left turn, and going straight through an intersection carries a penalty of 3, 2, and 1 units, respectively; and, all links are two-way.

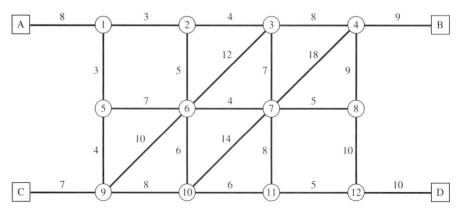

Problem 33

To From	A	B	C	D
A	0	900	400	700
B	200	0	700	300
C	600	800	0	400
D	100	200	500	0

34. A manufacturer produces two types of machines X_1 and X_2. The resources needed for producing these machines X_1 and X_2 and the corresponding profits are:

Machines	Labor (hrs/unit)	Capital ($/unit)	Profit ($)
X_1	10	40	40
X_2	20	30	50

There are 400 hours of labor and $1200 worth of capital available per day. How many machines of type X_1 and X_2 should be produced per day to maximize profits?

35. A company produces two kinds of septic tanks: a basic type A and a special type B. Each type B tank takes twice as long to produce as type A, and the company has the time to make a maximum of 2000 per week, if it produced only type A. The supply of materials per day is sufficient to produce 1500 tanks/week of both A and B types. The type B tank requires special fixtures of which there are 600 per week available. If the company makes a profit of $300 for an A type and $500 for a B type tank, how many of each should it produce per week in order to maximize profits? Solve this problem using the simplex method and then check your answer graphically.

36. A manufacturer produces two kinds of boxes, A and B. Their requirements are shown below.

Product	A	B	Constraint
Steel Sheets	8 units	10 units	80,000
Hinges	2.5 units	1 unit	20,000
Welding and paint	1 unit	4 units	30,000

Both types of boxes can be produced at the same time and 12 boxes can be put together per hour; 750 hours are available per week. There is a restriction that at least 3000 boxes of type A have to be produced per day. How many boxes of each type should be produced?

37. A concrete beam manufacturer produces two products. Type A requires 2 hours of preparation, 4 hours of casting, and 10 hours of finishing. Type B requires 5, 1, and 5 hours respectively. There are time constraints in hours for the two products as shown below.

$$2\,A + 5\,B \leq 40$$
$$4\,A + B \leq 20$$
$$10\,A + 5\,B \leq 60$$

The profit on type A is 24, and 8 for type B. How many of each type should be produced for maximizing profits?

38. A country suffering from famine wants to be assured that the people get the minimum daily requirements of three basic nutrients A, B, and C. Daily requirements are 14 units of A, 12 of B, and 18 of C. Product X_1 has 2 units of A and 1 unit each of B and C; Product X_2, has one unit of A and B, and 3 units of C. Products X_1 and X_2 cost \$2 and \$4 respectively. What is the least cost combination of X_1 and X_2?

39. Refer to Example 10.13. Because of improved manufacturing techniques, the firm is able to make a profit of \$10 on beams and \$15 on poles. How many beams and poles should be produced to maximize profits? Solve this problem using the graphical method.
  (a) Rework the problem using the simplex method.
  (b) How would you interpret the final tableau and the optimal solution?

40. Refer to Example 10.15. A new management has taken over this firm and changed the production schedule and the quality of the machines such that X_1 and X_2 reap profits of \$50 and \$30 each respectively. (a) What is the revised production for optimizing profits (solve the problem graphically and using simplex)? (b) Interpret the final tableau and the optimal solution.

41. Refer to Example 10.16. The management of the company estimates that it can bring in profits of \$30 and \$40 per gallon of the two products X_1 and X_2, respectively. (a) How many gallons of each product should be produced to gain the maximum profit? (b) How would you interpret the final tableau and the optimal solution?

42. Refer to Example 10.20. The farmer has revised his minimum requirements of carbohydrates and protein to 100 and 85 units respectively. Rework this problem graphically as well as using simplex to find the optimum combination of carbohydrates and proteins at a minimum cost.

11

Basic Hard Systems Engineering—Part II

11.1 INTRODUCTION

In Chapter 10 we examined a variety of methods of optimization ranging from the use of calculus, the application of the CPM, the program evaluation and review technique, and network flow analysis to linear programming. Some problems can best be solved graphically while others are best tackled through matrix applications, such as the simplex method. This chapter may be considered as a continuation of Chapter 10, as it deals with such topics as forecasting and decision analysis, techniques employed by planners and engineers in their day-to-day work.

11.2 FORECASTING

The ability to forecast or predict future events, such as the population of a city in the year 2010, or the traffic flow on Interstate 75 through Cincinnati, over the Ohio river in 2010, are examples of some of the work entrusted to engineers and planners. They use judgement, past experiences, and mathematical models coupled with intuition to predict the future. Although there are semantic differences in the use of such terms as projecting, predicting, and forecasting, we will use these terms interchangeably.

The science of forecasting covers an enormous field. We will cover just the basics to enable you to get a feel for the topic. As engineers and planners, we are concerned about two types of forecasts: long-range and short-range. Long-range forecasts are related to problems connected with building new facilities needing billions of dollars of capital. For instance, if we are planning the water supply facilities connected with the expansion of a city, we are looking at projections of population and water demand for a 50-year period. On the other hand, short-range forecasts could encompass periods from a year to five years. For example, a small construction company which has been in business for the past 15 years may like to project its likely profits for the next five years, based on past trends.

Forecasting methods can also be categorized in two groups: qualitative and quantitative. The former are usually non-statistical techniques using the techniques of Delphi and "brainstorming" sessions. Quantitative or statistical methods require appropriate historical data for their application. We will concern ourselves with some pertinent quantitative methods: the time-series method, and methods based on regression. In making decisions regarding forecasting, consider the following: What is to be forecast, why, and in what detail? How far into the future do you need to forecast and with what accuracy? What methods are you prepared to use? What prior information and data are needed to conduct a forecast, and are these available and reliable?

We will be dealing with some simple methods of forecasting commonly used in engineering and planning. It is a good idea to observe historical data available pertaining to your problem situation to learn whether it has any predominant characteristics such as a linear, cyclical, or exponential trend. In addition, you may like to note seasonal trends as well as irregular or erratic variations, connected with say, the weather or local floods, respectively.

11.2.1 Regularity

It is good practice to examine data presented to you to observe some degree of regularity in the numbers. A few common forms of regularity are illustrated through the following example.

Example 11.1

(a) The series 27, 27, 27, 28, 27, 27, 27 has no trend. The next observation will most likely be 27.

(b) The series 27, 29, 31, 33, 35 is equally predictable. The next observation is most likely to be 37, because the increase is linear.

(c) The series 9, 27, 81, 243, 729 is tripling each period, and so the most likely value of the next period is 2187. This is a case of exponential growth. By the same token, the series 64, 16, 4, 1, 0.25, 0.0625 appears to be an exponential "decay" series, and the next value is likely to be 0.015625.

(d) The series 39, 24, 50, 29, 40, 25, 51, 30 corresponding to the sale of a product in four quarters of a year for a two-year period appears to be cyclical for 4 periods at a time. It is likely that the next 4 periods may have values 41, 26, 52, and 31.

(e) There are possibilities where a linear and cyclical series may result from a combination of a linear series 32, 33, 34, 35, 36, 37, 38, 39 and a cyclical series 40, 45, 48, 50, 40, 45, 48, 50 resulting in 72, 78, 82, 85, 76, 82, 86, 89. The next value would likely be 40 + 40 = 80.

11.2.2 Use of Time Series

There are several cases in engineering and financial forecasting dealing with continuous though fluctuating demand. Such cases can be dealt with through the use-of-time series. A *time series* is a set of observations of a variable over a period of time. An example of a time series forecast could consist of considering the yearly consumption of gasoline by a family over the past five years in order to predict what the consumption is likely to be in the next two years. This problem could be solved very easily by plotting consumption per year as a graph and then drawing a freehand "curve" through the historical data and projecting it to the desired year. This result would undoubtedly be subjective, but may be sufficiently accurate for the family's requirements. However, for more accurate results we will describe three basic methods that are commonly used in practice: (1) moving average forecast, (2) trend projection models (linear, exponential, modified exponential), and (3) simple linear regression.

When historic data is available, one can detect a "trend" in the shape of a gradual long-term directional movement (either a growth or decline). Cyclical swings are long-term swings around a trend line, generally associated with business cycles. Seasonal effects and variations occurring during certain periods of the year can also be seen in data presented.

Simple Moving Average.   Let us start with the simple moving average method. It is calculated by adding up the last "n" observations and dividing by n. When the next observation is available, the oldest observation in the earlier calculation is dropped, the new one is added in, and a new average calculated. It is best to describe this procedure by solving a practical problem.

Example 11.2

A sales manager wants to forecast the demand for personal computers for the month of August based on a seven month record, January through July: 180, 215, 225, 220, 210, 205, 220. He wants to dampen the fluctuations in sales by using moving averages of 3 months at a time. What will be his sale in the month of August?

Solution:

The moving average is calculated for the 3-month period, which in this case is for the month of August, by considering the demand for the last 3 months in the sequence:

$$MA = (210 + 205 + 220)/3 = 635/3 = 211.667$$

The 3-month moving averages for April through July are also shown. This allows us to compare the forecasts with the actual demands. We could have solved this problem using a 4-month or 5-month moving average, which would have yielded smoother results.

Forecast Accuracy.   When one performs a forecasting exercise, the question that is always asked is, How accurate is your forecast? The difference between the forecast and the actual is called the "forecast error."

- The mean absolute deviation (MAD) is one of the more common measures of forecast error. It is the difference between the forecast and the actual demand as calculated by the expression.

$$MAD = \Sigma abs(D_t - F_t)/n$$

Where, t = the period number
D_t = demand in period t
F_t = forecast for period t
n = total number of periods
abs = absolute value (sometimes indicated by two vertical lines ||)

For our example, the computation is based on the period 4 through 7 (220, 210, 205, 220) and the forecast error for individual months is shown, and if the absolute value is taken, it amounts to 44.999 and dividing it by n = 4, we get 11.25.

- The mean square error (MSE) is derived by squaring each forecast error and dividing by n. Thus, $(13.333)^2 + (10)^2 + (13.333)^2 + (8.333)^2 = 524.98$. Dividing this by n = 4, we get 131.25
- The mean forecast error is the running sum of forecast error (taking positive and negative signs into account, divided by n). Thus,

$$-13.333 + 10 + 13.333 - 8.333 = 1.6667/4 = 0.4167$$

Period	Data	Forecast	Forecast error
1	180.000		
2	215.000		
3	225.000		
4	220.000	206.667	−13.333
5	210.000	220.000	+10.000
6	205.000	218.333	+13.333
7	220.000	211.667	−8.333
8		211.667	

Absolute value: 45
Mean absolute deviation: 11.2500
Mean square error: 131.2500
Mean forecast error: 0.4167

Weighted Moving Average (WMA).   The simple moving average method can be adjusted to reflect fluctuations in the data provided, by assigning weights to the most recent data. We will demonstrate the WMA method by amending the previous problem by assigning weights.

Example 11.3

With the same data but assigning weights of 0.5, 0.3, and 0.2 for periods 7, 6, and 5, respectively predict the sale in August (period 8). Apply all three tests and compare the results with those obtained before (for SMA).

Solution:

Here we apply the weights to the last three entries.

$$\text{WMA} = ((210 \times 0.2) + (205 \times 0.3) + (220 \times 0.5))/3 = 213.50$$

The other forecasts are also shown.

Period	Data	Forecast	Forecast error
1	180.000		
2	215.000		
3	225.000		
4	220.000	213.000	−7.000
5	210.000	220.000	10.500
6	205.000	216.000	11.000
7	220.000	209.500	−10.500
8		213.500	

The accuracy tests are:
(a) MAD for the period 4 through 7 is 39/4 = 9.75
(b) The MSE = 97.625, and
(c) The MFE = 4/4 = 1.0

Comparison	SMA	WMA
Forecast for August	211.667	213.000
MAD	11.25	9.75
MSE	131.24	97.625
Mean Forecast Error	0.4167	1.00

In this case, the WMA forecast is superior.

Exponential Smoothing.   This method of forecasting is really an averaging technique that weights the more recent past data point more strongly than the more distant data point. The method can be summarized as follows:

New forecast = old forecast + α (latest observation − old forecast), where α is a fraction between 0 and 1. Naturally, if $\alpha = 0$, the new forecast is always the same as the old forecast, regardless of all the latest observations. If $\alpha = 1$, then the new forecast = latest observation. We will apply this technique to the data given in Exercise 1 and use $\alpha = 0.2$. The simple exponential smoothing forecast is computed using the formula:

$$F_{t+1} = \alpha D + (1 - \alpha)F_t$$

Where, F_{t+1} = the forecast for the next period

D_t = actual demand in the present period

F_t = the previously determined forecast for the present period

α = a weighting factor called the "smoothing constant"

Example 11.4

Apply the exponential smoothing method to the data given in Example 11.2, with $\alpha = 0.2$, and apply all the tests of accuracy.

Solution:

Since $\alpha = 0.2$, it means that our forecast for the next period is based on 20 percent of recent demand (D_t) and 80 percent of past demand.

Forecast for period 2: $F_2 = (0.2)(180) + (0.80)(180) = 180$
Forecast for period 3: $F_3 = (0.2)(215) + (0.80)(180) = 187$
Forecast for period 4: $F_4 = (0.2)(225) + (0.80)(187) = 194.6$

And so on, until

Forecast for period 8: $F_8 = (0.2)(220) + (0.80)(202.395) = 205.916$

Period	Data	Forecast	Forecast error
1	180.000	180.000	
2	215.000	180.000	−35.000
3	225.000	187.000	−38.000
4	220.000	194.600	−25.400
5	210.000	199.680	−10.320
6	205.000	201.744	−3.256
7	220.000	202.395	−17.605
8		205.916	

The accuracy tests are:
(a) MAD for the period 2 through 7 is $(129.5808)/6 = 21.5968$
(b) The MSE $= 623.5322$
(c) The MFE is $(129.5808)/6 = 21.5968$

Least-Square Method.   Regression methods have already been dealt with in Chapter 9, but as a comparison we will demonstrate how regression methods can be applied in contrast to time series techniques.

Example 11.5

Refer to Example 11.2 and the data provided for 7 time periods. What is the projection for period 8 (August)?

Solution:

Refer to Chapter 9 to help you solve this problem. The equation is $Y = 198.5714 + 3.0357X$

Coefficient of determination: 0.1882

Correlation coefficient: 0.4338

Standard Error: 14.9224

Observation	Observed Value	Predicted Value	Residual
1	180.000	201.607	−21.607
2	215.000	204.643	10.357
3	225.000	207.679	17.321
4	220.000	210.714	9.286
5	210.000	213.750	−3.750
6	205.000	216.786	−11.786
7	220.000	219.821	0.179

MAD: 12.3810

Therefore, $D_8 = (3.0357 \times 8) + 198.57 = 222.86$ units

11.3 TRANSPORTATION AND ASSIGNMENT PROBLEM

11.3.1 Introduction

Part of management's problems are concerned with transporting goods from a number of sources to several destinations across the country, or even across a city. The overall objective is to minimize total transportation costs. Some basic assumptions are: (1) Transportation costs are a linear function of the number of units shipped; (2) all supply and demand are expressed in homogeneous units; (3) shipping costs per unit do not vary with the quantity shipped; (4) total supply must equal total demand, but if demand is larger than the supply, create a dummy supply and assign a zero transportation cost to it, and if supply is larger than demand create a dummy demand.

There are at least three methods for obtaining an initial solution: the Northwest corner method; the minimum cost method; and the penalty or "Vogel's" method. In all three cases the distribution uses a rectangular matrix, showing the demand requirements and supply availabilities. The costs associated with the route between the supply and demand points are indicated in the upper corner of the cells. The supply is allocated to meet the demand by writing down the number of units transported by a particular route from a supply source to a demand destination.

In all three methods, the solution procedure is iterative, beginning with an initial solution and improving it till a satisfactory feasible distribution has been achieved. This feasible solution may not be an optimal one. Since applying any one or all of the three methods does not necessarily guarantee an optimal solution giving the lowest total cost of shipment, there are at least two methods to test the solution for optimality using the initial basic solution as a starting point. Let us begin by describing the Northwest Corner method first, by working out an example.

11.3.2 Northwest Corner Method

Example 11.6

Steel factories A, B, and C need to supply 560 tons of steel products to their warehouses X, Y, and Z during the course of a day, demanding the same amount as shown in the matrix below. Assign the product from the plants to the warehouses, and find the total cost using the Northwest Corner (NW) method.

	Warehouses			
Steel Plants	X	Y	Z	Supply
A	24	15	18	240
B	45	30	36	160
C	9	27	30	160
Demand	300	140	120	560

Solution:

The NW method is a quick and systematic way of assigning the supply to the demand points, but is by no means scientific. However, it is a good start for an initial feasible solution. Simply put, you start from the northwest corner of the tableau, allocate as many units as possible into each cell, and work your way toward the southeast corner of the tableau. More specifically:

Steel Plants	Warehouses			Supply
	X	Y	Z	
A	24	15	18	240, 0
	240 (1)			
B	45	30	36	160, 100, 0
	60 (2)	**100 (3)**		
C	9	27	30	160, 120, 0
		40 (4)	**120 (5)**	
Demand	300, 60, 0	140, 40, 0	120, 0	560

(a) Assign as many units as possible to the NW corner cell AX from the total available in row A. Given the 240 units available in row A and the 300 unit demand in column X, the maximum number that can be assigned to cell AX is 240, and this is shown as 240 in cell AX and the demand column under row X is reduced by 240 to $(300 - 240) = 60$.

(b) Assign additional units of supply from row B, until the demand in column X is satisfied. This requires 60 units in cell BX, leaving 100 units of B yet to be assigned. The demand at column X has now been satisfied. It is a good plan to keep an arithmetical account of what is happening at each allocation, including the sequencing of the allocation, as indicated on the matrix. The number in parenthesis indicates the sequence of allocation.

(c) Column Y needs 140 units, of which row B can supply 100, the rest coming from row C. This exhausts the demands of columns X and Y. The balance remaining in row C of 120 units find their way through cell CZ to column Z.

(d) All the demand has now been satisfied and all the supply has been exhausted. The sequence of each allocation is also given.

(e) The total cost of supplying the steel as per our allocation is:

$$(240 \times 24) + (60 \times 45) + (100 \times 30) + (40 \times 27) + (120 \times 30) = \$16{,}140$$

Discussion:
Although the allocation has been made to obtain a feasible solution, satisfying supply and demand, it is highly unlikely that this answer is an optimal solution, and that it gives us the minimum cost. It is unscientific because we have not bothered to look at the cell costs. There is of course the possibility of tinkering with the figures and reallocating the products, but for now this is all we have.

11.3.3 The Minimum-Cost Cell Method

We will solve the same problem using a more rational method. As the name indicates, we should try to transport the product by the cheapest route possible, and this is done as follows:

(a) Select a cell having the lowest cost and allocate as much product as we can using that route.

(b) Continue by selecting the next cheapest route and repeat the procedure until the demand has been satisfied.

Example 11.7

Solve the steel plant problem described in Example 11.6 using the minimum-cell cost method.

Solution:

Steel Plants	Warehouses			Supply
	X	Y	Z	
A	24	15	18	240, 100, 0
		140 (2)	100 (3)	
B	45	30	36	160, 140, 0
	140 (5)		20 (4)	
C	9	27	30	160, 0
	160 (1)			
Demand	300, 140, 0	140, 0	120, 20, 0	560

(a) Inspection of cell costs indicates that CX is the cheapest route. Hence, allocate the maximum quantity of 160 in row C to column X, leaving 140 units to be yet supplied.

(b) The cell with the next cheapest cost is AY with a unit cost of 15. If we supply 140 units from A via AY to column Y, we will be left with 100 units in column A.

(c) The next cell is AZ where 100 units are supplied to column Z from row A.

(d) The next cell to consider is BZ with a unit cost of 36 and we therefore assign 20 units for column Z from plant B, exhausting the demand at Z. The balance of 140 units demanded in column X via route BX from row B exhausts all of the demand and supply.

The total cost is $(160 \times 9) + (140 \times 15) + (100 \times 8) + (20 \times 36) + (140 \times 45) = \$12,360$.

Discussion:

There is no question that the minimum-cost cell method is rational. Could there have been other combinations that could have lowered the cost? We cannot tell right away. Perhaps there is an optimal solution.

11.3.4 The Penalty or "Vogel's" Method

The Penalty method makes allocations minimizing the penalty or opportunity costs. We pay a penalty because of our failure to select the best alternative. The following steps briefly describe the method.

(a) Set up the tableau as usual.

(b) Calculate the penalty cost of each row and column.

(c) Select the row or column with the largest penalty and allocate as much as possible to the cell having the minimum cost.

(d) Eliminate rows and columns that are exhausted of their demand/supply.

(e) Recalculate the penalties in rows and columns and continue with the allocation until all supply and demand have been met.

We will apply the penalty method to the same problem, previously solved by the NW corner method and the Low-cost cell method. Notice that the tableau has an additional row and an additional column to take care of penalties.

Example 11.8

Solve the steel plant example described in Example 11.6 using the penalty method.

Solution

Steel Plants	Warehouses			Supply	Penalty
	X	Y	Z		
A	24	15	18	240, 100, 0	3
	140 (2)		**100 (3)**		
B	45	30	36	160, 20, 0	6
		140 (3)	20		
C	9	27	30	160, 0	18
	160 (1)				
Demand	300, 140, 0	140, 0	120, 20, 0	560	
Penalty	15, 21	12, 15	12, 18		

Calculate the penalties for rows and columns; for example, in the first row, cell AY has the lowest cost of 15 and the next higher cost is AZ of 18, indicating a penalty of 3. This is the penalty we would pay per unit if we allocate AZ instead of AY. In a similar manner, we calculate the penalty for the other rows and columns, as shown on the matrix.

The largest penalty is in row C, with a value of 18 and the cell with the lowest cost per unit is CX. To avoid paying this penalty, we allot the maximum we possibly can to this cell, which is 160 units, thus exhausting the entire supply. Therefore, we can eliminate row C from further consideration. The demand in column X is now $(300 - 160) = 140$.

Recalculation of the penalties in rows and columns is necessary to determine which penalty is the highest, and match the corresponding cell with the lowest cost. These new penalties are shown in the penalty row: 21, 15, and 18. Column X has the highest penalty of 21, and the lowest cell cost is 24 for cell AX. We can supply the maximum of 140 units from row A to column X, thus exhausting the demand. Eliminate column X from further consideration. This procedure is repeated over and over again until the demand is satisfied. Let us now calculate the total cost.

$$(140 \times 24) + (100 \times 18) + (140 \times 30) + (20 \times 36) + (160 \times 9) = \$11,520$$

Discussion:
Notice that $11,520 is an improvement over the low-cost method, which gave a figure of $12,360. But how are we to know whether this answer is the optimal or not? This question is dealt with in the following section.

11.3.5 How Do We Determine an Optimum Solution?

From the previous examples showing the application of the NW corner, least-cost cell, and the penalty methods, we were able to obtain feasible solutions of allocating units of products via combinations of routes, without being certain whether our solutions were optimum. Fortunately, there are some methods to evaluate our solutions, just for this objective. One of the popular methods is the Modified Distribution Method (MODI). An example will best demonstrate the procedure.

Example 11.9

Factory \ Warehouse	A	B	C	Supply
a	8	6	3	15
		13	**2**	
b	9	11	8	16
			16	
c	6	6	7	11
	4	**7**		
d	3	10	9	13
	13			
Demand	17	20	18	55

Suppose we would like to transport 55 units of goods from four factories a through d to three warehouses A, B, and C and shown in the tableau above. The unit costs are given in the right-hand top corner of each cell.

Solution:

We have allocated the units by the low-cost method and the cost works out to be:

$$(13 \times 6) + (2 \times 3) + (16 \times 8) + (4 \times 6) + (7 \times 5) + (13 \times 3) = \$310.$$

To check if there are alternative solutions with a net lower transportation cost, we need to examine in turn each unused route. If we send one unit along route aA, some modification has to be done to balance the supply and demand column of 17 and 15 units respectively, and one unit must be subtracted from either route aB or aC. If we reduce one unit from route aB, one unit must be added to route cB to maintain the column total of 20. Also, to keep the row total of 11 units for c, one unit must be subtracted from route cA, and this subtraction compensates for the initial modification of sending one unit by route aA. These changes will have no effect on the feasibility of the initial allocation.

Warehouse / Factory	A	B	C	Supply
a	8 (+1) $\longrightarrow$	6 13(−1)	3 2	15
b	9	11	8 16	16
c	6 4(−1) $\longleftarrow$	5 7(+1)	7	11
d	3 13	10	9	13
Demand	17	20	18	55

Revised total cost $= (8 \times 1) + (12 \times 6) + (2 \times 3) + (16 \times 8) + (3 \times 6)$
$$+ (8 \times 5) + (13 \times 3) = \$311.$$

This is unacceptable because this means an increase of \$1.

We could have come to the same conclusion by considering the cell costs as follows:

$$C_{aA} - C_{cA} + C_{cB} - C_{aB} = 8 - 6 + 5 - 6 = \$1,$$
where C_{aA} represents the cost of transport by that route.

Also, this inspection procedure could be repeated for each unused route in turn, to test whether we could improve the initial feasible solution.

  Another way to avoid this laborious procedure is by considering shadow costs. Shadow costs are obtained by assuming that the transportation cost for all used routes is made up of two parts—dispatch costs and receiving costs. So, the dispatch costs are a, b, c, and d, while receiving costs are A, B, C, and D. So, the unit cost of cell aA $= C_{aA} = a + A$. As per the initial feasible solution, the cost of transport of occupied cells are $c + A = 6$; $d + A = 3$; $a + B = 6$; $c + B = 5$; $a + C = 3$; and $b + C = 8$. There are six equations and seven unknowns. If A is assumed to be zero, we can find the values of the other unknowns to be a $= 7$, b $= 12$, c $= 6$, d $= 3$, and A $= 0$, B $= -1$, C $= -4$. These shadow prices are shown on the side and top of the matrix. The cell costs shown above:

  $C_{aA} - C_{cA} + C_{cB} - C_{aB}$ can also be written in terms of shadow costs as,

  $C_{aA} - (c + A) + (c + B) - (a + B)$ is equivalent to $C_{aA} - (a + A)$,

which is useful as a general result, because it illustrates that sending one unit along a previously unoccupied route increases the total cost by the unit transport cost of the new route, minus the sum of the shadow cost for that route. Thus, if this difference is negative for any unused route, a savings in cost will be made if each unit is transferred to this route.

  We can now calculate this difference for each unused route in the initial allocation as follows:

  $C_{aA} - (a + A) = 8 - (7 + 0) = 1$

  $C_{bA} - (b + A) = 9 - (12 + 0) = -3$ $\Leftarrow$ **we must examine this route!**

$$C_{bB} - (b + B) = 11 - (12 - 1) = 0$$
$$C_{dB} - (d + B) = 10 - (3 - 1) = 8$$
$$C_{cC} - (c + C) = 7 - (6 - 4) = 5$$
$$C_{dC} - (d + C) = 9 - (3 - 4) = 10$$

These results are entered in the top left-hand corner in the appropriate cells. Notice that a saving of \$3 can be made for each unit that can be sent along route bA, so we use this route as fully as possible to satisfy the requirements. The matrix illustrates how this is achieved. The arrows shown on the matrix indicate the modifications and illustrates that this in no way affects the feasibility of the solution.

Shadow → Costs	Warehouse / Factory	0 A		−1 B		−4 C		Supply
7	a	1	8		6		3	15
				13 − x ←		← 2 + x		
12	b	−3	9	0	11		8	16
		x →				→ 16 − x		
6	c	↑ 6		↓ 5		5	7	11
		4 − x ←		← 7 + x				
3	d		3	8	10	10	9	13
		13						
	Demand	17		20		18		55

Note also that the value of x should be so chosen that no allocation becomes negative and this is so when x = 4. The new matrix is:

Factory	Warehouse A		B		C		Supply
a		8	6		3		15
			9		6		
b		9	11		8		16
	4				12		
c		6	5		7		11
	0		11				
d		3	10		9		13
	13						
Demand	17		20		18		55

The new cost = $(9 \times 6) + (6 \times 3) + (4 \times 9) + (12 \times 8) + (11 \times 5) + (13 \times 3)$
= \$298

which shows that sending 4 units along a route whose potential saving is $3/unit reduces the total cost by $(3 \times 4) = \$12$.

If we wanted to determine whether further improvement to this solution is possible, new shadow costs can be calculated for a second feasible solution, and the test procedure can be repeated.

Shadow costs		0		2		−1		
	Warehouse Factory	A		B		C		Supply
4	a	4	8		6		3	15
							6	
9	b	0	9		11		8	16
			4				**12**	
3	c	3	6		5	5	7	11
				11				
3	d		3	5	10	7	9	13
			13					
	Demand	17		20		18		55

By arbitrarily assigning a value of zero to shadow cost A, the new shadow costs a, b, c, d, B, and C can be obtained by solving the following equations:

$$b + A = 9, d + A = 3, a + B = 6, c + B = 5, a + C = 3, b + C = 8$$

This works out to a $= 4$, b $= 9$, c $= 3$, d $= 3$, B $= 2$, and C $= -1$. Also, the differences between the unit cost and the sum of the shadow costs for the unused routes are:

$$C_{aA} - (a + A) = 8 - (4 + 0) = 4$$
$$C_{cA} - (c + A) = 6 - (3 + 0) = 3$$
$$C_{bB} - (b + B) = 11 - (9 + 2) = 0$$
$$C_{dB} - (d + B) = 10 - (3 + 2) = 5$$
$$C_{cC} - (c + C) = 7 - (3 - 1) = 5$$
$$C_{dC} - (d + C) = 9 - (3 - 1) = 7$$

Since none of these values are negative, no further improvement is possible. The minimum cost allocation is $298.

The MODI method for optimizing, just described, has been applied to the NW Corner results given in Example 11.6, and the optimal solution obtained, which works out to be $11,520.

Example 11.10

Find the minimum cost for the network given below, starting with the NW corner solution using the MODI method.

	D1	D2	D3	Supply
S1	24.0	15.0	18.0	240.0
S2	45.0	30.0	36.0	160.0
S3	9.0	27.0	30.0	160.0
Demand	300.0	140.0	120.0	560.0

Solution:

Initial solution by NW method.

	D1	D2	D3	Supply
S1	240.0	0.0	0.0	240.0
S2	60.0	100.0	0.0	160.0
S3	0.0	40.0	120.0	160.0
Demand	300.0	140.0	120.0	560.0

Therefore, the initial solution is $16140.00.
Net Cost Change Table (or cost-improvement) can be determined for the empty cells.

	1	2	3
1	0.0	6.0	6.0
2	0.0	0.0	3.0
3	−33.0	0.0	0.0

Solution after iteration 1

	D1	D2	D3	Supply
S1	240.0	0.0	0.0	240.0
S2	20.0 → 140.0→		0.0	160.0
S3	40.0 ↑	0.0	↓120.0	160.0
Demand	300.0	← 140.0 ←	120.0	560.0

Solution = $14820.00

Net Cost Change Table

	1	2	3
1	0.0	6.0	-27.0
2	0.0	0.0	-30.0
3	0.0	-33.0	0.0

Solution after Iteration 2

	D1	D2	D3	Supply
S1	240.0	0.0	0.0	240.0
S2	0.0	140.0	20.0	160.0
S3	60.0	0.0	100.0	160.0
Demand	300.0	140.0	120.0	560.0

Solution = $14220.00

Net Cost Change Table

	1	2	3
1	0.0	-24.0	-27.0
2	30.0	0.0	0.0
3	0.0	3.0	0.0

Solution after Iteration 3

	D1	D2	D3	Supply
S1	140.0	0.0	100.0	240.0
S2	0.0	140.0	20.0	160.0
S3	160.0	0.0	0.0	160.0
Demand	300.0	140.0	120.0	560.0

Solution = $11520.00

Net Cost Change Table

	1	2	3
1	0.0	3.0	0.0
2	3.0	0.0	0.0
3	0.0	30.0	27.0

Note, there are no negative numbers.
Optimal Solution by MODI

	D1	D2	D3	Supply
S1	140.0	0.0	100.0	240.0
S2	0.0	140.0	20.0	160.0
S3	160.0	0.0	0.0	160.0
Demand	300.0	140.0	120.0	560.0

Optimal Solution = $11,520.00

11.3.6 The Unbalanced and Other Transportation Problems

In most problems connected with transhipment, it would be rather rare that the supply and demand are exactly balanced. Two examples of imbalanced supply and demand are shown. In the first example, the demand is 200 units while the supply is 185, in which case a dummy supply of 15 units is introduced at zero cost.

From \ To	A	B	C	Supply
A	5	6	8	52
B	3	9	7	38
C	2	6	9	95
d (dummy)	0	0	0	15
Demand	120	35	45	200

Similarly, there can be supply that exceeds demand, as shown in the matrix below.

From \ To	A	B	C	D (dummy)	Supply
a	4	8	4	0	200
b	3	2	9	0	220
c	7	5	6	0	255
Demand	175	90	310	100	675

All three allocation methods can be used to find an initial problem solution. In the case of the NW corner or penalty method, the dummy row is treated as if it were one of the regular rows, but with the low-cost cell method it is better to leave out the dummy row until the very end.

Prohibited Routes.   The best way to handle the allocation of goods where prohibited routes are involved, due to government rules, or road construction is to assign an arbitrarily large unit cost of transportation to the route.

Maximization Problem.   In transportation problems it is possible to be confronted with tableaus giving profits instead of costs, in which case the distribution of supplies to meed demands is one to optimize (maximize) profits. An initial solution can be found by first converting the problem to a minimization case by subtracting each profit figure in the tableau from the largest. The solution is produced as before and the initial figures are used to calculate the final profit.

Degeneracy.   If "m" represents the number of rows and "n" the number of columns, there must be m + n − 1 number of occupied cells for us to evaluate the empty cells for solution improvement. If not, we have a case of degeneracy. The way to obviate this situation is to designate one of the empty cells as an occupied cell by assigning zero quantity, taking care that this cell connects all the missing links in evaluating the empty cells.

11.3.7 The Assignment Problem

The assignment problem is a special case of a transportation problem in that the supply at each source and the demand at each destination are each limited to one unit. The task is to minimize the total cost of the assignment. Say, you wanted to assign five machinists to five machines, where the capabilities of each worker on a particular machine varied. There would be $5 \times 4 \times 3 \times 2 \times 1 = 120$ ways of assigning the workers. The Hungarian Method is used for solving such problems, and the best way is to demonstrate it with the help of an example.

Example 11.11

Four workers a, b, c, and d are to be assigned four jobs A, B, C, and D and their capability to perform these jobs is understood as a measure of time needed to complete the jobs. The problem is to assign the workers the jobs so that the total time needed to finish the jobs is a minimum.

Solution:

Tableau 1

	Jobs			
	A	B	C	D
a	30	36	42	48
b	38	46	44	36
c	52	34	32	38
d	38	42	46	34

(Workers)

Tableau 2

	A	B	C	D
a	0	2	10	14
b	8	12	12	2
c	22	0	0	4
d	8	8	14	0

Tableau 3

	A	B	C	D
a	0	2	10	14
b	8	12	12	2
c	22	0	0	4
d	8	8	14	0

Tableau 4

	A	B	C	D
a	0	2	10	20
b	0	4	4	0
c	22	0	0	10
d	2	2	8	0

Tableau 5

	A	B	C	D
a	0	0	8	20
b	0	2	2	0
c	24	0	0	12
d	2	0	6	0

Step 1: Deduct the smallest non-zero time in each column from all entries in that column, thus obtaining at least one zero in each column. This is shown in Tableau 2.

Step 2: Deduct the smallest non-zero time in each row from all entries in that row, only if there is no zero in that row. This is shown in Tableau 3.

Step 3: Draw the minimum number of lines which will cover all the zeros in the matrix. In Tableau 3, we notice that three lines are enough. If there are as many lines as there are rows or columns, an optimum assignment is possible. If not, further adjustments are necessary. Because there are only three lines instead of four, we need to proceed further.

Step 4: Subtract the smallest uncovered entry in Tableau 3, which is 6 from all uncovered entries. Enter the results in Tableau 4. Then add the same number, that is 6, to the elements at which the lines of matrix 3 cross (6 in line a, and 6 in line c), obtaining 20 and 10 respectively. Enter these results in Tableau 4, and complete the tableau.

Step 5: In Tableau 4, it is again possible to cover all zeros with only three lines, and so we need to repeat Step 4, getting Tableau 5 in which four lines cover all the zeros. Hence, this is the optimal solution.

Step 6: Make the assignments, starting with the zeros, which are unique in each row or column. Notice, that in this example, two sets of assignments can be made.

Assignment I: cC, aA, bD, dB = 32 + 30 + 36 + 42 = 140 time units.
Assignment II: cC, aB, bA, dD = 32 + 36 + 38 + 34 = 140 time units.

Special Cases of Assignment

1. In cases of assignment, we may come across a situation where a worker cannot be assigned to a certain machine or to a certain job. In such cases these machines or jobs are marked with an M which implies that such an assignment is not permissible, because the cost is very high.

2. There are situations where five jobs need to be assigned to six machines. For making a minimum cost assignment, we need a square matrix for which a sixth

row, known as a dummy row, is added with zeros in all the row cells. In a similar way, if there were six jobs and five machines, we could add a dummy machine column to make up a square matrix.

3. Cases can also arise in assignment problems where an assignment needs to be made, which maximizes profit (instead of minimizing costs). In such cases, we transform the profits into opportunity losses. An example of such a case is shown below.

Example 11.12

A TV station has three programs that bring in high profits (in millions) as shown in the matrix below. Which program should be aired at what time to reap the largest profit?

	Program		
Hours	1	2	3
7 to 8 p.m.	56	54	61
8 to 9 p.m.	53	57	60
9 to 10 p.m.	58	55	57

Solution:

Tableau 1

	Program		
Hours	1	2	3
7 to 8 p.m.	56	54	61
8 to 9 p.m.	53	57	60
9 to 10 p.m.	58	55	57

Tableau 2

	Program		
Hours	1	2	3
7 to 8 p.m.	5	7	0
8 to 9 p.m.	7	3	0
9 to 10 p.m.	0	2	1

Tableau 3

	Program		
Hours	1	2	3
7 to 8 p.m.	5	5	0
8 to 9 p.m.	7	1	0
9 to 10 p.m.	0	0	1

Tableau 4

	Program		
Hours	1	2	3
7 to 8 p.m.	4	4	0
8 to 9 p.m.	6	0	0
9 to 10 p.m.	0	0	2

Show the third program at 7 p.m., the second program at 8 p.m. and the first program at 9 p.m. Profit = 61 + 57 + 58 = $176 million.

11.4 DECISION ANALYSIS

There is hardly a day that passes when we are not asked to make a decision. Of course, some of the results of these decisions are inconsequential, such as wearing the wrong color of socks with a pair of shoes. Other decisions can be more painful, such as buying a used car that turned out to be a bad deal.

11.4.1 Overview

Decision analysts distinguish among three different kinds of decisions:

(a) Decision making under certainty. These are decisions where you think you have all the necessary information to make an intelligent choice. However, this doesn't necessarily mean that you are likely to make the right decision. In simple cases it may depend on what your personal preferences are at the time of decision-making (e.g., buying a 3 – piece business suit for $300). In more complicated cases, you may need additional information (i.e., buying a single-family house).

(b) Decision making under uncertainty with constraints. These cases are quite common where resources, budgets, time, and legal constraints pose a problem. Various algorithms and techniques are available, such as linear programming to evaluate the available data and select the best outcome.

(c) Decision making under conflict. In such cases, apart from information regarding the problem-situation you may have to take account of what your competitor may do. For example, if you are responsible for fixing the price of a certain product that your company is producing, you would have to consider what your competitors are likely to charge for a similar product. These decisions are dealt with by game theory.

(d) Decision making under uncertainty with known probabilities (or under risk). In these cases you are taking into consideration the question of chance that is likely to play a part in your decision. We are not considering our competitors. In fact, pure chance is connected with nature, like a freak thunderstorm. Decision making under conditions of uncertainty naturally takes into consideration probabilities assigned to future outcomes. This category of decision-making is also known as "decision under risk." When a manager doesn't exactly know the probability, he can use subjective estimates.

(e) Decision making under uncertainty without known probabilities. These cases are similar to what is described under (d), where there is more than one possible state of nature, but the probability of a particular state is not known.

11.4.2 Decision Making under Conditions of Uncertainty

When probabilities of outcomes are unknown, the payoff for every decision and state of nature pair must be stated in the form of a matrix. The state of nature will determine the outcome of the decision. The decision-maker has no control over the state of nature. Payoffs are expressed in terms of profits or costs.

Decision makers operate based on their personality and style of their operation. For example, decision makers can be optimistic, even-handed, risk-taking or even pessimistic individuals. The following criteria are often used to describe decision types.

(a) The decision maker adopting the **maximax** criterion selects the maximum of the maximum payoffs from a matrix.

(b) If the maximum of the minimum payoffs is selected, we refer to this as the **maximin** criterion.

(c) In the **minimax regret** criterion (also known as the **Savage** criterion) the decision maker first creates a regret table and then chooses the payoff that contains the minimum of the maximum possible regrets.

(d) The **Hurwicz** criterion requires the decision maker to decide on a coefficient of optimism (α). Then, for each decision, we multiply the maximum payoff by α and the minimum payoff by $(1 - \alpha)$, and sum these to choose the decision with the largest sum.

(e) The **equal likelihood** criterion weights each state of nature equally. Here we multiply payoffs by weights for each state and choose the decision with the largest sum.

The example shown below will illustrate the application of all these criteria in a common setting.

Example 11.13

A developer has 10 million dollars to invest in one of four projects: school buildings (A), water and sewage projects (B), housing (C), or transport projects (D). The amount of profit depends on the market economy and employment situation for the near future. The possible states of nature are poor economy (P), normal growth (N), good economic conditions (G). The table below shows the payoff matrix. Determine the optimum action using the five decision criteria. The cell values indicate the profits.

Course of action	State of nature (economy)		
	P	N	G
A	−6	10	31
B	−29	21	42
C	0	8	12
D	−7	6	18

Solution:

An examination of the payoff matrix reveals that option D is in every way inferior to option A (cell by cell). Therefore, we will eliminate it from further consideration.

The revised matrix is as shown below:

Course of action	State of nature (economy)		
	P	N	G
A	−6	10	31
B	−29	21	42
C	0	8	12

(a) As per the maximin criterion, a decision maker who is pessimistic (or very cautious) about the outlook of a decision, considers the worst case scenario that might occur and is prepared for it. Such a person chooses C.

Course of action	State of nature (economy)			Minimum of each row
	P	N	G	
A	−6	10	31	−6
B	−29	21	42	−29
C	0	8	12	0 ← Choose C

(b) With the maximax criterion, on the other hand, a decision maker who is optimistic about the outcome, considers the best of all possible gains and expects the best from nature, chooses B.

Course of action	State of nature (economy) P	N	G	Maximum of each row
A	−6	10	31	31
B	−29	21	42	42 ← Choose B.
C	0	8	12	12

(c) Hurwicz Criterion: While the maximin is ultraconservative and the maximax is ultraoptimistic, the Hurwicz criterion is between the two extremes, using a weighted combination of the best and the worst consequences for each alternative. In calculating the weighted combination an optimism index (α) is used, depending on the decision makers attitude toward the state of nature. Alpha (α) ranges between 0 and 1. The weighted combination for alternative A_i is called the Hurwicz payoff H_i

$$H_i = \alpha M_i + (1 - \alpha)m_i$$

Where M_i and m_i are the maximum and minimum gains for alternative A_i. In this example if we adopt $\alpha = 0.6$, we get the following:

Alternative	Max gain	Min gain	Hurwicz Payoff
A	31	−6	$0.6(31) + 0.4(-6) = 16.2$ ← max
B	42	−29	$0.6(42) + 0.4(-29) = 13.6$
C	12	0	$0.6(12) + 0.4(0) = 7.2$

The value of α needs to be determined by the decision maker. If α were chosen to be 0.90 the payoffs would be

A $(0.9)(31) + (0.1)(-6) = 27.3$
B $(0.9)(42) + (0.1)(-29) = 34.9$ ← max
C $(0.9)(12) + (0.1)(0) = 10.8$

and the choice would be alternative B instead of A, when α was chosen to be 0.6.

(d) Minimax Regret Criterion: This criterion proposed by Savage illustrates the use of the concept of opportunity loss resulting from an incorrect decision. The best way to deal with this criterion is to set up a "Regret" matrix as shown below.

	State of nature			
Alternative	P	N	G	Max regret
A	6	11	11	11 ← Minimax regret
B	29	0	0	29
C	0	13	30	30
Max return	0	21	42	

Notice that if the decision maker had selected B and nature is G, he receives the maximum payoff of 42. However if he had selected C and nature is G the cost of the mistake is $(42 - 14) = 30$. The best way to set up the regret table is to have a row at the bottom of the matrix with the maximum return and then subtract cell by cell, the cell values from the column maximum return. Then, select the maximum regret in each row and select the minimum regret from this column, as indicated above. Since A is the row with the least regret, we choose alternative A.

(e) Laplace Criterion: This criterion is simple to apply. If the three states of nature are equally likely, we assign a probability of 1/3 to each cell value and find the expected value.

A : $(-6 + 10 + 31)(1/3) = 11.55 \leftarrow$ Max
B : $(-29 + 21 + 42)(1/3) = 11.22$
C : $(0 + 8 + 12)(1/3) = 6.66$

Choose alternative A, because it has the highest expected value.

Discussion:

Notice how a decision is guided by the criterion used as demonstrated in this example. How would you decide what to do under similar circumstances? The summary of outcomes is as follows:

Maximin	Alternative C
Maximax	Alternative B
Hurwicz	Alternative A if $\alpha = 0.6$; alternative B if $\alpha = 0.9$
Minimax regret	Alternative A
Laplace	Alternative A

11.4.3 Decision Making under Uncertainty with Probabilities

It is possible for a decision maker to assign preliminary values of probabilities to the state of nature, based on past records and current trends. Use is also made of two criteria, expected value and expected opportunity loss. To illustrate these concepts let us take up a simple case.

Example 11.14

A developer wants to diversify his investment through construction of either apartments (A), or bridges (B), or condominiums (C). He consults his economic adviser and comes up with probabilities of the state of nature for normal (N) conditions of 0.7 and depressed (D) economic conditions of 0.3 as shown in the following payoff matrix (in millions of dollars).

	State of nature (economy)	
	Normal (N)	Depressed (D)
Alternative	0.7	0.3
A	60	40
B	100	−50
C	20	10

Solution:

The expected value (EV) of each alternative is as follows:

$$EV(A) = (60 \times 0.7) + (40 \times 0.3) = 54$$
$$EV(B) = (100 \times 0.7) + (-50 \times 0.3) = 55 \leftarrow max$$
$$EV(C) = (20 \times 0.7) + (10 \times 0.3) = 17$$

Alternative B is the obvious winner, followed closely by A. All it means is that an average payoff of $55 million would result if this decision situation were repeated a large number of times. In a similar way, a decision maker can calculate the expected opportunity loss (EOL) for each decision outcome. Recall, that we used the concept of regret in the minimum regret criterion (after Savage). Here, we set up a table in very much the same way, which indicates the opportunity loss (or regret).

	States of nature (economy)	
	(N)	(D)
Alternative	0.7	0.3
A	40	0
B	0	90
C	80	30
Max. payoff	100	40

A: EOL $(40 \times 0.7) + (0 \times 0.3) = 28$
B: EOL $(0 \times 0.7) + (90 \times 0.3) = 27 \leftarrow$ minimum regret or opportunity loss
C: EOL $(80 \times 0.7) + (30 \times 0.3) = 65$

The best decision is minimizing the regret, and so we choose B, and this result corresponds to what we got from expected values.

Decision Trees.   It is useful to describe decision situations with the help of a decision tree, particularly in complicated cases. For example, the problem in the previous section can be converted to a decision tree. The circles and squares are the nodes, while the branches are the alternatives possible under normal and depressed conditions. Thus, the decision tree merely depicts the sequence of decision making. If we want to find the best decision, all we do is to work backwards from the ends of the branches toward node 1, by calculating the expected values of the payoffs.

$$EV \text{ (node 2)} = (60 \times 0.7) + (40 \times 0.3) = 54$$
$$EV \text{ (node 3)} = (100 \times 0.7) + (-50 \times 0.3) = 55$$
$$EV \text{ (node 4)} = (20 \times 0.7) + (10 \times 0.3) = 17$$

These expected payoffs are shown in Figure 11.1 below.

Expected Value of Perfect Information.   Referring to the example in the previous section, the question that one might consider is what additional information could the decision maker obtain regarding the future which would help in making a good decision, within certain limits? This information can be computed in terms of an expected value, and is called the expected value of perfect information (EVPI).

If we look at the payoff table, the most significant information that is driving our decision-making is the state of nature. If we were sure of these states, we would be in good shape. One way of working at this dilemma is to argue that normal condition prevail for 70 percent of time, while depressed conditions are likely to occur 30 percent of the time. Based on these conditions, it is reasonable to say that each of the decision outcomes obtained using perfect information must be weighted by its respective probability, shown below:

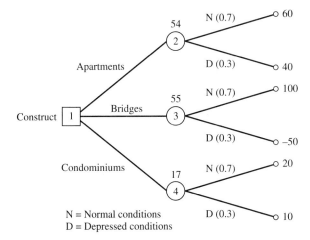

Figure 11.1   Tree diagrams for decision making.

	States of nature (economy)	
	Normal (N)	Depressed (D)
Alternative	0.7	0.3
A	60	40
B	100	-50
C	20	10

$(100 \times 0.7) + (40 \times 0.3) = \$82$ million (expected value given perfect information). This indicates that if we had perfect information, $82 million would be the value of the decision, by taking the maximum values from each of the columns. Now, we have already computed the value of the best decision (as calculated previously) that the expected value of alternative B is $55 million.

$$\therefore \text{ EVPI} = 82 - 55 = \$27 \text{ million.}$$

This is the maximum the decision maker would pay to obtain perfect information (or, near perfect information) from outside sources, such as an economic expert, although it is doubtful if such a large amount would ever be paid. Incidentally, it is interesting to note that this value of EVPI of $27 million corresponds to the expected opportunity loss (EOL) of $27 million obtained earlier.

Decision Making with Additional Information.   Although there are few instances of decision-makers paying huge sums of money to experts for perfect information, there are plenty of cases where decision makers have paid large sums of money to obtain additional information. For instance, geotechnical engineers have paid soil-boring experts to take additional samples of soil in addition to the ones they already have taken to make better choices on the site selection of facitilities such as an electrical power stations, costing billions of dollars.

In the case of our original problem, suppose the decision maker hires an economic expert to supply him with a report with conditional probabilities for each state of nature in the future as shown below:

$$N = \text{Normal economic conditions}$$

$$D = \text{Depressed economic conditions}$$

$$O = \text{Optimistic report}$$

$$P = \text{Pessimistic report}$$

If the conditional probabilities for each report outcome, given that each state of nature is:

Probability $(O/N) = 0.9$;   Probability $(P/N) = 0.1$

Probability $(O/D) = 0.2$;   Probability $(P/D) = 0.8$, which means that, if the future economic conditions are given as normal, the probability of an optimistic report is $p(O/N)$ is 0.9, and so on. The decision maker now has quite a good bit of information, although it is by no means perfect. Prior probabilities are also available:

$$p(N) = 0.7 \quad \text{and} \quad p(D) = 0.3 \text{ as noted before.}$$

With this information, he can calculate the posterior probabilities, using Bayes' rule. Looking at Figure 11.2, it is easy to compute these values!

$$p(N/O) = \frac{p(O/N)p(N)}{p(O/N)p(N) + p(O/D)p(D)}$$

$$= \frac{(0.9)(0.7)}{(0.9)(0.7) + (0.2)(0.3)} = 0.913$$

In a similar way:

$$p(N/P) = \frac{(0.1)(0.7)}{(0.1)(0.7) + (0.8)(0.3)} = 0.226$$

$$p(D/O) = \frac{(0.2)(0.3)}{(0.9)(0.7) + (0.2)(0.3)} = 0.087$$

$$p(D/P) = \frac{(0.8)(0.3)}{(0.1)(0.7) + (0.8)(0.3)} = 0.774$$

In addition, we can compute the probability of an optimistic (O) and pessimistic (P) report (see Figure 11.2).

$$p(O) = (0.9)(0.7) + (0.2)(0.3) = 0.69$$

$$p(P) = (0.1)(0.7) + (0.8)(0.3) = 0.31$$

As explained before, if we work backwards from the nodes on the right hand side towards the left, we can compute the expected values, and these are shown over nodes 4 through 9. We finally arrive at the expected value at node 1 of $74.0442 million, given the results of the report (see Figure 11.3).

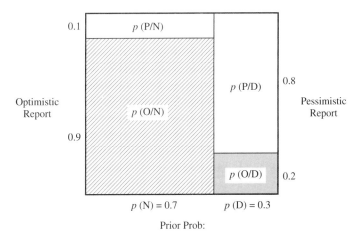

Figure 11.2   Block diagram.

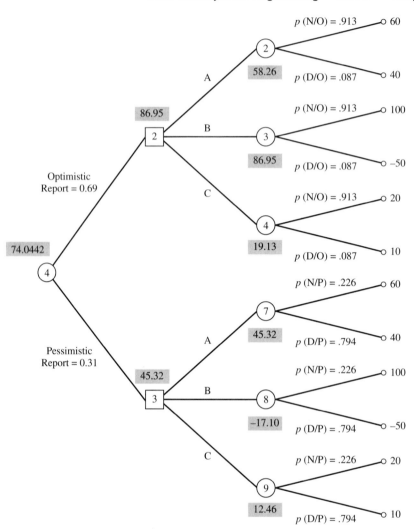

Figure 11.3   Tree diagram.

A summary of our computations is given below:

State of nature (1)	Prior probabilities (2)	Conditional probabilities (3)	Prior × conditional probabilities (4) = (2) × (3)	Posterior probabilities (5) = (4) ÷ (Σ4)
Normal (N)	0.7	p(O/N) = 0.90	p(ON) = 0.63	p(N/O) = 0.913
Depressed (D)	0.3	p(O/D) = 0.20	p(OD) = 0.06	p(D/O) = 0.087
			Σ0.69	Σ1.000

Going back to our original computation, we found that the expected value of our decision without any additional information was $55 million. Now that we have obtained additional information, the expected value has risen to $74.0442 million. The difference between these two figures is obviously the expected value of the sample information (EVSI).

$$\text{EVSI} = \text{EV(with additional information)} - \text{EV(without additional information)}$$
$$= \$74.0442 - \$55.00 = \$19.0442 \text{ million}$$

Does this mean that the decision maker would offer a consultant this huge amount for the additional information? This is an open question. One can also compute the efficiency of this sample information.

$$\text{Efficiency} = \text{EVSI/EVPI} = \frac{19.0442}{27.000} = 70.53\%$$

The report submitted by the expert containing the sample information is 70.53 percent efficient as perfect information.

11.5 QUEUING MODELS

11.5.1 Introduction

It is quite common to notice a queue formed in front of service counters in airports, hospitals, grocery stores, and scores of other places. Due to the irregularity with which customers arrive demanding service, coupled with the variability in time taken to satisfy customers, queues are likely to build up and dissipate from time to time.

The mathematical theories of queue are complex but they provide us with models of various types that help us to analyze and predict how a system dealing with queues would cope or fail with demand put upon it.

A general schematic diagram of a queuing system is shown in Figure 11.4. If a system has parallel service facilities, it is referred to as channels. If the service facilities are sequential, the steps are known as phases.

11.5.2 Characteristics of Queuing Systems

There are a number of operating characteristics of a queuing system. These are: (a) the probability of a specific number of customers in the system, (b) the mean waiting time for each customer, (c) the expected (mean) length of the queue, (d) the expected (mean) time in the system for each customer, (e) the mean number of customers in the system, and (f) the probability of the service facility being idle.

One of the features of a queuing system is queue discipline, that is, what happens between the moment of arrival of a customer wanting service till the time

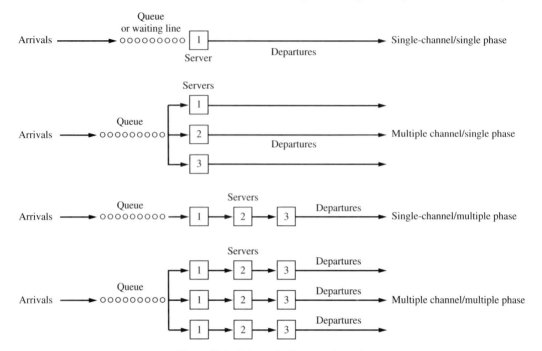

Figure 11.4   Schematic diagram of queuing systems.

he/she leaves the system. Two of the several options are most popular: first-in-first-out (FIFO), indicating that the first customer to arrive is the first to depart, and last-in-first-out (LIFO), indicating that the last customer to arrive is the first to depart. Sometimes, a customer may decide to leave the queue (balking) or he may join another queue, if he thinks he can better his chances of being served (jockeying).

Queuing models are generally identified by three alphanumeric values. The first value indicates the arrival rate assumption, while the second value gives the departure rate assumption. The third value indicates the number of departure channels. We will consider four models as detailed below:

1. D/D/1 queuing model, which assumes deterministic arrivals as well as deterministic departures, with one departure channel;
2. M/D/1 queuing model, which assumes exponentially distributed arrival times, deterministic departures, and one departure channel;
3. M/M/1 queuing model which assumes both exponentially distributed arrivals and departure times, with one departure channel;
4. M/M/N queuing model which is similar to M/M/1 except that it has multiple departure channels.

11.5.3 Model 1 (D/D/1) Deterministic Queuing Model

An excellent starting point is the D/D/1 queuing model. This model is the simplest waiting-line model, and assumes the following: (a) deterministic arrival, (b) deterministic service time, (c) single-channel server, (d) FIFO, and (e) infinite queue length. A simple queuing model's traffic intensity is important, where

$$\text{Traffic intensity } (\rho) = \frac{\text{mean rate of arrival } (\lambda)}{\text{mean rate of service } (\mu)}$$

also, mean inter-arrival time $= 1/\lambda$
and, mean service time $= 1/\mu$
Thus $\rho = 1/\mu/1/\lambda$
We will examine this model working out a couple of examples.

Example 11.15

Customers arrive at a movie theater ticket window at the rate of 10 per hour and are serviced at a constant rate of 12 per hour. Describe how this system will perform.

Solution:

Mean arrival rate, $\lambda = 10$ per hour
Mean service rate, $\mu = 12$ per hour
In this situation since $\lambda < \mu$ there will be no queue.

Example 11.16

Customers arrive at the ticket counter of a local movie theater at a rate of 240 persons/hour, at 5:30 p.m. After 10 min the arrival rate declines to 60 persons/hour and continues at that level for 20 min. If the time required to serve each customer is 20 seconds, describe the performance of the system.

Solution:

$$\lambda_1 = \frac{240 \text{ person/h}}{60 \text{ min/h}} = 4 \text{ persons/min t} \leq 10\text{min}$$

$$\lambda_2 = \frac{60 \text{ person/h}}{60 \text{ min/h}} = 1 \text{ persons/min t} > 10\text{min}$$

$$\mu = \frac{60 \text{ sec/min}}{20 \text{ sec/person}} = 3 \text{ persons/min for all t}$$

$\therefore$ Number of person arrivals at time $t = 4t$ for $t \leq 10\text{min}$
And, number of person arrivals $[40 + 1(t - 10)]$ for $t > 10\text{min}$
Also, the number of persons with tickets (departures) is 3t for all t.
These equations are depicted in Figure E11.16. Notice that when the arrival curve shown in the figure is above the departure curve, a queue will exist. The queue will dissipate at the time when arrival and departure curves intersect.

$$\therefore 40 + 1(t - 10) = 3t$$

$$\text{and } t = 15$$

Thus, the queue, which began to form at 5:30 p.m., will disappear at 5:45 p.m.
Longest queue will occur at $t = 10$ of 10 persons.

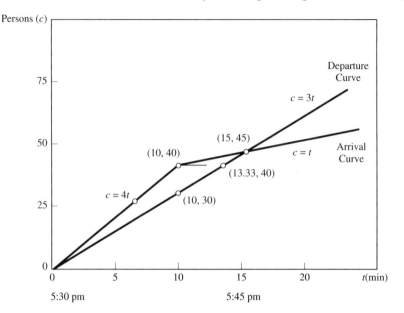

Figure E11.16   D/D/1 Queue.

and the longest delay will be $13.33 - 10 = 3.33\,\text{min}$.

$$\text{Total delay} = \frac{1}{2}(10 \times 10) + \frac{1}{2}(10 \times 5) = 75\,\text{person}-\text{min}$$

Number of persons encountering delay $= 45$

$\therefore$ Average delay/person $= 75/45 = 1.667\,\text{min}$.

11.5.4 Model 2 (M/D/1)

This model assumes that the arrival times of successive units in a queue are exponentially distributed (i.e., Poisson arrivals). However, departures are deterministically distributed. Such problems are best solved mathematically. Defining traffic intensity (ρ) as the ratio of average arrivals to departures (λ/μ) and assuming ρ is less than 1, it can be shown that for an M/D/1 queue with the following notation:

λ = mean arrival rate ($1/\lambda$ = mean time between arrivals)

μ = mean service rate ($1/\mu$ = mean service time)

n = number of customers (units) in the system (including those waiting and in service)

L = mean number in the system

L_q = mean number in the waiting line (queue length)

W = mean time in the system

W_q = mean waiting time (in the queue)

ρ = service facility utilization factor

I = percentage of server idle time

P_o = probability of number of units in the system

P_n = probability of n units in the system

$$\rho = \frac{\lambda}{\mu}$$

$$P_0 = 1 - \rho$$

$$L_q = \frac{\rho^2}{2(1 - \rho)}$$

$$L = L_q + \rho$$

$$W_q = \frac{L_q}{\lambda}$$

$$W = W_q + \frac{1}{\mu}$$

It is important to note that when the traffic intensity (ρ) is less than 1 (i.e., when $\lambda < \mu$) the D/D/1 queue will predict no queue formation. However, an M/D/1 model will predict queue formations under such conditions with randomness arising from the assumed probability distributions of arrivals.

Example 11.17

Consider the D/D/1 example worked out before, with the following changes. The arrival rate of customers is 165 per hour over the period till the movie starts, while the service rate is 3.25 persons/min. Compute the characteristics of this system.

Solution:

Mean arrival rate $\lambda = \dfrac{165}{6} = 2.75$ persons/min (exponential)

Constant service rate $\mu = 3.25$ persons/min $\rho = 0.846$

L_q = mean number of units in the waiting line = $\dfrac{\rho^2}{2(1 - \rho)}$ persons

$$= \frac{(0.846)^2}{2(1.154)} = 2.327 \text{ persons}$$

L = mean number of units on the system = $L_q + \rho = 3.173$ persons

W_q = mean time in queue = $\dfrac{L_q}{\lambda} = \dfrac{2.327}{2.75} = 0.846$ min

W = mean time in the system = $W_q + \dfrac{1}{\mu} = 0.846 + 0.308 = 1.154$ min

ρ = service facility utilization factor = 0.846 min

P_o = probability of no units in the system = $1 - \rho$ = 0.154.

11.5.5 Model 3 M/M/1

If we assume exponentially distributed arrival times as well as exponentially distributed departure times with one channel, we end up with a useful model with several applications. For example, if we look at the departure patterns of a movie theater booth, we find that some customers do not have the correct change, or have not decided on which movie to see. Under standard M/M/1 conditions, ρ is less than one and the equations for solving the characteristics of the queue are as follows:

$$\text{Mean number of units in the system: } L = \frac{\lambda}{\mu - \lambda}$$

$$\text{Mean number of units in the queue: } L_q = \frac{\lambda^2}{\mu - \lambda} = \frac{\rho^2}{1 - \rho}$$

$$\text{Mean time in the system (for each unit): } W = \frac{1}{\mu - \lambda}$$

$$\text{Mean waiting time: } W_q = \frac{\lambda}{\mu(\mu - \lambda)}$$

$$\text{Percentage of server idle time: } I = P_o = 1 - \frac{\lambda}{\mu} = 1 - \rho$$

Where P_o = probability of no customers in the system.

Example 11.17

A movie theater ticket booth has a mean arrival rate of 3 persons/min and the service rate is 4 persons/min. Calculate the characteristics of this queuing system applying the M/M/1 model.

Solution:

$$\lambda = 3; \mu = 4; \rho = \frac{\lambda}{\mu} = 0.75$$

$$L = \frac{\lambda}{\mu - \lambda} = \frac{(3)}{4 - 3} = 3 \text{ persons}$$

$$L_q = \frac{\rho^2}{1 - \rho} = \frac{(0.75)^2}{1 - (0.75)} = 2.25 \text{ persons}$$

$$W = \frac{1}{\mu - \lambda} = \frac{1}{1} = 1.00 \text{ min}$$

$$W_q = \frac{\lambda}{\mu(\mu - \lambda)} = \frac{3}{4(1)} = 0.75 \text{ min}$$

$$I = 1 - \frac{\lambda}{\mu} = 1 - 0.75 = 0.25 \text{ min}$$

11.5.6 The Economics and Operating Characteristics of Queuing Discipline

Engineers and managers making decisions regarding the level of service that needs to be maintained in handling goods, vehicles, and people, often have to consider the overall savings that would accrue if an additional worker were to be used. After all, saving customers time is highly important for a business that intends to increase its clientele. The cost trade-off relationship between the total cost of the service facility and the level-of-service is shown in Figure 11.5. The objective is to minimize the total cost of service and waiting time to achieve a respectable service level.

11.5.7 Model 4 M/M/N

If we extend model 3 (M/M/1) by considering multiple channels we get a more general formulation that can be applied in many cases of managerial decision making. We are still assuming Poisson arrivals and exponential service times. The mean service rate is determined by N (μ) where N is the number of services.

The following equations describe the operational characteristics of M/M/N queuing.

1. The probability of having no units in the system is

$$P_o = \frac{1}{\displaystyle\sum_{n_c=0}^{N-1} \frac{\rho^{n_c}}{n!} + \frac{\rho^N}{N!(1 - \rho/N)}}$$

where n_c is the departure channel number

2. The probability of having n vehicles in the system is

$$P_n = \frac{\rho^n P_o}{n!} \qquad \text{for n} \leq \text{N}$$

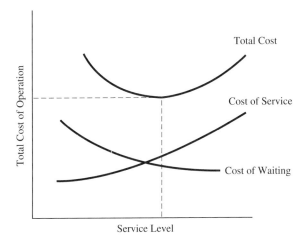

Figure 11.5   Service level vs. total cost.

$$P_n = \frac{\rho^n P_o}{N^{n-N}N!} \text{ for } n \geq N$$

3. The average length of queue (in units) is

$$L = \frac{P_o \rho^{N+1}}{N!N} \left[\frac{1}{(1 - \rho/N)^2} \right]$$

4. The average time spent in the system is

$$W = \frac{\rho + L}{\lambda}$$

5. The average waiting time in the queue is

$$W_q = \frac{\rho + L}{\lambda} - \frac{1}{\mu}$$

The probability of waiting in a queue (which is the probability that the number of units in the system, n, is greater than the number of departure channels, N) is

$$P_{n>N} = \frac{P_o \rho^{N+1}}{N!N(1 - \rho/N)}$$

Example 11.18

An entrance to a tollway has 4 toll booths. Vehicles arrive at an average of 1800 vehicles/hr and take 6.67 seconds to pay their tolls. Both arrivals and departures can be assumed to be exponentially distributed. Compute the average queue length, the time in the system, and the probability of waiting in a queue.

Solution:

$$\lambda = \frac{1800}{60} = 30 \text{ vehicles/min}$$

$$\mu = \frac{60}{6.67} = 9 \text{ vehicles/min}$$

$$\rho = \frac{30}{9} = 3.333$$

$$\rho/N = \frac{3.333}{4} = 0.8333 < 1$$

For four booths open

$$P_o = \frac{1}{1 + \dfrac{3.333}{1!} + \dfrac{3.333^2}{2!} + \dfrac{3.333^3}{3!} + \dfrac{3.333^4}{4!(0.1667)}} = 0.0213$$

$$L = \frac{0.0213(3.333)^5}{4!4} \left[\frac{1}{(0.1667)^2} \right] = 3.289 \text{ vehicles}$$

$$W = \frac{3.333 + 3.289}{30} = 0.2207 \text{ min}$$

$$P_{n>N} = \frac{0.0213(3.333)^5}{4!4(0.1667)} = 0.548 \text{ min}$$

Example 11.19

Refer to Ex. 11.18. The administration now feels that delays to vehicles are excessive and that a fifth booth should be opened. Compute the values of P_o, L, W, and $P_{n>N}$.

Solution:

$$P_o = \cfrac{1}{1 + \cfrac{3.333}{1!} + \cfrac{3.333^2}{2!} + \cfrac{3.333^3}{3!} + \cfrac{3.333^4}{4!(0.1667)} + \cfrac{3.333^5}{5!(1 - 3.333/5)}} = 0.032$$

$$L = \frac{0.032(3.333)^6}{5!5}\left[\frac{1}{(0.333)^2}\right] = 0.659 \text{ vehicles}$$

$$W = \frac{3.333 + 0.659}{30} = 0.133 \text{ min}$$

$$P_{n>N} = \frac{0.032(3.333)^6}{5!5(3.3334)} = 0.219 \text{ min}$$

Example 11.20

Compare the two systems with 4 and 5 booths as shown in Examples 11.18 and 11.19. If the value of time is $10 per hour and the wages and cost of operating a booth is $100/hr. What would be your advice to the administration?

Solution:

		4 booths	5 booths
P_o	Probability of having no vehicles in the system	0.0213	0.032
L	Average queue length	3.287 veh	0.659 veh
W	Average time spent in the system	0.331 min	0.133 min
$P_{n>N}$	Probability of having to wait in a queue	0.548	0.219

Opening a fifth booth reduces the queue length by $3.287 - 0.659 = 2.628$ veh

Average time saved in the system is $0.331 - 0.133 = 0.198$ min

$\therefore$ Since $\lambda = 20$ veh/min, $20 \times 0.198 = 3.96$ minutes

Total saving $3.96 \times 60 \times 10 = \$2376$/hour

Net saving $= \$2376 - 100 = \$2276$/hour

11.6 SIMULATION

11.6.1 Introduction

Many real-world decision problems are so complex that they are difficult, if not impossible, to solve by simply applying the usual optimization models described in previous sections. In such situations, engineers and managers conduct experiments. Simulation is one experimental technique commonly used. Simulation is a modeling technique consisting of experiments to evaluate a system's behavior or response over time. It is by no means an optimizing technique, but it does allow the experimenter to examine the problem for a possible solution. In short, to simulate is to imitate a real-world situation. For example, if a store manager using three cashier servers wanted to increase the efficiency of his outfit by reducing the length of the queues, he could simulate this situation and come up with a solution.

11.6.2 Random Numbers

Most simulations make use of random numbers. They can be generated by using a calculator, but statisticians have generated scores of pages of these numbers that have no discernable pattern, thus making them random. You can generate random numbers yourself by using a 100-sided spinner with a pointer, marked from 0 to 99, capable of producing a random number from 0 to 99. Flipping coins and rolling dice can also be used if necessary.

11.6.3 Simulations Using Known Probabilities

We will now demonstrate the use of simulation through some simple examples. First, empirical (actual) data is collected from the site of operation. Second, a probability distribution is developed and an interval of random numbers is assigned to each class of the distribution. Third, random numbers, derived from tables or otherwise, are applied to derive the results and lastly these are interpreted. A number of simple examples follow.

Example 11.21

Trucks arriving for unloading earth vary in length from 20 ft to 30 ft. The time needed to unload a 20 ft truck is 12 min, while a 30 ft takes 22 minutes. Using a uniform distribution, simulate the time needed to unload 6 trucks, on a random basis adopting the following random numbers 20, 31, 98, 24, 01 and 56. Assume that we don't know the distribution of the length of trucks.

Solution:

Let a = time needed for a 20 ft truck to unload = 12 min.

and b = time needed for a 30 ft truck to unload = 22 min.
RN = random number as a percentage.
Simulated value = $a + (b - a)(RN) = 12 + 10(RN)$

1. $12 + 10(0.20) = 14.0$ min.
2. $12 + 10(0.31) = 15.1$ min.
3. $12 + 10(0.98) = 21.8$ min.
4. $12 + 10(0.24) = 14.4$ min.
5. $12 + 10(0.01) = 12.1$ min.
6. $12 + 10(0.56) = \underline{17.6}$ min.

$$95.0 \text{ minutes}$$

Average time per truck = $95/6 = 15.83$ minutes
Certainly, 15.83 min is not the average time needed for unloading 6 trucks, but if we simulated a hundred trucks we would possibly get a more realistic answer.

Example 11.22

A professor spends time with students based on normally distributed times with a mean of 20 minutes and a standard deviation of 5 minutes. Using random numbers find the average time he takes for 5 students, adopting the following normally distributed random numbers $-0.25, 1.13, 0.35, 0.75, 2.09$.

Solution:

Let $\mu = 20\,\text{min}; \sigma = 5\,\text{min}$ and $RN = $ random number

Simulated value $= \mu + \sigma(RN) = 20 + 5(RN)$

$$
\begin{aligned}
20 + 5(-0.25) &= 18.75 \\
20 + 5(1.13) &= 25.65 \\
20 + 5(0.35) &= 21.75 \\
20 + 5(0.75) &= 23.75 \\
20 + 5(2.09) &= \underline{30.45} \\
& 120.35\,\text{min}
\end{aligned}
$$

Average time spent with each student $= 24.07\,\text{min}$

This answer is based on a sample of only 5 students. For realistic results, hundreds of students would need to be taken into account.

Example 11.23

Airplanes arrive at a small airport, described by a Poisson distribution, with a mean of three planes per hour. Simulate the number of plane arrivals for an 8-hour shift.

Solution:

First, set up a table connecting plane arrivals using the cumulative Poisson distribution.

$$
P(x) = \sum \frac{\lambda^x e^{-\lambda}}{x!}, \text{ where } \lambda = 3
$$

Plane arrival	0	1	2	3	4	5	6	7	8	9	10
Cum. P(x) prob.	.050	.199	.423	.647	.815	.916	.966	.988	.996	.999	1.0

Next, select 8 random numbers in sequence and match the plane arrivals to each of them.

853	540	985	903	266	373	920	164	
5	3	7	5	2	2	6	1	= 31 planes

Example 11.24

A life insurance salesman has kept good records for the past year regarding his performance. There is a 50 percent chance that when a client walks into his office there is a genuine interest in buying a policy. However, this by itself does not always end up in a sale. Fifty percent of the time there will be no sale, 1/3 of the time it will result in a sale of $100,000 and 1/6th of the time in a sale of $200,000. Using a simulation of 20 cases, determine the probability of a sale and the expected policy value. After you have completed the simulation, show your results in the form of a decision tree and compare your results with the theoretical tree. What is the expected value of your sale?

Solution:

There are two stages to this problem. In the first stage, there is a 50 percent chance that a prospective client will be interested in talking about buying a policy. In the second stage, the person who shows an interest will decide what he/she will do. Assign random numbers accordingly.

	1st stage		
	Probability	Cum. Probability	RN
Interest	0.50	0.50	00 – 49
No interest	0.50	1.00	50 – 99
	2nd stage		
No interest	0.50	0.50	00 – 49
Sale of $100,000	0.33	0.83	50 – 82
Sale of $200,000	0.17	1.00	83 – 99

Simulation of 20 Insurance calls.

Trial	1st Stage R. No.	Interest Yes	No	2nd Stage R. No.	No	Interest 10^5	2×10^5	Value
1	46	X		59		X		10^5
2	16	X		72		X		10^5
3	86		—	—				—
4	25	X		45	X			0
5	03	X		05	X			0
6	62		—	—				—
7	23	X		32	X			0
8	36	X		91			X	2×10^5
9	94		—	—				—
10	70		—	—				—
11	12	X		15	X			0
12	75		—	—				—
13	41	X		38	X			0
14	69		—	—				—
15	34	X		84			X	2×10^5
16	48	X		71		X		10^5
17	02	X		22	X			0
18	24	X		64		X		10^5
19	95		—	—				—
20	12	X		90			X	2×10^5
Result		13	7		6	4	3	10×10^5

For the theoretical tree,

$$\left(\frac{1}{4} + \frac{1}{6} + \frac{1}{12}\right) + \left(\frac{1}{2}\right) = 1.00$$

$$(25\% + 16.7\% + 8.3\%) + 50\% = 100\%$$

$$\text{No Sale} = 0.25 + 0.50 = 0.75\%$$

$$\text{Sale} = 0.167 + 0.083 = 0.25\%$$

$$\therefore \text{ Probability of selling } \$10^5/\text{given a sale} = \frac{0.167}{0.167 + 0.083} = 0.668$$

$$\text{Probability of selling } \$2 \times 10^5/\text{given a sale} = \frac{0.083}{0.167 + 0.083} = 0.332$$

Total = 1.000

Expected value of policy $= (0.668 \times 10^5) + (0.332 \times 2 \times 10^5) = \$133,200$

Theoretical Tree

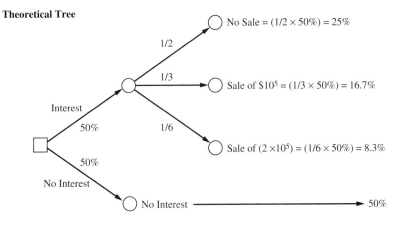

Simulated Tree

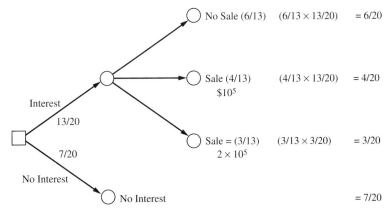

Figure E11.23   Theoretical and simulated trees.

For the simulated tree (see Figure E11.23),

$$\left(\frac{6}{20} + \frac{4}{20} + \frac{3}{20}\right) + \frac{7}{20} = 1$$

$$(0.30\% + 0.20\% + 0.15\%) + 0.35\% = 1$$

$$\text{No sale} = (0.30 + 0.35) = 0.65\%$$

$$\text{Sale} = (0.20 + 0.15) = 0.35\%$$

$$\text{Probability of selling } \$10^5/\text{given a sale} = \frac{0.20}{0.20 + 0.15} = 0.5714$$

$$\text{Probability of selling } \$2 \times 10^5/\text{given a sale} = \frac{0.15}{0.15 + 0.20} = 0.4286$$

$$\text{Total} = 1.000$$

Expected value of policy $= (0.5714 \times 10^5) + (0.4286 \times 2 \times 10^5) = \$14,286.$

Example 11.25

A one-man repair shop handles jobs as shown in the table below.

Time between jobs	Probability	Job time	Probability
10	0.10	8	0.15
20	0.15	16	0.30
30	0.35	24	0.25
40	0.20	32	0.20
50	0.15	40	0.10
60	0.05		
	1.00		1.00

Simulate the repair shop performance for 10 jobs and compute the following:
(a) the average turn around time per job
(b) the average number of jobs waiting to be done
(c) the idle time of the repair man

Solution:

Assign random numbers to time between jobs:

Arr. Interval Prob.	Probability	Cum. Prob. (P_x)	RN
10	0.10	0.10	00–09
20	0.15	0.25	10–24
30	0.35	0.60	25–59
40	0.20	0.80	60–79
50	0.15	0.95	80–94
60	0.05	1.00	95–99

Assign random numbers to repair time:

Repair Time (Y)	Probability (P_y)	Cum. Prob.	RN
8	0.15	0.15	00–14
16	0.30	0.45	15–44
24	0.25	0.70	45–69
32	0.20	0.90	70–89
40	0.10	1.00	90–99

Job	r_1	Arr. Int	Arr. Clock	Enter Service Clock	Waiting Time	Length of Queue	r_2	Service Time	Dep. Clock	Time in System
1	19	20	20	20	0	0	65	24	44	24
2	51	30	50	50	0	0	17	16	66	16
3	63	40	90	90	0	0	85	32	122	32
4	37	30	120	122	2	1	89	32	154	34
5	76	40	160	160	0	0	71	32	192	32
6	34	30	190	192	2	1	11	8	200	10
7	27	30	220	220	0	0	10	8	228	8
8	59	30	250	250	0	0	87	32	282	32
9	08	10	260	282	22	1	08	8	290	30
10	89	50	310	310	0	0	42	16	326	16
					26	6		72		219

$$\text{Average turn around time} = \frac{172}{10} = 17.2\,\text{min}$$

$$\text{Average waiting time} = \frac{26}{10} = 2.6\,\text{min}$$

$$\text{Average number of jobs waiting} = \frac{6}{10} = 0.6\,\text{jobs}$$

11.7 MARKOV ANALYSIS

Markov analysis is a technique used by engineers and managers to forecast future trends. The objectives of Markov analysis are to provide probabilistic information about a situation using the results of a just-previous experiment. For example, the probability of your car needing a major repair next year might depend on how many major repairs it had last year. Let us demonstrate Markov analysis by working out an example.

Example 11.26

A gas-station manager surveyed 900 customers who frequently fill gas at his pumps. Of those, 300 bought gas in the first week of March, while 600 did not in the same period. It is expected that in the second week 75 percent of those who bought gas will return, in addition to 20 percent of those who did not buy gas. What is the expected number of purchasers and non-purchasers in the second week? What is likely to happen in subsequent weeks?

Solution:

We can express this question in matrix form:

$$(300,600)\begin{bmatrix} .75 & .25 \\ .20 & .80 \end{bmatrix}$$

$$\text{Customers} = (300 \times 0.75) + (600 \times 0.20) = 225 + 120 = 345$$

$$\text{Non customers} = (300 \times 0.25) + (600 \times 0.80) = 75 + 480 = 555$$

$$\text{Total customers} = 900$$

This result can be expressed as:

$$(300,600)\begin{bmatrix} .75 & .25 \\ .20 & .80 \end{bmatrix} = (345,555) \text{ for the second week}$$

For the 3rd week the expected results are:

$$(345,555)\begin{bmatrix} .75 & .25 \\ .20 & .80 \end{bmatrix} = (370,530)$$

And, for the 4th week the expected results are:

$$(370,530)\begin{bmatrix} .75 & .25 \\ .20 & .80 \end{bmatrix} = (384,516)$$

If one works at the figures of purchasers and non-purchasers, it is evident that the number of purchasers is increasing, but at a slower rate as the weeks pass. Evidently the sales will reach a steady state in due time.

Example 11.27

Re-examine the problem in Example 11.26. What would the sales be in a steady state?

Solution:

$$\text{Let } X = (x, y) \text{ where } x = \text{purchasers}$$

$$y = \text{non-purchasers}$$

and $X = (x + y)$

$$(x, y)\begin{bmatrix} .75 & .25 \\ .20 & .80 \end{bmatrix} = (x \ y)$$

and $0.75x + 0.20y = x$ and $0.25x + 0.80y = y$
from which we find $x = 0.80y$ and since $x + y = 900$

$$\therefore (400,500)\begin{bmatrix} .75 & .25 \\ .20 & .80 \end{bmatrix} = (400,500)$$

In the steady state, there will be 400 buyers per week and 500 non-buyers. Let us interpret this transition matrix.

		Next period	
		P	N
This period	P	.75	.25
	N	.20	.80

The first row of numbers tells us what proportion of customers who buy gas in the first period will still buy gas in the next. Thus the 0.75 in row P, column P, means that of the customers who buy gas in the first period, 75 percent will still be buying gas in the next period. The second row gives us the same information about those who did not buy gas in the first period. This information could be put in the form of difference equations (with this period subscripted 1 and the next period 2).

$$P_2 = 0.75P_1 + 0.20N_1$$
$$N_2 = 0.25P_1 + 0.80N_1$$

and this is exactly what we did in the examples.

11.7.1 Characteristics of Markov Analysis

Now that we have solved some problems, we notice that Markov analysis is applicable to systems that exhibit probabilistic movement from one state to another, over time and this probability is known as a *transition probability*. The set of all transition probabilities when expressed in matrix form is called a *transition matrix*. For instance, (in Example 11.26)

$$\begin{bmatrix} .75 & .25 \\ .20 & .80 \end{bmatrix}$$

is a transition matrix. These matrices have the following characteristics:

(a) the probabilities for a given beginning state sum to 1.0
(b) the probabilities apply to all parties in the system
(c) the probabilities are constant over time, and
(d) the states are independent over time

If M is any square matrix and X is a vector such that XM = X, then X is called a "fixed vector" for M. The term fixed vector is also called *stationary vector* or *eigen vector* by some authors. In our example (400,500) is a fixed vector for M, where

$$M = \begin{bmatrix} 0.75 & 0.25 \\ 0.20 & 0.80 \end{bmatrix}$$

Also, if M is a Markov matrix, and X is a *probability vector*, such that XM = X, then X is called a *fixed probability vector* for M. If a matrix M has a fixed vector X, it is possible to find a fixed probability vector for M by dividing X by the sum of the elements in X. Thus,

$$\begin{bmatrix} 0.75 & 0.25 \\ 0.20 & 0.80 \end{bmatrix} = \left(\frac{400}{900}, \frac{500}{900} \right) = \left(\frac{4}{9}, \frac{5}{9} \right) = (0.444, 0.556)$$

Example 11.28

Show that the matrix $M = \begin{bmatrix} 0.75 & 0.25 \\ 0.20 & 0.80 \end{bmatrix}^n$ is equal to $\begin{bmatrix} 0.444 & 0.556 \\ 0.444 & 0.556 \end{bmatrix}$

Solution:

$$M^2 = \begin{bmatrix} 0.61 & 0.39 \\ 0.31 & 0.69 \end{bmatrix} \qquad M^3 = \begin{bmatrix} 0.54 & 0.45 \\ 0.37 & 0.63 \end{bmatrix} \qquad M^4 = \begin{bmatrix} 0.50 & 0.50 \\ 0.40 & 0.60 \end{bmatrix}$$

$$M^5 = \begin{bmatrix} 0.45 & 0.55 \\ 0.42 & 0.58 \end{bmatrix} \qquad M^6 = \begin{bmatrix} 0.444 & 0.556 \\ 0.444 & 0.556 \end{bmatrix}$$

These results tally with

$(300, 600)(M) = (345{,}555)$ 2nd week
$(300, 600)M^2 = (370{,}530)$ 3rd week
$(300, 600)M^3 = (384{,}516)$ 4th week

and eventually with

$(300, 600)M^6 = (400, 500)$ when the system reaches a steady state.

Example 11.29

Refer to Example 11.26. Using a decision tree, determine the probabilities of a customer purchasing or not purchasing gas in week 3, given that the customer buys in the present month. Summarize the resulting probabilities in a table.

Solution:

The situation is as follows:

	Next week	
This week	Buy	Not buy
Buy	0.75	0.25
Not buy	0.20	0.80

Figure E11.29 shows the two decision trees from which the following conclusions can be drawn

Starting state	Prob. of buy	Prob. of not buy	Sum
Buy	0.625	0.3875	1.00
Not buy	0.310	0.6900	1.00

11.7.2 Special Transition Matrices

We have seen that the use of Markov analysis can be used to determine the probability of being in a given state at some future time period. To find this probability we successively multiply the transition matrix by itself n times. When such a condition exists, the constant state probabilities are called steady-state probabilities.

If we want to generalize long-run probabilities we must consider three kinds of Markov chains: regular chains; absorbing chains; and cyclical chains.

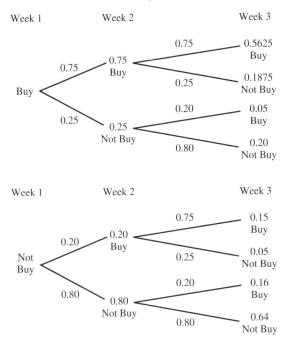

Figure E11.29   Week 1,2,3 diagram.

Regular Chains.   We have already looked at these chains before. In a regular chain, all states communicate with one another. For example matrix P, describes three states, W = well, S = sick for one week and V = sick for two weeks.

		Period 2		
		W	S	V
Period	W	0.75	0.25	0
1	S	0.50	0	0.50
	V	0.30	0	0.70

In this example for instance there are three zero entries. But the two-period matrix has no zeros.

		Period 3		
		W	S	V
Period	W	0.6875	0.1875	0.1250
1	S	0.5250	0.1250	0.3500
	V	0.4350	0.0750	0.4900

As noted, regular chains will lead eventually to an equilibrium distribution. This property may be useful when we are predicting the behavior of entire populations rather than the probabilistic movements of individuals.

Absorbing Chains.   In these cases, there are one or more absorbing states that the individual cannot leave once it is entered. To visualize what is meant by an absorbing state, examine the well/sick/very sick matrix given before and modify the very sick row to dead (D). If this matrix is modified to the following:

			Period 2	
		W	S	D
Period	W	0.80	0.19	0.01
1	S	0.50	0.47	0.03 = Q
	D	0	0	1

Notice that this is not a regular matrix, because a person cannot go from being dead to well or sick no matter how much time passes. Here, death is an absorbing state. Another example is a pollutant that may be transformed into a totally harmless substance. The opposite of an absorbing state is a transient state, which is the regular chain.

Cyclical Chains.   Sometimes an individual is trapped in a cyclical pattern that he cannot excape. For instance a judge may rotate his visitation to his four offices located in different parts of the state.

		N	S	E	W
	N	0	1	0	0
Period 1	S	0	0	1	0
	E	0	0	0	1
	W	1	0	0	0

In summary, with regular Markov chains one could draw two conclusions: (1) in the long-run, the probability of being in a particular state approaches equilibrium and is independent of the state that the individual is initially; (2) equilibrium probabilities may be interpreted as the percent of time spent in each state over the long run. With absorbing chains, we are not bothered by equilibrium as much as we are interested in knowing how quickly it will be trapped. With cyclical chains, the interest lies in finding how many periods are needed before completing a rotation.

EXERCISES

1. A car salesman would like to forecast the demand for Toyota trucks for next year based on sales this past year. His records indicate the following.

Month	Sales
January	10
February	12
March	15
April	16
May	20
June	22
July	20
August	15
September	12
October	12
November	10
December	9

   (a) Compute a 3-month moving average forecast for April of the current year through January of the next year.
   (b) Assigning weights of 2.0, 1.0, and 0.5 to the months in sequence, starting with the most recent month and forecast his sales for the month of January next year.
   (c) Compare the two forecasts using MAD and write your comments.
   (d) Compute the exponentially smoothed forecast ($\alpha = 0.3$) for January next year.
   (e) Conduct a least-square trend forecast for January and February of next year.

2. For the last 8 years, there have been a high number of accidents on a 20-mile stretch of freeway as shown below.

Year	Accidents
1	40
2	45
3	35
4	42
5	50
6	58
7	49
8	65

   (a) Compute a 3-year moving average forecast for years 4 to 9.

(b) Compute a 3-year weighted average forecast with weights of 3, 2, and 1 for the years.

(c) Compute the exponentially smoothed forecast with $\alpha = 0.3$ for the accident data.

(d) Using least-squares trend analysis forecast the likely accidents in the next two years.

3. A movie theater chain would like to know the patronage for their shows depending on the ticket price. In the last year, a record was kept for seven ticket rates and the corresponding patronage. (a) Set up a simple regression analysis equation for this data connecting ticket price with patronage (Y). (b) What patronage would be expected for tickets at $4.50 and $7.00?

Ticket price	Patronage (in 100s)
$3.00	52
$3.50	48
$4.00	47
$5.00	40
$5.50	24
$6.75	18

4. The manager of the movie chain is curious to know whether predictions of patronage can be made based on rating scores of movies. She has six cases, shown below:

Ratings	Patronage (100s)
5	52
6	48
8	47
6	40
5	24
8	18

Set up a regression equation and predict what patronage may be expected with a score of 7.

5. If in the previous problem, you consider the excellence ratings score given to films shown as well as the price, how would your answer change?

Price ($)	Patronage (100s)	Rating
3.00	52	5
3.50	48	6
4.00	47	8
5.00	40	6
5.50	24	5
6.75	18	8

6. A large shipping company needs to supply material from three sources a, b, c to four sources A, B, C, and D for unit costs shown in the matrix below.

To From	A	B	C	D	Supply
a	50	75	30	45	120
b	65	80	40	60	170
c	40	70	50	55	110
Demand	100	100	100	100	400

   (a) Find the initial feasible allocation using the NW corner, least-cost cell, and the penalty methods and compute the total cost.
   (b) Using the solutions found under part a, find the optimal solution.

7. Three production plants at locations I, II, and III supply steel goods to warehouses at A, B, and C as shown below, and have unit costs in dollars.

	A	B	C	Supply
I	20	28	16	40
II	24	20	24	60
III	16	24	20	80
Demand	80	60	40	180

   (a) Determine initial allocation using the NW corner, low-cost cell, and penalty methods, and find the total cost of shipment.
   (b) Use the initial allocation and find the optimal solution.

8. A manager has worked out a transhipment problem as shown in the tableau below.

Factory	A	B	C	Supply
a	24	20	12	12
b	8	30	6	8
c	18	14	M	6
d	22	16	12	16
e	0	0	0	4
Demand	18	10	18	46

(a) Does this tableau represent an unbalanced shipment problem, which has been rectified?
(b) Is this a degenerate solution? How would you correct this problem?
(c) Do you notice a prohibited route?
(d) Work through this problem by applying the NW corner, low-cost cell, and the penalty methods.
(e) Apply any method you know to find the optimum solution.

9. Three companies X, Y, and Z are bidding on three jobs A, B, and C. X can do 100 jobs/week and charges $6 for A, $5 for B, and $7 for C. Y can do 120 jobs and charges $9 for A, $6 for B and $10 for C. Z can do 100 jobs and charges $8 for A, $10 for B, and $9 for C. If 100 jobs of type A, 80 jobs of type B, and 90 jobs of type C are to be done, how would you assign jobs to each company using the NW corner, low-cost cell, and the penalty methods? Refine your answers by applying one of the optimization methods.

10. An electrical appliance can be produced at the rate of 100 per day throughout the year, but because of seasonal demand, only 40 per day are sold during the first three quarters of the year, but 160 per day are sold during the last quarter of the year. Storage costs amount to $200 per quarter and the expenses of production can rise at a rate of $100 per quarter. If the production costs are $4000 during the first quarter:
(a) Set up these data as a transportation problem.
(b) Find the production schedule that gives the minimum cost.

11. Find the minimum cost for supplying material as given below with unit costs in each cell. Start with the minimum cell cost solution and then use the MODI method to refine your answer.

	D1	D2	D3	Supply
S1	24.0	15.0	18.0	240.0
S2	45.0	30.0	36.0	160.0
S3	9.0	27.0	30.0	160.0
Demand	300.0	140.0	120.0	560.0

12. Find the minimum cost starting with Vogels solution for Exercise 11, and then use the MODI method to refine your answer.

	D1	D2	D3	Supply
S1	24.0	15.0	18.0	240.0
S2	45.0	30.0	36.0	160.0
S3	9.0	27.0	30.0	160.0
Demand	300.0	140.0	120.0	560.0

13. Four machinists are to be assigned to four jobs. The time taken by each job is shown below. Assign the machinists to the job in such a way that the total sum of the time needed is a minimum.

Machine Operator	1	2	3	4
A	20	23	10	12
B	7	20	9	12
C	13	15	13	20
D	16	16	12	10

Determine the assignment of machines to each operator to minimize the total number of hours and the optimal solution.

14. The manager of a shoe store has five salesmen who have varied capabilities to work in four stores. Their past records indicate that their sales profits in (1000s) are as shown in the matrix. Assign them to the four stores to bring in the highest overall profit.

Store Salesman	1	2	3	4
A	88	93	92	91
B	84	80	91	93
C	91	88	95	85
D	97	90	90	95
E	85	90	75	80

15. Refer to Exercise 14. After the manager makes the assignment as per the matrix, salesmen A, B, C, and D feel that they do not want to be assigned to stores 2, 4, 3, and 1 respectively for personal reasons. Reassign the salesmen and indicate the difference in total profits because of the new assignment.

16. If a large building, currently provided with the minimum fire protection, is not protected against fire, the total damage could be as much as $3 million in case of a fire whose probability is 60 percent. However, a fire protection engineer has estimated that if sophisticated equipment worth $0.75 million is provided, there is a probability that there would be no damage in case of a fire. (1) What are the states of nature, the alternatives, and their probability? (2) construct a matrix and decision tree using this information.

17. A person with an expensive equipment needs to replace its motor. He finds a used motor at a second hand outfit for $100, but finds that the testing is not reliable. 70 percent of the time it tests good motors as good and 40 percent of the time, it tests bad motors as good. From past experience, a used motor is good 20 percent of the time. The only other alternatives are to either order a brand new motor for $300, which is available only after six months and a loss of $100, or buy one from ready stock for $450. (a) Sketch a decision tree showing all options. (b) What is the best strategy?

18. A manufacturing company can produce three machines A, B, and C for third world countries depending on good, stable, and unstable conditions. The pay-off table below indicates profits/losses in millions per year.

	Market conditions		
	Good	Stable	Unstable
Machine	(0.2)	(0.7)	(0.1)
A	240	140	−60
B	120	80	40
C	70	60	60

(a) What would be the best machine to manufacture?
(b) Compute the opportunity loss table.
(c) Draw a decision tree diagram.
(d) What consulting fee would the company be willing to pay to obtain perfect information regarding market conditions to gain the best profit?

19. The manufacturing company described in exercise 18 is not satisfied with the results of its analysis and would like to hire a marketing company that knows about third world countries. Their reports indicate that there is a 0.6 probability of a positive report given good conditions, a 0.3 probability of a positive report given stable conditions and a 0.1 probability of a positive report given unstable conditions. There is a 0.9 probability of a negative report given unstable conditions, a 0.7 probability given stable conditions, and a 0.4 probability given good conditions. Using Baye's theorem and a decision tree, determine the best strategy the company can follow and the maximum sum of consulting fees that could be paid to the consulting company.

20. A company manufacturing bicycle parts has just acquired a new machine to produce axles. It was found that when the machine was set up correctly, there was a 10 percent chance of the item being defective; but if the machine were set up incorrectly, the chances of the item being defective rose to 40 percent. The information currently available is that the machine is set up incorrectly 50 percent of the time. What is the probability that the machine is set up incorrectly, if the sample is found to be defective?

21. A professor spends about 10 minutes with each student, although 12 minutes is scheduled for each student to be just on time. What is the average number of students waiting to be served, the average waiting time for a student and the mean time a student spends in the system (i.e., waiting and being served)?   (D/D/1)

22. In Example 11.16 worked out in the text, the service rate $\mu = 2.5$ persons/min.
   (a) Describe the performance of the system, all the factors remaining the same.
   (b) Draw a neat sketch of the system. (use D/D/1).

23. The local car-wash station has an automated system requiring 5 minutes to wash a car plus one minute to wipe it dry. Customers arrive at the rate of 8 vehicles/hr. If the system operates as per M/D/1, compute the characteristics of this operation.

24. The local airport in Walla Walla has a single runway with one traffic controller. It takes a plane 10 minutes to land and clear the runway with landing following an M/M/1 regime. According to Federal Aviation Administration (FAA) rules, the traffic controller must have at least 15 minutes rest time every hour. If two planes arrive per hour, then
   (a) What is the average number of planes that have to wait to land?
   (b) What is the average time a plane must be in the air before it can land?
   (c) Will the airport have to hire a second traffic controller to follow FAA rules?

25. (a) During the first few days of every semester, a student advisor takes 3 minutes to sign off on each student's schedule. Unfortunately he is the only authority to approve such schedules and when the arrival rate of students is 8 per hour, his work becomes pretty hectic. Compute the characteristics of this system.
   (b) The advisor feels that if some graduate student help is available his advising would go faster. If 5 minutes is a reasonable time for a student to wait, the help of 1 graduate student will reduce the waiting time by $1/2$ min how many graduate students should be hired. (Use M/M/1.)

26. A hardware store operates a single-server queuing system (with one cashier and one checkout counter) 12 hours per day. This system has the following details (1) infinite calling population (3) first come/first serve (3) M/M/1 system (4) 20 customers/hr arrive at the checking counter queue and 25 can be checked out. Compute P_o, L, L_q, W, W_q, and V.

27. Refer to problem 26. The manager of this store feels that if the queue is divided into two equal parts and a second checkout counter is operated, there would be greater efficiency, despite the cost of operating a second counter costing \$10/hr. Compute the characteristics of this proposal and estimate the probable savings per week, assuming the value of time of customers equal to \$10 per hour (because time spent in the queue represents a loss to the store).

28. Refer to problem 26. The manager of the store feels that it may be a good idea to hire a helper at \$5/hour. He tries out this arrangement and finds that because of a reduction of delay the arrival rate has correspondingly climbed to 38 customers/hour. Compute the characteristics of this arrangement, assuming customer time is worth \$10/hour and estimate the savings per week to the store.

29. Refer to problem 26. The manager of the store would like to try having two separate servers (counters) to speed up the queue. If the mean arrival and service rate remain as before and the cost of operating an additional counter is \$10/hr, compute the characteristics of this system and estimate the savings per week to the store.

30. A printing shop has two machines of equal speed serving customers. The arrival interval of customers is distributed as:

Arrival interval (A)	Probability (P)
2 min	0.2
4 min	0.5
6 min	0.3

Service time (S)	Probability (S)
5 min	0.3
6 min	0.5
7 min	0.4

Simulate these operations for 5 customers.

31. A CPM/PERT project shown below consists of the following activities and probabilities attached. For example, task $(1 - 2)$ can be completed in 5 weeks with a probability of 0.2 or in 6 weeks with a probability of 0.8. Simulate this network three times, determine the critical path, and compute the expected time of completion.

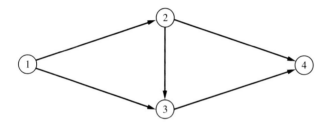

Problem 31   A CPM/PERT project.

Activity	Duration (x), weeks	Probability, p(x)
1–2	5	0.2
	6	0.8
1–3	9	0.4
	10	0.6
2–3	8	0.6
	9	0.4
2–4	3	0.8
	4	0.2
3–4	7	0.5
	9	0.5

32. If the trucks in the Example 11.21 worked out in the text vary between 20 and 40 ft, with 40-ft truck taking 35 minutes to unload, redo the simulation for 10 trucks.

33. If the professor in the Example 11.22 spends 15 minutes each on an average with a standard deviation of 4 min, rework the problem and simulate for 10 students, assuming normal distribution.

34. The airplanes in Example 11.23 are now arriving in the airport at 4 per hour. Simulate for a 10-hour shift.

35. A computer repair shop consists of an engineer and one machine. Clients come in to the shop at 9 a.m. at the following time interval.

Time	Interval
6	0.05
12	0.10
18	0.20
24	0.35
30	0.20
36	0.10

However, the problems are such that repairs can only be checked and done either by the engineer, or the mechanic, or sometimes by both. The distribution is as follows.

Engineer only	0.30
Mechanic only	0.60
Both engineer and mechanic	0.10

Simulate this operation for 10 customers assuming the following distribution.

Engineer	p(x)	Mechanic	p(y)	Both	p
10 min	0.2	20 min	0.3	10	0.1
20 min	0.4	30 min	0.5	30	0.7
30 min	0.4	40 min	0.2	50	0.2

36. A customer generally buys two brands of shoes P and Q changing brands as shown below:

		Next period	
		P	Q
This Period	P	0.55	0.45
	Q	0.60	0.40

(a) Determine the probabilities that a customer will buy shoe P or shoe Q in period 3 in the future given that the customer bought P or Q in this period.

(b) Draw decision trees to illustrate your answer.

(c) What would be the situation in the steady state?

37. An engineer has observed a particular machine's record regarding breakdown, as shown in the matrix, where O indicates that the machine operates and B indicates that there is a breakdown.

| | | Next day | |
		O	B
This day	O	0.4	0.6
	B	0.8	0.2

(a) Assuming that the machine operates on day 1, determine the probabilities that the machines will be operating or down on day 2 through day 6.

(b) Determine the steady state probability for this transition matrix.

38. A village of 20,000 people has a labor force of 10,000. In any particular month, there is a large number (E) who are gainfully employed and a small proportion who are unemployed (U). It has been observed that 95 percent of those employed in one year are still employed the following year. While 45 percent of the currently unemployed find jobs and are employed in the next year, and these percentages hold true year after year. Put down this information in the form of a transition matrix and interpret what it means.

39. A housing complex manager has observed that tenants pay their rents as per the transition matrix given below:

| | | Next month | |
		Pay	Not pay
This month	Pay	0.9	0.1
	Not pay	0.8	0.2

(a) If a renter did not pay his rent this month, what is the probability that she will not pay in any of the next 3 months?

(b) What is the steady state of this matrix?

40. It is said by sociologists that in general people tell the truth with a probability 'p' such that $0 < p < 1$. Then for a rumor (that could be either true or false) the probability that a person is likely to tell the truth can be represented by:

| | | What everyone told his friend | |
		True	false
What everyone was told	True	p	$1 - p$
	False	$1 - p$	p

Using this as a base and assuming $p = 0.9$, what is the probability that the fourth person who hears the rumor is hearing the truth?

41. In one of the Washington State counties it was found that in 1998, 0.07 of the rural population moved to the city and 0.04 of the city population moved to the rural area. (a) Describe this in the form of a Markov matrix; (b) What is the fixed probability vector of this matrix; (c) If this trend continued in future years what proportion of the population will end up in the city?

42. The manager of a college fund finds that of those members who did not donate last year, there is a strong probability that 10 percent of them will contribute a small gift this year. Of those that gave small gifts last year 20 percent will not give at all, but 10 percent will give large gifts this year. Also, of those who gave large gifts last year, 10 percent will skip contribution this year, 20 percent will give small gifts, and the rest will continue to give large gifts.

   (a) Describe the donation pattern by a Markov matrix.

   (b) If this pattern continues, what fraction of the alumni can eventually be expected each year to contribute large, small, and zero gifts.

12

Soft Systems Thinking and Analysis

12.1 INTRODUCTION

It has been widely acknowledged that the methods of decision-making currently used by engineers are proving to be progressively inadequate. Therefore, in a way it is fitting that the last chapter of this book should cover the subject of *soft systems thinking*. Fortunately, in the past 20 years or so, systems research has produced a vast array of methodologies to supplement the hard systems methodologies for tackling the ill-structured problems of the real world, so much less tidy than the ones posed by the natural and physical sciences. This chapter offers a brief description of systems thinking as it has developed in response to the demand for dealing with human systems.

First, we will take a preliminary look at what is meant by a system, and quickly make a comparison between hard and soft systems methodologies. We will then examine how systems engineers have shifted their attention from the process of optimizing to learning. Later, we will look at two case studies to find out how soft systems methodology is applied to real-world problem situations. Finally, we will close the chapter by discussing the various implications embedded in the hard and soft paradigms.

12.2 WHAT IS A SYSTEM? A PRELIMINARY LOOK

12.2.1 Scoping the Field

The term *system* has been in use for such a long time that most people have lost the significance of the word. Systems have come to be associated with anything and everything, from anthropology to zoology, and from communication to computation. With such a wide range of associations, it is useful to define the word. Weinberg (1975) describes a system as a set of objects together with relationships between the objects and their attributes. Churchman (1968) describes a system as a set of components that work together for the over-all objective of the whole. While there are differing definitions of a system, the one common strand through all these definitions is that "it is a selection of elements, relationships and procedures to achieve a specific purpose" (Wortman and Luthans, 1969). The elements and their interactions are almost always well defined and determinable, particularly in manmade systems like computers or machines. Problems occurring in such systems can often be solved using conventional techniques of problem solving, such as those mentioned in the previous two chapters. This is possible because these systems are predictable and repetitive in their behavior. In such instances, it is easy to engineer a solution using a structured, methodical, and systematic approach. This kind of an approach has come to be termed as the *hard systems methodology* (HSM). HSM is the application of the *hard systems paradigm* which includes operations research, systems engineering, cybernetics and general system theory. These varied and systematic techniques have their own niche in the domain of problem solving, and all of the techniques described in previous chapters fall under this category. They are best suited for dealing with problems that are most common among systems with certain attributes. These systems are termed *hard systems*. The question that naturally arises is, What is a hard system? This question and others pertaining to the soft systems paradigm will be taken up in this chapter.

12.2.2 Types of Systems

Systems are of two types, classified according to their behavior and the relationship between their elements along with the relationship with the environment. They are *hard* or *simple systems* and *soft* or *complex systems*. The irony of having the hard systems termed as simple and the complex systems as soft should not be lost on the reader.

   Hard systems.   Hard systems have certain unique characteristics. They are typically made up of a small number of elements with few interactions between these elements, to the point where these interactions are predetermined and highly organized. These systems have well-defined laws of behavior and are mostly immune to any changes in their environment.

Complex systems.   have a large number of elements with many interactions between these elements. Unlike the elements constituting the hard systems, those comprising a complex system have random attributes with highly unorganized inter-action. These systems also tend to evolve over time and have sub-systems, which may pursue their own goals. They are also subject to behavioral influence.

To solve the problems associated with hard systems, we focus on a predefined end and then select an efficient means to achieve that end. Hard systems have tradi-tionally been associated with real-world problems that make use of *problem-solving* techniques to tackle the problems associated with them. *Soft systems* techniques, on the other hand, *explore the plurality* embedded in problem situations, especially those associated with animate and human systems.

In this respect, these two systems make use of two different adjectives of the word system, namely, **systematic** and **systemic**. While systematic refers to the sys-tematic procedures adopted to achieve a predetermined end, systemic refers to holistic thinking about the system or the problem situation embedded in the system.

12.2.3 Hard Systems Methodologies

Hard systems methodologies can be conveniently classified into three distinct classes. These are *systems analysis*, *systems engineering*, and *operations research*. The aim of this section is to describe these three classes and note any commonalties that they possess.

Systems Analysis. Systems analysis is defined as an approach for "systematically examining the costs, effectiveness, and risks of alternative policies or strategies—and designing additional ones if those examined are found wanting" (Jackson, 1991). The development of systems analysis is in general associated with the RAND (Research and Development Corporation), a non-profit organization in the consulting business. Developed in response to war-time needs, this methodology gained prominence in the mid 1960s when the then Secretary of Defense, Robert McNamara, adopted its use in the Pentagon for systems and cost-benefit analysis. In the early 1970s, the International Institute for Applied Systems Analysis (IIASA) was set up to look into possible areas of application of systems analysis. The Institute came up with a seven-step procedure for effective systems analysis. These are:

1. Formulating the problem
2. Identifying, designing, and screening alternatives
3. Building and using models for predicting the consequences of adopting a par-ticular alternative
4. Comparing and ranking alternatives
5. Evaluating the analysis
6. Decision-making and Implementing, and
7. Evaluating the outcome.

The successful application of systems analysis is contingent on a well-defined problem situation along with the availability of feasible alternatives to choose from.

Systems Engineering. This branch of hard systems methodology is defined as "the set of activities that together lead to the creation of a complex, man-made entity and/or procedures, and the information flows associated with its operations" (Checkland, 1981). Since this methodology develops an engineering solution to a systems problem, it is known as systems engineering. While there have been many contributors toward the development of this methodology, perhaps the most significant has been A.D. Hall (1962). Hall's problem-solving tool was structured with the following sequence.

1. Problem definition
2. Choice of objectives
3. Systems synthesis
4. Systems analysis
5. Systems selection
6. Systems development
7. Current engineering

Most of Hall's work was developed in the Bell Telephone Laboratories where he often referred to his classic account of systems engineering as a part of "organized creative technology".

Operations Research (OR).   Operations Research (OR), was developed to tackle logistical problems encountered during World War II. A whole variety of quantitative techniques have since been developed, that fall under the umbrella of OR, for use in the civilian sector of manufacturing, production, and services. The step-by-step procedure involving the OR process is as follows:

1. Formulate the problem
2. Construct a mathematical model to represent the system under study
3. Derive a solution from the model
4. Test the model and the corresponding solution derived
5. Establish controls over the solution
6. Implement the solution, provided a budget can be worked out.

The three strands of the hard systems paradigm described above have helped in constructing a recurring theme with respect to problem solving. All three strands emphasize formulating an objective, to handle the problem situation successfully. Once the objective is identified, the appropriate solution can then be picked from a range of alternatives using a systematic approach. However, this kind of a means-ends approach runs into trouble when there is an element of complexity attached to the objectives and to the means themselves. The complexity in these cases can give rise to new issues and further complexity that needs to be resolved. The conventional techniques of problem solving have traditionally been unable to cope with

such issues. These problems gave the impetus for the development of a new paradigm, which would be able to deal with the complexity and plurality embedded in
problems with multiple unclear means and ends. This new focus resulted in the soft
systems paradigm, along with a wide range of methodologies developed to tackle
complex problem situations encountered in dealing with human systems.

12.2.4 Soft Systems Methodologies

The concept of complex systems and the problems associated with them were discussed briefly earlier in the chapter. This section looks critically at the nature of such
complex systems, the problems emanating from them, and the history of the
research that has led to the development of a system of methodologies to deal with
these problem situations.

Complex systems abound everywhere, ranging from those where no solution
seems quite right to those where every option seems both good and bad (Hutchins,
1996). The growing realization about the systemic nature of problems confronting
us, such as the elimination of hunger and poverty, world peace etc., has brought
about the need for a system of methodologies capable of tackling these diverse situations. This need for a system of methodologies is also the result of the inability of
conventional techniques such as PERT or CPM to cope with the organizational
dynamics in self-regulating systems, which adapt to ever-changing environments. In
the past, the concept of reductionism was used and continues to be applied to solve
many an intricate problem. This approach fails in the case of complex systems
because of the nature of the system being analyzed. Breaking a complex system into
smaller components does not necessarily make it easier to comprehend, because the
smaller component may not necessarily be less complex in nature. Such problem situations, which when broken down into smaller units, give rise to new sets of problems, are termed as "messy problems" by Russell Ackoff (1974). He suggests that
the best way to deal with such messy problems is to harness the ideas of holistic
thinking. Accounts of his contribution towards the development of systems science,
along with other major contributions in this area are given in the next section.

Researchers like R.L. Ackoff (1974), C. W. Churchman (1968), and P. B.
Checkland (1981) have pioneered some of the original work with the soft systems
paradigm. While Churchman's five basic considerations regarding systems thinking
are outlined in an earlier chapter in the book, Russell Ackoff has contributed to
interactive planning.

Interactive Planning.   Interactive planning is the main operating tool of Ackoff's (1978) Social Systems Sciences (S3). There are three ways of tackling a problem
situation. One way is by ***resolving the problem***; a "satisficing" approach, in which the
objective is to choose a course of action which is good enough, reminiscent of Herb
Simon's (1960) work. The next is by ***solving a problem***; an optimizing approach, and

lastly by ***dissolving a problem***, which is the idealized approach. Interactive planning (IP) is all about dissolving a problem. The principles of IP are:

    1. *Participative*, which implies that the process of planning is more important than the plan itself and that the process needs to be enriched by the participation of those who are affected by the plan.

    2. *Continuous*, to account for any unexpected changes and

    3. *Holistic*, to simultaneously and interdependently plan for many different parts and levels of the system as possible.

    The five phases of Interactive Planning are:

    1. Formulating the mess
    2. Ends planning
    3. Means planning
    4. Resource planning
    5. The design of implementation and control.

Once the design is implemented, there has to be constant monitoring with a feedback process from the output to the planning process in order to ensure continuous learning.

    Checkland's Soft Systems Methodology (SSM).   SSM emerged as a result of dissatisfaction with the limitations of traditional HSM. Partially as a result of this feeling, Checkland and his colleagues at Lancaster University in the United Kingdom began an action research program designed to extend systems ideas to ill-structured management cases. Their aim was to produce a systems methodology capable of dealing with soft problems (Jackson, 1987).

    Checkland (1985) introduced the idea of emergence as a corner stone in systems thinking. The principle of emergence states that whole entities exhibit properties that are meaningful only when attributed to the whole. For example, the wetness of water is a property of that substance and has no meaning in terms of its components, hydrogen and oxygen. This concept of emergence has even passed into everyday language in the notion that the whole is more than the sum of its parts. In addition, he added three more ideas to assemble the core concepts on which systems thinking is based: hierarchy, communication, and control. Hierarchy means that entities are themselves wholes, and so on; communication simply means the transfer of information. In the formal systems model, the decision-making process ensures that controlled action is taken in light of the systems' purpose or mission and the observed level of the measures of performance. Collectively, then, the ideas of emergence, hierarchy, communication, and control provide the basic systems image or metaphor of a whole entity, which may itself contain smaller wholes or be part of a larger whole in a hierarchical structure, possessing processes of communication and control as well as adapting itself to strive in an environment undergoing change.

In applying systems ideas to human activity systems, it is evident that the most difficult part is the learning component. For example, in the case of natural or physical systems, accounts of real-world manifestations are publicly testable (if it is said that a car has four wheels, this fact can be easily checked). However, a group of people could be described as *terrorists* by one observer and as *freedom fighters* by another. Every observation could be considered valid according to a particular *Weltanschauung* or world outlook. Indeed, the concept of human activity systems is to consider a variety of *Weltanschauungen* in considering a problem situation. The essence of SSM can be simply expressed as a way of getting from finding out about a problem situation to taking action in that situation (Checkland, 1985).

Checkland's soft-systems methodology has been continuously improved since it was first formulated in the early 1970s. It can be described, with reference to Figure 12.1, in the following way:

1. SSM is an inquiring system for tackling ill-structured problems.
2. Users of SSM can learn their way to improve a problematic situation.
3. The background and history of the problem is always useful.
4. SSM consists of two interesting streams of analysis: logic-driven and culture-driven. The latter stream examines the social and political context of the problem situation. Eventually, the logic-driven stream and the culture-driven stream will interact, each informing and supporting the other.

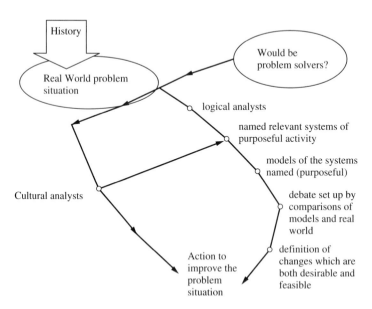

Figure 12.1   Learning Cycles of Soft-Systems Methodology.

5. Some systems of purposeful activity that appear relevant to debating the problem situation can be chosen.

6. The debate is structured by comparing models of the selected activity system with perceptions of the real world; these models express *Weltanschauungen* and serve as vehicles for structuring debate.

7. The debate seeks changes that are systemically and systematically desirable as well as culturally feasible.

8. Ultimately, action to improve the problem situation appears feasible.

It is pretty obvious that SSM developed because the traditional methods of systems engineering, based on defining goals and objectives, simply did not work when applied to messy, ill-structured, real-world problems, particularly related to human activity systems. The problem of defining objectives is the problem.

Over the last decade, Checkland has crystallized SSM, and his general framework is illustrated in Figure 12.2. Regarded as a whole, Checkland's SSM is a learning tool that uses the system's ideas to organize four basic mental processes: perceiving (stages 1 and 2), predicting (stages 3 and 4), comparing (stage 5), and determining needed changes and actions (stages 6 and 7). The output and utility of SSM is quite different from that of hard-systems engineering. It is recognition, learning, and insight. Six elements — customers, actors, transformation, Weltanschauung, owner, and environmental constraints — help to structure SSM. The definitions of these six elements, which form the mnemonic CATWOE, are:

- **C**ustomers. Who are the victims or beneficiaries of this system, i.e., clients?
- **A**ctors. Who would perform the activities of this system, i.e., agents?

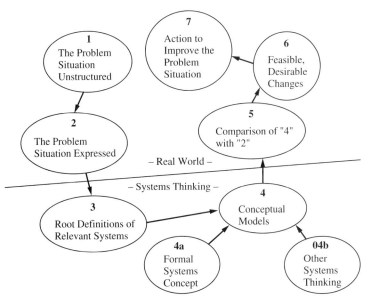

Figure 12.2 Soft Systems Methodology.

- **T**ransformation process. What input is transferred into what output by this system, i.e., the core of the purposeful activity?
- **W**eltanschauung. What image of this world makes this system meaningful, i.e., world view?
- **O**wner. Who could abolish or stop this activity, i.e., ownership?
- **E**nvironmental constraints. What external constraints, does this system take as given, i.e., environmental propositions?

In SSM, the real-world situation to be analyzed is expressed in non-systems language using the concepts of structure and process, plus the relation between the two. This constitutes a relevant system and encapsulates various specific viewpoints expressed as root definitions (RDs). An RD is a concise description of a human activity that states what the system is. From the RD a conceptual model of the necessary activities in the system is built. This conceptual model of the human activity system may then be compared to the real world. The model is the formal vehicle for exploring dysfunctions and needed changes in the real world, involving both system analysts and clients. The products of SSM should provide the basis for needed changes and such changes can fall into three categories: structural changes, procedural changes, and attitudinal changes. The entire process is done interactively between clients and key informants.

12.3 THE PATH FROM OPTIMIZATION TO LEARNING

12.3.1 Paradigms of Inquiry

It is a well established fact that when physicists or chemists perform laboratory experiments for investigating a phenomenon, the results of their experiments are repeatable and can be publicly tested. Indeed, the scientific method can be described as being based on at least three fundamental principles which characterize it and lend it power and authority: reductionism, repeatability, and refutation (Checkland, 1981). Scientists, in general, select a small portion of the world for investigation and carry out experiments over and over again, until they are satisfied with their results. These results are then added to the body of existing knowledge. Thus, scientific knowledge is accumulated, unless a particular body of knowledge is refuted by another scientific experiment. This replicability of experimental results stems from the fact that the phenomenon under investigation must be "homogenous through time" (Keynes, 1938).

For a number of compelling reasons, the social sciences sought from the outset to copy the methods and practices established by scientists in the natural sciences. But this practice led to various problems. As it is well known, there is an ontological unity assumed in the scientific method, in the sense that all objects in the universe, whether these are inert, living, conscious, or rational beings, are taken to be fundamentally and qualitatively to be the same. There has fortunately been a growing awareness that the social world is qualitatively different from the natural world, and in consequence, it was soon realized that the methodological assumptions of the scientific assumptions were untenable in applications to social problems. Thus, it is not surprising that new systems methodologies, predominantly in real-world problem solving, have been developed (Oliga, 1988).

12.3.2 System Typologies

Checkland (1981) describes a *system typology* consisting of three basic system types: natural systems, physical systems, and human activity systems. The first two are distinctly described and can be characterized as hard systems, where the well known methodologies of the scientific method and systems engineering have been and continue to be successfully applied. Essentially, the hard systems approach defines the objectives to be achieved, then engineers the system to achieve them. The third system type, the human activity system, is quite ill defined, and cannot be described by its state. In such case the analyst must concede to its purposeful activity, human values, and non-physical relationships. This is because human activity systems can be expressed only as perceptions of people who attribute meaning to what they perceive. There is therefore no "testable" account of a human activity system, only possible accounts, all of which are valid according to a particular world-view (or *weltanschauung*) (Checkland, 1981, 1984).

In contrast to hard systems engineering, soft systems methodology does not seek to mechanically design a solution as much as it orchestrates a process of learning. These differences between hard systems engineering and soft systems methodology will be elaborated further on in this chapter.

12.3.3 Action Research

We have already seen that the scientific method which has been practiced by the natural scientists, based on testing hypotheses, is extremely powerful. However, when scientists and engineers began to apply the scientific method (and the hard systems methodologies that eventually followed) to social and human phenomena, the results were far from satisfactory. A question that constantly cropped up was: If the scientific method including the hard system methodologies are not truly applicable to social and human activity systems because they are not homogenous through time, thus making complete replicability impossible, what else can be done? This is the context in which Action Research emerged. In fact, Checkland and his colleagues at Lancaster University (UK) have consistently presented their development of soft systems methodology under the umbrella of Action Research (Checkland and Scholes, 1990; Checkland and Holwell, 1998).

The roots of Action Research date back at least to the time of Kurt Levin (1890–1947), when researchers became interested in human group dynamics. There were scores of researchers who would immerse themselves in human activity problems and pursue them along whatever path it took till the problem unfolded through time. The only principal object of research in human activity systems is the change process.

At the cost of some repetition let us compare the scientific method where hypothesis-testing is the main objective of the natural sciences and the Action Research process which embraces the soft systems methodologies. Figure 12.3 shows a rich picture of how a researcher wants to test a hypothesis using the conventional hard systems methodology. In contrast, Figure 12.4 (after Checkland and

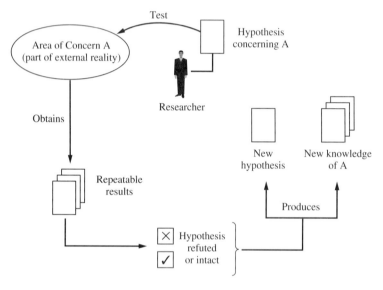

Figure 12.3

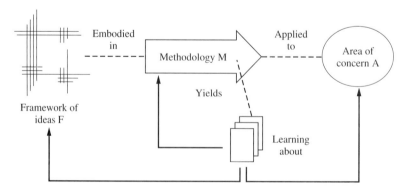

Figure 12.4

Holwell, 1997) shows F, a framework of ideas used in a methodology M to investigate an area of interest A. Using the methodology M may in fact teach us not only about A but about the adequacy of F and M. For example, the application of systems engineering through the use of a hard systems methodology (F) for tackling an area of interest A in a human activity problem was found to be inadequate, because of the use of systematic thinking. On the other hand, it was the very use of this process that the inadequacy was brought forth and the learning process led to the birth of a new M, based on systemic thinking (F), in the form soft systems methodology. The emphasis on change in F, M, and A in which the researcher becomes immersed and involved in the flux of the real-world problem situation is probably the hall-mark of Action Research. (See Figure 12.5.)

The crucial elements of Action Research are:

- A collaborative process between researchers and people in the situation,
- A process of critical inquiry
- A focus on social practice, and
- A deliberate process of reflective learning.

This process can best be described as shown in Figures 12.3 and 12.4. Note that the Action Research process substitutes themes for hypotheses.

There are several areas of explanation that one may like answers at this point, such as the question of verification, recoverability, etc., but these are best left to be discovered by those who would like to examine the philosophical implications of

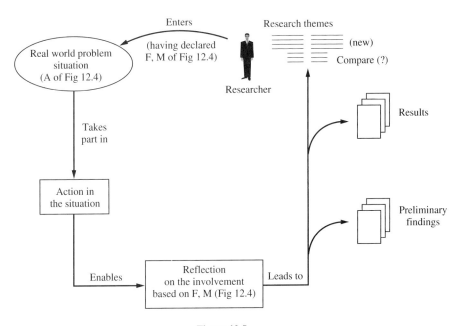

Figure 12.5

Action Research, and the references at the end of this chapter indicate such sources (Checkland 1981, Flood and Jackson 1991, Jackson 1991, Khisty 1993, 1995).

12.4 CASE STUDIES

12.4.1 Case Study 1. Reduction of Pedestrian Accidents

Pedestrians cross the streets wherever they please in the downtown area of a major city. This act of random street crossing not only endangers the pedestrians but also causes severe traffic problems. The city wants to find a solution to this problem and has called upon you as the expert to handle the situation. Make use of Checkland's soft systems methodology to formulate root definitions and conceptual models in order to analyze the problem. Make appropriate assumptions where necessary.

Solution

Step 1: Draw a rich picture to reflect the situation.
Step 2: Develop root definitions to fit the situation.
    The appropriate root definition in this case is that of a "well-disciplined, law-abiding citizenry that obeys traffic rules and does not take to jay-walking in the city".

Based on this root definition, the CATWOE mnemonic is developed to facilitate the construction of the conceptual model.

C (customers)	- The citizens of the city (the victims or beneficiaries of the system)
A (Actors)	- Pedestrians, Government officials, etc. (agents who would perform the activities of the system)
T (Transformation)	- Jay-walking pedestrians into law-abiding citizens (the core of the purposeful activity)
W (Weltanschauung)	- It is beneficial to have this law enforced (worldview)

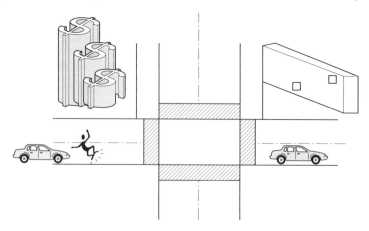

Figure E12.1a   Picture depicting the problem situation.

O (Owners)   -   Government and its citizens (who could abolish or stop the activity)

E (Environment)   -   The drivers in the area and other pedestrians, along with the businesses in downtown (external constraints).

Step 3: Build conceptual models.

Step 4: Compare the conceptual model to the root definition.

The conceptual model developed above is compared with the root definition formulated in Step 1, to better understand the tasks that need to be completed in order to ameliorate the situation and make the root definition true.

In this example, the city council needs to look at the existing situation, and then compare it with the conceptual model to identify those activities that are not present in reality. By doing so, they may find that the increase in police surveillance and the levying of heavier penalties are necessary to improve the current situation. The conceptual model also suggests a more active participation, from both the violators and those affected, in the planning process. There may be other viewpoints also.

The difference between this process and any conventional planning solution is the fact that SSM looks at the whole picture and takes into account the differing

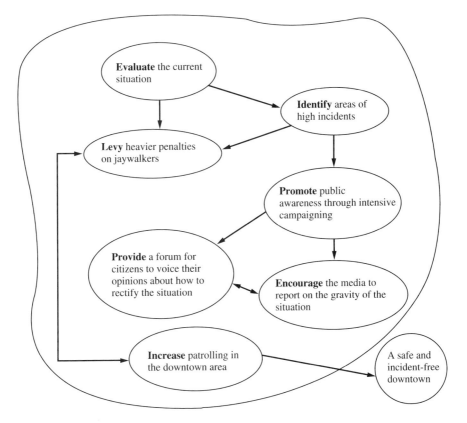

Figure E12.1b   Conceptual model.

viewpoints associated with a given problem situation. Thus, in this case, the view of the citizens and other motorists are taken into account along with that of the media even as the decisions to implement certain alternatives are being finalized.

12.4.2 Case Study 2: Resolving a Conflict Situation With a City

A small city (population 30,000) served by a city municipal committee had a problem in deciding whether one segment of its regular street network, Jackson Street, deserved to be converted to a shared street, so as to introduce the concepts of traffic calming (Klau, 1990). Accidents involving bicyclists, children, and the elderly were on the rise, primarily because of increased through traffic. Accident records maintained by the city appeared to be incomplete and inaccurate, and were not readily shared with individual citizens.

The shared-space and traffic calming concepts for pedestrians and motor vehicles is the most recent approach to enhance the safety and environmental qualities of local streets. The major characteristics of these concepts are as follows: rearranging the street into wall-to-wall sidewalk space that is equally shared by pedestrians and motorists; planting trees, designating play areas for children, and providing benches and flowerbeds; forcing motorists to slow down to speeds of 8 to 16 km/h (5–10 mph); and providing just enough on-street parking to serve local residents. The idea is to eliminate or reduce to the very minimum conflicts between cars and pedestrians, providing street use for pedestrians, bicyclists, and children as well as giving them first preference.

Implementation of a shared street project was a difficult problem. There were citizens in other neighborhoods who believed that automobile mobility reduction on Jackson Street would result in a corresponding overloading of adjacent streets. In addition, members of the city council were ambivalent in allowing this change to happen. Finally, the city budget was burdened with implementing higher priority projects, according to city officials. The neighborhood surrounding Jackson Street did not have a citizen advisory committee. Much of the decision-making process was done directly by the city administration on an ad-hoc basis. There was little citizen input at any stage. Citizens in general were frustrated with city administrators. The situation was corrected by following the stages in SSM.

Stages 1 and 2.   A rich picture representing the current situation is shown in Figure E12.2a

The following themes emerged as a result.

1. The need to organize a citizens' action committee (CAC) representing Jackson Street residents and other observers.
2. The need for CAC to organize itself to make decisions regarding converting Jackson Street to a shared street.
3. The importance and need to collect information (existing and additional) regarding Jackson Street, plus other similar streets, to convince city officials and help them make necessary changes. City administration was called on to help in furnishing information needed by CAC, including what budget constraints were anticipated.

4. CAC was determined to press its case for a shared street, in light of safety, convenience, and health of its citizens.

5. CAC would actively help in planning the shared street.

6. CAC recognizes budget constraints while it develops alternatives and will check the cost-effectiveness of alternatives by working jointly with city officials.

7. CAC would help select the best alternative along with city officials.

Stages 3 and 4.   Root Definition and Conceptual Models

This is a model of a system that can explore the problem situation and lead to action. This is Stage 3. In Stage 4, the core of the language for modeling activity system is very simple, yet it can be very sophisticated. The model is one of a system that can adapt and survive via processes of communication and control in a changing environment. Because of these features, it was necessary to add a monitoring and a control subsystem. One possible basic question is how the system could fail. At least three answers result: Failure could occur from doing the wrong thing, which boils down to performing a test for effectiveness of the system; if the selected strategy does work, then one could test the efficacy of the system; and efficacy of the system could be tested based on the economy of the resources used.

These three "E"s cover just the most basic means of monitoring and control. Consideration of such features as ethical or political issues could be added, if appropriate. Stage 4 named relevant systems that encapsulated all the problem themes along with their root definitions. Two particularly relevant systems emerged and both are normative in that they are expressing a version what ought to be rather than what is. The first was the Jackson Street community system Figure E12.2b. It is obvious that such a system is necessary if the community wants to get anything done. The second was the city-council system Figure E12-2c. People needed to be able to communicate with the city administration. The root definitions and a mnemonic were used to work out the two conceptual models, as shown in the following.

Jackson Street Community System.   The root definition of the Jackson Street community system is a community action committee to plan, control, and manage Jackson Street and the neighborhood by introducing improvements to the environment and safety through transformation of Jackson Street to a shared street for convenience of the pedestrians, bicyclists, and residents, as well as inhibiting through-vehicular traffic.

A mnemonic device, "CATWOE," was used for both conceptual models. In this case, CATWOE means:

- C = customers/clients (pedestrians, bicyclists, children, and residents).
- A = actors (elected members of CAC).
- T = transformation (transforming a regular street to a shared street).
- W = Weltanschauung (a shared street is worth having because of safety and improvement in well-being).

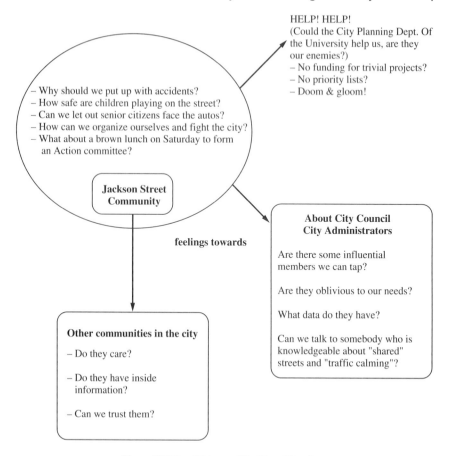

HELP! HELP!
(Could the City Planning Dept. Of
the University help us, are they
our enemies?)
– No funding for trivial projects?
– No priority lists?
– Doom & gloom!

– Why should we put up with accidents?
– How safe are children playing on the street?
– Can we let out senior citizens face the autos?
– How can we organize ourselves and fight the city?
– What about a brown lunch on Saturday to form
   an Action committee?

Jackson Street
Community

feelings towards

About City Council
City Administrators

Are there some influential
members we can tap?

Are they oblivious to our needs?

What data do they have?

Can we talk to somebody who is
knowledgeable about "shared"
streets and "traffic calming"?

Other communities in the city

– Do they care?

– Do they have inside
  information?

– Can we trust them?

Figure E12.2a   Picture of Problem Situation.

- O = ownership (the elected members of CAC).
- E = environment constraints (budget constraints and lack of data).

City Council System.   In parallel to the Jackson Street Community System, the City-Council System was examined. The root definition of the city council system (including administration and elected members of the council) is that the system develops and enhances a sense of community, then uses it effectively to handle issues connected with the development of projects all across the city. This is achieved by setting up and maintaining communication arenas, both formal and informal, that facilitate the negotiation of projects and the participation of all stakeholders in tackling issues connected with prioritizing, funding, and implementing such projects. In this case, CATWOE is:

- C = customers (the city council members and administration).
- A = actors (the city engineer and staff).
- T = transformation (ad hoc community development, prioritizing, and funding projects).
- W = Weltanschauung (issue handling requires being "just and fair" with all communities).

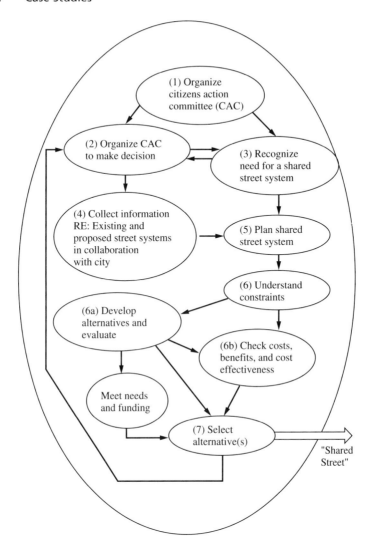

Figure E12.2b   Conceptual Model: Jackson Street Community System.

- O = ownership (the city council).
- E = environmental constraints (time, staff, and expertise).

Stage 5.   Comparison

Comparing models and reality can be both an exciting experience and a painful one, with several ways of conducting comparisons being recorded. One way is to simply record differences that stand out between the models and current perceptions. A more formal method would be to detail every set of differences for which specific answers are sought. Another approach is to resort to writing scenarios, describing how things might be resolved given the RD in question. At Stage 5, a comparison was made between the conceptual models and the problem situation so that one could draw up an agenda to debate the issues. Comparison of the Jackson Street

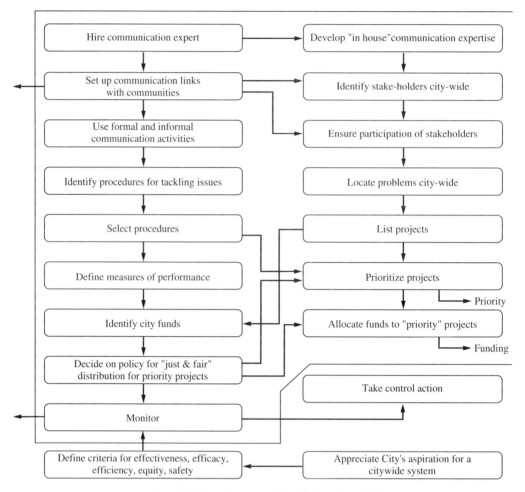

Figure E12.2c Conceptual Model: City-Council System.

community-system model with the problem situation indicated that, for example, collection of data is an important issue and should be taken up immediately with the city. Understanding the budget constraints of the city was also considered an important issue. This interaction is shown in Figure E12-2(d).

Comparison of the city-council system model with the real world showed the vital importance of good communication between the city officials and all of the communities involved. Regular reporting procedures as a consequence of monitoring and control could resolve the issues of secrecy and coverup leveled against city administrators. Lines of open communication between the city and Jackson Street CAC removed feelings of animosity because funding and priority issues were discussed openly.

Stage 6. Debate

The differences between models and reality provide a fertile field to discuss possible changes which could result in the problem situation. Two points were addressed during the debate: Changes should be systemically desirable (i.e., making sure resources

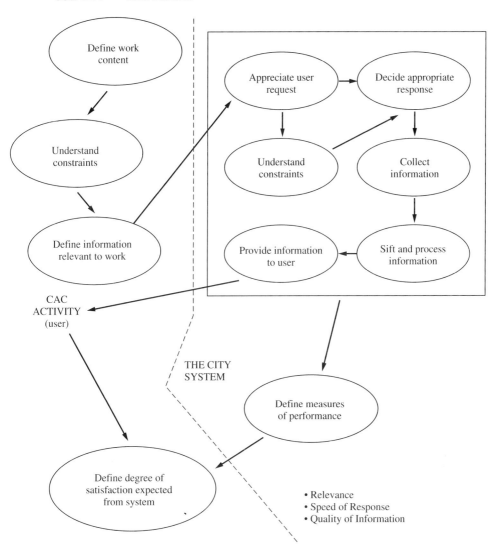

Figure E12.2d   Interaction between Jackson Street CAC and City Administration Regarding Supply of information.

are adequate and logical, and creating mechanisms for assessing effectiveness are in place), and the changes must be culturally feasible (and not driven merely by logic). Because the city officials needed to decide whether or not to implement this shared street, the questions asked were: "Given the budget constraints, is it possible to provide a shared street, as requested by CAC? How does this project stack up with other priority activities needed to be implemented?" Armed with appropriate data and a cost-effective working plan, CAC made a pitch for effecting change.

It took several months to come to an equitable solution. Two parallel streets (Oak and Pine) on either side of the Jackson formed their own CACs, because they were afraid that if the Jackson street CAC eventually got what it wanted, the excess traffic demand would be taken up by the other two streets. Also, based on sheer observation and scrutiny of the data, a four-lane arterial located nine blocks north of Jackson (with a current level of service of D) would be able to absorb the traffic from Jackson, Oak, and Pine if the shared street concept were adopted. In summary, the following ideas emerged from the debate:

- Parking on both side of the arterial should be removed.
- A continuous turning lane should be added to the arterial.
- The intersection capacities on the arterial should be improved through progressive signaling.
- Jackson and Oak must be shared streets as well as a one-way pair.
- Pine Street should be left as is. A decision on converting it to a shared street will be taken at a later date.
- Speed-restricting devices such as bumps and humps were recommended for Jackson and Oak streets.

Stage 7.   Taking Action

When contending actors come to accept changes as systemically desirable and culturally feasible, it is a sign that the SSM cycle is completed. Relevant systems will eventually take over to implement the defined changes. The Jackson Street community was now taking on a new image and a confidence it could be proud of. The strategies for action developed in the debate with respect to cost effectiveness and priority helped CAC convince the city council to include this shared street project for implementation. A decision-making hierarchy was put in place and the process iterated that allowed for communication structuring and community development by participative problem solving.

Reflection

The essential difference between HSM and SSM can be stated as follows: Whereas HSM is concerned with achieving objectives, SSM is a process of learning and enquiry. The learning is about complex, problematic human activity systems, eventually leading to taking purposeful action aimed at improvement. SSM is also a process of managing, where managing is interpreted very broadly as a process of achieving organized action. It is evident that in most real-world situations the application of both HSM and SSM may be appropriate to organize a debate in which a spectrum of needs, interests, and values can be teased out and discussed. This combination embraces systematic as well as systemic thinking involving publicly testable facts, data, logic, and cultural myths and meaning. SSM especially records the elements of the structure of the situation, the elements of the process, and the relationship between the two or the climate of the situation. It also examines the crucial roles of actors in the situation, the behavior expected in the roles (norms), and the values by which performance is judged.

More important, an understanding emerges of how power is acquired, exercised, retained, and passed on. There are no right or wrong descriptions of human activity systems—only multiple possible descriptions based on different images of the world. Also noteworthy is that, in general, conceptual models of human activity systems describe what goes on in the system of concern, whereas at the comparison stage how these *whats* can be achieved becomes a subject for discussion. If necessary, these models are expanded at levels of higher resolution. The process can go through several cycles for further refinement.

SUMMARY

This chapter presents a brutally short account of the soft systems methodology (SSM), together with a description of its implications in dealing with human activity systems. As we have discussed before, SSM developed in the shadow of well-developed methodologies in systems engineering and management science, generally covered by what is termed as the hard systems methodologies (HSM). These HSMs were highly effective in dealing with natural, physical and engineering systems to achieve defined goals and objectives. Does this mean that we have to throw away the HSMs we have learned through the window and clasp on to SSMs? Of course not. HSMs are truly powerful methods and there are few substitutes for them when it comes to well-defined problems in the real world. SSMs are learning processes that can supplement HSMs, as will be apparent through the case studies.

It is possible to map real-world natural and physical systems and find solutions through the use of HSMs. Many of these physical systems, such as bridge building systems, chemical plants or automobile manufacturing establishments require designing, and this designing can also be done using HSMs. However, it was very quickly realized that real world problems containing concepts of human activity could not be described, leave alone solved, unless an explicit *weltanschauung* (W) was defined. For instance, a human activity system concerning education, safety, rehabilitation, urban planning, or justice needed to examine clusters of "W"s for using the notion of systemicity.

It was also realized that SSM emerges as a learning system through various stages, particularly at the debate stage, which sets into motion an hermeneutic (interpreting) process.

A summary of the HSM versus SSM approaches is appropriate at this stage. The main difference is as follows: HSM considers goal-seeking to be an adequate model of human behavior and relies heavily on the language of problems and solutions to eliminate problems. SSM does not consider goal-seeking to be an adequate model for representing and solving human activity problems. SSM is therefore relevant to arguing and debating about real-world problems, and not merely models of the world. And this posture leads to learning and not just to optimizing or "satisficing". This results in the language of issues and accommodations rather than mere "solutions". SSM is also a process of managing, where managing is interpreted very broadly as a process of achieving organized action (Khisty 1993, 1995).

It is evident that in most real-world situations, the applications of both HSM and SSM would be appropriate to structure a debate in which a spectrum of needs, interests, and values could be teased out and discussed. This combination embraces systematic as well as systemic thinking involving publicly testable facts, data, logic, and cultural myths and meaning. SSM essentially records the elements of the structure of the situation, the elements of the process, and the relationship between the two. It also examines the crucial roles of actors in the situation, the behavior expected in the roles, and the values by which performance is judged. An overview of HSM and SSM is given in Table 12.1 (Khisty, 1995).

It must be remembered that unlike natural and physical problem solving, there are no right or wrong descriptions of human activity systems—only multiple possible descriptions based on different images of the world, as seen and perceived by different groups or individuals. Also noteworthy is that conceptual models of human

TABLE 12.1   HARD SYSTEMS VERSUS SOFT SYSTEMS METHODOLOGIES

Attributes	HSM	SSM
Orientation	Systematic Goal Seeking	Systemic Learning
Roots	Simplicity Paradigm	Complexity Paradigm
Beliefs	Systems can be "engineered"	Systems can be "explored"
	Models are of the world (ontologies)	Models are intellectual constructs (epistemologies)
	Closure is needed	Inquiry is never-ending
	"Finding" solutions to problems	"Finding' accommodation to issues
Human content	Non-existent	High
Questions	How?	What and How?
Suitability	Well-Structured problems	Ill-Structured problems
Advantages	Uses powerful methods but needs professionals to run the programs	Available to owners and practitioners
Disadvantages	Not transparent to the public	Transparent & understood by the public
Principles	Reductionism	Participants part of the research inquiry
	Replicability	Allows reflective learning
	Refutation possible	Process is "recoverable"
	Results homogenous through time	Results may not be homogenous through time

activity systems describe what goes on in the system of concern, whereas at the comparison stage how these 'whats' can be achieved becomes subject for discussion. If necessary, these models can be expanded at levels of higher resolution, through several cycles of refinement.

The dilemma of dealing with highly complex types of human activity systems, where both ends and means are uncertain and fuzzy, is most perplexing, particularly for engineers and scientist, who are used to dealing with neat and tidy looking problems, or at least ones that can be transformed into tidy problems through reductionism. There is, however, no alternative but to resort to a wide range of tools for coping with messy problems. The spirit of this dilemma is captured by Donald Schön (1987) as follows:

"In the swampy lowland, messy, confusing problems defy technical solution. The irony of this situation is that the problems of the high ground tend to be relatively unimportant to individuals or society at large, however great their technical interest may be, while in the swamp lie the problems of greatest concern. The practitioner must choose. Shall he remain on the high ground where he can solve relatively unimportant problems according to prevailing standards of rigor, or shall he descend to the swamp of important problems and non-rigorous inquiry?"

Soft systems inquiry and Action Research are ways of dealing with messy, confusing, and complicated problems residing in the swampy lowlands.

REFERENCES

ACKOFF, R. L., (1974), Redesigning the Future, John Wiley and Sons, Inc., New York.

ACKOFF, R. L. (1978), The Art of Problem Solving, John Wiley and Sons, Inc., New York.

CHECKLAND, P. B. (1981). Systems Thinking, Systems Practice, John Wiley and Sons, Inc., Chichester, UK.

CHECKLAND, P. B. (1984). "Systems Thinking in Management: The Development of Soft Systems Methodology and its Implications for Social Sciences" In H. Ulrich and G.J.B. Probst (Ed.) Self-Organization and Management of Social Systems: Insights, Promises, Doubts, and Questions, Springer-Verlag, Berlin, Germany.

CHECKLAND, P. B., and Scholes, J. (1990). Soft Systems Methodology in Action, John Wiley and Sons, Chichester, UK.

CHECKLAND, P. B., and HOLWELL, S. (1998). "Action Research: Its Nature and Validity", Systems Practice and Action Research, 11:1, pp. 9–21.

CHURCHMAN, C. W., (1968), The Systems Approach, Dell Publishing, New York.

FLOOD, R. L., and JACKSON, M. C. (1991). Creative Problem Solving, John Wiley and Sons, Chichester, UK.

HALL, A. D., (1962), A Methodology for Systems Engineering, Van Nostrand, Princeton, New Jersey.

JACKSON, M. C. (1991). Systems Methodology for the Management Sciences, Plenum Publishing Corp. London, UK.

KEYNES, J. M. (1938). Discussion of R. F. Harrod's Presidential address to the Royal Economic Society, In Moggridge, D.E. (Ed) (1976) Keynes, Fontana/Collins, London, UK.

KHISTY, C. J. (1993). "Citizen Participation using a Soft Systems Perspective", Transportation Research Record 1400, Transportation Research Board, Washington, D. C. pp. 53–57.

KHISTY, C. J. (1995). "Soft Systems Methodology as Learning and Management Tool", Journal of Urban Planning and Development, American Society of Civil Engineers, 121:3. pp. 91–107.

KLAU, C. H. (1990). An Illustrated Guide to Traffic Calming: The Future Way of Managing Traffic, Friends of the Earth, London, U. K.

LEWIN, K. (1947). Frontiers in Group Dynamics 11: Channels of Group Life; Social Planning and Action Research, Human Relations 1, pp. 143–153.

OLIGA, J. C. (1988). "Methodological Foundations of Systems Methodologies", Systems Practice, 1:1, pp.87–112.

SCHÖN, D. (1987). Educating the Reflective Practitioner: Towards a New Design for Teaching and Learning in the Professions, Jossey-Bass, San Francisco, CA.

SIMON, H. A., (1960), The New Science of Management Decision, Harper.

EXERCISES

1. Mrs. Smith, the owner of a newly built house, wants to put up a fence around her house, which is located in a beautiful part of the city. Although she is paying for the fence, it appears that the neighborhood housing association has an influence on her decision to select the type and color of the fence. She resents this interference, but is willing to go along with the association's wishes. Formulate the root definitions and draw appropriate rich pictures to illustrate this situation using the CATWOE mnemonic.

2. Refer to the case study concerning traffic calming. As a systems engineer, what information and data would you collect and analyze to supplement the SSM application described? Are there specific HSMs that you can think of that would be particularly helpful in this case?

3. An estate manager in charge of 2000 housing units has been asked to investigate how to curb motor-vehicle speeds on the estate property. Accidents (and near accidents) have been increasing in the last five years. There are at least three vocal groups of housing owners: [a] those who favor speed bumps, [b] those who favor imposing severe fines on those who do not comply with speed regulations, but who resent the use of speed bumps because it ruins their vehicles, and [c] those who don't care. The manager is perplexed and has sought your advice. [1] From a hard systems standpoint, what information and data will you gather and analyze [2] What relevant root definitions and rich pictures will you formulate, using the CATWOE mnemonic, just to understand the situation, and [3] How will you combine the results of the HSM and SSM analysis to take appropriate action.

4. Examine a typical facilities problem afflicting your university, such as a shortage of parking for students, staff, and faculty. Find out who the stake-holders are, who are the people who have the power to do anything, and who could be the victims of decisions that could be taken, and then draw a flow chart, rich pictures, and apply appropriate action research to deal with the problem.

5. A brilliant student comes to you along with his parents for resolving an apparently simple problem. The parents feel that their daughter should study the biological sciences and then shoot for going to medical school. The student wants to study chemical engineering first, and then decide later to enter medical school if she still feels the urge to do so. How would you deal with this situation from a HSM and SSM point of view?

Appendix A

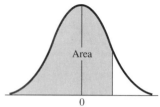

Area

0

TABLE A.1 AREAS UNDER THE NORMAL CURVE

	.00	.01	.02	.03	.04	.05	.06	.07	.08	.09
-3.4	0.0003	0.0003	0.0003	0.0003	0.0003	0.0003	0.0003	0.0003	0.0003	0.0002
-3.3	0.0005	0.0005	0.0005	0.0004	0.0004	0.0004	0.0004	0.0004	0.0004	0.0003
-3.2	0.0007	0.0007	0.0006	0.0006	0.0006	0.0006	0.0006	0.0005	0.0005	0.0005
-3.1	0.0010	0.0009	0.0009	0.0009	0.0008	0.0008	0.0008	0.0008	0.0007	0.0007
-3.0	0.0013	0.0013	0.0013	0.0012	0.0012	0.0011	0.0011	0.0011	0.0010	0.0010
-2.9	0.0019	0.0018	0.0017	0.0017	0.0016	0.0016	0.0015	0.0015	0.0014	0.0014
-2.8	0.0026	0.0025	0.0024	0.0023	0.0023	0.0022	0.0021	0.0021	0.0020	0.0019
-2.7	0.0035	0.0034	0.0033	0.0032	0.0031	0.0030	0.0029	0.0028	0.0027	0.0026
-2.6	0.0047	0.0045	0.0044	0.0043	0.0041	0.0040	0.0039	0.0038	0.0037	0.0036
-2.5	0.0062	0.0060	0.0059	0.0057	0.0055	0.0054	0.0052	0.0051	0.0049	0.0048
-2.4	0.0082	0.0080	0.0078	0.0075	0.0073	0.0071	0.0069	0.0068	0.0066	0.0064
-2.3	0.0107	0.0104	0.0102	0.0099	0.0096	0.0094	0.0091	0.0089	0.0087	0.0084
-2.2	0.0139	0.0136	0.0132	0.0129	0.0125	0.0122	0.0119	0.0116	0.0113	0.0110
-2.1	0.0179	0.0174	0.0170	0.0166	0.0162	0.0158	0.0154	0.0150	0.0146	0.0143
-2.0	0.0228	0.0222	0.0217	0.0212	0.0207	0.0202	0.0197	0.0192	0.0188	0.0183
-1.9	0.0287	0.0281	0.0274	0.0268	0.0262	0.0256	0.0250	0.0244	0.0239	0.0233
-1.8	0.0359	0.0352	0.0344	0.0336	0.0329	0.0322	0.0314	0.0307	0.0301	0.0294
-1.7	0.0446	0.0436	0.0427	0.0418	0.0409	0.0401	0.0392	0.0384	0.0375	0.0367
-1.6	0.0548	0.0537	0.0526	0.0516	0.0505	0.0495	0.0485	0.0475	0.0465	0.0455
-1.5	0.0668	0.0655	0.0643	0.0630	0.0618	0.0606	0.0594	0.0582	0.0571	0.0559
-1.4	0.0808	0.0793	0.0778	0.0764	0.0749	0.0735	0.0722	0.0708	0.0694	0.0681
-1.3	0.0968	0.0951	0.0934	0.0918	0.0901	0.0885	0.0869	0.0853	0.0838	0.0823
-1.2	0.1151	0.1131	0.1112	0.1093	0.1075	0.1056	0.1038	0.1020	0.1003	0.0985
-1.1	0.1357	0.1335	0.1314	0.1292	0.1271	0.1251	0.1230	0.1210	0.1190	0.1170
-1.0	0.1587	0.1562	0.1539	0.1515	0.1492	0.1469	0.1446	0.1423	0.1401	0.1379
-0.9	0.1841	0.1814	0.1788	0.1762	0.1736	0.1711	0.1685	0.1660	0.1635	0.1611
-0.8	0.2119	0.2090	0.2061	0.2033	0.2005	0.1977	0.1949	0.1922	0.1894	0.1867
-0.7	0.2420	0.2389	0.2358	0.2327	0.2296	0.2266	0.2236	0.2206	0.2177	0.2148
-0.6	0.2743	0.2709	0.2676	0.2643	0.2611	0.2578	0.2546	0.2514	0.2483	0.2451
-0.5	0.3085	0.3050	0.3015	0.2981	0.2946	0.2912	0.2877	0.2843	0.2810	0.2776
-0.4	0.3446	0.3409	0.3372	0.3336	0.3300	0.3264	0.3228	0.3192	0.3156	0.3121
-0.3	0.3821	0.3783	0.3745	0.3707	0.3669	0.3632	0.3594	0.3557	0.3520	0.3483
-0.2	0.4207	0.4168	0.4129	0.4090	0.4052	0.4013	0.3974	0.3936	0.3897	0.3859
-0.1	0.4602	0.4562	0.4522	0.4483	0.4443	0.4404	0.4364	0.4325	0.4286	0.4247
-0.0	0.5000	0.4960	0.4920	0.4880	0.4840	0.4801	0.4761	0.4721	0.4681	0.4641

TABLE A.1 *(continued)*   AREAS UNDER THE NORMAL CURVE

	.00	.01	.02	.03	.04	.05	.06	.07	.08	.09
0.0	0.5000	0.5040	0.5080	0.5120	0.5160	0.5199	0.5239	0.5279	0.5319	0.5359
0.1	0.5398	0.5438	0.5478	0.5517	0.5557	0.5596	0.5636	0.5675	0.5714	0.5753
0.2	0.5793	0.5832	0.5871	0.5910	0.5948	0.5987	0.6026	0.6064	0.6103	0.6141
0.3	0.6179	0.6217	0.6255	0.6293	0.6331	0.6368	0.6406	0.6443	0.6480	0.6517
0.4	0.6554	0.6591	0.6628	0.6664	0.6700	0.6736	0.6772	0.6808	0.6844	0.6879
0.5	0.6915	0.6950	0.6985	0.7019	0.7054	0.7088	0.7123	0.7157	0.7190	0.7224
0.6	0.7257	0.7291	0.7324	0.7357	0.7389	0.7422	0.7454	0.7486	0.7517	0.7549
0.7	0.7580	0.7611	0.7642	0.7673	0.7704	0.7734	0.7764	0.7794	0.7823	0.7852
0.8	0.7881	0.7910	0.7939	0.7967	0.7995	0.8023	0.8051	0.8078	0.8106	0.8133
0.9	0.8159	0.8186	0.8212	0.8238	0.8264	0.8289	0.8315	0.8340	0.8365	0.8389
1.0	0.8413	0.8438	0.8461	0.8485	0.8508	0.8531	0.8554	0.8577	0.8599	0.8621
1.1	0.8643	0.8665	0.8686	0.8708	0.8729	0.8749	0.8770	0.8790	0.8810	0.8830
1.2	0.8849	0.8869	0.8888	0.8907	0.8925	0.8944	0.8962	0.8980	0.8997	0.9015
1.3	0.9032	0.9049	0.9066	0.9082	0.9099	0.9115	0.9131	0.9147	0.9162	0.9177
1.4	0.9192	0.9207	0.9222	0.9236	0.9251	0.9265	0.9278	0.9292	0.9306	0.9319
1.5	0.9332	0.9345	0.9357	0.9370	0.9382	0.9394	0.9406	0.9418	0.9429	0.9441
1.6	0.9452	0.9463	0.9474	0.9484	0.9495	0.9505	0.9515	0.9525	0.9535	0.9545
1.7	0.9554	0.9564	0.9573	0.9582	0.9591	0.9599	0.9608	0.9616	0.9625	0.9633
1.8	0.9641	0.9649	0.9656	0.9664	0.9671	0.9678	0.9686	0.9693	0.9699	0.9706
1.9	0.9713	0.9719	0.9726	0.9732	0.9738	0.9744	0.9750	0.9756	0.9761	0.9767
2.0	0.9772	0.9778	0.9783	0.9788	0.9793	0.9798	0.9803	0.9808	0.9812	0.9817
2.1	0.9821	0.9826	0.9830	0.9834	0.9838	0.9842	0.9846	0.9850	0.9854	0.9857
2.2	0.9861	0.9864	0.9868	0.9871	0.9875	0.9878	0.9881	0.9884	0.9887	0.9890
2.3	0.9893	0.9896	0.9898	0.9901	0.9904	0.9906	0.9909	0.9911	0.9913	0.9916
2.4	0.9918	0.9920	0.9922	0.9925	0.9927	0.9929	0.9931	0.9932	0.9934	0.9936
2.5	0.9938	0.9940	0.9941	0.9943	0.9945	0.9946	0.9948	0.9949	0.9951	0.9952
2.6	0.9953	0.9955	0.9956	0.9957	0.9959	0.9960	0.9961	0.9962	0.9963	0.9964
2.7	0.9965	0.9966	0.9967	0.9968	0.9969	0.9970	0.9971	0.9972	0.9973	0.9974
2.8	0.9974	0.9975	0.9976	0.9977	0.9977	0.9978	0.9979	0.9979	0.9980	0.9981
2.9	0.9981	0.9982	0.9982	0.9983	0.9984	0.9984	0.9985	0.9985	0.9986	0.9986
3.0	0.9987	0.9987	0.9987	0.9988	0.9988	0.9989	0.9989	0.9989	0.9990	0.9990
3.1	0.9990	0.9991	0.9991	0.9991	0.9992	0.9992	0.9992	0.9992	0.9993	0.9993
3.2	0.9993	0.9993	0.9994	0.9994	0.9994	0.9994	0.9994	0.9995	0.9995	0.9995
3.3	0.9995	0.9995	0.9995	0.9996	0.9996	0.9996	0.9996	0.9996	0.9996	0.9997
3.4	0.9997	0.9997	0.9997	0.9997	0.9997	0.9997	0.9997	0.9997	0.9997	0.9998

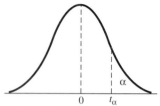

TABLE A.2   CRITICAL VALUES OF THE *t*-DISTRIBUTION

ν	α						
	0.40	0.30	0.20	0.15	0.10	0.05	0.025
1	0.325	0.727	1.376	1.963	3.078	6.314	12.706
2	0.289	0.617	1.061	1.386	1.886	2.920	4.303
3	0.277	0.584	0.978	1.250	1.638	2.353	3.182
4	0.271	0.569	0.941	1.190	1.533	2.132	2.776
5	0.267	0.559	0.920	1.156	1.476	2.015	2.571
6	0.265	0.553	0.906	1.134	1.440	1.943	2.447
7	0.263	0.549	0.896	1.119	1.415	1.895	2.365
8	0.262	0.546	0.889	1.108	1.397	1.860	2.306
9	0.261	0.543	0.883	1.100	1.383	1.833	2.262
10	0.260	0.542	0.879	1.093	1.372	1.812	2.228
11	0.260	0.540	0.876	1.088	1.363	1.796	2.201
12	0.259	0.539	0.873	1.083	1.356	1.782	2.179
13	0.259	0.537	0.870	1.079	1.350	1.771	2.160
14	0.258	0.537	0.868	1.076	1.345	1.761	2.145
15	0.258	0.536	0.866	1.074	1.341	1.753	2.131
16	0.258	0.535	0.865	1.071	1.337	1.746	2.120
17	0.257	0.534	0.863	1.069	1.333	1.740	2.110
18	0.257	0.534	0.862	1.067	1.330	1.734	2.101
19	0.257	0.533	0.861	1.066	1.328	1.729	2.093
20	0.257	0.533	0.860	1.064	1.325	1.725	2.086
21	0.257	0.532	0.859	1.063	1.323	1.721	2.080
22	0.256	0.532	0.858	1.061	1.321	1.717	2.074
23	0.256	0.532	0.858	1.060	1.319	1.714	2.069
24	0.256	0.531	0.857	1.059	1.318	1.711	2.064
25	0.256	0.531	0.856	1.058	1.316	1.708	2.060
26	0.256	0.531	0.856	1.058	1.315	1.706	2.056
27	0.256	0.531	0.855	1.057	1.314	1.703	2.052
28	0.256	0.530	0.855	1.056	1.313	1.701	2.048
29	0.256	0.530	0.854	1.055	1.311	1.699	2.045
30	0.256	0.530	0.854	1.055	1.310	1.697	2.042
40	0.255	0.529	0.851	1.050	1.303	1.684	2.021
60	0.254	0.527	0.848	1.045	1.296	1.671	2.000
120	0.254	0.526	0.845	1.041	1.289	1.658	1.980
	0.253	0.524	0.842	1.036	1.282	1.645	1.960

TABLE A.2 *(continued)* CRITICAL VALUES OF THE *t*-DISTRIBUTION

ν	α						
	0.02	0.015	0.01	0.0075	0.005	0.0025	0.0005
1	15.895	21.205	31.821	42.434	63.657	127.322	636.590
2	4.849	5.643	6.965	8.073	9.925	14.089	31.598
3	3.482	3.896	4.541	5.047	5.841	7.453	12.924
4	2.999	3.298	3.747	4.088	4.604	5.598	8.610
5	2.757	3.003	3.365	3.634	4.032	4.773	6.869
6	2.612	2.829	3.143	3.372	3.707	4.317	5.959
7	2.517	2.715	2.998	3.203	3.499	4.029	5.408
8	2.449	2.634	2.896	3.085	3.355	3.833	5.041
9	2.398	2.574	2.821	2.998	3.250	3.690	4.781
10	2.359	2.527	2.764	2.932	3.169	3.581	4.587
11	2.328	2.491	2.718	2.879	3.106	3.497	4.437
12	2.303	2.461	2.681	2.836	3.055	3.428	4.318
13	2.282	2.436	2.650	2.801	3.012	3.372	4.221
14	2.264	2.415	2.624	2.771	2.977	3.326	4.140
15	2.249	2.397	2.602	2.746	2.947	3.286	4.073
16	2.235	2.382	2.583	2.724	2.921	3.252	4.015
17	2.224	2.368	2.567	2.706	2.898	3.222	3.965
18	2.214	2.356	2.552	2.689	2.878	3.197	3.922
19	2.205	2.346	2.539	2.674	2.861	3.174	3.883
20	2.197	2.336	2.528	2.661	2.845	3.153	3.849
21	2.189	2.328	2.518	2.649	2.831	3.135	3.819
22	2.183	2.320	2.508	2.639	2.819	3.119	3.792
23	2.177	2.313	2.500	2.629	2.807	3.104	3.768
24	2.172	2.307	2.492	2.620	2.797	3.091	3.745
25	2.167	2.301	2.485	2.612	2.787	3.078	3.725
26	2.162	2.296	2.479	2.605	2.779	3.067	3.707
27	2.158	2.291	2.473	2.598	2.771	3.057	3.690
28	2.154	2.286	2.467	2.592	2.763	3.047	3.674
29	2.150	2.282	2.462	2.586	2.756	3.038	3.659
30	2.147	2.278	2.457	2.581	2.750	3.030	3.646
40	2.125	2.250	2.423	2.542	2.704	2.971	3.551
60	2.099	2.223	2.390	2.504	2.660	2.915	3.460
120	2.076	2.196	2.358	2.468	2.617	2.860	3.373
	2.054	2.170	2.326	2.432	2.576	2.807	3.291

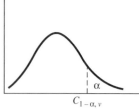

$C_{1-\alpha,\,v}$

TABLE A.3 CRITICAL VALUES OF THE CHI-SQUARE DISTRIBUTION

v	α									
	0.30	0.25	0.20	0.10	0.05	0.25	0.02	0.01	0.005	0.001
1	1.074	1.323	1.642	2.706	3.841	5.024	5.412	6.635	7.879	10.827
2	2.408	2.773	3.219	4.605	5.991	7.378	7.824	9.210	10.597	13.815
3	3.665	4.108	4.642	6.251	7.815	9.348	9.837	11.345	12.838	16.268
4	4.878	5.385	5.989	7.779	9.488	11.143	11.668	13.277	14.860	18.465
5	6.064	6.626	7.289	9.236	11.070	12.832	13.388	15.086	16.750	20.517
6	7.231	7.841	8.558	10.645	12.592	14.449	15.033	16.812	18.548	22.457
7	8.383	9.037	9.803	12.017	14.067	16.013	16.622	18.475	20.278	24.322
8	9.524	10.219	11.030	13.362	15.507	17.535	18.168	20.090	21.955	26.125
9	10.656	11.389	12.242	14.684	16.919	19.023	19.679	21.666	23.589	27.877
10	11.781	12.549	13.442	15.987	18.307	20.483	21.161	23.209	25.188	29.588
11	12.899	13.701	14.631	17.275	19.675	21.920	22.618	24.725	26.757	31.264
12	14.011	14.845	15.812	18.549	21.026	23.337	24.054	26.217	28.300	32.909
13	15.119	15.984	16.985	19.812	22.362	24.736	25.472	27.688	29.819	34.528
14	16.222	17.117	18.151	21.064	23.685	26.119	26.873	29.141	31.319	36.123
15	17.322	18.245	19.311	22.307	24.996	27.488	28.259	30.578	32.801	37.697
16	18.418	19.369	20.465	23.542	26.296	28.845	29.633	32.000	34.267	39.252
17	19.511	20.489	21.615	24.769	27.587	30.191	30.995	33.409	35.718	40.790
18	20.601	21.605	22.760	25.989	28.869	31.526	32.346	34.805	37.156	42.312
19	21.689	22.718	23.900	27.204	30.144	32.852	33.687	36.191	38.582	43.820
20	22.775	23.828	25.038	28.412	31.410	34.170	35.020	37.566	39.997	45.315
21	23.858	24.935	26.171	29.615	32.671	35.479	36.343	38.932	41.401	46.797
22	24.939	26.039	27.301	30.813	33.924	36.781	37.659	40.289	42.796	48.268
23	26.018	27.141	28.429	32.007	35.172	38.076	38.968	41.638	44.181	49.728
24	27.096	28.241	29.553	33.196	36.415	39.364	40.270	42.980	45.558	51.179
25	28.172	29.339	30.675	34.382	37.652	40.646	41.566	44.314	46.928	52.620
26	29.246	30.434	31.795	35.563	38.885	41.923	42.856	45.642	48.290	54.052
27	30.319	31.528	32.912	36.741	40.113	43.194	44.140	46.963	49.645	55.476
28	31.391	32.620	34.027	37.916	41.337	44.461	45.419	48.278	50.993	56.893
29	32.461	33.711	35.139	39.087	42.557	45.722	46.693	49.588	52.336	58.302
30	33.530	34.800	36.250	40.256	43.773	46.979	47.962	50.892	53.672	59.703

TABLE A.4   CRITICAL VALUES OF THE KOLMOGOROV-SMIRNOV TEST[1]

α / n	0.20	0.10	0.05	0.01
5	0.45	0.51	0.56	0.67
10	0.32	0.37	0.41	0.49
15	0.27	0.30	0.34	0.40
20	0.23	0.26	0.29	0.36
25	0.21	0.24	0.27	0.32
30	0.19	0.22	0.24	0.29
35	0.18	0.20	0.23	0.27
40	0.17	0.19	0.21	0.25
45	0.16	0.18	0.20	0.24
50	0.15	0.17	0.19	0.23
>50	$1.07/\sqrt{n}$	$1.22/\sqrt{n}$	$1.36/\sqrt{n}$	$1.63/\sqrt{n}$

[1] Hoel, P.G., *Introduction to Mathematical Statistics,* 3rd Ed., J. Wiley and Sons, New York, 1962

TABLE A.5 CRITICAL VALUES OF
THE F-DISTRIBUTION

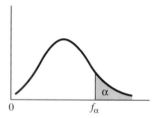

$$f_{0.025}\,(V_1,V_2)$$

v_2	v_1								
	1	2	3	4	5	6	7	8	9
1	647.8	799.5	864.2	899.6	921.8	937.1	948.2	956.7	963.
2	38.51	39.00	39.17	39.25	39.30	39.33	39.36	39.37	39.39
3	17.44	16.04	15.44	15.10	14.88	14.73	14.62	14.54	14.47
4	12.22	10.65	9.98	9.60	9.36	9.20	9.07	8.98	8.90
5	10.01	8.43	7.76	7.39	7.15	6.98	6.85	6.76	6.68
6	8.81	7.26	6.60	6.23	5.99	5.82	5.70	5.60	5.52
7	8.07	6.54	5.89	5.52	5.29	5.12	4.99	4.90	4.82
8	7.57	6.06	5.42	5.05	4.82	4.65	4.53	4.43	4.36
9	7.21	5.71	5.08	4.72	4.48	4.32	4.20	4.10	4.03
10	6.94	5.46	4.83	4.47	4.24	4.07	3.95	3.85	3.78
11	6.72	5.26	4.63	4.28	4.04	3.88	3.76	3.66	3.59
12	6.55	5.10	4.47	4.12	3.89	3.73	3.61	3.51	3.44
13	6.41	4.97	4.35	4.00	3.77	3.60	3.48	3.39	3.31
14	6.30	4.86	4.24	3.89	3.66	3.50	3.38	3.29	3.21
15	6.20	4.77	4.15	3.80	3.58	3.41	3.29	3.20	3.12
16	6.12	4.69	4.08	3.73	3.50	3.34	3.22	3.12	3.05
17	6.04	4.62	4.01	3.66	3.44	3.28	3.16	3.06	2.98
18	5.98	4.56	3.95	3.61	3.38	3.22	3.10	3.01	2.93
19	5.92	4.51	3.90	3.56	3.33	3.17	3.05	2.96	2.88
20	5.87	4.46	3.86	3.51	3.29	3.13	3.01	2.91	2.84
21	5.83	4.42	3.82	3.48	3.25	3.09	2.97	2.87	2.80
22	5.79	4.38	3.78	3.44	3.22	3.05	2.93	2.84	2.76
23	5.75	4.35	3.75	3.41	3.18	3.02	2.90	2.81	2.73
24	5.72	4.32	3.72	3.38	3.15	2.99	2.87	2.78	2.70
25	5.69	4.29	3.69	3.35	3.13	2.97	2.85	2.75	2.68
26	5.66	4.27	3.67	3.33	3.10	2.94	2.82	2.73	2.65
27	5.63	4.24	3.65	3.31	3.08	2.92	2.80	2.71	2.63
28	5.61	4.22	3.63	3.29	3.06	2.90	2.78	2.69	2.61
29	5.59	4.20	3.61	3.27	3.04	2.88	2.76	2.67	2.59
30	5.57	4.18	3.59	3.25	3.03	2.87	2.75	2.65	2.57
40	5.42	4.05	3.46	3.13	2.90	2.74	2.62	2.53	2.45
60	5.29	3.93	3.34	3.01	2.79	2.63	2.51	2.41	2.33
120	5.15	3.80	3.23	2.89	2.67	2.52	2.39	2.30	2.22
	5.02	3.69	3.12	2.79	2.57	2.41	2.29	2.19	2.11

TABLE A.5 *(continued)*

$$f_{0.025}(V_1, V_2)$$

v_2	\(v_1\) 10	12	15	20	24	30	40	60	120	
1	958.6	976.7	984.9	993.1	997.2	1001	1006	1010	1014	
2	39.40	39.41	39.43	39.45	39.46	39.46	39.47	39.48	39.49	39.50
3	14.42	14.34	14.25	14.17	14.12	14.08	14.04	13.99	13.95	13.90
4	8.84	8.75	8.66	8.56	8.51	8.46	8.41	8.36	8.31	8.26
5	6.62	6.52	6.43	6.33	6.28	6.23	6.18	6.12	6.07	6.02
6	5.46	5.37	5.27	5.17	5.12	5.07	5.01	4.96	4.90	4.85
7	4.76	4.67	4.57	4.47	4.42	4.36	4.31	4.25	4.20	4.14
8	4.30	4.20	4.10	4.00	3.95	3.89	3.84	3.78	3.73	3.67
9	3.96	3.87	3.77	3.67	3.61	3.56	3.51	3.45	3.39	3.33
10	3.72	3.62	3.52	3.42	3.37	3.31	3.26	3.20	3.14	3.08
11	3.53	3.43	3.33	3.23	3.17	3.12	3.06	3.00	2.94	2.88
12	3.37	3.28	3.18	3.07	3.02	2.96	2.91	2.85	2.79	2.72
13	3.25	3.15	3.05	2.95	2.89	2.84	2.78	2.72	2.66	2.60
14	3.15	3.05	2.95	2.84	2.79	2.73	2.67	2.61	2.55	2.49
15	3.06	2.96	2.86	2.76	2.70	2.64	2.59	2.52	2.46	2.40
16	2.99	2.89	2.79	2.68	2.63	2.57	2.51	2.45	2.38	2.32
17	2.92	2.82	2.72	2.62	2.56	2.50	2.44	2.38	2.32	2.25
18	2.87	2.77	2.67	2.56	2.50	2.44	2.38	2.32	2.26	2.19
19	2.82	2.72	2.62	2.51	2.45	2.39	2.33	2.27	2.20	2.13
20	2.77	2.68	2.57	2.46	2.41	2.35	2.29	2.22	2.16	2.09
21	2.73	2.64	2.53	2.42	2.37	2.31	2.25	2.18	2.11	2.04
22	2.70	2.60	2.50	2.39	2.33	2.27	2.21	2.14	2.08	2.00
23	2.67	2.57	2.47	2.36	2.30	2.24	2.18	2.11	2.04	1.97
24	2.64	2.54	2.44	2.33	2.27	2.21	2.15	2.08	2.01	1.94
25	2.61	2.51	2.41	2.30	2.24	2.18	2.12	2.05	1.98	1.91
26	2.59	2.49	2.39	2.28	2.22	2.16	2.09	2.03	1.95	1.88
27	2.57	2.47	2.36	2.25	2.19	2.13	2.07	2.00	1.93	1.85
28	2.55	2.45	2.34	2.23	2.17	2.11	2.05	1.98	1.91	1.83
29	2.53	2.43	2.32	2.21	2.15	2.09	2.03	1.96	1.89	1.81
30	2.51	2.41	2.31	2.20	2.14	2.07	2.01	1.94	1.87	1.79
40	2.39	2.29	2.18	2.07	2.01	1.94	1.88	1.80	1.72	1.64
60	2.27	2.17	2.06	1.94	1.88	1.82	1.74	1.67	1.58	1.48
120	2.16	2.05	1.94	1.82	1.76	1.69	1.61	1.53	1.43	1.31
	2.05	1.94	1.83	1.71	1.64	1.57	1.48	1.39	1.27	1.00

TABLE A.5 *(continued)*

$$f_{0.025}(V_1, V_2)$$

v_2	v_1 1	2	3	4	5	6	7	8	9
1	161.4	199.5	215.7	224.6	230.2	234.0	236.8	238.9	240.
2	18.51	19.00	19.16	19.25	19.30	19.33	19.35	19.37	19.38
3	10.13	9.55	9.28	9.12	9.01	8.94	8.89	8.85	8.81
4	7.71	6.94	6.59	6.39	6.26o	6.16	6.09	6.04	6.00
5	6.61	5.79	5.41	5.19	5.05	4.95	4.88	4.82	4.77
6	5.99	5.14	4.76	4.53	4.39	4.28	4.21	4.15	4.10
7	5.59	4.74	4.35	4.12	3.97	3.87	3.79	3.73	3.68
8	5.32	4.46	4.07	3.84	3.69	3.58	3.50	3.44	3.39
9	5.12	4.26	3.86	3.63	3.48	3.37	3.29	3.23	3.18
10	4.96	4.10	3.71	3.48	3.33	3.22	3.14	3.07	3.02
11	4.84	3.98	3.59	3.36	3.20	3.09	3.01	2.95	2.90
12	4.75	3.89	3.49	3.26	3.11	3.00	2.91	2.85	2.80
13	4.67	3.81	3.41	3.18	3.03	2.92	2.83	2.77	2.71
14	4.60	3.74	3.34	3.11	2.96	2.85	2.76	2.70	2.65
15	4.54	3.68	3.29	3.06	2.90	2.79	2.71	2.64	2.59
16	4.49	3.63	3.24	3.01	2.85	2.74	2.66	2.59	2.54
17	4.45	3.59	3.20	2.96	2.81	2.70	2.61	2.55	2.49
18	4.41	3.55	3.16	2.93	2.77	2.66	2.58	2.51	2.46
19	4.38	3.52	3.13	2.90	2.74	2.63	2.54	2.48	2.42
20	4.35	3.49	3.10	2.87	2.71	2.60	2.51	2.45	2.39
21	4.32	3.47	3.07	2.84	2.68	2.57	2.49	2.42	2.37
22	4.30	3.44	3.05	2.82	2.66	2.55	2.46	2.40	2.34
23	4.28	3.42	3.03	2.80	2.64 5	2.53	2.44	2.37	2.32
24	4.26	3.40	3.01	2.78	2.62	2.51	2.42	2.36	2.30
25	4.24	3.39	2.99	2.76	2.60	2.49	2.40	2.34	2.28
26	4.23	3.37	2.98	2.74	2.59	2.47	2.39	2.32	2.27
27	4.21	3.35	2.96	2.73	2.57	2.46	2.37	2.31	2.25
28	4.20	3.34	2.95	2.71	2.56	2.45	2.36	2.29	2.24
29	4.18	3.33	2.93	2.70	2.55	2.43	2.35	2.28	2.22
30	4.17	3.32	2.92	2.69	2.53	2.42	2.33	2.27	2.21
40	4.08	3.23	2.84	2.61	2.45	2.34	2.25	2.18	2.12
60	4.00	3.15	2.76	2.53	2.37	2.25	2.17	2.10	2.04
120	3.92	3.07	2.68	2.45	2.29	2.17	2.09	2.02	1.96
	3.84	3.00	2.60	2.37	2.21	2.10	2.01	1.94	1.88

TABLE A.5 *(continued)*

$$f_{0.025}\,(V_1,V_2)$$

V_2	V_1									
	10	12	15	20	24	30	40	60	120	
1	241.9	243.9	245.9	248.0	249.1	250.1	251.1	252.2	253.3	254.
2	19.40	19.41	19.43	19.45	19.45	19.46	19.47	19.48	19.49	19.50
3	8.79	8.74	8.70	8.66	8.64	8.62	8.59	8.57	8.55	8.53
4	5.96	5.91	5.86	5.80	5.77	5.75	5.72	5.69	5.66	5.63
5	4.74	4.68	4.62	4.56	4.53	4.50	4.46	4.43	4.40	4.36
6	4.06	4.00	3.94	3.87	3.84	3.81	3.77	3.74	3.70	3.67
7	3.64	3.57	3.51	3.44	3.41	3.38	3.34	3.30	3.27	3.23
8	3.35	3.28	3.22	3.15	3.12	3.08	3.04	3.01	2.97	2.93
9	3.14	3.07	3.01	2.94	2.90	2.86	2.83	2.79	2.75	2.71
10	2.98	2.91	2.85	2.77	2.74	2.70	2.66	2.62	2.58	2.54
11	2.85	2.79	2.72	2.65	2.61	2.57	2.53	2.49	2.45	2.40
12	2.75	2.69	2.62	2.54	2.51	2.47	2.43	2.38	2.34	2.30
13	2.67	2.60	2.53	2.46	2.42	2.38	2.34	2.30	2.25	2.21
14	2.60	2.53	2.46	2.39	2.35	2.31	2.27	2.22	2.18	2.13
15	2.54	2.48	2.40	2.33	2.29	2.25	2.20	2.16	2.11	2.07
16	2.49	2.42	2.35	2.28	2.24	2.19	2.15	2.11	2.06	2.01
17	2.45	2.38	2.31	2.23	2.19	2.15	2.10	2.06	2.01	1.96
18	2.41	2.34	2.27	2.19	2.15	2.11	2.06	2.02	1.97	1.92
19	2.38	2.31	2.23	2.16	2.11	2.07	2.03	1.98	1.93	1.88
20	2.35	2.28	2.20	2.12	2.08	2.04	1.99	1.95	1.90	1.84
21	2.32	2.25	2.18	2.10	2.05	2.01	1.96	1.92	1.87	1.81
22	2.30	2.23	2.15	2.07	2.03	1.98	1.94	1.89	1.84	1.78
23	2.27	2.20	2.13	2.05	2.01	1.96	1.91	1.86	1.81	1.76
24	2.25	2.18	2.11	2.03	1.98	1.94	1.89	1.84	1.79	1.73
25	2.24	2.16	2.09	2.01	1.96	1.92	1.87	1.82	1.77	1.71
26	2.22	2.15	2.07	1.99	1.95	1.90	1.85	1.80	1.75	1.69
27	2.20	2.13	2.06	1.97	1.93	1.88	1.84	1.79	1.73	1.67
28	2.19	2.12	2.04	1.96	1.91	1.87	1.82	1.77	1.71	1.65
29	2.18	2.10	2.03	1.94	1.90	1.85	1.81	1.75	1.70	1.64
30	2.16	2.09	2.01	1.93	1.89	1.84	1.79	1.74	1.68	1.62
40	2.08	2.00	1.92	1.84	1.79	1.74	1.69	1.64	1.58	1.51
60	1.99	1.92	1.84	1.75	1.70	1.65	1.59	1.53	1.47	1.39
120	1.91	1.83	1.75	1.66	1.61	1.55	1.50	1.43	1.35	1.25
	1.83	1.75	1.67	1.57	1.52	1.46	1.39	1.32	1.22	1.00

TABLE A.5 *(continued)*

$$f_{0.025}(V_1, V_2)$$

V_2	1	2	3	4	5	6	7	8	9
					V_1				
1	4052	4999.5	5403	5625	5764	5859	5928	5981	
2	98.50	99.00	99.17	99.25	99.30	99.33	99.36	99.37	99.39
3	34.12	30.82	29.46	28.71	28.24	27.91	27.67	27.49	27.35
4	21.20	18.00	16.69	15.98	15.52	15.21	14.98	14.80	14.66
5	16.26	13.27	12.06	11.39	10.97	10.67	10.46	10.29	10.16
6	13.75	10.92	9.78	9.15	8.75	8.47	8.26	8.10	7.98
7	12.25	9.55	8.45	7.85	7.46	7.19	6.99	6.84	6.72
8	11.26	8.65	7.59	7.01	6.63	6.37	6.18	6.03	5.91
9	10.56	8.02	6.99	6.42	6.06	5.80	5.61	5.47	5.35
10	10.04	7.56	6.55	5.99	5.64	5.39	5.20	5.06	4.94
11	9.65	7.21	6.22	5.67	5.32	5.07	4.89	4.74	4.63
12	9.33	6.93	5.95	5.41	5.06	4.82	4.64	4.50	4.39
13	9.07	6.70	5.74	5.21	4.86	4.62	4.44	4.30	4.19
14	8.86	6.51	5.56	5.04	4.69	4.46	4.28	4.14	4.03
15	8.68	6.36	5.42	4.89	4.56	4.32	4.14	4.00	3.89
16	8.53	6.23	5.29	4.77	4.44	4.20	4.03	3.89	3.78
17	8.40	6.11	5.18	4.67	4.34	4.10	3.93	3.79	3.68
18	8.29	6.01	5.09	4.58	4.25	4.01	3.84	3.71	3.60
19	8.18	5.93	5.01	4.50	4.17	3.94	3.77	3.63	3.52
20	8.10	5.85	4.94	4.43	4.10	3.87	3.70	3.56	3.46
21	8.02	5.78	4.87	4.37	4.04	3.81	3.64	3.51	3.40
22	7.95	5.72	4.82	4.31	3.99	3.76	3.59	3.45	3.35
23	7.88	5.66	4.76	4.26	3.94	3.71	3.54	3.41	3.30
24	7.82	5.61	4.72	4.22	3.90	3.67	3.50	3.36	3.26
25	7.77	5.57	4.68	4.18	3.85	3.63	3.46	3.32	3.22
26	7.72	5.53	4.64	4.14	3.82	3.59	3.42	3.29	3.18
27	7.68	5.49	4.60	4.11	3.78	3.56	3.39	3.26	3.15
28	7.64	5.45	4.57	4.07	3.75	3.53	3.36	3.23	3.12
29	7.60	5.42	4.54	4.04	3.73	3.50	3.33	3.20	3.09
30	7.56	5.39	4.51	4.02	3.70	3.47	3.30	3.17	3.07
40	7.31	5.18	4.31	3.83	3.51	3.29	3.12	2.99	2.89
60	7.08	4.98	4.13	3.65	3.34	3.12	2.95	2.82	2.72
120	6.85	4.79	3.95	3.48	3.17	2.96	2.79	2.66	2.56
	6.63	4.61	3.78	3.32	3.02	2.80	2.64	2.51	2.41

TABLE A.5 *(continued)*

$$f_{0.025}(V_1, V_2)$$

v_2	v_1 10	12	15	20	24	30	40	60	120	
1	6056	6106	6157.	6209	6235	6261	6287	6313	6339	
2	99.40	99.42	99.43	99.45	99.46	99.47	99.47	99.48	99.49	99.50
3	27.23	27.05	26.87	26.69	26.60	26.50	26.41	26.32	26.22	26.13
4	14.55	14.37	14.20	14.02	13.93	13.84	13.75	13.65	13.56	13.46
5	10.05	9.89	9.72	9.55	9.47	9.38	9.29	9.20	9.11	9.02
6	7.87	7.72	7.56	7.40	7.31	7.23	7.14	7.06	6.97	6.88
7	6.62	6.47	6.31	6.16	6.07	5.99	5.91	5.82	5.74	5.65
8	5.81	5.67	5.52	5.36	5.28	5.20	5.12	5.03	4.95	4.86
9	5.26	5.11	4.96	4.81	4.73	4.65	4.57	4.48	4.40	4.31
10	4.85	4.71	4.56	4.41	4.33	4.25	4.17	4.08	4.00	3.91
11	4.54	4.40	4.25	4.10	4.02	3.94	3.86	3.78	3.69	3.60
12	4.30	4.16	4.01	3.86	3.78	3.70	3.62	3.54	3.45	3.36
13	4.10	3.96	3.82	3.66	3.59	3.51	3.43	3.34	3.25	3.17
14	3.94	3.80	3.66	3.51	3.43	3.35	3.27	3.18	3.09	3.00
15	3.80	3.67	3.52	3.37	3.29	3.21	3.13	3.05	2.96	2.87
16	3.69	3.55	3.41	3.26	3.18	3.10	3.02	2.93	2.84	2.75
17	3.59	3.46	3.31	3.16	3.08	3.00	2.92	2.83	2.75	2.65
18	3.51	3.37	3.23	3.08	3.00	2.92	2.84	2.75	2.66	2.57
19	3.43	3.30	3.15	3.00	2.92	2.84	2.76	2.67	2.58	2.49
20	3.37	3.23	3.09	2.94	2.86	2.78	2.69	2.61	2.52	2.42
21	3.31	3.17	3.03	2.88	2.80	2.72	2.64	2.55	2.46	2.36
22	3.26	3.12	2.98	2.83	2.75	2.67	2.58	2.50	2.40	2.31
23	3.21	3.07	2.93	2.78	2.70	2.62	2.54	2.45	2.35	2.26
24	3.17	3.03	2.89	2.74	2.66	2.58	2.49	2.40	2.31	2.21
25	3.13	2.99	2.85	2.70	2.62	2.54	2.45	2.36	2.27	2.17
26	3.09	2.96	2.81	2.66	2.58	2.50	2.42	2.33	2.23	2.13
27	3.06	2.93	2.78	2.63	2.55	2.47	2.38	2.29	2.20	2.10
28	3.03	2.90	2.75	2.60	2.52	2.44	2.35	2.26	2.17	2.06
29	3.00	2.87	2.73	2.57	2.49	2.41	2.33	2.23	2.14	2.03
30	2.98	2.84	2.70	2.55	2.47	2.39	2.30	2.21	2.11	2.01
40	2.80	2.66	2.52	2.37	2.29	2.20	2.11	2.02	1.92	1.80
60	2.63	2.50	2.35	2.20	2.12	2.03	1.94	1.84	1.73	1.60
120	2.47	2.34	2.19	2.03	1.95	1.86	1.76	1.66	1.53	1.38
	2.32	2.18	2.04	1.88	1.79	1.70	1.59	1.47	1.32	1.00

TABLE A.6   MULTIPLE RANGE TEST VALUES

(Studentized rp)

	least significant studentized ranges r_p						least significant studentized ranges r_p				
	$\alpha = 0.05$						$\alpha = 0$				
	P						P				
r	2	3	4	5	6	r	2	3	4	5	6
1	17.97	17.97	17.97	17.97	17.97	1	90.03	90.03	90.03	90.03	90.03
2	6.085	6.085	6.085	6.085	6.085	2	14.04	14.04	14.04	14.04	14.04
3	4.501	4.516	4.516	4.516	4.516	3	8.261	8.321	8.321	8.321	8.321
4	3.927	4.013	4.033	4.033	4.033	4	6.512	6.677	6.740	6.756	6.756
5	3.635	3.749	3.797	3.814	3.814	5	5.702	5.893	5.898	6.040	6.065
6	3.461	3.587	3.649	3.680	3.694	6	5.243	5.439	5.549	5.614	5.655
7	3.344	3.477	3.548	3.588	3.611	7	4.949	5.145	5.260	5.334	5.383
8	3.261	3.399	3.475	3.521	3.549	8	4.746	4.939	5.057	5.135	5.189
9	3.199	3.339	3.420	3.470	3.502	9	4.596	4.787	4.906	4.986	5.043
10	3.151	3.293	3.376	3.430	3.465	10	4.482	4.671	4.790	4.871	4.931
11	3.113	3.256	3.342	3.397	3.435	11	4.392	4.579	4.697	4.780	4.841
12	3.082	3.225	3.313	3.370	3.410	12	4.320	4.504	4.622	4.706	4.767
13	3.055	3.200	3.289	3.348	3.389	13	4.260	4.442	4.560	4.644	4.706
14	3.033	3.178	3.268	3.329	3.372	14	4.210	4.391	4.508	4.591	4.654
15	3.014	3.160	3.250	3.312	3.356	15	4.168	4.347	4.463	4.547	4.610
16	2.998	3.144	3.235	3.298	3.343	16	4.131	4.309	4.425	4.509	4.572
17	2.984	3.130	3.222	3.285	3.331	17	4.099	4.275	4.391	4.475	4.539
18	2.971	3.118	3.210	3.274	3.321	18	4.071	4.246	4.362	4.445	4.509
19	2.960	3.107	3.199	3.264	3.311	19	4.046	4.220	4.335	4.419	4.483
20	2.950	3.097	3.190	3.255	3.303	20	4.024	4.197	4.312	4.395	4.459
24	2.919	3.066	3.160	3.226	3.276	24	3.956	4.126	4.239	4.322	4.386
30	2.888	3.035	3.131	3.199	3.250	30	3.889	4.506	4.168	4.250	4.314
40	2.858	3.006	3.102	3.171	3.224	40	3.825	3.988	4.098	4.180	4.244
60	2.829	2.976	3.073	3.143	3.198	60	3.762	3.922	4.031	4.111	4.174
120	2.800	2.947	3.045	3.116	3.172	120	3.702	3.858	3.965	4.044	4.107
	2.772	2.918	3.017	3.089	3.14		3.643	3.796	3.900	3.978	4.0406

Abridgement of H. L. Harter's "Critical Values for Duncan's New Multiple Range Test", *Biometrics*, Vol. 16. No. 4 (1960). With permission from the Biometric Society.

TABLE A.7 WILCOXON SIGNED-RANK TEST

One-sided	Two-sided	n = 5	n = 6	n = 7	n = 8	n = 9	n = 10
$P = .05$	$P = .10$	1	2	4	6	8	11
$P = .025$	$P = .05$		1	2	4	6	8
$P = .01$	$P = .02$			0	2	3	5
$P = .005$	$P = .01$				0	2	3
One-sided	Two-sided	n = 11	n = 12	n = 13	n = 14	n = 15	n = 16
$P = .05$	$P = .10$	14	17	21	26	30	36
$P = .025$	$P = .05$	11	14	17	21	25	30
$P = .01$	$P = .02$	7	10	13	16	20	24
$P = .005$	$P = .01$	5	7	10	13	16	19
One-sided	Two-sided	n = 17	n = 18	n = 19	n = 20	n = 21	n = 22
$P = .05$	$P = .10$	41	47	54	60	68	75
$P = .025$	$P = .05$	35	40	45	52	59	66
$P = .01$	$P = .02$	28	33	38	43	49	58
$P = .005$	$P = .01$	23	28	32	37	43	49
One-sided	Two-sided	n = 23	n = 24	n = 25	n = 26	n = 27	n = 28
$P = .05$	$P = .10$	83	92	101	110	120	130
$P = .025$	$P = .05$	73	81	90	96	107	117
$P = .01$	$P = .02$	62	69	77	85	93	102
$P = .005$	$P = .01$	55	61	68	76	84	92
One-sided	Two-sided	n = 29	n = 30	n = 31	n = 32	n = 33	n = 34
$P = .05$	$P = .10$	141	152	163	175	188	201
$P = .025$	$P = .05$	127	137	148	230	171	183
$P = .01$	$P = .02$	111	120	130	141	151	162
$P = .005$	$P = .01$	100	100	118	128	138	149
One-sided	Two-sided	n = 35	n = 36	n = 37	n = 38	n = 39	
$P = .05$	$P = .10$	214	228	242	256	271	
$P = .025$	$P = .05$	195	208	222	235	250	
$P = .01$	$P = .02$	174	186	198	211	224	
$P = .005$	$P = .01$	160	171	183	195	208	
One-sided	Two-sided	n = 40	n = 41	n = 42	n = 43	n = 44	n = 45
$P = .05$	$P = .10$	287	302	319	336	353	371
$P = .025$	$P = .05$	264	279	295	311	327	344
$P = .01$	$P = .02$	238	252	267	281	297	313
$P = .005$	$P = .01$	221	234	248	262	277	292
One-sided	Two-sided	n = 46	n = 47	n = 48	n = 49	n = 50	
$P = .05$	$P = .10$	389	406	427	446	466	
$P = .025$	$P = .05$	361	379	397	415	434	
$P = .01$	$P = .02$	329	345	362	380	398	
$P = .005$	$P = .01$	307	323	339	356	373	

Reprinted with permission from W. H. Beyer (ed.), *CRC Handbook of Tables for Probability and Statistics,* 2d ed., 1968, p. 400. Copyright CRC Press, Inc., Boca Raton, Florida.

TABLE A.8 WILCOXON RANK SUM TEST

$m = 3(1)25$ and $n = m(1)m + 25$
$P = .05$ one-sided; $P = .10$ two-side

n	m = 3	m = 4	m = 5	m = 6	m = 7	m = 8	m = 9	m = 10	m = 11	m 12	m = 13	m = 14
n = m	6,15	12,24	19,36	28,50	39,66	52,84	66,105	83,127	101,152	121,179	143,208	167,239
n = m + 1	7,17	13,27	20,40	30,54	41,71	54,90	69,111	86,134	105,159	125,187	148,216	172,248
n = m + 2	7,20	14,30	22,43	32,58	43,76	57,95	72,117	89,141	109,166	129,195	152,225	177,257
n = m + 3	8,22	15,33	24,46	33,63	46,80	60,100	75,123	93,147	112,174	134,202	157,233	182,266
n = m + 4	9,24	16,36	25,50	35,67	48,85	62,106	78,129	96,154	116,181	138,210	162,241	187,275
n = m + 5	9,27	17,39	26,54	37,71	50,90	65,111	81,135	100,160	120,188	142,218	166,250	192,284
n = m + 6	10,29	18,42	27,58	39,75	52,95	67,117	84,141	103,167	124,195	147,225	171,258	197,293
n = m + 7	11,31	19,45	29,61	41,79	54,100	70,122	87,147	107,173	128,202	151,233	176,256	203,301
n = m + 8	11,34	20,48	30,65	42,84	57,104	73,127	90,153	110,180	132,209	155,241	181,274	208,310
n = m + 9	12,36	21,51	32,68	44,88	59,109	75,133	93,159	114,186	136,216	159,249	185,283	213,319
n = m + 10	13,38	22,54	33,72	46,92	61,114	78,138	96,165	117,193	139,224	164,256	190,291	218,328
n = m + 11	13,41	23,57	34,76	48,96	63,119	80,144	100,170	120,200	143,231	168,264	195,299	223,337
n = m + 12	14,43	24,60	36,79	50,100	65,124	83,149	103,176	124,206	147,238	172,272	199,308	228,346
n = m + 13	15,45	25,63	37,83	52,104	68,128	86,154	106,182	127,213	151,245	177,279	204,316	234,354
n = m + 14	15,48	26,66	39,86	53,109	70,133	88,160	109,188	131,219	155,252	181,287	209,324	239,363
n = m + 15	16,50	27,69	40,90	55,113	72,138	91,165	112,194	134,226	159,259	185,295	214,332	244,372
n = m + 16	17,52	28,72	42,93	57,117	74,143	94,170	115,200	138,232	138,266	190,302	218,341	249,381
n = m + 17	17,55	29,75	43,07	59,121	77,147	96,176	118,206	141,239	167,273	194,310	223,349	254,390
n = m + 18	18,57	30,78	44,101	61,125	79,152	99,181	121,212	145,245	171,280	198,318	228,357	260,398
n = m + 19	19,59	31,81	46,104	62,130	81,157	102,186	124,218	148,252	175,287	203,325	233,365	265,407
n = m + 20	19,62	32,84	47,108	64,134	83,162	104,192	127,224	152,258	178,295	207,333	237,374	270,416
n = m + 21	20,64	33,87	49,111	66,138	86,166	107,197	130,230	155,265	182,302	211,341	242,382	275,425
n = m + 22	21,66	34,90	50,115	68,142	88,171	109,203	133,236	159,271	186,309	216,348	247,390	280,434
n = m + 23	21,69	35,93	52,118	70,146	90,176	112,208	136,242	162,278	190,316	220,356	252,398	285,443
n = m + 24	22,71	37,95	53,122	72,150	92,181	115,213	139,248	166,284	194,323	224,364	257,406	291,451
n = m + 25	23,73	38,98	54,126	73,155	94,186	117,219	142,254	169,291	198,330	229,371	261,415	296,460

$m = 3(1)25$ and $n = m(1)m + 25$
$P = .05$ one-sided; $P = .10$ two-sided

n	m=15	m = 16	m = 17	m = 18	m = 19	m = 20	m = 21	m = 22	m = 23	m = 24	m = 24
n = m	192,273	220,308	249,346	280,386	314,427	349,471	386,517	424,566	465,616	508,668	552,723
n = m + 1	198,282	226,318	256,356	287,397	321,439	356,484	394,530	433,579	474,630	517,683	562,738
n = m + 2	203,292	232,328	262,367	294,408	328,451	364,496	402,543	442,592	483,644	527,697	572,753
n = m + 3	209,301	238,338	268,378	301,419	336,462	372,508	410,556	450,606	492,658	536,712	582,768
n = m + 4	215,310	244,348	275,388	308,430	343,474	380,520	418,569	459,619	501,672	546,726	592,783
n = m + 5	220,320	250,358	281,399	315,\??\	350,486	387,533	427,581	468,632	511,685	555,741	602,798
n = m + 6	226,329	256,368	288,409	322,452	358,497	395,545	435,594	476,646	520,699	565,755	612,813
n = m + 7	231,339	262,378	294,420	329,463	365,509	403,557	443,607	485,659	529,713	574,770	622,828
n = m + 8	237,348	268,388	301,430	336,474	372,521	411,509	451,620	494,672	538,727	584,784	632,843
n = m + 9	242,358	274,398	307,441	342,486	380,532	419,581	459,633	502,686	547,741	594,798	642,858
n = m + 10	248,367	280,408	314,451	349,497	387,544	426,594	468,645	511,699	556,755	603,813	652,873
n = m + 11	254,376	286,418	320,462	356,508	394,556	434,606	476,658	520,712	585,769	613,827	662,888
n = m + 12	259,386	292,428	327,472	363,519	402,567	442,618	484,671	528,726	574,783	622,842	672,903
n = m + 13	265,395	298,438	333,483	370,530	409,579	450,630	492,684	537,739	584,796	632,856	682,918
n = m + 14	270,405	304,448	340,493	377,541	416,591	458,642	501,696	546,752	593,810	642,870	692,933
n = m + 15	276,414	310,458	346,504	384,552	424,602	465,655	509,709	554,766	602,824	651,885	702,948
n = m + 16	282,423	316,468	353,514	391,563	431,614	473,667	517,722	563,779	611,838	661,899	712,963
n = m + 17	287,433	322,478	359,525	398,574	438,626	481,679	526,734	572,792	620,852	670,914	723,977
n = m + 18	293,442	328,488	366,535	405,585	446,637	489,691	534,747	581,805	629,866	680,928	733,992
n = m + 19	299,451	334,498	372,546	412,596	453,649	497,703	542,760	589,819	639,879	690,942	743,1007
n = m + 20	304,461	340,508	379,556	419,607	461,660	505,715	550,773	598,832	648,893	699,957	753,1022
n = m + 21	310,470	347,517	385,568	426,618	468,672	512,728	559,785	607,845	657,907	709,971	763,1037
n = m + 22	315,480	353,527	392,577	433,629	475,684	520,740	567,798	615,859	666,921	718,986	773,1052
n = m + 23	321,489	359,537	398,588	439,641	483,695	528,752	575,811	624,872	675,935	728,1000	783,1067
n = m + 24	327,498	365,547	405,598	446,652	490,707	536,764	583,824	633,885	684,949	738,1014	793,1082
n = m + 25	332,508	371,557	411,609	453,663	498,718	544,776	592,836	642,898	694,962	747,1029	803,10

TABLE A.8 WILCOXON RANK SUM TEST *(continued)*

m = 3(1)25 and n = m(1)m + 25
P = .025 one-sided; P = .05 two-sided

n	m = 3	m = 4	m = 5	m = 6	m = 7	m = 8	m = 9	m = 10	m = 11	m = 12	m = 13	m = 14
n = m	5,16	11,25	18,37	26,52	37,68	49,87	63,103	79,131	96,157	116,184	137,214	160,246
n = m + 1	6,18	12,28	19,41	28,56	39,73	51,93	66,114	82,138	100,164	120,192	141,223	165,255
n = m + 2	6,21	12,32	20,45	29,61	41,78	54,98	68,121	85,145	103,172	124,200	146,231	170,264
n = m + 3	7,23	13,35	21,49	31,65	43,83	56,104	71,127	88,152	107,179	128,208	150,240	174,274
n = m + 4	7,26	14,38	22,53	32,70	45,88	58,110	74,133	91,159	110,187	131,217	154,249	179,283
n = m + 5	8,28	15,41	24,56	34,74	46,94	61,115	77,139	94,166	114,194	135,225	159,257	184,292
n = m + 6	8,31	16,44	25,60	38,78	48,99	63,121	79,146	97,173	118,201	139,233	163,266	189,301
n = m + 7	9,33	17,47	26,64	37,83	50.104	65,127	82,152	101,179	121,209	143,241	168,274	194,310
n = m + 8	10,35	17,51	27,68	39,87	52,109	68,132	85,158	104,186	125,216	147,249	172,283	198,320
n = m + 9	10,38	18,54	29,71	41,91	54,114	70,138	88,164	107,193	128,224	151,257	176,292	203,329
n = m + 10	11,40	19,57	30,75	42,96	56,119	72,144	90,171	110,200	132,231	155,265	181,300	208,338
n = m + 11	11,43	20,60	31,79	44,100	58,124	75,149	93,177	113,207	135,239	159,273	185,309	213,347
n = m + 12	12,45	21,63	32,83	45,105	60,129	77,155	96,183	117,213	139,246	163,281	190,317	218,356
n = m + 13	12,48	22,66	33,87	47,109	62,134	80,160	99,189	120,220	143,253	167,289	194,326	222,365
n = m + 14	13,50	23,69	35,90	49,113	64,139	82,166	101,196	123,227	146,261	171,297	198,335	227,375
n = m + 15	13,53	24,72	36,94	50,118	66,144	84,172	104,202	126,234	150,268	175,305	203,343	232,384
n = m + 16	14,55	24,76	37,98	52,122	68,149	87,177	107,208	129,241	153,276	179,313	207,352	237,393
n = m + 17	14,58	25,79	38,102	53,127	70,154	89,183	110,214	132,248	157,283	183,321	212,360	242,402
n = m + 18	15,60	26,82	40,105	55,131	72,159	92,188	113,220	136,254	161,290	187,329	216,389	247,411
n = m + 19	15,63	27,85	41,109	57,135	74,164	94,194	115,227	139,261	164,298	191,337	221,377	252,420
n = m + 20	16,65	28,88	42,113	58,140	76,169	96,200	118,233	142,268	168,305	195,345	225,386	256,430
n = m + 21	16,68	29,91	43,117	60,144	78,174	99,205	121,239	145,275	171,313	199,353	229,395	261,439
n = m + 22	17,70	30,94	45,120	61,149	80,179	101,211	124,245	148,282	175,320	203,361	234,403	266,448
n = m + 23	17,73	31,97	46,124	63,153	82,184	103,217	127,251	152,288	179,327	207,369	238,412	271,457
n = m + 24	18,75	31,101	47,128	65,157	84,189	106,222	129,258	155,295	182,335	211,377	243,420	276,466
n = m + 25	18,78	32,104	48,132	66,162	86,194	108,228	132,264	158,302	186,342	216,384	247,429	281,475

m = 3(1)25 and n = m(1)m + 25
P = .025 one-sided; P = .05 two-sided

n	m = 15	m = 16	m = 17	m = 18	m = 19	m = 20	m = 21	m = 22	m = 23	m = 24	m = 25
n = m	185,280	212,316	240,355	271,395	303,438	337,483	373,530	411,579	451,530	493,683	536,739
n = m + 1	190,290	217,327	246,366	277,407	310,450	345,495	381,543	419,593	460,644	502,698	546,754
n = m + 2	195,300	223,337	252,377	284,418	317,462	352,508	389,556	428,606	468,659	511,713	555,770
n = m + 3	201,309	229,347	258,388	290,430	324,474	359,521	397,589	436,620	477,673	520,728	565,785
n = m + 4	206,319	234,358	264,399	297,441	331,486	367,533	404,583	444,634	486,687	529,743	574,801
n = m + 5	211,329	240,368	271,409	303,453	338,498	374,546	412,596	452,648	494,702	538,758	584,816
n = m + 6	216,379	245,379	277,420	310,464	345,510	381,559	420,609	450,662	503,716	547,773	593,832
n = m + 7	221,349	251,389	283,431	316,476	351,523	389,571	428,622	469,675	512,730	556,788	603,847
n = m + 8	227,358	257,399	289,442	323,487	358,535	396,584	436,635	477,689	520,745	565,803	612,863
n = m + 9	232,363	262,410	295,453	329,499	365,547	403,597	443,649	485,703	529,759	575,817	622,878
n = m + 10	237,378	268,420	301,464	336,510	372,559	411,609	451,662	493,717	538,773	584,832	632,893
n = m + 11	242,388	274,430	307,475	342,522	379,571	418,622	459,675	502,730	546,788	593,847	641,909
n = m + 12	248,397	279,441	313,486	349,533	386,583	426,634	467,688	510,744	555,802	602,862	651,924
n = m + 13	253,407	285,451	319,497	355,545	393,595	433,647	475,701	518,758	564,816	611,877	660,940
n = m + 14	258,417	291,461	325,508	362,556	400,607	440,660	482,715	526,772	572,831	620,892	670,955
n = m + 15	263,427	296,472	331,519	368,568	407,619	448,672	490,728	535,785	581,845	629,907	679,971
n = m + 16	269,436	302,482	338,529	375,579	414,631	455,685	498,741	543,799	590,859	638,922	689,986
n = m + 17	274,446	308,492	344,540	381,591	421,643	463,697	506,754	551,813	599,873	648,936	699,1001
n = m + 18	279,456	314,502	350,551	388,602	428,655	470,710	514,767	560,826	607,888	657,951	708,1017
n = m + 19	284,466	319,513	356,582	395,613	435,667	477,723	522,780	568,840	616,902	666,955	718,1032
n = m + 20	290,475	325,523	362,573	401,625	442,679	485,735	530,793	576,854	625,916	675,931	727,1048
n = m + 21	295,485	331,533	368,584	408,636	449,691	492,748	537,807	584,868	633,931	684,996	737,1063
n = m + 22	300,495	336,544	374,595	414,648	456,703	500,760	545,820	593,881	642,945	693,1011	747,1078
n = m + 23	306,504	342,554	380,606	421,659	463,715	507,773	553,833	601,895	651,959	703,1025	756,1094
n = m + 24	311,514	348,564	387,616	427,671	470,727	515,785	561,846	609,909	660,973	712,1040	766,1109
n = m + 25	316,524	353,575	393,627	434,682	477,739	522,798	569,89	618,922	668,988	721,1055	775

TABLE A.9 RANDOM NUMBERS

Random Number Table

39 65 76 45 45	19 90 69 64 61	20 26 36 31 62	58 24 97 14 97	95 06 70 99 00
73 71 23 70 90	65 97 60 12 11	31 56 34 19 19	47 83 75 51 33	30 62 38 20 46
72 18 47 33 84	51 67 47 97 19	98 40 07 17 66	23 05 09 51 80	59 78 11 52 49
75 12 25 69 17	17 95 21 78 58	24 33 45 77 48	69 81 84 09 29	93 22 70 45 80
37 17 79 88 74	63 52 06 34 30	01 31 60 10 27	35 07 79 71 53	28 99 52 01 41
02 48 08 16 94	85 53 83 29 95	56 27 09 24 43	21 78 55 09 82	72 61 88 73 61
87 89 15 70 07	37 79 49 12 38	48 13 93 55 96	41 92 45 71 51	09 18 25 58 94
98 18 71 70 15	89 09 39 59 24	00 06 41 41 20	14 36 59 25 47	54 45 17 24 89
10 83 58 07 04	76 62 16 48 68	58 76 17 14 86	59 53 11 52 21	66 04 18 72 87
47 08 56 37 31	71 82 13 50 41	27 55 10 24 92	28 04 67 53 44	95 23 00 84 47
93 90 31 03 07	34 18 04 52 35	74 13 39 35 22	68 95 23 92 35	36 63 70 35 33
21 05 11 47 99	11 20 99 45 18	76 51 94 84 86	13 79 93 37 55	98 16 04 41 67
95 89 94 06 97	27 37 83 28 71	79 57 95 13 91	09 61 87 25 21	56 20 11 32 44
97 18 31 55 73	10 65 81 92 59	77 31 61 95 46	20 44 90 32 64	26 99 76 75 63
69 08 88 86 13	59 71 74 17 32	48 38 75 93 29	73 37 32 04 05	60 82 29 20 25
41 26 10 25 03	87 63 93 95 17	81 83 83 04 49	77 45 85 50 51	79 88 01 97 30
91 47 14 63 62	08 61 74 51 69	92 79 43 89 79	29 18 94 51 23	14 85 11 47 23
80 94 54 18 47	08 52 85 08 40	48 40 35 94 22	72 65 71 08 86	50 03 42 99 36
67 06 77 63 99	89 85 84 46 06	64 71 06 21 66	89 37 20 70 01	61 65 70 22 12
59 72 24 13 75	42 29 72 23 19	06 94 76 10 08	81 30 15 39 14	81 33 17 16 33
63 62 06 34 41	79 53 36 02 95	94 61 09 43 62	20 21 14 68 86	84 95 48 46 45
78 47 23 53 90	79 93 96 38 63	34 85 52 05 09	85 43 01 72 73	14 93 87 81 40
87 68 62 15 43	97 48 72 66 48	53 16 71 13 81	59 97 50 99 52	24 62 20 42 31
47 60 92 10 77	26 97 05 73 51	88 46 38 03 58	72 68 49 29 31	75 70 16 08 24
56 88 87 59 41	06 87 37 78 48	65 88 69 58 39	88 02 84 27 83	85 81 56 39 38
22 17 68 65 84	87 02 22 57 51	68 69 80 95 44	11 29 01 95 80	49 34 35 36 47
19 36 27 59 46	39 77 32 77 09	79 57 92 36 59	89 74 39 82 15	08 58 94 34 74
16 77 23 02 77	28 06 24 25 93	22 45 44 84 11	87 80 61 65 31	09 71 91 74 25
78 43 76 71 61	97 67 63 99 61	30 45 67 93 82	59 73 19 85 23	53 33 65 97 21
03 28 28 26 08	69 30 16 09 05	53 58 47 70 93	66 56 45 65 79	45 56 20 19 47
04 31 17 21 56	33 73 99 19 87	26 72 39 27 67	53 77 57 68 93	60 61 97 22 61
61 06 98 03 91	87 14 77 43 96	43 00 65 98 50	45 60 33 01 07	98 99 46 50 47
23 68 35 26 00	99 53 93 61 28	52 70 05 48 34	56 65 05 61 86	90 92 10 70 80
15 39 25 70 99	93 86 52 77 65	15 33 59 05 28	22 87 26 07 47	86 96 98 29 06
58 71 96 30 24	18 46 23 34 27	85 13 99 24 44	49 18 09 79 49	74 16 32 23 02
93 22 53 64 39	07 10 63 76 35	87 03 04 79 88	08 13 13 85 51	55 34 57 72 69
78 76 58 54 74	92 38 70 96 92	52 06 79 79 45	82 63 18 27 44	69 66 92 19 09
61 81 31 96 82	00 57 25 60 59	46 72 60 18 77	55 66 12 62 11	08 99 55 64 57
42 88 07 10 05	24 98 65 63 21	47 21 61 88 32	27 80 30 21 60	10 92 35 36 12
77 94 30 05 39	28 10 99 00 27	12 73 73 99 12	49 99 57 94 82	96 88 57

Index